THE PRICE

THE PRICE OF VIGILANCE

THE PRICE OF VIGILANCE

VIGILANCE

Attacks on American Surveillance Flights

Larry Tart
and
Robert Keefe

BALLANTINE BOOKS
NEW YORK

Additional photo credits:
Nisei linguists: Samuel S. K. Hong; S.Sgt. Donald G. Hill: James Smestad; RB-50 flying: Tom Short; Quonset huts (both photos): Jackie Price; Capt. John E. Simpson: Mark Simpson; 1st Lt. Ricardo M. Villarreal: James Edds; S.Sgt. Laroy Price: Marion Barnett; T.Sgt. Arthur L. Mello: The Mello family; A/2C Harold T. Kamps: Luther Tarbox; A/2C James E. Ferguson Jr.: The Ferguson family; A/2C Gerald C. Maggiacomo: Luther Tarbox; A/2C Joel Fields: Jackie Price; A/2C Robert Oshinskie: Robert Sprankle; Airborne intercept operator position 10: O. T. Johnson; C-130 60528 in Bödo, Norway: Del Johannsen; Armenian *khachkar* with Lorna Bourg: Lorna Bourg

Library of Congress Catalog Card Number: 2001117399

ISBN 0-8041-1911-2

Manufactured in the United States of America

First Edition: June 2001

10 9 8 7 6 5 4 3 2 1

To the crew of C-130 60528:
Capt. Paul E. Duncan
Capt. John E. Simpson
Capt. Rudy J. Swiestra
Capt. Edward J. Jeruss
1st Lt. Ricardo M. Villarreal
M.Sgt. George P. Petrochilos
T.Sgt. Arthur L. Mello
S.Sgt. Laroy Price
A/1C Robert J. Oshinskie
A/2C Archie T. Bourg Jr.
A/2C James E. Ferguson Jr.
A/2C Joel H. Fields
A/2C Harold T. Kamps
A/2C Gerald C. Maggiacomo
A/2C Clement O. Mankins
A/2C Gerald H. Medeiros
A/2C Robert H. Moore

In memory of Donald "Wimpy" Belmont, Horace "Red" Haire, and
Thomas Short—former Security Service airborne voice intercept
operators who would have enjoyed this book

For our wives, Diane Tart and Jan Keefe

Stoop Angels, hither from the skies
There is no holier spot of ground
Than here where defeated valor lies
By mourning beauty crowned.
—HENRY TIMROD

If, begrudging the outlay of ranks, emoluments, and a hundred pieces of gold, a commander does not know the enemy's situation, his is the height of inhumanity. Such a person is no man's commander, no ruler's counselor, and no master of victory.
—SUN-TZU

CONTENTS

—

PREFACE

The idea for *The Price of Vigilance* evolved while I was researching the 528 shootdown incident, at the time of the creation of the Aerial Reconnaissance Memorial at the National Security Agency's National Vigilance Park. Because I sensed a deep yearning for details about the incident from family members whom I contacted, I resolved to document the shootdown and began to research and organize the facts. In January 1997, I located Robert Keefe, and we bonded immediately: We speak the same language on the shootdown tragedy; we're both former Air Force Russian linguists and airborne voice intercept operators; we had both served in the home unit of the men who perished aboard 60528. Keefe had flown recon missions with the lost crew in 1957–58 and participated in the search for 60528 subsequent to the shootdown. I flew airborne communications intelligence reconnaissance missions aboard the same fleet of C-130 aircraft in the 1960s and 1970s. Feeling deep sympathy for the families of the lost men, we vowed during the memorial dedication in 1997 to honor them and their families with this book.

I am deeply indebted to family members of the lost crew and to Air Force veterans who have made available much of the detailed information in the book, and who have shared anecdotes that add the human dimension to our story. I am especially grateful to Mark Simpson (son of copilot Capt. John E. Simpson), Theresa Durkin (sister of recon airborne mission supervisor M.Sgt. George P. Petrochilos), and Raymond Kamps (brother of airborne voice intercept operator A/2C Harold T. Kamps). They opened their hearts and shared their Air Force casualty correspondence files with me. Luke Mankins (father of airborne voice intercept operator A/2C Oscar O. Mankins) wrote me a short helpful note about his son; a commendable effort by Mr. Mankins, who is ninety-three years old. In addition, I would like to acknowledge the multitude of relatives of all the family members I have located: You have graciously welcomed me into your families, and you are my friends for life.

Others meriting special mention include Kenneth A. Minihan (Lt. Gen., USAF, Ret.), Col. Wyatt C. Cook (USAF), Thomas H. Tennant (CM.Sgt., USAF, Ret.) and Luther A. Tarbox (Lt. Col., USAF, Ret.). As Director of the National Security Agency, General Minihan took a bold, major step by creating the Aerial Reconnaissance Memorial, bringing closure for family members during the memorial dedication:

> We are honored to host the family members of the reconnaissance crew who were shot down over Armenia September 2, 1958. . . . And we want to publicly acknowledge to the families and to the nation that we will never forget their sacrifice.

I credit Colonel Cook—at the time, commander of the Air Force Air Intelligence Agency's 694th Intelligence Group—with marshalling the resources that made it possible to develop National Vigilance Park and the Aerial Reconnaissance Memorial. Our story would be incomplete without coverage of the recognition that the memorial and dedication ceremony brought to 60528's lost crew and their families.

Tom Tennant, a close personal friend, was serving as an airborne voice intercept operator in the squadron with the eleven recon crew members when their plane was shot down. I am deeply indebted to him for using his phenomenal recall to provide, authenticate, and elaborate on names, dates, locations, and unique events that occurred more than forty years ago. He also served as my sounding board during the research and development of this book.

As operations officer of the Air Force Security Service squadron to which the eleven recon crew members were assigned (and as acting commander when the tragedy struck), Luther Tarbox was intimately involved in all aspects of European airborne communications intelligence reconnaissance operations during 1957–1960 and has provided me with meticulous detail on airborne operations during that era. His assistance and technical inputs have been invaluable in re-creating events surrounding the shootdown and its aftermath.

Finally, I thank Eugene Willard, himself a former recon flyer. As a librarian in the Philadelphia Public Library, Gene helped me locate many significant related documents that I would not have uncovered otherwise.

LARRY R. TART
State College, Pennsylvania
October 24, 2000

I have little to add to what Larry has said, except one thing. Forty years ago, I felt it my duty to pay my condolences to the families of the men who died. Bureaucratic, largely senseless, security considerations prevented me and my friends from taking that simple human step, which seemed so natural, so necessary to me and to the others. This book has finally given me that chance.

Moreover, after nearly half a century, I feel that I finally have a reasonable understanding of just what happened and why it happened. A knowledge of history doesn't really heal anyone, but telling the truth—to others and to oneself—is nevertheless a human necessity. For me, for the men of our outfit, and I hope for the families of the men who died, this book is at the very least a large step in the direction of truth.

ROBERT KEEFE
Northampton, Massachusetts
March 27, 2001

AUTHOR'S NOTE

———

The average American citizen could not even spell SIGINT (pronounced *sig' int*) and had no clue about signals intelligence on April 1, 2001. But when I heard a news flash that date about a U.S. Navy P-3 aircraft in an emergency landing on Hainan Island, China, I considered it a dire situation—I hoped it was not an EP-3 surveillance plane. Learning that the crew survived provided some relief, but further identification of the plane as an EP-3E Aries II signals intelligence reconnaissance aircraft affected the most significant project of my career, this book.

As originally planned, this book focused on one incident, the shoot-down of an Air Force C-130 SIGINT reconnaissance aircraft in 1958 with the loss of seventeen crewmen. That tight focus soon developed into a much broader consideration of the dangers of aerial reconnaissance throughout the Cold War. Having described incident after incident in which a peacetime aerial reconnaissance platform was blown out of the sky over international waters, we were now confronted with yet another incident, this time involving only one death, as opposed to those times in the past when an entire crew had died. There have always been inherent dangers associated with manned airborne reconnaissance missions—yet the missions were and still are necessary.

The recent encounter over the South China Sea between the Navy

EP-3E aircrew and two Chinese air force fighter pilots clearly shows that today's surveillance flights are every bit as perilous as the recon missions of our airborne recon pioneers more than fifty years ago. From the beginning of the Cold War, one of the primary results of aerial reconnaissance was to allow the U.S. to hold down military spending because the country had a very accurate idea of potential enemies' ability to carry out hostile actions, and, simultaneously, that knowledge allowed the United States to avoid other potential Pearl Harbors. At the dawn of the twenty-first century, the United States employs the world's most sophisticated intelligence surveillance satellites, but these satellites complement rather than replace manned intelligence collection platforms. Airborne reconnaissance, working in tandem with surveillance satellites, is still necessary to forewarn America of the military capabilities and intents of its adversaries.

Operating in excess of sixty miles from Chinese shores, the EP-3E crew was engaged in signals intelligence surveillance against China, a completely legal mission similar to the thousands of other peacetime aerial reconnaissance program (PARPRO) flights flown by U.S. Air Force and U.S. Navy crews each year—in all areas of the world. Unlike covert overflight reconnaissance missions that intentionally violate foreign airspace, PARPRO missions are "peripheral," they file flight plans, bear U.S. markings, and operate overtly in international airspace, well outside the twelve-mile territorial zones claimed by China and other nations. Many countries—China and Russia included—conduct similar aerial recon missions against potential adversaries. China operates its own electronic surveillance fleet of auxiliary ships and aircraft that patrol along the coasts of Vietnam, Malaysia, Taiwan, South Korea, and Japan.

The goal of any national intelligence is to provide a factual basis for political decision making. To take the most obvious example, the downed EP-3 and its sister aircraft have always played a large role in American decisions on precisely what weapons to provide to Taiwan. The ultimate considerations, correct or incorrect, are political, but they must be based on accurate estimates of the nature of the threat.

The vast majority of airborne reconnaissance missions are completed without incident, but the U.S.-Chinese collision on April 1, 2001, demonstrates one of the myriad dangers confronting reconnaissance crews.

Because of the extraordinary skill of its pilot, the twenty-four EP-3 crew members survived a midair collision and are safely home. This time it was the fighter pilot who died. In part, ironically enough, he died because China did not want to create an incident with the United States. Shadowing the plane with his wingman, creating turbulence by flying directly beneath the recon plane, and then suddenly starting a climb immediately in front of it, he misjudged his distance. He performed that dangerous maneuver precisely because China does not officially consider the United States its enemy. Had we been enemies, in the sense that the Soviet Union was an enemy even in peacetime, he would have destroyed the American plane from a safe distance. Nowadays, it seems, the opponent pesters the recon plane. In the Cold War, in too many cases, the approved method was to kill it.

This book is about those kills.

LARRY TART
April 20, 2001

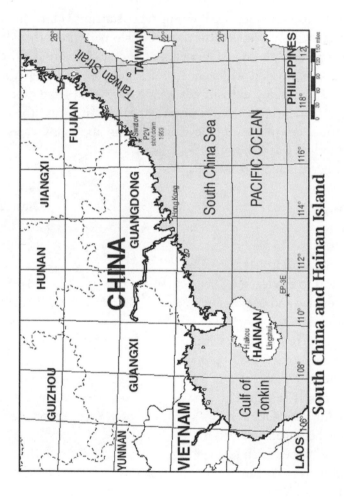

South China and Hainan Island

INTRODUCTION:
U.S.-CHINESE AIR INCIDENTS

During the Cold War, the rules of engagement for pilots of American peacetime aerial reconnaissance program missions were the same for all areas of the world, including China. At whatever cost, an aircraft commander was to evade enemy attackers and avoid compromising his reconnaissance crew and onboard intelligence-gathering systems. But the rules of engagement (or more appropriately "rules of disengagement") had changed by April 1, 2001, when U.S. Navy Lt. Shane Osborn was faced with the decision of his life.

Lieutenant Osborn was the mission commander aboard a Navy EP-3E Aries II signals intelligence reconnaissance plane that departed Kadena Air Base, Okinawa, on a routine patrol flight on Sunday, April 1. The crew belonged to Fleet Air Reconnaissance Squadron One (VQ-1) based at Whidbey Island Naval Air Station, about fifty miles from Seattle, Washington. At the time of the accident, they were on temporary active duty at Kadena.

EP-3E Aries II

The EP-3E Airborne Reconnaissance Integrated Electronics Suite II (Aries II) is a four-engine turboprop electronic warfare and reconnaissance system—the Navy's only land-based signals intelligence (SIGINT) reconnaissance aircraft. Derived from the P-3 Orion (a military variant of the long out-of-service Lockheed Electra passenger aircraft), the original EP-3Es (Aries I) were fielded in the late 1960s and early 1970s. The current Aries II variant that replaced the worn-out Aries I during the last decade has a twelve-hour endurance and a 3,000-nautical-mile range.

The EP-3E Aries II aircraft has twenty-four seating positions, twenty of which are numbered crew stations; the other four seats (ditching stations) are located in the rear of the plane and are used for extra crew members. Stations 1, 2, 3, 5, and 6 are flight crew positions and the

EP-3E Aries II
Crew Stations

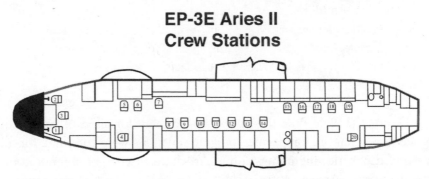

remaining stations make up the mission or reconnaissance crew. Station 4 is the secure communications operator and station 7 is the recorder operator/flight technician. Stations 8 through 13 are electronic intelligence (ELINT) positions that exploit electronic signals; station 14 (special systems evaluator) functions as the coordinator for the mission crew; and stations 15 through 19 are COMINT (communications intelligence) positions used to intercept and exploit communications signals. The last station, 20, is a scientific-technical operator charged with special signals tasking.

By some estimates the EP-3E aircraft—tail number 156511 (PR-32)—that the crew left behind in China is valued at eighty to one hundred million dollars. But the real value to the Chinese may be how well Chinese engineers can reverse-engineer the plane's surveillance suite. With sensitive receivers and high-gain dish antennas, the EP-3E exploits a wide range of electronic and communications emissions from deep within targeted territories, providing near real time tactical direct support to appropriate command and control authorities. The U.S. Navy has eleven EP-3Es to meet worldwide fleet and theater requirements. Interpreting and reporting tactically significant radar and communications signals, an EP-3E mission crew supports battle groups in indications and warning, targeting, and suppression of air defenses and strike sortie execution. An official Navy description of the EP-3E:

> *Operating in international airspace either independently or in conjunction with other U.S. forces, the EP-3E provides the Fleet Commander with a real-time assessment of the tactical posture of potentially unfriendly military forces. While providing intelligence for the fleet in a multithreat open environment, the reconnaissance crew must rapidly determine the evolving tactical scenario by analyzing available information. Disseminating this information directly to the National Command Authority allows decision makers at all levels to respond to key developments.*

The U.S. Navy has two squadrons of EP-3E aircraft, VQ-1 with home base at Whidbey Island NAS and VQ-2, based at Rota Naval Base, Spain. The two squadrons also operate from detached locations at Kadena and Atsugi, Japan; Souda Bay, Crete; and a number of other locations.

Midair Collision over the South China Sea

The EP-3 crew was flying in international airspace over the South China Sea when a pair of Chinese People's Liberation Army Air Force Shenyang F-8 "Finback" fighter pilots intercepted them. Sixty to seventy miles south of Hainan Island, China, one of the F-8 pilots bumped into the port (left) wing of the EP-3 aircraft—not a direct or head-on collision, but any midair collision is life-threatening. Among other damage to Lieutenant Osborn's four-engine propeller aircraft, the collision severely damaged the propeller on engine No. 1. The collision also caused damage to the underside of the plane's wing and aileron, and sheared off the radome from the front of the EP-3; the fighter aircraft broke in half and crashed.

With his life and the lives of his twenty-three crew members hanging in the balance, Lieutenant Osborn had, in that region of the world, just three options in accordance with U.S. Navy operating instructions: (1) bail out his crew; (2) ditch his aircraft and crew at sea; (3) land at an enemy airfield. He chose the third option, declared an inflight emergency, began transmitting Mayday calls on the international distress frequencies, and headed for the nearest available landing strip—Lingshui airport—a military airfield on Hainan Island.

The EP-3 crew was horror-struck in the harrowing minutes after their midair collision. The plane was vibrating horribly; the altimeter was out; warning lights were flashing, and whistling noise caused by depressurization of the aircraft made it extremely difficult to hear. Many were certain they would die, according to a *New York Times* story datelined Oak Harbor, Washington, April 15.

> *"The first thing I thought of was, 'Oh my God,'" said Avn.Mach.M. 2C Wendy S. Westbrook, the navigator. "All I could see was blue water."*
>
> *"All the crew members were scared at that point," said Lt.(j.g.)Jeffrey R. Vignery.*
>
> *The mission commander and pilot Shane J. Osborn, a hulking lieutenant from Norfolk, Nebraska, changed to the seat on the left, where landing procedures are generally conducted, and began working the controls to try to stabilize the plane.*
>
> *"I was hoping and praying he was going to get us out of this," Lieutenant Vignery said. "I didn't think we were going to make it. I had already accepted Jesus Christ as my Savior, but I said another prayer at that time in case I didn't get it right the first time," he said.*
>
> *As the seconds passed, Lieutenant Osborn gave the order to prepare to bail out by parachute. But he was able gradually to pull the plane out of its dive, and he rescinded the command, telling the crew instead to prepare to ditch, which meant he intended to land on the water.*
>
> *For people in the rear [reconnaissance crew], that meant strapping in, facing the back of the plane to minimize any injury upon impact. Even as the plane was about to land on Hainan Island, Lieutenant Honeck said, "People in the back thought we were going into the water. . . ."*
>
> *Lieutenant Osborn regained enough control of the plane that Lieutenant Honeck moved to the back to study maps to see where the plane*

might land. They quickly ruled out a run for Okinawa, which was four and a half hours away, or the Philippines, which was farther. . . . .

[The damaged No. 1 propeller was spinning so wildly that they were afraid it would lose all of its oil, come loose, and shear the EP-3E's fuselage. In addition, following the collision, there was no time for the crew to use oxygen masks, and for a short time, until the plane got down to about 12,000 feet, it was somewhat difficult to breathe.]

Once the plane landed safely, Lieutenant Osborn said that as commander, he wanted to be the first to walk off. A small group of armed Chinese military, including an interpreter, approached.

"He told us not to move and don't do anything," the lieutenant said. "I asked if I could use a phone to call the U.S. ambassador to let him know we were safe on deck, but he said they had already taken care of that. Then they told us to get off the plane, and they were pretty adamant about it. We dropped a ladder, and I got off first."

The crew certainly did not look forward to what lay ahead, but they were all alive, and Hainan was better than the alternative. Later, while discussing his first impressions of their emergency landing, Cr. Tech. Josef Edmunds said, "When the plane landed and the Chinese authorities approached, I was so happy to be alive, I had a big grin on my face."

To Land or Ditch?

Some members of the press, and more than a few former airborne reconnaissance crew members from the Cold War era, have questioned Lieutenant Osborn's decision to land his critically crippled aircraft at a Chinese airfield. (During the Cold War, operational guidance for an aircraft commander engaged in a PARPRO surveillance mission directed him to avoid permitting his reconnaissance platform to fall into enemy hands. But with the end of the Cold War, the rules have changed.) When asked by a TV reporter if he had any misgivings about his decision to land on Hainan Island instead of denying the Chinese access to one of the Navy's most sensitive reconnaissance platforms, Lieutenant Osborn smiled and said, "None whatsoever; ask my crew members what the decision should have been."

Flight safety and the lives of the crew come first. Speaking anonymously, an Air Force NCO who flies similar reconnaissance missions aboard the U.S. Air Force's analogous RC-135 recon platform said that crews no longer try to destroy the aircraft if it is possible to get it down safely.

Navy EP-3E–Chinese Air Incident

Unable to establish communications with Lingshui's airfield controller, the EP-3 crew entered Chinese airspace and landed at the airfield without verbal authorization, a perfectly legal maneuver under international law but a point the Chinese government would argue against vehemently during negotiations to release the crew. The twenty-four person EP-3 crew[1] consisted of Lieutenant Osborn and the flight crew (six crew members who flew the aircraft) and eighteen reconnaissance crew members who were performing a surveillance flight against China. The crew included three female officers, plus a U.S. Marine sergeant and an Air Force senior airman.

Miraculously, none of the crew suffered any serious injuries; a few minor scratches at worst. The only casualty was the PLAAF (naval air force) fighter pilot who is missing and presumed dead.

On the ground, the Chinese soldiers offered the crew water and cigarettes, and the interpreter told them not to worry. They herded the Americans into vans and took them to what they perceived as officers' quarters on the Lingshui military base. "Their best barracks," Lieutenant Osborn said. "But by American standards, they were poor. Lots and lots of bugs and mosquitoes. But it was livable."

The Chinese provided them with basics: toothpaste and electric shavers—no razors. Brig. Gen. Neal Sealock, American military attaché in Beijing, was finally permitted to visit the crew on their second day of detention, bringing them clean socks and underwear. He assured the crew their families had been notified and that efforts were being made at the "highest level" of the Bush administration to secure their release.

For two days, the PLA housed them on Lingshui, then moved them to a nearby base lodge in Haikou, the capital of the Hainan province. In the new quarters, described as "Chinese resort-type" facilities, the three female crew members were provided a room together while most of the men were housed two to a room. Lieutenant Osborn had a room to himself, and all crew members were permitted to dine together.

The rooms had television sets without cable and phones that had been disconnected. Except for meals, the crew members were allowed to mingle only with those with whom they shared a room. They assumed their rooms were bugged. The crew subsequently described their quarters and food—including "lots of rice"—as adequate. "It was Chinese food, but definitely not Americanized," said Lieutenant Vignery, adding that their Chinese hosts served them fish heads "until they realized we weren't into fish heads." They received three meals per day.

Interrogations (always videotaped) were conducted at various times—day and night—sometimes for as long as five hours. Crew members have not shared the nature of their interrogations with the public. Interrogation was their only activity the first few days; later some of the guards brought them decks of cards and a newspaper in English. The newspaper included no coverage of their situation. Although each detainee was deprived of sleep and interrogated extensively, none of the crew members accused the PLA of mistreatment.

Lieutenant Osborn said that early in his detention, he thought about the Iranian hostage situation in which Americans were held in the American Embassy in Teheran for 444 days. He did not expect a similar fate, but the thought nagged him:

We knew it might take a while; this was definitely going to be a touchy situation. But there was no wavering. I was confident we were going to get home.

Completing the Checklists

The EP-3E reportedly radioed home after landing on Hainan. According to an April 13 *Chicago Tribune* story, they communicated with the NSA (National Security Agency) facility located in Hawaii, letting them know they had landed safely on Hainan Island and were surrounded by Chinese troops shouting at them to leave the aircraft: "That message was immediately flashed to NSA headquarters at Fort Meade, Maryland (probably as a "CRITIC"), and thence to the White House."

In U.S. Intelligence, a CRITIC report is used to forward time-sensitive critical information to the National Command Authority. Transmitted in secure sensitive compartmented information channels at the highest— flash—precedence, a CRITIC arrives at the White House within just minutes of its sending.

En route to the emergency landing, the crew began the execution of an emergency destruct plan, destroying classified mission equipment and materials to keep sensitive information, cryptographic codes, and intelligence-producing capabilities from falling into enemy hands. The mission's "special communicator" would have sent the CRITIC report as an encrypted message, with destruction of the encryption devices being accomplished after the last message was sent. The extent to which the Chinese gained access to classified holdings is unknown.

The crew had only a few frantic minutes to try and destroy everything they could before they were "invited" off the aircraft by armed Chinese soldiers. Encounters with Chinese pilots flying aggressively against American planes had continued in recent months despite American protests to the Chinese, and finally, on April 1, what everyone had feared happened.

The U.S. diplomats in Beijing said they couldn't confirm the second Chinese fighter pilot's claim, broadcast on state television, that he requested permission to shoot down the American plane. They had no evidence that shots were fired.

Without getting into sensitive details, a senior diplomat suggested the crew had completed the crew's emergency destruct plan. However, anonymous government sources leaked reports on April 25 that the crew "had not been able to destroy as much of the secret materials on board as originally believed, and some of it could be exploited by Beijing." "It's pretty bad; they weren't able to get a lot of it," claimed a source said to be knowledgeable about a secret damage assessment being conducted by the

Pentagon. "It was serious." The source said the crew did not have the ability to destroy everything in an expeditious manner so as "to not subject it to compromise." In some cases the crew was not able to physically destroy the material, and in others, what they tried to destroy was not destroyed to the extent that rendered it useless.

A senior anonymous U.S. Navy official said the situation was not necessarily worse than was believed in the very beginning.

> . . . We knew that there would be computer disks and drives, even though smashed, that could be compromised by a determined investigator. They got through the checklist, but we never intended to imply that there was no loss. We knew from the outset that this was not going to be complete. We knew there were going to be compromises and that there was going to be a significant windfall for the Chinese.

Negotiations

Tense negotiations between the U.S. and Chinese governments to free the crew began within hours of the landing on Hainan. From the start, U.S. spokesmen maintained that the midair collision was an accident that occurred in international airspace. Initially, a Chinese spokesperson claimed that the collision occurred "inside Chinese territorial airspace."

On Monday, April 2, U.S. ambassador Joseph Prueher demanded immediate access to the crew of the Navy surveillance plane who, by that time, had been held incommunicado for thirty-two hours. Later in Washington, Secretary of Defense Rumsfeld cited instances where military aircraft of both the Soviet Union and China had made emergency landings at American facilities without incident. According to Rumsfeld, the United States had facilitated the repair of the out-of-commission planes, had assisted the foreign crews in contacting their governments, and had permitted the aircrews and their aircraft to depart expeditiously.

The Chinese Foreign Ministry told the Ambassador Prueher that U.S. diplomats would not be allowed to meet with the crew until Tuesday night, Chinese time (Tuesday morning in the United States), prompting a demand from President George W. Bush on Monday for "immediate access" to the crew. President Bush also demanded that the aircraft be returned "without further damaging or tampering." The Chinese government ignored the request for the return of the aircraft and refused to release the crew while its investigation progressed, and while search and rescue teams attempted to locate the missing fighter pilot. A former U.S. airborne reconnaissance crew member from the Cold War era commented:

> The Chinese are surely holding the trump, considering they have the airplane and crew. I wonder who they want to blame the whole thing on?

An answer to his question appeared promptly and unequivocally in a news release. On April 4, a Chinese Foreign Ministry spokesman announced the Chinese version of the midair collision and stated China's stance on the incident:

> On the morning of April 1, a U.S. EP-3 electronic surveillance plane flew southeast of China's Hainan Island. At 8:36 Beijing time, the U.S. surveillance plane approached the airspace over China's territorial waters off the city of Sanya to conduct reconnaissance. The Chinese Navy sent two F-8 fighters to follow and monitor the U.S. plane. At 9:07, the Chinese planes made a normal flight in an area 104 kilometers from the baseline of China's territorial waters. The course of the Chinese planes was at 110 degrees, and the U.S. plane was flying parallel with the right side of the Chinese planes in the same direction.
>
> The U.S. plane suddenly veered at a wide angle toward the Chinese planes, which were closer to the baseline of the Chinese side. The U.S. plane's nose and left wing rammed the tail of one of the Chinese planes, causing it to lose control and plunge into the sea. The pilot, Wang Wei, parachuted from his stricken plane, while the other Chinese plane returned safely and landed at 9:23. The U.S. plane entered Chinese airspace without approval, and landed at Lingshui Airport in Hainan at 9:33. The Chinese side made proper arrangements for the twenty-four crew members aboard, in the spirit of humanitarianism.

After the incident, relevant Chinese departments immediately sent search and rescue planes and ships to look for pilot Wang Wei. President Jiang Zemin is deeply concerned about Wang's safety and has instructed time and again to search for and rescue him at any cost. . . . The search and rescue mission is still going on.

It should be pointed out that it was proper and in accordance with international law for Chinese military fighters to follow and monitor the U.S. military surveillance plane within airspace over China's exclusive economic waters.

By veering and ramming the Chinese jet at a wide angle in violation of the flight rules, the U.S. surveillance caused the crash of the Chinese jet. The surveillance flight conducted by the U.S. aircraft overran the scope of "free overflight" according to international law. The move also violated the United Nations Convention on the Law of the Sea, which stipulates that any flight in airspace above another nation's exclusive economic zone should respect the rights of the country concerned. Thus, the U.S. plane's actions posed a serious threat to the national security of China. Meanwhile, such an action was also against the consensus reached by the two countries in May last year on avoiding risky military actions in sea areas. According to the consensus, when military airborne vehicles encounter each other in international airspace, both sides should properly observe the current international law and practices, and take into consideration the flight safety of the other side so as to avoid dangerous approaches and possible collisions. It should also be pointed out that after the incident, the U.S. surveillance plane intruded China's airspace and landed at a Chinese airport without permission from the Chinese side, a move that further violated the regulations set forth by international and Chinese law, thus constituting a gross encroachment upon China's sovereignty and territorial airspace.

The Chinese Foreign Ministry lodged a solemn representation and protest to the U.S. government on April 1 concerning the U.S. plane's act of crashing into the Chinese warplane and infringing upon China's sovereignty and airspace. The Foreign Ministry has pointed out that the U.S. should bear full responsibility for the incident, and demanded that the U.S. government make an explanation to the Chinese government and people on the U.S. plane's actions. China also demanded that the U.S. take effective measures to prevent such an incident from recurring. The Chinese Foreign Ministry lodged a solemn representation once again on April 2.

In response to a U.S. representation, the Foreign Ministry spokesman stressed:

First, the incident had occurred in airspace "near China's coastal areas and China's exclusive economic waters. . . ."

Second, it was illegal for the U.S. military surveillance plane to enter China's territorial space and to land at a Chinese airport without China's approval. . . .

Third, it is a fact that the U.S. surveillance plane rammed the Chinese warplane. After the collision, the front part of the nose of the U.S. plane dropped off, and the propeller of its second left engine was deformed, evidence that the U.S. plane veered into, approached, and collided abruptly with the Chinese plane, which cannot be denied. The U.S. side should face up to the facts, bear full responsibility, apologize to China, and not seek any excuse to shirk its responsibility. . . .

Fourth, according to both international law and Chinese domestic laws, China has the right to investigate the plane which caused all this trouble, and the incident as a whole, as China is the victim, the country where the incident occurred and the country where the culprit aircraft landed. Taking into consideration the suddenness and complexity of the incident, China needs sufficient time to conduct the investigation. Even under such circumstances, the Chinese Foreign Ministry still called in the U.S. ambassador to China, and lodged a representation with him at 9:30 P.M. on the evening of the day the incident took place. . . . It also needs to be pointed out that the U.S. plane is not a civilian aircraft, but a military spy plane. . . . The Chinese side reserves the right to lodge further representations in line with the investigation results. . . .

Fifth, the most urgent matter for the U.S. side is not to table all manner of requests, but to make a thorough review of the incident, apologize to the Chinese side, and respond to China's concerns and demands.

At present, the Chinese side is conducting an investigation into the incident. Although the process is not yet complete, China lost no time in allowing U.S. diplomats in China to meet the U.S. plane crew members in question, after taking into consideration humanitarian concerns and the relevant agreements between China and the U.S.. This demonstrates China's sincerity and humanitarian spirit in handling the issue. China will deal properly with the U.S. crew and plane in accordance with the law and the results of the investigation.

Wang Wei's Comrades' Views of the Incident

The comrades-in-arms of Wang Wei, the lost Chinese pilot, spoke out to the press about the "provocative tactics of U.S. reconnaissance aircraft."

Xinhua Net, Hainan, April 4, by Sha Zhiliang and Liu Jianxin

After the U.S. military used a reconnaissance aircraft to smash into the fighter of their comrade Wang Wei, leaving Wang dead or missing, Wang's fellow naval aviators in righteous anger revealed the provocative tactics of the U.S. reconnaissance aircraft.

Zeng Cheng, the vice regimental commander, said that in recent years he has often been ordered to monitor U.S. reconnaissance aircraft that had snuck into airspace along China's coast. Zeng said that suddenly reducing airspeed to make use of the performance differences between the reconnaissance aircraft and the interceptor was one tactic the U.S. aircraft use. Chinese jet aircraft do not handle well at low speed so the U.S. aircraft would cut its airspeed from 300 kph down to 250 kph. Another tactic was rapid climbs or descents to make it harder for the interceptors to monitor the U.S. aircraft. The U.S. aircraft often made sharp turns to the right or to the left. The U.S. aircraft would do a quick series of these maneuvers in order to intimidate the Chinese pilots and make it harder for them to monitor the U.S. aircraft.

Zeng Cheng said that over the past two years he has been the command aircraft in over ten interceptions. In early 1999, he and Wang Wei followed a U.S. interceptor as it made a series of very dangerous maneuvers. When the U.S. aircraft realized that it couldn't shake the Chinese, it went away, said Zeng.

Zeng said that the United States still has a Cold War mentality. This can be seen in their provocative flights along China's seacoast. The U.S.

aircraft make many maneuvers that make the Chinese pilots angry. Despite this, while Chinese aircraft need to keep close control over the course of the U.S. aircraft, they strive to maintain separation and altitude difference with them. There is ironclad evidence that the accident occurred because the U.S. aircraft made a turn into the path of the Chinese aircraft. The responsibility for the collision is entirely on the U.S. side.

All Chinese Citizens Do Not Agree with Their Government

Although many Chinese people, who have limited access to non-Chinese news services, frequently believe whatever the *People's Daily* and other Communist media tell them, others with more open access, such as some who appear on Internet forums, speak out against blind allegiance to the party system. One such forum[2] on April 16, 2001, cast doubt on the PRC government version of the midair collision.

> *(Author: Visionary Wang Mang)*
> *[Author's note: I do not entirely agree with the views of the author of the essay copied below. However, I do believe the kind of cool analysis presented in this essay is just what we need. Yelling cheap slogans is no use.]*
> *. . . Here we have to consider a matter of common sense. According to an article by a Chinese author in the March–April issue of* World Military Affairs (Shijie Junshi), *a Mach-2 fighter plane, should keep a safe separation of between 300 and 1,500 meters in order to avoid colliding with friendly aircraft. So the key question is, "Did the two aircraft maintain a safe separation?" Which aircraft disregarded the safe separation?*
> *Although the U.S. was a bit ungentlemanly to send a reconnaissance plane to the vicinity of the Chinese seacoast, we should admit that it is allowed to do so according to the rules of the game. It is like playing a basketball game; as long as I don't stay too long in the three-second zone, I can stand wherever I like for as long as I like without breaking the rules. How is it then that the U.S. side, in what cannot be called honest or glorious circumstances, dared before the midair collision to complain about and negotiate with the Chinese side concerning the "frequent provoca-*

tions by Chinese aircraft against U.S. aircraft?" Why is it that China and the United States two years ago came to an agreement about preventing accidents at sea? Why is it that the U.S. side has broadcast many videos containing photographs of Chinese fighters in level flight closely approaching U.S. aircraft? The video broadcast on April 13 showed the Chinese fighter #85119 very clearly. This kind of U.S. action cannot be explained away by saying that the U.S. is a bully.

The plane on the U.S. side, according to the United States, was an unarmed aircraft that had reconnaissance as its principal mission. On the Chinese side was a fighter aircraft that had interception as its principal mission. The place the midair collision occurred was 105 kilometers from the Chinese coast, a considerable distance from the twelve-nautical-mile territorial limit claimed by China.

The interceptor certainly can monitor the U.S. aircraft but at such a distance. The issue of driving the U.S. plane out of the area or out of Chinese airspace did not arise. American pilots [fighter pilots] like to play games, yes; but these are mostly the single seat or two seat fighters and always in nonthreatening circumstances.

I have flown on Chinese military aircraft several times, and I have a relative who is a deputy squadron commander. Our Chinese pilots play around to the extent that even someone like myself who doesn't admit to being frightened was badly shaken.

Thus the principal question is not whether the U.S. aircraft changed its direction. The U.S. side says that the U.S. aircraft changed direction only after the collision (although this statement is not entirely plausible). However, the Chinese side has not presented any evidence or data. There has been no announcement of the discovery of the flight recorder of the Chinese aircraft. He who makes a charge should also present evidence. As long as the Chinese side does not have sufficient evidence, relying on a few words of testimony to put the blame on one side is unscientific.

Why is it that the rhetoric on the Chinese side was not much tougher? Although Wang Wei did not return, Zhao Hong did. All the U.S. crew members were in Chinese custody. The Chinese side therefore must have had a much clearer idea of the flight paths of the two aircraft than did the American side.

This logic doesn't apply just to airplanes. If a car on the highway speeding at over one hundred kph crashes into the back of a truck carrying a load of rocks, the car might be knocked a half meter or a meter into the next lane. If a vehicle does not stay in the proper lane and cuts into the lane of another car so that it is just a half meter or meter away from the other car or even closer, the decision on who is at fault in any resulting accident would depend upon which car was traveling in the proper lane. This is even more important in midair since there are air currents.

To make a simple analogy, if one side drives a bread truck and the bread truck stops on the street outside a marketplace to observe customer traffic, window displays, and other commercial intelligence, you might think that the people in the truck are very dishonest, but they haven't broken the rules of the game. They haven't gone into your market to take pictures. You might detest them. You can send two guards on motorcycles to bother them and disrupt their monitoring, but if there is a collision between the motorcycles and the truck, it must be objectively analyzed and handled as a traffic accident.

We all know that an aircraft changes direction differently from an automobile. An automobile remains horizontal when it turns, but an aircraft must bank as it turns. According to the statement of the Chinese side, the accident was caused by "the sudden turn of the U.S. aircraft." Therefore, if we assume that the Chinese plane was trailing several hundred meters behind, the U.S. plane must have been executing its turn when the collision occurred. Moreover, a very sharp turn would mean that the U.S. plane would have to bank nearly horizontally so that its wings would be at right angles to the earth.

According to information the Chinese side released on the damage to the U.S. plane, its left wing and nose were damaged in the collision. Please calculate the wingspan of the U.S. plane (more precisely the distance between the collision on the wing and the collision on the nose of the aircraft) and the vertical height of the tail of the Chinese aircraft (or even of the entire aircraft) and determine if it could have collided with these two points. If that is not possible, that might mean that the U.S. aircraft was in level flight at the time of the collision. That is, it was not turning and was flying straight ahead.

The video clips of Chinese fighter #85119 showing the fighter within feet of a Navy EP-3 on an earlier mission were released to the media by the U.S. Defense Department, and Chinese officials would not dare show this footage on Chinese TV. Thus the person who made this assessment obviously has access to cable television news—perhaps at a hotel for Westerners.

U.S. Policy on Reconnaissance

The United States readily admits that the EP-3 crew was engaged in reconnaissance, but U.S. policy took a different approach during the Cold War. Declassified archival material from the first year of the Nixon administration sheds light on Cold War policy regarding reconnaissance flights near Chinese territory. Under a policy in effect prior to April 1969, U.S. reconnaissance aircraft could fly as close as twenty miles to the Chinese coasts. Moreover, the traditional U.S. policy was to not acknowledge reconnaissance flight activity.

After North Korean MiGs shot down a Navy EC-121 over the Sea of Japan killing the thirty-man crew, President Richard Nixon temporarily halted reconnaissance flights in the region. In May, after a risk assessment had been performed, the flights resumed under new rules. For future flights, the closest point of approach to China (and North Korea) became fifty miles rather than twenty. In addition, to protect the reconnaissance missions, the U.S. Air Force deployed fighter aircraft to Taiwan on strip alert in the event of an incident—American fighters had not operated regularly from Taiwan since 1958.

Though fearful that the new policy "risks a clash between U.S. and Chinese Communist aircraft," the State Department reluctantly approved the plan. There were no incidents.

Toward the end of 1969 there were signals on both sides that the U.S. and China desired to improve relations. In October, the State Department suggested redeploying the Air Force fighters from Taiwan, noting that the U.S. reconnaissance aircraft were, at the time, flying about seventy-five miles from the Chinese coasts and that "the Chinese never threaten U.S. reconnaissance aircraft in the Taiwan Strait area even when they fly closer than seventy-five miles." The Air Force concurred, and the fighters left Taiwan. (The EP-3E in the 2001 incident was flying more than sixty miles from the Chinese coast, well beyond a range that could be considered provocative.)

In December 1969, Beijing and Washington agreed to resume formal discussions between their ambassadors to Poland. (This was before the U.S. and the PRC established diplomatic relations.) Being cautious, the State Department asked the military to take "special precautions" to avoid naval or aerial activities that could trigger an "incident" off the Chinese coast. On the day that the first round of talks began, the Pentagon assured the State Department that "current operating rules" were in order to keep U.S. forces away from "incident prone" areas near China.

Shortly thereafter a minor incident did occur, but it did not involve a reconnaissance aircrew—a malfunctioning American drone (pilotless plane) intended to fly over North Vietnam fell to earth on Hainan Island on February 10, 1970. The State Department prepared to address a formal complaint but nine days later there had still been no complaint. The State Department did not know what had happened, but speculated that Beijing was not going to "make a major issue of the incident." Another round of Sino-American talks resumed in Warsaw. In the event the Chinese did complain, a State Department official recommended that the U.S. hold its "traditional" stance of not acknowledging reconnaissance flights. He also urged our ambassador in Poland to make no apologies because that would set the wrong precedent; an apology could lead to explanations and Chinese demands that the United States stop flying reconnaissance missions near China.

Eventually, claiming to have shot down the drone, the Chinese government used the incident for internal propaganda. According to an uncorroborated source,[3] two Chinese naval officers, Qi Deqi and Zhou Xingcheng, of the Naval Air Force 4th Regiment, Division 8, claimed to have downed a drone on February 10, 1970, at Ledong on Hainan Island. On February 16, the Chinese press publicized the incident, including coverage of festivities on the island. The local populace rejoiced in the air defense unit's victory over "American imperialism," beginning the event with the song "The East Is Red" and concluding with "Sailing the Sea Depends on the Helmsman."[4] Celebrations not withstanding, the Chinese government did not formally complain about the incident.

Recently declassified National Archives records[5] reveal the true story. The drone was a Ryan 147SK—generally known as the SK-5—which failed as it was heading toward North Vietnam, not the PRC. The U.S. Navy used SK-5 drones for battle damage assessment, to evaluate targets before and after they had been bombed. An account of the incident prepared for veterans of the program in 1982 states that during a mission on February 10, 1970, the SK-5's beacon failed and its U.S. Navy operators, flying in a Navy E-2 Hawkeye aircraft, could not fly the drone properly. The drone ran out of fuel, and after its operators deployed its parachute, it landed on Hainan Island.

Apologize? No Way!

The requests for an apology from individual crew members came as often as their steady diet of rice; they were pressed repeatedly to apologize for their actions. The interrogator told them they would not be allowed to go home until they apologized. Lt.(jg) Richard Payne commented on the Chinese interrogators' attempts to obtain an apology at the crew's homecoming at Whidbey Bay NAS:

> They asked us for an apology the same as they asked the United States government. By the time they made their requests, we had already spoken to General Sealock [American Defense Attaché in China], who told us what President Bush's response was and we used those same words.

An apology would have amounted to capitulation and opened the door for a rogue nation to seize an American surveillance plane and crew from international airspace in some other part of the world. The tone of the Chinese note offered cautious optimism that the twenty-four EP-3 crew members would be released quickly. Yet, the state of Sino-American relations was extremely tense, and the thought of hostages no doubt entered some American minds. Not since the seizure of the USS *Pueblo* by

North Korea in 1968 had the United States been confronted with a similar potential hostage situation involving a detained U.S. reconnaissance crew.

Extremely strained diplomatic relations with China had only recently been repaired after a U.S. bomber on a NATO mission destroyed the Chinese Embassy in Belgrade, Serbia. That accidental bombing sparked bitter anti-American street protests in Beijing, and the Chinese military appeared to be attempting to stir up similar sentiment in response to this recent confrontation between the U.S. military and the PLA. (Despite the fact that the bombing of the Chinese embassy was clearly the fault of the United States, caused by a targeting error, it should not be overlooked that standard procedure of nonbelligerent countries in war zones is to remove their personnel, or at the very least their nonessential personnel, from harm's way. Without trying to ameliorate the American error, it must be noted that the Chinese were forcing their people to remain in a city where most of the other foreign embassies had been evacuated.)

To the Bush Administration and a majority of Americans, the Chinese demand for an apology and acceptance of full responsibility for what was clearly an accident, was unacceptable. In addition, the U.S. would never agree to give up its right to operate freely in international airspace adjacent to coastal China as the Chinese were demanding.

We're Very Sorry

In the end on April 11, Ambassador Prueher delivered to the Chinese Foreign Ministry a one-page letter that allowed each side to save face:

> . . . Both President Bush and Secretary of State Powell have expressed their sincere regret over your missing pilot and aircraft. Please convey to the Chinese people and to the family of pilot Wang Wei that we are very sorry for their loss.
>
> Although the full picture of what transpired is still unclear, according to our information, our severely crippled aircraft made an emergency landing after following international emergency procedures. We are very sorry the entering of China's airspace and the landing did not have verbal clearance, but very pleased the crew landed safely. . . .

The use of "very sorry" instead of "sorry" in the letter made the difference; prior to "very" being penned into the document twice, Chinese negotiators had rejected it. The U.S. side emphatically states that the letter is *not* an apology; Foreign Ministry spokesman Sun Yuxi called it a "letter of apology." An editorial in the Communist Party newspaper, the *People's Daily*, informed the Chinese people:

> *The firm struggle by the Chinese government and people against U.S. hegemony has forced the U.S. government to change from its initial rude and unreasonable attitude to saying "very sorry" to the Chinese government.*

After eleven tension-filled days in China, the EP-3 crew departed Hainan Island on April 12 aboard a chartered U.S. commercial Boeing 737 jet, bound for Guam, Hawaii, and ultimately Whidbey Island Naval Air Station, Washington, their home base.

The Chinese Media

The Communist Party controls the news media in the country, defining the Party line for general consumption. Immediately after the midair collision on April 1, Chinese media attention focused on charges of American responsibility for the incident. Three days later, state media focus began shifting to the fate of the missing Chinese pilot, Wang Wei, and the exhaustive efforts to search for him at sea. Several newspapers carried photographs of him standing by his aircraft in his flight suit, identifying him as a thirty-three-year-old squadron leader. The rhetoric whipped up a frenzy among the populace. Interviewed on Hainan Island, Zhang Qi expressed typical sentiment:

> *Of course we are angry with America. You bombed our embassy and killed three Chinese and said it was an accident. And now you have destroyed one of our planes and killed another Chinese off our coast, and say it was an accident. How would you feel if we did that to you?*

By April 11, media attention had shifted to condition public opinion regarding release of the crew. The Associated Press reported on April 12 that the crew's departure from Hainan "left some ordinary Chinese feeling that China had to settle for an inadequate end to another episode of American abuse."

> *Outside the military hostel where the crew were sequestered for most of their stay, Mao Yunzao, thirty-two, a laborer who spoke with the staccato accent of Mao Zedong's native Hunan Province, said: "America came and struck on our doorstep, but we can't strike back. If Mao were still around there would have been a war. . . ."*
>
> *Word spread Wednesday that the crew would be released after Chinese journalists, who are mid-ranking Communist Party members and above, were called to attend secret meetings at which they were ordered to stick to official New China News Agency accounts when reporting.*
>
> *The message, according to people who attended one meeting, was that America should be blamed for the incident and that the struggle would continue because the surveillance aircraft would remain on Chinese soil.*

On April 9, Asia specialists Bruce Elleman and S.C.M. Paine cited the U.S.-Chinese air incident as the most recent sign that Beijing seeks sovereignty over the entire South China Sea:

> *. . . Chinese leaders calculate that a foreign policy victory in the South China Sea will prop up the regime's waning authority. Faced with domestic opposition by disaffected intellectuals on the one hand and the Falun Gong movement on the other, the government aims to make nationalism a new rallying point to compensate for the declining ability of communism to unite the population in support of the government.*
>
> *Tensions between civilian and military leaders in China may be complicating the handling of the spy plane incident. It is unclear whether there is a consensus on what to do. . . .*
>
> *. . . The leadership may see the crisis as a way to rally the population, and so seek to prolong it. But the result would be to provoke additional U.S. arms sales to Taiwan and reprisals in the U.S. Congress that would undermine the trade on which continued Chinese economic development depends.*

Who's in Charge?

A *Washington Times* editorial sees that indecisiveness in Beijing: Their [EP-3E surveillance flights] very presence provokes the other country to turn on, or "light" up, its air defense and communication nets—all info the EP-3 is designed to collect. The editorial went on to note that the incident had created "hesitancy and confusion in the Chinese political decision-making mechanism," prompting the editors to ask "who's in charge?"

Repatriation: The China Rescue Mission

During negotiations for release of the crew the Chinese government insisted that a civilian aircraft be used to repatriate the EP-3E crew. The U.S. government negotiated a contract with Continental Airlines to fly a commercial jet to Hainan Island on what was later dubbed the "China Rescue Mission": Capt. Guy Greider was one of three Continental pilots who headed up the crew that carried out the repatriation. This description of the rescue mission is based on Captain Greider's comments on the trip to China.

Continental Airlines was chosen for the mission because of its Guam base and its ability to launch such an operation on a moment's notice. Continental's director of Micronesia Flight Operations began assembling a crew on Saturday, April 7, 2001. The selected crew (three pilots, five flight attendants, two onboard mechanics, and a load planner) remained on standby until Wednesday evening, April 11, 2001, when they were asked to report to the airport for a briefing. The U.S. and Chinese governments were close to an agreement to release the detained Navy EP-3E crew.

Continental provided a 155-passenger Boeing 737 for the mission. A Repatriation Team of Navy, Marine Corps, and Air Force specialists— fourteen persons including doctors, psychologists, and communications experts—accompanied the Continental crew to China. Not knowing the condition of the twenty-four detained crew members, the Repatriation Team carried with them two full stretcher kits bolted in over rows of seats, complete with oxygen tanks and IV bottles. They were prepared for all eventualities.

In approving the mercy mission, the Chinese stipulated that the civilian airliner should arrive in China—at Haikou Airport on Hainan— no earlier than 6:00 A.M. Planning accordingly, the Continental flight departed Guam at 2:15 A.M. In addition to the stretcher kits and medical gear, Continental had loaded an additional navigational data file in the onboard flight management computer to allow the crew access to navigation information needed for flying within China. In addition, the Repatriation Team carried sophisticated equipment to communicate with the military and government officials that would monitor progress throughout the flight.

After flying west toward the Philippines—remaining well outside Taiwanese airspace to avoid offending the Chinese—the Continental crew turned north directly toward Hong Kong. Approaching the Chinese coastline, they contacted Hong Kong radar control; Hong Kong gave them a shortcut to expedite traffic flow. The unplanned turn cut off considerable distance, causing their onboard computer to project an early arrival at Haikou. The crew compensated by slowing their airspeed until their computer projected a 6:00 A.M. arrival. The turn also caused concerns among the onboard Repatriation Team. The instant the plane made the unplanned turn, the team asked for an explanation over the aircraft interphone. With the adjusted speed, the flight touched down at Haikou at 6:07, daybreak.

An English-speaking Air China employee came onboard, the only Chinese person to board the plane. He announced that he would act as a translator between the American group and the Chinese military. He asked that each person onboard fill out both arrival and departure documents and collected everyone's passports. Only one person was allowed off the airliner at a time. One of the Continental mechanics deplaned and supervised the refueling and aircraft servicing, followed by Captain Greider, who left the plane to conduct the captain's walk-around inspection. During the walk-around, he noticed a skirmish with Chinese police as unidentified persons attempted to climb a wall to photograph the aircraft. [A CNN TV crew managed to carry live coverage of the arrival and departure of the repatriation flight.]

With the plane serviced and ready to go, the waiting process began; there was still no sign of buses carrying the twenty-four detainees. Momentarily, U.S. Army General Sealock, military attaché in Beijing, arrived on the scene and stormed on the Boeing 737 demanding to speak with the captain. There was a paperwork problem, and the entire mission was in jeopardy. In completing a "general declaration" document—a standard form on all international flights—the Continental crew had listed their destination as China R.O.C. The Chinese were very upset; R.O.C. stands for Republic of China (Taiwan). The Continental captain crossed out R.O.C. and wrote in P.R.O.C. (People's Republic of China). This seemed to satisfy the Chinese officials.

With the minicrisis resolved, two buses arrived and twenty-four smiling U.S. service personnel saluted as they bolted up the stairs. After the last detainee came aboard, the Air China employee returned all passports and left the aircraft. The crew closed the cabin door, started engines, and departed. As they headed straight south and departed the Chinese coast, an announcement over the interphone that they were over international waters brought a great cheer from the back of the plane.

Moments later the Continental flight received a telephone call over their HF radio from Joseph Prueher, U.S. Ambassador to China. The ambassador wanted to speak to Lt. Shane Osborn, mission commander of the EP-3E crew. Lieutenant Osborn took the call using a pair of headsets in the airliner cabin. On behalf of the president of the United States, the ambassador welcomed the crew home and thanked them for an outstanding job.

The repatriated crew received VIP treatment during the five-hour trip to Anderson AFB, Guam. Following a first-class meal, they were treated to the movie *Men of Honor*. Unbeknownst to anyone on the plane, hundreds of people turned out to welcome everyone home upon arrival at Anderson. The twenty-four EP-3E crew members and the Repatriation Team deplaned to the cheers of military and civilians waving small American flags.

After a brief stop on Guam, the EP-3E crew boarded an Air Force C-17 jet transport and continued to Hickam AFB, Hawaii. Another warm welcoming committee and a debriefing awaited them in Honolulu.

Aloha: The Crew Arrives in Hawaii

The huge gray C-17 transport plane ferrying the EP-3's crew touched down at Hickam Air Force Base on April 12 at first light, about 6:20 A.M. Fifteen minutes later, the C-17 taxied toward a mass of television cameras, and one by one, the crew members in their flight suits appeared in the doorway, saluted, and made their way to a receiving line of welcoming VIPs. A crowd of several hundred—people in uniform as well as crew members' families—had gathered. There was a brass band and a color guard of sailors, an airman, and a marine. Amid handmade cardboard signs reading "Pride" and "Honor," the crowd cheered and waved little American flags. Adm. Thomas B. Fargo, the Pacific Fleet commander, welcomed the crew with a hearty aloha.

All are very proud of you and the way you conducted yourselves. Welcome back and well done for this great crew.

Reuters covered Lt. Shane Osborn's brief remarks during the ceremony at Hickam.

"The first thing I'd like to say on behalf of the crew is we are definitely glad to be back. But we obviously have some business we have to take care of. On that note, I'd like to start so we can go home."

He assured the crew members' families that his fellow crew members "miss them very much—they're all healthy and would like to get home." He said the crew planned to be home by Easter, and added, "On behalf of Combat Reconnaissance Crew No. 1, I'd like to thank you, and God bless America."

President Bush, speaking with reporters at the White House, offered a warm welcome home to the twenty-four Americans, calling them "a reminder of the debt all Americans owe" to men and women in uniform. Then he had tough words about the entire episode, asserting that the United States plane had been in international airspace "and did nothing to cause the accident. . . ."

During the welcoming ceremony, the crew members were read a letter from Defense Secretary Donald Rumsfeld. "Throughout your days in detention you conducted yourself with honor and professionalism," the letter said. "You put your lives at risk in the service of the citizens of a grateful nation so they can live their lives in peace and freedom. We welcome you back to the United States."

Debriefings by a dozen teams of specialists began about 10:00 A.M. A naval officer familiar with the debriefing plan said the Repatriation Teams represented a wide range of organizations from different parts of the country, many cloaked in the acronyms beloved by the military.

One group, for instance, is from SERE, which stands for Survival, Escape, Resistance, and Evasion. This is a kind of training given to troops who might fall into enemy territory, to help them avoid capture— and, if they are captured, teach them to resist interrogation.

The SERE team will want to know how effective its training was and how the Chinese behaved toward the Americans. And when it comes to the electronic eavesdropping and other intelligence devices on the plane and what the Chinese might have learned from or about them, the discussions will take place in a SCIF, or Sensitive Compartmented Information Facility, a special soundproof room immune to bugging. The plane is still on the tarmac in Hainan, and the Chinese are presumed to be taking it apart.

Hopefully SERE training had made the crew's eleven-day stay in Chinese custody more tolerable.

Interception and Harassment

After two days of rest and debriefing, Lieutenant Osborn spoke on behalf of his crew at a news conference before they departed Hickam AFB en route to an open-house welcome home party at Whidbey Island NAS, Washington, on April 14. For the first time in public, he talked about the midair collision. He reiterated parts of the story he had told Captain Greider, the Continental Airlines pilot, in the cockpit of the Boeing

737 en route from China to Guam. In pilot-to-pilot discussions with Greider, he described how the Chinese F-8 fighter bumped their EP-3E.

The fighter came up under their left wing. Earlier, the Chinese pilot had made two very close passes, intercepting at an angle from the rear. On his final pass, the F-8 pilot apparently misjudged his closure rate and closing distance. His vertical stabilizer struck the outboard left (No. 1) propeller on the EP-3. At the time, Osborn's crew was flying straight and level on autopilot. The collision knocked the EP-3 off autopilot, and the aircraft rolled to the left. The fighter broke into two pieces and plunged into the sea.

After the Chinese fighter struck the propeller, it raked across the fuselage and tore off the EP-3's nose radome, causing Osborn's plane to buffet wildly. When the radome broke away, it collided with and damaged the EP-3's No. 4 propeller on the right wing and knocked off the pitot tubes on the forward fuselage—eliminating airspeed and altitude indications in the cockpit. In addition, the collision caused the aircraft cabin to depressurize, bringing forceful winds and noise into the aircraft. It also dislodged the forward bracket of the HF radio antenna, and the antenna ended up wrapped around the EP-3's tail.

The episode began late into a ten-hour mission, while the EP-3 was lumbering along at 200 mph. The collision caused the EP-3 to lunge to an almost inverted angle of about 130 degrees before Lieutenant Osborn and his copilot regained control. "Another few seconds and it would have been unrecoverable," Osborn said. He finally managed to regain straight and level flight at about 8,000 feet altitude. Crew members had donned their parachutes.

Osborn gave the command to ditch the plane but later retracted it. Ditching would almost certainly end in loss of life. In the end, Osborn chose to head for the nearest airfield, on Hainan Island.

The crew made numerous Mayday radio calls on internationally recognized emergency frequencies, but Osborn admits that he may not have been able to hear a reply due to the holes in the pressure bulkhead that brought winds and shrilling, loud noise into the aircraft. Somehow, they managed to get the EP-3 on the ground safely. As the crew worked frantically to destroy sensitive electronic surveillance equipment and classified materials aboard the aircraft, Chinese military approached and yelled at them through loudspeakers to deplane.

As it turned out, they fared better in the hands of the Chinese than most expected. Their food was adequate, sort of like three meals a day in a Chinese restaurant. By the fourth day, the Chinese served them coffee, and on the fifth day, they were provided Cokes.

The Chinese later identified the pilot who collided with the EP-3E as Wang Wei, a naval air force fighter pilot.

The Real Story Emerges

With the crew safely out of Chinese custody, Pentagon officials began openly discussing the midair collision. They portrayed the pilot Wang Wei as something of a showoff who had repeatedly flown dangerously close to American surveillance planes, at times coming within three to five feet of the intercepted aircraft.

The Chinese government received little support in the international press regarding its claims that the American aircraft banked sharply immediately before the collision and ran into the Chinese jet. A Dutch "P-3 Orion Research Group" completed an analysis of the collision.

". . . Obviously the F-8 and EP-3E were so close to each other that the vertical stabilizer of the F-8 came into the propeller. Exactly the same thing happened when a Soviet Flanker [SU-27 interceptor] tried to accelerate from his position below the right wing of a Norwegian P-3B."

A Norwegian airman aboard the P-3B in the September 1987 incident reported that the Flanker [SU-27 interceptor] flew less than five meters from the P-3 and moved slightly outward, diving back in just below the right wing. Igniting his jet's afterburners, the Flanker pilot pulled up too close. His right vertical stabilizer struck the No. 4 propeller on the P-3, causing damage very similar to the damage on the Navy EP-3E's No. 1 propeller in the midair collision with the Chinese F-8 fighter.

Comparing photographs of the Norwegian P-3's damaged propeller and the beaten-up propeller on the EP-3E, the researcher found it quite plausible that the F-8's stabilizer may have impacted with the propeller. And that collision may have caused the Chinese pilot to lose control momentarily, swerving to the right and immediately in front of the EP-3 where his jet struck and dislodged the nose radome from the EP-3.

Based on a photograph of the EP-3E aircraft provided by the Chinese, antenna mounts on the left wing appear to be bent forward, suggesting that whatever tore the antennas from the mounts may have been coming from the back of the aircraft and traveling forward. In other words, the Chinese F-8 pilot would appear to have zoomed in for an intercept, approached way too close, and struck the EP-3's left wing. In the photograph, a black antenna on the front side of the wing is not damaged, but two similar antennas seem to have been ripped out by the collision; the antenna mounts remained on the wing. In addition, a cut is evident in the aileron on the left wing. Comparing photographs, damage to the Norwegian P-3—struck by the stabilizer of a Soviet fighter approaching from the rear—is quite similar to damage to the EP-3E on Hainan Island. This comparative analysis lends credence to claims that the Chinese pilot ran into the American EP-3 while intercepting the slower flying plane from the rear.

Another captioned photograph in the researchers' report provides evidence of a similar incident of the interception and harassment of EP-3E crews. That photo shows a Soviet MiG-23 interceptor very close to and banking away from the left wing of another EP-3E two years ago.

Discussing events leading up to the EP-3 and F-8 collision, one of the EP-3 pilots, Lt. Patrick Honeck said that the Chinese pilot, Wang Wei, saluted the American crew on his first pass and "mouthed something to us" on the second. Commenting on the third interception that resulted in the collision, Honeck noticed the Chinese F-8 jet pull up under the port wing; "It was kind of surreal—like slow motion." At the time, their mission commander, Lt. Shane Osborn, was in the right pilot's seat, writing notes about the earlier midair harassment, a practice that had long been commonplace during electronic surveillance missions.

Causing the No. 1 engine to lose power and vibrate severely, the collision forced the EP-3 off autopilot, and the plane plunged suddenly to the left in a sharp dive. Chaos reigned as Lieutenant Osborn worked to regain control. Recovering from possible disaster, mission navigator

Lt. (jg) Regina Kauffman set a course for Hainan Island, a harrowing fifteen-minute flight for the frightened crew.

According to remarks attributed to an experienced P-3 pilot, an EP-3E aircraft operating on three engines cannot sustain altitudes above 18,000 feet (slightly higher toward the end of a mission when the plane is lighter). Loss of the engine may explain in part the rapid loss of about 8,000 feet of altitude by the EP-3 on April 1. The experienced P-3 pilot reportedly told the Dutch researcher that loss of the nose radome was no big deal, claiming it had happened many times on a P-3. He did, however, consider the loss of the engine a big deal, especially since the No. 1 propeller appeared to have jammed in the flight range instead of the feathered position. This would explain the reported severe vibrations, and if the e-handle [emergency shutdown handle] were pulled, that could make things worse with the propeller in the flight position.

Adding to the problems, Lieutenant Osborn reportedly landed without functional flaps and without an airspeed indicator. EP-3 pilots are said to practice no-flap landings and don't consider the loss of flaps a serious problem—depending on center of gravity, aircraft, weight, length of runway, etc.

The loss of the ASI is a further complicating factor that can be compensated for under certain conditions. An experienced pilot can use Doppler indicated speed corrected for wind speed and be able to estimate air speed for the approach, although this is ground speed instead of air speed. In addition, a seasoned pilot can fix power settings equating to a certain speed, but the missing radome would create extra drag. Thus this technique might not be effective with a damaged airframe. Finally, the pilot could fly the approach "guessing" the speed across the ground visually while adding a "comfort factor." This guessing approach would definitely be the last choice. The expert pilot reportedly told the Dutch researcher that any one of these anomalies by itself was not critical, but taken collectively, Lieutenant Osborn's crew did a great job of getting their aircraft on the deck safely.

Midair Harassment

According to the Department of Defense (and Taiwanese officials), the interception of the EP-3 mission on April 1 represented a continuation of harassing interceptions that had been occurring in international airspace off China during the past year. On April 28, 2000, a Taiwanese general stated that two Chinese F-8 jets intercepted a U.S. Air Force RC-135 reconnaissance aircraft operating in international airspace at 28,000 feet over the East China Sea the previous day. The general added, "This was the first time in three years that the People's Liberation Army air force scrambled to intercept aircraft out of its airspace." The *Washington Times* reported that the Chinese jets closed to within two miles of the American reconnaissance aircraft. U.S. officials claim such intercept missions have become more frequent during the past year.

Subsequent to the midair collision, Secretary of Defense Rumsfeld described at a press conference how Chinese fighter pilots had been harassing other U.S. flights in international airspace near China. He played audio and video tapes of what were said to be previous encounters with Chinese jets. The video tapes, recorded by a different EP-3 crew on a mission prior to the April 1 incident, clearly show a Chinese fighter aircraft passing within a few feet of the intercepted American plane—an American pilot aboard the intercepted EP-3 is heard saying: "We got thumped." Discussing thumping and possible causes of the midair collision, a former RC-135 reconnaissance pilot recently discussed real world surveillance operations under adversarial fighter escort.

As an RC-135 aircraft commander, Robert Hopkins flew peacetime aerial reconnaissance missions around the world, in many cases being escorted by various fighter/interceptors from nations ranging from the USSR to Israel. He found that the escorts broke the monotony; some were "quite enjoyable." On one occasion, he recalled flying an RC-135S COBRA BALL mission over the North Pacific in formation with a Soviet TU-16 Badger for over three hours; the TU-16 escort even watched Hopkins's RC-135 rendevous with a KC-135 tanker and refuel.

Reconnoitering the reconnaissance mission, the Badger crew kept its distance from the American plane, but on other occasions, some interceptor pilots were aggressive to the point of endangering flight safety, usually trying to "shoo" the U.S. recon missions away or to establish their "pilot bona fides."

Hopkins found the North Korean and North Vietnamese to be the most aggressive; they were automatic "get out of town" intercepts due to outright hostility toward the United States and the unpredictability of their controllers. The Israelis were indignant at having U.S. surveillance planes flying along their borders, and he considered Israeli pilots the most dangerous in their attempts to discourage reconnaissance.

He also reminsiced about war stories passed on to him by U.S. Navy F-4 and F-14 pilots who often revel in their tales of how close, how long, and how risky they could get during intercept missions. He used the tales from his Navy F-4 and F-14 colleagues to point out that all the possible causes of the collision between the Navy EP-3 and the Chinese F-8 are common environments in the escort world. According to Hopkins, a high-speed interception from the rear and above (or below) at near Mach is extremely routine and is called "thumping." As the fighter passes the heavier intercept aircraft, the fighter pilot pulls up abruptly, causing shock waves to beat upon the bigger plane.

In a variation on this theme, the fighter pilot pulls in front of an engine—average pilots go for an outboard engine and "hot dogs" go for an inboard—and turns on the afterburner in an effort to cause cavitation of the engine. If successful, the reconnaissance crew must abort and leave the area. On other occasions, the fighter pilot might slow down in front of the heavier plane to the point where the recon crew may leave the area to avoid ramming the interceptor. Of course, these maneuvers are more difficult for the interceptor pilot since a fighter plane is increasingly unstable at high angles and slow speeds—more so than the heavier reconnaissance aircraft. Part of the interceptor's goal is to approach as close as possible, but this does not absolve the interceptor pilot of the responsibility for flight safety.

In one video frame series covering prior interceptions by Chinese pilots, the jet fighter is so close to the cameraman aboard the U.S. aircraft that the fighter pilot can be seen waving and holding up a sheet of paper with an unidentified message on it. Some press reports claim the waving Chinese fighter pilot was Wang Wei, and that he was displaying his e-mail address.

Acknowledging that its air force pilots scramble to follow and intercept foreign aircraft operating over international airspace, the Chinese military denies that its pilots approach closer to intercepted planes than authorized by international law or that its pilots harass surveillance flights operating outside Chinese airspace. Under international law addressing the interception of foreign aircraft over international airspace, fighter-interceptor pilots must remain at sufficient range from their intercepted target aircraft to avoid infringing on flight safety. Secretary Rumsfeld's video footage shows otherwise.

After the EP-3 crew was released, two U.S. diplomats who played central roles in negotiations to win the crew's release said, on condition their names not be used, there is some doubt that the landing at Lingshui had been a total surprise to the base.

> . . . They said a second Chinese tracking jet, after witnessing the collision, had landed at the same field ten minutes earlier. They also said that the runway appeared to have been cleared for the ailing craft's arrival and that the Americans signaled their intent to land with a 270-degree "clearing turn" above the airbase.
>
> The diplomats also reasserted the firm United States belief—contradicting Beijing's claim—that reckless flying by the Chinese jet pilot caused the collision, leading to the first crisis in relations between the Bush Administration and China. The claim of reckless flying was supported in Washington by Defense Secretary Donald H. Rumsfeld, who said at a news conference: "The Chinese pilots have been maneuvering aggressively against our pilots for months. The F-8 pilot clearly put at risk the lives of twenty-four Americans."

Asked about his thoughts at the moment of the midair collision, Lieutenant Osborn replied emphatically, "This guy just killed us." Faced with a life and death situation, Osborn recovered quickly, executed emergency procedures flawlessly that he and his crew had practiced often but hoped they would never have to use. Experience gained in prior emergency procedures training exercises paid off on April 1. To a person, Lieutenant Osborn's crew credit him with saving their lives by recovering from what could have been disaster and safely landing their critically damaged plane. They left their EP-3E aircraft behind at Lingshui, China; negotiations are underway to bring it home.

Getting Her out of China

Defense Department official Peter Verga headed a team who commenced meetings with Chinese diplomats in Beijing on April 18, 2001, to discuss issues related to the U.S.-Chinese air incident. Upon arrival, Verga told the press, "We are here to meet with the Chinese government to exchange information regarding the incident with our reconnaissance aircraft and that is all." He cited four items that the Bush administration wanted to discuss and resolve:

- the cause of the collision
- how to avoid such accidents in the future
- Chinese intercept practices
- the return of the EP-3E

The Chinese insist that the United States end surveillance missions near its shores, while the U.S. has announced plans to resume such reconnaissance missions, suspended in the aftermath of the crash. The Chinese regard the flights as humiliating as well as a threat to national defense. Meanwhile, Chinese diplomats have lodged countercharges, claiming U.S. Navy carrier-based fighter pilots have buzzed Chinese aircraft over the Chinese seas, approaching their fighters too close for flight safety. They have provided their own video clips, purportedly showing these close encounters. And discussions on the return of the EP-3E drag on.

Welcome Home

The twenty-four members of Combat Reconnaissance Crew 1, who had been detained in China two weeks earlier, ended their long journey home on April 14—stepping off a plane at Whidbey Island NAS, Washington, into the arms of loved ones as 7,000 well-wishers welcomed them home. Clad in flight suits, the crew disembarked from a Navy jet one at a time, led by their mission commander, Lt. Shane Osborn. Osborn, who landed their disabled plane in China two weeks earlier, addressed the assembled crowd:

> *I'd like to thank God for allowing myself and my crew to be here because it was definitely Him flying that plane.*

The crew waved back to a sea of flag-wavers who had been waiting hours for their plane to land. Of their welcome home, Lt.(jg) Jeffrey Vignery expressed his American pride:

> *"I had no idea what kind of welcome we would receive. I can say I've never felt so proud to be an American in my life."*

The crowd interrupted the hour-long arrival ceremony several times with hearty applause. The town of Oak Harbor, where sixty percent of the 21,000 residents are affiliated in some manner with the base, was proud to have its men and women back. Oak Harbor's mayor said the town and base are so inextricably linked that probably neither could function well without the other.

> *We take pride in the relationship. When these folks walk off the base, they're our soccer coaches and our softball coaches, and their spouses are our deacons and our teachers. They define who we are as a community.*

If only momentarily, the crew's return home raised the spirit of many Americans throughout the world. What might have ended in tragedy became a national homecoming.

Other U.S.-Chinese Air Incidents

During the Cold War, more than 200 other U.S. military "Silent Warriors," who were involved in airborne intelligence gathering missions, were not as fortunate. They became KIA and MIA statistics.

Twenty-two of these losses (four KIAs and eighteen MIAs) resulted from attacks by Chinese air defense forces against U.S. Navy surveillance missions. These losses involving Chinese forces are in addition to Navy losses in U.S.-Soviet Cold War air incidents—twenty-one missing in action (MIA) in four Soviet shootdowns—and two killed in action (KIA) and twenty-eight MIAs in the shootdown of a Navy EC-121 by North Korean fighters in April 1969. The U.S.-Soviet air incidents are discussed in chapter two.

Other U.S government surveillance losses included thirty-five KIAs (mostly Navy men), killed during the Cold War in two separate attacks on intelligence collection ships. One sailor was killed in 1968 when the USS *Pueblo* was attacked and captured by the North Koreans, and thirty-four men died in 1967 when the Israeli Defense Forces attacked the USS *Liberty* in the Mediterranean Sea. The Israeli government apologized, claiming that in the heat of battle the IDF had misidentified the *Liberty* as an Egyptian ship.

Each of these losses occurred while American crews were engaged in peacetime reconnaissance, highlighting the dangers that surveillance crews routinely face. The dangers increase immensely when an adversarial relationship, such as that between the United States military and the People's Liberation Army of China, exists.

Relations with Taiwan and China

A quick history lesson helps, at least in part, to explain the tense relationship between the military forces of the United States and China. Relations between the United States and the People's Republic of China have not been good since the Chinese Communist Party came to power in 1949. The ideology of the two countries—democracy versus communism (autocracy)—creates friction and mistrust; American support for

China's archrival, the Nationalist Chinese on Taiwan, further worsens the relationship.

The rift between the Nationalists and the Chinese Communists dates back to the early twentieth century. Sun Yat-sen formed the Kuomintang (Nationalist Party) and created the Republic of China in 1912. The Chinese Communist Party was formed in 1921 and initially shared power with the Nationalists. Assuming control of the Nationalists upon Sun's death in 1925, Chiang Kai-shek purged his party of its Communist membership, forcing the Communist movement underground.

Faced with Japanese aggression, the Nationalists and the Communists formed a united front against the Japanese in 1937. During World War II, the Nationalists suffered more serious military losses than the Communists; the Communists expanded their territorial bases, military forces and party membership. Thus the Communists emerged from WW II a far larger and stronger force than the Nationalists, and fighting broke out between the two sides over the reoccupation of Manchuria shortly after Japan surrendered in 1945.

The conflict expanded into a civil war. Finally unable to continue their resistance, Nationalist forces sought refuge on the island of Taiwan, formally moving the government of the Republic of China to Taipei, Taiwan, on December 8, 1949. Meanwhile on October 1, 1949, the Communists created the People's Republic of China (PRC) on the mainland, with its capital in Beijing.

The United States and most of its Western allies did not recognize the legitimacy of the "People's" government. Instead, the United States rearmed Chiang Kai-shek's forces on Taiwan, and the PRC signed a treaty of friendship and alliance with the Soviet Union in 1950. Sino-American relations were further inflamed in 1950 when the U.S. foiled the People's Liberation Army plans to invade Taiwan by sending naval forces to defend the island.

One China Policy

On coming to power, the Communists began initiatives to regain areas the PRC considered to be within the historic boundaries of China. Chou En-lai officially established the "liberation" of Taiwan as one of his country's primary objectives. And, from time to time, Chiang Kai-shek asserted his intention to reconquer the mainland. In 1954 the Communists began bombarding offshore islands held by Chiang's government in the Taiwan Strait (Quemoy, Tachen, Matsu, etc.); Taiwan retaliated with air and naval raids against the mainland in 1955. Skirmishes continued for three years. A cease-fire in 1958 has been generally observed by both sides, but from time to time the Communist regime threatens to take Taiwan by force.

Both the People's Republic of China (mainland) and the Republic of China (Taiwan) contend that there is only one China. The PRC considers Taiwan a renegade province, and the ROC would like to replace the PRC's Communist government with Taiwan's elected Republican government. Throughout the 1960s Taiwan enjoyed wide diplomatic relations throughout the world. But by the early 1970s, Taiwan's international situation changed drastically as countries began shifting their formal relations to the PRC on the mainland.

The People's Republic of China was admitted to the United Nations in 1971, replacing the Republic of China (Taiwan). President Richard Nixon made an official visit to China in 1972, leading to the eventual withdrawal of U.S. troops from Taiwan and the opening of liaison offices in Beijing and Washington in 1973. The PRC established full diplomatic relations with Japan in 1972 and with the United States in 1979. While establishing diplomatic relations with the PRC and breaking formal ties with Taiwan, most nations, including the U.S., maintain informal relations and trade agreements with the island nation. The United States also maintains a defense pact with Taiwan, a continuing barrier to better relations between the U.S. and China.

The Taiwanese government formulated a long-term, three-phase plan in 1991 for reunification with mainland China. In 1993 representatives from Taiwan and China met in Singapore to discuss a relationship and establish a schedule for subsequent meetings between the two governments. The Singapore meeting was the first high-level contact between China and Taiwan since 1949. These PRC-ROC relations deteriorated in 1995 as the Chinese military was allowed to flex its muscles in military exercises near Taiwan, seen by many as intimidation and threats against pro-independence movements on the island. While a shaky status quo continues, the United States remains committed to provide Taiwan with adequate defensive weapons to defend against forced reunification with the mainland government.

Chinese Signals Intelligence Capabilities

Some have questioned why the United States would conduct surveillance missions off the coast of China, never mind that the Navy aircraft was operating legally in international airspace. As stated in a Chinese government protest note, the Navy EP-3E was flying 104 kilometers from Chinese territory when the Chinese sent two F-8 fighters "to follow and monitor the U.S. plane." The fact is that the United States, China, and all nations conduct intelligence gathering, some with more sophisticated means than others and for different purposes.

Signals intelligence (SIGINT)—monitoring and exploiting an adversary's electronic and communications activities—is one of the most popular and lucrative of all intelligence operations. China focuses its SIGINT activities primarily within its neighborhood, which is not to say that it does not snoop on the United States. It does.

But territorial clashes have resulted in mistrust and adversity between China and its neighbors. Since coming to power in 1949, the Communist regime has attempted to regain areas it considers to be within China's historic boundaries. In the late 1990s, it regained control of Hong Kong and Macao, and would have taken Taiwan by force fifty years ago if the United States had not defended the island nation. While maintaining a status quo vis-à-vis Taiwan, the Chinese leadership has increased its military might and expanded its influence in Asia.

In 1950 it invaded Tibet and forced the Tibetans to live under Chinese rule. The same year, China and the Soviet Union signed a treaty of friendship and alliance, but a decade later the two neighbors would be competing for leadership of the world Communist movement. Soviet influence over Outer Mongolia affects Sino-Russian relations to this day. In 1969, Chinese troops attacked Soviet border guards along the Ussuri River—the border between China and the USSR—creating an explosive situation.

Later in March 1974, according to an uncorroborated Russian source,[6] a Soviet Border Guards MI-4 helicopter crew on a scouting mission along the Sino-Soviet border became disoriented and accidentally overflew the border south of Belesha village in the Altay Kray and landed in China when it ran out of fuel. Despite numerous Soviet protests to the Chinese government, the three MI-4 crewmen were imprisoned until December 1975, when both the crew and the helicopter were returned. The authors of the Russian articles were unable to find accounts of other similar incidents in Soviet or foreign press archives. However, they mentioned an incident on August 25, 1990, in which a Chinese MiG-19 crossed the Soviet border and landed at Knevichi, a Soviet naval air force base near Vladivostok. On August 30, 1990, the Soviets returned the Chinese pilot and aircraft. The tense Sino-Soviet rift continued throughout the 1970s and 1980s, easing somewhat in 1989 after then Soviet leader Mikhail Gorbachev patched up the relationship during a visit to Beijing.

Chinese troops also occupied thousands of miles of disputed territory on the Indian border—in 1959. Fighting between China and India ended in 1962, and China later withdrew to the pre-1959 borders. Indonesia, another Asian neighbor, forced the Chinese to withdraw its embassy staff from Djakarta in 1965 because the embassy had been actively fomenting a communist revolution in the Indonesian archipelago.

During the 1970s relations between China and Vietnam also became strained. In 1974, China seized the Paracel Islands in the South China Sea from Vietnam. Later in 1978, Vietnam expelled thousands of ethnic Chinese, resulting in China closing its border with Vietnam. Then when Vietnam invaded Cambodia and toppled its Chinese-backed government in January 1979, China retaliated by sending PLA troops into Vietnam in February. It withdrew the PLA forces a month later but the incident precipitated the expulsion of hundreds of thousands of ethnic Chinese from Vietnam, causing international concern over the expelled "boat people" during the 1980s. Finally, China, Vietnam, the Philippines, Malaysia, and Brunei lay claim to the disputed Spratly Islands in the South China Sea. China recently warned Vietnam that China has "indisputable sovereignty" over the Spratlys and adjacent waters, and cautioned Manila that the Scarborough Shoals, in the South China Sea off the Philippines, are China's "innate territory."

Signals intelligence plays a major role in China's military operations vis-à-vis its neighbors. Professor Desmond Ball of the Australian National University described China's SIGINT operations a decade ago. China reportedly had (and, no doubt, still has) dozens of SIGINT ground stations deployed throughout its country to monitor signals from Russia, Japan, Taiwan, Southeast Asia, and India. The mission of these intercept sites would be to monitor its adversaries in order to create and maintain a database defining its adversaries' military capabilities, operating procedures, and intentions—the same type of mission the U.S. Navy EP-3 crew was performing when tragedy struck on April 1, 2001. In addition, with internal unrest intensifying, the Chinese no doubt employ extensive SIGINT resources to monitor Falun Gong and other dissident activities.

Professor Ball identified the two largest SIGINT stations as the main Technical Department SIGINT net control in Beijing and a large complex near Lake Kinghathu in the extreme northeast corner of China. Intercept sites at Jilemutu and Jixi in the northeast, and at Erlian and Hami near the Mongolian border, are said to be oriented to intercept and exploit Russian signals. Two more sites—in Xinjiang, at Qitai, and Korla—are in a special category. They have reportedly been operated by China jointly with the U.S. Central Intelligence Agency's Office of SIGINT Operations since the late 1980s. These sites were originally tasked to monitor Soviet missile tests and space launches, but their current status is uncertain.

A large station at Chengdu, supplemented by the nearby facility at Dayi and numerous smaller posts along the Indian border, reportedly covers SIGINT operations against India, while a major complex at Kunming mainly covers Indochina—most notably Vietnam. Other significant facilities are located near Shenyang, near Jinan, and in Nanjing and Shanghai. Additional stations are in the Fujian and Guangdong military districts opposite Taiwan. Two more large SIGINT facilities are said to be on Hainan Island, a large complex mainly monitoring signals activity in and around the South China Sea, and a ground station believed to be capable of intercepting and decrypting signals transmitted through U.S.

and Russian communications satellites. While the Navy EP-3 crew were detained on Hainan, there were rumors that Lingshui, where the crew made its emergency landing, was home to a large Chinese "intelligence complex."

According to Professor Ball's treatise, "half a dozen ships, truck-mounted systems, airborne systems, and a limited satellite collection capability" supplement the capabilities of the Chinese SIGINT ground stations, serving as mobile electronic intelligence (ELINT) signal collection platforms. The ships and aircraft operate under the command of the South Sea Fleet, headquartered at Zhanjiang, immediately north of Hainan.

Little is known publicly about China's airborne SIGINT reconnaissance systems. According to Ball, the four engine turboprop EY-8, an indigenous variant of the Russian AN-12 (NATO nickname Cub), was China's main ELINT surveillance aircraft a decade ago; subsequently the PLA may have acquired four or more locally modified TU-154M jet transports for airborne SIGINT reconnaissance. The Antonov-12 Cub is a high-winged airframe similar in appearance to the U.S. Air Force C-130 shot down over Armenia in 1958, and variants of the C-130 still serve as SIGINT collection platforms for the U.S. and its allies. Intelligence analysts speculate that the People's Liberation Army (PLA) TU-154M ELINT platform has capabilities similar to the Soviet four engine turboprop IL-20 Coot, the primary Soviet SIGINT airborne platform since the late 1970s. The IL-20, a variant of the IL-18 used as a commercial passenger aircraft, has a flight crew of four or five and twenty "mission specialists," i.e., intelligence technicians (a crew composition similar to the U.S. Navy EP-3).

Chinese PLA naval SIGINT capabilities appear more extensive. At least eight specialized ships were operational a decade ago, and their number has since grown to at least ten intelligence-gathering auxiliary vessels. The extent to which PLA ships and aircraft shadow U.S. operations in the Pacific appears to be minimal; U.S. sources in Honolulu noted three years ago that Chinese submarines had never sought to mirror Soviet surveillance of U.S. Pacific Command facilities in Hawaii. And unlike the Soviet navy that often used IL-20 Coot SIGINT platforms to snoop on U.S. and NATO exercises, similar Chinese missions are not known to have shadowed U.S. naval operations at sea with either air-borne or shipborne surveillance systems, concentrating instead on their Asian neighbors.

The extent to which access to the surveillance gear aboard the detained EP-3E airplane will influence future Chinese SIGINT capabilities is unknown. However, according to the testimony of U.S. experts, Chinese engineers have expertly reverse-engineered and copied illicitly obtained, highly sensitive U.S. guided missile and nuclear technology. If Professor Ball is correct in his assessment that jointly operated Chinese and CIA collection sites have existed at Qitai and Korla for a decade, any signals intelligence collection technology provided by the CIA for those sites has in all probability already found its way into other Chinese intelligence collection systems. Thus without accounting for Chinese access to the surveillance systems aboard the EP-3, the Chinese military probably has a formidable SIGINT capability, albeit the technology may be dated.

Korean War: First Confrontation between the U.S. and China

The outbreak of the Korean War set the stage for the first hostilities between American and Chinese forces. The U.S. Eighth Army and its United Nations allies counterattacked after the North Korean army invaded South Korea in June 1950, eventually chasing the North Korean troops northward toward the Yalu River—the North Korean/Chinese border. Hordes of Chinese People's Liberation Army soldiers charged across the Yalu in November 1950 and drove the U.N. forces southward to the Seoul area. Seesaw battles ensued, generally in the vicinity of the 38th parallel that still separates the two Koreas, until an armistice terminated hostilities in July 1953. Casualties included 33,629 American KIAs, 415,000 South Korean KIAs, and an estimated two million Communist casualties.

At the dawn of the 21st century, the American public is generally aware of the American casualties from the Korean and Vietnam Wars. But few know about the sacrifices made by American reconnaissance aircrews in nonwar confrontations during the Cold War. We discuss a few U.S.-Chinese air incidents because of their relevance to the recent downing of the U.S. Navy EP-3 aircraft on Hainan Island.

P2V Shot Down over the South China Sea: January 18, 1953

The inflight emergency experienced by Lt. Shane Osborn's EP-3E crew on April 1, 2001, had many similarities to another U.S.-Chinese air incident that occurred five decades ago.

April 1, 2001—U.S. Navy surveillance mission over South China Sea	January 18, 1953—U.S. Navy surveillance mission over South China Sea
EP-3E crew struck in flight by Chinese F-8 pilot; recon aircraft critically damaged.	P2V crew hit by shore-based Chinese artillery; recon aircraft critically damaged.
Damage: No. 1 engine disabled by crash; radome torn off aircraft nose, airspeed indicator and flaps inoperative; cabin depressurization; winds blowing in.	Damage: two gaping holes in vertical stabilizer; radar out; starboard engine smoking; port engine on fire; landing gear door dropped off.
Mayday, Mayday; gave "Prepare for Ditching" command; rescinded command; landed in China; notified U.S. of safe landing and capture by PLA soldiers.	Transmitted SOS, DITCHING message and aircraft position report; ditched aircraft about six miles off Chinese coast; most crew members reached life raft safely.

While the outcome of these two missions were vastly different—American lives were lost in the P2V ditching and spared in the EP-3 emergency landing—both incidents illustrate the perilous nature of airborne reconnaissance.

The Sino-American confrontation in January 1953 was one of the most challenging and contentious air incidents of the Cold War. The P2V crew was conducting reconnaissance over water near the Chinese port of Swatow, when Chinese PLA shore batteries on an offshore island opened fire on it, forcing the P2V to ditch at sea. Swatow is located on the south China coast, where the Taiwan (formerly Formosa) Strait flows into the South China Sea. Having made a water-landing and brought the rescued crew members aboard, a U.S. Coast Guard flying boat crashed during takeoff from the water and sank. Another SAR aircrew and navy surface vessels moved in and completed the rescue efforts. All the while, the search and rescue forces were being fired on by Chinese shore-based forces and aircraft.

In 1954, U.S. Navy Lt. Clement R. (Bob) Prouhet, the patrol plane commander, described how their inflight emergency and subsequent aircraft ditching was handled:

> *Sunday, January 18, 1953, started as a normal patrol day for Crew Seven of Navy Patrol Squadron 22. We were flying our P2V Neptune at about 1,000 feet altitude on a routine flight in the South China Sea. About one o'clock in the afternoon we were off the China coast opposite the city of Swatow, headed in a northerly direction toward the Formosa Strait.*
>
> *The crewmen were at their stations and all hands were starting to think seriously about food in the form of the usual cold box lunches. I was checking the power settings to make certain we weren't burning too much gas.*
>
> *Suddenly one of the crew reported seeing flashes of gunfire from a small island off our port beam. Seconds later the plane bucked and a burst of flame shot through the flight compartment behind the cockpit. I immediately wrapped the plane into a turn and, jamming on power, climbed the airplane into some low-hanging clouds.*
>
> *My plane captain, Dan Ballenger, who sits just behind the pilots, reported that Byars, the radar operator was hit. By this time we were in the protection of the clouds, flying on instruments. I asked all stations to report battle damage. The top crown turret reported two gaping holes in the vertical stabilizer. Checking the controls, I noticed no effect on the maneuverability of the plane. Further reports revealed the radar out of commission, the fuel gauges pages flipping rapidly from zero to the normal reading, and smoke coming from the starboard engine. All these reports over the plane's intercommunication system were made in a matter of moments while we were flying on instruments.*

Lt. Verl Varney, who was copilot, and I decided the best course to follow would be to attempt to fly to a friendly field on Formosa. Then a loud banging noise was heard from the starboard engine. The after station, registering considerable concern in his voice, reported the two doors covering the retracted main landing gear wheel had broken off. I still had good control of the airplane and the engines were running fine. We finished drafting a message to our home base: "Fired up by shore batteries. Moderate damage. Amplifying report to follow. Latitude 23 degrees north, Longitude 117:30 degrees east."

After the message went out I turned the controls over to Lieutenant Varney and headed aft to check casualties among our thirteen-man crew and damage to the plane. I found that Byars, the radar technician, had been knocked out of his seat by the explosion. He had a four-inch cut on his neck and a piece of shrapnel through his shoulder. Plane Captain Ballenger had administered first aid by sprinkling sulfa powder on his wounds. Byars, though not unconscious, was suffering from shock.

While inspecting the flight deck, I saw a sheet of flame shoot out of the port engine. I jumped back into the pilot's seat in short order. Up to now the port engine had been our good engine. Pushing the propeller feathering button, I shut down the engine and engaged the emergency disconnect valves stopping all fuel, oil, hydraulic fluid, and alcohol from being supplied to the engine. These emergency procedures did not stop the fire.

Over the intercom now came the report that the wing was in danger of dropping off due to the intensity of the flames. We were still on instruments, flying in the "soup" at about 2,500 feet, with one engine out and the other smoking. I ordered French, the radioman, to send "SOS— DITCHING" and our position report. After the message was out he tied the transmitter key down in case any direction-finder stations were taking bearings on us.

So far, about fifteen minutes had elapsed since that first jolt of the AAA shell—it was a fast fifteen minutes for crew seven from that initial shot of adrenaline after the hit to the present frantic preparations to ditch. Each crew member has an assigned station for ditching: each man provides a specific piece of equipment and has a designated escape route after the plane stops in the water. There was no hesitation—every man knew from repeated drills what to do and was ready and eager to get out of that burning plane.

Varney and I were still flying on instruments with an engine feathered and the fire burning briskly. Heading the plane in a northerly direction we began letting down rapidly. Just under 900 feet [altitude] we broke out of the clouds and spotted two small islands northwest about twenty miles away. As usual the seas in the Formosa Strait were very rough—waves ten to fifteen feet high. Should we head for the islands and thereby increase our chances of making a successful ditch? The relatively calmer seas nearer the island would make it easier to survive in a rubber life raft, but the islands could belong to the unfriendly comrades who had just shot up our airplane.

Just as we decided to head for the islands, the radioman reported desperately that he had been burned on the face and hands when he jettisoned the port waist escape hatch. Flames from the burning wing engine were being sucked into the after station, spreading fire to that area. Men in the after station reported that the wing or engine might burn off. There was no doubt now—we would have to ditch here.

Flaps full down, power on our good engine, nose high, I established a slow rate of descent heading nearly into the wind. We touched down on the rough water and decelerated abruptly to a stop.

The yoke bounced around considerably but there were no severe bumps. The shock was great enough to tear equipment out of the hands of the men still at their ditching stations. Copilot Varney was hit in the forehead by a piece of flying glass from a crack in the windshield and Chief MacDonald, our photographer, was struck in the head by flying debris. Fortunately, these were our only immediate casualties on ditching. I scrambled out through the pilot's escape hatch as water was filling the cockpit. That Formosa Strait water is cold! I started swimming to get clear of a possible explosion, but the plane came floating down upon me. My arms went into high gear, and I swam the fastest fifty-foot dash I've ever logged to get clear of that still burning wing and engine.

Clear of the wing tip, I inflated my Mae West life jacket and looked around for the rest of the crew. No one was in sight—until a big wave picked me up on its crest and I spotted heads and the uninflated life raft nearby. I paddled over to help inflate the seven-man life raft.

As we unfolded the eight-foot raft our hearts took a nosedive when we saw charred and burned areas in one end. Pulling the CO_2 inflation bottle, we were relieved to find that two of the three compartments in the raft were filling. Byars was the most seriously injured man so we put him aboard while the rest of us clung to the sides.

I counted eleven noses; we were missing two men: Smith, the second mechanic, and McClure, the photographer. They had been seen downwind of the raft, Smith with his Mae West inflated and McClure calling for help to get his jacket inflated. These two men were not seen or heard from again. It was almost impossible for them to swim upwind to the rest of us against the fifteen-foot swells. We searched as best we could, but in vain.

A short time later two paddles and several exposure suits came drifting by; rescuing this equipment we decided to try rowing and kicking the raft toward the two small islands I had observed from the air. While under way, plane Captain Ballenger climbed on the raft to try on one of the exposure suits. It is watertight if donned before one gets into the water, but Ballenger got into the suit accompanied by quantities of cold water. He left the suit on but the rest of us decided it wasn't such a hot idea. (I believe now we all should have put them on since they were some protection.)

The next hour passed rather quickly while we took turns climbing in the half submerged raft and paddling toward the islands to the west. As about every fifth wave broke over us, it was impossible to bail out the raft and those taking turns resting were almost as wet as those in the water.

Byars was resting as comfortably as possible in a waterlogged life raft. Varney and MacDonald, who had superficial cuts on the forehead, were both in good shape. Checking back over those last frantic minutes in the plane, we believed the "SOS—DITCHING" message had gone out so we were expecting help eventually. Morale was good; everyone was cold.

The most wonderful sight we could hope to see was our squadron's number three plane when it appeared on the horizon headed for us. Crew three had been flying a patrol east of Formosa about 300 miles away. When they intercepted our first damage report they turned around and headed for our position in order to escort us. Although they had not received our SOS, they had heard our transmitter key when it was tied down.

As they passed nearby our copilot fired a life jacket flare. Miraculously, the crew three radioman sighted the flare and the big blue plane wheeled around to come help us. Immediately they radioed our plight to home base and proceeded to drop one of their two life rafts. Unfortunately, the drop was too far away and because of the high swells, we could do nothing to rescue it. Our shipmates continued circling and we settled back into our wet existence in and out of the raft.

Another clammy hour passed, but now we were buoyed by hope as well as stiff Mae Wests. Far away we heard a new sound of engines and finally spotted a PBM seaplane approach our position. Even though we didn't believe the plane could land in the rough seas, our spirits soared once again.

The plane was overhead and we identified it as a Coast Guard Air-Sea Rescue aircraft. We hoped the PBM could drop us a new life raft and keep us in sight until surface vessels arrived. It circled once and then executed a beautiful open-sea landing. We felt that we had it made; our damp spirits started drying out. We didn't know the trouble that lay ahead.[7]

Despite the heavy seas the PBM landed alongside, and after several attempts, threw a line to the hands of one of the downed crew by the raft, and drew the raft alongside the seaplane. Lieutenant Prouhet's crew clambered aboard the plane—exhausted and suffering from five hours of exposure in the cold waters. The PBM pilot, Lieutenant Vukic, questioned Prouhet about the two missing crewmen and taxied around looking for them. Regretfully, they were not found.

A lead story in the New York Times, January 19, 1953, described the incident in graphic detail:

U.S. PLANE DOWNED NEAR CHINA COAST; RESCUERS IN CRASH

Naval Craft Fired on by Reds 6 Miles off Swatow during Formosa [Taiwan] Strait Patrol

11 OF 13 ABOARD ARE SAVED

Then Mercy Flight Is Wrecked in Takeoff—7 Survivors Picked Up by Warship

TAIPEI (AP)—Monday, January 19—Official United States reports said a Navy Neptune patrol plane was shot down yesterday by Communist antiaircraft guns off the coast of South China and a United States Navy Mariner amphibian plane sank while taking off. . . .

Hours later, Navy rescue planes and warships operating in the darkness with flares sent word that several survivors of the second crash had been picked up.

[A spokesman at Pacific Naval headquarters in Honolulu said Sunday the Mariner had picked up eleven of thirteen persons from the Neptune, then crashed on takeoff, and burned and sank. The spokesman said a destroyer had picked up seven survivors of the Mariner crash, including five from the Neptune and two from the Mariner's crew. A search was under way for fourteen men, he added.]

SEIZURE BY REDS FEARED

There was the danger that other survivors, if any, might fall into Communist hands.

Five British and American warships were sent to the crash scene, about six miles northeast of the big Chinese Communist port of Swatow.

United States authorities on Formosa [Taiwan] disclosed that the two-engine P2V Neptune reported by radio yesterday afternoon that it had been damaged moderately by Communist antiaircraft fire from Namoa, a Communist-held island east of Swatow. Complete silence followed this report. . . .

The United States Seventh Fleet was assigned to guard the Chinese Nationalist island of Formosa from Communist invasion on June 27, 1950, by a Presidential directive issued two days after the outbreak of the Korean War. On November 6, 1950, a bomber with twelve persons aboard failed to return from a combat patrol over the Strait of Formosa. Its fate was never learned.

In another incident, a Navy patrol bomber was damaged by gunfire from *an unidentified trawler one hundred miles southeast of Shanghai on April 4, 1952. No one was hurt and the plane returned safely to Formosa.*

Another *New York Times* article dated January 19, 1953, provided additional details on the P2V incident:

A Pacific Fleet headquarters spokesman today said that the Chinese Communists, who shot down a Navy Neptune patrol bomber, had fired on a United States destroyer attempting to rescue survivors in the Strait of Formosa. The destroyer was not damaged by the Red shore batteries. . . .

The Navy said ten crewmen had been rescued and eleven were missing from two plane disasters growing out of the firing incident. . . .

A United States Coast Guard PBM Mariner set down in the choppy waters and picked up eleven of the thirteen Neptune crewmen. But it splashed in on takeoff, burned, and sank.

Aircraft and surface vessels of the United States and Britain converged on the area and swept the waters by the light of flares. A destroyer (USS Halsey Powell—DD686) picked up seven men, five from the Neptune and two from the Mariner. Three others were rescued later, two from the Neptune and one from the Coast Guard plane. A search for the others was continuing, the Navy said.

The spokesman said he did not know whether the destroyer had returned fire on the Red shore batteries.

SEARCH PLANE IS CHASED

TAIPEI (AP)—Tuesday, January 20—Official United States quarters said today an unidentified hostile aircraft, presumably Communist, fired at a United States plane yesterday as it searched for survivors of a Navy patrol bomber shot down by Red antiaircraft guns Sunday off the coast of China, and a rescue plane that crashed.

Fragmentary reports indicated the United States search plane had been fired on and chased by the attacking craft while it was circling over the scene of Sunday's double crashes. . . .

American sources on Formosa were unable to say whether the search plane had returned safely to its base. However, there was nothing to suggest that it was missing. . . .

In 1995, the USS *Halsey Powell's* chief engineer, Harold (Smitty) Schmidt, answered a letter to retired Coast Guard Commander Michael Perry regarding the destroyer's involvement in the rescue. In his letter, Schmidt talked about the search for the crew being a "hairy" situation and was amazed they were able to save eleven of the twenty-one men in very trying conditions. Schmidt went on to ask how "a P2V on a routine patrol [could] get shot down" but answered his own question when he found out the aircraft carried a chief photographer—"hardly a normal crewman for a routine patrol. So I guess the patrol was not too 'routine,' but rather a mapping exercise." This was made all the more apparent to him when they landed in Hong Kong for some R&R and found themselves front page news as nearly having started World War III.

The USS *Halsey Powell's* deck log for January 18, 1953, documented recovering seven survivors at latitude 23:24.3N longitude 117:12.2E at 20:25 hours, and three survivors at latitude 23:22.5N longitude 117:07.0E at 23:40 hours. None of the survivors had serious injuries.

At the end of the search and rescue, six crewmen from the P2V patrol craft and five from the Mariner amphibian were MIA and presumed dead. They have never been factually accounted for.

Given the closeness of the crash scene to the port of Swatow—about six miles—and the ferocity with which the Chinese intervened in the search and rescue efforts, there is speculation that some of the MIAs may have been recovered by the Chinese PLA. Richard L. Jones, a retired Air Force colonel lost a friend in the incident and commented on the search and rescue effort in September 1999.

> . . . My interest is focused on the people who were lost, especially the copilot of the PBM-5G, a friend from my hometown. There is reason to believe he survived the crash, and the nearness to the Chinese islands and coast made it possible for him and others to survive. Or worst case, their bodies made it to the coast and were identified by the Chinese. Letters to the State Department asking them to query the Chinese have met with no response.[8]

The Search and Rescue Mission

Retired U.S. Coast Guard Comdr. Michael A. Perry, one of the amphibian pilots who participated in the SAR efforts off Swatow, China, remembered pilot "Big John" Vukic.[9]

They were stationed in the Philippines at Sangley Point U.S. Naval Station. Their two primary missions were search and rescue (SAR) and logistics support. When the call came in that a Navy P2V had gone down, Vukic was sent out in SAR PBM-5G to attempt to rescue the downed crew floating in the sea just off Swatow.

An experienced pilot, Vukic landed his seaplane in the fading light and picked up the P2V crew. Using four JATO rockets to assist with the takeoff, the PBM gained speed as Vukic sought to get airborne. As he did, the right engine quit and the PBM cartwheeled and broke apart. Now there were two crews in the water that needed rescue.

A second PBM piloted by Perry dropped parachute flares in the growing dark to assist a U.S. Navy destroyer that had arrived on the scene to help in the rescue. In the end, the P2V crew, Vukic, and his flight engineer were pulled from the waters, the rest of the PBM's crew was never found. They were posthumously awarded the Coast Guard Gold Life Saving Medal.

The loss of eleven flyers in the January 1953 incident shows the inherent dangers involved in both airborne reconnaissance and search and rescue. The incident also illustrates the tenacious determination of the Chinese PLA to defend China's territorial waters. The loss of this P2V crew may have been the first loss of a U.S. Navy crew to Chinese hostile fire. [The authors can not confirm the loss of a bomber over the Taiwan Strait on November 6, 1950, that a wire service reporter reported in 1953. That reporter may have confused that loss with a Navy P2V that Soviet fighters shot down off the coast of Siberia on November 6, 1951.]

P4M Shot Down Near Wenchow, China: August 22, 1956

The U.S. Navy suffered twelve more MIA casualties on August 22, 1956, when Chinese fighters shot down a P4M Mercator patrol aircraft over the East China Sea off the Chinese coast near Wenchow—about

160 miles north of Taiwan. Search and rescue efforts recovered four of the sixteen crew members' bodies: a U.S. SAR force recovered two sets of remains, and the Chinese recovered and returned two additional sets. The fate of the other twelve men has not been determined.

An uncorroborated report[10] identifies the Chinese pilot who shot down the P4M as Zhongwen Song, who at the time was assigned to the PLA Air Force 6th Regiment of Division No. 2. The same report states that the incident occurred thirty-two miles off the Chinese coast of China (by Shengsi Island near Wenchow), and provides identifying data on the downed patrol bomber—P4M-1Q Mercator tail number 124362 from Fleet Reconnaissance Squadron One (VQ-1). VQ-1 is the home unit of the EP-3 crew that made the emergency landing on Hainan Island after the midair collision with the Chinese F-8 fighter on April 1, 2001. Other claimed shootdowns by People's Republic of China pilots, as provided by the report, include: one U.S. Navy PBM-5A at Qianlidao on November 7, 1953, and eighteen "drones" between 1964 and 1970 over various Chinese locations, including two drone shootdowns in May and August 1965 over Lingshui, where the Navy EP-3E crew made its emergency landing in April 2001. The claimed drone shootdowns, if true, offered good target intercept practice for the PLAAF fighter pilots. In addition, the Chinese could have exploited confirmed shootdowns for propaganda purposes.

Fecteau and Downey—First Chinese Cold War Prisoners

The first documented Chinese shootdown of an American Cold War intelligence gathering mission occurred in 1952. Two American civilians, Richard George Fecteau and John Thomas Downey, survived the crash of their downed aircraft, were captured by the Chinese, and served long prison sentences in China. In 1951 Fecteau and Downey were recruited by the CIA to run a CIA agent-infiltration program designed to report on the flow of Chinese Communist men and materiel into Korea. Following in-house training that included a six-month paramilitary program, the agency posted them abroad in Seoul, Korea.

On November 29, 1952, Fecteau and Downey and nine Taiwanese guerrilla agents boarded an unmarked C-47 "Gooney Bird" aircraft at

Seoul, Korea, for a covert flight to Manchuria. Their instructions: set down at a secret airstrip, disgorge the nine agents, pick up agents who had been on assignment in Manchuria, and return to Seoul. According to the *Washington Post*, the mission was doomed from the outset; the Chinese had captured the agents and forced them to send an SOS message that brought the C-47 on the mission. PLA antiaircraft guns were waiting and quickly shot down the plane; only Fecteau and Downey survived the crash. They were captured and taken to Tsao Lan-Tze Prison in Beijing.

Placed on trial in 1954, Downey was convicted of espionage and sentenced to life in prison. Fecteau received a twenty-year sentence. Downey was twenty-two years old, Fecteau twenty-five. Their trial and conviction drew strong protests and denials of spying charges from President Eisenhower's administration. When the Chinese government published photos of Fecteau and Downey, U.S. officials insisted that they were not associated in any way with espionage. For years, while they sat in prison in Beijing, the U.S. government stuck to its story: The two were civilian Army employees lost at sea in an accident on a "routine flight" from Seoul, Korea, to Japan. Embarrassed by the capture and imprisonment of the two agents, the CIA denied any relationship with the men.

An article in the *Battle Creek Enquirer* (Battle Creek, Michigan) on April 5, 2001, details sensitive discussions in 1971 that helped free the men:

> *Washington (AP)—Richard Nixon had a sensitive item on his agenda as he began reaching out to China in the spring of 1971: the release of four Americans held by the communist government.* . . .
>
> *Months before Nixon's historic trip to China in February 1972, his national security advisor, Henry Kissinger, took a nonconfrontational approach, asking the Chinese to free the four men as a favor on humanitarian grounds.*
>
> *"We would consider it an act of mercy if the People's Republic of China could pardon all or some of them whenever, in the judgment, it felt that conditions were right," according to a transcript of Kissinger's meeting with former Chinese premier Chou En-lai in July 1971.*
>
> *"This is not a request. I'm asking it as a favor."*

Chou was noncommittal, but noted that a reduction of a sentence was possible in cases of good behavior.

"We shall continue to study this matter."

Among the detainees was John T. Downey. . . .

"Downey is a confessed spy, and the PRC has been very lenient in commuting his life sentence to five more years," an undated briefing memo on the China trip said about Downey, who was released in March 1973, thirteen months after Nixon's visit to China.

Downey was released after Nixon admitted he was on a CIA spy operation. . . .

The documents indicate that Richard George Fecteau was released after Kissinger's initial visit to Beijing in 1971 but before Nixon's visit. . . .[11]

Nixon dispatched Kissinger to Beijing to talk to the Chinese before he made his historic visit, which eventually led to renewed diplomatic relations with the communist power. . . .

In a surprise announcement on July 15, 1971, Nixon told the world about Kissinger's visit and how he planned to formally open dialogue with China in his own trip there months later.

In a July 14, 1971, memo to Nixon, Kissinger called his first talks with the Chinese—more than twenty hours over two days—the "most searching, sweeping and significant discussions I have ever had in government."

He told Nixon there were challenges, however, in dealing effectively with the Chinese whom he described as a "tough, idealistic, fanatical, single-minded and remarkable people." Success in relations, he wrote would "transform the very framework of global relationships. . . ."

But Kissinger said he found negotiating with the Chinese more agreeable than talking with the Russians. "There was none of the Russian ploymanship, scoring points, rigidity, or bullying," Kissinger said. "They do not turn everything into a contest."

Downey arrived in his hometown, New Britain, Connecticut, on March 12, 1973. He was released secretly with the second to last group of American POWs who were returned from captivity in Vietnam. Three days later, Air Force Maj. Phillip E. Smith and Navy Lt. Robert J.

Flynn—pilots who had been shot down on combat missions over Vietnam and imprisoned in China—were released. Smith and Flynn were the other two POWs that Kissinger has asked Premier Chou to release in July 1971.

At a March 13 news conference, Downey described his twenty-year imprisonment as "to a large extent wasted. I don't see that it benefited anybody." He noted that his captors questioned him closely during the first eight or nine months in jail and "I revealed about every bit of information I had."

Downey and Fecteau waited twenty-five more years before finally being honored by the agency that had disowned them in 1952. On June 19, 1998, U.S. Congressman Porter J. Goss from Florida read a proclamation in the U.S. House of Representatives, recognizing the "extraordinary service and sacrifice for this nation of two officers of the Central Intelligence Agency, Mr. Richard G. Fecteau and Mr. John T. Downey."

On June 25, 1998, George Tenet, the Director of the Central Intelligence Agency, will present the Director's Medal to Dick Fecteau and Jack Downey for reasons that, to some extent, I am able to describe in this forum today.

Except for their kind indulgence in allowing me to commemorate this event on the floor of the House, Dick Fecteau and Jack Downey will receive their awards as privately and as quietly as they served, and sacrificed for, our country.

In 1951, fresh from college, Mr. Fecteau and Mr. Downey joined the clandestine service of the Central Intelligence Agency. After a period of training, they were sent to east Asia to conduct agent resupply and pickup operations over China as part of our war effort in Korea.

In such operations, Mr. Fecteau and Mr. Downey were to drop supplies and to retrieve agents for debriefing by flying in low, among the trees, and literally snatching agents from the ground. These operations are extremely difficult and demanding in peacetime. Needless to say, in war zones, they are outright perilous.

In November 1952, Mr. Fecteau and Mr. Downey were part of a crew that was to fly into China, swoop to tree level, and snatch an agent from the ground. As their plane descended and approached the snatch site, it was hit by machine-gun and small arms fire. The plane crashed and burned, killing the two pilots. Mr. Fecteau and Mr. Downey survived, but they were captured by the forces of the People's Republic of China.

In 1954, two years later, China sentenced Mr. Fecteau and Mr. Downey to life in prison. Their sentencing was, I understand, the first time that the families of the two learned that they were alive. Over the next twenty years, Mr. Fecteau and Mr. Downey were subjected to extensive and aggressive interrogations and to long periods of solitary confinement. Year after year the two endured this suffering and deprivation and they did so with dignity and courage and an abiding faith in our country.

The nation ultimately did not fail them. In December 1971, nearly twenty years later, our government finally obtained the release of Dick Fecteau. And in March of 1973, we obtained the release of Jack Downey.

Dick Fecteau returned to the agency and continued his career. In 1976 he retired and joined the staff of Boston University, his alma mater, as assistant director of athletics. He retired from BU in 1989. . . .

Jack Downey retired from the agency in 1973. Some of us feel that a baccalaureate from Yale is perfectly serviceable; but Jack, however, went on from there to Harvard Law School, and in 1976 he entered legal practice. In 1990 he was appointed to the bench in Connecticut and became a senior judge in the state system. . . .

These, Mr. Speaker, are the extraordinary stories of two extraordinary people. Their awards, it seems to me, are most properly for the totality of their lives, for answering their country's call; for engaging in perilous operations under fire; for enduring unimaginable hardship in Chinese prisons; and perhaps most of all, for returning to their families, to their communities, and to their country, and continuing to contribute and give and make a difference in their communities.

Back in America, Downey met and married a Chinese textile designer studying in America, and they have a son. In 1983 on the tenth year of his release from prison, the Beijing regime invited him and his family back to China. They accepted the invitation, and Downey is positive about the trip.

As reported in the *St. Louis New Press*, July 3, 1998, the CIA honored the two men more than twenty-five years after their release from a Chinese prison as part of the agency's fiftieth anniversary celebrations.

> *WASHINGTON (AP) In a private ceremony not announced by the CIA, retired spies John "Jack" T. Downey and Richard G. Fecteau received a prestigious Director's Medal for surviving two "dark decades" in Chinese prisons—the longest any CIA officers have been held captive abroad and lived to tell about it.*

CIA Director George Tenet called them "true legends." Finally, Downey and Fecteau were recognized formally by their peers. In a related note, officials from the Pentagon's office of POW/MIA affairs continues to pursue leads regarding two other Americans involved in the shootdown incident in which Fecteau and Downey were captured and imprisoned. The People's Liberation Army has insisted that Korean War losses are a closed issue, while the Ministry of Foreign Affairs has declared wartime records to be classified. Declassified U.S. military records indicate some American POWs were taken into China and some never returned.

It had been generally believed that Downey and Fecteau were the only Americans aboard that C-47 shot down on November 29, 1952. But a June 1998 Defense Department document—a cable to the U.S. Embassy in Beijing—identified the two pilots as Americans Robert Snoddy and Norman Schwartz. The cable said they were killed and presumed buried at the crash site. The Pentagon wants China to provide any information it might have about the pilots' remains. And as late as January 2001, the U.S. POW/MIA office was making plans for six U.S. veterans of the Korean War to fly to Beijing at China's invitation to discuss their experiences with Chinese veterans—an unprecedented encounter that officials hope will lead eventually to new information about the fate of Americans still missing from that war.

This incident is one of the very few covert air operations conducted during the Cold War that the American government has finally acknowledged. The number of other covert air operations—both successful missions and those that met with enemy fire or encountered other unintended fates—are still classified, as is the success of such missions. Unlike the peacetime aerial reconnaissance program (PARPRO)—peripheral missions like the EP-3E flight on April 1 that fly in international airspace—covert missions typically entailed the planned overflight of denied territory, such as U-2 flights over China.

Unmarked U-2s—Taiwanese Pilots

One extensive covert flying program involved high altitude intelligence collection missions over China and other targeted countries in the Far East, Southeast Asia, and East Asia—flown by Taiwanese pilots in unmarked U-2 aircraft from airfields in Taiwan, the Philippines, Thailand, South Korea, and other friendly countries in the area. This was a CIA-managed operation. An uncorroborated report[12] on the Republic of China Air Force (ROCAF) U-2 operations names thirty ROCAF pilots who received U-2 training in the United States. Twenty-seven of the pilots reportedly completed their U-2 training at bases in America.

As described in the report, ROCAF U-2 operations occurred during the 1960s. The first two U-2s arrived in Taiwan in July 1960. Two more arrived in December 1962. From January to June 1961, the ROCAF flew eleven missions over China; pilot Huai-Sheng Chen flew the first overflight, entering China at Fujian and completing the mission in eight hours and forty minutes. The third mission overflew southwest China, Vietnam, and Burma.

During the fourth mission, flown by Tai-Yow Wang in March 1961, more than thirty Chinese fighters attempted unsuccessfully to intercept it. During a March 1962 overflight, a Chinese surface-to-air missile guidance radar locked on to and tracked Tai-Yow's U-2 aircraft. He took evasive action and escaped without harm. Others encountered similar SAM SA-2 responses to their flights; SAM battalions fired as many as three SA-2 missiles at some flights. Most missiles missed their targets; others did not. Between 1962 and 1969, six Taiwanese-piloted U-2s were shot down by Chinese SAMs. Four of the downed pilots perished in the shootdowns, the two others were captured in 1963 and 1965, respectively, and released from Chinese prisons in 1982. The report lists nine U-2s destroyed during training sorties, with the loss of three pilots. Overall, according to the source document, Taiwanese pilots flew at least one hundred overflights of the Chinese mainland from 1961 to 1970. Based on an estimate by a retired U.S. Air Force master sergeant (a photo processing specialist), significantly more flights were flown during that period:

> After I reenlisted I had the opportunity for a tour with the 67th Reconnaissance Technical Squadron, Yokota Air Base, Japan, the film processing facility for U-2 overflights of China, flown by Chinese pilots out of Taiwan. The time frame was 1963–1966.
>
> The U-2 has two cameras, or did at that time. One flight produced a minimum of 5,000 feet of film per camera; normal procedures produced 10,000 feet times two equaling 20,000 feet, or around four miles of film per flight. In the beginning we produced twenty-seven copies for all the various agencies; 108 miles of film processed and reproduced per mission in a twenty-four-hour period. The norm was one flight per week.
>
> After things cranked up in Vietnam, the aircraft were diverted to cover that area of concern. Missions again produced a minimum of 10,000 feet per flight, the average was closer to 20,000 feet. We initially produced the twenty-seven copies. Our workload increased to three to four flights a week and we started round-the-clock processing, working twelve-hour shifts. Every fourteen days we got a three-day break and then started over again.
>
> After processing facilities were installed in-country, our workload was reduced to the overflow that the in-country facility could not handle. Also facilities were installed at Hickam Field and we only produced the number of copies needed in the Pacific region. Hickam Field then produced worldwide distribution from a copy we forwarded to them.
>
> A large number of our personnel then began thirty-day TDYs to Vietnam to help out. I never got picked to go before my tour ended and I rotated back to the 2d Reconnaissance Technical Squadron, Barksdale AFB, where I again handled some of the film we produced at Yokota; this time in the production of up-to-date maps for the region. I extended my tour for six months because a large number of us were scheduled to rotate at the same time and this would have left the facility undermanned.

Little is known publicly about the intelligence produced from the miles of film exposed from U-2 flown over China and Southeast Asia, or the sacrifices made by the Taiwanese pilots. During the 1960s, rumors attributed the loss of what was viewed as an excessive number of Taiwanese pilots and U-2 aircraft to the less than stellar skills of the U-2 pilots. What the rumormongers did not know was the large number of missions that were being flown and the difficulty involved in flying the U-2. Nor did they appreciate the dangerous nature of airborne reconnaissance missions.

And it is precisely that issue that this book addresses.

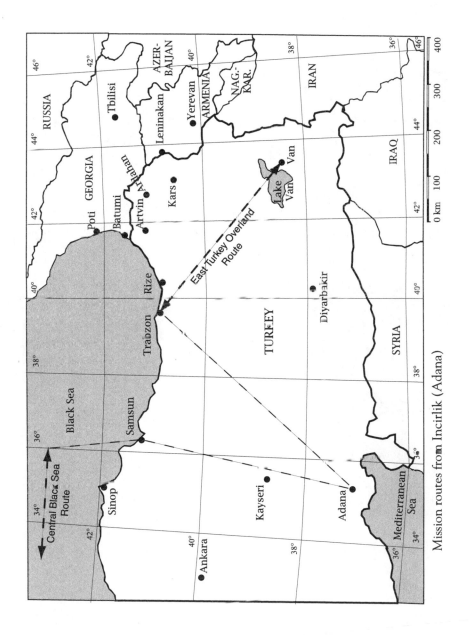

Mission routes from Incirlik (Adana)

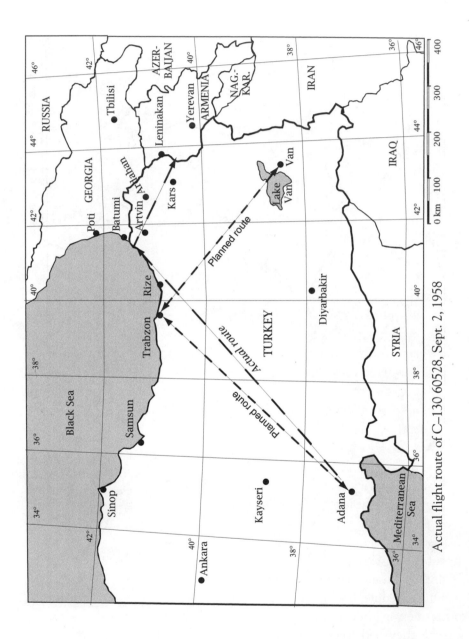

Actual flight route of C–130 60528, Sept. 2, 1958

ONE

—

THE SHOOTDOWN

Three A.M. is a miserable time to get up. By three-thirty on September 2, 1958, the crew of the C-130 was sitting in the dining hall. Nothing ever tasted good in the mess halls at Incirlik Air Base, Turkey, but breakfast, particularly at that time of the morning, was even worse than the other meals. Powdered eggs, powdered milk, even the coffee (prepared to what they thought were American standards by cooks who were used to a quite different, much stronger Turkish brew) were terrible. The seventeen men, deprived of proper sleep by their strange schedule, looked as if they had been up for days.

In those days, duty in Turkey was awful at the best of times. There was nothing to do in the evening but drink and play cards, and the food inevitably gave at least part of the crew dysentery. This group was special, though, so perhaps they didn't yet feel ill. The eleven enlisted men who made up the reconnaissance section on the crew were almost all athletes, members of their unit's softball team, one that had nearly won the Rhein-Main Air Base tournament several days earlier. Because of their hectic playing schedule, they hadn't flown as much in the previous month as the other men in their unit, but they were in excellent physical condition. Maybe they had fought off the local microbes that seemed to have a fondness for American bodies. Though most of them drank, none of

1

them was a really heavy drinker by the standards of their outfit. Besides, even suffered together, a hangover and the runs couldn't keep a man from flying.

After breakfast the men climbed into the waiting truck and headed out to their plane parked on the west side of the tarmac, the side of the Turkish army base reserved for Americans.

The aircrew consisted of six flight crew members (the "front-enders," who actually flew the aircraft) and eleven recon specialists (the "back-enders," who monitored Soviet bloc communications). The front-enders and their RB-50 and C-130 recon aircraft were assigned to the 7406th Support Squadron, U.S. Air Forces, Europe (USAFE), and the recon crewmen belonged to Detachment 1, 6911th Radio Group Mobile—a U.S. Air Force Security Service (USAFSS) unit. Both the 7406th and Detachment 1 were based at Rhein-Main Air Base near Frankfurt, Germany.

Although the two units flew together daily, their relationship was uncomfortable. The men in the plane that day reported to two different headquarters with different and, at times, conflicting goals. Under such circumstances, cooperation was useful, but hardly inevitable.

The small detachment of the 6911th was composed primarily of Russian and Soviet-satellite language specialists who were responsible for aerial reconnaissance of the Soviet Union and Eastern Europe from the Baltic Sea in the north to the southernmost reaches of Soviet Armenia in the south. The 7406th maintained and flew the planes. However, although the flight crews possessed secret or top secret clearances, and the common sense to guess what the back-ender recon crewmen were doing, they did not officially know who their passengers were or why the aircraft flew their specific routes. The front-enders (all officers except for an enlisted flight engineer) had no need to know the details of what the back-enders did, and the back-enders (all enlisted) were forbidden to tell.

The two halves of the crew were completely separate, in the air and on the ground. In fact, the men of the 7406th were forbidden even to mention to outsiders the 6911th or its Rhein-Main detachment; they referred to the back-enders simply as "sailors." The head sailor (the NCO who was the airborne mission supervisor) was the "admiral."

In reality, Detachment 1's back-enders came by their name logically.

When the 7406th and Detachment 1 were being formed in 1955–56, the RB-50 recon aircraft assigned to the 7406th Support Squadron was dubbed the "Dream Boat"—a nickname used in unclassified conversations and messages. It followed that the recon crews would become "sailors."

Some of the 7406th pilots resented the fact that they seemed to be treated like chauffeurs by a group of enlisted men. Questioned years later about that relationship, one pilot had this to say:

> I came to the '06th out of TAC [Tactical Air Command] with the usual heavy indoctrination from flight training of the position of the officer over the enlisted troops and the leadership qualities for which I had been chosen. . . . [It] took some getting used to when I found that enlisted personnel had such a measure of control over operational aspects of the mission. Over time, I came to realize that I wasn't dealing with "typical" enlisted troops, but for the whole time that I was flying in the '06th, I was going on blind faith that [those] guys knew what they were doing. There was the vague discomfort from time to time when I thought about mission success and crew survival.

These strangely split crews, with enlisted men who often gave directions to officers, normally rotated into Incirlik for a stay of two weeks every two months, flying eleven hours a day in RB-50s, three days a week. That schedule changed in the late summer of 1958 because of heightened Middle East political tensions, and the resulting American apprehension about a possible Soviet attack on Turkey. In normal times, crews took off before dawn, spent eleven hours flying along the Soviet border, then landed and drove to a hangar where they stored the classified tapes on which they had recorded Soviet military communications. The rest of the evening was free. But because of the political tensions in the summer of 1958, the five language specialists specially chosen for an August 5 deployment remained in Turkey for an extended period and, after each day's flight, spent several extra hours in the hangar reviewing what they had taped. Thus, their workday often lasted from 3:00 A.M. until 11:00 P.M. or midnight.

The intelligence specialists on the September 2 mission expected to remain in Turkey for well over a month but probably looked forward to improved working conditions, at least while in the air: the 7406th had received a consignment of new C-130s to replace the RB-50s, worn-out relics of the Korean War era that had been retrofitted for reconnaissance work. Since the new planes were expected to be more reliable and carried twice as many intelligence operatives, both the 7406th and Detachment 1 were anxious to place them into service as quickly as possible, in Turkey as well as Germany.

Fresh out of the factory, the C-130s were outfitted with a galley, a real toilet (the RB-50 had a bucket), and a heating system that worked. They even had red carpeting. The large pods under the tip of each wing, built to look like auxiliary fuel tanks, were actually crammed with radio antennas. Powered by four turboprop engines, they took off at what for the 1950s was a steep angle, and they could land on unbelievably short runways.

Arriving at their aircraft before dawn on the morning of September 2, 1958, the crew for the local mission over Turkey was informed by the 7406th maintenance chief that the plane wasn't ready to fly. C-130 tail number 60528, which had arrived in Turkey the previous day, would not be ready until late morning. Like the other new C-130s in the squadron, 528 was a spanking-new aircraft with less than two hundred total flying hours, most of them in transition training for the flight crews and recon crews—nonmission flights to familiarize the men with their new equipment. For its time, the C-130 was a state-of-the-art machine, with hundreds of new, unfamiliar systems and components; neither the maintenance crews nor the aircrews were yet completely comfortable with the new gear. And 528 was the most trouble-prone of the new aircraft.

So both crews, front-end and back-end, had a few extra hours before the new scheduled takeoff time. M.Sgt. George Petrochilos had brought a crew down from Germany on 25 August for an extended stay, and Petrochilos's crew was living in the unit's Quonset hut. They were flying the local mission from Incirlik on September 2. While 528 was being prepared for a late takeoff, Pete's recon crew may have returned to the unit's hut, but it is doubtful that they had time to catch more than a few minutes sleep before they had to report back for takeoff.

The flight crew stayed at the plane, talking with the ground maintenance men about the minutiae of the repair and some of the hundreds of other details they would need to learn about the new craft in the course of the coming year. 1st Lt. Ricardo Villarreal, lead navigator, spent his time discussing the C-130's navigation system and the day's flight route with Capt. Edward Jeruss, second navigator. Lieutenant Villarreal had extensive experience on the unit's Turkish routes—he had logged more hours in 1958 than any other navigator in the squadron, but nearly all of his missions in general, and every one of his Turkish missions, had been in RB-50s. He was considered the best young navigator in the unit, but like everyone else in the 7406th, he was still getting used to the new C-130 equipment.

He did have more experience on the new planes than most of the navigators in his outfit. He had ferried 60528 from the depot at Greenville, Texas, to Rhein-Main, Germany; had flown several transition training missions in the plane; and had been the lead navigator on the previous day's mission from Rhein-Main to Adana. But the September 2 mission would be his first in a C-130 on the eastern Turkish route.

The aircraft's pilot, Capt. Rudy Swiestra, was a highly skilled veteran flier, but like the others, he had relatively little experience on the C-130, and none at all flying in the Turkish mission area. A more senior pilot, Capt. Paul Duncan, was "standboarding" him, checking him out in order to upgrade him to aircraft commander in Turkey. Swiestra had long since received that designation for the German missions. The copilot, 1st Lt. John Simpson, was one of the most impressive men in the 7406th; the senior officers felt sure that he would make general before he retired. Captain Duncan would also be taking a look at Lieutenant Simpson. Later in the week, he was scheduled to evaluate Lieutenant Simpson and in all probability upgrade Simpson's status from copilot to aircraft commander.

The crew was scheduled to fly an "overland" mission on September 2. That is, instead of flying out over the southern half of the Black Sea in order to listen in on Soviet air force pilots and ground forces in the Crimean Peninsula area, the aircraft would fly along the eastern border of Turkey—concentrating on Soviet military communications from Soviet Georgia and Armenia. With Soviet and American tensions rising over Lebanon and Soviet saber-rattling against Turkey, the crew's primary mission that day was to listen for Soviet ground communications involving new Soviet SS-4 SCUD surface-to-surface missiles suspected of being in that area.

But it had other missions as well. Soviet radar operators, tracking the path of the Trabzon-Van leg of the recon flights out of Incirlik, referred to the normal American procedure as "painting" the Soviet border. As the American aircraft hugged the Soviet border, it would be picked up and tracked by one Soviet air defense radar station after another. As the radar stations tracked airborne targets, Soviet operators used Morse code (and to a lesser extent, voice) to report tracking data via radio to air defense centers and command posts. Using the tracking data, updated minute by minute on a large map of the area, Soviet tactical aircraft controllers could direct fighter pilots by voice-command radios during intercept missions. Monitoring those communications was a handy way for the Americans to keep track of the "air order of battle" and modus operandi in the front-line Soviet air force and air defense units. Order of battle data are the identification, command structure, strength, and disposition of personnel, equipment, and units of an armed force.

Incirlik Air Base is located a few miles outside of Adana, a medium-size city in south-central Turkey. The plane would fly north-northeast from Incirlik, passing over or abeam the Kayseri beacon in east-central Turkey, and then head for Trabzon, on the Black Sea coast about a hundred miles west of the Soviet border. From there it would fly southeast to a point near the east coast of Lake Van, opposite the border of Soviet Armenia. The overland mission called for "orbiting" between Trabzon and Van in a figure-eight pattern (always turning away from Soviet territory) until heading back to Incirlik eight hours after takeoff. The C-130A-II had adequate fuel onboard to fly about three orbits between Trabzon and Van before returning home to Incirlik.

In the end, instead of taking off at dawn as they had planned, they weren't in the air until 11:21 A.M. Incirlik time. The pilot rescheduled their return to Incirlik for 19:40 that evening—projecting an eight hour and twenty minute mission. For that group, used to flying eleven hours at a time on ancient, uncomfortable RB-50 aircraft, those were bankers' hours.

After take off Lieutenant Simpson contacted Incirlik tower with his departure report: "Off at :21 [11:21], outbound course 040 . . . Roger, contact Ankara control on HF . . . Ankara control, this is Air Force 60528, departed Incirlik at :21, outbound 040 . . . Roger (I am to) report over Trabzon." It was time to report to "Homeplate," 7499th Support Group flight-following post at USAFE [United States Air Forces, Europe] Headquarters, in Wiesbaden, Germany. The 7499th monitored the progress of the missions of the 7406th and its other two squadrons.

Switching his AIC-10 interphone/comms control knob to the right, Lieutenant Simpson used HF #1 radio to pass a message to the Frankfurt Flight Service Center for relay to Homeplate, "Sky King, Sky King. This is a Steel Girder message . . ."

Proceeding as planned, Lieutenant Simpson again contacted Ankara control at 12:42, reporting that 60528 was over Trabzon at 12:42, at flight level 255 (i.e., at an altitude of 25,500 feet).

The Transcaucasian Air Defense Corps guarded the western frontiers of Soviet Georgia on the southeastern coast of the Black Sea and Soviet Armenia to the south. Radar stations assigned to the 29th Radio Technical Regiment had their radars pointing westward scanning the skies of the southeastern Black Sea and eastern Turkey for would-be intruder aircraft. The mission of the 29th Regiment, as of all such border units, was to detect and track all airborne aircraft within range of its radar stations—the primary objective being to detect non-Soviet aircraft at maximum distance from Soviet territory, identify each radar "blip" as either friendly or hostile, and pass resulting tracking data up the air defense chain of command. As plotters charted on a map board the individual tracks of airborne targets, radio operators, some using Morse code and others using voice, transmitted the tracking data on air defense radio frequencies. On the receiving end, other radio operators and plotters took in the tracking data and plotted each track on a board where tactical aircraft controllers could use the data to vector fighter pilots on intercept missions.

When Lieutenant Simpson reported that C-130 60528 was over Trabzon at 12:42, Soviet air defense forces in both Georgia and Armenia had already been tracking the C-130's flight path for ten minutes—and they had pinpointed its *actual* position, well off course to the east. Radar stations belonging to the 29th Regiment had detected the C-130 at 12:32 in an area fifty kilometers south of Rize, Turkey; that meant that it was fifty to sixty kilometers southeast of Trabzon on a northeasterly heading *away* from Trabzon.

Ultimately, seven Soviet radar stations tracked the C-130—passing each target plot to the 236th Fighter Air Division command post. The command post assigned target number 7845 to the C-130 track, identifying it as a single foreign aircraft at an altitude of 7,500 meters (24,600 ft). Track 7845 proceeded northeasterly toward the Soviet city of Batumi on the Black Sea coast—immediately north of the border between Turkey and Georgia. Twenty kilometers south of Batumi (perhaps shortly after Lieutenant Simpson had reported being over Trabzon), track 7845 turned and with a climb began flying along the Soviet state border. The Soviets watched on their radar screens as it painted the border; they tracked it as it passed Artvin, then Ardakhan, then Kars, Turkey; they treated it as a potential threat to their border, but the plane was not yet in danger, because the border doesn't jut westward at those points. But just beyond Leninakan, Armenia, the border changed shape.

Southwest of Leninakan, a salient, with Yerevan at its southeastern end, juts out from the otherwise southeasterly Armenian border. The American plane was headed toward the Yerevan "parrot's beak" of the Armenian border. As the C-130 gained altitude and headed toward the Soviet border on a course of 140 degrees, Major Kulnikov, the zonal command and control post duty officer, initiated actions to place "alert duty" pilots of the 117th Fighter Aviation Regiment (IAP) at Leninakan airfield, and the 25th Fighter Regiment at Yerevan on readiness for immediate takeoff.

Meanwhile, Captain Romanyuta, ground-controlled intercept site controller at Leninakan, and his plotters were working at the vector plotting board. Using data provided by the reports from the radar stations, the plotter put the cross bearings that defined the movement of track 7845 on the board. The cross bearings appeared on the map overlay at specific time intervals, annotations next to them showing altitude, speed, and azimuth.

Evaluating the situation in which a non-Soviet track was approaching the Soviet state border, Captain Romanyuta passed a fighter aircraft scramble order to the alert pilot center at Leninakan airfield: "201, scramble as a pair." But the Leninakan airfield was in the midst of a transient dust storm, and the fighters couldn't immediately take off. Switching his command radio to another channel, Captain Romanyuta therefore passed the scramble order to Yerevan airfield: "582, scramble in a pair."

It was a hot day at Yerevan, without a breath of air, and the two duty pilots, Senior Lieutenants Lopatkov and Gavrilov, both rated Senior Pilots, were in the shade of the "alert pilot" tent playing dominoes when the alarm sounded. Instantly, at 12:47 Incirlik time, Lieutenant Lopatkov using call sign 582 and his wingman, Lieutenant Gavrilov, call sign 583, scrambled from the runway in MiG-17 fighters. Seven minutes later at 12:54, when the dust storm had subsided at Leninakan airfield, Senior Lieutenant Kucheryaev, call sign 201 and his wingman, Senior Lieutenant Ivanov, call sign 218, scrambled in a pair. Thus, by 1:00 P.M., four MiG-17s were in the air on the track of the C-130.

Vectoring the Yerevan fighters to their patrol zone northwest of Yerevan, Romanyuta told them the target was at an altitude of 10,000 meters (32,800 feet) and directed them to climb above it, to an altitude of 11,000 meters, a position from which they could blindside the American plane. He directed the Leninakan pair to the same patrol area twenty kilometers south of Leninakan where the foreign aircraft was approaching Soviet territory.

Meanwhile, the data from the radar stations were streaming into the regimental control post, and a set of three lines was taking shape on the plotting board showing the flight courses of both the two pairs of fighter aircraft and the target. Those lines were approaching one another toward a point of intersection inside the Soviet border. Captain Romanyuta commended his plotters and operators—the tracking of the target was reliable and without gaps. Steadily the two pairs of fighters approached their combat air patrol stations. Captain Romanyuta directed the fighters into an initial position advantageous for attack.

It was just past 1:00 P.M. on the Turkish/Armenian border, at a time of day when men who had been awakened before dawn were normally fighting off drowsiness. It had probably been an uneventful flight, and both the flight crew and the recon crew sailors would have been settling into a comfortable routine.

At 1:07 the lines on the plotting board intersected. From an altitude of 11,000 meters, "582" told Captain Romanyuta at 1:07 that he saw the target—"a large one at 10,000 meters, as you said." In another exchange one of the pilots identified the foreign aircraft as "a large four-engine transport." The C-130 had "violated" the state border a moment earlier, twenty kilometers south of Leninakan in the region of Mastara (Marzik) on a course of 120 degrees at a reported altitude of 10,000 meters.[13] In other words, the four fighters had the American plane in their sights the moment it crossed the border. The Soviet air defense system was working beautifully.

The two pairs of MiGs swooped down on the C-130 from the northwest. Beneath the terse Russian communications (see the transcript in appendix C) we can visualize the deadly encounter. The first pair of MiGs (582 and 583) suddenly materialized out of the blinding glare of the afternoon sunlight before the American crew noticed its mistake. The Yerevan flight leader (call sign 582) made a quick pass, opening fire on the American plane, and the C-130, instead of obeying that command to land, banked sharply to the right, diving and turning west. Two minutes later, at 1:09, the second pair of MiGs (call signs 201 and 218) had been vectored into the interception. Making sure that they stayed on the Soviet side of the border—"I can see the fence"—the Soviets then began their kill.

In the area where the C-130 crossed into Soviet territory and was attacked, the Arpa-Chaj River that forms a natural boundary between Turkey and Armenia should have been at least partially visible with a reported cloud cover of ten to thirty percent and visibility at fifteen to twenty kilometers. The MiG pilots used a fence along the border as a reference, referring to it in several of their air-to-ground reports.[14] It was familiar turf for the Soviet pilots. For the crew of the C-130, it was terra incognita; they had no knowledge at all of the terrain below them since it was eighty-five to one hundred miles off their planned flight path.

The Yerevan team took up positions on each side of the plane to herd it away from the border, while the Leninakan team—who had first rights on the enemy, since they were there first to spot him—positioned themselves to the rear and above the intruder. The first attacker fired a

rocket that severely damaged the vertical stabilizer on the tail of the
enemy aircraft.

"Attack, attack, 218, attack," the Leninakan flight leader shouted to
his wingman, at one point, urging him on to an already fatally crippled
target.

It was unusual for four fighters to participate in an attack on one
plane; had the dust storm not delayed the Leninakan team, only two
would have been involved. Perhaps Romanyuta improvised the "box"
configuration to avoid the possibility of the four fighters inadvertently
hitting one another, or perhaps it was a tactical maneuver that had been
practiced before. If by some luck the C-130 had managed to avoid the
first pair of MiGs, the second pair would have been available to complete
the mission.

Like sadistic hunters surrounding a trapped game animal, each fighter
took its turn at making killing runs at the much slower, unarmed cargo
plane. In just eight minutes, several fighters even found time for a second
pass.

The damage to the tail section had taken away much of the pilot's
ability to handle the plane. Still, Captain Swiestra tried to corkscrew
down into a sickly power dive, desperately trying to turn the plane west
at the same time ("The target is burning . . . it's heading toward the
fence"). The MiGs followed him down, each one raking the doomed
plane with every weapon it had. Then a shell struck the right inboard engine, setting the right wing on fire.

"Look at him, he won't get away, he's already falling."

"Yes, he's falling . . . I'll finish him off, boys; I'll finish him off on the
run."

"The target has lost control; it's going down."

One hunter made a final, joyous, utterly gratuitous charge at the defenseless craft, emptying his guns. Its controls blown away, its right wing
ablaze, the C-130 reacted like a huge, grotesque toy. It spun vertically
down toward the ground, burning fiercely. Then, somehow, its nose
lifted; at the last second it pancaked down flat onto its belly, and the entire structure exploded on impact, blowing the cockpit partially clear. By
the time the one-sided dogfight was finished, the carcass of the plane lay

forty-five kilometers inside the Armenian border, twenty-six miles south of Leninakan in the foothills of the Aragat Mountains near the village of Sasnashen.

Without even time for a Mayday call, seventeen men, the majority of them in their late teens or early twenties, had been blasted out of the sky and burned to cinders.

TWO

——

ATTACKS ON OTHER RECON PLATFORMS

Reconnaissance and intelligence operations played a major role in avoiding armed conflict with the Soviet Union during the Cold War, but at a grave cost in American lives. Most of those who paid the ultimate price were involved in airborne reconnaissance aboard U.S. Air Force, U.S. Navy, and U.S. Army aircraft although two deadly incidents involved U.S. Navy shipborne signals intelligence collection platforms. During the Cold War, American reconnaissance crews suffered casualties at the hands of the Soviets, Chinese Communists, North Koreans, North Vietnamese, Cubans, and even the Israelis. Collectively, 264 Americans were killed in action or declared missing in action (105 KIAs and 159 MIAs) in thirty-six reconnaissance incidents during the Cold War. Twelve of the incidents (forty-one KIAs and nine MIAs) occurred in Southeast Asia in support of the Vietnam War, and thirty-four men were killed in the Israeli attack on the USS *Liberty* in the Mediterranean Sea north of the Egyptian coast. The *Liberty* incident can be legitimately considered a Cold War casualty because the Soviet Union was very much involved in the Arab-Israeli conflict as the major supplier of combat arms and military advisers to Iraq, Syria, and Egypt. Additionally, the USS *Liberty* mission included the collection of signals intelligence on Soviet Fifth Ehskadra naval operations in the Mediterranean Sea.

Twenty-three of the recon missions that incurred losses (29 KIAs and 150 MIAs) occurred under peacetime conditions while U.S. Air Force and U.S. Navy crews conducted reconnaissance against the Soviet Union, Cuba, China, and North Korea in incidents not related to the Vietnam War. Ironically, only one U.S. airman was lost in the many intentional American overflights of the Soviet Union and other communist countries during the Cold War[15]—the twenty-two other missions that incurred losses were Peacetime Aerial Reconnaissance Program (PARPRO) missions that were not authorized to overfly territory that the U.S. recognized as "enemy airspace." The Vietnam War losses, forty-one KIAs and nine MIAs, break down as follows: six Air Force EC-47 signals intelligence recon missions suffered losses (five missions shot down and one fatal crash due to nonhostile causes), and two intelligence specialists were killed in separate Viet Cong ground attacks on Air Force Security Service ground facilities in Vietnam. As well, there were four U.S. Army signals intelligence-related incidents in which nine soldiers were killed and five are missing in action. In other words, for airborne reconnaissance personnel, the Cold War was every bit as "hot" in nonhostile areas as it was in Vietnam.

Other Cold War signals intelligence reconnaissance casualties included the shootdown of an American U-2 on a reconnaissance mission over Cuba and the crash from nonhostile causes of two Strategic Air Command RC-135 recon aircraft involved in monitoring Soviet missile tests. A Cuban SA-2 missile downed the U-2 on October 27, 1962, killing U.S. Air Force Maj. Rudolf Anderson. On June 5, 1969, an Alaskan-based SAC Rivet Amber RC-135 disappeared over the Bering Sea after the flight crew reported severe aircraft vibrations.[16] The entire aircrew (nineteen men) was listed as Missing in Action, Presumed Dead after search crews were unable to locate the crash site. In the other SAC signals intelligence recon loss—returning from a recon mission off Kamchatka—six aircrew members died in the crash landing of a Cobra Ball RC-135 on Shemya Island on March 16, 1981.[17]

The fact that the two SAC recon mission losses were attributable to nonhostile causes in no way detracts from the dangers associated with Cold War reconnaissance. Nor were military personnel the only casualties of the airborne espionage duel. When a Soviet SU-15 "Flagon" fighter pilot shot down Korean Air flight 007, a commercial Boeing 747 airliner, near Sakhalin Island on August 31, 1983, the Soviet government accused the Korean crew of being on a recon mission for the United States and some commentators speculated that Soviet air defense authorities mistakenly believed that the airliner was actually a U.S. Air Force RC-135 when they ordered the KAL 007 shot down.[18]

By September 1958 when Soviet MiGs downed C-130 60528 over Armenia, Soviet air defense forces had already shot down ten U.S. recon aircraft; the Communist Chinese had shot down two U.S. Navy recon flights; and one U.S. recon mission had simply disappeared on a recon mission over the Sea of Japan. Over the years there has been speculation that some of the missing in action from these losses, especially some of those shot down near or within Soviet borders, survived and were imprisoned in the Soviet Union. However, a bilateral U.S.-Russian Joint Commission on POW/MIAs has been investigating details surrounding the MIAs from Cold War reconnaissance missions since March 1992, and has found no proof to date that any of the MIAs survived the incidents in which they were lost. During an early assessment of the incidents, the commission agreed to investigate ten incidents in which there were crew members missing in action who had not been accounted for:

Date	Incident
8 Apr 1950	USN PB4Y-2 "Privateer" shot down over Baltic Sea—ten crewmen/all MIA
6 Nov 1951	USN P2V "Neptune" shot down over Sea of Japan—ten crewmen/all MIA
13 Jun 1952	USAF RB-29 shot down over Sea of Japan—twelve crewmen/all MIA
7 Oct 1952	USAF RB-29 shot down north of island of Hokkaido, Japan—eight crewmen/seven MIA and one KIA

29 Jul 1953   USAF RB-50 shot down over Sea of Japan—seventeen crewmen/Capt. John Roche survived/thirteen MIA and three KIA

18 Apr 1955   USAF RB-47 shot down off coast of Kamchatka (over Pacific Ocean)—three crewmen/all MIA

10 Sep 1956   USAF RB-50 disappeared over Sea of Japan during typhoon—sixteen crewmen/all MIA

2 Sep 1958   USAF C-130 60528 shot down near Yerevan, Armenia—seventeen crewmen/six KIA and eleven MIA

1 Jul 1960   USAF RB-47 shot down over Barents Sea—six crewmen/two survivors, one KIA and three MIA

14 Dec 1965   USAF RB-57 disappeared over Black Sea—two crewmen/both MIA

Because of the relevance to the C-130 shootdown in which eleven crew members have not been accounted for, several of these incidents are discussed below.

PB4Y-2 Shot Down Over Baltic Sea—April 8, 1950

Joseph Mishkofski enlisted in the army in July 1947, right after graduating from high school in Hazelton, Pennsylvania. Mishkofski attended school in Hazelton with Angeline Petrochilos, younger sister of M.Sgt. George Petrochilos who perished aboard C-130 60528 on Sept. 2, 1958. In 1949, Mishkofski had transferred from the Army Security Agency to the U.S. Air Force Security Service. As a Morse intercept operator assigned to the Air Force Security Service 2d Radio Squadron Mobile in Darmstadt, Germany, in September 1949, Mishkofski became involved in the squadron's monitoring of U.S. recon missions along the Soviet and European satellite borders—primarily U.S. Navy missions flown in PB4Y-2 "Privateer" aircraft that, although based in Morocco, operated out of Wiesbaden Air Base, Germany. He vividly recalls the U.S. Navy "Pixie" (a term borrowed from the British for a highly sensitive "ferret" or recon mission) mission that Soviet naval fighter aircraft shot down near Bornholm Island over the Baltic Sea on April 8, 1950, the first Soviet shootdown of a U.S. aircraft during the Cold War. Ten men died or disappeared in the incident.

It was normally a fairly routine operation with the mission aircraft using a fixed call sign (Metro-43 implying a weather mission) and broadcasting unencrypted in-flight reports in Morse code on a fixed frequency of 1002 Kilohertz. One of Mishkofski's intercept assignments was to copy the Morse traffic from Pixie missions.

Mishkofski was on duty when the Soviet fighters shot down the recon aircraft on April 8. He had copied several earlier in-flight reports, but the mission aircraft failed to send its next report as scheduled.

The 2d RSM also monitored Soviet communications related to recon missions. Its highest priority intercepts during recon missions were the Soviet air defense (PVO) nets that passed information regarding the recon missions. The Soviet air defense controllers used a very elementary system to differentiate between friendly (Soviet) and hostile (non-Soviet) targets. A list of all scheduled friendly flights for the day was passed in advance. Then, when the PVO forces observed an airborne flight, if the flight was not listed on the preflight schedule, the Soviets assumed the flight to be non-Soviet and therefore, by definition, hostile. As a general rule, the U.S. Navy recon missions flew in international airspace and the Soviets, for their part, respected the rights of the American aircrews as long as the U.S. aircraft did not violate Soviet state borders. But this time, they shot one down.

As with other similar U.S.-Soviet air incidents, Soviet authorities claimed that the intruder aircraft on April 8 had violated Soviet territory, a claim the American government vehemently denied. A search and rescue effort was launched when the crew failed to call in an in-flight report and contact with the mission was lost. The fate of the ten crew members, who were declared MIAs after the shootdown, has never been determined.

Declassified U.S. and Soviet documents elaborate on the incident, but provide few additional details regarding the fate of the MIAs. The American records relate simply that on April 8, 1950, a PB4Y-2 Privateer tail number 59645 assigned to squadron VP-26, Port Lyautey, Morocco, was shot down over the Baltic Sea by Soviet fighters. Search and rescue efforts were unsuccessful—two lifeboats from the aircraft were eventually recovered as well as some wreckage, but all ten crew members remain un-accounted for.

The Soviet government acknowledged that its fighters attacked the Privateer, but justified its actions with the claim that the American plane was flying in Soviet airspace and had fired on the Soviet fighters when they attempted to signal it to land. The Soviet government stated at the time and subsequently that it had no information about survivors from the flight.

As with most similar incidents, the American position reveals a fun-damental disagreement with the Soviet government concerning both the location of the incident and the question of who fired first. There are no known American eyewitnesses to the shootdown and no indications that any of the crew bailed out and survived. No one actually saw the aircraft crash or break up; thus, the possibility of survivors cannot be ruled out. The only known witnesses are the Soviet fighter pilots themselves.

Declassified handwritten statements from the Soviet pilots involved in the shootdown and from others in the chain of command provide the prevailing Soviet views. Senior Lt. Boris Pavlovich Dokin, the group commander of two pairs of intercepting fighters, described the intercep-tion in detail:

> Being in the duty flight on readiness condition one, I received the order to take off. After take-off, I received the command to assume an altitude of 4,000 meters on a course of 360 degrees. I flew for four minutes on this course. At 17:33 hours, I received the command from the control point to take a course of 340 degrees. At 17:37 hours I received the com-mand to take a course of 360 degrees. At 17:39 hours I made contact with a four-engine aircraft with American markings on a course of 135 degrees—south of Liepaya, eight kilometers from the settlement of Tsenkon'. After I sighted the aircraft, my pair approached from behind

*and to the right, and I told the second pair, led by Senior Lieutenant
Gerasimov, to force the violator to land. Gerasimov flew ahead and
sharply rocking his wings, turned to the left. The violator took a course of
270 degrees toward the sea and did not follow Senior Lt. Gerasimov's
pair. I then gave a 12-shot warning burst. The violator began firing at
me. Seeing this, my wingman, Lt. Tezyaev, fired at the violator. The violator steeply descended and entered the clouds at an altitude of 500
meters. Presumably, the aircraft crashed 5-10 kilometers from the shore.*

All four interceptor pilots provided handwritten statements describing the incident, with each pilot corroborating the other pilots' reports.
In June 1994 former Lieutenant Gerasimov commented on the incident
to the United States–Russian Joint Commission on POW/MIAs:

*It was on 8 April 1950, about 12:00 noon. We got word that a U.S.
B-29 was approaching from Wiesbaden. Tezyaev and I went up, took a
left and were about 70 kilometers from shore. I had my radar on. Every
day this happened, the U.S. planes were there. We were told to come
west toward shore. There was a second pair of MiGs sent up as well. I
got under the tail. I figured maybe he was lost. I waggled my wings and
indicated that he was to fly toward land. He tried to get out to sea. It was
a little foggy. I reported this to the ground. I was told to give warning
shots, which I did. Then we got the codeword "Molniya" (lightning),
which was the codeword to open fire on the plane. My comrades did. The
plane caught fire, exploded in the air and fell in pieces into the sea. I was
ordered to circle around awhile in the area and then to return to Liepaya.
My opinion is that the plane exploded and no one survived. Sailors patrolled and did not find anybody.*

Additional Soviet fighter aircraft from Kaliningrad also attempted to
locate the American plane, but were called back due to foggy conditions.
None of the interceptor pilots reported observing the crash of the American aircraft. The Privateer crew apparently followed standard evasive
procedures—turn away from hostile territory and attempt to escape. The
reported firing of warning shots may well have happened, and been

intended as "warning shots." But, given the belligerent confrontational state of the relations between the United States and the Soviet Union, if you were aboard the American aircraft being "warned" with bursts of cannon fire, your thought would probably be "Those bastards are firing on us." Defending themselves by returning fire would have been the instinctive response.

An interview with Col. Jurus Vectrans, Chief of the Latvian Police in 1992, revealed that the fighters that shot down the Privateer in April 1950 were operating from the local airfield in Liepaya, on the Latvian coast. He recalled that upon their return from the mission, the Russian pilots were reported to have been laughing because they "shot down a big plane and it was easy." Vectrans reported that for a week following the incident all roads in the coastal area were closed and the local area was searched—an apparently standard operating procedure in case parachutists had been dropped from the intruding aircraft before it was intercepted. Vectrans stated that the KGB played the leading role in the road closure and search effort.

The destruction of the American aircraft over the Baltic Sea in April 1950 got the personal attention of Joseph Stalin who ordered an extensive search in an effort to recover equipment from the downed aircraft to prove that it was spying on the Soviet Union. A declassified message found in naval archives and addressed to Comrades Stalin and Bulganin in June 1950 describes the search undertaken by Soviet naval forces:

> I report that the search conducted by the 4th Navy for the American plane that sank on April 8 of this year to the west of Liepaya did not yield positive results. During the period 22 April to 14 June the search employed 45 different vessels, 33 of which were trawlers. There were 160 divers involved in the underwater portion of the search. The area where the aircraft was assumed to have sunk, a general area of 166.4 square kilometers, was patrolled and investigated by trawlers and metal detectors. . . . In spite of the large effort and resources spent on the search for the American plane, no pieces of it were found. Discovery of the aircraft by additional searches also appear unlikely. . . . I consider it expedient to discontinue the search for the American plane in the area of Liepaya.

Many of the documents describing the interception and shootdown of the U.S. PB4Y-2 Privateer aircraft came from the Baltic Military District's "Air Observation, Warning and Communications Troops" command file in the archives at the Podolsk archival center outside Moscow. The archived records indicate a degree of confusion regarding the incident. For example, some reports identify the intruder aircraft as a B-29. In response to an inquiry from the U.S. State Department in 1975, an internal Communist Party report signed by Chairman of the Committee for State Security Andropov in November 1975 suggests that the Soviets had no knowledge about the fate of the ten missing crew members. The report states, in part:

> . . . The American propaganda organs have recently published a number of reports on the crew of an American plane shot down over our country in 1950. The crew members are allegedly imprisoned in the USSR. . . . Official documents on hand testify that on 8 April 1950 an American B-29 violated the airspace of the USSR over the Baltic Sea and was driven off by Soviet fighters. The crew observed radio silence while approaching the state border and while in Soviet airspace. The subsequent fate of the plane is unknown. As has been established, none of the crew members the Americans are looking for were prosecuted or held in prisons in the USSR. The U.S. Embassy in Moscow appealed for an explanation concerning the fate of the crew members. They received the appropriate answers.

Retired Soviet General Shinkarenko, who had commanded the Soviet aircraft involved in the downing of the Privateer, could shed no additional details regarding the fate of the lost crew, but pointed out that the Soviet air force always produced a "Lessons Learned" file of reports, and that copies of those reports were always forwarded to Moscow. Retired Col. Nikolai Ryzhov, former assistant to General Shinkarenko, recalled that he personally supervised destruction of local files on the incident, but that there should be more information in the Soviet air force "Bulletins on Lessons Learned from the Downing of U.S. Aircraft Violating Soviet Borders" archives. The Russians located and provided to the Americans in late 1992 such a "Lessons Learned" file on the C-130 shootdown over Armenia in 1958. No such files have surfaced for the 1950 Privateer downing.

Records dated December 1949 showed the chaotic status of Soviet air defense at the time, and point to a buildup of tensions immediately before the Privateer was shot down. As late as 1949, U.S. aircraft were violating Soviet airspace at will, not only over the sea but well inland as well, and there was little Soviet authorities could do about it. At the time, Soviet aircraft and bases had no radar devices, and many officers were reprimanded for allowing the Americans to violate the Soviet state borders. On March 7, 1950, a decision was made to transfer special aircraft to Palanga in the Lithuanian republic not far from the Baltic coast to put a stop to the violations. Tensions were high in the Baltic air defense network on April 8, 1950, when the Privateer arrived in the Baltic area on what its crew assumed would be a routine recon mission over international waters. Did it intentionally violate Soviet airspace? No. Did it unintentionally violate Soviet territory? We have no way of knowing. It was foggy over the southeastern Baltic; it might have accidentally strayed from its flight path.

P2V Shot Down Over Sea of Japan—November 6, 1951

The U.S. Navy experienced the loss of another reconnaissance crew on November 6, 1951, when Soviet Naval fighter aircraft shot down a P2V Neptune aircraft, tail number 124283, near Cape Ostrovnoj over the Sea of Japan in the Soviet Far East. When the shootdown occurred, the aircraft and crew assigned to squadron VP-2, Atsugi Air Base, Japan, were on detached duty under the control of Gen. Matthew Ridgway's United Nations Command in Korea. The aircrew transmitted no distress signals and none of the ten crew members has ever been accounted for.

A declassified top secret report signed by the admiral of the Pacific Fleet, Adm. N. G. Kuznetsov, on November 6, 1951, was found in 1992 in Russian presidential archives, *Arkhiv Prezidenta RF*, at Podolsk, Russia. Kuznetsov's report informed Comrade Joseph Stalin about the incident and included one enclosure depicting the flight route of the American aircraft and another providing general tactical and technical data for the Neptune recon aircraft:

I report:

According to a report from the Commander of the 5th Navy, during the morning of 6 November an A-20-J (Boston) aircraft conducted reconnaissance of a 12 nautical mile frontier area to the southwest of Cape Ostrovnoj. It [the frontier] was protected by two LA-11 fighters from the 5th Navy. At 10:10 hours Vladivostok time, our aircraft detected the American aircraft within the boundaries of our territorial waters, 10-15 kilometers from the shore. When they spotted the intruder, our two fighters (the flight leader was Lykshov and the wingman was Shchukin) closed on and identified the American patrol aircraft. It was a "Neptune" type bomber. Upon approach of our fighters, the American plane opened fire on them. The intruder was shot down by return fire from our fighters. At 10:18 hours it fell, burning, into the water and exploded 32 kilometers from the shore. Our fighters returned to their airfield undamaged. Three torpedo cutters that were sent to the crash site did not find any remains of the aircraft.

After the crash, according to 5th Navy signals intelligence resources, American and Japanese radio stations on Hokkaido Island persistently called the aircraft on the radio. (The plane evidently did not manage to report in.) As established by radio intercepts, the plane was Number Five and belonged to the 6th Patrol-Bomber Aviation Squadron based at Atsugi airfield (Honshu Island). I believe that the actions of our fighter planes were proper, considering that the American plane violated our territorial waters and opened fire on our planes first.

Kuznetsov's report was the equivalent of a "critic follow-up" in the American Intelligence reporting cycle—the initial Critic Report provides the bare essentials to the president immediately when a critical event occurs, and additional details appear in follow-up reports. Admiral Kuznetsov provided further information to Stalin on November 7:

As a supplement to my report on the American plane shot down on 6 November 1951 near Cape Ostrovnoj, I report:

Radio intercepts from our stations have established that the American "Neptune" aircraft Number Five from the 6th Patrol-Bomber Aviation

Squadron took off from Atsugi airfield at 06:26 hours on 6 November Vladivostok time. It flew to the northern part of the Sea of Japan for reconnaissance. Toward the end of the day, the American Air Force command gave orders to aircraft of the 2nd Group of the 96th Operation Group (aircraft carriers) to conduct a search for "Neptune" Number Five in the Sea of Japan between the 40th and 44th parallels. At the same time, ships of the 77th and 95th Operational Groups located near the coast of Korea were informed that "Neptune" Number Five was missing.

According to the Americans, the last time that aircraft Number Five was noticed was 08:40 hours on 6 November, 30 miles to the west of Oku-Shiri Shima Island. On the night of the sixth, two "Mariner" aircraft and one "Neptune" aircraft flew to the Sea of Japan to search for the American plane. On 7 November five "Neptunes," five "Mariners," two "B-29s" and two helicopters were noted searching for the downed American plane. The American planes conducting the search did not come closer than 180 kilometers to our shores. Based on this, I conclude that the downed American plane did not manage to report the incident with our fighters.

The Soviet Union lodged an immediate demarche (i.e., formal protest) with the American Embassy in Moscow on November 7, but said nothing publicly about the incident. Neither did the U.S. government announce the loss of the aircraft to the press until November 23 when facts about the incident and the Soviet demarche were made known. The Soviet demarche followed standard diplomatic protocols:

> *The Government of the Union of the Soviet Socialist Republics considers it necessary to announce the following to the Government of the United States of America.*
>
> *According to confirmed information received by the Government of the USSR, at 10:10 hours Vladivostok time, on 6 November 1951, an American twin-engined "Neptune" type bomber violated the state border of the USSR near Cape Ostrovnoj. Two Soviet fighters approached the American aircraft that had violated the border with the intent to force it to land at a Soviet airfield. The American aircraft opened fire. The Soviet*

aircraft were forced to return fire, and the American aircraft turned off
toward the sea and disappeared.

Bringing this to the attention of the U.S. government, the Soviet gov-
ernment is announcing a strong protest against this new, flagrant viola-
tion of the state border of the USSR by an American military aircraft.
The Soviet government insists that those responsible for this violation be
made to answer for this act and expects that the U.S. government will
immediately take appropriate actions to ensure that there are no violations
of the state borders of the USSR in the future.

When word of the loss of an American aircraft and ten crew members leaked to the press, the U.S. Navy provided scant details on November 23. The same day the Soviet *Pravda* newspaper declared that the
Presidium of the Soviet Union had awarded the Order of the Red Banner
to two Soviet naval aviators for "exemplary fulfillment of their service
duties" and stated that American aviators had been "impudent fellows"
who had received a "proper lesson."

The United States tacitly conceded defeat in a battle of words with
the Soviets regarding culpability for the incident. During the more than
two weeks that the U.S. kept the loss of the aircraft under wraps, a debate
raged within the State Department about the advisability of a direct
protest to the Soviet government: the lost aircraft was, after all, actually
assigned to the United Nations Command. The initial U.S. public position
when expressed on November 23 by the U.S. Navy was only that the aircraft had been on a weather reconnaissance patrol and was missing —no
mention was made that it was shot down, nor was the location of the incident mentioned.

The State Department followed up with an announcement that the
aircraft had been missing since November 6, 1951, after being fired upon
by Soviet fighters, and that Moscow had protested the incident claiming
that the aircraft had violated Soviet airspace and was "last seen disappearing toward the sea." The U.S. response to the Soviet demarche
charged that the missing Neptune was "attacked without warning" by Soviet fighters while over international waters over the Sea of Japan.

In 1955, a U.S. Air Force study on Cold War shootdowns concluded that "The United States did not request a United Nations (U.N.) investigation, nor did it give any indication that the Soviet government would be asked to discipline those responsible for the incident, pay damages or give assurances against a repetition of the incident. . . . U.N. Secretary Lie indicated that no action would be taken by the U.N. unless the Soviets or the United States demanded a Security Council debate. . . . The matter was dropped by both sides." An internal State Department document dated December 17, 1951, sheds additional light on the failure to pursue the matter, concluding that "The American fliers were lost in the performance of duty and, as much as we dislike it, there is little we can do to obtain redress. . . . In the circumstances, I think it is probably more in accord with realities of the situation if we take no further action in this case." The lack of American eyewitnesses was a hindrance to making a strong American case to protest the incident.

RB-29 Shot Down Over Sea of Japan—June 1952

On June 13, 1952, American reconnaissance fliers suffered their next loss when a Soviet air force MiG-15 pilot shot down an RB-29 south of Valentin Bay in the Sea of Japan, 105 miles east of the city of Vladivostok. The plane, tail number 44-61810, was assigned to the 91st Strategic Reconnaissance Squadron at Yokota Air Base, Japan. While on a reconnaissance mission, it disappeared from friendly radar coverage one hundred miles north of Hokkaido Island, Japan—approximately one hundred miles from the Soviet coast. An empty six-man life raft similar to the type carried on RB-29s was sighted near that location; however, no wreckage or survivors were found. The entire twelve-man crew was lost, and the fate of the crew has never been factually determined.

The American Embassy in Moscow delivered a demarche to the Soviet foreign ministry on June 18, 1952, protesting the shootdown. On June 25, the Deputy Minister of State Security of the Soviet Union, N. Stakhanov, referred to the U.S. protest note in a declassified top secret message to the Soviet deputy foreign minister, V. A. Zorin. Stakhanov's message implies that the Soviets accepted the American's estimated location, and had searched that area themselves.

Top Secret

We report that the American Embassy's demarche No. 689 dated 18 June 1952 says essentially the following: A U.S. B-29 aircraft was shot down by a MiG-15 aircraft of the Air Force of the Soviet Army over our territorial waters south of Valentin Bay at 17:35 hours on 13 June 1952.

The location of the unidentified aircraft's wreckage is listed in the American Embassy's demarche as 41:03.9' N 133:05.5' E. This [point] is 80 miles south of Valentin Bay—105 miles east of Vladivostok. No wreckage of the aircraft, pieces of equipment or crew members were found by either the coast guard or the shore patrol.

Another declassified Soviet message from sources in the field to the Soviet ministry of state security (KGB) provides the Soviet version of the shootdown:

On 13 June of this year at 17:05 hours local time, an anti-air defense radio-technical station of the 5th Navy fixed on an American aircraft twenty-two kilometers south of the Bay of Valentin in the Primorskij Kraj.

Two MiG-15 aircraft of the 165th Air Division of the Naval Air Force stationed at Unashi airfield were scrambled. According to targeting by the main station for target control of fighter aviation for Naval Air Defense, at approximately 17:33 hours, south of Cape Ostrovnoj, on the border of our waters and at an altitude of 1,500 meters, those aircraft met with a B-29 American aircraft. On the MiG-15s' approach, the American aircraft was the first to open fire, after which the MiG-15s attacked the B-29 and shot it down. At 17:35 hours the burning B-29 crashed into the sea.

The aircraft's crash is confirmed by photographs taken from the MiG-15s and by questioning the pilots. One of the MiG-15s has a 12.7 mm bullet hole and a hole made by a fragment from the downed American aircraft. . . .

Presumably the MiG-15 photographs were taken by a gun camera on each fighter. Gun camera photographs showing the shootdown of Air Force C-130, tail number 60528, over Armenia in 1958 were located in 1992 in a "Lessons Learned" file in the air defense archives at Podolsk, Russia, but no gun camera photos for any of the other air incidents have been found. An additional Soviet report which included a map indicated that the American B-29 was engaged ten miles from the Soviet coast and "crashed in flames" at a distance of about eighteen miles offshore.

In reference to a message from the American Embassy, a declassified message from the deputy minister of state security to the foreign ministry on June 25, 1952, states that the border guards' search party had found no debris, equipment, or crew members at the geographical coordinates provided by the embassy as being the crash site.

To the present, the Russians deny that any crew members from the RB-29 crash on June 13, 1952, were rescued and incarcerated in a Soviet prison. The crew of that aircraft would have been a lucrative target for the Soviet intelligence services that would have done their utmost to pick up any survivors. There is no substantial proof that any of the crew survived the crash. One possible clue does exists, however. On July 3, 1952, a B-29 bomber was shot down on a bombing mission against the Yalu River bridge at Sinanju, North Korea. Some of the crew bailed out and were captured and interrogated at Mukden, China. Two of those POWs later testified that their Chinese interrogators suddenly shifted the focus of their investigation and queried them about Maj. Sam Busch, aircraft commander of the RB-29 shot down over the Sea of Japan on June 13, 1952. They were repeatedly queried about Major Busch in a manner that suggested the questions were posed on behalf of Soviet intelligence officers. The former POWs are convinced that the Soviets must have been holding Busch. On the other hand, it would have been easy for the KGB to have obtained the names of the downed RB-29 aircrew from press reports.

Compared to other shootdowns, the information on the incident provided by the Russians from Soviet archives has been scant, and absent any eyewitnesses or distress call, the U.S. had little information to go on in 1952. Consequently, the known facts of the incident are sketchy. The possibility of there having been survivors is slim.

RB-29 Shot Down North of Hokkaido, Japan—October 7, 1952

Another RB-29 from the 91st Strategic Recon Squadron was shot down by Soviet fighters while conducting a reconnaissance mission northeast of the Island of Hokkaido, Japan, on October 7, 1952. A U.S. search and rescue effort was mounted immediately, but found no trace of the eight crew members aboard the downed recon aircraft. The shootdown occurred near Yuri Island[19] in the vicinity of the Kurile Island chain. The incident occurred in a border area consisting of Soviet and American zones of occupation in post–World War II Japan. The Soviet Union occupied the former Japanese controlled Kurile Islands at the end of World War II and claimed the airspace around the islands as sovereign Soviet territory. This time there were plenty of witnesses to the shootdown, including Japanese fishermen, the Soviet pilots who attacked the RB-29, and Soviet border guards.

One Soviet report located the crash site as 1.5 kilometers southwest of Demina Island (latitude 43 degrees 24.3 minutes north, longitude 146 degrees 08.5 minutes east). Several Japanese fishermen witnessed the incident although none actually saw the RB-29 fall into the sea. According to the Japanese witnesses, the RB-29 was flying in the vicinity of the Kurile/Habomai Islands when fighters appeared and attacked it. The RB-29 was trailing thick black smoke as it disappeared from sight. Claiming that the American aircraft fired first on two Soviet LA-11 fighters scrambled to intercept the intruder inside Soviet airspace, the Soviets admitted that they shot down the aircraft.

The Soviets did not acknowledge at the time that Soviet border guards sent to the crash site recovered aircraft debris and the body of one of the RB-29's eight crew members—1st Lt. John Robertson Dunham. Without ceremony or notification to the U.S. government, the Soviets buried the body—a headless corpse in a black flight suit containing Lieutenant Dunham's identification card—on the small island of Yuri. None of the other crew members has ever been accounted for.

Declassified U.S. and Soviet documents shed additional light on the incident. On October 8, the commander of the Soviet Far East Military District provided a wrap-up on the shootdown incident to Marshal Vasilevskij, Soviet defense minister. In turn, Marshal Vasilevskij informed Stalin and the Communist Party Central Committee of the shootdown in a top secret summary report:

> *Top Secret*
> *Copy No. 1 to Comrade Stalin*
> *We report:*
>
> Two LA-11 fighters from the 368th Air Defense Fighter Aviation Regiment shot down an American B-29 on 7 October of this year, at 15:30 hours Khabarovsk time, in the southeastern part of the Malaya Kuri'lskaya Island chain. It violated our state border 12–15 kilometers southwest of Yuri Island.
>
> The B-29 aircraft was discovered by a radio-technical [air surveillance] post at 14:31 hours in the immediate proximity of our state border. Consequently, a pair of fighters that was on duty at Yuzhno-Kuril'sk airfield was scrambled. The fighters were piloted by Senior Lieutenant Zheryakov and Senior Lieutenant Lesnov.
>
> At 15:29 hours, the B-29 aircraft violated the border and flew over the territorial waters of the USSR in the direction of Yuri Island. Since the violator fired first, it was attacked by our fighters at 15:30 hours. As a result of the attack, the B-29 aircraft caught on fire, fell, and sank in our territorial waters three kilometers southeast of Yuri Island. A headless corpse wearing a deployed parachute was picked up by cutters of the 114th Frontier Guard Detachment in the area where the aircraft went down. A map of Hokkaido Island and the Kurile Islands, a ripped piece of an unidentified document with the signature of James Smith— Captain, Intelligence Officer, U.S. Armed Forces—four fuel tanks, and a torn inflatable rubber boat were also picked up. Documents with the name First Lieutenant Dunham, John Robertson, American Army, were found in the corpse's clothes.
>
> From dawn until midday on 8 October, American F-86 fighters patrolled along our state border southwest of Yuri Island in groups of four to eight. Individual aircraft violated the border three times at high speed and flew past the area where the aircraft went down. Measures have been taken to heighten the combat readiness of all systems in the Sakhalin-Kurile border region of air defense.

The Far East Military District commander also pointed out that their low performance LA-11 fighter aircraft were too slow to intercept the faster American fighters that were violating their borders on October 8. Although those facts were excluded from the summary that Stalin received, the Soviet military leaders were no doubt agitated by this disparity.

U.S. airmen in the U.S. Air Force Air Defense Center at Nagoya, Japan, were tracking the RB-29 when the attack occurred. They saw the RB-29s track merge with the track of an unidentified aircraft. Shortly thereafter, the RB-29 crew broadcast one final transmission, "Mayday!!! . . . Let's get the hell out of here." U.S. records indicate that the RB-29 was shot down about 14:30 local (15:30 Vladivostok) time on October 7, 1952. U.S. aircraft and ships conducted search and rescue operations in the general crash area until October 12, but being hampered by bad weather, found no debris or survivors. U.S. investigators claimed at the time that the RB-29 was on the U.S. side of the so-called "MacArthur Line," the dividing line between Soviet and American zones of occupation—Japan was still an occupied country. Later analysis, however, revealed that the RB-29 probably did unintentionally violate Soviet airspace shortly before it was shot down.

On October 12, and again on November 24, 1952, the Soviet government delivered diplomatic messages to the U.S. ambassador in Moscow, protesting the violation of their state border in the Kurile Islands. The United States denied violating the Soviet border and disputed Soviet claims to ownership of Yuri Island and other islands in the area. Later in September 1954, the U.S. government presented a formal claim against the Soviet Union for $1.6 million for loss of the aircraft and crew, and took the case to the International Court of Justice in the Netherlands in May 1955. The American legal position centered on questions of sovereignty over islands in the Kurile chain. The Soviet Union refused to pay the damages and reasserted its claim to the disputed territories. In a top secret memo on December 29, 1954, to the Central Committee, Soviet Foreign Minister Molotov said:

> . . . On 25 Sep of this year [1954], the U.S. government sent a demarche that once again raised the question of this incident. The demarche

extensively sets forth the American version of this incident. It expresses the unsubstantiated supposition that the crew members of the aircraft may have been picked up by a Soviet vessel and that they are in Soviet custody. As far as the substance of the incident is concerned, this demarche contains nothing new in comparison with previous American demarches.

The U.S. government points to a sum of claims in connection with the loss of the aircraft and members of its crew and suggests, in the event of the USSR's refusal to satisfy these claims, that this matter be turned over to the International Court of Justice for consideration.

The USSR's right to ownership of the Malaya Kurile Island chain (Habomai), which includes Yuri Island, was once again disputed in the demarche. In connection with this, a number of demagogic declarations were made alleging that the USSR was trying to bring the Japanese people to ruin, by impeding Japan's normal commerce, by intimidating the government and the Japanese people, etc. The text of the demarche was published by the State Department and at the request of the American representative to the U.N. was circulated to the members of the security council.

The foreign minister of the USSR considers it advisable to send a demarche in reply to the U.S. government, attaching an extract from the report on the circumstances of the violation of the state border by an American "B-29" aircraft in the Yuri Island area on 7 Oct 52. As the position of the USSR on the USSR's ownership of the Malaya Kuril'skaya Island chain was stated in demarches from the Soviet government dated 24 Nov 52 and 12 Oct of this year, the Soviet foreign minister considers it advisable, in the given demarche, not to touch on the substance of this matter and only to refer to our two aforementioned demarches.

As concerns the demagogic statements of the U.S. government about the USSR's relations with Japan, an appropriate response to these statements should be given in the demarche. Taking into account that this incident happened over two years ago and that at the present time it is not necessary to draw the public's attention to this incident, it is the opinion of the foreign ministry that it is not advisable to publish said demarche. A draft of the resolution is attached.

Please review. V. Molotov

The Central Committee answered with orders for an official response to be delivered by Molotov. Excerpts from the Central Committee's memo to Molotov dated December 31, 1954, follow:

> On the reply to the demarche from the U.S. government dated 25 Sep 54. Approve the draft of the demarche made by the MID . . .
>
> . . . The circumstances of this incident, set forth in the aforementioned demarches of the Soviet government, and also in the aforementioned report, show that the American aircraft violated the state border of the USSR on 7 Oct 52 in the area of Yuri Island and opened unprovoked fire on Soviet fighters that were protecting the state border of the USSR.
>
> The Soviet government, in its demarche dated 24 Nov 52, has already reported that it does not have any information on the fate of the American "B-29" aircraft or its crew. . . .
>
> As it is firmly established that the American military aircraft violated the border of the USSR and for no reason opened fire on Soviet fighters, the responsibility for the incident that took place and its consequences falls completely on the American side. Under these conditions the Soviet government is not able to discuss the pretension contained in the U.S. government's demarche dated 25 Sep of this year. The U.S. government's suggestion to transfer this matter to the International Court is considered unwarranted.
>
> As concerns the U.S. government's attempt to use the incident of 7 Oct 52 to present the USSR's position with respect to Japan and the Japanese people in a false light, the Soviet government considers it necessary to point out that the USSR's relations with Japan and the Japanese people are well known. The position of the USSR was in particular echoed in kind in the Joint Declaration of the Government of the USSR and the Government of the KNR [China] dated 12 Oct 52 on relations with Japan. In this declaration it is pointed out that although 9 years have passed since the end of the war, Japan has not gained independence and remains a partially occupied country. The territory of Japan is covered with a multitude of American military bases, Japan's industry and finances are dependent on American military purchases, and her external commerce is under the control of the United States of America. All of this

has caused the difficult economic situation that continues to exist in Japan.

In the aforementioned declaration, the USSR expressed sympathy for Japan and the Japanese people as they are in a difficult situation owing to the San Francisco Treaty and other agreements that were thrust upon them by the United States. The USSR announced its readiness to take steps to normalize relations with Japan. Moreover, the USSR noted that Japan will be given full support in its attempt to establish political and economic relations with the USSR, just as any steps taken by the Japanese directed at providing the conditions for Japan's peaceful and independent development will be given full support.

In May 1955, the United States filed a claim in the International Court of Justice in The Hague, Netherlands, against the Soviet government for $1,620,295.01 plus interest for damages incurred in the incident.

As with most other shootdown incidents during the Cold War no progress was made regarding a settlement of issues. Russia continues to occupy the Kurile Islands, and discussions between Russia and Japan continue aperiodically regarding the ownership of the islands. The end of the Cold War did make it possible to readdress the missing in action issues associated with this and other U.S.-Soviet air incidents. After acknowledging that the body of Lieutenant Dunham had been recovered at the crash site and buried on Yuri Island on October 10, 1952, Russian President Boris Yeltsin's government assisted in exhuming Captain Dunham's[20] remains in 1994.

The fate of the other seven crew members remains a mystery although indications are that they perished in the crash. In response to appeals in the Russian press and on TV in 1993, a sixty-four-year old former sergeant in the Soviet maritime border guards and current resident of Rostov-on-Don, Vasili Ivanovich Saiko, came forward and returned the 1950 U.S. Naval Academy class ring that he had removed from Dunham's corpse in 1952. The ring was returned to Dunham's widow in 1993. At a ceremony on December 16, when Mrs. Mary Dunham Nichols was presented the ring, she commented publicly on what the return of the ring meant to her:

It brought back happy memories of an optimistic time of youth and pleasure and young love, expectation of life in the peace-time United States Air Force. It also symbolizes the humanity of a former enemy who kept the ring all these years with the hope of returning it to the family in person. My thanks go to the senators who established the Joint Commission with Russia and especially all the dedicated men and women in Washington and Moscow who work so hard and with such compassion for families of the missing. They treat us with dignity, respect, consideration and understanding.

Finally, additional closure was made for the Dunham family on 1 August 1995 when Capt. John Dunham received full military honors and his remains were interred at Arlington National Cemetery in Virginia. At the ceremony, Malcolm Toon, former American ambassador to the Soviet Union and cochairman of the United States–Russian Joint Commission on POW/MIAs, read a portion of a letter from the daughter of a crew member of the downed plane:

I am finally finishing my own grieving . . . . It is important to me that you understand that the efforts you have put forth to recover Captain Dunham's body have helped more than just his family. You have made it possible for me to heal what I thought was permanent unresolved daily grief. Like a pebble thrown into the pond, the results of your cooperation and efforts have rippled out in unknown and unexpected ways.

Significant East-West Air Incidents in March 1953

East-West air incidents made front-page column one and two headlines in the *New York Times* on March 18, 1953. On March 10, a Czechoslovakian air force MiG-15 shot down a U.S. Air Force F-84 fighter along the Czech–West German border; the pilot bailed out and survived. In a strong protest to the Czech government defining the attack as a "provocative incident," the U.S. government claimed the F-84 was flying over the United States zone of Germany when attacked.

On March 12, a Soviet MiG-15 shot down a British Royal Air Force bomber in the Berlin-Hamburg air corridor and the crew of seven perished. British Prime Minister Winston Churchill admitted that the unarmed bomber might temporarily have strayed into East Germany by error, but claimed that it definitely was flying over West Germany when "mercilessly destroyed" by Soviet MiGs.

A related headline in the *New York Times* on March 18, 1953, showed the U.S. sending both Hungary and the Soviet Union a bill for $637,894 for damages related to a forced landing of a U.S. Air Force C-47 transport aircraft in Hungary on November 18, 1951. Soviet MiG-15 pilots in Hungary forced the C-47 crew to land in that country after the American plane was blown off course by a strong tailwind while on a routine flight from West Germany to Belgrade, Yugoslavia. The damage claim included restitution for a fine of $123,605.15 that the U.S. had been required to pay the Hungarian government before it would release the four crew members.

Not to be left out, on March 14 a single-engine Soviet air force biplane from East Germany landed on a small airfield at Irmelshausen, West Germany,[21] after its pilot apparently became disoriented and inadvertently crossed the border between the two Germanys. Realizing he was at the wrong airfield, the pilot quickly took off and returned to East Germany before West German border police could arrive to question him.

The more significant *Times* headline on March 18 read U.S. PLANE FIRED ON BY MIG OFF SIBERIA; REPLIES TO ATTACK. Smaller headlines read WEATHER RECONNAISSANCE CRAFT IS ENGAGED BY RUSSIAN 25 MILES FROM KAMCHATKA . . . NEITHER SUFFERS DAMAGE and SENATORS SUGGEST INQUIRY INTO 'CHIP ON SHOULDER' ATTITUDE BY AMERICANS IN AREA. What all this amounted to was that a Soviet MiG-15 had attempted to shoot down a Strategic Air Command RB-50 bomber that according to the Air Force was on a "weather reconnaissance" over international airspace twenty-five miles east of the Kamchatka peninsula. The incident occurred on March 15. Claiming that the MiG fired first, the RB-50 returned the fire and took evasive actions; neither plane was damaged in the encounter.

The U.S. Air Force gave the location of the engagement as 54:02 north latitude 161:04 east longitude, i.e., over the Pacific Ocean twenty-five nautical miles east of Zhupanovo, Kamchatka. The Air Force spokesman added that as a matter of policy all weather reconnaissance missions[22] were flown no closer to Kamchatka than twenty-five miles. The Strategic Air Command RB-50 was operating from Eielson AFB, Alaska, on one of what was said to be almost daily weather flights throughout the arctic and subarctic areas. It landed at Shemya after the incident. A spokesman explained that constant weather information is considered essential to the command's continuous alert status since SAC is charged with delivering retaliatory attacks against the Soviet Union should the United States be bombed.

That the RB-50 crew had been performing a highly sensitive electronic intelligence (ferret) reconnaissance mission was known by very few outside the crew's home squadron at Forbes AFB, Kansas. The Forbes-based crews also flew "weather reconnaissance" missions while on temporary duty at U.S. Air Force bases in England, Germany, and Japan. While President Eisenhower had approved the missions and a few of his key advisers had been briefed on the intelligence missions, Congress and the Senate were kept pretty much in the dark on such matters. In almost comical fashion, Senator Ralph Flanders of the Senate Armed Services Committee wanted his committee to study whether there was "an element of chip on the shoulder" in the weather plane's flying close to Kamchatka. He said the Air Force might have been "a little reckless" in venturing so close to Soviet territory and he wondered if the weather could not be observed at a safer distance. Senator Warren Magnuson noted solemnly that there could be no excuse for the MiGs opening fire first, but added that since the RB-50 was six hundred miles west of the nearest United States territory in the Aleutians, he could understand why the Soviet planes might want to challenge it.

The incident might have been dropped at that point, but the Air Force had demanded that State issue a protest. So the U.S. State Department "vigorously" protested the incident to the Soviet Foreign Office on March 18. The protest note said the U.S. "expects to be informed at an early date of the disciplinary action taken with regard to the Soviet personnel responsible for the attack." The note also wanted assurances of steps taken to prevent a recurrence of such incidents. Two days later, on the floor of the Senate, Senator Flanders charged the Air Force with "waging psychological warfare on the people of the United States" by its account of the attack the previous Sunday by Soviet MiGs on an Air Force RB-50 engaged in a "routine weather reconnaissance" flight off Kamchatka. "The story is preposterous," he told the Senate. "There is no need to go within twenty-five miles of Kamchatka to look for weather . . . There is just as much weather fifty miles out or one hundred miles out."

In commenting on the senator's speech, the Air Force issued the following statement:

> *The Air Force has nothing to add to its statement except to emphasize that the fact that at no time was the RB-50 closer than twenty-five miles to Kamchatka, and so was not in airspace claimed to be under any national jurisdiction.*

Senator Flanders told the senators he had information he considered reliable that weather reconnaissance flights normally were made from the Bering Straits to Attu at the end of the Aleutian Island chain, and that their course did not come within four hundred miles of Kamchatka. "That reconnaissance bomber just was not there on weather business," the senator declared. "It may nevertheless have been engaged on a useful mission.

"The serious thing about this incident is the false report given to the American people by the Air Force," Senator Flanders continued:

> *It tended and probably was intended to influence public opinion by making the incident into an act of aggression. In publishing this false report the Air force has been guilty, in effect, of waging psychological warfare on the people of the United States. This must stop. There are two honest and honorable courses open in a case of this sort. One is for the Air Force to tell the truth. The other is for it to say nothing. It had better do one or the other.*

The Pentagon, State Department, and President Eisenhower's press secretary declined to comment on Senator Flander's fight with the Air Force. The senator's comments apparently had an impact on Air Force policy, however—shortly thereafter, intelligence reconnaissance missions, when talked about at all, were described as *navigational training missions*.

Meanwhile, the Soviet government rejected the U.S. charge that the Soviet MiG fired first, and countercharged that the American aircraft made two "premeditated" violations of the Soviet state border:

> . . . *In accordance with verified data, it has been established that an American bomber of the B-29 type violated on 15 March at 11:57 time in the district of Cape Krestovoj [the southern part of Kamchatka] the state frontier of the USSR and flew over the territory of Kamchatka up to seventy kilometers over a distance of 15 to 17 kilometers from the edge of the shore only a short distance from Mutnovskaya Height and turned in the direction of the sea.*
>
> *At 12:28 the American aircraft B-29 type appeared again and violated the state frontier of the USSR northeast of the town of Petropavlovsk-Kamchatki in the area of the village of Zhupanovo.*
>
> *Good weather, which in both cases enabled the crew of the aircraft to carry out visual reconnaissance on a large scale, excluded the possibility of loss of orientation and confirmed that the above two cases of violation of the state frontier of the USSR were of a clearly premeditated character.*
>
> *When the two Soviet fighter aircraft, which had taken off, approached the American bomber aircraft, which was in the process of a second violation of the Soviet state frontier, the American aircraft opened fire against the Soviet fighter aircraft.*
>
> *For the purpose of self-defense, one of the Soviet aircraft had to open fire after which the infringing aircraft turned around, left the Soviet coast and disappeared in an eastern direction.*
>
> *The above facts show that the protest made by the Government of the USA in a note of 18 March is without foundation and therefore the Soviet government rejects the protest.*
>
> *In view of the fact that the above-quoted data confirm the fact of violation of the state frontier of the USSR by an American military aircraft, the Soviet government sends a protest to the Government of the USA against the above-mentioned infringement and expects that the Government of the USA will take due measures to prevent in the future violation of the state frontier of the USSR by American aircraft.*

A State Department spokesman said on March 23 that the Soviet Union's reasons for rejecting the U.S. protest were "directly contrary to facts known here." In a press release, the State Department countered that the Soviet Union in a typical attempt to avoid responsibility for the action of its military personnel, had resorted to "the device of fabricating an unfounded version of the affair."

RB-50 Shot Down Over Sea of Japan—July 29, 1953

On July 29, 1953, the Strategic Air Command's 91st Strategic Recon Squadron suffered its first loss of an RB-50 recon aircraft when Soviet MiG pilots shot down Yokota Air Base, Japan–based bomber serial number 47145 near Askol'd Island in the Sea of Japan southeast of Vladivostok, Soviet Union. This incident was unique from a couple of perspectives. First of all, aircraft and flight crew belonged to the 343rd Strategic Reconnaissance Squadron, 55th Strategic Reconnaissance Wing at Forbes AFB, Kansas; they were on temporary duty with the 91st to perform electronic intelligence recon missions in the Far East. Second, one of the seventeen men survived: a U.S. Navy destroyer recovered Capt. John Roche at the crash site on July 30, 1953.

Captain Roche, copilot on the mission, reported that he and the pilot, Captain Stanley O'Kelley, managed to bail out, but that Captain O'Kelley died in Roche's presence in the water while awaiting rescue. Capt. O'Kelley's body and two other corpses from the crew were later recovered, leaving thirteen crew members missing in action. Two Air Force Security Service Russian linguists, S.Sgt. Donald G. Hill and A/2C Earl W. Radlein Jr. from the 1st Radio Squadron Mobile, Johnson AB, Japan, were among the MIAs—the first Security Service personnel lost in the line of duty.

The loss of the two 91st Strategic Reconnaissance Squadron RB-29s earlier in June and October 1952 had played a role in the decision to include a Security Service voice intercept position aboard 91st reconnaissance bombers. Russian linguists flying as voice intercept operators served dual roles on the recon missions—tipping off the recon bomber's pilot about approaching Soviet fighters and collecting intercepted Russian communications to update Soviet air order of battle databases.

Members of an SB-29 search and rescue crew reported sighting survivors at the crash site on July 29, and dropped lifeboats near them. As the search and rescue aircrew departed the crash scene at dusk, they sighted a number of small Soviet surface craft heading toward the crash site. When an American search and rescue craft reached the site the following day, it found only Captain Roche—no additional survivors were found, and Soviet authorities denied picking any up.

Although the American government preferred to maintain silence about its reconnaissance missions, the Air Force released a short statement on the incident after the Soviet government publicly protested an intrusion into its airspace and claimed that an intruding bomber had fired first against a Soviet jet sent out to investigate a border violation. The *Chattanooga Daily Times*, A/2C Earl Radlein Jr.'s hometown newspaper, carried a UPI article— datelined Washington, July 31—stating that the United States had protested "in the strongest terms" against the shooting down of an American bomber in the Sea of Japan, and had demanded an immediate report on what was being done to release surviving crew members.

The State Department announced its protest twelve hours after Moscow charged that the plane violated Soviet territory on the Siberian coast. The department said the plane was forty miles off the coast when it was attacked and disabled by Russian MiG fighters. The U.S. spokesman offered no explanation why it had withheld its version of the incident until long after the Russians had broadcast their border violation charge.

Capt. John Roche said one, possibly two Russian MiG jet fighters had attacked "without provocation." He stated at a news conference in Tokyo that he did not see any Russian ships in the area or anything to indicate that any of the sixteen other American crewmen had been rescued by the Russians. How many other crew members survived was not known, but the State Department stated that Russian ships were sighted in the area where survivors were seen on life rafts. The U.S. protest note, handed to Deputy Foreign Minister Andrei Gromyko by Ambassador Charles Bolen, said the B-50 was on a routine navigational training mission. Moscow had charged that the plane was over Siberia near the big naval base at Vladivostok.

In a later UPI wire service dispatch datelined Tokyo, August 2, the

rescued copilot said the chances were "very good" that some of the sixteen other Americans parachuted into the water. He told a press conference that he believed the engineer, navigator, and probably the waist and
tail gunners parachuted out as well as the pilot.

U.S. rescue planes, which scoured the area where the B-50 was
downed, reported several Russian motor torpedo-type boats had been
sighted in the area and might have picked up other members of the crew.
Despite reported sightings of crew members in life rafts at the crash site,
there is no firm evidence today that anyone other than Captain Roche
survived the crash.

As was the situation with all over-water air incidents, the U.S. and
Russia disagreed on the location at which the incident occurred. Roche
claims to this day that his crew was flying in international airspace at
least forty miles from Soviet territory when attacked without provocation
or warning. Soviet authorities, on the other hand, claim that the American aircraft violated the Soviet state border and that the American aircraft opened fire on two approaching Soviet fighter aircraft. His aircraft
damaged by the RB-50's fire, the fighter pilot claimed to have returned
the fire and ordered his wingman to attack the intruder aircraft. An internal report informed the Soviet leadership of the incident on July 30:

> On 29 July of this year at approximately 07:00 hours Vladivostok
> time, an American B-50 type four-engine bomber violated the state bor-
> der of the USSR in the area of Cape Gamov and Askol'd Island not far
> from Vladivostok. The American aircraft opened fire on two approaching
> Soviet fighters inflicting serious damage on one of them. The American
> bomber was shot down by return fire from the Soviet fighters and crashed
> into the sea.

The Soviets lodged a protest with U.S. ambassador Charles Bolen in
Moscow. The demarche stated in part:

> Upon approach of two Soviet fighters whose mission was to indicate to
> the American aircraft that it was within the borders of the USSR and to
> order it to leave Soviet airspace, the American aircraft opened fire and in-
> flicted serious damage to one of the Soviet fighters by piercing the fuselage

and left wing, and also by breaking the hermetic seal of the cockpit. The Soviet fighters were forced to return fire, after which the American aircraft withdrew in the direction of the sea.

The U.S. government in turn protested that the downed RB-50 was in international airspace over the Sea of Japan when attacked: "The copilot of the American aircraft, who was rescued by a U.S. ship approximately forty kilometers from the Soviet coast south of Cape Povorotnyj, verified that his aircraft with a crew of seventeen was attacked by one or more Soviet MiG-17 aircraft." The Soviet government rejected that contention, insisted on strict accountability of the people responsible for the border violation and added that it had no information on the downed crew. Another declassified Soviet report—from the Pacific Fleet's Admiral of the Fleet Kuznetsov to the Soviet minister of defense—was more detailed than the earlier report to Premier Khrushchev:

Top Secret

According to a report of the Pacific Fleet Headquarters on 29 July at 07:16 hours Vladivostok time, an American "B-50" violator was shot down over our territorial waters 15 kilometers to the south of Askol'd Island by two MiG-17 fighter aircraft of the Pacific Fleet under the following circumstances:

At 06:44, fleet radar stations detected an unidentified aircraft 130 kilometers to the south of Cape Gamov heading in the direction of Cape Gamov, Vladivostok.

At 06:56, two MiG-17 fighters on alert-duty were scrambled from Nikolaevka airfield and sent to provide cover for Vladivostok.

At 07:01, the fleet radar stations, continuing to track the movement of the unidentified aircraft, detected it over our territorial waters. The violator was headed in the direction of Askol'd Island at an altitude of 10,000 meters.

At 07:06, our two fighters were ordered to intercept the violator in order to determine its nationality and its reason for being over our territorial waters.

At 07:11, the leader of the fighter pair (pilot Captain Rybakov) detected the violator at a distance of 10 kilometers from Askol'd Island. It turned out to be an American "B-50" with red stripes on the vertical stabilizer and USAF identifying markings.

Upon closing for identification, our aircraft were fired upon by the violator. The left wing surface and the forward portion of the lead fighter's fuselage were damaged.

Having felt the hit in the fuselage and the loss of cabin pressure, Captain Rybakov opened fire at an altitude of 7,000 meters and ordered his wingman, Senior Lieutenant Yablonkovsky, to likewise open fire on the violator.

At 07:16 hours, the violator, while breaking into pieces, fell in flames into the water 15 kilometers (8 miles) to the south of Askol'd Island.

Our fighters returned to their airfield. Shell hits were discovered in the left wing surface and fuselage, and there was damage to the undercarriage of the lead aircraft.

According to information received from radio intercept, at 14:20 hours four American aircraft from the rescue squadron at Misawa Air Base (Japan), were scrambled and flew off in the direction of the incident. Heavy fog over the sea in the area of Vladivostok and over the aircraft crash site is complicating the search of the area.

I consider the actions of our pilots justified, since in accordance with the conditions of Article 7 of the defense minister's order No. 00117-1953 the violator was fired on when it was over our territorial waters, i.e., it was located over our territory and took hostile action by firing on our aircraft.

The reference to "radio intercept" confirms that Soviet intercept operators (English linguists) were monitoring and intercepting the communications of the American search and rescue team. Admiral Kuznetsov also sent a message on those operations to the Soviet Minister of Foreign Affairs, V. M. Molotov:

. . . According to radio intercept data from Pacific Fleet Headquarters, Admiral Clark, Commander of U.S. Naval Forces in the Far East, gave an order to send ships to an area 55 kilometers to the southeast of Askol'd Island to search for an aircraft that did not return to base.

At 20:00 hours on 29 July, an American "SB-29," having flown to the area of the supposed downed "B-50," reported to base that they had detected "B-50" debris, a lifeboat, and seven persons swimming near the lifeboat.

Two American destroyers and one cruiser, which were escorting a destroyer, were given an order by American headquarters to go to an area fifty-five kilometers to the southeast of Askol'd Island to look for the lifeboat and the people from the "B-50" that the aircraft had discovered.

Later, in another follow-up message to the minister of defense, Admiral Kuznetsov provided additional details and rationalized the impact point where the RB-50 crashed versus the location where the border violation occurred. (The point of impact was indeed in international waters.)

I am reporting that since July 30, 04:00 hours Vladivostok time, five American naval vessels, including one cruiser and four destroyers have been conducting a search for a "B-50" aircraft in the area 55 kilometers southeast of Askol'd Island.

According to radio intercept of the Pacific Ocean Fleet, on 30 July at 06:00 hours, an American cruiser in the search area reported to its command that one of the destroyers participating in the search had recovered copilot John Roche from the water. He allegedly reported that he and the aircrew fell [landed] into the water after the aircraft broke up and that remaining crew are in the search area.

Around 04:00 hours, 45 kilometers to the south of Cape Povorotnyj, two American destroyers approached Soviet fishing trawler No. 423 that was fishing in the area. American and Japanese officers, on a launch lowered from one of the destroyers, attempted to obtain information from the trawler regarding the "B-50." No information could be obtained however, as they did not have a Russian translator. Fishing trawler No. 423 arrived in Port Nakhodka at 11:00 hours.

At 04:04 hours, the group commander of the American vessels conducting the search for the aircraft reported to his command staff that one of the destroyers spoke with a Soviet trawler. No survivors or aircraft debris were found on the trawler. He explained that conversation was not possible due to the lack of a translator.

The area where the Americans located the debris and the approximate area where the B-50 copilot was recovered is 40–45 kilometers southeast of the place where the violator was shot down by our fighters.

These circumstances give full grounds to the belief that the aircraft was fired on while over our territorial waters—and in a steep glide angle to the southeast at 400 KPH—impacted after 6–7 minutes in an area 55 kilometers to the southeast of Askol'd Island.

Kuznetsov's final paragraph directly contradicts his earlier message to the minister of defense in which he reports the B-50 "broke into pieces" and crashed into the sea fifteen kilometers from Askol'd.

Of special note, a colored map appended to this report showed a total of ten Soviet ships in the search area—nine navy cutters and one border guards patrol cutter. This is the first documentary proof from the Russian archives that Soviet vessels were active in the shootdown area.

Both sides agreed that an air incident occurred and that the American aircraft was shot down. Beyond that point, they generally disagreed on all other specifics. For one thing, the two sides had their own perspectives of what constituted an intrusion—they disagreed on the width of the Soviet Union's territorial waters. In a diplomatic message dated October 9, 1954, the United States sought financial reimbursement for loss of the aircraft and crew, and raised the issue of the width of Soviet territorial waters. Contrary to international law, the Soviets claimed territorial waters of twelve nautical miles of width while the U.S. "does not recognize the Soviet government's claim to territorial waters beyond three miles from its shore." (There was no universally accepted international law establishing sovereignty over coastal sea waters and airspace in 1958 although the "twelve-mile rule" was claimed by most countries. The *United Nations Convention on the Law of the Sea* (1982) establishes a twelve nautical mile definition, with sovereignty extending "to the airspace over the territorial sea as well as to its bed and subsoil.") The Soviets responded with a demarche that said in part:

The U.S. government's demarche dated 9 October asserts, as if it is international law, that there is a limit on the width of territorial waters to three nautical miles. In connection with this, the Soviet government con-

siders it necessary to turn the U.S. government's attention to the widely known fact that no common measures of international law exist establishing the width of territorial waters. The establishment of territorial waters is dependent on the competence of the coastal government that determines the width in consideration of their national interests and also in the interests of international maritime navigation. It is known that more than 30 governments currently have territorial waters with a width of more than three nautical miles. Thus, the U.S. government's assertion that the establishment of Soviet territorial waters to twelve nautical miles is contradictory to the norms of international law does not have any basis.

The point of contention was whether the B-50 violated Soviet airspace. The Soviets maintained the "intrusion" occurred at 42:39.3 north longitude 132:20.9 east latitude (near Askol'd Island); not forty miles south of Cape Povorotnyj as the U.S. government claimed. Declassified secret messages from the 91st Strategic Recon Squadron provided progress reports on search and rescue efforts for July 29, 30, and 31, and reported the sighting of survivors at the coordinates of 42:12 north latitude, 132:59 east longitude at 17:50 "I" [Japanese] time on July 29. In other words, the crash area was outside Soviet territorial waters. The 91st messages read in part:

Search Progress Report pertains to Capt. Stanley Keith O'Kelley, AO776002 and 16 others. (Ref my Msg GX 1530 PERS.) 2 SB-29 searched area 41:42 north and 42:30 north 132:00 east to 133:20 east with 90 percent coverage. A-3 boat dropped to 4 survivors at 42:14 north 132:59 east at 17:50 "I" time. Positive sighting of 2d group of 3 survivors approximately 1/2 mile east of boat drop. Positive sighting of debris and/or possible sighting of survivors 1 and 1/2 miles east of boat drop area. Pilot reports seeing the survivors making way to A-3 boat but did not see actual boarding due to fog bank. Both craft performed concentrated search of immediate area but were restricted by fog banks and darkness. 4 Navy destroyers estimated to arrive at 24:00 hours 29 July "I" time in search area. 12 boats, PT Type, nationality unknown, sighted at 42:18 north 132:30 east. 9 of these boats were heading toward crash area. 3 of these boats were proceeding north.

Search Progress for 30 July 53. 3 SB-29 and 2 RB-29 covered search area with negative sightings. In north search area encountered radar and VHF jamming throughout search.

Search Progress for 31 July 53. 1 SB-29 proceeded to search area but search impossible due to undercast covering complete area. Search suspended 10:00 hours "I" 31 July 53.

The sightings by the search and rescue aircraft were "yellow objects" in the water and could have been "Mae West" life vests that spilled from the aircraft wreckage. A *New York Times* article datelined Tokyo, Friday, July 31, reported that "the Air Force said today that it had abandoned the search for sixteen missing crewmen of a B-50 bomber that went down Wednesday off the coast of Siberia." The article also reported that the U.S. Navy had abandoned its search as well. "Fleet headquarters said the cruiser *Bremerton* radioed that the search had been abandoned at 4 P.M. Thursday, Korean time." The *Bremerton* led six destroyers, including one Australian, two helicopters, and several Air Force and Task Force 77 planes in the search.

The tight-lipped Far East Air Forces gave out few details except that the copilot had been picked up south of Cape Povorotny, only fifty miles east of Vladivostok. The article went on to say, "United States planes have figured in at least two other clashes with Soviet aircraft in the Pacific in the last ten months . . . Last February 15, two United States jet fighters fired on two Soviet planes that flew over northern Japan and damaged one . . . A B-29 bomber was shot down by Soviet planes in the same area last October 8 [October 7 Eastern Standard Time]."

The shootdown of a Soviet IL-12 transport aircraft by U.S. fighter aircraft in the Korean theater on July 27 was reported in the *New York Times* August 1, 1953 issue. The Soviets described the attack on their transport aircraft as "piratelike," and they reserved the right to demand compensation for those who died. The question begging an answer is whether a "tit for tat" was involved in the RB-50 shootdown two days later, on July 29. A Soviet protest over the shootdown of the Soviet transport by Korean-based U.S. Air Force fighters presented the Soviet Union's views on their loss:

*On July 27, 1953 at 06:28 Moscow time four American fighters, af-
ter crossing the border of the Democratic Republic of China, attacked and
shot down a Russian IL-12 transport aircraft that was flying from Port
Arthur to Vladivostok. This occurred near the city of Khuadyan', 110
kilometers from the Sino-Soviet border. The aircraft burned up, and the
six crew members and 15 passengers on board were killed.*

The Soviets also informed the government of the Democratic Republic of Korea and the Chinese government that the Soviet Union had
sent the two latest demarches, and recommended that the Chinese government protest to the Americans this violation of the Korean/Chinese
border, tying in other Korean border violations by American aircraft. A
number of heated diplomatic exchanges ensued without reaching any
mutual agreements between the aggrieved parties.

In a later diplomatic exchange on the downing of the RB-50 the Soviets refuted an American claim that Soviet "PT"-type boats allegedly
were observed picking up surviving crew members. No declassified messages have been found in Soviet archives that discuss surviving crew
members being picked up by the Soviets. A Russian witness who came
forward in May 1993 claims to have witnessed the shootdown and to
have seen crew members bail out of the burning aircraft. Georgij
Yakovlevich Kravchenko, a former Soviet antiaircraft artillery sergeant,
stated that he witnessed the shootdown while on duty with an AAA bat-
tery on Russkij Island near Vladivostok. According to Kravchenko, as
two Soviet jet fighters approached what he believes was a four-propeller
intruding aircraft, the intruder opened fire, hitting and damaging one of
the Soviet fighters. The damaged fighter reversed course while the other
fighter attacked the intruder. The intruder's tail caught fire, and the intruder descended in the direction of Russkij Island. Within two minutes
of the attack, he saw seven crew members bail out of the burning intruder
aircraft that hit the water a couple of minutes later.

Whether RB-50 crew members were taken prisoner by Soviet authorities remains an open question. Kravchenko's testimony appears
credible, if for no other reason than because his story is consistent with
other facts about the incident (time of day, two Soviet jets, one damaged,

etc.). According to Captain Roche, Captain O'Kelley sounded the bailout alarm at about 18,000 feet altitude and both managed to bail out—suggesting that others could have jumped.

The search and rescue aircrews observed what were believed to be survivors in the water at the crash site, and any such survivors would have been vulnerable to capture by Soviet patrol boats that had access to the crash site for eight hours or so before the U.S. Navy destroyer that picked up Captain Roche arrived on the scene. A retired Soviet officer stationed in Vladivostok at the time said in 1992 that rumors after the shootdown had it that Soviet maritime forces had apprehended some survivors from the flight.

Parachutes, seven American fliers in the water, lifeboats, Russian torpedo boats, and vague rumors of captives: the evidence is tantalizing. The shootdown would have given Soviet intelligence agencies an excellent opportunity to gain access to American Intelligence personnel.

Many Americans familiar with the case believe that some survivors from that aircraft shootdown were picked up and imprisoned in the Soviet Union, but the U.S. government has no solid evidence of that. Russia has opened some of its archives (some air defense, naval, and presidential archives), but KGB files for the most part remained sealed. Access to closely held KGB archives would no doubt clarify the issue of survivors. Any survivors from the RB-50 shootdown on July 29, 1953, (or any other shootdown incident) taken into Soviet custody would without doubt have ended up being interrogated and incarcerated within the highly compartmented KGB system. And that is a system to which not even the U.S.-Russian Joint Commission on POW/MIAs has direct access.

In July 1999, forty-six years after the RB-50 shootdown, Ms. Anne Radlein, the aunt and one of two known surviving relatives of Earl Radlein Jr., was interviewed during the research for this book. Even at the age of eighty-two, Ms. Radlein remembered Earl Jr. and his comrades vividly. But she had not been made aware that the U.S. government was still attempting to determine the fate of Earl Jr. and others who went missing in action during the Cold War. Over the years, Earl Jr.'s immediate family members passed away as have family members concerned with other Soviet-American air incidents that occurred during the Cold

War—never knowing what happened to their missing loved ones. Official records read "*Missing in action, presumed to have died in the crash.*"

P2V Shot Down over Sea of Japan—September 4, 1954

On September 4, 1954, a pair of Soviet air force MiG-17 aircraft shot down a U.S. Navy P2V Neptune aircraft in the vicinity of Vladivostok in the Primorskij (Maritime) area of the Soviet Far East. The ten-man crew and aircraft were staging from Atsugi Naval airfield, Japan, and performing a reconnaissance mission over the Sea of Japan. A naval search and rescue task force saved nine of the ten crew members on September 5; the tenth was killed in the incident, his body not recovered. A report from the border guards to the interior ministry provides the Soviet version of events:

> . . . *At 19:10 hours, holding a course in the direction of our shore, the above mentioned aircraft entered our airspace in an area 11.5 miles southwest of Cape Ostrovnoj (42 degrees 37 minutes north latitude 133 degrees 35 minutes east longitude). At 19:12 hours at an altitude of 3000 meters, the aircraft was attacked by two Soviet aircraft, "MiG-17s" that were patrolling at the time in the region of Uglovaya airfield.*
>
> *When attacked by our aircraft, the violating aircraft opened fire with all cannons and machine guns and turned toward the sea. Our pilots observed that both left and right engines of the plane had caught fire. At 19:16 hours the American plane fell into the sea at the approximate location of 42 degrees 30 minutes north latitude and 133 degrees 45 minutes east longitude.*
>
> *After the air battle a torpedo boat section was sent to the area, but found no trace of the downed aircraft.*
>
> *Commencing on 5 September of this year at 06:00 local time, flights of American aircraft (in groups of 2, 3, and 4 planes) have been recorded 35-40 miles south of Cape Ostrovnoj. Two American destroyers, which were located 50 miles south of Askol'd Island, moved toward this region.*
>
> *Over the course of 5 September of this year, fleet radio intercept established that a complement of the crew of the "Neptun" [sic] was picked up from the sea 50 miles south of Cape Povorotnyj. The rescued crew,*

numbering 5-7 individuals, it seems, were located in a raft, [and were] taken by seaplanes. The rescue effort ended at approximately 10:00 local time on 5 September. According to the [intercepted] data, however, the commander of the aircraft was not found.

At 17:30, 5 September of this year, the American destroyers and aircraft left the region of Cape Povorotnyj.

An examination of the coastline indicates that the border was not violated.

This may be the first time a Soviet report acknowledged that a Soviet fighter pilot fired first. The Soviet report does not indicate whether the Soviet pilot attempted to warn the U.S. crew that they were intruding in Soviet airspace although it points out that the border violation occurred 11.5 miles from the Soviet coast (i.e., within the twelve-mile buffer zone claimed by the Soviet Union).

The U.S. immediately protested to the Soviets and brought the incident before the United Nations Security Council. At first, the U.S. Navy Department and the State Department claimed that the American aircrew did not fire on the attacking Soviet MiGs. Later, after the crew told the press that they had indeed returned fire, an apologetic correction was issued. TASS [the official Soviet press agency] gleefully reported the U.S. government's error:

On the American Provocation in the Far East

New York, 7 Sep (TASS). A Washington correspondent for The New York Times *newspaper reports that on 6 September the Department of the Navy revealed that an American patrol bomber shot down near the Siberian coast on 4 September by two Soviet fighters had opened return fire, but only after it was attacked. . . . The announcement by the Department of the Navy caused some confusion in the State Department since the second of the two demarches of protest to Moscow maintained the assertion that the "American naval aircraft never opened fire on the Soviet aircraft." As officials here point out, this declaration was based on the initial report of this incident that the Pentagon received from the Far East. It was only after the nine surviving crew members were thoroughly debriefed, that the Department of the Navy was able to estab-lish that one of the gunners on the aircraft opened return fire on the Rus-sian pilot. . . .*

(TASS, 7 Sep 54, l. 21-d)

That the Soviet border guards reported sending a section of torpedo boats out to search the crash site after the air battle, "but found no trace of the downed aircraft," is curious. Apparently, either the boats were sent to the wrong area, or they did a lackadaisical job of searching for intrud-ers. It would be interesting to know if any of the border guards staff in-volved in the search were punished for not capturing the nine crew members who were picked up only hours later by a U.S. Navy search and rescue team.

That downed crew was lucky. They could easily have become an-other MIA statistic, leaving behind only lingering fears that the crew had been picked up and imprisoned by the Soviet Union.

RB-47 Shot Down Off Kamchatka—April 18, 1955

On April 18, 1955, Soviet MiG fighters shot down a Strategic Air Command RB-47E photo reconnaissance aircraft over the Pacific Ocean west of the Kamchatka peninsula. The aircraft belonged to the 4th Strategic Recon Squadron, 26th Recon Wing, Eielson AFB, Alaska. Al-though the U.S. government suspected that the plane had been shot down, it had no proof of hostile actions until 1992 when Russian Presi-dent Boris Yeltsin's government provided the U.S.-Russian Joint Com-mission on POW/MIAs with declassified documents revealing details. After declaring the RB-47 crew to be missing, the U.S. Air Force launched an intensive search and rescue effort, but searched in the wrong area—U.S. signals intelligence stations were not intercepting Soviet air surveillance tracking of the recon mission at the time, and the Air Force knew only that the RB-47 had failed to return. In the Air Force official presumptive finding of death—*Missing in action, presumed to have died in the crash*—there is no indication that the aircraft was shot down or where the incident occurred.

The Soviet documents show that Soviet air surveillance stations began tracking the RB-47 in the vicinity of Cape Lopatka at the southern end of the Kamchatka peninsula about 09:30 Khabarovsk [Soviet Far East Military District] time. At 10:57 Soviet tracking showed the aircraft to be about forty-three miles southeast of Cape Vasiliev, and although it had not violated Soviet state borders, the local air defense command center on Kamchatka scrambled a pair of MiG-15 fighters to intercept it.

The MiGs intercepted the recon aircraft thirty-two miles east of Cape Kronitski (approximately 55:00 degrees north 164:00 degrees east) at an altitude of 39,000 feet. The documents claim that the RB-47 opened fire on the MiGs, resulting in the MiG pilots attacking the RB-47 between 11:25 and 11:27. The RB-47 vanished from Soviet radar screens at 11:40 hours. Soviet fishermen noted an explosion and a column of black smoke at 11:50 hours, thirteen kilometers west of Nikol'skoe on Soviet-owned Bering Island—at approximately 55:50 degrees north 165:50 degrees east—in Soviet-claimed territorial waters).

Soviet "OSNAZ" [signals intelligence] units monitored the communications of the U.S. forces involved in the search and rescue efforts—twenty sorties over a four-day period—and concluded that the Americans did not know where the aircraft crashed. "From the nature of the search, one can suppose that the Americans do not know the place, cause, and time of the aircraft's destruction." With no definitive information on the fate of the RB-47, the American government filed no protests about the incident with the Soviet government. For its part, the Presidium of the Central Committee of the Soviet Communist Party approved the recommendations of Soviet Foreign Minister Molotov and Minister of Defense Zhukov that details of the shootdown be withheld from the American government. Their message reads in part:

> . . . The engagement area between the Soviet fighters and the American aircraft is being determined. At the present, it cannot be determined whether the engagement took place in the USSR's airspace or over neutral waters.
>
> According to available information, it can be surmised that the Americans do not have information regarding the location or cause for loss of their aircraft. This conclusion is corroborated by the following:

The American aircraft was obviously conducting a special mission [re-connaissance] and did not maintain radio communications with the ground. In addition, our radio intelligence did not notice any transmissions from the aircraft during its flight, upon encountering the Soviet fighters or after the engagement. It is also noteworthy that American searches for the aircraft were not in the region of the supposed point of impact of the aircraft, but along the aircraft's flight route and especially intense in a region 500-600 kilometers from the aircraft's supposed impact point.

While it can not be confirmed that radars on an American ship, which could have been located in that region, did not follow the flight of the American aircraft and the Soviet fighters, it should also be taken into account that American ships could not have visually observed the engagement with the Soviet fighters, as the flight of the aircraft took place above a dense cloud cover.

Considering the above, the MID USSR and ministry of defense consider it inadvisable to make any kind of statement at the present time to the U.S. government as regards the flight on 18 April of this year of the American B-47 military aircraft near the Kurile Islands and Kamchatka Peninsula.

Moreover, the MID USSR and the ministry of defense are of the opinion that the Americans obviously do not consider it possible to raise this matter with us. Under these conditions, notifying the Americans would be premature and could damage us.

Request consideration.

V. Molotov, G. Zhukov
22 Apr 55 No. 602/M

The level of deception revealed by the Soviet hierarchy's decision not to raise the issue of the air incident with the American government is not surprising. The fact that the issue was raised of where the Soviet attack on the RB-47 occurred (within or outside Soviet airspace) is interesting. First of all, if Soviet air surveillance tracking had shown the RB-47 violating Soviet airspace, field commanders most assuredly would have pointed out the violation in their messages to the Kremlin. Second, to have Soviet airspace addressed in a message from the foreign minister and defense minister to the Communist Party Central Committee shows the importance that Soviet leaders placed on defending their borders.

A declassified summary report from a Soviet navy chief of intelligence in the Far East to Admiral Sokolovskij of the Soviet Fleet in the Kremlin illustrates the vast blanket of coverage that Soviet signals intelligence units had on American military communications.

Top Secret

To: Comrade Sokolovskij, 2nd Department, Main HQs, Naval Force
Enciphered Telegram No. 1495, 1496
Copy No. 1 Comrade Sokolovskij
Received 13 hours 05 minutes, 25 Apr 55
To: Acting Chief of Intelligence, VMS Captain 1st Rank Comrade Shashenkov

I am reporting supplementary and generalized information on the RB-47 aircraft. According to intercepted radiograms to the Commander of the 10th Air Rescue Group and the 5010th Air Base Wing, on 18 April an RB-47 aircraft of the 4th Aviation Squadron, 26th Reconnaissance Wing disappeared. It was flying along the route Eielson-Unalaklit-Attu in an area 100 miles east of Hokkaido-Unalaklit-Eielson. The last time the aircraft was noted was at 08:10 hours, 18 April in an area 100 miles southwest of Attu, after which contact was lost. All bases in the Aleutian Islands were queried about the aircraft. Answers were negative. A search for the RB-47 aircraft began on 19 April. The Commander of the Joint Search and Rescue Center (Elmendorf AFB) ordered the Commander of the 3rd Search and Rescue Region (Elmendorf AFB) to assign four SA-16s and one SC-54 for search and "not to raise unnecessary noise about it." A notice was transmitted to the Chief of Search and Rescue, Johnson AFB, requesting a search by forces of the 3rd Rescue Aviation Group. The commander of the 4th Search and Rescue Region (Adak) was responsible for conducting the search mission in the region of the

Aleutian Islands. The region was ordered to carry out a watch on emergency frequencies and to plan a wide search using aircraft of the 3rd Region.

The search was conducted with the following number of aircraft: 19 April, four SB-29s about 260-240 miles east of the Kurile Islands to the 100th parallel, one "Neptune" in the region of Adak-Attu; on 20 April, three "Neptunes" along the Aleutian Islands to a region 120 miles east of Cape Lopatka, three "Neptunes" in the eastern section of the Bering Sea, two "Neptunes" in the western section of the Bering Sea, and one RB-47 along the missing aircraft's flight route. In addition, on 20 April, one B-36 was noted at Attu at an altitude of 5000 meters on a west-southwest course and one B-29 at an altitude of 3000 meters on a southwest course. Possibly these aircraft were en route to the search area. On 21 April, five "Neptunes" in the central section of the Bering Sea; 22 April, the Adak Region; 23 April, one "Neptune" noted at 08:38 at 5515N 17040E and at 09:40 at 5325N 17210E eastern, and one "Neptune" in the region of the central section of the Bering Sea. In addition to the aircraft, the icebreaker "Burton Island" and the tug "Takelma" participated in the search. On 21 April, an unidentified official ordered the commander of the Neptune flights conducting the search "not to fly over the Komandors [Soviet islands]."

On 22 April, five "Neptunes" flew from Adak to Kodiak, suggesting that the search had ended. Conclusion: results from the analysis of the radio communications and the character of the search would suggest that the Americans do not know where, the reason, or the time the aircraft was lost.

Chief of Intelligence, TOF, Captain 1st Rank Razumnyj

The level of detail provided by the Soviet intelligence services about the American search and rescue efforts in this shootdown incident illustrates the capabilities of Soviet signals intelligence units to monitor and intercept American military communications during the Cold War. Undoubtedly, the Soviets employed far more voice intercept operators than did the U.S. signals intelligence services at that time. The U.S. Air Force

Security Service would have been profoundly disturbed had they seen that Soviet report. After its primary mission of intercepting enemy military communications, the secondary mission of the Security Service was to monitor U.S. Air Force communications (communications security) to ensure that the classified information the Soviets were intercepting was not being transmitted on open communications systems that could be intercepted.

On April 26, Soviet border guards found RB-47 aircraft debris, a life jacket, maps, and an RB-47 aircraft manual that washed ashore on Bering Island [one of the Soviet-owned Komandorskij Islands in the vicinity of the crash site]. A further search was conducted along the shore without any further discoveries.

The interval between the attack (11:27) and disappearance of the RB-47 from Soviet radar screens (11:40) provided ample time for the crew to bail out, but the chances of survival would have been slim; the crew would have succumbed to hypothermia in the 38 degree Pacific waters unless the men were picked up almost immediately by a Soviet boat. There are no indications that the Soviets rescued the crew.

P2V Attacked over Bering Strait—June 22, 1955

On June 22, 1955, Soviet MiG fighter aircraft attacked a U.S. Navy P2V Neptune reconnaissance bomber over the Bering Strait that separates northwestern Siberia and Alaska—another of the many air skirmishes during the Cold War, but with a different ending. Critically damaged in the attack, the Neptune crashlanded on St Lawrence Island, Alaska. The Neptune was destroyed but, miraculously, the twelve crew members survived. Almost as miraculously, the Soviet government agreed to reimburse the United States for 50 percent of the claimed damages incurred in the incident.

Like earlier confrontations between Soviet fighter aircraft and American aircrews, the incident occurred over water. In previous incidents both sides invariably disagreed on where the encounter took place, and in most cases, on who fired first. In turn, charges and countercharges followed each incident. But the location of the June 22 attack and the

political climate at the time combined to result in a more amicable resolution. The confrontation occurred over the Bering Strait, along the
international boundary between the United States and the Soviet
Union. Moreover, neither side appeared to want to disrupt the coming
conference in Geneva. The East and West had recently relinquished
four-power control over Austria, with Austria gaining full sovereignty
on May 15. The U.S. had rejected a similar Soviet proposal for Germany,
but the U.S., British, French, and Soviet heads of state were meeting in
a summit conference on German reunification and disarmament in
Geneva in July, and neither side wanted the incident to contaminate the
summit.

Rather than lodge a typical demarche requesting that those responsi-
ble for the "unprovoked attack without warning" be disciplined and that
compensation be paid for resulting damages and injuries, Secretary of
State John Foster Dulles protested quietly to the Soviet ambassador to
America for the MiG attack on an American aircraft over American airspace. Much to the surprise of Samuel Klaus, State Department Special
Assistant who litigated air incident cases against the Soviet Union in the
International Court of Justice, the Soviets offered to share the costs for
damages resulting from the attack. On March 17, 1956, the Soviet Union
sent a note and a check for $724,947.68 to the State Department—
covering half the amount claimed by the U.S. for incurred damages. The
note was in response to a United States note of January 6 that pressed the
Soviets to make good on a promise of at least compensation in part for
the incident. The State Department placed the cost of the incident at
$1,449,895, including $924,700 as the value of the aircraft.

Even partial reimbursement for damages constituted a tacit admission of partial culpability; however, the note accompanying the compensation check insisted, as the Russians had all along, that the U.S. plane
had violated Soviet airspace. Just as adamantly, the U.S. maintained that
the Navy Neptune bomber never approached closer than twenty-four
nautical miles to the nearest Soviet land. Either Secretary Dulles's quiet
diplomacy had paid off or the Soviet compensation was part of a Soviet
strategy to soften American views vis-à-vis Soviet policy in the upcoming summit conference in Geneva. A priority diplomatic message from

the Soviet ambassador in Washington to Foreign Minister Molotov in
Moscow in late June 1956 clearly lacks the vitriolic wording seen in
other Soviet diplomatic messages on shootdown incidents:

> *On 24 June, [Secretary of State] Dulles invited me to his office and de-
> clared the following:*
>
> *The day before yesterday an American aircraft was attacked by Soviet
> fighters over the strait dividing the American Lawrence Island and Soviet
> Kamchatka. The aircraft was damaged and made a forced landing on
> Lawrence Island. There were wounded who were sent to the hospital.
> The aircraft, according to Dulles' assertion, was flying exactly in the cen-
> ter of the strait, which has a width of 50 miles. This means that it al-
> legedly did not violate the 12-mile zone that the USSR observes as a
> border to its territorial waters, and that, by the way, the United States
> does not recognize. Dulles casually said that, of course, with the speeds of
> contemporary aircraft it is possible that there could have been some devia-
> tion of the aircraft.*
>
> *The incident that took place was kept secret from the press by the State
> Department; however, according to a message received by Dulles in
> Washington today, news is starting to be leaked to the press from the fliers
> who are in the hospital. It is not ruled out that corresponding reports have
> already appeared in today's papers.*
>
> *Dulles said that President Eisenhower hopes that the Soviet govern-
> ment will give appropriate attention to this incident, will thoroughly
> investigate it, and after the investigation will take measures toward com-
> pensation for the damaged aircraft and for the wounds inflicted on the
> American crew members.*
>
> *I am fearful, said Dulles, of the bad impression that this incident can
> make on public opinion, especially in light of the upcoming conference in
> Geneva. Both sides must elect the correct form of action in order to block
> turning this incident into an object for heated debate between both sides.*
>
> *I said that I am hearing about this incident for the first time from
> Dulles and, therefore, I cannot say anything as to its substance. I added
> that I express sympathy concerning this incident regardless of what comes
> to light in the future regarding the circumstances of the incident. I prom-*

ised Dulles to immediately inform Moscow about this conversation with him and, upon receipt of an answer, to report to him what becomes known to me.

The State Department confirmed that the compensation by the Soviet Union was the first ever paid by the Russians or their satellites for planes they had shot down. Secretary of State John Foster Dulles was surprised, when, immediately after the incident, at a meeting commemorating the tenth anniversary of the United Nations, Soviet Foreign Minister Vyachaslav M. Molotov expressed regret that the shootdown had occurred and offered to pay half of the damages. The Soviet Union actually paid the damages only after the U.S. pressed it, in January 1956, making good on Molotov's promise. It was the last time the Soviet government reimbursed America for damages incurred in Soviet attacks on U.S. aircrews involved in reconnaissance missions along Soviet borders.

RB-50 Missing Over Sea of Japan—September 10, 1956

The disappearance on September 10, 1956, of an RB-50 aircraft on a reconnaissance mission over the Sea of Japan is perhaps the most baffling loss of the Cold War. Recently arrived at Yokota Air Base, Japan, from Greenville, Texas, where it had been configured as a communications intelligence reconnaissance platform, RB-50G-2 tail number 47133 was on its first operational communications intelligence recon mission when the aircraft and its sixteen-person crew simply disappeared. The aircraft and crew were based at Yokota. A very powerful storm –Typhoon Emma— was active in the area and may have been a contributing factor. No distress signals were received from the RB-50, and the sixteen crew members remain unaccounted for. On November 13, 1956, in response to a U.S. request dated October 13, the Soviet government informed the American ambassador in Moscow that it had no information on the aircraft or its crew. A declassified Air Force "Report of Aircraft Accident" provides most of the relevant details that are known about the mission:

The crew was briefed on 9 September 1956 at 11:00I ["I" time zone is Japan time] to fly RB-50-G-2, #47133A on a top secret reconnaissance mission at 20,000 feet over the Sea of Japan. The route is top secret and was omitted from this report to keep from classifying the report top secret. The entire mission was to be flown over international waters. The briefing was conducted by Major Lloyd L. Holdcroft, the Squadron Operations Officer. Included in the briefing were all aspects of the mission, weather, route, communications, normal and emergency procedures. The crew reported for first stations at 02:30I, 10 September 1956, received their final weather briefing at 03:00I, and departed at 04:30I on the mission. Takeoff was routine, a report was made to Tokyo departure control over Kamagaya homer [beacon] at 04:41I. An IFF parrot check [Identification, Friend or Foe radar check] was made with Palace Radar site at 04:45I. An HF radio check was accomplished at 05:07I. The air defense radar net monitored the flight on its departure until it faded at 05:49I, 10 September 1956.

The last radar position fix was 38 degrees, 34 minutes north, 135 degrees, 03 minutes east [approximately 250 miles northwest of Niigata, Honshu, Japan and 375 miles southeast of Vladivostok, Russia]. The mission was to be conducted in radio silence after the initial calls after takeoff, until the aircraft was 100 miles out from the coast of Japan on its return. The estimated time this radio report was expected was 12:05I. When this call was not received a request was made that communications agencies try contacting the aircraft on "CW" [Morse] emergency frequency. The extended communications search was begun at 13:05I although the estimated time of arrival of the aircraft at Yokota was 13:30I. Fifth Air Force was advised and they in turn alerted Air Sea Rescue at 13:05I. An RB-50 assigned to the 6091st Reconnaissance Squadron departed on a search mission at 15:40I with two more squadron aircraft joining the search later that day. As indicated on the clearance, a total of 17 hours of fuel placed the fuel exhaustion time at approximately 21:30I. A Missing Aircraft Report was sent out at 22:30I. Subsequent investigation revealed the actual fuel on board versus the flight plan profile would provide 14 to 15 hours of flight. Therefore, the fuel exhaustion time would have been 19:30I or 20:30I. The search was continued through 18 September 1956 without any confirmed reports of debris or leads to possible location of the missing aircraft. The search was officially discontinued at 23:30I, 18 September 1956.

The aircrew included nine flight crew members from the 6091st Recon Squadron (pilot, copilot, three navigators, flight engineer, aircraft radio operator, and two gunners) and seven U.S. Air Force Security Service personnel assigned to Detachment 1, 6924th Security Squadron—five airborne intercept operators (four Russian linguists and one Morse operator), one airborne maintenance technician, and Maj. Loren Disbrow, the commander of Detachment 1.

When the mission disappeared, it was described as a weather flight that had been sent out to check on Typhoon Emma. The approach to the Soviet government in October 1956 was in the form of an information request, not a demarche, and an Air Force spokesman discounted the idea the RB-50 might have been shot down. The typhoon registered extremely high wind speeds—140 miles per hour when weather gauges were blown away on Okinawa—and undoubtedly hampered search and rescue efforts. Moreover, the storm could have forced the crew to deviate from the planned course. It would certainly have impacted the men's ability to survive at sea even if they managed to abandon the RB-50 before it sank.

This constituted America's first loss of a communications intelligence reconnaissance platform; earlier losses of recon missions had involved either electronic recon or photo recon platforms. For security reasons—special intelligence security restrictions applied to communications intelligence—the Air Force issued only a small news release and informed family members that their loved ones had disappeared while conducting a weather reconnaissance mission. The loss was not reported in large U.S. newspapers like the *New York Times*.

S.Sgt. Duane Kolilis had been flying recon missions as an airborne intercept operator (Russian linguist) with the Air Force Security Service detachment at Yokota AB for a couple of years when the RB-50G disappeared. One of six Russian linguists in the unit at the time, Duane was originally scheduled for the mission, but was replaced by S.Sgt. Theodorus Trias at the last minute. Sergeants Kolilis and Trias were the detachment's two Russian transcribers. One of them usually flew a mission and the other met the crew when the mission returned to transcribe communications signals intercepted during the mission.

The mission on September 10 was special for Sergeant Trias; it was to be his last. He would surrender his special intelligence security clearance[23] to marry his Japanese girlfriend. In fact, their commander, Major Disbrow, had received a message from Headquarters Air Force Security Service directing that Sergeant Trias be "debriefed" and denied access to operations immediately. For a combination of reasons—he was the most qualified intercept operator in the unit; there was a severe shortage of qualified Russian linguists; it was the first flight in a RB-50 communications intelligence recon platform; and he had a simple wish to reward Sergeant Trias's outstanding career with one more flight—Major Disbrow authorized Trias to fly the mission. Sergeant Kolilis, who had only recently assumed duties as the NCO in charge of operations (NCOIC of Operations) from Sergeant Trias, agreed to be replaced on the mission by Trias.

Kolilis was friendly with all the Security Service enlisted men on the mission. He had attended Russian language school with two of the airborne intercept operators, Raymond Duane Johnson and Paul Swinehart, and had flown missions with Leo Sloan (Russian linguist), William Ellis, and Harry Maxwell (airborne maintenance technician and Morse intercept operator, respectively). Kolilis, Johnson, and Swinehart had served a one-year tour as Russian voice intercept operators and transcribers on Paeng-Yang Do ("P-Y Do") Island, Korea, before being reassigned to the new Security Service airborne recon unit at Yokota in 1954. Duane Johnson was Kolilis's best friend.

The Air Force had been extremely closemouthed about the disappearance of the mission. Kolilis remembers being told at the time that the plane was definitely not shot down because Intelligence had determined that there were no foreign aircraft in that area. He recalled reading either in the Yokota base newspaper or in *Stars and Stripes* [the American military newspaper] a short blurb on the downing. The article stands out in his mind because, although the article said it was a weather plane, they called it an "RB-50" rather than a "WB-50." The U.S. government finally admitted in 1992 that the RB-50 lost on September 10, 1956, was performing an intelligence gathering mission.

Kolilis also remembers seeing a photograph in *Life* magazine of some Japanese throwing a wreath of flowers into the Sea of Japan as a memorial to the crew on the lost RB-50. He tried over the years to find additional accounts of the incident, but was unsuccessful. Like others associated with similar losses, Duane Kolilis says that he was in a state of shock and denial when the aircraft with his friends, including Duane Johnson, his very best friend, disappeared. He went through a long period of grief and depression, and could not force himself to contact Duane Johnson's mother until many years later. Family members and friends of all the crews involved in Cold War air incidents were affected in similar ways.

C-118 Shot Down Over Armenia—June 27, 1958

The page one headline in the *New York Times* for Sunday, June 29, 1958, read: SOVIET PLANES FORCE DOWN U.S. TRANSPORT IN ARMENIA . . . RUSSIANS HOLD 9 ABOARD—"GROSS VIOLATION" OF AIRSPACE CHARGED. The lead sentence of the article datelined Moscow, June 28, read "A four-engine United States Air Force plane was forced down yesterday more than 100 miles inside the Soviet Union's southern frontier with Turkey, the government announced tonight." So began one of the Cold War's most incredible shootdown incidents—incredible in hindsight—because it shows how Soviet intelligence services captured and, not appreciating who their detainees were, released one of its single most significant spy catches during the Cold War.

On June 27, 1958, a pair of MiG-17s[24] attacked and forced down a C-118 transport aircraft deep within Soviet airspace. The border violation began at the Turkish-Armenian border and ended with the American plane crash landing in Azerbaijan.

In prior incidents there is no proof that the Soviets rescued and took into custody any U.S. crew members; in this incident the Soviet KGB detained the nine-man crew, but released them ten days later. The evidence indicates that the C-118 had indeed not intended to violate the Soviet state border. But there was much more to the story than that. They were indeed "off course," but some of the nine detained men were CIA operatives, and the aircraft's cargo included highly sensitive special intelligence documents that, fortunately, burned in the crash. Unfortunately for the KGB but to the relief of the downed American crew and the U.S.

Central Intelligence Agency, Soviet interrogators did not comprehend the true identity of the nine captured American aircrew members or the complete significance of their mission.

The downed C-118 aircraft belonged to the 7405th Support Squadron, or more precisely to Flight "C" of the 7405th. Flight C—also known as the "Special Project"—provided special courier support flights for the Central Intelligence Agency.

T.Sgt. James G. "Jim" Holman, who had entered the Army Air Corps in 1940, was a C-118 flight engineer assigned to the 7405th from 1955 to 1959. During an earlier assignment flying in and out of Prestwick, Scotland, he had met and married a Scottish woman named Molly. Jim retired from the Air Force as a senior master sergeant in 1971 after a thirty-one-year career and died in 1977.

Mrs. Holman recently commented that the 7405th was the strangest unit that Jim served with during his Air Force career:

> On prior assignments he traveled a lot, and I always knew where he was going on TDY and when to expect him to return. In the 7405th at Wiesbaden, I only knew where he'd been when he returned home—he would not tell me where he was going when leaving on trips. I knew in general terms where he was going based on what he asked me to pack—if he asked for short-sleeved shirts, I knew that he was not heading for Alaska. And, when he'd return home, I did not even have to ask him where he'd been; I could figure it out based on the foreign currency he'd bring home in pocket change—if he returned home with small change in Greek, Turkish and Iranian money, it was a good indication of where he'd been. Later, he fouled up my logic when he stopped bringing his loose change home with him. Jim was very secretive about his assignment with the 7405th—much more so than with any of the other assignments during the years after we married. Jim's trip on June 26, 1958, began normally. He flew out of Wiesbaden with his crew; I did not know where he was going, but I expected him home in about a week.

On June 27, 1958, while on a flight from Cyprus to Tehran, Iran, the C-118 flew into Soviet airspace and was forced down in Azerbaijan. In statements to the press after the aircraft was forced down, the U.S. Air

Force stated that the C-118 was on a bimonthly "embassy run" from home base at Wiesbaden to Karachi, Pakistan, with planned intermediate stops at Wheelus Air Base, Libya; Nicosia, Cyprus; and Tehran, Iran.

Departing Cyprus as planned, the flight plan called for the crew to fly north to Turkey and then continue eastward along an internationally recognized commercial air route via Adana, Diyarbakir, and Lake Van, Turkey, to Iran—a route that would have taken them along an air corridor immediately south of the Iranian-Armenian border. Instead, the C-118 violated the Armenian border, and was intercepted by a pair of Soviet MiG fighters. One of the MiGs attacked the four-engine transport—hitting a wing fuel tank inboard of the number two engine. The fuel tank erupted into flames that engulfed the fuselage in the vicinity of the wings.

Maj. Luther W. Lyles, the aircraft commander, ordered everyone to abandon the aircraft, and five of the nine on board (Col. Dale D. Brannon, Maj. Robert E. Crans, Major Bennie A. Shupe, A/2C Earl H. Reamer and A/2C Peter N. Sabo) successfully bailed out. Blocked by flames raging in the center of the fuselage, Major Lyles chose to crash-land the aircraft rather than attempt to go through the flames to reach the exit doors in the rear. He, Capt. James T. Kane (navigator), Jim Holman, and 1st Lt. James N. Luther crash-landed the shot-up aircraft on a half-finished airstrip that had about 2,000 feet of usable runway—an airfield that Major Lyles saw at the last minute after his C-118 had taken a hit. One of the MiGs conducted another firing pass against the crippled transport but missed as the C-118 was making the crash landing. The aircraft stopped in the rough beyond the airstrip, and the four airmen scrambled out. A minute later, there was a loud explosion, and when last seen, the C-118 "was burning pretty good." The landing occurred about seventy-five miles east-southeast of Lake Sevan, Armenia (inside Azerbaijan, approximately fifty miles from the Azerbaijani-Iranian border). Major Shupe claimed to have been the copilot, and Major Crans professed to have been a third pilot on his stan/eval check-ride—that is, he was being upgraded to aircraft commander status.

Miraculously, all nine American airmen escaped serious injury although Airman Sabo had suffered second-degree burns charging through the flaming fuselage to reach an exit. The five who bailed out parachuted onto a Soviet collective farm. Drifting down not too far apart, the five men had barely assembled when they were descended upon by what appeared to be a hundred peasants—none of whom spoke English. Shouting excitedly in a language the airmen did not recognize, the peasants tied the Americans' hands behind their backs, guarded them with pitchforks, and hauled them in a truck to a local village. Thinking that the parachuting airmen were members of the hated Turkish army that had massacred thousands of Armenians and Azerbaijanis decades earlier, the peasants beat up four of them—all except Sabo, who had injuries. The peasants put a noose around Bennie Shupe's neck, threw it over a crossbar on a telephone pole, and were about to string him up in front of a crowd of shouting, pummeling peasants when Shupe finally got his point across to them that he was an American. Somebody in the crowd said the words "New York" and "Chicago," and Shupe called out the names of every American city he could think of. Realizing he was an American, the peasants removed the noose from his neck. Later, Shupe remarked, "I had no doubt they were going to hang me."

Soviet military troops arrived in the village a couple of hours later and rescued the five parachutists from the peasants. Other Soviet military authorities took the four who were involved in the crash landing into custody almost immediately as they exited the burning aircraft. The Soviet captors readily recognized the men as American airmen and treated them civilly without abusing them.

Soviet Foreign Minister Andrei Gromyko delivered the following note to United States ambassador Llewelyn Thompson Jr. in Moscow. At the same time, TASS, the official Soviet news agency, made the note public:

> On June 27 this year, at 18:30 hours Moscow time, a four-engine military plane with the identification marks of the United States Air Force violated the state frontier of the USSR south of Yerevan and penetrated the Soviet airspace to the depth of 170 kilometers.
>
> The American plane was met by two Soviet fighters that signaled it to follow them to a near-by airfield. The intruder did not comply and the Soviet fighters compelled it to make a landing.

It landed on Soviet territory 240 kilometers from the place where it violated the state frontier of the USSR and burned up.

Nine members of the crew were detained after the landing of the intruder aircraft. All were dressed in American military uniform.

Their testimony and the documents they carried show that all the persons detained are in the service of the Air Force of the United States of America.

Deliberate Violation

These facts are evidence of a deliberate violation of the state frontier of the USSR by an American warplane.

It is known that similar violations have taken place in the past, but the Government of the United States, notwithstanding the full substantiation of the information given by the Soviet government and in face of facts, denied the American planes violated the state frontier of the USSR. The circumstances of the violation of the state frontier of the USSR by an American military plane on June 27 are such that now it should be believed, the Government of the United States will not deny the fact of violation.

The Government of the USSR protests vigorously to the Government of the United States against this gross violation of the Soviet frontier by an American military plane.

The Soviet government has repeatedly called the attention of the Government of the United States of America to the facts of violations of Soviet airspace by American military planes and pointed to the grave consequences that such violations might produce. It insisted on measures by the Government of the United States to prevent such violations.

Effect on Relations

Unfortunately, it should be noted that the Government of the United States of America did not follow this road.

One cannot fail to see that this position of the Government of the United States does not conduce to the easing of tension in the relations

*between our countries even though the Government of the USA has de-
clared more than once that it, like the Government of the USSR, wishes
for an improvement of these relations. This position of the Government
of the United States is at variance with its peaceful professions and not
only leads to the aggravation of relations between the USSR and the
United States but hampers the improvement of the international situation
in general.*

*The Soviet government insists that the Government of the USA take
effective measures to prevent violation of the state frontier of the USSR
by American military planes.*

In saying that the U.S. plane had "burned up," the note did not make
clear whether it burned as a result of a crash landing, whether it had been
fired on or whether the crew itself destroyed the aircraft to protect secret
equipment or cargo. The most important aspect of the relatively mild
note was what it lacked—there was no accusation of espionage.

Ambassador Thompson asked only one question: "Are all members
of the crew alive?" The answer was yes. The Soviet Union's most recent
charges of menacing flights by United States planes had been in connection with Strategic Air Command's "alert" flights in the Arctic regions
near the North Pole. Moscow had protested the previous spring about
flights of U.S. Air Force SAC B-52 bombers carrying atomic weapons flying across the North Pole toward Soviet Siberia and reversing course
abruptly a couple of hundred miles short of penetrating Soviet airspace in
the Arctic. Given the speed of the B-52, Soviet air defense commanders
had only a few minutes each time American bombers were spotted on the
radar heading toward them to decide whether or not a cross-polar flight
represented a training mission or an attack. Moscow's complaints included the quite realistic argument that catastrophic consequences could
result if a patrolling bomber were mistaken for an attacker and that error
set off a "retaliatory" attack.

The mild tone of the protest note on June 28 suggests that the Soviet
government, despite its claim to the contrary, believed that the border
violation was indeed unintentional, and that the captured crew members
were who they professed to be—an innocent air transport crew on a

"milk run" servicing American embassies in North Africa, the Middle East, and Western Asia. It was obvious that the Soviets had no evidence to the contrary. All sensitive cargo and equipment had, after all, burned beyond recognition and recovery.

The U.S. Defense Department announced the Saturday night of June 28 that an Air Force transport with nine persons aboard was "unreported" on a flight from Nicosia, Cyprus, to Tehran, Iran, via Turkey.

American newspapers began to speculate about where the incident occurred and what it meant. "Why would an American aircraft be flying from Cyprus to Tehran? . . . The border between Turkey and Armenia is about two hundred miles north of the probable air route from Cyprus to Tehran—any U.S. flight in the border area would be most unusual." The UPI press service also commented that military planes are equipped with devices by which the crew can destroy them to keep them from falling into enemy hands.

The U.S. press also pointed out that another air incident involving U.S. aircraft had occurred less than three weeks earlier when a U.S. Army helicopter became lost on a training flight, ran out of gas, and landed in East Germany near Zwickau. Eight U.S. Army officers and a sergeant were seized by the East Germans and were still being held. After seizing the men, the East German authorities delivered them to Soviet forces in East Germany. In a political maneuver the Soviets handed the Americans back to the East Germans, and then insisted that the American government negotiate directly with the East German government—which the U.S. did not recognize as a sovereign entity—for the release of the detained soldiers.

On June 27 the U.S. sent a stiff aide-mémoire to the Soviet Embassy in Washington declaring that it regarded "with grave concern" the prolonged detention of the nine army personnel. After several weeks of haggling with the Soviet government and refusing to recognize the legitimacy of the East German regime, the East Germans handed the nine army men back to the Soviets, who promptly returned the men to American control.

On June 30 the U.S. government delivered a response to the Soviet foreign ministry in Moscow denying that the C-118 had deliberately

violated Soviet airspace. The State Department note is written in a notably quiet tone, accusing the Soviets of nothing. It merely asks for the
return of the airmen:

> It has been ascertained that an unarmed military transport Air Force
> plane of the DC-6 type, with destination Tehran via Turkey, is missing.
> It is undoubtedly the plane that the USSR charges crossed the border of
> Soviet territory and was forced to land near Yerevan, USSR.
>
> This was a routine flight, on a regular bimonthly schedule, carrying
> cargo consigned to United States military and diplomatic missions in Iran
> and Pakistan.
>
> The flight originated in Wiesbaden for Tehran and Karachi. Its last de-
> parture point was Nicosia, Cyprus, with destination Tehran by the pre-
> scribed international civil airways route.
>
> It was last reported over Adana, Turkey at 13:23 local time on June 27
> (7:23 E.D.T., Friday morning).
>
> This commercial airlane to Tehran passes within about fifty miles of
> the Soviet border. The weather was overcast. Due to high mountains
> along the route, it is presumed that the aircraft flying above the overcast,
> on instruments and on radio beacon guidance, had no visual reference to
> ground checkpoints.
>
> The usual request for diplomatic clearance had been made to Tehran,
> Iran and had been granted.
>
> There is no basis whatsoever for the Soviet charges that there was de-
> liberate violation of the airspace of the USSR.
>
> The Department of State is instructing the United States ambassador
> to Moscow to seek the prompt return of the crew consisting of six officers
> and three airmen.

Like the Soviet protest note, the American response was conspicuous
for the points that it did not address. It treated the incident as a regrettable mistake but did not comment on the Soviet claim that the aircraft
had penetrated 105 miles (170 km) into Soviet airspace or that the plane
had flown 45 additional miles (70 km) farther into Soviet airspace after
being ordered by two Soviet jets to land. Moreover, the note avoided
high-level policy questions or sources of international tension.

On Sunday, June 29, the Soviet military newspaper *Krasnaya Zvezda* (Red Star) gave a brief description of the incident. Two jet fighters had been dispatched to intercept an intruder that had been spotted on radar. When signaled to land, the plane failed to respond, then turned sharply toward the south. The Soviet fliers forced the plane down, and it began to burn upon landing. The nine crew members leaped out and were detained, uninjured and in normal health. Other pseudo unofficial Soviet reports intimated that the detainees had been involved in intelligence work and that the flight over Soviet territory had been a deliberate provocation. However, the evidence available to the Soviets obviously did not justify that claim.

The C-118 incident had occurred around dusk. All nine American airmen were reunited at a military facility about 10:00 P.M. and immediately driven several hours to Kirovabad, Azerbaijan. From there, the nine airmen were flown the following morning in two Soviet air force LI-2 transport aircraft to Baku, capital of Azerbaijan. Held for the next week at the Baku Air Defense District Headquarters, they were questioned about their military duties. Their interrogators (those who spoke directly with the Americans) spoke excellent English and were generally friendly. No one suffered any physical mistreatment, and all were provided adequate medical care. The interrogators wore civilian clothes, but displayed military decorum and generally worked as a team during questioning.

From the beginning the men were treated better in Soviet hands than they had expected. The airmen were brought one at a time before an interrogation team and asked general questions about their jobs in the Air Force, the nature of their flight, and why they violated Soviet airspace. They had anticipated more severe grillings. A pecking order among the interrogators was obvious.

Major Bob Crans recently described his strategy for dealing with his captors. The senior person who attended and was in charge of the interrogations did not speak English—he asked his questions through an English-speaking interpreter. In a casual conversation with one of the interpreters Crans asked the Soviet leader's rank. He was said to be a colonel. The next time he was summoned before the interrogation board, Crans faced the colonel and saluted smartly. Speaking through the interpreter, the colonel asked Crans why he had saluted. Crans explained that he saluted out of respect for the colonel's rank. The colonel nodded, smiled, and said, "Khorosho" (okay). From that point on, Crans always saluted when entering the interrogation room and was asked very few questions. Apparently, the Soviet interrogators believed the American airmen's cover stories because they barely touched on the subject of espionage.

The rank-conscious Soviet group readily accepted Colonel Brannon as the leader of the captured Americans. Toward the end of the first week in captivity (on July 3), one of the interrogators told Colonel Brannon that they would be released in a day or two. On July 7, the nine men were driven in a truck from Baku to the Caspian seaside town of Astara, Iran, on the Azerbaijani-Iranian border and delivered into the hands of Col. John W. Baska, U.S. air attaché from the American Embassy in Tehran. No U.S. representatives had been permitted to interview the nine men while they were held by the Soviets. TASS, the official Soviet news agency, announced the transfer in a brief statement, naming all nine airmen.

Back in American hands, they were flown to Tehran. After an overnight rest, an Air Force C-118 flew them home to Germany on July 8, arriving at Wiesbaden around 14:00 local time, where they were greeted by their wives. Molly Holman was especially happy; it was also her birthday. She teased Jim about his not bringing her a birthday present. In a matter of minutes the nine men were hustled aboard a waiting bus and driven to the Wiesbaden Air Force Hospital. They made no public statements, and no reporters were allowed to interview them.

The U.S. public learned only after the nine airmen had been released by the Soviets that Soviet MiG fighters had shot up the C-118 during the forced landing. A news conference was scheduled at USAFE HQ for the following afternoon, but delayed an extra twenty-four hours, till July 10.

At the news conference, the men described their treatment as "considerate." Colonel Brannon pointed out that they had not been accused of espionage. He described the entire incident in a carefully worded statement. They were on a "normal cargo run." While flying at 15,000 feet after passing Adana, Turkey, they began to encounter extremely turbulent thunderstorms. Major Lyles, the aircraft commander, turned slightly north to dodge around the storms. A short time later, two unidentified fighter planes appeared, which the crew initially believed to be Turkish, or perhaps Iranian.

> *One of the aircraft fired a short burst off the wing of our aircraft. At that time we recognized the aircraft to be MiGs with Soviet markings. Major Lyles lowered the landing gear in an attempt to indicate clearly that we were on a non-provocative flight [that is, signaling their readiness to land]. Then the fighters fired upon the aircraft with the apparent intent to shoot it down. We were hit in the wing tank, just behind the left No. 2 engine.*

It was at that point that Major Lyle gave the bailout order and five men bailed out; he decided to attempt an emergency landing when the other three who remained aboard told him the flames made their escape by parachute impossible.

The U.S. Congress had already reacted angrily upon learning on July 8 that the unarmed C-118 had been shot down by Soviet jet fighters. Representative James E. Van Zandt, Republican member of the House Armed Services Committee, called the incident "typical" of the Soviet Union, adding, "You're dealing with a gangster type of government and must expect gangster treatment." Democratic representative Overton Brooks, another House Armed Services Committee member, said, "It sounds to me very serious and we should treat it accordingly." Senator Mike Mansfield declared that it was "not understandable" why a Soviet fighter plane had shot down the unarmed United States plane. "It appears in view of the new turn of events that we ought to be more grateful than ever that these fliers have been released and are now back with our forces."

Later, on July 9, the State Department got into the act by denouncing the "inhumane attacks." The State Department spokesman noted that the circumstances of the assault by Soviet MiG interceptors were being studied and that "further action" in the case was under consideration. The Defense Department weighed in with an announcement that the five airmen who parachuted from their burning aircraft were "mistreated" by Soviet civilians before local authorities took them into custody. These comments presaged a very strong formal protest to the Soviet government.

On July 11 the U.S. formally demanded that the Soviet Union pun-ish the fighter pilots who shot down the C-118. The American protest read in part:

> *The facts determined by investigation are these:*
>
> *An unarmed C-118 transport-type aircraft, while on a routine flight on the established commercial air route to Tehran, inadvertently crossed the Soviet frontier near Yerevan owing to circumstances beyond its con-trol. Following interception by Soviet fighter aircraft, which fired a burst off the wing of the United States transport, the American aircraft lowered its landing gear, indicating innocent intent. In spite of this action, the So-viet fighters shot directly at the transport, setting it afire. After five of the crew had parachuted from the transport, the four remaining crew mem-bers, whose exit was prevented by fire, endeavored to land the transport. The Soviet fighters made no attempt to point out a safe landing area to the burning aircraft. While the C-118 was on its final approach to an emer-gency landing, the Soviet fighters made another firing run on the crippled transport . . .*
>
> *. . . The United States government expects that those guilty of the at-tacks on the plane will be punished in a degree commensurate with their offense.*

Moscow responded "unofficially" in the *Krasnaya Zvezda* (Red Star) army newspaper, charging on July 12 that the United States government was using "inexcusable lies" and "threats" to cover up the "rude viola-tion" of Soviet airspace. While not denying outright that Soviet fighters shot down the aircraft, the article used the term "imaginary shooting down," and denigrated the American descriptions of the incident as mere allegations. *Krasnaya Zvezda* insisted that the Americans had failed to obey the command of Soviet fighters, and attempted to evade capture.

Finally, the Soviet government responded officially to the U.S. note on July 21, rejecting as "unfounded and inappropriate" the U.S. demand that the responsible Soviet airmen be punished. The Soviet note insisted anew that the fighters had signaled the transport to land but that the plane tried "to flee"—adding that as in other countries instructions are in force under which Soviet airmen "are obliged to utilize all means at their command in order to compel a violator airplane to land at a local airdrome." Whom to believe? At their news conference at Wiesbaden on July 10, the returning airmen had insisted that the Soviet fighters ignored their signal of readiness to land—the lowering of their landing gear while remaining aloft. And an official U.S. Air Force spokesman stated on July 12 that the Defense Department stood by every word of its original statement.

The Americans called the mission "routine," and the Soviets believed them. But then why is the official record of the plane and its mission so scanty? Details about the Soviet shootdown of the C-118 and detainment of its nine-man crew for ten days are not included in the official 7405th Support Squadron history for 1958 (or, for that matter, any other year). The operations section of the unit history makes no mention of the incident. The maintenance officer addressed the issue laconically: "On 27 June 1958, the attached C-118A type aircraft, serial number 51-3822, was transferred." A subsequent maintenance entry in the unit history shows that on July 17, 1958, C-118A serial number 53-3278 was assigned to the unit—no doubt replacing the aircraft that the nine airmen left burning in Armenia the previous month.

The men in that plane were engaged in a mission that was far from routine, though it is certainly true that the plane was unarmed. Over the years, the crew members of 3822 have talked very little about the incident. Decades later, Colonel Brannon said, when reminded that the Soviets released them after only ten days in captivity, "I cried like a baby; I never expected to get out of there alive."

Colonel Brannon discussed the mission with Larry Tart in early 2001. At eighty-six years of age, he is exceptionally spry, plays golf often, takes no medications, and has few ailments. He recalled the incident vividly. Although they had two navigators on their aircrew and an outstanding aircraft commander, he believes that the navigators locked onto the wrong beacon, resulting in the inadvertent border violation. He recalled that a Soviet beacon in the area transmitted on a frequency that differed by only a couple of kilocycles from the frequency used by one of the Turkish radio beacons, and that this probably played a part in their getting off course and into Soviet airspace.

He vehemently denied that their aircraft was equipped with cameras or other reconnaissance equipment, calling it "clean as a whistle." Colonel Brannon said, "That aircraft belonged to the chief of mission in the company that I worked for." According to Brannon, the aircraft's mission was precisely as stated: it hauled passengers and cargo, and was not used in clandestine activities. Who the passengers were officially remains a mystery, and cargo included typical fare for embassies and special mission locations—classified intelligence plans and products, storage safes and encryption equipment, and other items that traveled in diplomatic pouches. Even refrigerators and lots of booze were hauled into U.S. overseas embassy compounds. When the Russians investigated the C-118's wreckage, they found no classified or incriminating materials among the smoldering debris.

Like two others on the crew—Majors Bennie Shupe and Robert Crans—Colonel Brannon told the American press that he was Major Lyle's copilot, and Capt. James Kane and Lt. James Luther professed to have been navigators on the fateful mission. Likewise, the two junior enlisted men, A/2C Earl Reamer and Peter Sabo, claimed to be flight engineers along with T.Sgt. James Holman. A nine-member cockpit crew! Their cover story makes one wonder how the Russians could have been so gullible.

A report from Soviet air defense authorities to the Central Committee of the Communist Party of the Soviet Union provides a more detailed description of how the American aircraft had been forced down. It reads in part:

> The state border of the USSR was violated by an American military aircraft in the region south of Yerevan from the direction of Turkey on 27 June 58 at 18:30 hours. The violator at an altitude of 5,500 meters and a speed of 500 KPH penetrated 170 kilometers into Soviet territory.
>
> The [American] aircrew did not obey the demands of the fighters to "follow me for landing," and continued to fly on a course toward Baku.
>
> The central command post of the PVO Forces ordered the forced landing of the aircraft. The fighters opened defensive fire at 18:48 hours in the execution of this order.
>
> Afterwards, the violator attempted to depart toward Iran.

*Seeing that the violator was not obeying the demands of the fighters and
based upon orders of the CP [command post], they opened fire on the aircraft, setting it on fire.*

*Five personnel parachuted from the aircraft and four landed in the
burning aircraft at an auxiliary airfield in the area of Gindarkh (105 kilometers southwest of Kyurdamir).*

*The remains of the surface sections and tail unit are those of a four-
engine C-118 military transport with USAF markings and tail number
13822. The remains of the burned aircraft are being investigated.*

*Of the nine American servicemen, two received minor burns . . .
[After naming the servicemen aboard the violator aircraft, the report
continues] . . .*

*At the time, the weather in the region south of Lake Van was 60-90%
cloud cover at 600-1,000 meters with visibility of 10 kilometers. The detained American servicemen were taken to the city of Kirovabad where
they are being interrogated.*

With no evidence to the contrary, sixty to ninety percent cloud
cover may well have swayed the decision of the interrogators to accept
the American crew's story. And the fact that, as Major Lyle said, the
C-118 "was burning pretty good" no doubt helped the crew's case by
eliminating if not "evidence" certainly material that would have proved
an embarrassment and that might have caused the interrogators to return
to their trade with enthusiasm. Obviously, any sensitive classified materials had been burned beyond recognition. Whatever the deciding factors,
the situation could not have turned out better for the nine Americans—
to a man, they all expected a more grievous ending to their odyssey.

And what happened to the forced down C-118 aircraft? The Soviet
military quickly grew tired of providing guards to watch the burned-
out hulk at the crash site. Summarizing the incident in a report to
the Central Committee of the Communist Party of the Soviet Union
in August 1958, a ministry of defense official provided the committee
a recommended solution. Concluding that the nine American servicemen from the violator aircraft had been transferred to a representative
of the American military mission in Iran on 7 July 1958, the report
continued:

. . . The wreckage of the aircraft is currently under guard by troops detached from the Baku Air Defense District.

Considering that the American side up to this time has not inquired about the return of the downed aircraft remains, and also that it is inadvisable to guard it further, the Ministry of Defense of the USSR considers it expedient to:

1. *Destroy the downed aircraft remains and draw up a destruction certificate.*
2. *Transfer the aircraft remains for re-processing in industry.*

Should the Americans ask, give them the document regarding the destruction of the aircraft.

A draft decision of the CC CPSS is attached. Please review.

Talk about micro management. The ministry of defense apparatchiki didn't even dare to dispose of the remains of an adversary's aircraft without approval from the highest levels in the Soviet government. And, just what had the KGB and PVO (air defense) interrogators given away when they allowed the Americans to be returned to the American government?

In 1993, a *U.S. News & World Report* exposé on Cold War espionage identified the C-118 that the Soviets forced down in Armenia in June 1958 as a "specially designated courier aircraft" on a mission for the Central Intelligence Agency. The report continued, "There is no question that the C-118 was carrying sensitive intelligence information. . . . What remains unclear is what it was—and whether the Soviets got their hands on it." The article identified Colonel Brannon as the highest ranking of three CIA officers among the nine men aboard the C-118 when it was shot down—three CIA officers who worked on the U-2 program. Colonel Brannon denied that the aircraft was carrying information about the U-2 program but conceded that it was carrying documents detailing another top-secret intelligence operation—"papers that could have told the Russians what we were doing." Samuel Klaus, a State Department lawyer who investigated the C-118 shootdown incident with the intent of filing a claim against the Soviets in the International Court of Justice, wrote in a memo classified as secret, "It was fortunate [both] that the crew lived and [that] the plane was destroyed." Bennie Shupe was confident that the Soviets did not get their hands on any of the secret documents in his possession. While drifting down to Earth after bailing out, he ripped materials that he had with him into tiny pieces and ate them— one by one.

This Soviet-American air confrontation along the Turkish-Armenian border in late June in all probability had an impact on the way the Soviet air defense forces in Armenia reacted to U.S. Air Force C-130 60528 when it inadvertently crossed the Soviet frontier into Armenia only two months later. It is reasonable to assume that the local air defense leadership was severely chastised for permitting the U.S. C-118 to penetrate 240 kilometers (150 miles) into Soviet airspace before being forced down on June 27. And it is more than mere coincidence that the Soviet minister of defense issued order number 0049 on July 4, 1958—a death warrant of sorts for aircrews who violate Soviet state borders. Under order number 0049 Soviet air defense forces were "obliged to utilize all means at their command to compel a violator airplane to land at a local airdrome."

RB-47 Chased from Caspian Sea—July 26, 1958

A month after the C-118 incident, Soviet air force fighters from the same air defense district were scrambled to defend Soviet state borders against yet another intruding U.S. aircraft. On July 30, the Soviet foreign ministry filed protest notes with both the American and Iranian Embassies in Moscow, charging that a U.S. RB-47 from Iran had deliberately violated airspace over the Caspian Sea and been forced to flee on July 26, 1958. The foreign ministry claimed that the American military plane flying from the direction of Iran had crossed the Soviet border over the Caspian Sea 130 miles east-southeast of Astara (a coastal city on Azerbaijani-Iranian border). The protest notes claimed that the border violator intruded fifteen miles inside Soviet airspace before being driven off by Soviet fighters. The notes did not say whether the fighters opened fire.

In the note to the Iranians, the Soviet government drew attention "to the fact that such violations had occurred before and that the facts do not tally with Iranian government statements that no foreign troops will be stationed in Iran and that Iran will never be used as a base for attacks against the Soviet Union." An Iranian government spokesman denied that Iran had any knowledge of any such flight from Iranian territory, and no immediate response was available from the U.S. government. The Soviet notes specifically mentioned ongoing tensions in the area—the Soviet government regarded the violation as "particularly serious in view of the fact that the violation took place at a moment when the armed intervention of the United States and Britain in the Near and Middle East has created a most tense situation in this area."

Distrust on both sides had added to the tensions along the southern periphery of the Soviet Union and in the Middle East. In late 1956 in response to Egypt's nationalization of the Suez Canal, Britain, Israel, and France had intervened militarily to crush the Egyptian military and retake control of the canal. In response, Soviet Premier Nikita Khrushchev threatened to use Soviet long-range surface-to-surface missiles to defend Egypt. The United States and the Soviet Union, who were fighting each other diplomatically at the time over Soviet intervention in anticommunist uprisings in Hungary, were caught off guard by the Suez crisis and had to join diplomatic forces to defuse the situation. As a compromise, the British and French withdrew their forces that were protecting the Suez; Israel withdrew from the Sinai Peninsula; Egypt regained control of the Suez Canal and Sinai; and a United Nations peacekeeping force deployed in the canal zone.

Notwithstanding that interim solution, tensions remained high. In the summer of 1958, there was an outbreak of religious strife and a small civil war in Lebanon, resulting in a request for assistance from Lebanese President Camille Chamoun. Fearing a spread of the Lebanese fighting to neighboring countries, U.S. President Dwight Eisenhower landed a 14,000 Marine task force on the beaches south of Beirut on July 15. The presence of the U.S. Marines brought stability and the civil war ended by early August, but tensions remained high as the Soviet Union was backing the Arabs against Israel, which the United States supported.

With the communists tightening control in the East European countries and Khrushchev threatening to "bury the West," President Eisenhower considered it paramount to obtain intelligence about Soviet capabilities and intentions. Airborne reconnaissance such as the RB-47 mission over the Caspian Sea on July 26 provided the only way of gathering strategic and tactical intelligence (order of battle and operational data) from Soviet-controlled areas not accessible to other intelligence gathering means.

At the same time, the Soviet Union was determined to deny access to such information. With at least two recent earlier overflights by the Americans alone, the southwestern border of the Soviet Union had been shown to be dangerously porous. With possible severe punishments hanging over them, the authorities in the air defense command center at Leninakan, Armenia, near the Turkish border, would have been more determined than ever to stop another intruding aircraft. That rather desperate resoluteness was evident in the savage manner in which the MiG pilots attacked the C-130 on September 2d.

RB-47 Shot Down Over Barents Sea—July 1, 1960

One more shootdown should be mentioned, despite the fact that it occurred nearly two years after the September 2, 1958 incident. Next to the Gary Powers's U-2 shootdown on May 1, 1960, the shootdown of an RB-47 over the Barents Sea on July 1, 1960 is perhaps the most memorable Soviet-American air incident of the Cold War—memorable to the average American because two crew members survived and received a hero's welcome home from President John F. Kennedy in early 1961 after they were released from Lubyanka prison in Moscow.

In June 1960, Maj. Willard G. Palm (aircraft commander) and his crew—Captains Freeman B. Olmstead (copilot) and John R. McKone (navigator), plus three electronic warfare officers (Maj. Eugene E. Posa and Captains Dean B. Phillips and Oscar L. Goforth)[25] deployed on temporary duty from Forbes AFB, Kansas, to Royal Air Force (RAF) Base Brize Norton near Oxford, England. Assigned to the 343rd Strategic Recon Squadron of the Strategic Air Command's 55th Strategic Recon Wing at Forbes, they would be flying electronic intelligence reconnaissance missions against the Soviet Union, pinpointing the locations of Soviet air defense radars and gathering other radar order of battle data that SAC needed to maintain a SIOP (single integrated operations plan) in the event of war with the Soviet Union.

On July 1, Major Palm's crew departed Brize Norton at 10:00 A.M. aboard RB-47H tail number 53-4281 on an intelligence mission code-named "Boston Casper" along the Arctic coastline of the northwestern Soviet Union. The SAC recon crews called such twelve-hour missions "milk runs"—a run up the Barents Sea along the Kola Peninsula, a left turn up toward Novaya Zemlya (often referred to as banana island because of its shape), and back to Brize Norton. The signals environment was relatively sparse in that area, and at no time were they to fly closer than fifty miles from the Soviet landmass. Flying due north along the prime (zero degree) meridian over the North Sea, they reached the Arctic Circle at noon, and by 12:30, Major Palm had refueled—taking on 50,000 pounds of fuel from a KC-135 tanker—over the Norwegian Sea about 300 miles west of Bodö, Norway. Bodö, a NATO base on the Norwegian coast about fifty miles north of the Arctic Circle, had been Gary Powers's intended destination exactly two months earlier, when he was shot down over Sverdlovsk, Russia. Ironically, Bodö would serve as the search and rescue staging center for the extensive SAR efforts that ensued when Major Palm's RB-47 crew failed to return to Brize Norton from their mission.

At 1:30 P.M. the RB-47 crew reached a point north of Norway where they turned east into the Barents Sea. A few minutes and 150 miles later, they assumed a southerly heading on a route toward the point where the Norwegian and Soviet borders intersect on the Barents Sea. Prior to reaching the next turning point, McKone, the navigator, used his radar to "fix" his location relative to the Norwegian headland—the northern part of Norway that juts out into the Barents Sea. On their intercom, he and Palm, the pilot, discussed seeing the headland prior to reaching their turning point thirty-five miles north of the Norwegian coast at a point close to the Soviet border. Later, McKone would comment that he always used his radar to take fixes off land points in the Arctic although it was easier to determine the aircraft's location by taking fixes on radio stations—radios in the area were intermittent and deemed unreliable. By 1960, American fliers had learned—at a high cost—the dangers of relying on radio beacons as navigational aids near the Soviet border.

As they reached their turning point and took up a southeasterly heading to parallel the Soviet Kola Peninsula, McKone took another radar fix when they were located directly north of the Rybachiy Peninsula, a well defined Soviet landmass jutting out into the Barents Sea northeast of Murmansk. At that point McKone estimates that they were no closer than forty-five nautical miles from the Soviet landmass, and he asked Major Palm to correct their heading to the left, away from Soviet territory, to bring them back on their planned route—at least fifty miles from the Soviet coast. That leg of their route covered about 220 miles, about thirty minutes of flight; they were flying southeast on a 120 degree heading. About halfway to their next point, McKone took another radar fix on the Kola Peninsula to their right; his radar showed them exactly fifty miles—midway between the forty-mile and the sixty-mile marker rings on his radarscope—from the nearest Soviet beaches.

Shortly after the RB-47 had passed abeam and north of Murmansk, Bruce Olmstead, the copilot, observed an aircraft contrail to their right. The contrail, which was paralleling their flight path, turned out to be the track of a MiG fighter that suddenly took a 90-degree turn and closed to within two to three miles of the RB-47 before breaking off and disappearing toward the Soviet coast. McKone noted the time as 2:57, three minutes before their scheduled left turn at their next checkpoint. It was time for another radar fix.

His new point of reference was Cape Holy Nose (Mys Svyatoi Nos in Russian), an unmistakable finger of land that juts out into the sea near the area where the Barents and White Seas join. McKone zeroed in on Cape Holy Nose and saw by his radar range marker that their aircraft was located more than sixty miles from the coast. He also noted that they were approaching their checkpoint two minutes early (they had a good tailwind). Other instruments showed that they were flying at an altitude of 30,000 feet at a true air speed of 425 knots (490 mph).

That was exactly their planned distance from Cape Holy Nose at that point—an important fact because for seven months while he was in solitary confinement in Lubyanka prison, Soviet interrogators would try without success to get McKone to say that the RB-47 had violated Soviet airspace twelve nautical miles (twenty-two kilometers) from Cape Holy Nose. At 14:58 McKone told Bill Palm that they were at their checkpoint, and Palm put the aircraft into a gentle left turn, taking them away from Soviet territory.

Suddenly Olmstead spotted a MiG off the right wing, so close that he could see the red star on the MiG-19's tail and the pilot in the cockpit. To say that it got Olmstead's blood flowing was an understatement—it was his first reconnaissance mission in the Arctic, and the first time he'd ever seen a MiG up close. Olmstead and McKone heard Palm say, "Where the hell did that guy come from." The MiG pilot broke away, turned, reapproached from the rear, and opened fire with his cannons.

Seeing the flashes from the cannons, Olmstead, who controlled the bomber's defensive systems, returned fire with the RB-47's 20 mm cannons. The first attack wiped out two of the three engines on the left wing and caused the RB-47 to go into an uncontrolled spin, diverting Olmstead's attention to try to help Major Palm gain control of the aircraft while the MiG pilot opened fire again. While Palm and Olmstead wrestled with the rudder attempting to bring the aircraft out of a spin, the MiG struck a third time. There was a loud explosion, and the RB-47's canopy blew away from the aircraft, at which point Palm shouted, "Standby, Standby," and a few seconds later yelled, "Bail Out! Bail Out!" and activated the alarm bell and red bailout warning lights.

The pilot, copilot, and navigator—Palm, Olmstead, and McKone—managed to eject from the out-of-control RB-47, but only Olmstead and McKone survived the bailout. The three electronic warfare officers (affectionately known as ravens in SAC) were in a separate, special compartment built into the bomb bay of the RB-47H. After departing Brize Norton, they had crawled through a tunnel to their compartment where their job was to intercept active radar signals during the mission. Using an interphone communication system the ravens could communicate with the pilot, copilot, navigator, and each other. Although they were busy monitoring radar signals, including airborne signals emanating from the attacking MiG during the attack, each raven was most likely monitoring their flight crew's conversation on intercom. The three raven positions were equipped with emergency ejection seats, but it is not known if any of them managed to eject.

A Soviet trawler picked up Olmstead and McKone, and Bill Palm's body. Olmstead and McKone were transferred to a Coast Guard (KGB border police) cutter, taken to a small airstrip and flown the following day to Moscow, where they would spend the next seven months as special guests of the Soviet secret police, in the infamous Lubyanka prison at KGB Headquarters on Dzerzhinsky Square, central Moscow. On July 11, 1960, the Soviet government filed a protest with the American Embassy in Moscow for "another American violation of Soviet state borders" and announced that Olmstead and McKone were being held for trial on espionage charges.

McKone suffered no serious injuries during the bailout. Olmstead was not as fortunate. Suffering a crushed vertebra as he and his ejection seat were catapulted from the aircraft, he had to endure the pain without serious medical help until a Soviet doctor put him in traction in his cell about July 15. He remained in traction about seven weeks except during the frequent interrogations. The three ravens were unaccounted for.

Olmstead and McKone realized they were in deep trouble at their first interrogation session—both were kept in solitary confinement and interrogated separately. Their interrogator asked why they had violated the Soviet state border twenty-two kilometers (twelve nautical miles) north of Cape Svyatoi Nos and each was shown a map depicting the spot where the interrogator claimed the violation had occurred. Both contended that they were a full fifty miles off the Soviet coast when a MiG attacked their RB-47 without provocation, and that they had not violated Soviet airspace.

Meanwhile, on July 2, the U.S. Air Force notified the families of the six missing crew members that the aircraft had failed to return from a mission over the Barents Sea and that search and rescue efforts were under way. Almost from the start news leaks and rumors resulted in confusion, half truths, and in some cases, outright lies about the RB-47's mission and the status of search efforts. The Air Force said that the crew was performing an "electromagnetic survey" mission, announcing that the missing plane carried instruments to chart the earth's magnetic field in the Arctic area. "The data is used to make 'magnetic maps' to assist aircraft commanders in navigating on long flights."

In a news release to the press the U.S. Air Forces in Europe said it was "unlikely" that the plane had approached Soviet territory. According to unnamed "informed sources," it was not scheduled to fly overland. The

Air Force spokesman added that the mission bore no similarity to the discontinued U-2 espionage flights over the Soviet Union that had ended in Gary Powers's U-2 shootdown just two months earlier. (Following the U-2 shootdown, President Eisenhower had officially announced that reconnaissance flights over the Soviet Union had been stopped.)

A Norwegian air force spokesman at Bodö, Norway, stated that the RB-47 pilot had last reported his location over the Barents Sea the previous night as 73 degrees 30 minutes north latitude and 35 degrees west longitude—adding that this point was between Murmansk and Spitzbergen Island about 300 miles off the Soviet coast. [This was almost certainly *disinformation* since the RB-47 crew was flying under rules of radio silence that prohibited the crew to transmit except during an emergency, and there had been no opportunity to transmit even a mayday when the MiG attacked.] The U.S. Air Force's Europe Headquarters announced that twenty to twenty-five search planes were scouring the Barents Sea around the clock, thanks to the daylight provided by the midnight sun in the Arctic. Unfortunately, the search crews did not search in the area of the Barents Sea where the RB-47 had disappeared.

As word of the lost RB-47 appeared in the news, reporters speculated about the plane's mission. The Associated Press accurately described the RB-47 as a version of the combat B-47 with "all bomb carrying equipment removed and packed instead with electronic equipment for checking sites and frequencies of aircraft direction systems."

In another report, a coastal station at Vardö, Norway [on the coast of the Barents Sea near the Soviet border], reported that the Soviet rescue cruiser *Kapitan Afanasiev* had stated that it was steaming at full speed to help in the search. Either the Soviets were engaged in their own disinformation or the Soviet ship's captain had not learned that the KGB was already interrogating the two surviving crew members.

Even Soviet Premier Nikita Khrushchev, who together with Soviet Foreign Minister Andrei Gromyko was on a state visit to Austria in early July, 1960, appears not to have learned about the shootdown incident until days after the air confrontation occurred. On July 2, in response to a question about the missing RB-47 from an American reporter, Gromyko responded, "We know nothing of such a plane. Plane? What plane?"

The following day when another reporter asked Khrushchev the same question, Khrushchev looked puzzled and said, "I know absolutely nothing of the plane, and I wish you would stop bothering me with your damned planes." Realistically, Khrushchev probably was playing games with the U.S. press. He ended his nine-day state visit to Austria on Friday, July 8, and there were no discussions between the U.S. and the Soviet Union about the incident until he returned to Moscow. While in Austria, Khrushchev drew very small crowds and appeared in a bad mood much of the time. Attempting to win over the neutralist Austrian government, he would try to woo them one day and then threaten them the next. He hinted on July 4 at increased Soviet-Austrian trade, then on July 5 commented, "Life is short and I want to see the Red Flag fly over the whole world in my lifetime." The following day he warned Austria that her neutrality would be imperiled if the United States used its rocket bases in northern Italy against the communist world. He also embarrassed his hosts more than once by verbally attacking President Eisenhower during speeches in Austria.

Arriving back in Moscow on Friday, July 8, Khrushchev and the Presidium of the Soviet Communist Party settled on a plan for dealing with this most recent U.S.-Soviet air incident. On July 11, Gromyko delivered a note of "strong protest" to the American Embassy, charging a new gross violation of Soviet airspace. Gromyko also handed protest notes to the British and Norwegian ambassadors, accusing Britain and Norway of complicity by permitting their bases to be used by American reconnaissance planes. A copy of the note to the U.S. provided to Western newsmen by the Soviet authorities presented the Soviet side of the incident:

> . . . An unidentified military aircraft heading for the frontier of the USSR was sighted by the aerial observation service of the Soviet anti-aircraft defense forces over the Barents Sea in the vicinity of the Kola Peninsula on 1 July 1960. A fighter plane was sent up to identify the nationality of the plane and prevent it from invading the territory of the USSR.
>
> The pilot of the Soviet fighter plane established that the unidentified plane was a bomber with the markings of the United States Air Force.

The American plane violated the state frontier of the USSR twenty-two kilometers north of Svyatoi Nos Cape and was moving in the directions of the city of Arkhangelsk.

Advanced Despite Signals

Despite the signals given by the Soviet fighter plane to follow it and to prepare for landing, the violating plane continued moving into the airspace of the USSR. In accordance with the order issued to the armed forces of the USSR on safeguarding the Soviet frontiers, the violator plane was shot down at 18:03 hours [6:03 p.m. Moscow time] over Soviet territorial waters east of Svyatoi Nos Cape.

Some time later, a Soviet ship picked up in the territorial waters of the USSR two members of the crew of the American plane that was shot down. They were the plane's navigator, Air Force Lieutenant John Richard McKone of Missouri, born in 1932, and the copilot, Air Force First Lieutenant Freeman Bruce Olmstead of New York, born in 1935.

As McKone and Olmstead testified during the interrogation, the plane in which they had flown—a six-engine RB-47 reconnaissance bomber—belonged to an air unit of the American Military Strategic Reconnaissance group included in the 55th Wing and fulfilled special military reconnaissance missions. The plane was armed with two twenty-millimeter guns and a set of shells, and had a compartment encompassing special reconnaissance photo and radio electronic equipment.

According to Olmstead and McKone, the plane had a crew of four men besides themselves: the commander of the plane, Captain [Willard G.] Palm and three officer-specialists in photo and radio-electronic equipment, Captain [Eugene E.] Posa and First Lieutenants [Oscar L.] Goforth and [Dean B.] Phillips. The body of the first pilot, Captain Palm, was discovered by a Soviet vessel in a rubber boat and taken aboard. The search for other members of the plane's crew yielded no results.

According to the testimony of Olmstead and McKone, the RB-47 plane on which they flew took off on 1 July 1960 at 10:00 hours Greenwich time from an American military base situated in Brize Norton, England, on a route lying along the northern frontiers of Norway and the USSR. It was under instructions to return after fulfilling its assignment to the same base in Britain where the United States Air Force unit to which the plane belonged was stationed.

Flight was Top Secret

Before the take-off, the crew of the plane had been warned by their unit commander at Brize Norton base, Major DeBelle, that the flight had to be kept top secret and the crew were therefore forbidden to maintain regular radio communications with the base.

It is only two months ago that the aggressive actions of the United States, which found expression in the predetermined intrusion of an American military aircraft into the USSR on a spy mission and in the proclamation of such provocative acts to be a matter of the national policy of the United States, led to the wrecking of the summit conference by the United States government—[acts that] were unanimously condemned by the public opinion of the world.

The new violation of the frontier of the USSR by an American aircraft proves that the United States is still following the same course dangerous to peace. Everybody sees now what is the real worth of the solemn assurances by the United States government and by President Eisenhower in person about the president's alleged order to discontinue American spying overflights of the territory of the USSR.

U.S. Policy Questioned

The question arises what purpose does the United States government have in continuing the policy of aggressive incursions in the airspace of the USSR? There can be only one answer. The actions of the United States government constitute a deliberate violation of the generally accepted norms of international law, a policy of deliberate provocations aimed at aggravating the situation; at increasing the war danger.

In so doing, as formerly, the United States of America continues using for its aggressive actions against the USSR the military bases the United States has set up in the territories of other countries, its allies in military blocs.

Even if the fate of American fliers, whose life apparently is of little value to the United States government and is deliberately sacrificed for organizing espionage flights over the USSR, can be regarded as the internal affair of the United States, this can by no means be said about the tremendous threat to world peace created by the provocative activities of the United States government.

This is a matter that can not be treated with indifference either by the USSR or by any other nation earnestly concerned with preserving peace.

Considering that the violation of the frontier in this case was stopped in its early stage, the Soviet government found it possible to confine itself to destroying the intruder plane and having the surviving members of the crew brought to trial under the full vigor of the Soviet laws.

At the same time, the Soviet government warns the United States government in full earnest against the dangerous consequences to which the continuation of the provocative activities of the American Air Force will lead and the responsibility that will rest with the United States government.

Warned of Consequences

The Government of the United States is certainly aware of the consequences its policy of deliberate provocations against the USSR may entail. It may for some or other reasons withhold them from its people. But, the Government of the USSR deems itself in duty bound to warn the United States government that it has no right to gamble with the destinies of the world.

This warning must be made known to the American people too as well as the fact that the USSR has been and is doing everything in its power to save the people from the horrors of another war and that the blame for the hard ordeals to which the world is now being subjected fully rests with the Government of the United States.

The Soviet government deeply regrets to have to state that the government of certain countries, the United States allies in the military blocs, have still not drawn the due conclusions from the well known facts connected with the aggressive actions of the United States Air Force. By allowing the American military bases in their territory to be used, they

continue this policy of complicity in the aforementioned aggressive ac-
tions, thereby inviting a great danger on the peoples of their countries. . . .

This lengthy demarche [as translated into English by the Russians]
was more a protest against continued U.S. reconnaissance of Soviet borders than one against this specific incident. It lacked the usual accusa-
tions that the U.S. aircraft had fired first—McKone and Olmstead were,
after all, still alive and knew the details. It was also significant that the
protest justified the shootdown not on the basis that the aircraft had tried
to evade and leave Soviet airspace, but that the Soviet fighter pilot shot
it down because it continued *into* Soviet airspace, an improbable situation even if McKone and Olmstead had not survived. The Soviet government announced on July 11 that Premier Khrushchev would hold a news
conference on July 12 to discuss the latest violation in more detail.

At his news conference, Khrushchev accused the United States and
its allies of "provoking serious military conflict" by continuing to send reconnaissance missions over the Soviet Union. He declared that the Soviet Union had withheld its announcement of the shootdown to hear
what the Americans would say about it. "It was an attempt to trap Washington into making conflicting statements about the flight similar to
those that arose out of the downing of the U-2 reconnaissance plane in
the Urals on May 1," Mr. Khrushchev claimed, and added: "To a degree,
we succeeded." It was apparent that he had called the news conference,
attended by 300 correspondents, to embarrass the United States. He
added no new details about the shootdown or about the status of the two
survivors. Only written questions were accepted, and questions as to the
exact spot where the RB-47 was shot down and why a Soviet cruiser
joined in the search two days after the incident went unanswered.

The Soviet protest did indeed succeed. British Prime Minister
Harold MacMillan promised British opposition political leaders that he
would discuss with President Eisenhower modification or improvement of
the agreement on United States air bases in Britain. The Norwegian foreign ministry rejected the assertion by the Russians that the lost RB-47
had used Norwegian territory in its flight. The same day, July 11, the
Japanese foreign ministry announced in Tokyo that all U-2 aircraft had

been removed from Japan. The Soviets would do whatever it took to stop the recon missions along their borders, and America was just as determined to maintain its right to fly in international airspace.

After a review by the State and Defense Departments, the United States sent a strongly worded response to Moscow:

> . . . The Ministry's note cannot, in view of the nature of the circumstances concerned, represent other than willful misinterpretation and misstatement of fact.
>
> The United States Air Force plane in question, with a crew of six, was proceeding on an entirely legitimate mission over international waters and at no time penetrated Soviet territory or even areas that have been claimed at one time or another as territorial waters or airspace of the USSR. At no time was the airplane closer to Soviet land territory than about thirty miles (approximately forty-eight kilometers).
>
> It is therefore evident that pursuant to instructions of the Soviet government, airplanes of the Soviet air force wantonly attacked the American airplane over international waters with the admitted loss of that aircraft and of the lives of at least one of the members of its crew. Two other members of the crew have, according to the Soviet note, been taken into custody without any legal basis and are to be subjected to trial under what is called "full severity of Soviet law." The three other members of the crew remain unaccounted for.
>
> The Ministry's note attempts to establish some kind of link between the flight of an American Air Force airplane over international waters with the incident that occurred over Soviet territory on May 1. These flights were, as must be known to the Soviet government, entirely different in character. The Air Force flight on July 1 was one of a continued series of electromagnetic research flights well known to the Soviet government to have taken place over a period of more than ten years. Instructions to the crews of these airplanes rigidly require that the aircraft remain well outside the airspace of Soviet territory.
>
> The Government of the United States of America rejects the completely unfounded allegations contained in the Ministry's note under reference. It solemnly and vigorously protests the unwarranted shooting down of an American airplane over international waters and the eventual

failure of the Soviet government to make its action known for a period of days during which a search for the missing men was known to be in course in which the Soviet government was voluntarily participating in what was apparently good faith.

It demands release to its custody of the two United States Air Force officers admitted to be in Soviet custody. It further demands that a representative of the United States Embassy in Moscow be permitted to see these men without delay. Additionally, it demands that the body of Captain Palm be returned to the custody of United States officials immediately.

The Government of the United States is prepared to undertake in cooperation with the Government of the Union of Soviet Socialists Republics and such other authority as might be acceptable to both sides, a thorough search for the downed aircraft and the missing members of its crew and examination of such remains of the aircraft as may be located.

The Government of the United States of America reserves its right to demand full compensation from the Government of the Union of Soviet Socialist Republics for its unjustified action in this matter. It should be clear to the Soviet government that a repetition of acts of this nature cannot fail to have the most serious consequences, responsibility for which would rest upon the Soviet government alone.

The Soviet government transferred Major Palm's body to the American Embassy on July 25, 1960, but was not about to acquiesce to a joint search for remains of the RB-47 and its three missing crew members since such a search would acknowledge that the attack occurred in international waters. Recalling the shootdown of another RB-47 off Kamchatka in April 1955, when America obviously had no details about where or how the RB-47 disappeared, Soviet Foreign Minister Gromyko probably surmised that the U.S. again had no knowledge of where the shootdown over the Barents Sea occurred. A note from Gromyko dated July 15 rejected the U.S. protest over the shootdown on July 1 and challenged the U.S. to prove its allegations that the incident occurred over international waters:

. . . The question arises on what basis the United States government permits itself to assert that the plane did not once enter Soviet territory,

and even did not once approach nearer to it than a distance of forty-eight kilometers (thirty miles) if this plane was shot down when it violated the border of the USSR and was in its territorial waters? The United States does not have any basis to assert that the American bomber was located outside Soviet territorial waters.

The note stressed that, when the plane was first reported missing, United States authorities had said they lost radio contact with the aircraft and did not know its position.

Asked at a special news conference at which the U.S. note was released how the U.S. was certain that the RB-47 had not flown closer than thirty miles to Soviet territory, press secretary Lincoln White said that he did not have a detailed explanation. The *New York Times* explained, "Other sources said that planes engaged in the research and mapping missions over northern waters were tracked by specially equipped radio outposts . . . The same is true of most planes flying anywhere near the Soviet frontier." The *Times* article continued, "It was believed in official circles here [Washington] that the Soviet government had deliberately ordered the shooting down of the RB-47 to further embarrass the United States and its allies from whose bases United States planes fly." By intercepting tracking reports transmitted on Soviet air defense air surveillance radios, U.S. Air Force Security Service listening posts in England and Germany monitored the progress of the RB-47 mission along the northern Soviet frontier as well as the tracking of the Soviet MiG that intercepted and shot down the reconnaissance aircraft. A third-party (non-American) source also intercepted voice communications involving ground controllers and the MiG pilot who shot down the RB-47. But if the U.S. had released that information, it would have compromised extremely important, ongoing sources; therefore, it had no choice but to withhold its evidence.

Keeping the incident in the headlines, on July 13, Soviet newspapers printed a photograph of Soviet air force Captain Vasili Polyakov and said that the Soviet Union had awarded him the Order of the Red Banner for shooting down the American RB-47 on July 1. Polyakov said he believed the RB-47 was on a photo recon mission and was heading straight toward a new, secret Soviet nuclear submarine base.

Following the U-2 shootdown just two months earlier, the Soviet Union gained both significant exposure as the victim of U.S. spy flights before the United Nations Security Council and a promise from President Eisenhower that United States aircraft would no longer overfly Soviet territory. Now, the Soviet Union attempted a similar ploy. It requested an airing of the RB-47 incident before the U.N. Security Council—hoping to again embarrass the U.S. into canceling reconnaissance missions along its borders.

On July 14, a *New York Times* reporter hypothesized Soviet intentions in this fashion: "One of the purposes of the Soviet exploitation of the incident is clear . . . Having ended the U-2 program, the Russians now hope to halt United States reconnaissance flights around the Iron Curtain . . . These flights with instructions to remain thirty miles off Soviet territory have continued in many parts of the world since the 'Cold War' started and have provided a watch against surprise attack and invaluable electronic and other information."

President Eisenhower agreed to a full review before the council. NATO allies in Paris reacted in "complete solidarity" with the U.S. on the RB-47 incident. A French official called "scandalous" the shooting down of a plane well outside even the Soviet definition of territorial airspace, and the attempt of Premier Khrushchev to justify it.

In late July the Soviet Union and the U.S. made their cases before the U.N. Security Council. On July 25, 1960, United States ambassador Henry Cabot Lodge used a map overlaid with information derived at least in part from Soviet air defense tracking data to show the flight route of the RB-47 over the Barents Sea and the point where the MiG attack allegedly occurred. His map overlay showed that the recon aircraft never approached closer that approximately thirty miles to the Soviet coastline.

Emphasizing that the RB-47 remained "over international waters" at all times, Lodge surprised his U.N. audience by alluding to his source, "United States personnel who monitored this flight could pinpoint its precise location at all times by means of 'scientific devices.' " The British Ambassador to the United Nations was even more emphatic. "Her Majesty's government in the United Kingdom has reliable evidence to show that the aircraft never went within thirty miles—I repeat, never within thirty miles—of the Soviet coast. We were able to determine the position of this aircraft, and our information fully tallies with the United States estimate just explained to the Council by Mr. Lodge."

Concluding his presentation, Lodge stated categorically that the attack occurred over open seas outside Soviet territorial waters. No definitive resolutions came out of the security council meetings. Later on October 13, 1960, unbeknownst to the U.S. at the time, the body of Maj. Eugene Posa was recovered by Russian fishermen in the Barents Sea. A handwritten report from the Soviet fishing trawler *Yalta* describes the recovery of the body:

> *From Captain Poliashov of RT-194 [fishing trawler]* Yalta.
>
> *EXPLANATION [report]*
>
> *While fishing on 13 Oct 60 at 10:45 hrs we raised the trawl from the depth of 130 meters and brought it aboard. In the stern wing of the trawl we discovered a parachute of foreign manufacture. In the parachute shroud we found part of a human leg (foot and part of the shin) with one shoe and a dark blue wool sock. Since the leg was badly decomposed, we threw the leg and the sock into the sea. We also discovered items of unknown purpose:*
>
> *Small canisters [possibly oxygen tanks], jacket, metal box without a lid, and a bag containing documents.*
> *The trawl was raised in quadrant #946, 69:12 degrees north latitude, 40:04 degrees east longitude. We were on a heading of 310 degrees, +17 degrees with the trawl and covered the distance of approximately 8 miles. There was a foreign trawler about 1 mile ahead of us following the same course.*
>
> *25 Oct 60 [signed] Poliashov*

This discovery led to a further Soviet search and recovery of other shootdown-related materials. The fishing fleet recovered parts of the RB-47. KGB Chief Alexandr Shelepin described the recovered items in a message to Premier Khrushchev on October 17, 1960:

Especially Urgent
17 Oct 60
To Comrade Khrushchev N.S.

I report that on 14 October of this year, while fishing, trawlers of the Murmansk Economic Council raised parts of an aircraft. They were located at coordinates 69:12 degrees north latitude, 40:11 degrees west longitude; 69:15 north latitude, 40:26 west longitude at a depth of 60-140 meters. This was 60-70 miles north of the Cape Svyatoi Nos (35-40 miles from territorial waters). The following was found:

A wingtip 12 meters long with U.S. Air Force markings, wreckage of the tail unit 1 meter long, an ejection seat, a metal frame and plastic with stenciling (presumably from a camera), a small turbine with a radiator, a damaged conduit and many small pieces of aviation equipment. Many of the pieces found have factory markings.

In addition, a human skeleton outfitted with a parachute was raised. Upon examination of the clothing, documents were discovered in the name of the USAF flier POZ, Evgenij Ehrnest [POSA, Eugene E.], born 1922: ID No. AO 2088613 with a photograph, fingerprint and a description of distinctive marks; identification card and instructions (probably about the use of the parachute).

On 17 October the remains of the pilot and the parts of the plane that were recovered will be delivered to Severomorsk.

Measures are being taken toward furthering the search for the remainder of the plane.

Chairman of the Committee for State Security
(A. Shelepin)

The location of Major Posa's remains and the aircraft debris—sixty to seventy miles north of Cape Svyatoi Nos and thirty-five to forty miles outside Soviet territorial waters by the KGB's own reckoning—unequivocally locates the RB-47 in international waters when it was attacked and shot down. The Soviet government could not tell the U.S. government that it had located and recovered aircraft debris and Major

Posa's remains without admitting that the shootdown occurred over international airspace. Khrushchev, Shelepin, and others in the Soviet hierarchy lied and conspired to force Olmstead and McKone to admit that they had violated Soviet airspace.

Honoring the fighter pilot who cold-bloodedly shot down the RB-47 with a medal (Order of the Red Banner) and then declaring him a hero in the Soviet press indicates the emphasis Soviet leaders placed on publicizing the shootdown. We will probably never know with absolute certainty the actual details of the shootdown, but Soviet actions subsequent to the shootdown clearly show Soviet attempts to force an end to U.S. airborne reconnaissance along Soviet borders. Coming on the heels of the U-2 debacle that caused President Eisenhower to publicly renounce U.S. overflights of Soviet territory, the Soviet government was gambling that world opinion over the RB-47 shootdown would force a similar fate on U.S. recon missions in international airspace adjacent to the Soviet Union. A "show trial" of the two detained American flyers would end American spy missions against the Soviet Union—at least, that was the goal of the Soviet leadership.

As chairman of the KGB, Alexandr Shelepin was probably surprised—even disappointed—that two crew members survived the shootdown. It would have been much easier to cover up a conspiracy without witnesses, but Olmstead and McKone not only survived a bailout from a spiraling, out-of-control plane; they were miraculously rescued by a Soviet fishing trawler. So, Shelepin's people had to try to obtain a false confession from them.

Both Olmstead and McKone refused to confess to anything—they irritated their interrogators repeatedly by insisting that they had been in international airspace, and that they were shot down illegally. Under the Soviet system of "justice," prosecutors generally did not try cases in a court of law without a confession—the KGB simply extended the authorized thirty-day investigative periods a month at a time until a detainee confessed. From the first interrogation session, it was obvious that the interrogators wanted information that would embarrass President Eisenhower personally. Several years after being released and permitted to return home Olmstead said:

*They [the interrogators] wanted two things; they wanted us to admit
that we crossed the border and to admit that Eisenhower had ordered us to
cross it, the reason being that Eisenhower had said after the U-2 incident
that he would never again order a U.S. aircraft to violate Soviet airspace.
Our reaction to their questions was pretty simple. We weren't ordered to
cross the border, and we didn't cross the border. They very often said to
me that the only way I could help myself was to give frank, honest answers and a complete confession. I said, "What's more important, a confession or an honest answer?"*

*The KGB interrogators wore civilian clothes, the same suit and necktie
every day. The interpreter spoke good English. He had been in the Soviet
Embassy in London. He wore a Rolex watch, wrote with a Parker 51
pen, told me that he shaved with Gillette Blue Blades and that he had an
extensive English library from which he would eventually let me read
books. The interrogators claimed not to speak any English, and I believed
that was the case.*

*I was confined in a small cell six feet wide and eight feet long with a
10-foot ceiling. The cell had a Judas hole in it—a little glass window that
had a squeaky metal gate on it—so you knew when they were looking in
on you. A light bulb burned constantly. If you covered your head with a
blanket, they took it away. That was the idea. They wanted you to know
that you'd lost everything, even your privacy. That's probably as tough a
thing to deal with as anything. Eventually, I read books, but early on, I
prayed a lot. I counted the hairs on my arm. I built a house in my mind,
a nail and board at a time. I was certain that everything that could be
done was being done, but I often thought I would probably never get out
of there. Only three Americans ever went in and came out of Lubyanka.
John McKone and I are two of them, and Gary Powers was the third.*

*Though we never went on trial, they did take us individually before
Rodion [sic] Rudenko, the Prosecutor [sic] General of the USSR one day,
and he asked us privately, "Do you understand the charges against you?"
We both said, "Yes." And, when he asked me, "Are you guilty?" I said,
"No," and he flew into a rage, and I was taken out of the room. I guess
he really got all over the staff there because they came out sweating bullets, and they said, "You've got to realize, you can't talk to big people like*

that . . . We've got to go back and start all over again." So, I figured,
well, I've been here for six months; now its gonna be another six months
before we get out.

Attempting to coerce confessions from Olmstead and McKone, the
KGB brought them face-to-face with the MiG pilot who had shot them
down. In August not long after Francis Gary Powers had been convicted
of spying during his fateful U-2 shootdown, McKone was led into a room
full of new faces. He was introduced to a Russian in air force uniform who
wore air force wings and the Order of the Red Banner medal—Capt.
Vasili Polyakov, a name he had not heard before. Thinking it was
expected, McKone extended his hand for a handshake, but Polyakov
would not even look at him. The interpreter explained that Captain
Polyakov had shot them down. While maintaining eye contact with the
senior Soviet air force officer at the table, Polyakov stiffly recalled the
events of July 1—quoted herein from *The Little Toy Dog* by William L.
White:

> *I took off from my base with orders to make an identification pass. I
> came back to the mainland, and flew parallel, in Soviet airspace, to the
> intruder aircraft, and I could see the coast line quite easily. As I was fly-
> ing parallel to the intruder aircraft, before it crossed our border, I was
> called by our radar tracking station and told to arm my weapons. After
> the intruder aircraft had entered Soviet airspace, and had passed Holy
> Nose Cape on the Kola Peninsula, on which I took a fix, I came abreast
> of the intruder aircraft, which was headed in the direction of Arkhangelsk,
> and signaled it to follow me. After this signal, the intruder aircraft started
> to turn away from the Soviet air-sea border, to the left. Since it had vio-
> lated my instructions, I shot it down. Then, since I was short on fuel, I
> returned to my base.*

In 1996, the Russian magazine *Aviation World (Mir Aviatsii)* claimed,
in a series of articles on foreign overflights of the Soviet Union, that Captain Polyakov acted on his own, firing on the American reconnaissance
aircraft without first obtaining permission from his controller, and was
placed under arrest as soon as he landed. However, after learning of the

incident, Khrushchev had the pilot promoted, given a medal, and reassigned from the 171th Guards Fighter Aviation Regiment to a more comfortable assignment in the Ukraine.[26]

Did Polyakov provide a valid "follow-me" signal? Olmstead and McKone claim they saw no signal and were attacked without provocation or warning. Allowed to question the MiG pilot through an interpreter, McKone asked Polyakov which follow-me signal he gave. Polyakov responded, "I waggled my wings." While discussing that face-to-face meeting later with the author of *The Little Toy Dog*, McKone pointed out that, if indeed Polyakov had given any signal at all, he had given the wrong one. A flight leader waggles his wings in a flying formation as an order for others in the group to follow the leader in single file. If a fighter pilot wants to order another aircraft to follow him for a landing, the international signal is to come abreast and in full view of the other pilot, and fire a warning burst. This incongruity could explain the conflicting Soviet and American positions on a warning before the attack, but the matter of the location of the RB-47 when attacked remains a critical factor.

The follow-me signal (a fighter pilot fires a warning burst in front of an intercepted aircraft) is only valid when issued within the intercepting fighter pilot's airspace; it has no legal authority when given in international airspace. During his meeting with Polyakov, McKone was shown a map depicting the tracks of the RB-47 and Polyakov's MiG, tracks supposedly created from Soviet air defense tracking data. One track showed the MiG taking off from Murmansk and swinging far out over international waters during Polyakov's identification pass on the RB-47, then returning to Soviet airspace marked on the map by a line clearly drawn twenty kilometers (twelve miles) from the shore over water along the Soviet coastline. The track for the RB-47 showed an interesting deviation from what McKone knew as their actual flight route. The bomber was shown flying southeasterly along a track approximately fifty miles north of and adjacent to the Kola Peninsula, then suddenly about midway down the peninsula, making a twenty-five-degree turn to the right. Such a turn would have taken them into Soviet airspace. Then just as suddenly, the map showed the RB-47 making a hairpin left turn while in Soviet airspace immediate north of Cape Holy Nose.

Polyakov claimed in the presence of McKone that the bomber had made the sharp left turn indicated on the map, attempting to escape him after he had given the follow-me signal. To this day, Olmstead and McKone adamantly state that the "twenty-five-degree turn" depicted on the Soviet map never occurred; in fact, all their turns—even minor course changes—had been to the left away from the Soviet landmass. Further, they were executing their planned left turn when attacked, not attempting to escape as Polyakov claimed.

On October 8, quoting an East European "diplomatic source," a message reached Washington indicating that the Soviet government was experiencing difficulties in the RB-47 case. The Soviets had been unable to obtain confessions from Olmstead and McKone, without which they would "have difficulty in placing them on public trial." Two days later, McKone had a second face-to-face confrontation with Polyakov, this time in the presence of a major general from the military procurator general's office. The general, whom McKone had not seen previously, was strictly business. He seemed intent on getting down to facts by clearly asking pointed questions about the incident of both McKone and Polyakov. McKone got the idea that the Soviets had now decided the whole incident might have been a mistake, and the general seemed to be trying to sort out the facts.

Running through his recitation—this time without a map showing the aircraft tracks—Polyakov claimed that at no time had he left Soviet airspace. This was an important shift from the previous meeting when a track on the Soviet map had shown the fighter going far out over international waters to intercept the RB-47. Having not participated in the last session, the general did not catch the tracking anomaly. He asked McKone, "Do you, as the navigator of the RB-47, know that you crossed the Soviet sea border?" McKone's response: "If we did, it would have been an accident. But I am sure we did not." And McKone vigorously explained why he had known exactly where they were: he had two magnetic and three gyroscopic compasses, a precision navigational radar, and a computer that gives a latitude/longitude readout on two dials as the plane flies, all the while compensating for wind and magnetic variation. He also pointed out that he had just taken a precision radar fix on land and had found that the computer readout was accurate.

Acknowledging, the general asked, "Have you any questions for Captain Polyakov?" "Yes. Captain Polyakov has said that he was in contact with his ground station. My question to him is: Was he in contact with that ground station, which was doing his radar tracking for him, at the exact moment that he shot us down?" The question precipitated lots of conversation in Russian that McKone did not understand, but Polyakov seemed unable to answer. So the general responded, "But I understand the question. Let me rephrase it for him." Polyakov finally answered, "No, I was not. Just prior to the time the intruder aircraft crossed our borders, I got bad static in my radio and so was receiving no messages." That ended the interrogation for the day; the general rose to leave, and this time, Polyakov shook McKone's hand.

It was about this time that the Soviet government began squirming and looking for a way to backtrack on its commitment to subject Olmstead and McKone to a public trial for spying with the least loss of prestige. On November 15, McKone was escorted to the office of Roman Rudenko, Procurator General of the Soviet Union (the Soviet equivalent of the Attorney General of the United States). Rudenko had conducted the prosecution of Francis Gary Powers. After some small talk—"Are you feeling well? How have you been treated?" etc.—Rudenko asked:

Are you familiar with the accusation?

Yes.

How do you plead?

I plead guilty to part of it, but not to all.

To what part do you object?

To that part which says we crossed the Soviet sea border. I don't think we ever did.

You have seen the evidence of the Soviet People's Republic.

If we ever crossed your border, we did it accidentally.

Why do you say that, when you know you were ordered to overfly our border and for the purpose of collecting intelligence on the radar defenses of our country? The leaders in America are continuing the Cold War policy of brinkmanship.

I got no such orders, and I don't think we did cross your border. According to my navigation, we were shot down more than 50 miles north of Holy Nose Cape.

But we have proof that you have already seen [Rudenko pointed to a chart which lay on the table] that you crossed the sea border.

If that is your evidence, I cannot dispute it. But so far as I am concerned, it is not correct.

Were you ordered to cross our sea border?

No.

Is it possible that you accidentally crossed our border?

My job was to keep the plane on its course, and it was all I had to do. Your evidence shows that, in the middle of the last leg, our plane suddenly turned to the right at least 25 degrees, and flew a distance in time of about seventeen minutes, which then would be my estimated time of arrival at our scheduled turning point. But I can't resolve all that with what I saw in the plane. We made no such turn in the middle of that leg.

They tried unsuccessfully to get McKone to change his story. Finally, Rudenko said:

Well, we have our proof that you did cross our border. This chart

*shows the course of your plane. It was made by our radar tracking sta-
tions two weeks after you gave your original testimony.*

In response to the question "Do you regret what you have done?",
McKone answered, "I regret that we were shot down." That was not the
answer Rudenko wanted to hear. Getting very emotional, he pounded on
the table between him and McKone and began shouting about the mis-
deeds of U.S. leaders—"the American warmongers who had ordered
McKone's crew to cross Soviet borders." Rudenko ended the meeting by
asking, "Would you like to see a copy of the Powers trial? I shall see that
you get one." A few days later an English translation of Powers trial was
delivered to McKone's cell.

Two days after McKone's encounter with Rudenko, Olmstead found
himself in the same ornate office of Procurator General Rudenko.
Shelepin, the head of the KGB, was there to assist Rudenko with the interrogation. Olmstead answered the same questions. "I plead not guilty.
We did not cross the Soviet sea border. Our plane was attacked without
warning. I saw no follow-me signals from the fighter pilot. I did not say
that the fighter pilot did not signal; I said I did not see them." At this
point, Shelepin chimed in with an offer to arrange a meeting between
Olmstead and Polyakov. Overall, the meeting did not go well; Rudenko
was obviously dissatisfied. During an interrogation the following day
by his regular interrogator and interpreter, Olmstead sensed that his
interrogator had been chewed out for Olmstead's performance before
Rudenko because, the interrogator said, "Don't you know that I am responsible for everything you say to these big people? You should not con-
tradict a man like Rudenko, or complain to him." It was at this point that
the interrogator said, "Now I shall have to begin the investigation all
over again—just as though it were July 1st."

Olmstead had his eye-to-eye confrontation with Polyakov on November 21 in the office of a Soviet army colonel-general of justice within
Lubyanka Prison. Describing the incident of July 1, Polyakov again said
that he was a pilot on duty with the Soviet army air defense command at
Murmansk when an unidentified aircraft appeared and was approaching
the Soviet border. Receiving orders to investigate the intrusion, he was

directed by a Soviet radar ground station to the point where he visually sighted the intruder in the vicinity of Cape Holy Nose. No maps were used at this meeting, and Polyakov left out all details about flying out into international airspace to make the interception. Instead, he concentrated on other details:

> Since I had received instruction as an air navigator, I knew at all times where I was. I recognized the intruder aircraft as a B-47 of the USAF. I then approached it from the rear, waving my wings. This is the international "follow-me" signal. I then flew ahead of the aircraft on its left, so that the pilot could see me, then dropped back and took up a position on its right wing.
>
> As soon as the B-47 crossed the Soviet sea border—which I knew from my training as a Soviet pilot—it tried to escape by turning toward the north. Two minutes after I sighted it, I shot it down, in accordance with the directive of the Soviet minister of defense issued in early May 1960.

Olmstead acknowledged that he understood a translation of Polyakov's testimony. After a contentious discussion about the follow-me signal which Olmstead denied seeing, Polyakov continued:

> I shot the intruder plane down when it tried to escape from a forced landing in the Soviet Union, after it had crossed our borders. It had been given signals.

Sensing a sticky situation, the colonel-general of justice turned to Olmstead and asked:

> Why did you not follow the signals of the Soviet fighter to land?

Because I did not see any signals.

> Were you flying the aircraft at the time?

No.

Then your answer should more accurately be, you did not follow the signals because your were not flying the aircraft. We feel that Major Palm did not follow the signals of the fighter because he was afraid to land on Soviet territory.

Olmstead sensed that the interrogators were looking for a way out. They would let him off the hook if he blamed everything on Bill Palm, because they had murdered him and he could not defend himself. He tried to answer the question calmly.

I don't think Major Palm saw any signals either, or he would have told me about them.

The court will not be interested in your opinions.

Does this mean that your opinion about what Major Palm saw would be valid evidence in that court, while mine would not?

Olmstead admits that he blew his stack. The colonel-general of justice stood up, ending the meeting with the remarks, "The fact is, your airplane did turn away, after the Soviet pilot had given the signals." That ended the confrontation.

Several months after Olmstead and McKone were released, the news media learned the real reason that they had not been released earlier. During a one-on-one session with American columnist Drew Pearson in the summer of 1961, Nikita Khrushchev told Pearson that he had "refused to release the RB-47 flyers during last year's U.S. election because it might help elect Richard Nixon."

After the Soviet KGB had held McKone and Olmstead incommunicado in Lubyanka prison for the remainder of 1960, the Soviet hierarchy decided it had gained all possible political mileage from detaining the two American fliers. Kennedy had defeated Nixon in a very close election in November, and the Eisenhower administration—a Soviet nemesis for the previous eight years—was coming to an end. Returning Olmstead and McKone to Kennedy's incoming administration as a good will gesture would look good in the world press.

On January 25, 1961, just two days after Kennedy was inaugurated as America's 35th president, the head of the Soviet KGB, Alexandr Shelepin, personally awoke Olmstead and McKone at 4:00 A.M. to inform them to expect a "big day today." Later at 10:00, Olmstead and McKone were taken to a conference room where Shelepin sat at the end of a long table with lower officials sitting along each side. Although their cells were only four doors apart in Lubyanka, that was the first time Olmstead and McKone had seen each other since arriving in Moscow. Shelepin announced that they would be sent to America later that day and asked Olmstead as the senior officer if he cared to make any comments. Olmstead's response, "Yes, sir, I certainly hope we don't miss that airplane."

The resolution of the Presidium of the Supreme Soviets of the USSR, which was not released to the world press, reads as follows:

Resolution

. . . *Having reviewed the documents of criminal case No. 45 against the accused McKone, John Richard, born 1932 in Kansas City, Missouri, America, U.S. citizen, First Lieutenant, U.S. Air Force, navigator, and Olmstead, Freeman Bruce, born 1935 in Elmira, New York, U.S. citizen, First Lieutenant, U.S. Air Force, copilot—The Chief Investigator of the Investigation Department of the KGB of the Council of Ministers of the USSR found that:*

McKone, J.R. and Olmstead, F.B. intruded into the airspace of the USSR, on 1 July 60 in a USAF RB-47 military reconnaissance aircraft. The RB-47 was shot down by a Soviet fighter. Saved by parachutes, McKone and Olmstead were arrested and criminal proceedings were instituted according to Article 2 of the Law of the USSR "Criminal Proceedings for Espionage."

The investigation of the case established that McKone and Olmstead flew in a RB-47 over a frontier region of the USSR on 1 July 60. They violated the Soviet state border 22 kilometers north of Cape Svyatoi Nos [Cape Holy Nose] to collect military intelligence information about radar installations and other military sites of the USSR.

The RB-47 aircraft was equipped with special intelligence gathering radio-electronic equipment and armed with two cannons.

In the course of the investigation it was also established that in 1959, McKone made a series of flights in a RB-47 aircraft over border areas of the Soviet Black Sea and Baltic Sea coasts in order to gather information about military strategic sites of the USSR.

Guided by the desire to improve relations between the USSR and the United States of America, the Presidium of the Supreme Soviet of the USSR on 24 January 1961 declared that McKone, J.R. and Olmstead, F.B. are to be released from criminal responsibility and be transferred into the custody of American authorities.

On the basis of the aforementioned and guided by Article 5, Paragraph 4 of the RFSR [Russian Federated Socialist Republic] Code of Criminal Procedure, it is RESOLVED:

To close the criminal case and drop charges against McKone, John Richard, and Olmstead, Freeman Bruce.

On January 25, 1961, at his first news conference as President of the United States, John F. Kennedy announced that McKone and Olmstead were on their way home. Kennedy also informed the airmen's wives. In a news release in Moscow, the Soviet government put the news this way:

The Soviet government, guided by a sincere desire to lay down a basis for a new stage in the relations between the Soviet Union and the United States, has decided to meet halfway the wishes of the American side with regard to the freeing of two American airmen who were members of the crew of the United States Air Force plane RB-47, and has petitioned the Presidium of the USSR Supreme Soviet to release these two airmen from criminal responsibility.

The statement went on to claim: "The Soviet government has been informed that the United States president had issued an order forbidding American aircraft to violate the airspace of the Soviet Union."

What the Soviet press release did not say was that President Eisenhower—not Kennedy—had ordered American aircraft not to *overfly* Soviet territory. President Eisenhower had made that commitment before the Soviets illegally shot down the RB-47 over international airspace. Reconnaissance missions along the periphery of the Soviet Union, however, similar to the planned RB-47 mission on July 1, 1960, would continue throughout the Cold War.

Olmstead and McKone did not miss their plane from Moscow, but suffice it to say that they were more than a bit anxious as their departure was delayed at Moscow Sheremetevo Airport—their commercial flight from Moscow to Amsterdam was delayed several hours to replace a flat tire. They were welcomed home on January 27 as heroes. An entourage that included President Kennedy and their wives met them at Andrews Air Force Base, Maryland. Later, the president hosted the two airmen and their wives at a coffee in the White House. Both Olmstead and McKone completed careers in the Air Force, but the Air Force forbade them to again fly reconnaissance missions.

The three electronic warfare officers, Posa, Goforth, and Phillips, remain unaccounted for. In 1993 the Russian government handed over former KGB Chief Shelepin's declassified report dated October 17, 1960, informing Premier Khrushchev about the discovery of Capt. Eugene Posa's remains and miscellaneous aircraft debris at a point in the Barents Sea sixty to seventy miles north of Soviet territory. No additional information has surfaced on Goforth or Phillips, but witnesses indicate that Major Posa's remains were interred in an as yet unidentified grave on the Kola Peninsula. The U.S.-Russian Joint Commission on POW/MIAs has followed all possible leads, including exhuming several bodies in the Severomorsk area, but has not yet found Posa's remains. The search continues.

The freeing of Olmstead and McKone in January 1961 resulted in false hopes for the families of missing crew members from the C-130 shootdown over Armenia in September 1958. Of the seventeen men aboard 60528, the Soviets returned six bodies—eleven of the C-130 crew members remained unaccounted for. As only four of the returned bodies were identified, thirteen families still did not know the fate of their loved ones.[27] After Olmstead and McKone were released, the Soviet foreign ministry again denied having any information on the eleven airmen missing from the C-130 incident.

RB-57 Missing Over Black Sea—December 14, 1965

On December 14, 1965, an RB-57F with two crew members disappeared from radar after being observed flying erratically and losing altitude over the Black Sea. Assigned to the 7407th Support Squadron at Rhein-Main Air Base, Germany, the crew and aircraft were operating out of Incirlik Air Base, Turkey, on temporary duty—conducting a reconnaissance mission along the southern borders of the Soviet Union. Radars of the Soviet Southwestern Air Defense District were tracking the RB-57 when it began losing altitude and gradually disappeared from the radar screens. No Soviet fighter aircraft were observed near the RB-57 when it disappeared, and an aircraft mechanical failure is suspected. No mayday calls were received from the crew, which remains unaccounted for.

Flying at high altitude—in the 80,000 feet range—at the time, the crew may have experienced an oxygen system malfunction causing them to lose consciousness. Another possibility is that the pilot suffered a heart attack. Even if conscious, the onboard electronic warfare officer would have had no way to control or to fly the aircraft. At any rate, the aircraft spiraled down to about 50,000 feet where it orbited in a circular pattern for a while, after which it spiraled at a faster rate to approximately 20,000 feet altitude, and from there plunged quickly below radar coverage. Centrifugal force may have caused the wings to separate from the aircraft at 20,000 feet, causing the quick plunge to the water.

Search and rescue operations commenced almost immediately, supported by search and rescue aircraft, reconnaissance crews aboard C-130 aircraft, and a Turkish destroyer. Searching in grid patterns at altitudes as low as 300 to 500 feet in the area where the RB-57 disappeared, aircrews flew daily search missions through December 23. They spotted aircraft debris, but saw no signs of the missing crew members. Pieces of an RB-57 wing and part of the fuselage were winched aboard the Turkish destroyer. The recovered wreckage showed no signs that the plane had been shot down and contained no clues as to the status or whereabouts of the crew. The C-130 recon crews also observed Soviet trawlers and a couple of submarines in the search area. Operating just below the surface, the Soviet submarines were as easy to spot as the trawlers.

On December 24 (the day after search operations had ended), Soviet Deputy Foreign Minister Kuznetsov summoned the U.S. ambassador to the Soviet Union to the foreign ministry and lectured him about U.S. reconnaissance flights near Soviet borders, including the RB-57 mission over the Black Sea on December 14. When asked for specific information about the missing RB-57, Kuznetsov would not elaborate on his prepared remarks.

That was the first serious incident involving a U.S. recon aircraft near Soviet borders in more than five years. Very quickly, Security Service C-130 recon crews searched for the two missing RB-57 crewmen in 1965 in the same manner that their predecessors had searched for the seventeen C-130 crew members that the Soviets had shot down over Armenia in 1958. Using the 7406th Support Squadron's cargo C-130A (tail number 41637) and one of the C-130A-II recon aircraft, two recon crews searched the general area over the Black Sea where Soviet air defense radars had last tracked the missing aircraft. In 1999, John Fitton, a former Security Service airborne intercept operator at Rhein-Main, reminisced about his participation in search missions aboard the cargo C-130 aircraft:

> We launched and flew over the Black Sea at a general search altitude of about 1000 ft but at times dropping down to 300–500 feet looking for both survivors and wreckage. We flew with the tail ramp down and rear side doors open. Crew members wore their parachute harnesses with chest packs and were tethered with cargo straps clipped into the D-rings on the harness seat so we could stand in the doors or on the ramp without fear of falling. Whenever we spotted anything that was orange we notified the aircraft commander who would then bring us down to between 300 and 500 feet for identification.
>
> After several hours we spotted what I think was the only piece of wreckage ever found. It was a section of one of the wings, probably about 1/2–2/3 since I didn't see the characteristic RB-57 engine nacelle. We orbited over the wing until a Turkish destroyer was able to come into the area and safeguard the wreckage until it could be recovered. We then returned to Incirlik after continuing our search for a while longer. Other

crews on TDY took over for the next few days of search missions until the search was called off.

The recon crews searched fruitlessly for their missing Air Force brothers—not knowing at the time that they had flown their last airborne communications intelligence reconnaissance platform mission over the Black Sea.

Indirectly, Soviet demands that Turkey deny America the use of airfields in Turkey for airborne reconnaissance against the Soviet Union paid off. Turkey placed a temporary moratorium on further U.S. airborne communications intelligence recon flights from Turkish bases. Unwilling to meet Turkish demands for exorbitant military and financial aid as payment for use of its bases for reconnaissance, the United States decided to forgo further airborne reconnaissance missions from Turkish soil.

In 1994, the Russian government handed over to the American side of the U.S.-Russian Joint Commission on POW/MIAs two declassified Soviet documents on Soviet search activities related to the missing RB-57 in 1965. Both documents detail the search efforts made by Soviet vessels which found parts of the plane in international waters of the Black Sea on 18 March 1966. The recovered aircraft debris was sent to a Soviet aircraft design bureau for detailed analysis. Neither document mentions survivors. No additional details have surfaced on the two missing crew members.

Other Attacks on Recon Platforms—Summary

These and the other incidents involving American reconnaissance platforms during the Cold War share many common traits. Of necessity, reconnaissance—and in particular, signals intelligence reconnaissance—has been and remains one of the most highly secretive operations within all military forces, domestic and foreign. The effectiveness of communications intelligence and electronic intelligence as means of learning about an enemy's capabilities and intentions depends on secrecy. Even the identification of the source of intelligence can result in the loss of further intelligence.

The Soviet Union knew that America was intercepting and exploiting its communications and radar transmissions; it was doing the same thing against the West. The Soviet Union also knew that the photo recon platforms were providing us intelligence that it was able to deny us otherwise. What the Soviet Union did not know—and this is where the need for secrecy comes in—was precisely where and how the U.S. was obtaining information on Soviet capabilities and how effective the United States was in its signals intelligence and photo recon operations.

Almost all U.S. aircraft involved in an air incident with Soviet air defense forces were conducting reconnaissance regardless of statements to the contrary made to the press by U.S. officials. Much like human intelligence operatives "leading normal lives" while surreptitiously spying to obtain otherwise denied intelligence, reconnaissance units typically obscured their operations with cover stories—navigational training, weather reconnaissance, electromagnetic surveys, etc.

All of the recon aircraft that the Soviets shot down—excluding Gary Powers's U-2 in May 1960—were being conducted as legal missions flying in international airspace. Some strayed into Soviet airspace, but the flight plan for each showed them operating in internationally recognized airspace. A number of overflight missions (i.e., missions planned to actually overfly Soviet territory) were indeed flown prior to May 1960, but Francis Gary Powers's U-2 mission was the only one shot down during the Cold War.

To claim legitimacy for the actions of its pilots in attacks on foreign aircraft, the Soviet Union alleged in each shootdown incident that the attacked aircraft had violated Soviet airspace. The Soviet government claimed ownership of airspace out to twenty-two kilometers (twelve nautical miles) beyond its borders. In declassified reports related to most of the shootdowns, Soviet pilots asserted that the American aircraft fired first, and that the incident occurred in Soviet airspace; however, such evidence is totally one-sided since in most cases, none of the U.S. crewmen survived.

In one incident (the shootdown of the RB-47 in Barents on 1 July 1960), declassified Soviet documents show that the Soviets lied about where the attack occurred. At precisely the same time that KGB interrogators were attempting to obtain a confession from John McKone and

Freeman Olmstead in October 1960 for violating Soviet airspace in the RB-47 incident, the head of the KGB informed Premier Khrushchev that a body and aircraft wreckage from that shootdown was recovered sixty to seventy miles from the Soviet shore. In other words, the shootdown had occurred over international waters. Coming on the heels of the shootdown of Powers's U-2 in May 1960 that ended overflights of Soviet territory, the Soviet leadership may have ordered the RB-47 shot down in July in an effort to force President Eisenhower to discontinue recon missions along the Soviet borders.

Five years earlier in the shootdown of another RB-47 off Kamchatka in April 1955, declassified Soviet documents indicate that the Soviets were uncertain whether the bomber was in Soviet airspace when the attack occurred. In that incident, the U.S. knew only that the RB-47 failed to return, and not knowing where or how it disappeared, did not even bother contacting the Soviet foreign ministry. The Soviets, for their part, intercepted U.S. communications associated with the search for the missing RB-47, determined that America had no inkling of where or why their recon aircraft disappeared, and kept silent about the incident.

The safeguarding of classified information under stringent security guidelines frequently caused U.S. government officials to be less than forthright and truthful with the press and family members of men killed or missing in action during attacks on reconnaissance platforms. Reconnaissance crew members could not discuss their jobs with anyone outside their place of work, where a special access security clearance was typically required for entrance, leaving family members with absolutely no understanding of their loved one's job.

Such work was stressful on both the worker and the families even under "normal" circumstances. One could argue that in such work, circumstances were never really normal. This situation was exacerbated when a crew member failed to return from a mission. The security clearance issue created a barrier between commanders and friends on the one side, and family members that the crew member left behind and the press on the other. Security guidelines forbade releasing any meaningful details regarding reconnaissance missions, leaving family members feeling abandoned, frustrated, and often bitter toward their government.

The truth of the matter was that the U.S. government had no real leverage to force cooperation from the Soviet government in explaining the fate of missing crew members. A statement included in an internal State Department document in December 1951 regarding the shootdown of a U.S. Navy P2V over the Sea of Japan could be applied in most of the air incidents: "The American fliers were lost in the performance of duty and, as much as we dislike it, there is little we can do to obtain redress." There were few options for dealing with a brutal Soviet regime that snubbed its nose at international public opinion, especially in matters dealing with punishment that they meted out to recon crews on missions along their borders.

Another factor important to the fates of the recon crews was a result of conflicting military philosophies and operating orders for the Soviet air defense forces and United States reconnaissance aircrews. The Soviet military was charged with defending Soviet state borders and its pilots were specifically ordered to force intruders to land at a Soviet airfield; if the intruder refused to comply, they were commanded to shoot it down, whether it was an armed enemy aircraft, an unarmed plane, or—as happened in at least two cases—even a civilian airliner. America took the position, and rightfully so, that it was perfectly legal to perform airborne reconnaissance over international airspace adjacent to the Soviet Union. The U.S. reconnaissance pilot had orders to turn away from enemy territory if attacked, and to avoid landing at an enemy airfield at all costs. Two such differing command philosophies were sure to result in tragic clashes.

THREE

—

COLD WAR
AERIAL RECONNAISSANCE

With the Russians attacking so many reconnaissance aircraft during the Cold War, why did the United States continue airborne reconnaissance along Soviet borders? Simple: America and most of the Western allies did not trust—nor should they have trusted—Soviet leaders. Soon after becoming president, Dwight Eisenhower put it this way:

> *Without intelligence you would have only your fears on which to plan your own defense arrangements and your whole military establishment. Now if you're going to use nothing but fear and that's all you have, you are going to make us an armed camp. So this kind of knowledge is vital to us.*[28]

Intelligence gathering was essential, and human intelligence (HUMINT) from within communist countries was very hard to obtain, frequently unreliable, and almost always difficult to confirm. At the time, airborne reconnaissance was the only collection platform available from which the government could collect photo intelligence (PHOTINT), electronic intelligence (ELINT) and communications intelligence (COMINT) on enemy military forces. The interception and exploitation of enemy communications (COMINT) and enemy radars (ELINT) is known collectively as signals intelligence (SIGINT). An airborne platform can photograph targets and intercept enemy radio and radar signals and telemetry that are well beyond the range of ground-based intercept sites. During the Cold War, access to information about military capabilities and intentions in Eastern Europe, Russia, China, and Southeast Asia became the number one priority of intelligence agencies in the West.

Eisenhower was well aware that the numerous overflights—many of which he personally approved—undertaken during his administration by the British and the Americans were both an infringement on the sovereignty of the Soviet Union, and thus illegal under international law, and a provocation that was bound to stir up further animosity between the Russians and the Americans. Nevertheless, it was ultimately safer than military blindness, as far as he was concerned. And indeed the overflights constituted one of his most effective weapons in holding the arms race in bounds.

HUMINT and PHOTINT often demanded illegal operations. SIGINT, however, did not usually require a penetration of Soviet territory and, moreover, it was on the whole the most effective form of intelligence.

Lt. Gen. Marshall S. Carter, having served both as assistant director of the CIA (April 1962–May 1965) and director of the NSA (June 1965–August 1969), was one of the few people knowledgeable enough about all three of the primary categories of intelligence gathering to make a fully informed opinion of their relative worth. In his opinion, SIGINT won hands down.

> HUMINT is subject to all of the mental aberrations of the source as well as the interpreter of the source. SIGINT isn't. SIGINT has technical aberrations that give it away almost immediately if it does not have bona fides, if it is not legitimate. A good analyst can tell very, very quickly whether this is an attempt at disinformation, at confusion, from SIGINT. You can't do that from HUMINT; you don't have the bona fides—what are his sources? He may be the source, but what are his sources? . . . Photo interpretation can in some cases be misinterpreted by the reader or intentionally confused by the maker in the first place— camouflage, this sort of thing. SIGINT is the one that is immediate, right

*now. Photo interpretation, yes, to some extent, but you still have to say
"Is that really a fake, have they confused it?" It is better than HUMINT,
it is more rapid than HUMINT [but] SIGINT is right now; its bona
fides are there the minute you get it.*[29]

In World War II, the allied intelligence services used aerial photo reconnaissance extensively in both the European and Pacific theaters, offensively as a means of pinpointing potential targets, and defensively to
identify potential threats to their bombers, but the need for aerial signals
intelligence reconnaissance was slower to catch on. Since most military
radios transmitted in the high frequency (HF) band that could be intercepted at great distances by ground sites, aerial SIGINT reconnaissance
seemed an unnecessary luxury.

Cold War—Dearth of Intelligence

Immediately after World War II, America demobilized rapidly, with a
sense both of relief and of urgency. The country had built planes, ships,
and tanks for more than four years; it was time now to build civilian auto-
mobiles, to supply the country with necessary consumer goods, and to allow a generation of young men to go back to school. In our urgency to
move from a war footing to a peacetime economy most of the intelligence hardware was scrapped and nearly all of that hard-won experience
allowed to dissipate, to the extent that in the late 1940s, the intelligence
"wheel" would have to be practically reinvented.

The Western allies were overly optimistic about the intentions of
Stalin and the other Soviet leaders. At the Yalta Conference in February
1945, U.S. President Franklin Roosevelt and British Prime Minister
Winston Churchill gave Soviet leader Joseph Stalin carte blanche domi-
nation over the East European countries that the Red Army occupied at
the time in return for a pledge that Stalin would allow democratic governments to rise within those countries. They divided Germany into Soviet and Allied occupation zones, with Berlin, deep in the Soviet zone,
jointly administered. An analogous situation existed in Austria until
1955, when it regained its independence. The Soviet Union also gained
certain possessions in the Far East and rights in Manchuria, lost to the

Japanese in 1905, in exchange for Soviet assistance in the invasion of Japan that, as it turned out, was not needed. With Stalin installing puppet regimes in Eastern Europe and cutting off access to the Soviet Union, Poland, East Germany, Czechoslovakia, Hungary, Romania, and Bulgaria, it became obvious that the "democratic" governments in Eastern Europe were a sham.

When Japan surrendered, the United States, under General Douglas MacArthur, occupied Japan and rearranged its internal constitution and economy to fit the capitalist mold, while the Soviets occupied the Kurile Islands and, until they relinquished control to Communist China a few years later, Manchuria. Thus, the political boundaries were established for the Cold War.

Henceforth as the Soviets and Americans interpreted each other's actions, charges and countercharges flew back and forth. The Soviets set up communist governments in each of the East European countries that they occupied, and powerful communist movements threatened the stability of Turkey, Greece, other Western European countries, and other countries of the world. After a series of East-West crises, most dramatically the Berlin Blockade of 1948–49, the West created the North Atlantic Treaty Organization in April 1949. Under the NATO alliance America became linked militarily to Western Europe, including Greece and Turkey—an attack against one member would constitute an attack against all. Much later, in 1955, the Soviet Union and the East European satellite nations countered with their Warsaw Treaty Organization (Warsaw Pact). With Stalin declaring capitalism incompatible with communism and Churchill coining the phrase "Iron Curtain" to describe an Eastern Europe cutoff from the West, the Cold War had begun.

The Soviet Union had established the Iron Curtain in part to block military intelligence from reaching the West. The Berlin Blockade in 1948, the early detonation of the first Russian atomic bomb in 1949—several years ahead of U.S. Intelligence estimates—and our exaggerated evaluations of Soviet progress in rocketry made the U.S. and its allies realize that they had to have a way to obtain much more intelligence than they were currently receiving. Finally, the West's incorrect assumption that the Soviets had precipitated the Korean War led U.S. policy makers to conclude that the Soviets were intent on conducting a "hot" war with its capitalist enemies.

Ferret Flights vs. Overflights

The advent and deployment of ground-based air defense radars during World War II created a need for airborne electronic intelligence (ELINT) reconnaissance. Radar (radio detection and ranging) works by transmitting pulses of high-frequency radio signals. As the pulses hit a target (for example, an airborne aircraft), they are reflected back as echoes that are detected (received) by an antenna and displayed as blips on an operator's radar screen. The time it takes a pulse to travel from the transmitting antenna to the target and return to the receiving antenna indicates how far away a target is. In addition, the direction from which the pulse is returned and changes in frequency provide the target's relative speed and heading. During the Cold War radar technology was quickly adapted to mobile platforms (aircraft, ships, satellites, ground vehicles, etc.). Today, radars serve in a multitude of military and civilian applications (target acquisition, location, tracking, and selection; navigation, air traffic control, highway speed control; etc.).

Early on, Allied engineers and intelligence analysts developed defensive measures against enemy radar systems by exploiting the characteristics of deployed radars. Each radar has a signature (set of parameters) that can be intercepted and measured by sensitive receivers and recorded on tape and other media for later analysis. Significant parameters include frequency, pulse repetition frequency, pulse repetition interval, pulse length or duration, and beam width. A radar's signature determines its purpose: early warning, search, acquisition, or fire control, for example. Understanding an enemy radar's signature permits one to develop countermeasures, including electronic countermeasures. In fact, simply knowing where specific types of ground-based radars are located (electronic order of battle) is the first step in planning both offensive and defensive military operations.

Early warning radars came into general use during World War II. Radars played a major role in helping the British ward off attacks by

Hitler's Luftwaffe, and the Germans and Japanese were deploying radars to warn of approaching Allied bombers by 1943. The planning of bombing raids took into account the location of known radars—targeting radar sites and taking advantage of known gaps in radar coverage to plan ingress and egress routes to targets. The evolution of rudimentary electronic order of battle databases to support mission planning resulted in the need for airborne electronic intelligence reconnaissance.

In March 1943, a U.S. Army Air Forces RB-24D crew using mission call sign "Ferret-One" conducted America's first ELINT reconnaissance mission—against a Japanese radar located on Kiska Island in the Aleutian Island chain. "To ferret" literally means to uncover and bring to light by searching (as in "to ferret out"); a ferret is a weasel-like mammal related to the polecat that is often used to hunt rats by entering the rats' burrow and chasing them out into the open where they can be killed. The intelligence community quickly adopted the term—reconnaissance missions were dubbed "ferret missions" for decades, and for good cause. During the Cold War it was a common ploy for ELINT missions to antagonize an adversary's air defenses; sometimes by penetrating a radar's area of coverage at an altitude too low to be detected then suddenly "popping up" to a detectable altitude. At other times, the ferret mission might suddenly descend below radar coverage—the objective in either case being to entice the radar operators to activate their equipment since the radar's operating parameters cannot be observed and exploited if the radar is not operating. Although photo intelligence recon missions were sometimes referred to as "ferrets," and some photo recon aircraft indeed included an ELINT collection capability, the term *ferret* generally applied only to ELINT recon missions.

In the early 1950s, the Western Allies were concerned that the Soviet Union was intent on starting World War III with attacks against Western Europe and the United States. U.S. presidents and British prime ministers authorized U.S. and British reconnaissance aircraft to overfly Soviet Long-Range Air Force bases, fighter bases, missile test facilities, and other military complexes to collect order of battle data that could be used to plan retaliatory bombing missions against the Soviet Union. A limited number of photo intelligence and electronic intelligence overflight missions were approved and flown. Some missions such as Francis

Gary Powers's U-2 mission included both cameras and signals intelligence receivers and recorders—collecting PHOTINT and SIGINT (i.e., ELINT and COMINT) on the same mission.

Convinced that the Soviet leadership intended to launch a nuclear attack against the West—most probably from Soviet airfields in Siberia—United States reconnaissance missions probed Soviet air defenses throughout the Arctic area. The Alaskan Air Command was assigned responsibility to obtain AOB (air order of battle) and EOB (electronic-order of battle) information for vast reaches of northern Siberia. An RB-17 flew the first Cold War ferret mission in September 1946 against Siberia. A top secret order to the Alaskan Air Command in 1947 defined ELINT recon requirements for northern Siberia.

> *Electronic reconnaissance flights [over Siberia] should be made as often as possible with the equipment and personnel available. First priority of search missions should be assigned to locations and characteristics of radar stations in order to establish radar chains as well as operating schedules.*[30]

Naval reconnaissance aircrews shared the reconnaissance workload with the Air Force during the Cold War—conducting missions over the Sea of Japan, Black Sea, Arctic and northern Siberia, and Baltic Sea areas. Often flying what the Soviets undoubtedly considered aggressive flight profiles, U.S. Navy aircrews suffered many casualties in catastrophic shootdown incidents against Soviet, North Korean, and Chinese air force interceptors. The U.S. Navy also suffered the loss of the USS *Pueblo*, a signals intelligence collection platform that the North Korean navy seized in international waters off the Korean coast in 1968. One of the Pueblo's crew members was killed during the Korean attack on the ship. The North Koreans ultimately released the *Pueblo's* crew after months in captivity. Adding to the animosity created by military overflights, the Central Intelligence Agency on occasion conducted illicit overflights over parts of the Soviet Union and the communist satellite countries to drop intelligence agents.

American statistics on Cold War overflights are classified. One overflight that the U.S. government officially acknowledged occurred on

August 30, 1962, when a U-2 pilot flew north over Hokkaido, Japan, into airspace over the Sea of Okhotsk. Heading north of the Kurile Islands on a counterclockwise route, the pilot flew along the east coast of the Kamchatka Peninsula and eastward across the northern Sea of Okhotsk before turning due south and paralleling the east coast of Sakhalin Island.

The Air Force Security Service shift on duty in the surveillance and warning center at Wakkanai Air Station, Hokkaido, Japan, monitored the progress of the U-2 mission. As the U-2 headed south, it gradually veered westward into Soviet airspace and overflew Sakhalin for a few minutes before reentering Japanese airspace over Hokkaido.

The U-2 flew directly over SA-2 launch sites and an air defense fighter base on Sakhalin, but no surface-to-air missiles were launched; they were possibly restrained to avoid the shootdown of airborne Soviet fighters that were attempting in vain to intercept the U-2.

The Soviet Foreign Ministry formally protested the violation of Soviet airspace. The United States issued an apology and a statement that an American aircraft on a *weather reconnaissance* mission had been blown off course by unanticipated high winds aloft. Two months later, a Soviet-made SA-2 missile shot down an American U-2 over Cuba.

Of course, obtaining complete statistics on Soviet claims of border crossings is very difficult. However, in 1995 and 1996, the Russian magazine *Aviation World (Mir Aviatsiyi)*, published a series of articles titled "Hot Skies," in which it laid out some of the Soviet-era statistics, couching them cautiously and pointing out the difficulty in obtaining reliable information.

For example, *Aviation World* cites 113 border-crossings by U.S. aircraft between 1953 and 1956 and describes in some detail overflights from 1950 through November 7, 1958, for which the Soviets attempted twenty-one intercepts against more than thirty-seven aircraft.

Date of Activity	Number of Border Crossings	Comments
Aug. 1962	1	In the Far East by U-2
Sept. 1962	1	In the Far East by U-2
1967–1970	10	
1982	5	
1983	10	Through beginning
1988	10+	of September
1989	15+	

Citing only the official accounts published in Soviet newspapers, *Aviation World* says that between August 1951 and May 1954, seven U.S. Air Force transport aircraft crossed the Soviet border to drop twenty agents. The article states that these statistics are based only on the publicly available data, implying that there may have been many more such flights. (Although we have no way of determining whether the statistics are correct, it is a matter of historical record that the U.S. attempted to infiltrate agents into the Soviet Union in this manner.)

To the Soviet, Chinese, and North Korean leaders, all foreign aircraft (and ships) that approached their borders were up to no good—pure and simple. They considered all intruders to be *spy missions,* and responded with hostile actions. Even civilian airliners that inadvertently violated Soviet airspace were not immune to deadly force. The Soviets shot down two Korean civilian airliners during the Cold War—a Boeing 707 over Siberia in 1978 and Korean Air flight 007 (a Boeing 747), near Sakhalin Island in August 1983. In both civilian aircraft shootdowns, Soviet fighter aircraft intercepted and shot down a commercial airliner loaded with civilian passengers that had simply strayed off course and overflown Soviet territory.

Soviets Force Down an Airliner Carrying U.S. Servicemen

Another well-publicized Soviet interception of a civilian airliner occured on June 30, 1968, when Soviet fighters forced a Seaboard World Airways jet airliner to land on Iturup Island in the Kurile Islands. Iturup is approximately 200 to 250 miles southwest of the southern Sakhalin Island area where Soviet fighters shot down the KAL 007 Boeing 747 in 1983.

The incident was especially memorable for the 214 U.S. servicemen aboard the DC-8, which had been chartered by the Air Force Military Airlift Command to transport them from the United States to South Vietnam. The *New York Times* reported on July 1, 1968, that the chartered airliner may have strayed into Soviet airspace. The U.S. Defense Department said the jet "apparently strayed off course and was intercepted and escorted" to a landing in the Kuriles. (The commercial air lane used by the airliner skirted the southeastern side of the Kurile Island chain in international airspace over the North Pacific Ocean, about 80 to 100 miles outside Soviet-controlled airspace.)

In air-to-air communications with a second World Airways pilot in the area, the DC-8 pilot said he was being escorted by two Russian MiGs toward what appeared to be a Soviet fighter base in the Kuriles. He later reported landing without damage to the plane and without injury to crew or passengers. The airliner was reportedly a new DC-8, being flown by a "check pilot and crew," testing out the plane on its maiden flight for World Airways.

The *Times* article commented that the incident occurred at a time when relations between the Soviet Union and the United States appeared to be making important new strides toward improvement, especially in the arms reduction field—perhaps explaining the timely release of the aircraft and detained Americans. After the U.S. State Department expressed regret to the Soviet Union over the violation of Soviet airspace, the Soviet government released the airliner, its seventeen-person crew, and the 214 U.S. servicemen on July 2. Looking weary but cheerful, the Americans arrived at Yokota Air Base, Japan, later in the afternoon:

> *Specialist 5 Franklin Campbell Jr. of Dayton, Ohio, described how Soviet fighters had intercepted the chartered airliner in the Kuriles area:*
>
> *"We were sitting on the left-hand side of the plane looking out the window when a MiG appeared suddenly near the wingtip and fired a couple of bursts in front of the plane.*
>
> *"The pilot of the MiG began making hand motions with his thumb pointing down, apparently ordering our pilot to land. Ten minutes later the second MiG appeared on the right-hand side of our plane to the rear and close to the tail. . . .*
>
> *"The Russians we met on the ground seemed friendly but they made us stay in the plane, except for the stewardesses who were allowed to debark last night," Private Stevens said.*
>
> *Specialist Campbell said that the food aboard the plane ran out while the aircraft was on Iturup Island and that the Soviet authorities furnished meals consisting only of bread, butter, cheese and coffee.*
>
> *Members of the disembarked group here said the pilot had to sign a statement that he was off course before the plane was released.*

An uncorroborated source credits four Soviet pilots, Captains Alexandrov, Igonin, Yevtushenko, and Moroz, with the interception and forced landing.[31]

Other U.S.-Soviet Air Incidents

The same uncorroborated source credits a Yak-9 pilot, Junior Lieutenant Zizevskii, with damaging and forcing a U.S. Air Force B-29 to land on August 29, 1945, suggesting that the Cold War began heating up immediately following the end of World War II. The location of the incident is not identified. If the report is correct, this could be the first instance of a Soviet pilot forcing a U.S. military pilot to land on Soviet territory during the Cold War. The report also claims that Soviet pilots downed seven Iranian aircraft (mostly civilian aircraft) between 1963 and 1981 along the Soviet-Iranian border; in one case, the Soviet MiG-21 pilot, Capt. Gennadii Yeliseyev, is said to have destroyed an Iranian "T-33 or F-4" by ramming it on November 28, 1973. Yeliseyev was reportedly killed in the incident.

Another Soviet ramming incident allegedly occurred on July 18, 1981, when Capt. Valentin Kulyapin, a SU-15 Flagon pilot, rammed an Argentinean-registered Canadair CL-44 transport that had inadvertently violated Soviet-Azerbaijanian airspace. Author James Oberg discusses the border violation and ramming in *The Bloody Border*.[32] According to Oberg, after delivering a load of arms to Iran during the Iran-Iraq War, the transport aircrew departed Tehran for Cyprus and flew inside the Soviet side of the Iran-Azerbaijan border for several minutes before being intercepted Kulyapin. Oberg describes in vivid detail how Kulyapin claims to have intentionally rammed the intruder at the last moment to prevent the transport from escaping into Turkish airspace. As reported, whether the ramming was intentional or a cover-up to mask an accident caused when the fighter pilot approached too close to his target is unknown. In either event, Kulyapin's fighter collided with the CL-44, causing the transport to crash in Azerbaijan, killing its four occupants; Kulyapin bailed out of his crippled jet and survived:

Western aviation experts who have examined Kulyapin's account of the encounter are highly skeptical. Pilots who have flown the CL-44 report that air turbulence behind the engines is so violent that it would have been impossible to control a throttled-down jet to hold a position directly behind and below one wing. The consensus is that Kulyapin misjudged a turn and hit the airliner by accident, afterward deciding to make up a story of glorious self-sacrifice.

The cargo plane was quickly reported overdue by the Argentine company, and a check with Turkish air traffic controllers revealed that radar had shown the aircraft disappearing into Soviet airspace. Still, the Soviets were at something of a loss to account for the event, and they took four days to announce that the foreign plane had crashed into a Soviet jet— and then blamed it for the collision. Said TASS: "The crew of the plane did not respond to any inquiries by Soviet ground air traffic control services and to attempts to render help to it, [but] continued the flight over the Soviet territory, performing dangerous maneuverings. Some time later the plane collided with a Soviet plane, was destroyed, and burned." Officially, at least at first, it was a negligent accident. Oddly, TASS never identified the nationality of the aircraft.

Airborne Reconaissance—Satisfying Intelligence Needs

While there were numerous incidents between U.S. reconnaissance aircrews and non-Soviet adversaries, most Cold War shootdowns and attacks on American recon missions involved Soviet air defense forces. Denied access to military intelligence by the "Iron Curtain" the U.S. military began an aggressive aerial reconnaissance program against the Soviet Union shortly after the end of World War II. Commencing in 1946, U.S. Army Air Forces reconnaissance aircraft—converted bombers that still retained their defensive air-to-air cannons—began flying recon missions along the borders of the Soviet Union and its European satellite countries.

Flying under "PARPRO" (Peacetime Aerial Reconnaissance Program) guidelines, early photo and electronic intelligence recon missions remained outside Soviet airspace. But, with their field of view limited to peripheral areas and hounded by mission planners for more complete Soviet order of battle data, the U.S. Air Force and U.S. Navy obtained permission on a mission-by-mission basis to penetrate Soviet borders, and in some cases to actually overfly Soviet territory. "Overflight"—intentionally traversing the territory of another state in peacetime without that other state's permission—was obviously illegal, but it was deemed necessary to obtain critical intelligence about Soviet intentions. PARPRO missions, on the other hand, operated in accordance with international law by flying outside internationally recognized borders of denied countries. (The C-130 shot down over Armenia in 1958 was a PARPRO mission and overflew Armenia unintentionally.)

In 1948, the U.S. Joint Chiefs of Staff turned down initial requests from Strategic Air Command commander Gen. Curtis E. LeMay to conduct overflight recon missions over the Soviet Union. In fact, after the Soviet foreign ministry vigorously protested the intrusion of American bombers over Soviet territorial waters in 1948, the U.S. Department of State limited PARPRO missions to flying no closer than forty miles from Soviet territory. In October 1950, the Air Force Director of Intelligence, Maj. Gen. Charles P. Cabell, while denying a request from SAC to conduct an overflight mission, added, "I am looking forward to a day when it becomes either more essential or less objectionable."

That day was approaching quickly. International tensions increased significantly when the Soviets exploded an atomic device in 1949 and the communists came to power in China the same year. Then in June 1950, the North Korean Army marched into South Korea—starting the Korean War. The start of the Korean War, and Chinese entry into the war in November 1950, increased the tensions further. Many in the West believed the Korean War to be a diversionary tactic; in fact many military planners feared that the Soviet Union might, as a second step, launch atomic attacks against Western Europe and the United States.

Led by the U.S. military, United Nations forces counterattacked the North Korean Army troops in South Korea in July 1950. Declaring a national emergency in December 1950 following Chinese entry into the war, President Truman called up national guard and reserve military units to active duty and extended the tours of many military active duty personnel.

Shortly thereafter, the Joint Chiefs of Staff recommended and President Truman approved overflight reconnaissance missions of communist territory—on a mission-by-mission basis. The British government likewise authorized its Royal Air Force to overfly the Soviet Union on recon missions.

When the Korean War started, the U.S. Far East Air Forces had limited airborne (photo) recon capabilities. To support the war effort and beef up Air Force aerial recon capabilities in the Far East, the Strategic Air Command rushed its 91st Strategic Recon Squadron from Barksdale AFB, Louisiana, to Yokota AB, Japan, in July 1950. Bringing RB-45C and RB-29 bombers to Yokota, the 91st SRS began conducting photo recon missions over the Korean peninsula, the Soviet maritime district near Vladivostok, and parts of China and Manchuria. The recon capabilities of the 91st SRS were later enhanced with the arrival of ELINT collection-equipped RB-29 and RB-50 aircraft. In addition, an Air Force Security Service Russian linguist sometimes collected communications intelligence aboard RB-45 missions in the Far East.

Three British Royal Air Force crews piloting RB-45Cs carried out the first overflights of the European Soviet Union in April 1952. Staging from RAF Sculthorpe Air Base, England, and flying separate routes, the three crews photographed Soviet Long-Range Air Force bases and air defense facilities in Estonia, Latvia, Lithuania, Belarus, and the Ukraine, before returning home safely.

Meanwhile, between April and June 1952, a U.S. Naval P2V ELINT recon aircraft and a U.S. Air Force RB-50 PHOTINT recon bomber conducted coordinated recon missions over Kamchatka peninsula and eastern Siberia while staging from Kodiak and Shemya air bases in Alaska. Later in October 1952, a SAC crew flew the first RB-47 overflight of the Soviet Union from Eielson AFB, Alaska—overflying Wrangel Island, Ambarchik, and Provideniya in the Soviet Arctic. All recon crews completed their missions unscathed.

In 1953 current events caused the issue of overflights to be reassessed. In January, Eisenhower replaced Truman as President of the United States and new Soviet leaders came to power in the Soviet Union upon the death of Joseph Stalin. In his memoirs, Soviet Premier Nikita

Khrushchev described Soviet paranoia toward American overflights of Soviet airspace:

> *When Stalin died we felt terribly vulnerable . . . The Americans had the Soviet Union surrounded with military bases and kept sending reconnaissance planes deep into our territory, sometimes as far as Kiev. We expected an all-out attack any day.*[33]

As former Supreme Allied Forces commander during World War II, President Eisenhower understood the importance of strategic airborne reconnaissance. He was also aware that the armistice that he'd secured to end the Korean War eliminated any legal justification for overflights of the Soviet Union and China. But, from a national security perspective, overflights could alert him to a potential surprise atomic attack. That in itself was worth the political risks, and he chose to continue overflights, but on a mission-by-mission basis. Occasionally, he disapproved requests for overflights.

In some cases, intelligence collected on missions justified obtaining approval for additional overflights. Such was the situation with "Project Sea Horse" under which a SAC RB-47E (photo) crew and an RB-47H (ELINT) crew conducted a series of missions over Siberia in the spring of 1955 while staging from Eielson AFB. The information collected during the missions was critical to SAC's integrated target mission planning.

British Prime Minister Winston Churchill faced similar decisions on overflights. Western intelligence sources indicated a rapidly evolving Soviet missile program at Kapustin Yar —a missile test range east of Stalingrad (Volgagrad). Churchill approved an overflight mission, and in August 1953 a Royal Air Force (RAF) Canberra flew a photo recon mission over Kapustin Yar. Soviet radars tracked the Canberra, and MiG pilots attacked it. Damaged by the MiGs, the Canberra escaped, headed south and landed safely in Iran. In April 1954, one additional British overflight was flown. Three RB-45Cs bearing RAF markings flew essentially the same routes over the Soviet Union that a trio of RB-45s had flown earlier in April 1952. Soviet air defense facilities tracked the three sorties, and MiGs attempted to shoot them down, damaging one of the aircraft. All three crews returned home safely. Three U.S. Air Force RB-45C crews flew overflight missions over the same routes in 1955. They recovered safely in West Germany. The RB-45 aircraft were painted black and the crews flew the missions at night—making it more difficult for Soviet fighter pilots to detect the intruders.

On May 8, 1954, U.S. Air Force Capt. Harold Austin's crew conducted one of the first overflights of the northwestern Soviet Union in an RB-47E, photographing Soviet Long Range Air Force airfields from which Soviet bombers could be launched on nuclear bombing missions against America and Great Britain. Along their planned route, the crew flew over Murmansk, Arkhangelsk, and several airfields. MiGs pursued the RB-47 in the vicinity of Murmansk, but at an altitude of 40,000 feet and a speed of 440 knots, the bomber left the MiGs behind. A half-dozen MiG-17s awaited the RB-47 as it approached Arkhangelsk, one of them attacking the bomber with cannon fire, hitting it with a shell in the port wing, but not crippling it. The RB-47 crew escaped across Finland and returned safely to RAF Fairford Air Base, England, from which they had launched the mission.

Photographs brought back by Captain Austin's crew reassured Western leaders that no long-range bombers were deployed on the Kola Peninsula. General LeMay, SAC commander, decorated the crew with a pair of Distinguished Flying Crosses although he made it clear that he'd rather have decorated them with a Silver Star. However, approval authority for a Silver Star award was in Washington, and those who'd have to approve the award of the Silver Star were not authorized to know about overflights. Such was the reward (or lack thereof) for extraordinary performance by recon crews.

Other overflights were conducted in 1954 and 1955, some of which involved Tactical Air Command Far East Air Forces RF-86 recon fighters that overflew Vladivostok, Sakhalin Island, the Soviet airfield at Sovetskaya Gavan, and Dairen and Shanghai, China. The last and longest of the RF-86 missions occurred on February 19, 1955. Operating from Chitose airfield on Hokkaido, Japan, Maj. Robert E. Morrison overflew the Soviet airfield at Khabarovsk on the Amur River along the border between the Soviet Union and Manchuria. One of Major Morrison's wing tanks failed to separate initially, causing drag and added weight that consumed valuable fuel. While he was maneuvering over the target airfield at Khabarovsk, the recalcitrant wing drop tank fell free and he hightailed it back to Hokkaido. As he landed and exited Chitose's concrete runway onto the parking apron his engine flamed out—his fuel tanks were empty.

Genetrix—Balloon Recon Platforms

Given the distrust and lack of knowledge of Soviet intentions and capabilities, the Eisenhower administration was constantly weighing risks against need and payoff relative to intelligence collection strategies. Most initiatives paid off; others did not. Project Genetrix—a high altitude photo recon initiative—was one of the less successful programs. The idea was to launch balloons in Western Europe or Turkey where air currents would drift them eastward across the Soviet Union. Each balloon that successfully traversed Russia released a gondola and parachute near Japan where an Air Force C-119 cargo aircraft retrieved the gondola in midair. During one four-week period in early 1956, the Strategic Air Command launched 516 balloons, of which only 44 were recovered. It is assumed that Soviet air defense forces shot down many of them.

In 1996, the Russian magazine *Aviation World (Mir Aviastii)* claimed, in a series of articles on foreign overflights of the Soviet Union, that between 1956 and 1977, Soviet air defense forces tracked 4,112 "freefloating" balloons launched into its airspace by Finland, France, Norway, Sweden, Turkey, West Germany, and the United States, but were successful in knocking down just 793. In some years, the article says, the U.S. launced, on average, 600 such balloons—300 by the U.S. Navy, 150 by the U.S. Air Force, and 150 by unnamed civilian institutions. The Soviets expended considerable effort to bring up the level of intercept effectiveness. *Red Star,* the official newspaper of the Red Army, is cited in the *Aviation World* article as claiming that between August 11 and September 14, 1975, eleven balloons crossed Soviet borders: eight were destroyed, two lost their payloads, and one recrossed the Soviet border. Missions against each of the balloons were flown by from one to sixteen aircraft, and the destruction of each ballon required, on average, 1.4 air-to-air guided missiles, 26 unguided missiles, or 112 antiaircraft artillery rounds.[34]

Project Home Run

Officially ending the Genetrix balloon overflights in 1956, President Eisenhower approved Project Home Run under which SAC RB-47s would overfly and map the northernmost reaches of the Soviet Union from the Kola Peninsula to the Bering Strait—3,500 miles of rugged Arctic territory. Staging from Thule AFB, Greenland, between March and May 1956, RB-47 recon bombers reconnoitered the entire northern Soviet frontier, completing 156 overflights of Soviet territory.

Sixteen RB-47E PHOTINT aircraft, five RB-47H ELINT aircraft, and twenty-eight KC-97 tankers participated in the project. Taking off and landing from ice-covered runways, the crews navigated across the North Pole and carried out aerial refuelings in complete radio silence.

They divided the area to be mapped into three sectors: (1) from Kola Peninsula to Dikson, (2) Dikson to Tiksi, and (3) Tiksi to the Bering Strait. The recon missions showed that the northern regions were poorly defended. Very few Soviet fighters scrambled in response to the overflights, and none of the fighter pilots successfully intercepted an intruding aircraft.

On the final mission, six RB-47Es flew a final "massed overflight" on May 6, 1956. Departing Thule, the six photo recon crews crossed the North Pole to the Soviet landmass at Ambarchik. Flying abreast at 40,000 feet altitude, they headed south, then swung east and exited Soviet territory at Anadyr on the Bering Strait, recovering at Eielson, Alaska.

The project was deemed a total success—not one person or aircraft was lost during the deployment although everyone worked in subzero temperatures on exposed aircraft. The intelligence obtained from the missions was invaluable. The Soviet government protested the American overflights, but—apparently embarrassed that its air defenses had been ineffective—did not specifically mention the "massed overflight" of Anadyr, a major Soviet Long-Range Air Force forward area staging base.

Top Eisenhower administration officials met with the president on May 28, 1956, to assess the Soviet demarche. Wanting to encourage the Soviet leadership to move in peaceful directions, they drew up a carefully worded lie, explaining in part:

> *Navigational difficulties in the Arctic region may have caused unintentional violations of Soviet airspace, which, if they in fact had occurred, the U.S. State Department regretted.*

Top Priority—Soviet Long-Range Air Force

At a Four-Power Summit Conference in Geneva, Switzerland, in July 1955, President Eisenhower proposed an "open skies" disarmament proposal under which the Soviets and Western nations would be permitted mutually to overfly one another's territories to see for themselves which weapons systems each country was developing and deploying. At the time, Lockheed engineers were feverishly testing the first U-2 recon aircraft in the Nevada desert. After Soviet Premier Khrushchev cast a "Nyet"(no) vote to "open skies," President Eisenhower authorized U-2 overflights of the western Soviet Union.[35] The Central Intelligence Agency would conduct U-2 reconnaissance missions—initially from U.S. air bases in England and West Germany.

The most sought-after information involved the Soviet strategic bomber force. How many long-range bombers did the Soviet Long Range Air Force (SAC's counterpart) have in its inventory, and where were they deployed? There was controversy within Eisenhower's administration on how many Soviet LRAA strategic bombers existed. Many pointed to a critical "bomber gap" in which the Soviets allegedly had significantly more long-range bombers than did America's Strategic Air Command.

Proponents of the bomber gap theory cited the appearance of significant numbers of Soviet Myacheslav-4 (aka "Mya-4"; NATO code-name "Bison") intercontinental bombers in a military parade flyover of Red Square as supporting evidence. The U-2 would be used to count Soviet bombers parked at their home airfields.

The first U-2 overflight of the western Soviet Union occurred on July 4, 1956. Soviet air defense radars tracked the U-2, but Soviet MiGs could not fly high enough to intercept it. A second U-2 overflight on July 5 provided photographs that ended—or should have ended—the "bomber gap" controversy.[36] Only a single Mya-4 bomber was parked on the ramp at its airfield near Saratov.

The Soviets had used chicanery to dupe Western observers at the military parade. The aircraft flyovers involved different types of Soviet aircraft flying over Red Square in trail formation. In addition to the flyovers, there were troop formations, tanks, artillery, etc.—a typical Soviet May Day Parade in Red Square. Intelligence officers from the American Embassy photographed an Mya-4 overflying the square several times without realizing that a single Mya-4 was making multiple appearances. Analysis of the officers' Mya-4 photographs showed that the bomber in each photograph had the same identification number painted on its fuselage. It had merely flown a box pattern after exiting Red Square, reappearing over the reviewing stands every ten minutes for the duration of the parade.

Overflights Heightened Soviet-American Tensions

Unable to intercept the U-2 overflights, the Soviet foreign ministry lodged a sharp protest almost immediately—the Soviet leadership's only defense against high altitude overflights at the time. Fearing an international incident, President Eisenhower felt increasingly uncomfortable about the overflights of Soviet territory but continued to accede to the recommendations of his Joint Chiefs of Staff.

In the fall of 1956, he approved an overflight of the Soviet Far East maritime district. Staging from Yokota Air Base, Japan, Air Force RB-57D crews flew simultaneous photo recon missions over three different target areas at altitudes of 60,000+ feet. Unable to bring down the intruding spy flights militarily, the Soviet protest was loud and speedy.

On December 11, 1956, between 13:07 and 13:21 hours Vladivostok time, three American B-57 jet planes coming from the Sea of Japan south of Vladivostok violated the airspace of the Soviet Union. Good weather prevailed in the violated area with good visibility that precluded any possibility of the loss of orientation by the fliers during their flight. The Government of the USSR insists that the government of the USA take measures to punish the guilty parties and to prevent any future violations of the boundaries of the USSR by American planes.

During the earliest overflights that Presidents Truman and Eisenhower had approved, the Soviet military possessed only limited capabilities to shoot down intruding aircrews. In some areas—for example, in vast stretches of the Arctic wastelands—there were gaps in radar coverage where Allied (American and British) aircraft could and did overfly areas of the Soviet Union without being detected. (The intelligence collected by those missions was invaluable for planning ingress and egress routes should hostilities start between the Soviet Union and the West.) The fact that those earliest overflights operated more or less with impunity added to the frustrations of Soviet authorities.

Officially, intentional overflights never happened. Flying in communist airspace violated international law, and clandestine overflights would be embarrassing if acknowledged publicly. At the same time, many Americans naively believed that their government did not engage in *spying*. But, what else does one call intentional reconnaissance overflights of an adversary's airspace?

Aircrew members on ferret and PARPRO missions—legal missions flown within international airspace—were provided cover stories in the event that they fell into enemy hands. Initially, Air Force aircrews were authorized to tell interrogators that they were conducting weather reconnaissance—until a crew member raised the point that interrogators could readily determine that there were no qualified weather specialists aboard their aircraft. The *weather mission* gave way to the *long-range navigation training mission* in 1949. Later, the cover story for RB-50 and C-130 airborne communications intelligence recon aircrews became *electromagnetic wave propagation research*—the announced mission of C-130 tail number 60528 on September 2, 1958.

There were major similarities and differences between the RB-50/C-130 airborne COMINT recon mission and missions of its ELINT and PHOTINT recon cousins. The ELINT (ferret) aircraft and photo birds tended to fly more provocative and less predictable flight routes. The COMINT recon aircraft, on the other hand, was more predictable, and flew on planned routes at an adequate distance (at least forty miles) from the sovereign territory of targeted nations—unless the aircraft got off course due to a weather diversion or through inadvertent crew error. For airborne communications intelligence reconnaissance crews, intentional overflight of denied territory was strictly forbidden. Accidental, inadvertent overflights such as the incident that resulted in the shootdown of Air Force C-130 60528 over Armenia in September 1958 did, however, occur.

To the Soviet hierarchy, *all* aircraft that violated Soviet airspace—intentionally or unintentionally—were "hostile" and were dealt with accordingly. Intentional overflights of Soviet territory—often traversing widespread inland military complexes—undoubtedly added to Soviet determination to appropriately punish offending aircrews. Soviet policy was to warn an intruder aircraft that it was violating Soviet airspace and to force it to land at a Soviet airfield, the accepted international policy outside combat zones. In a number of incidents the Soviet government claimed its fighter pilots used international signaling (for example, turned on navigation lights, waggled the fighter's wings, or fired warning shots) to warn the intruder.

There are no documented instances wherein Soviet warning shots were fired and an intruding aircraft obeyed the warning and followed the intercepting Soviet fighter to a landing at a Soviet airfield. But that is not to say that warning shots did not occur; to an American recon crew, warning shots from a Soviet fighter would most likely have been interpreted as a hostile attack. An immediate problem involves actions used to force compliance; how far should a defending fighter pilot go to force an intruder aircraft to land? What if the intruding aircraft is clearly an unarmed transport or a commercial airliner?

Should a Soviet fighter shoot down an intruding aircraft if the intruder refuses to land at a Soviet airfield? The Soviet dictatorship's answer was an unequivocal *Yes*.

On the allied side, recon aircraft commanders had quite different guidelines; handing over an aircraft's sophisticated intelligence collection gear and crew of intelligence specialists was not considered an option—recon aircraft commanders were to avoid surrendering their aircraft and crew at all costs.

In many of the incidents, Soviet pilots claimed to have attacked an intruder only after the intruder failed to obey warning shots. In other cases, Soviet fighter pilots claimed to have returned fire after having been fired on by a recon bomber's guns. RB-50s and other converted bombers retained their tail guns and did in fact fire on attacking Soviet fighters. With distrust on both sides, warning shots by a fighter pilot could easily be construed as an attack, resulting in return fire by a bomber's tail gunner. Further complicating the issue, there are usually no independent witnesses to verify either the attacker's or the intruder's story. Most Soviet-American air incidents resulted from situations in which diametrically opposing political and military views produced a tragic confrontation.

Soviet Airborne Reconnaissance

The Soviets had their own intelligence operations in the West, including airborne reconnaissance missions against Alaska in the northwest, along the east coast of the United States, and against the Western countries in Europe. In the Far East, Soviet Long-Range Air Army recon bombers operating from forward area staging bases at Mys Schmida and Anadyr in northwest Siberia conducted aperiodic photo and electronic intelligence missions against Alaska. Some of the LRAA missions overflew Alaskan territory and were intercepted and escorted.

According to an article appearing in VFW *Magazine* in April 1998, Soviet violations of Alaskan airspace were first detected in March 1958, and U.S. Air Force fighters intercepted two LRAA TU-16 Badgers over the Bering Sea in 1961. Alaskan-based fighters intercepted Soviet reconnaissance bombers in U.S. airspace frequently throughout the Cold War.

Intercepts peaked in the 1980s with thirty-three Soviet aircraft intercepted in 1987 and fifteen Soviet violations of U.S. airspace recorded during the last year of the Cold War (1991). Between 1961 and 1991, U.S. Air Force fighters conducted 306 intercepts of intruding Soviet aircraft, often escorting them from American airspace but never attacking them.[37]

Soviet airborne reconnaissance along the east coast of the United States was conducted primarily by Soviet heavy TU-95 "Bear" recon platforms on transit missions between the Soviet Union and Havana, Cuba. Remaining outside U.S. airspace, these Soviet ferret missions typically skirted along the Atlantic coastline enroute to and from Cuba, and occasionally conducted round-robin reconnaissance missions out of Cuba. U.S. air defense fighters routinely intercepted and escorted the TU-95 Bears without incident.

Monitoring the Enemy

Aware that pre–World War II Germany had used airborne photography of Soviet airfields and military complexes to plan the German invasion of the Soviet Union, Stalin was paranoid about giving foreigners access to Soviet military capabilities. Although America had sided with the Soviets and provided the Red Army with thousands of aircraft and tanks, a huge amount of other military equipment, and food during World War II, U.S. pilots were seldom permitted to overfly Soviet territory—even to deliver aircraft that Russia needed to beat back Hitler's invading German armies. (In the late phases of the war, U.S. bombers sometimes landed in the Ukraine after bombing runs against Germany, but these were the exception rather than the rule.) Under a U.S.-Soviet lend-lease program, American pilots ferried aircraft from factories in the U.S. to Alaska. From there, Soviet pilots ferried the aircraft from Alaska to military destinations in the Soviet Union. After World War II, the descent of the Iron Curtain in Europe and of the bamboo curtain that denied access to Communist China and North Korea caused near panic in many military circles in the West.

Soviet military facilities were spread over vast territories with an almost nonexistent telephone landline infrastructure. Command and control were accomplished by radio. Thus, although the Soviets minimized their vulnerability to human and photo intelligence gathering by keeping foreigners out, they were still highly vulnerable to signals intelligence exploitation. Anyone with a receiver and within detection range could monitor Soviet radio transmissions. Immediately after World War II, the

Soviet military used high frequency (HF) radios almost exclusively, making it possible for distant ground-based intercept sites to listen in on Soviet communications because HF radio signals traveling through the atmosphere can be received hundreds, even thousands, of miles away, depending on the power of the signal and on atmospheric conditions.

The Soviet military was determined to prevent the West from gathering intelligence on its forces, and the West was just as determined to keep abreast of Soviet military capabilities and intentions. Averting a surprise military attack was paramount. With human intelligence capabilities severely restricted by the closed nature of Soviet society and with the acquisition of photo intelligence being severely restricted, at the time, by the East bloc's closed borders, the U.S. turned more extensively to signals intelligence to fill intelligence gaps on the location, capabilities, and state of readiness of Soviet military units at any given time.

The types of intelligence sought by the signals intelligence community on communist military forces included operational activities, order of battle data, and deployment status that could reveal intentions. A major objective was to understand and exploit the command, control, and communications structure of enemy forces. Training in specific tactics or by specific units could reveal operational capabilities and weaknesses, or preparations for planned missions, while the movements of large groups of aircraft or special purpose aircraft could be an indicator of impending activity. For example, the deployment of a regiment of heavy bomber and tanker aircraft to an Arctic staging base had to be assessed as a preparatory act for possible nuclear attack on North America. Air order of battle data ("AOB," i.e., the number and types of aircraft by unit and deployment base) and electronic order of battle data ("EOB," number and types of radars and other emitters in use and where they are deployed) are essential elements of information for strategic air combat planners. Faced with the possibility of Soviet nuclear attack on U.S. and British retaliatory air forces and a potential Soviet conventional invasion of Western Europe, General LeMay's Strategic Air Command required accurate AOB and EOB databases to locate strategic targets and develop air operations plans. Signals intelligence was often the only available source for that critical data on the enemy's military forces.

At the height of World War II the Red Army (redesignated the "Soviet Army" in 1946) had a peak strength of 12.5 million troops. The role of the Soviet military changed after World War II with several army divisions occupying Poland, East Germany, Hungary, and Czechoslovakia. While America and the West reduced their military forces in the immediate postwar period, Stalin's government continued pouring funds into the military despite the massive rebuilding campaign needed to repair the devastation caused by the German invasion and its own defensive scorched earth policy. Moving on from producing copies of American weapons under lend-lease during the war (for example, the TU-4 bomber was a Soviet version of the U.S. B-29 that the Soviets had confiscated and copied part by part, down to the smallest details), the Soviet government began fielding new Soviet-designed weapons and expanding its military—creating fear in the West that the Soviet leadership was preparing for a conventional war in Europe. New Soviet military facilities proliferated, and by the early 1950s the Soviets ringed the periphery of the Soviet Union and Eastern Europe with air defense radar stations and the latest fighter aircraft, an air defense shield analogous to its ground-based Iron Curtain.

The air defense shield consisted of a deployed network of air-surveillance radars, fighter regiments, ground-controlled intercept (GCI) controllers, and a command and control center to orchestrate the defense of airspace within a designated air defense zone. Each radar station used a combination of target acquisition and height-finding radars to determine air target location and altitude—the acquisition radar measured range and azimuth from the radar and identified the target (friendly or hostile plus type), and the height-finder showed each target's altitude. Each individual radar station detected and tracked all aircraft flying within its radar detection range, transmitting target identification and tracking data to a filter center that received similar radar station inputs from each radar site within the filter center's zone of responsibility. The filter center combined tracking data from its individual radar stations and transmitted a continuous flow of messages showing the composite air situation within its air defense zone.

Recipients of the air surveillance tracking data included the air defense zone command and control center, fighter regimental controller, and GCI controllers. The air defense zone command and control center, regimental controllers, and GCI controllers used the tracking data as a basis for scrambling fighters and directing the airborne fighters during target intercept missions. Using declassified Soviet documents and an article in *Soviet Aviation* magazine in 1958, the interception and shootdown of C-130 tail number 60528 serves as a good illustration of how the Soviet air defense system operates.

Soviet radar stations and filter centers generally used HF radios[38] to transmit tracking data—primarily as Morse code, but some tracking data was passed by voice. In the case of the pilots who shot down the C-130, the aircraft controllers communicated with the MiG-17 pilots by voice on VHF radios.[39] The earlier generations of Soviet aircraft (those prior to the MiG-15bis) had HF radios only, and most communications with aircrews in those older aircraft were accomplished using Morse code. The MiG-15bis with its four channel VHF radio set was introduced in August 1952, and all Soviet aircraft fielded subsequent to the MiG-15bis were capable of communicating in the VHF frequency range.

The physics of HF radio transmissions is such that Soviet air defense tracking data transmitted on an HF radio in Armenia could be received by an air defense center in Moscow. In an ironic way, HF transmission is thus a perfect mode of communication for a centralized state; there could be no purely "private" radio conversations. However, from a Soviet perspective HF had a downside: U.S. intercept sites in Europe, including the Air Force Security Service sites at Darmstadt, Germany, and Chicksands, England, could monitor Soviet air defense activities throughout the European Soviet Union. Those sites and others monitored Soviet communications around the clock, seven days per week. (In 1958, one of the ten intercept positions onboard the doomed C-130 60528 also had HF intercept receivers capable of monitoring targeted HF communications; however, prior to the shootdown of 60528, Detachment 1, 6911th intercept operators aboard recon aircraft did not routinely track the location of their reconnaissance aircraft. The other nine intercept positions aboard the airborne intercept platform included receivers capable of intercepting the conversations of the MiG pilots that shot down the aircraft.)

The introduction of VHF radios for Soviet tactical communications in 1952 was a problem for the U.S. signals intelligence community—

intercept sites had no VHF intercept receivers or antennas. Some problems were easily solved and others warranted totally new solutions. Unlike HF signals that can be intercepted up to thousands of miles from the transmitter, VHF communications usually work "line-of-sight" (typically 100 to 125 miles maximum for ground sites intercepting airborne targets). Thus, only a few Air Force Security Service ground intercept sites (e.g., Berlin, Germany; Wakkanai, Japan; and a detached intercept team in Korea) were within intercept range of new Soviet VHF-equipped aircraft.

Security Service quickly installed VHF receivers and antennas at those sites. At the same time, the command sought out additional locations suitable for new ground-based VHF intercept sites. Wherever friendly territory permitted—from Norway and West Germany, through Turkey and Iran, around to Taiwan, Japan, and of course Alaska—the U.S. and its allies created ground-based listening posts to monitor the other side's military activities continually.

Nonetheless, there were vital areas under communist control from which VHF communications could not be intercepted from ground stations. To gather intelligence from those areas, it was quite clear that airborne communications intelligence reconnaissance was the only answer. Security Service would solve this problem by transforming bomber aircraft into airborne COMINT collection platforms.

Air Force Signals Intelligence—The Early Years

In 1947 the United States reorganized its military—the old War Department became the Department of Defense, made up of the Army, Navy, Air Force, and Marine Corps. Concurrently, on September 18, 1947, the Army Air Forces—"the brown-shoe corps" as later troops referred to it—became the U.S. Air Force. Overnight, AAF soldiers in olive-drab uniforms became airmen in the new blue-suit Air Force. To accomplish its special intelligence mission the Air Force created the U.S. Air Force Security Service command on October 20, 1948, and on February 1, 1949, four Army Security Agency units (1st Radio Squadron Mobile in Japan, 2d RSM in Germany, 8th RSM at Vint Hill Farms, Virginia, and

136th Communications Security Detachment at Fort Slocum, New York) were transferred to USAFSS.

In the reorganization the Air Force received the charter within the Department of Defense for airborne reconnaissance. Headquarters Air Force tasked the Strategic Air Command ("SAC") with airborne photo intelligence and electronic intelligence reconnaissance. When the Korean War started, photo recon was the main source of intelligence, and SAC was expanding its ELINT reconnaissance capabilities. Air Force Headquarters gave Air Force Security Service the job of creating an aerial communications intelligence reconnaissance capability, but that would come later. First, as a new command, the U.S. Air Force Security Service had to create an operational plan for using its newly acquired ground-based intercept sites to meet Air Force special intelligence needs.

USAFSS tasked its 1st Radio Squadron Mobile in Japan with intercepting Soviet air force communications in the Far East (east of the Ural Mountains), and the 2d RSM at Darmstadt, Germany, with intercept coverage of Soviet and East European air force targets in Europe (west of the Urals). Later, USAFSS would activate the 3d RSM in Alaska to cover Soviet air force targets in the Arctic area. The 8th RSM moved to Brooks Air Force Base, Texas, and became the technical training squadron for USAFSS. The other arm of the USAFSS was the 136th CSD, in charge of American mission security—monitoring U.S. Air Force communications to detect security compromises. Realizing that potential enemies will monitor its communications, the Air Force practices strict COMSEC; aircrews often conduct missions in strict radio silence.

The 1st and 2d RSMs operated as fixed ground intercept sites although as "radio squadron mobile" implies, each unit operated in trailer-mounted shelters that could be deconfigured, deployed, and reconfigured for operations at a new location in a matter of hours. Prior to 1949, Security Service had only Morse intercept operators—no Russian linguists or other voice intercept operators. The Soviet military, which communicated primarily in Morse code, had only recently started communicating by voice (by radio-telephone).

Early USAFSS Operations in Europe

The Air Force Security Service began expanding its intercept capabilities the moment it inherited its intercept squadrons from the Army Security Agency. Initial expansion efforts were devoted to creating direction-finding capabilities to locate targets. In DF work at ground sites, a DF control station operates in a network with one or more remotely located DF stations. Each station is equipped with a direction-finding receiver that displays a "line of bearing" showing the direction from which an intercepted signal is received. Under management of the control station, each station attempts to intercept transmissions from the same transmitter. Drawing the lines of bearing from each DF intercept station toward the intercepted transmitter on a map, the DF controller uses triangulation to locate the transmitter.

In mid 1949, the 2d Radio Squadron Mobile sent 1st Lt. Hollis Benson on temporary duty to Rothwesten, Germany, as the officer in charge of the squadron's first DF station (Detachment A). 1st Lt. Buster Beadle activated the second DF station (Detachment B) at Schleissheim, Germany, a few weeks later, and still later in late 1949, Lieutenant Benson activated Detachment C at Bremerhaven, Germany. Each of the DF sites included one or two intercept positions in addition to the direction-finding position.

With Russian radio operators switching from Morse code to voice more frequently to pass messages, Security Service had a serious problem—the command had no intercept operators who understood Russian. In mid 1949, the 2d RSM sent two Morse operators, Sergeants Virgil Fordham and Robert Draughon, on temporary duty to the army's Russian Liaison Agent and Interpreters School at Oberammergau, Germany, to learn Russian. Sergeants Fordham and Draughon became the 2d RSM's first Russian voice intercept operators, activating the first USAFSS voice intercept section in Europe within the 2d RSM in November 1949. Later on July 4, 1950, Staff Sergeant Fordham and 1st Lt. Kenneth Pearsall opened a new covert ground intercept site—Detachment D—at Tempelhof Airport in the Western Sector of occupied Berlin. Still later, the 2d RSM activated additional detachments at Linz and Vienna, Austria.

To avoid Soviet protests—Berlin was deeply within East Germany and jointly administered by the Allies, including the Russians—Detachment D's men were officially assigned on temporary duty with the 7350th Air Base Complement Squadron at Tempelhof Airport, and their relationship with the 2d RSM at Darmstadt was classified. They worked in a couple of secured rooms within the airport, and no one in Berlin knew what they did. Flying in and out of Berlin on C-47 courier flights, Lieutenant Pearsall traveled to Wiesbaden weekly to brief the U.S. Air Forces, Europe Chief of Intelligence.

As an army corporal, Fordham had been a Morse intercept operator with the Army Security Agency's Detachment Six at Herzo Base, Herzogenaurach, Germany, in 1948. The ASA sought volunteers among Detachment Six's soldiers to transfer to the 2d RSM for ultimate transfer to the Air Force Security Service. Corporal Fordham volunteered, transferred to the 2d RSM, and moved with the 2d RSM from Herzo Base to Darmstadt in late 1948. He transferred to Air Force Security Service in early 1949.[40] Attempting to get a grip on its signals intelligence mission, the U.S. Department of Defense created the Armed Forces Security Agency (precursor of the National Security Agency) on May 20, 1949, and the AFSA became the NSA on November 4, 1952.

Unlike the other detachments, Detachment D in Berlin had a primary mission of collecting Soviet air force voice communications so it did not have a direction-finding capability for its first eighteen months of operations. In January 1952, S.Sgt. William Baker flew into Tempelhof Airport with a camouflaged DF system housed in a standard HO-17 hut mounted on a deuce and a half (2½-ton, 6' x 6'-foot) truck. Engineers had mounted a regular aircraft radio compass on the HO-17's roof; the intercept receiver was inside the hut. With the HO-17 hut parked along the Tempelhof flightline, they were quickly in business. Forty-eight years later, Bill Baker recalled some events that illustrate the tense situation in Berlin during the early years of the Cold War.

We had a recon flight that came over practically every evening. It was a twin jet (probably light bomber), and I'm sure it was taking photos to see if anything had changed at Tempelhof since the day before. I'm sure they had quite a conference when they got the first picture of our little

HO-17 out by the runway!! Anyway, that was frustrating too since we were not allowed to have any combat aircraft at Tempelhof or even fly them up the corridors. I think the first years of the "Cold War" were probably the most trying for the military folks, especially in places like Berlin. Of course they told us when we volunteered to go up there that we were expendable.

The light bomber was probably one of the Soviet air force IL-28 Beagle bombers that the Soviets brought to East Germany in the early 1950s. Bill Baker also recalled another incident that illustrates the viciousness of the Soviet military toward Western aircraft overflying Soviet-controlled territory:

An Air France DC-6 was shot at coming up the south corridor in April 1952. That was my first experience at seeing the size of hole a 20 mm cannon shell can put in an airplane, and there were quite a few of them. I wish I could explain the anger and frustration I felt when I looked over that airplane.

This was one of the many air incidents occurring over the Allied air corridors linking Berlin to West Germany during the Cold War.

Expanding its signals intelligence capabilities in Europe, the USAFSS deployed the 6910th Security Group to Wiesbaden, Germany, in 1951, and activated several new squadrons. All the squadrons except the 31st Communications Security Squadron were communications intelligence intercept squadrons; the 31st CSS monitored U.S. Air Force communications in performing a communications security mission. The 6910th, to which the squadrons in Europe reported, co-located small subordinate units called "operating locations" (OL's) with most of the intercept squadrons. The mission of the 6910th was twofold: second-echelon processing (analyzing traffic intercepted by the squadrons) and managing the squadrons.

The 6910th moved from Wiesbaden to Landsberg, Germany, in May 1953. During the following August, Air Force Security Service (USAFSS) Headquarters and its Air Force Special Communications Center (new third-echelon analysis center) moved from Brooks AFB to the new

FIGURE ONE—USAFSS EUROPEAN UNITS IN EARLY 1950S *

Unit	Location	Active Dates
2d Radio Squadron Mobile	Darmstadt, Germany	1949–55
Detachment A, 2d RSM	Rothwesten, Germany	1949–52
Detachment B, 2d RSM	Schleissheim, Germany	1949–51
Detachment C, 2d RSM	Bremerhaven, Germany	1949–51
Detachment D, 2d RSM	Berlin (Tempelhof), Germany	1950–54
6910th Security Group	Wiesbaden, Germany	1951–53
	Darmstadt, Germany	1952–56
	Landsberg, Germany	1953–56
Flight A, 6910th SG	Wasserkuppe, Germany	1953–54
Flight F, 6910th SG	West Drayton, England	1953–54
10th Radio Squadron Mobile[41]	RAF Chicksands, England	1950–55
Detachment 101, 10th RSM	RAF Stracathro, Scotland	1952–53
Detachment 102, 10th RSM	RAF Kirknewton, Scotland	1952–52
12th Radio Squadron Mobile	Landsberg, Germany	1951–55
Detachment 1, 12th RSM	Linz, Austria	1951–55
Detachment 2, 12th RSM	Schleissheim, Germany	1951–53
Detachment 4, 12th RSM	Vienna, Austria	1953–55
Detachment 2, 12th RSM	Hof, Germany	1955–55
41st Radio Squadron Mobile	Bremerhaven, Germany	1951–55
Detachment 1, 41st RSM	Fassberg	1954–55
34th Radio Squadron Mobile[42]	Wheelus Air Base, Libya	1951–55
Flight A, 34th RSM	Ankara, Turkey	1953–54
OL 1, Flight A, 34th RSM	Samsun, Turkey	1953–55
OL 2, Flight A, 34th RSM	Trabzon, Turkey	1953–55
Detachment 1, 34th RSM	Ankara, Turkey	1954–55
Detachment 2, 34th RSM	Iraklion, Crete	1954–55
Detachment 3, 34th RSM	Diyarbakir, Turkey	1955–55
37th Radio Squadron Mobile	RAF Kirknewton, Scotland	1952–55
85th Radio Squadron Mobile	Darmstadt, Germany	1953–54
85th RSM Operations	Grunstadt, Germany	1954–55
85th RSM Headquarters	Sembach, Germany	1954–55
Detachment 1, 85th RSM	Berlin (Tempelhof), Germany	1954–55
Detachment 2, 85th RSM	Kassel, Germany	1954–56
Detachment 3, 85th RSM	Wasserkuppe, Germany	1954–55
31st Comms Security Squadron	RAF Bushy Park, England	1953–55
Flight A, 31st CSS	RAF Burtonwood, England	1953–55
Detachment 2, 31st CSS	RAF Bushy Park, England	1953–55
Detachment 3, 31st CSS	Wiesbaden, Germany	1953–55
Detachment 4, 31st CSS	Wheelus Air Base, Libya	1953–55
6900th Security Wing	Landsberg, Germany	1953–54
	Frankfurt, Germany	1954–61
6901st Special Comms Group[43]	Landsberg, Germany	1955–56

*The squadron designators changed in May 1955; reference figure two.

FIGURE TWO—USAFSS EUROPEAN
UNITS EFFECTIVE MAY 1955*

Unit Designator when activated	Location	Unit Designator from May 1955
2d Radio Squadron Mobile	Darmstadt, Germany	6911th RSM
2d RSM detachments were re-subordinated to other units.		
Detachment 1, 6911th RSM	Rhein-Main Air Base, Germany	activated Feb. 1956
Detachment 1, 6911th RGM**	Rhein-Main Air Base, Germany	RGM Sept. 1956
Detachment 1, 6911th RGM	Rhein-Main Air Base, Germany	6916th RSM 1960
6910th Security Group	Landsberg, Germany-1953	6910th SG
Detachments at several European locations.	Sembach, Germany-1956	
10th Radio Squadron Mobile	RAF Chicksands, England	6951st RSM in 1955
6950th Radio Group Mobile	RAF Chicksands, England	6950th RGM 1956
12th Radio Squadron Mobile	Landsberg, Germany-1951	6912th RSM***
	Bingen, Germany-1955	
	Berlin, Germany-1959	
Detachment 1, 12th RSM	Linz, Austria	Det 1, 6912th RSM
Detachment 2, 12th RSM	Hof, Germany	Det 2, 6912th RSM
Detachment 4, 12th RSM	Vienna, Austria	Det 3, 6912th RSM
Detachment 2, 12th RSM	Hof, Germany	6915th RSM 1959
41st Radio Squadron Mobile	Bremerhaven, Germany	6913th RSM
Detachment 1, 41st RSM	Fassberg	Det 1, 6913th RSM
34th Radio Squadron Mobile	Wheelus Air Base, Libya	6934th RSM
Flight A, 34th RSM	Ankara, Turkey	6933rd RSM 1955–57
OL 1, Flight A, 34th RSM	Samsun, Turkey	Det 2, 6933rd RSM
OL 2, Flight A, 34th RSM	Trabzon, Turkey	Det 1, 6933rd RSM
Detachment 3, 34th RSM	Diyarbakir, Turkey	Det 4, 6933d RSM
6933d Radio Group Mobile	Karamursel, Turkey	6933d RGM 1957
Detachment 2, 34th RSM	Iraklion, Crete	6930th RSM
37th Radio Squadron Mobile	RAF Kirknewton, Scotland	6952d RSM
85th RSM Operations	Grunstadt, Germany	6914th RSM
85th RSM Headquarters	Sembach, Germany	6914th RSM
Detachment 1, 85th RSM	Berlin (Tempelhof), Germany	Det 1, 6914th RSM
31st Comms Security Squadron	RAF Burtonwood, England	6931st CSS
Flight A, 31st CSS	RAF Burtonwood, England	Det 1, 6931st CSS
Detachment 2, 31st CSS	RAF Bushy Park, England	Det 2, 6931st CSS
Detachment 3, 31st CSS	Wiesbaden, Germany	Det 3, 6931st CSS
Detachment 4, 31st CSS	Wheelus Air Base, Libya	Det 4, 6931st CSS
6900th Security Wing	Frankfurt, Germany	6900th SW
6901st Special Comms Group	Landsberg, Germany-1955	6901st SCG
	Zweibrücken, Germany-1956	

*Air Force Security Service unit designators changed in May 1955 to 69xx series.
**USAFSS men lost aboard C-130 60528 were assigned to Det 1, 6911th RGM.
***6912th RSM moved to Bingen, Germany in 1955 and to Berlin in 1959.

USAFSS Headquarters building on Kelly AFB, Texas—on the southwest side of San Antonio.[44] At Landsberg the same month, USAFSS activated the 6900th Security Wing as its intermediate headquarters in Europe. The 6900th SW relocated from Landsberg to the I.G. Farben Building in downtown Frankfurt, Germany, in 1954, just months before USAFSS moved the 6901st Special Comms Group from Kelly AFB, Texas, to Landsberg in 1955. The 6901st assumed second-echelon processing responsibilities from the 6910th Security Group.

Most, though not all, of the European-based USAFSS units that existed in 1955 are depicted in Figure One, where it can be seen that, by the mid-1950s, USAFSS was collecting communications intelligence at European-based intercept sites from northern Germany to Libya. In May 1955, the USAFSS updated its worldwide organizational structure. A major part of the restructuring involved re-designating the command's one- and two-digit squadrons as four-digit squadrons in the 69xx series—for example, the 2d Radio Squadron Mobile became the 6911th RSM. Figure Two shows the deployment of Air Force Security Service (USAFSS) units in Europe in the late 1950s.

An overview of significant organizational changes from 1955 to 1960 follows. In 1955, the USAFSS detachments in Austria were deactivated when Austria regained its independence; the 6912th RSM transferred from Landsberg to Bingen am Rhein, and a new squadron, the 6933d RSM, stood up at Ankara, Turkey, in 1955—with subordinate detachments at Trabzon and Samsun. In late 1956, the remaining USAFSS units left Landsberg Air Base: the 6901st moved to Zweibrücken, Germany, and the 6910th moved to Sembach—absorbing the 6914th that was deactivated. Three years later in 1959, the 6912th RSM moved from Bingen to Berlin, and the detachment at Hof, Germany, became the 6915th RSM.

Finally and most important for our story, the 6911th Radio Squadron Mobile activated Detachment 1, 6911th at Rhein-Main Air Base, Germany, as Security Service's first airborne communications intelligence reconnaissance unit in Europe in early 1956. A brief history of Detachment 1—later known as the 6916th Security Squadron—is included in chapter five.

By the late 1950s, USAFSS had grown phenomenally since Headquarters Air Force authorized its creation in 1948 with an authorized strength of 156 personnel. When the Korean War broke out in June 1950, its authorized strength was 3,050, and by the time the armistice ending the war was signed in July 1953, authorized USAFSS strength was 17,143. Growth leveled off, and USAFSS was authorized 18,124 personnel in June 1958. Security Service peaked at the height of the Vietnam War with 28,637 slots.

Soviet air force strength grew probably at even greater rates. The MiG-17 was the Soviet air force's frontline interceptor by 1958. At that time, MiG-17 pilots defended Soviet state borders from Ashkhabad and Mary in Turkmenistan (north of Iran) in the south, westward around the Soviet borders to Murmansk in the north, eastward across Siberia to the Bering Strait, and south along the Soviet Union's Pacific shores to Vladivostok. The only USAFSS ground intercept sites in Europe within tactical (VHF) intercept range of the Soviet air force communications were those at Trabzon and Samsun, Turkey, and Hof and Berlin, Germany. Airborne reconnaissance therefore provided the only means to collect Soviet air order of battle and electronic order of battle data for most areas of the Soviet Union—data that were considered essential to America's defense.

Early USAFSS Operations in the Far East

U.S. Air Force Security Service operations began and evolved in the Far East in a manner similar to that which occurred in Europe. The U.S. Army Security Agency moved the 1st Radio Squadron Mobile to Johnson Air Base, Japan, in late 1947 and handed the squadron over to USAFSS in February 1949. The 1st RSM was severely understaffed with 11 officers and 176 airmen in February 1950. The unit borrowed twenty-five Morse operators from the Army Security Agency (ASA) to relieve its shortage. By June 30, staffing had increased to 11 officers and 243 enlisted men. With the outbreak of the Korean War in June 1950, the squadron's authorized staffing levels increased from 285 enlisted men and 17 officers to 500 enlisted men and 36 officers—numbers that would remain more a dream than a reality.

At the outbreak of the war, the squadron's mission was almost exclusively Morse traffic; the squadron had only one linguist—Sgt. Robert T. Hauch, a Russian linguist who had completed the first twelve-month Russian language course at the Army Language School, Monterey, California, in late 1949. Adding to the weak position of United Nations forces in Korea, none of the signals intelligence services had any Korean or Chinese linguists. The U.S. Navy Security Group also had one Russian linguist in the Far East: Lieutenant Gray, a second generation American of Russian descent, was based at Yokosuka Naval Base, Japan. PFCs Donald G. Hill, William R. Peer, and Hugh A. Bishop graduated from a six-month Russian course at Monterey and had just arrived at Brooks AFB for intercept operator training in June 1950 when the Korean War started.

Curtailing their training, USAFSS rushed Hill, Peer, and Bishop to Johnson AB, Japan, where they joined Hauch as the 1st RSM's initial Russian intercept cadre. Navy Lieutenant Gray trained the airmen in intercept and transcription to expedite creation of a functioning USAFSS voice intercept section in the Far East. Nationally, the Armed Forces Security Agency (forerunner of NSA), was in no better shape; no U.S. SIGINT units had any Korean or Chinese linguists. For that matter, the entire U.S. military establishment was ill prepared for war.

In 1950, the 1st RSM had Detachment A (aka Detachment 11), a direction-finding site at Misawa Air Base, Honshu Island. This was one of only two U.S. DF networks in the Far East. The other belonged to the Navy. In late 1950, the 1st RSM activated Detachment B (Detachment 12) at Ashiya AB, Japan, to support the Korean War, and detached a mobile Morse intercept team to Pyongyang, North Korea, just in time for the team (Detachment C/13) to beat a spirited retreat southward ahead of several hundred thousand Communist Chinese soldiers who entered the war in November.

By early January 1951 the Chinese army had forced the U.N. forces southward to positions south of Seoul. On January 25, 1951, the U.S. Eighth Army took the offensive, reoccupying Seoul on March 14. By April 22 U.N. forces, led by the 8th Army, occupied positions just north of the 38th parallel that separated North and South Korea when the war started. Periods of heavy fighting—largely static ground battles with significant losses on both sides—continued generally along the 38th parallel with extensive air combat in "MiG Alley" over the North Korean/Chinese border until July 1951, when negotiations began to end the conflict. Negotiations dragged on for two years before a truce was finally signed in July 1953.

The impact of signals intelligence support to U.N. air force operations during the Korean War was immediate and immense. Located on a mountaintop above Kimpo Air Base in tandem with an Air Force radar unit, a small Air Force Security Service signals intelligence intercept team monitored enemy air force communications and tipped off Air Force warning and control officers of potential threats to Allied fighter crews operating over MiG Alley. In a single air engagement on November 27, 1951, F-86 pilots shot down eleven MiGs while sustaining no losses and only four damaged F-86s. Due in large part to the SIGINT-based tip-offs, the F-86 to MiG kill ratio in the Korean War was approximately thirteen to one. Lt. Gen. O. P. Weyland, Far East Air Forces commander, awarded the 1st RSM a Meritorious Unit Commendation in August 1951 for outstanding signals intelligence support.[45]

> . . . *exceptionally meritorious conduct in performance of outstanding service from 26 November 1950 to 18 July 1951.*

At the time, the Soviet government denied any direct involvement in the Korean War, but intercepted communications by the 1st RSM showed otherwise. The squadron history for the period January–March 1951 contains this typically oblique remark:

> *The 1st Radio Squadron Mobile made one of the most important contributions to [signals intelligence] in its history during the month of March. No details of that "Scoop" can be given in this document; however, only a few days after receipt of a wire from USAFSS stating that this particular item was number one priority with [voice intercept], the 1st Radio Squadron Mobile sent a FLASH wire with the answer. . . . It is interesting to note that about three days after our report was sent, Speaker of the U.S. House of Representatives, Sam Rayburn, made statements on the floor of the House that he had just returned from a*

White House briefing on Korean War developments and in a veiled way
indicated that he was aware of the particular intelligence involved.

In some respects, the solution of that particular problem lessened the
urgency for airborne reconnaissance mentioned in paragraph one [above,
referring to plans for airborne communications recon] since it proved that
the desired material was available through existing facilities. However, the
work of the airborne project is continuing in hope that the information we
now have can be broadened and further exploited . . .

The 1st RSM historian was alluding to interception of Russian voice
communications confirming Soviet involvement in the Korean War. In
September 1999, Burton R. Knotts, former Air Force sergeant and 1st
RSM Morse intercept operator, recalled intercepting Russian communications shortly after he arrived in Korea in August 1951.

I found and recorded a very important radio transmission from North
Korea about my second or third night on the mountain north of Kimpo. I
heard a voice broadcast that sounded like Korean, so I started recording.
As soon as the first man stopped talking, I heard the reply spoken by a
man with a deep, guttural voice; the first speaker's voice was fairly high
pitched. I made a note on my log of the time and a statement about the
two different voices that I had recorded on tape. I also entered the radio
frequency. The time was during the period 2:00-3:00 a.m. I recorded the
same broadcast each night, and about three days later, Lt. Holbert [offi-
cer in charge] told me that the colonel at 5th Air Force was excited about
the recorded messages. I had recorded a North Korean and a Russian ex-
changing messages—proof of Russian involvement in the war effort.

Airlifted to Korea from Japan aboard a C-119 Flying Boxcar with 1st
Lt. George Holbert and two others as a self-contained four-man intercept
team, Sergeant Knotts soon learned the real purpose of his team. Desperate for linguists during the first year of the war when U.S. airmen were
still studying Chinese and Korean at American colleges, the Air Force
Security Service had bent security rules and permitted the 1st RSM to
use South Korean airmen as voice intercept operators at its USAFSS de-

tachment in Korea. Later, in the fall of 1951, Security Service would, as we shall see, bend them even further—break them, in fact. Sergeant Knotts continued:

A few days later—prior to 17 August 1951—we found out a lot more about why we were sent to South Korea. A 5th Air Force colonel drove up to our mountain site one morning, bringing several Japanese civilians with him. The men were all middle-aged or older. Only one could speak passable English. They were there to help with our mission; they were fluent in Russian and several Chinese dialects. The colonel told me to teach them how to use our radios and tape recorders, and they were to monitor radio networks that I would find for them, copying and recording the Russian and Chinese messages.

The Colonel lectured us about treating the Japanese with respect although they recently had been waging war against us; World War II was still fresh in our minds. We were really shocked and worried about working with these Japanese. We were also responsible for their safety, as they had no weapons. . . .

A Mr. Hirota, who spoke passable English, was their leader. He told me later that he had been a 3-star general in charge of the Japanese Naval Air Force; all had been Japanese military officers and had fought in World War II . . . They were so smart and took to their intercept work so easily that it scared me. I felt strange about our former enemies learning so much about our security methods and procedures . . .

On 19 August 1951, we moved across the Han River into Seoul, past Ewha High School for Girls and to the shell-damaged buildings of Chosen Christian College. The 5th Air Force has given us clearance papers for the Japanese so that the guards at the Han River bridge would let us cross. Our U.S. Army's 440th Signal Corps was occupying the Ewha school buildings located around the mountain and about 1.5 miles by road from Chosen Christian College where we set up operations in the main building. We constructed a barbed-wire fence around the entire complex with two barbed-wire gates. The 5th Air Force assigned some South Korean (ROK) soldiers to us for guard duty. We were instructed to keep the Japanese in our compound at all times; not let them outside our barbed-wire fencing.

As their NCO in charge, Sergeant Knotts got along well with the Japanese, and they honored him with a Christmas card in December 1951, signed by all twelve.

Elated at the speed and quality of the intelligence on enemy operations that the Air Force was by then providing his United Nations Command Headquarters, Gen. Matthew Ridgway, the U.N. forces commander who had replaced General MacArthur, congratulated the Air Force for the unique, timely intelligence reports provided to his G2 intelligence staff. Later, when he inquired about the source of the intelligence and was told about the use of the Japanese nationals, he immediately ordered them to be spirited out of the country, completely overruling Air Force generals who interceded on behalf of retaining the unique signals intelligence collection team.

Ridgway did not want his reputation stained by an international incident, should the communist propaganda machines learn about the Japanese national intercept operators. He was willing to endure the loss of the special intelligence if necessary. Fortunately, the first U.S. Air Force graduates of a Mandarin Chinese class at Yale University (thirty-three airmen) arrived in Korea in early 1952 and replaced the Japanese nationals as Security Service's first Chinese voice intercept operators.

In July 1951, USAFSS activated the 15th Radio Squadron Mobile at Ashiya to assume signals intelligence support to U.N. forces in Korea. At the same time, the 1st RSM closed its Detachment 12 at Ashiya then reactivated it as an intercept and DF site at Wakkanai on August 18, 1951. The 15th RSM activated Detachment 15-1, eventually replacing Detachment 13 of the 1st RSM in Korea.

Capt. Russell E. (Hop) Harriger, a former World War II B-17 pilot, arrived in Korea in the first half of 1951 to replace Capt. Reginald G. M. Gilbert as Detachment 13's operations officer. Gilbert, a former World War II P-51 pilot, had deployed with the detachment to Pyongyang six months earlier. PFCs Donald C. Falkner and Jay Botschen—Botschen later flew missions aboard RB-29 290—accompanied Gilbert to Korea as Morse intercept operators.

Having no linguists who understood Korean, Security Service hand-picked a contingent of Republic of Korea—South Korean—airmen to form a voice intercept section within Detachment 13. Lieutenant Cho of the ROK air force commanded the group of Koreans and reported directly to the detachment operations officer, Captain Harriger. Later, as a major general, Cho commanded the South Korean air force security service.

Harriger and Cho have remained lifelong friends, and retired General Cho visited Harriger at the Harriger farm in Pennsylvania in 1998. In addition, Cho is a personal friend of Samuel Hong, who had pioneered airborne communications intelligence reconnaissance with the Army Air Corps in 1945.

When Harriger arrived in Korea, Detachment 13 had recently occupied the facilities at Ewha University, a women's college near Seoul that had ceased operations due to the war. Detachment 13's airmen shared the facilities with Lieutenant Cho's ROK military linguists. Harriger demonstrated his wit and command of the English language in the unit history for July–September 1951:

> The early part of July was a busy one for Detachment 13. A majority of the time was spent getting things firmed up and various offices relocated in more advantageous areas. The detachment experienced the usual confusion that always accompanies a unit when moving to a new site. The "loose" tactics peculiar to 5th Air Force alone, added more than a few problems to our already overflowing list. If you have seen it, there is no use recapping it; if you never have seen it, you never would believe it. Since we are sick about it we won't talk about it here.
>
> The backward and forward movement of Detachment 13 along the countryside between Seoul and Taegu reminds one of the definition of "jiggle," as applied to a voluptuous woman. It goes something like this.
>
> A jiggle occurs when one part of the body, which is in motion (while the main part of the body is at rest), suddenly finds itself without support of the main part of the body. In its anxiety, it hurriedly retires too far to the rear, whereupon, a secondary jiggle ensues. We might say that for many reasons, 5th Air Force and Detachment 13 are still "jiggling."
>
> On 2 July, our Detachment 13 commander, Captain Robert W. Karnan, returned to Japan after seven months in Korea. He came in with the original unit in November of last year. After the evacuation of Sinanju, Pyongyang and Seoul, the Detachment settled down for the winter in

Taegu. Upon the return to Seoul in mid-June, our new commander, Captain Clarence Wilhelm, took charge.

Approximately 12 July, the rear echelon of the outfit, earmarked for space at Ewha University, arrived in the Seoul area. Final space allocations were made at this time . . . we were granted the downstairs floor of our building previously used by 440th Signal Supply. This has alleviated the housing problem to some extent.

Due to the lack of windows, the mosquitoes have caused trouble for both airmen and ROK's (Republic of Korea airmen). Headquarters, 1st RSM air-shipped us enough mosquito nets, DDT and other repellents to whip the problem. At present all airmen and ROK's have mosquito netting. The average ROK airman never heard of mosquito netting or DDT until he saw the Americans with this equipment. We have tried insofar as possible to treat all as equals and it has worked out to everyone's satisfaction. . . .

Touching on detachment morale Captain Harriger took a potshot at the unit's "comfort" facilities:

Morale was shattered last week when our "one holer" was condemned by the sanitation inspector (as we figured it would be). It seems there should be a lid on the thing. We assured the inspector that someone was sitting on it 24 hours a day, but still, he insisted we close her up. 440th Signal Battalion promised to build a new one that would meet proper specifications.

Harriger kept detachment morale high by intermingling levity with Detachment 13's day-to-day tasking.

On September 1, 1951, Security Service activated the 6920th Security Group at Johnson AB to manage USAFSS intercept units in the Far East. The following year, the 6920th activated the 29th RSM in the Philippines to monitor non-Soviet communist communications in Southeast Asia. In August 1954, USAFSS created the 6902d Special Communications Center in the Philippines to provide second-echelon analysis and reporting to user commands.

With the 15th RSM picking up more of the USAFSS responsibilities in Korea in 1951, the 1st RSM redirected its attention to Soviet Far East military activities outside the war zone. With the advent of newer Soviet aircraft with VHF radios, new VHF voice intercept sites were critically needed adjacent to peripheral areas of the Soviet Far East and Communist China. In late 1952, the 6920th added a VHF intercept capability at Wakkanai Air Station, Japan, and opened a new VHF intercept site on Oku-Shiri Shima, a small island off the southwestern coast of Hokkaido, Japan. The Wakkanai detachment became the 6986th Radio Squadron Mobile in 1958, and the Oku-Shiri Shima site was deactivated in 1957, with VHF collection capabilities concentrated at Wakkanai.

Maj. Paul Tisdale, a World War II glider pilot who supported the Normandy Beach landings in 1944, was one of the first officers assigned to Air Force Security Service and played key roles in USAFSS operations in the Far East in the early 1950s. Completing a twelve-month Russian language course in 1949, he transferred from the Army Security Agency to the Air Force Security Service and helped set up USAFSS operations at Brooks AFB, Texas. When the Korean War started, the Air Force assigned Tisdale as the Air Force special security officer at Far East Air Forces Headquarters in Tokyo. He often briefed USAFSS plans and interests to General Weyland and other FEAF senior staff and coordinated the plan whereby Security Service voice intercept operators in Korea passed MiG alert tip-offs to Air Force aircraft control and warning officers for immediate relay to airborne F-86 pilots. In addition, in late 1951, Tisdale made arrangements with the Strategic Air Command's 91st Strategic Recon Squadron at Yokota to permit USAFSS voice intercept operators to fly recon missions aboard 91st recon aircraft.

When Major Tisdale was reassigned to the 6920th Security Group in 1952, its commander assigned him to set up an intercept detachment on the island of Formosa (Taiwan). Subordinate to the 29th RSM in the Philippines, the Taiwan detachment later became the 6987th Radio Squadron Mobile at Shu Lin Kou Air Station, Taiwan.

A year later in 1953, Colonel Sawyer called upon Major Tisdale to activate another pair of communications intercept detachments—one at Da Nang, Vietnam, and another at Pelawan in the northeastern Indonesian islands. Those two direction-finding stations, built to monitor enemy communications in Southeast Asia, would be of significance a few years later as the U.S. slowly moved toward a military commitment in Vietnam.

By September 1956 when the Air Force Security Service lost its first airborne recon crew, the 1st Radio Squadron Mobile had been redesignated as the 6924th RSM and transferred from Johnson AB, Japan, to Shiroi AB, Japan, along with its headquarters unit, the 6920th Security Wing. The seven crew members lost aboard the RB-50 airborne communications intelligence recon platform over the Sea of Japan on September 10, 1956, were assigned to Detachment 1, 6924th. That USAFSS flying detachment at Yokota AB became Detachment 1, 6920th Security Wing in 1957, was redesignated Detachment 1, 6988th RSM in September 1958, and finally became the 6988th RSM in January 1959.

FOUR

—

BIRTH OF THE ACRP

Airborne communications intelligence reconnaissance traces its roots to World War II in the Pacific. At least two U.S. Army Air Corps radio squadrons mobile used airborne voice intercept operators flying aboard Air Corps RB-24 recon aircraft to collect signals intelligence on Japanese air defenses in the Pacific theater. Nisei (second-generation Japanese American) linguists assigned to the 8th Radio Squadron Mobile flew as voice intercept operators on missions operating along the main Japanese islands while 1st Radio Squadron Mobile nisei linguists flew similar missions against Japanese air defense targets on Formosa (Taiwan).

The Flying Eight Ball—First Airborne COMINT Recon

The Army Signal Corps activated the 8th Radio Squadron Mobile in November 1942. Activated as the 958th Signal Radio Intelligence Company (Aviation) at Drew Field,[46] Florida, the unit trained at Camp Pinedale, California (near Fresno), in 1943–44. Tom Ito, a nisei and former 8th RSM voice intercept operator, provided Larry Tart a copy of the 8th RSM's unit history: "The Story Behind The Flying Eight Ball."[47] The unit history sums up changes in the unit's mission before it deployed overseas.

*The original mission of the 958th was to provide a group of highly spe-
cialized men for gathering radio intelligence for the Air Forces. Then
came a change in which we were designated as a Japanese intercept unit.
This necessitated additional training, which consisted of monitoring Japanese Army nets for three months, and then having the entire group of
[Morse] radio operators study Japanese Kata Kana Radio Code. . . .*

The Signal Corps also decided to include a voice intercept section in
the unit—to intercept Japanese air force voice communications. Reori-
enting the unit as a "Japanese intercept unit" and adding a voice intercept section later proved to be a wise decision.

In March 1944, the 958th, a Japanese intercept unit, was redesignated
the Provisional 1st Radio Squadron Mobile. Finally, the army transferred
the squadron from the Army Signal Corps to the Army Air Corps and redesignated it the 8th Radio Squadron Mobile.

The 8th RSM arrived for operational duty on Guam in November
1944. Ed Bradfield, Morse intercept operator and unit historian, described his first observations of Guam:

*The trip through the ruined city of Agana is one we'll never forget.
There didn't seem to be a single house that hadn't been damaged, and yet,
wherever there was even a part of a roof left, the natives had returned and
were living there. The shoreline had been battered by naval gunfire, and
the palms were all broken and bare, and leaning in every which way. The
last things that we noticed as we left town were the damaged tanks, half-
tracks and "ducks" [amphibious vehicles] that were strewn over the beach
or abandoned in the surf. Quite a sight!*

Joining forces with the U.S. Navy, the 8th RSM began intelligence
operations in early December 1944, operating in a secure compound
called "The Joint Communications Activity." The 8th deployed a direction-finding platoon to outlying islands in order to get closer to the lower
power transmitters that the Japanese were using. With DF network control on Guam, the squadron set up DF stations on Palau, Saipan, and—
after the island was liberated from the Japanese in March, 1945—on Iwo
Jima.[48]

The mission of the 8th and its deployed DF platoons was to intercept Japanese air force air-to-ground and ground communications to forewarn 5th Air Force Headquarters of pending Japanese air raids and other air force activities. Although small in number, nisei voice intercept operators played a major role in the squadron's intercept and direction-finding missions. In addition to the voice intercept section that operated on Guam, two to three nisei linguists deployed with each DF team to the outlying islands.

James Iwatsubo, a nisei linguist who deployed onto Iwo Jima a couple of weeks after the U.S. Marines captured the island, discussed his involvement in December 1999:

> Mail call was a highlight of the day on Iwo Jima; we had mail call almost every day. We also had beer and cigarettes there, too. Beer was rationed, but some who did not drink traded beers for the candy bars that others got in their C-rations. I thought I did something good for my country. I believe we shortened the war significantly with our intelligence efforts. I felt happy that I was able to make a contribution.

He cited Admiral Nimitz's surprise attack on a Japanese aircraft carrier task force near Midway Island in June 1942 to show the value of communications intelligence. Nimitz wrote of the victory, "Midway was essentially a victory for intelligence."

Francis B. Waggenspack and Frank Diamond are two of a very limited number of non-nisei Japanese linguists who worked in signals intelligence during World War II. They both learned Japanese at the University of Washington, Seattle—one of the earliest American military language training programs. Waggenspack recently described his language training as rigorous.

> We studied Japanese eight hours per day, six days per week, and had three hours of supervised study hall each night. However, that living in a fraternity house during school beat the hell out of living in army tents.

Waggenspack worked as a cryptanalyst on Guam, sometimes served as an intercept operator with the nisei, and considered briefly the idea of flying reconnaissance missions with them. But when a B-29 loaded with bombs exploded on the runway during takeoff, his desire to be an airborne voice intercept operator vanished.

Getting Their Wings

Born in Honolulu and grown up in Hawaii as a Korean American, Samuel S. K. Hong studied Japanese at Camp Savage, Minnesota, in 1943 and served with the Army Air Corps as a Japanese linguist. As the only officer of Asian heritage in the 8th Radio Squadron Mobile, he was placed in charge of the enlisted nisei contingent of intelligence specialists assigned to the squadron. Now eighty years old and leading an active life in Hawaii, Hong is casual—almost cavalier—in describing America's intelligence capabilities at the start of World War II and how the idea to use airborne voice intercept operators came about.

> We [in American Intelligence] were just babes in the woods at the start of World War II. The Army Air Corps sent some guys over to England to learn from the Brits who were the pros in communications intelligence. The 8th RSM was formed and trained at Camp Pinedale in COMINT before shipping out to Guam in late 1944. We were still learning toward the end of the war and got into airborne communications intelligence reconnaissance by accident.

Using native Japanese-speaking nisei linguists in the war in the Pacific to intercept Japanese voice communications was a novel concept that grew out of a desperate need for tactical intelligence. Of the more than 4,000 men who learned Japanese at military-sponsored language schools during World War II, only a handful ended up being used to intercept voice communications. The linguists with no Japanese heritage— a very small minority—qualified for a top secret clearance and worked in cryptanalysis jobs. The nisei—the overwhelming majority of the graduates—were denied top secret clearances and, as a result, worked in combat intelligence as translators, interrogators, and in similar jobs not requiring a special clearance.

Reporting operationally on Guam to the U.S. Navy cryptanalysis group that had no prior experience with intercepted tactical voice communications, Lieutenant Hong's nisei section was maligned initially; the navy viewed the nisei as "gofers" and used them more extensively for menial chores than as contributors to the war's intelligence efforts. In recent discussions, Hong commented on an acrimonious relationship with the U.S. Navy on Guam.

> On Guam, we [Lt. Hong and the nisei Japanese linguists] were on loan to the navy. There were bad relations between us and the navy; they did not trust us entirely and treated us as second-class citizens. At the intelligence compound, the navy had a tall fence around the compound, and we could not enter; they built a little hut outside the compound and put another fence around our hut. We were fighting not only the Japanese, but the U.S. Navy.

Hong recalls that the navy finally authorized him access to the compound [Joint Communications Activity] after an intelligence flap in which his nisei men were not provided necessary tip-offs to properly do their intercept jobs. Subsequently, the navy cleared him; he could enter the compound, read the message files and brief his nisei intercept operators.

The nisei linguists felt insulted that the army did not trust them with cryptographic secrets. Mamoru Ishii,[49] one of the nisei linguists who is now eighty years old, commented on the matter with mixed feelings of sadness and incongruity in December 1999:

> There was a big 12-feet fence around the operations complex, and the complex was guarded by army and navy security guards 24 hours per day. We Japanese boys did the voice intercepts in a little bungalow outside the fence. Everyone else in the 8th RSM—the Morse intercept operators, communicators, DF operators and others—worked inside the compound. That upset me somewhat; kinda griped me then, but I laugh about it today.

The nisei received more equal treatment as members of direction-finding teams. Each team worked its Morse, voice intercept, and DF missions as a team in the same facility.

Tom Ito, a nisei who served with a DF team on the island of Palau, commented on working with the navy on Guam:

The navy was in charge of our squadron's operations. At first, the navy was skeptical about using nisei as intercept operators. When we arrived on Guam, the navy kept us busy on garbage detail and other non-intelligence related duties. After the nisei began intercepting Japanese voice communications and providing transcripts to the navy, the navy was surprised at the results and wanted more.

Lieutenant Hong, ever on the lookout for ways to make the men under his command more a part of the mainstream 8th RSM mission, learned by chance about electronic intelligence reconnaissance missions against Japan that were being flown from Guam.

The 21st Air Force Recon Wing on Guam was using a modified B-24 with ELINT intercept equipment installed in its bomb bay to fly recon missions off the Japanese coast. Delving farther into these missions, Lieutenant Hong learned that the mission of the RB-24 was to intercept Japanese radar signals during B-29 raids on Japan. The recon wing used ELINT data collected by the RB-24 to update an order of battle database, and the updated database was used in planning subsequent bombing missions.

Hong reasoned to the ELINT analysts of the 21st Recon Wing that his nisei operators could intercept valuable associated voice communications if the wing would provide his men a couple of intercept receivers aboard the airborne reconnaissance platform. He cited recently intercepted Japanese voice air defense air-to-ground and ground-to-ground communications that his nisei operators were copying on Guam as examples of what could be accomplished by airborne voice intercept operators. He recently commented on the involvement of the nisei in airborne reconnaissance:

It was just sheer luck that I found out that an ELINT reconnaissance aircraft was flying missions off the coast of Japan. I suggested that the Air Corps put a couple of our receivers on the aircraft so our nisei boys could intercept Japanese air defense communications.

The 21st Recon Wing bought into Hong's suggestion and modified their RB-24 to accommodate two nisei voice intercept operators. The recon wing removed the RB-24's nose gun turret and replaced it with an enclosure that was barely large enough for two receivers and two nisei operators. Almost immediately, the 8th Radio Squadron Mobile became known as "The Flying Eight Ball."

The squadron history praises nisei contributions to the unit's intelligence mission, with special mention of the airborne nisei voice intercept operators:

> The nisei group proved invaluable in all phases of our work with which they came in contact. They were assigned voice intercept missions, and occasional tasks of interpretation, interrogations of prisoners, and translation of documents. When volunteers were requested for dangerous flight missions near the Japanese homeland, they all offered to go. However, only ten were needed, and those chosen were: [Herbert] Kawashima, [Maseo] Deguchi, [Yoshio] Kimoto, [T. M.] Ishisaka, [Mamoru] Ishii, [H.] Tanouye, Jimmy [James] Yoshioka, [Yoshio] Hoshide, [George] Hanafusa and Johnny [James] Okada.
>
> Although most of the group had been trained for Combat Intelligence, they quickly adapted themselves to the intricacies of our type of work, and performed their duties remarkably well. The nisei boys proved themselves praiseworthy time and again, and we who worked with them will always respect their loyalty and devotion to duty.

Lieutenant Hong flew one mission "just to see what it was like and because my men were flying missions." The nisei voice intercept operators flew about two missions per month and were happy to be flying because they were paid extra flight pay amounting to about half of their regular enlisted pay. Most of the nisei airborne voice intercept operators have passed on, but at least two—George Hanafusa and Mamoru Ishii— are still alive. Hanafusa is too feeble to discuss his wartime years, but Ishii talks about his airborne missions with justifiable pride.

> Samuel Hong was the lieutenant in charge of the Japanese boys in the 8th Radio Squadron Mobile. I knew Hong when we were both

students at the University of Hawaii before the war, and he was in ROTC.

We flew intercept missions on a modified B-24 Liberator that had the nose turret and nose guns removed.[50] *They [the Air Corps] installed two receivers in a metal enclosure that replaced the turret, and for an antenna, we had a long wire about 50 yards long that trailed behind the aircraft. There was room for two Japanese boys who had to crawl by the pilots to the aircraft's nose to work. Radar [ELINT intercept] operators had other equipment in the bomb bay to intercept Japanese radar signals, and we [nisei voice intercept operators] copied Japanese air defense communications.*

I flew about seven or eight missions. I probably was on the first Liberator mission that carried nisei operators. I definitely was on the last Liberator reconnaissance mission flown the day that the surrender was announced. We were approaching Iwo Jima to refuel after the mission when we heard over the radio that President Truman had announced that Japan had surrendered. That was also the last bombing raid, and there must have been 700 to 800 B-29's in the raid. Some of the flights were long—up to about 18 hours including refueling stops at Iwo Jima.

Our missions were planned to be in place along the Japanese coast during bombing raids. We had to be there when the first B-29 went in on its raid, and we stayed until the last B-29 made its raid. Missions were flown under radio silence.

We copied mostly ground communications; by that time the Japanese air force was depleted, and [Japanese] fighters were used mostly for reconnaissance. I never felt threatened. On one flight, our pilot said that a picket ship near Bonin Island fired on us, but we were not hit.

The best thing about the flights was the steak dinner for aircrews at the end of the flights. I really looked forward to that.

Ishii said there were lots of rumors after the war. Others joked that the nisei were being sent to Japan—"You Japanese boys are going to have to go to Japan for three or four years." In reality, he did go to Hokkaido Island for a short time—as an interpreter with the first Americans to arrive on Hokkaido after the war.[51] He completed college on the G.I. bill and became a professor of agriculture in Hawaii.

The 8th RSM received numerous accolades from field commanders whose operations they supported throughout the Pacific. After the seizure of Iwo Jima in March 1945, AAF B-29s began an intense bombing campaign against Japanese cities, and a fierce battle raged from April to June for Okinawa. During the Okinawan campaign the 8th received a "Well Done" commendation from Adm. Richmond "Kelly" Turner who commanded that battle's amphibious operations. Later, the 8th was commended for missions accomplished in support of Third Fleet operations in Japan's home waters in a terse message sent to Admiral Nimitz's Headquarters, "Please pass to Captain Layton from Commander Emory . . . Hope you note that the army—in the form of the 8th RSM is carrying the ball." Finally, Major Mundorff, 8th RSM Commander, received a laudatory message from Lt. Comdr. Robert B. Seaks, officer in charge of the joint radio analysis group, for the work of the 8th's analysts and translators directly engaged in processing and exploiting intercepted Japanese communications of all types. The message said in part:

> The contribution made by the Voice Intercept [Section] provided by the 8th RSM side of the joint radio analysis group deserves special mention. Its potentialities were just beginning to be realized as hostilities ceased. Not too much was known about Jap use of voice in air/ground traffic; what was known was developed by the joint group. Jap voice for air/ground communications was close to a virgin field, and one that the 8th RSM was almost alone endeavoring to exploit. Records and transcripts of voice activity during B-29 missions were provided by the XXI [21st] Bomber Command. Nisei operators were continually provided for ferret missions.

Unlike the Cold War operators who came after them, the World War II nisei operators had no recorders on which to record and play back intercepted traffic. Mamoru Ishii recently commented that each operator developed his own style of writing down intercepted communications in shorthand, and after returning from airborne missions, the operator would use his hand logs to type out a transcript. With their native speaker understanding of Japanese, the nisei quite naturally produced commendable transcripts. Lieutenant Commander Seaks concluded his message by stating that the 8th RSM had "produced intelligence reports in quantity and quality that far surpassed all other RSMs in the Pacific."

Finally, Admiral of the Fleet Chester W. Nimitz sent a message on the contributions of the 8th RSM to the Commanding General, U.S. Army Strategic Air Forces:

> CINCPAC/CINCPOA desires to express appreciation for the contribution of the 8th Radio Squadron Mobile to joint radio analysis group from the date of organization of that activity on 28 December 1944 until the Japanese surrender.
>
> . . . The proficiency developed by the officers and men of the 8th RSM in their field of signals intelligence, and hence their share in the victory over Japan, can well be a source of pride to them.

With the surrender documents signed on September 2, 1945, President Truman's proclaimed "VJ Day"—Victory over Japan. While administrators were closing out the books on the 8th Radio Squadron Mobile and the squadron historian was going to press with the unit history, the historian received a Letter of Commendation dated October 16, 1945, from the chief of staff, Headquarters, United States Army Strategic Air Forces.

> The 8th Radio Squadron Mobile during its period of operation from December 1944 through September 1945 had as its mission the processing and exploitation of intercepted Japanese communications. The cessation of hostilities found this exploitation at peak effectiveness with the production of intelligence of immediate tactical value to the Air Forces. Possession of this information placed our forces at a definite advantage over the enemy and, therefore, the contribution of the 8th Radio Squadron Mobile in this war cannot be overemphasized . . . The splendid record achieved by this squadron has been due in large measure to the resourcefulness and excellent cooperative spirit of the personnel involved. Keen analysis and thorough knowledge of Japanese communications have characterized their work.

The war over, it was time to pack up and go home. The job was done. Very few people anticipated a need for military intelligence in peacetime. And regrettably, the lesson learned by the surprise attack by the Japanese at Pearl Harbor and the value of airborne communications intelligence reconnaissance were forgotten. America was tired of war; demobilization was the order of the day. The 8th Radio Squadron Mobile was deactivated in late 1945. It would take another surprise attack—the North Korean invasion of South Korea on June 25, 1950—and saber rattling by the Soviet Union and China to rekindle interest in airborne communications intelligence reconnaissance.

1st Radio Squadron Mobile Airborne Recon in World War II

As had been the case with the 8th Radio Squadron Mobile, the Army Signal Corps activated the 1st RSM in 1942 as a signal company— the 138th Signal Radio Intelligence Company. Trained in Spokane, Washington, for duty in Europe, this 299-man company was diverted to Australia, arriving in the fall of 1943. Targeted against Japanese air force communications to support the U.S. Army Air Corps's 5th Air Force Headquarters, the 138th was resubordinated to the Army Air Corps in 1944 and redesignated the 1st Radio Squadron Mobile.[52]

While 8th RSM nisei airborne voice intercept operators were supporting Army Air Corps bombing operations against the main Japanese islands in late 1945, nisei soldiers from the 1st Radio Squadron Mobile were supporting similar Air Corps operations in the Philippines, over Formosa, and in other areas of the southwest Pacific. Bennett Ikeda, one of the nisei voice intercept operators, recently wrote about their operations:

> After graduating from Camp Savage, Minnesota Military Intelligence Service Language School and completing radio intelligence training at MacDill Air Force Base in Florida in mid-1944, we headed to Camp Pinedale, California, as the first group of nisei soldiers to return to the West Coast. The 26 nisei members[53] assigned to the 1st Radio Squadron Mobile (RSM), 5th AAF, landed at Tacloban Bay on Leyte Island, Philippines in late 1944.

As its principal duties, the team intercepted enemy radio transmissions and translated decoded messages intercepted by other analysts. In early 1945, the team split into two groups, with one remaining in Leyte and the other advancing to Tarlac Province in central Luzon after landing at Lingayen Gulf. The latter group split into message interception and message translation units. The Leyte group later joined the advanced group at Tarlac. Shiochi Nakahara was killed at Tarlac while returning from an assignment in Manila.

Between April and July 1945, Yoshito Kawabe, George Okamoto, Kazuo Oshiki and others flew on B-24 bombing missions over Formosa and Kyushu to intercept enemy radio transmissions. . . .

Kazuo Oshiki recently recalled his involvement as a voice intercept operator with the 1st RSM. His nisei class studied "Heigo" (Japanese military terminology) only at Camp Savage. He flew his intercept mission aboard an RB-24 on April 30, 1945. He was the only nisei operator aboard; his intercept position was in the bomb bay of the aircraft, and an officer from the 1st RSM worked in the bomb bay with him. For their participation in support of the bombing campaigns, Sergeant Oshiki and the other airborne intercept operator received the Bronze Star device for their Western Pacific Campaign ribbons. A declassified 1st RSM letter and endorsements dated November 1945 describe their missions:

Under the provisions of Paragraph 21, AR 260-10 and Circular 195, WD 1944, it is requested that the following named officer and enlisted man be authorized to wear a bronze service star on the Asiatic Pacific ribbon for the Western Pacific Campaign.

1st Lt. John J. Frey
Sgt. Kazuo Oshiki

The above named personnel, on 30 April 1945, flew an airplane number 976 of the 19th Squadron, 22nd Bomb Group, with a bombing mission over Toshien Oil Works, Formosa. A total of seven aircraft participated in the mission, dropping forty six general purpose (M-65) bombs. Two aircraft were damaged by heavy, accurate anti-aircraft fire.

Personnel flew on authority of assistant chief of staff, Fifth Air Force, APO 710. Purpose of flight was to attempt interception of enemy radio-telephone communications (VHF) controlling enemy aircraft and anti-aircraft fire . . .

Endorsement—addressed to Commanding General, 5th Air Force

Subject personnel were part of cited bombing mission—to attempt to intercept enemy radio telephone communications. Additional radio equipment was installed in plane number 976 and subject personnel monitored very high frequencies with the hope of hearing enemy fighter and anti-aircraft control stations. Personnel were to intercept, translate and relay information to pilot and flight leader. Enlisted man was a voice interceptor and officer mentioned was a qualified radio technician. Duties had to be performed during actual strike and within VHF radio wave propagation range.

This was the first attempt in the theater of airborne radio interception. Four other flights of similar nature followed with personnel of 1st Radio Squadron Mobile participating. Plan was subsequently dropped for reasons not pertinent to above subject.

During discussions in early 2000, Oshiki could not recall intercepting any Japanese voice communications during his missions. The tone of the 1st RSM letter and endorsements ("attempt to" intercept without mention of positive results) suggests that the 1st RSM airborne recon missions may have been discontinued due to lack of success. The statement about Oshiki's being the "first attempt in the theater of airborne radio interception" is probably incorrect; as we have seen, nisei Japanese linguists from the 8th RSM commenced flying airborne voice intercept missions from Guam at approximately the same time and continued such missions with positive intercept results until the last day of the war. In any event, the Army Air Corps's use of airborne voice intercept operators ended in August 1945. Five years later, the U.S. Air Force Security Service faced new signals intelligence collection requirements that the command could not solve at ground-based intercept sites.

Air Force Security Service Gets Wings

Understanding the significance of airborne reconnaissance, Security Service managers began looking for ways to get signals intelligence intercept operators aboard reconnaissance missions in the early 1950s. The 1st Radio Squadron Mobile unit history for January–March 1951 says:

> The matter of airborne COMINT intercept has been kicked around by many people for a long period of time. Air Force Security Service sent a wire about the middle of March that suggested we try to get one position installed on the aircraft used by the 91st Strategic Reconnaissance Sqdn. This possibility was investigated and found unfeasible. However, the problem of procuring an aircraft was presented to Generals Banfill, Crabb, Craigie and Stratemeyer, Headquarters, Far East Air Forces by Captain Tisdale, and they immediately bought the idea. A request was drafted by General Banfill and signed by General Stratemeyer for two C-54 type aircraft for this purpose.
>
> As an interim measure, they authorized the modification and use of one C-46 to be under the operational control of the 1st Radio Squadron Mobile. Modification is now underway, and the aircraft should be available for operational flights by the end of April.
>
> As usual, this project has the effect of "spreading ourselves thin" as does every other project at its outset. No additional people or equipment are available . . . Previous attempts at airborne COMINT met with little success, but it is hoped that this effort will prove more fruitful.

Being "spread too thin" and the immediate needs of the Korean War apparently killed these initial attempts, but eventually USAFSS (Captain Tisdale) did manage to arrange to install a voice intercept position on some 91st Strategic Recon Squadron electronic reconnaissance bombers. In late 1951, S.Sgt. Donald G. Hill, one of the four Russian linguists assigned to the 1st RSM, became the first Security Service intercept operator to fly recon missions—aboard 91st SRS ELINT recon aircraft. The following year, Hill flew missions aboard the Security Service prototype airborne communications intelligence recon platform—RB-29A 44-62290.

RB-29A 44-62290—First USAFSS Recon Aircraft

On September 15, 1945, the U.S. War Department reorganized the army's cryptologic (signals intelligence) organizations, combining the Army Signal Security Agency and the army's cryptanalytic field units to form the Army Security Agency. The new agency reactivated the 8th Radio Squadron Mobile, and when the U.S. Air Force Security Service was created in 1948, the 8th RSM was transferred to USAFSS control and relocated from Vint Hill Farms, Virginia, to Brooks AFB, Texas. The new Air Force mission of the 8th Radio Squadron Mobile was to train airmen in communications intelligence operations, a legacy mission similar to the squadron's mission at Camp Pinedale, California in 1943–44.

Graduating from Trimble High School in west Tennessee in 1949, Felix C. Shoffner Jr. wanted to be a pilot in the U.S. Air Force, to join the Air Force and see the world. He had already acquired his commercial pilot's license and had had his fill of the Shoffner cotton fields in Trimble. His local Air Force recruiter sold Felix on a three-year enlistment: "During your first operational assignment after basic training, you can apply for Aviation Cadets and become an Air Force pilot." When Felix graduated from Morse radio operator school at Keesler AFB, Mississippi, in May 1950, the Air Force paid him three cents per mile to travel by privately owned vehicle to his next assignment, with the 8th RSM—a unit Felix and fellow airmen at Keesler had never heard of. That was his introduction and welcome to the U.S. Air Force Security Service.

Morse intercept operator training in the 8th RSM was cut short by the outbreak of the Korean War. Per orders dated June 30, 1950, Private First Class Felix Shoffner was directed to report to the 1st Radio Squadron Mobile (USAFSS), Johnson Air Base, near Tokyo, Japan. For a nineteen-year-old Tennessee plowboy, chasing "dots" and "dashes" as a Morse intercept operator for USAFSS was not as exciting as flying, but Felix was certainly seeing the world.

Meanwhile, in October 1950, Fred Smith, having served in the Army Air Force during World War II, was thriving in his electrical engineering studies at the University of Texas. It was a shock, to say the least, when he received notification of recall to active duty in the Air Force: "Report to Headquarters USAFSS, Brooks AFB, Texas." The following month, noting Lieutenant Smith's engineering background, Colonel Travis (Tex) Hetherington, USAFSS commander, said, "Welcome aboard," and handed the lieutenant a folder labeled AIRBORNE OPERATIONS. Inside the folder, Smith found just two pieces of paper: a staff study showing the theoretical feasibility of performing a USAFSS intercept mission from an airborne platform, and a letter directing him to make it happen. After creating a specification of sorts and basic engineering drawings, Smith studied the characteristics and availability of various aircraft, made a few scientific WAGs (wild-ass guesses), and asked Headquarters Air Force for four B-50 bombers. Headquarters, in typical military fashion, responded, "We'll give you one old B-29 out of the bone yard, and if you make the airborne reconnaissance operations work, then we'll consider the B-50s." Thus was born in 1950 the program to develop Security Service's airborne communications intelligence reconnaissance platform (ACRP).[54]

The worn-out B-29 Super Flying Fortress, tail number 44-62290, was found in "mothballs" at Davis-Monthan AFB, Arizona. Two complete flight crews (four pilots, two navigators, two flight engineers, and two aircraft radio operators) were assigned to Air Force Security Service's airborne reconnaissance prototype development project. As the ranking member of the flight crews, Major Paul H. V. Swanson served as the officer in charge of the project.[55]

Major Swanson, a former B-26 pilot in World War II who had recently been recalled to active duty, performed double duty, serving as both aircraft commander and project officer for Project 502-50, the name assigned to the program. In 1958, Major Swanson would be the 7406th Support Squadron commander when the Soviets shot down C-130 60528. Two other USAFSS officers, Captain Morris O. Beck and Lieutenant Smith, served as operations staff officer and project systems engineer. Richard N. McKenzie, a USAFSS radio maintenance technician, became the project's airborne maintenance technician. In October 1951, Headquarters USAFSS handpicked six 1st RSM Morse intercept operators to be USAFSS's first airborne intercept operators: T.Sgt. Robert J. Jones; S.Sgts. Jay A. Botschen, Claude B. Fisher, George W. Rubel; and Airmen First Class Harold J. Hess and Felix C. Shoffner Jr. As his recruiter had promised, Felix Shoffner was going to fly—but not as a pilot.

Starting with the outdated World War II B-29, the USAFSS team turned an area on the flight line at Kelly Field (now Kelly AFB, Texas) into a repair depot—inspecting and replacing parts on the B-29 as needed, and adding the necessary intercept equipment to transform it into RB-29A number "Two-Niner-Nothing," as the aircraft radio operator identified the plane in radio comms. The intercept equipment for five operator positions—essentially jury-rigged receivers and MC-88 typewriters borrowed from the 8th RSM at Brooks AFB, as well as a couple of surplus World War II radar receivers and scopes—were housed in the aft pressurized compartment, which was connected to the cockpit area by a tunnel. Some called the tunnel the "pickle barrel"; the intercept operators considered it a cavern. Thus they were "bats" flying around the cavern—Technical Sergeant Jones, the lead intercept operator, was "Bat One," operator number two was "Bat Two," etc. And so was born the "nom de guerre" for USAFSS airborne intercept operator positions on 44-62290 and other airborne communications intelligence reconnaissance aircraft assigned later to Yokota Air Base, Japan. With several intercept antennas protruding from the fuselage, Two-Niner-Nothing took on the looks of a menacing warrior.

Major Swanson and his men quickly developed the close-knit rapport of a seasoned combat crew. Sergeants Botschen and Shoffner served as scanners, monitoring the aircraft engines through blister windows adjacent to their intercept positions, in addition to searching for and copying targeted Morse signals. Prior to deploying to Eglin AFB in April for mission training, the crew completed mandatory "physiological training"—at that time, not much more than a few turns in a high altitude chamber—at Randolph AFB in March. By flying a few operational training missions from Eglin, they got the kinks out of their equipment and fine-tuned their procedures in preparation for USAFSS's first operational airborne communications intelligence reconnaissance mission.

Getting pretty good at spotting oil leaks streaming from laboring engines, and becoming familiar with airborne reconnaissance, Felix Shoffner had enjoyed his Air Force career, but looked forward to discharge and college. His discharge plans were interrupted when President Truman extended his enlistment (and the enlistments of thousands of others) by executive order in June 1952.[56] Later, on June 20, 1952, Major

Swanson and 290's crew deployed on temporary duty (TDY) for seventy-five days to the 91st Strategic Recon Squadron, Yokota AB, Japan, on Project 502-50, Phase II. A third navigator accompanied the crew from Eglin to Travis Air Force Base, California, where, after claiming a fear of flying, he left the crew and returned to USAFSS Headquarters, San Antonio, Texas—by train. Major Bozarth and Lieutenant Benaquis would navigate without a backup on all missions.

Staging from Yokota, they flew operational missions over the Sea of Japan along the Soviet Far East periphery and in the combat zones over Korea. On the missions over the Sea of Japan, S.Sgt. Donald G. Hill and A/1C Jimmie L. Justice, Russian linguists assigned to the 1st RSM, complemented the basic crew, monitoring Soviet voice communications from Vladivostok and other coastal areas. Later, on July 29, 1953, Staff Sergeant Hill and A/2C Earl W. Radlein Jr., would be part of an RB-50 crew of the 91st Strategic Reconnaissance Squadron that the Soviets shot down over the Sea of Japan—becoming the first USAFSS men killed in the line of duty.

With an extra fuel tank installed in the forward bomb bay, long eighteen-to-twenty-hour missions were the norm. The men worked hard and played just as hard. When not flying missions, they relaxed on rest and recuperation visits to the U.S. Army Nikko Rest Area, Fuji, Yokohoma, or to Tokyo. Many referred to the R&R duty as I&I (intercourse and intoxication). In some ways, navigating drunkenly around Japanese binjo ditches—open sewers—in the dark alleys of Tokyo was as exciting as their combat missions.

On August 25, Major Swanson and crew checked out of the 91st Strategic Reconnaissance Squadron on a continuation of their extended overseas temporary duty assignment. They flew a mission along the Kurile Island chain en route to the island of Shemya, Alaska. On Shemya, the crew spent some downtime repairing one of the aircraft's long-wire antennas and continued on to a twenty-day deployment at Elmendorf AFB, Alaska. Hill and Justice flew along on the Elmendorf stay to cover Soviet voice targets on their missions in the Alaska area. S.Sgt. Ralph L. Pittenger, a 1st RSM Morse operator, also participated in the airborne recon missions in the Alaskan area. Their plan called for a series of local missions from Alaska to determine airborne intercept effectiveness against Soviet targets on the Kamchatka peninsula and in the Soviet arctic area adjacent to Alaska. After a couple of missions the inevitable happened: one of their engines broke down. An entire replacement engine had to be requisitioned from Eielson AFB, Alaska; maintenance support and spare parts were difficult to come by at Elmendorf.

Stuck in backwoods Alaska for three weeks, with no payday and no women in sight, there was not much for the men to do. Attached to the Security Service 3d Radio Squadron Mobile at Elmendorf, the crew spent more ramp time awaiting a replacement engine and spare parts than they did flying. Bored, broke, and craving a drink, Shoffner hit upon the idea of "borrowing" a bottle of Lieutenant Benaquis's private champagne cache. In a cubbyhole aboard the aircraft, Benaquis had hidden several cases of premium champagne purchased at giveaway prices from the Class VI liquor store at Yokota, and Shoffner figured he'd never miss a bottle. Besides, the lieutenant had already lost a couple of bottles from popped corks due to pressurization differential during a steep climb to avoid thunderstorms, so Shoffner assumed Benaquis wouldn't know precisely how many bottles remained.

Unfortunately, the first bottle led to another, and another, and another. . . . By the next morning, when the crew departed Elmendorf for Minneapolis en route to Kelly Field, the guys had pretty much wiped out Benaquis's special champagne supply. He was not pleased—the enlisted troops had to call him "sir" all the way home.

On their way back to Texas, a typical military "mishap" occurred. Approaching Minneapolis, where Major Swanson happened to have relatives, an engine acted up, and they had to lay over in Minneapolis while it was checked out before they continued on home to San Antonio.

While departing Minneapolis a couple of days later, the crew accidentally popped a life raft located in an external compartment in the left wing and had to circle the airport and land to retrieve the raft, which contained morphine in first aid kits and a survival rifle with ammo. After that they had an uneventful flight to San Antonio, arriving back at Kelly Field none the worse for their three-month odyssey. They'd worked hard and proved that performance of the USAFSS communications intelligence collection mission aboard an airborne platform was not only feasible, but highly valuable.

Each air crew member was awarded an Air Medal for meritorious achievement between June 14 and August 25, 1952. One citation read in part:

> During that period, despite the imminence of enemy attack, hazardous operational requirements, and long distances flown over water, Sergeant SHOFFNER demonstrated exceptional professional ability in performing his duty. He was instrumental in obtaining intelligence material of great value to the successful prosecution of the Korean campaign.

Those were the first Air Medals awarded to USAFSS aircrew members. So far, so good. After IRAN (inspection and replacement as necessary) at their depot at Kelly Field, the crew would fly RB-29 290 to Europe to evaluate USAFSS airborne recon operations in the denser European airspace.

By then Staff Sergeants Harold Hess and Felix Shoffner (promotions were easier in those days) had completed their overseas assignments with the 1st RSM and were reassigned to the 6923rd Personnel Processing Squadron (USAFSS), Brooks AFB, for eventual discharge. Unable to qualify by that time for Aviation Cadet training without a college degree (the requirements had changed), Shoffner was discharged. After graduating from the University of Tennessee, he again visited his local Air Force recruiter. Determining that Shoffner had married, the recruiter gave him the sad news: "Aviation Cadets can no longer be married." Undeterred, Shoffner reenlisted, eventually completing a twenty-year Air Force career as an airborne radio operator on transports and search and rescue aircraft—he might not have been a pilot, but he flew. After retiring from the Air Force, he completed a second flying career as a corporate pilot.

In November 1952, Major Swanson and his crew deployed from Brooks AFB (USAFSS Headquarters) back to Eglin AFB to participate in Project 502-50, Phase III—reconnaissance in the European theater. Having attended scanning school at Randolph AFB, S.Sgt. George Rubel replaced Shoffner as the scanner/intercept operator for the European deployment.

On November 28 the crew continued from Eglin to Wiesbaden Air Base, Germany. Only three intercept operators, T.Sgt. Robert Jones and Staff Sergeants Rubel and Jay Botschen, accompanied the recon platform to Europe—USAFSS would augment the intercept operators with linguists, a maintenance technician, and another Morse operator assigned to USAFSS ground sites in Europe. The augmentee intercept operators included: S.Sgts. John A. Dailey, Floyd L. Foltz Jr., Henry P. "Hank" Stacewicz; Airmen First Class Phillip E. Eckel, Donald H. Riedmiller, Humberto J. Pieroni, and Thomas E. Shipp; plus A/1C Conrad D. Chenault, a maintenance technician. These were the first USAFSS airborne recon crew members in Europe

RB-29 290's crew remained in Europe six months. Operating from Wiesbaden Air Base, RAF Lakenheath, England, and Wheelus Air Base, Libya, they flew missions against Soviet targets in the Baltic Sea area, along the East European satellite border, and in the Black Sea area. Then, leaving the borrowed European intercept operators in Germany, Major Swanson flew 290 and its crew back to Kelly AFB in June 1953. Despite having been kicked out of Wiesbaden early because Major Swanson would not compromise security and brief the Headquarters USAFE staff on his aircrew's purpose and mission in Europe, the deployment was a resounding success. During the missions, the crew collected unique intelligence data identifying Soviet and East European satellite targets that the West had not previously observed. Lt. Fred Smith and the USAFSS Headquarters airborne operations staff would use results from those missions to sell the concept of a fleet of RB-50 recon aircraft to the Headquarters USAF air staff and to the newly created National Security Agency.

Over the next several months, Captain Beck, Lieutenant Smith, and the Headquarters USAFSS airborne operations staff created a master plan for deploying a fleet of RB-50 recon aircraft. They briefed their plan at Headquarters USAF and the National Security Agency, receiving especially high marks at NSA for intelligence that had been collected aboard RB-29 290 over Korea, in the Far East, and in Europe. NSA controlled the cryptologic budget that would fund the airborne platforms. In the end, a budget was approved for ten RB-50s—five each for Europe and the Far East. The USAFSS and NSA would jointly control operational mission tasking for these new aircraft.

Under Air Force Project 502-50, USAFSS had created a much needed aerial communications intelligence reconnaissance platform. RB-29A 290 was an ACRP that could gather intelligence from remote areas that were otherwise inaccessible to NSA's conventional ground-based intercept sites.

But the USAFSS specialized in intelligence; its men did not operate aircraft. Providing cockpit crews, maintaining the aircraft, and operating an ACRP fleet was a job for a traditional Air Force line organization. In an arrangement that would later prove tragically complicated, USAFSS would have responsibility for the intelligence part of the mission only (that is, for the recon crews and recon equipment paid for by the crypto-logic budget); the aircraft and cockpit crews would be assigned to a new support squadron at Rhein-Main Air Base, Germany, under operational control of Headquarters U.S. Air Forces, Europe, or to the 6091st Strategic Reconnaissance Squadron (Far East Air Forces), Yokota AB, Japan.

In December 1955 the Air Force awarded a contract to the TEMCO Aircraft Corp., Majors Field, Greenville, Texas, to modify one government-furnished B-50 for the newly defined airborne COMINT reconnaissance mission. Later, the initial contract was amended to provide for the con-version of, in all, ten B-50s to a recon configuration under the Air Force "Big Five" project. In the interim, while the B-50s were being trans-formed into special reconnaissance configurations, RB-29A 290 was to be permanently assigned to the 6091st Strategic Reconnaissance Squadron at Yokota AB, where it would serve as the nucleus of the new USAFSS airborne recon operation in the Far East.

By October 1953, USAFSS had run RB-29 290 through the IRAN process (inspecting and replacing as necessary) to bring the prototype air-borne communications intelligence platform up to the latest Air Force standards. The recon equipment housed in the aft compartment was up-dated, while keeping the basic design of five intercept operator positions. Though the aircraft was originally conceived and equipped as a Morse intercept platform, the shakedown missions in Korea, the Far East, and

Europe had demonstrated an urgent need to increase the platform's VHF (very high frequency) voice intercept capabilities—the single VHF intercept receiver in the original 290 recon suite was inadequate to cover the new Soviet VHF-equipped MiGs then being deployed.

Senior voice intercept operators—S.Sgt. Donald Hill in the Far East and S.Sgt. Hank Stacewicz, et al., in Europe—demonstrated that the real intercept mission for an ACRP was voice communications, not Morse code. Newly deployed Soviet MiG pilots communicated with their ground controllers using voice, rather than Morse code, on four-channel (R-800) VHF radios. The major selling point of 290 was that an airborne communications intelligence reconnaissance platform could intercept VHF voice communications that were well beyond the range of most USAFSS ground sites. Retaining limited HF Morse intercept capabilities but dispensing with the clumsy typewriters, combination HF/VHF intercept receivers were integrated into each intercept operator position. Voice intercept operators would "hand-scan" intercepted data on pads of paper laid out in three columns titled: TO, FROM, and TEXT. RB-29A 44-62290 was once again ready to go, leaky engines and all.

Completing his overseas assignment with the 1st RSM at Johnson Air Base, Japan, after spending much of his three-year tour on temporary duty supporting Project 502-50, Staff Sergeant Rubel was assigned to the then newly activated 6960th Headquarters Support Group, located next to USAFSS Headquarters, Kelly Field, San Antonio, Texas—USAFSS had recently moved its headquarters into a brand new facility (Building 2000) on "Security Hill," a newly developed area on the southwest corner of Kelly Field. As one of USAFSS's original six airborne intercept operators, Rubel was selected as the airborne operations expert who would deploy with RB-29 290 once again, and train USAFSS's cadre of new airborne intercept operators at Yokota AB, Japan.

In October 1953, George Rubel was designated a flight scanner with the USAFSS Flight Section; the following month, he was sent with Capt. Herbert Fielding, 1st Lt. Faran A. R. McClimans, and M.Sgt. Benjamin Faulkner to Randolph AFB for forty-five days of four-engine transitional training. For two years they had flown as an integrated USAFSS crew on RB-29A 44-62290 in Korea, the Far East, and Europe, and after all that, the Air Force had suddenly decided it was time to train them!

Some things never change—if the capability is not documented on your AF Form 7, you are not qualified.

Later, in January 1954, that crew, supplemented by Major Swanson, 1st Lt. Fred Smith, 2d Lts. Thomas C. Amick and Edward W. Ryan (navigators), S.Sgt. Roger C. Buley (aircraft radio operator), and three supporting airmen (all assigned to USAFSS units at Security Hill), flew RB-29A 44-62290 on a training flight to Ramey AFB, Puerto Rico. During that three-day TDY trip, the crew had a chance to "shakedown" 290's equipment after it emerged from IRAN maintenance as a preparatory step toward declaring 290 a mission-ready reconnaissance platform. At the same time, Major Swanson passed along last-minute advice to his crew, and reported to USAFSS commander, Maj. General Roy H. Lynn, that RB-29A 44-62290 and its crew were ready to perform as a mobile USAFSS intercept station.

On March 8, 1954, Captain Fielding and his USAFSS crew flew 290 from Kelly AFB to Travis AFB, California, and from there to the 91st Strategic Reconnaissance Squadron, Headquarters FEAF, Yokota AB, Japan, for six months. Their mission was to deliver RB-29A 44-62290 to the 91st SRS and train Yokota-based cockpit and recon crews to fly operational aerial recon missions aboard the plane. The crew was to return to Kelly AFB when it had completed the mission; however, 290 would remain with the 91st SRS.

USAFSS Headquarters gave 6920th Security Group, recently activated at Johnson AB, Japan, responsibility for USAFSS airborne recon operations from Yokota AB. Maj. James (Jim) Brady, 6920th SG operations officer, and Capt. Robert O. Brooks, his assistant, created the operations concept and supervised the start-up of USAFSS operations at Yokota.

On March 24, 1954, the 6920th Security Group sent eleven airmen on temporary duty to the 91st SRS at Yokota AB for ninety days "for the purpose of accomplishing a classified mission in connection with this headquarters." Those eleven airmen—S.Sgts. John W. Fitzpatrick and Dale S. Williams; Airmen First Class John P. Corryn, Leo J. Sloan, Konstantinos Conto; and six Airmen Second Class: Richard M Hain, Theodorus J. Trias, Frederick C. Jacobites, Richard H. Davis, Henry M. Taylor, and Wilber O. Bell—formed the nucleus of the first USAFSS flying contingent at Yokota Air Base. Ten of the airmen were linguists—mostly Russian voice intercept operators. Conto was a Chinese linguist, and Corryn was an electronics maintenance technician.

Two of the airmen, Corryn and Hain, would spend many years of their twenty-plus-year Air Force careers flying USAFSS recon missions from Yokota AB. Two others, Sloan and Theodorus Trias—both Russian linguists—would lose their lives on September 10, 1956, aboard an RB-50 over the Sea of Japan when the plane disappeared on its first operational mission.

During initial operational orientation flights on RB-29 290, Captain Fielding and his USAFSS flight crew performed cockpit duties and introduced the Yokota-based USAFSS recon crewmen to onboard equipment and flying operations. In addition to his scanner duties (monitoring the engines for oil leaks, etc.), Sergeant Rubel taught the intercept operators how to don their parachutes, power up their equipment, and search for and record targeted signals. Demonstrating a weakness that would dog the USAFSS aerial recon squadrons for years, the linguists were on their own insofar as the military terminology of the target language was concerned; Sergeant Rubel only spoke English (and that with a southern drawl) and a half-dozen words of Japanese he'd learned from the girls on the Ginza in Tokyo.

Although not totally unexpected, the first operational training mission was pretty much a disaster for the USAFSS recon crew. Setting a tradition that would prove prophetic of what to expect with delivery of new recon aircraft from the depot, the operators identified several latent hardware problems. The acceptance tests performed by engineers who installed the equipment at TEMCO in Texas, while thorough, did not catch all the problems that could conceivably be encountered in the various equipment configurations in the field, not to mention that it could not anticipate exactly how the prolonged in-flight vibration might loosen equipment cabling.

On the first mission, Sergeant Rubel needed to be everywhere at once—performing his "scanning" duties and training the intercept operators. As always, scanning the engines through the blister windows on the left and right sides of the fuselage was a constant requirement, and he'd be training intercept operators who manned the positions by the windows to look for engine problems. At the same time, he showed the operators how to turn on their equipment. Some of the receivers and recorders did not seem to be working properly; Perry Hain figured out how to turn on his receivers, but for some reason did not seem to have any signal input to the receiver. Airman Corryn got his indoctrination as an airborne maintenance technician on that first flight. He determined that Hain's VHF antenna connection to the receiver was bad; it had apparently been vibrated loose during the trip to Japan.

However, despite the problems, during the mission each linguist recorded at least a few minutes of voice signals, more to practice using the equipment than for its intelligence value, since the flight crew had not ventured far from Yokota. On the ground after landing they'd play back the tapes they had recorded, to type a transcript on six-ply paper of recorded conversations of interest. Noting that overall the first mission had gone pretty smoothly for the flight crew, Captain Fielding while en route back to base checked in with A/1C Ron Belky on the aircraft interphone. Belky, the tail gunner, was the only non-USAFSS crew member on the mission. Other than being cold in the tail gunner area—a systemic problem that would keep a series of tail gunners' teeth chattering throughout the era of the B-50s—Belky was fine; he had seen no MiGs during the mission.

Truth be known, Belky had never fired a .50 caliber tail gun in anger, but he did look forward to getting off a few rounds at the end of missions. In the airborne communications intelligence reconnaissance platform specification that USAFSS had developed, there was no mention of weapons for self-defense. The CONOP (concept of operation) called for overt USAFSS aerial recon missions only over international (presumably friendly) territory. Violating international borders by flying into denied air space was strictly prohibited. However, the twin .50 caliber machine guns remained intact in the tail gunner's nest on RB-29A 290, a carry-over from the armed photo intelligence and electronic intelligence recon RB-29s that sometimes flew provocative covert missions—some of which skirted enemy airspace—and had fired on attacking enemy fighters in self-defense.

But to a MiG pilot, all B-29s looked alike, all carried menacing .50 caliber tail guns, and were the enemy—period. If RB-29 290 was attacked, tail gunner Belky would have to return fire, so he was allowed to maintain some claim to proficiency by periodically firing the tail guns over water en route home. Since he had no target to aim at, the chances that he could defend the plane effectively were slim, but regulations were regulations. The plane was a B-29, and B-29s carried tail guns, and gunners to fire them.

Arriving back at Yokota, Hain and the other young operators were anxious to listen to some of the tapes they had recorded during the mission. On the ground they'd have more time to figure out what was being said on the tapes—unlike in real time, in playback mode they could stop and start their recorders at will and, through use of a foot pedal, replay tape segments if necessary to make sense of difficult transmissions. Playing back their tapes, they were surprised. On the track that was supposed to contain the recorded signal, they found nothing except operator comments, primarily "time hacks"—operators used their interphone microphones to record time announcements on the tape between target transmissions. Time hacks were useless without the transmissions they were supposedly timing.

Corryn, the maintenance man, had his greatest challenge of the day—figure out why none of the five operators' recorders on the aircraft had captured the signals the operators thought they had recorded. It was doubtful that all five operators had simply screwed up somehow—was it an "operator malfunction" or an equipment malfunction? After hours of testing, Corryn discovered that someone had inadvertently misrouted the time code signal cable within the recon compartment—instead of recording a target signal on the recorder's channel one, and the time code and operator comments on channel two, the recorders recorded the time code signal on both channels, and target signals were not recorded at all. Rerouting the cable to the proper connection solved the problem.

Training progressed very well over the summer. During one thirty-day period in mid-1954, Captain Fielding's crew earned special, though intentionally vague, recognition. A group photograph of the aircrew and ground crew together with a news article in the Yokota AB newspaper noted:

An RB-29 of the 91st Strategic Recon Squadron has turned in a recent remarkable achievement. This aircraft, with Capt. Herbert Fielding as its commander, flew 106 hours over a one-month period. The missions were of a variety of reconnaissance types.

The article noted that the 91st had recently observed its thirty-seventh anniversary, having participated in World War I, World War II, and the Korean War as a combat photographic unit in all three conflicts. Though neither USAFSS nor RB-29 290 and its stealthy mission were mentioned, the article went in the "kudos" file in the airborne operations section at USAFSS Headquarters, San Antonio.

The kudo file would grow throughout the Cold War as USAFSS "Silent Warriors" flying aboard aircraft of other Air Force commands earned many well-deserved outstanding unit awards and "Travis Trophy" awards—at the time, the Travis Trophy was awarded annually by the NSA to the U.S. cryptologic unit with the most significant intelligence contributions during the year. Although the far more numerous USAFSS ground sites, Navy Security Group (NSG) units, and Army Security Agency (ASA) units also competed for the Travis Trophy, one or another of the USAFSS airborne units won the trophy frequently during the Cold War. Later, as a means of leveling the field for the competition, the Travis Trophy became an award for ground sites only, and the Director of the National Security Agency created the Director's Trophy for mobile platforms.

Their training tasks accomplished, on September 5, 1954, Captain Fielding and his USAFSS crew departed Japan from Tachikawa Air Base, bound for home in San Antonio, Texas. They left RB-29A 44-62290 with the 91st Strategic Reconnaissance Squadron and traveled home via a Military Air Transport Service aircraft.

Several years later Sergeant Rubel would be part of the 6911th Radio Group Mobile, Darmstadt, Germany, where he served as a Morse intercept operator, awaiting another opportunity to fly missions as a member of a USAFSS recon crew. That opportunity would come in 1958: he would be scheduled to fly on 528 the day it was shot down—missing that mission only because his Turkish visa didn't come through on time.

USAFSS crews assigned to Detachment 1, 6920th Security Group,

Yokota AB continued flying recon missions from Yokota aboard RB-29 290 for two more years. They flew recon missions along the periphery of China, Korea, and the Soviet Far East, in the same general mission areas initially exploited aboard 290 by Major Swanson and a different USAFSS crew in 1952. In the second half of 1956 a fleet of RB-50s was assigned to the 6091st Strategic Recon Squadron from the depot at Greenville, Texas, taking some of the flying workload off RB-29 290.

Transitioning to airborne operations aboard the RB-50s was not difficult since an RB-50 was a derivative of the original B-29, with more powerful engines and airborne recon equipment. The USAFSS electronics on RB-29 290 were jury-rigged equipment originally designed for ground site use, but the system engineers at TEMCO had had enough time to design a more rugged recon module for the RB-50, and some of the equipment was designed especially for use on the RB-50. The recon module consisted of five operator positions and one maintenance position.

The USAFSS plan to decommission RB-29 44-62290 when RB-50s were delivered to the 6091st was changed by the unfortunate loss of one of the new RB-50s on September 10, 1956, on a mission over the Sea of Japan. Short one RB-50, USAFSS decided to keep 290 in commission as long as maintenance crews deemed it airworthy. Finally, in May 1957, a ground mechanic while servicing 290 observed some corrosion that warranted more detailed examination. An inspection of the plane's surface skin identified corrosion damage so severe that the inspector could poke his fingers through the skin in some places. RB-29A 44-62290 had flown its last mission.

On May 9, 1957, the aircraft was decommissioned. Parked in an obscure area off the runway at Yokota AB, 290 served the Air Force in a new capacity. Yokota Air Base firemen practiced their fire fighting techniques, using the carcass of 290 as a simulated "crashed aircraft," where the firemen practiced putting out the postcrash fires and retrieving "injured airmen and charred bodies" from the crash site. Taxiing to the end of the runway for takeoff aboard an RB-50, Perry Hain and the other Detachment 1 airmen who had earned their wings on 290 always felt a twinge of nostalgia as they rolled past her charred hulk.

Project Blue Sky

The Blue Sky airborne communications intelligence reconnaissance platform evolved as a means of extending the intercept range of U.S. Air Force Security Service ground-based collection sites operating in Korea in 1952. USAFSS intelligence support was a major factor in helping the United Nations forces maintain air superiority during the Korean War. Charged with supporting Allied air forces, USAFSS put its 1st Radio Squadron Mobile on alert on June 27, 1950, and pulled students from the training pipeline for immediate reassignment to the 1st RSM, Johnson Air Base, Japan.

In November 1950 the 1st RSM sent a detached force (Detachment C, later redesignated Detachment 13)[57] to Pyongyang, North Korea, where the detachment began operations just behind the front lines. The detachment had barely set up operations at Sinanju, Korea, near the Chinese border, when the Chinese Peoples Liberation Army charged across the border. After just three days of intercept operations, the Detachment C team barely managed to pack up and scurry south ahead of hordes of attacking Chinese soldiers. The Chinese army chased the United Nations soldiers and the Detachment C intercept team southward to the Taegu area, where successful counterattacks forced the Chinese and North Korean forces to retreat. By mid-1951, Detachment 13 (formerly Detachment C) was settling into a more or less stable operating environment near Seoul, Korea. By January 1952, the 15th RSM's Detachment 1 was also operating in Korea, supplementing and ultimately replacing the 1st RSM detachment.

The 1st Radio Squadron's Detachment 13, and later Detachment 1, 15th RSM, played a major role in tilting the air war in favor of the United Nations allies. The detachment intercept operators kept the 5th Air Force apprised of enemy air operations—using intercepted air defense communications to forewarn U.S. crews of counter–air operations. American F-86 pilots were enjoying a thirteen-to-one kill ratio vis-à-vis MiG-15 pilots. The enemy was taking a beating offensively and defensively, and in need of countermeasures.

Discovering the New Signal Environment

Countermeasures arrived in August 1952 in the form of the new MiG-15bis aircraft variant that the Soviet Union introduced to combat over Korea. Replacing the early version of the MiG-15, which was equipped with an HF radio, pilots of the new MiGs communicated in a manner that the USAFSS operators could not intercept initially. Overnight—to Detachment 13's Korean, Russian, and Chinese intercept operators at Ewha University—it was as if the enemy fighter pilots were practicing radio silence. Unable to derive warning tip-offs from enemy communications, the air combat advantage evaporated for a time.

The enemy pilots had to be communicating with their controllers, but in what frequency spectrum? Neither USAFSS Headquarters nor the NSA had the answer. The Ewha detachment's existing intercept equipment covered the HF spectrum only (up to 30 megahertz). Air forces of the western world had used VHF radios for years, and were equipping newer aircraft with UHF radios, while the Soviets had steadfastly stayed with World War II HF technology. Was the new Soviet MiG-15 equipped with a VHF radio, a UHF, or both? The USAFSS detachment did not have the receivers and antennas to find out. Using jury-rigged receivers and antennas to cover both the VHF and UHF spectrums, Air Force Security Service operators discovered the answer. The Soviet air force had rotated a new fighter division into the war zone—the new division's pilots were flying the MiG-15bis variant equipped with an R-800 four-channel VHF radio.

Solving the VHF Intercept Problem

Like his contemporaries who had been mustered out of the Army Air Corps at the end of World War II, Maj. Leslie J. Bolstridge was recalled to active duty in February 1951 and assigned to Air Force Security Service. In late 1951 he was sent to the new 6920th Security Group in Japan to be the group communications-electronics officer. Major Bolstridge and Maj. Oakley Stockton of the 15th RSM cobbled together some VHF intercept equipment, replacing existing intercept receivers and antennas. The detachment at Ewha University (now Detachment 1, 15th RSM) could intercept signals from MiGs in an area within a hundred miles or so of its site—good, but not good enough. The MiGs did not typically venture that far south from their sanctuary in Manchuria.

Seeking a VHF intercept site closer to the battle lines, the 15th RSM opened an operating location (Detachment 2) on Cho Do (Cho Island), off the northwest coast of Korea—north of the line of battle. The site was protected by a British naval contingent of the U.N. forces. Detachment 2 remained on Cho Do until hostilities ceased in mid-1953, at which time Detachment 2 moved to Paeng Yang Do (P-Y Do)—an island to the south below the DMZ line. The Demilitarized Zone was established roughly along the final truce line.

P-Y Do was just south of and out of 37mm artillery range of another island occupied by the North Korean Army. Detachment 2 was collocated on P-Y Do with the U.S. Air Force 608th Air Control & Warning Squadron, whose radar stood on the tallest peak on the island. The Detachment 2 operations site was directly on line with the North Korean mainland, in front of the aircraft control and warning squadron's radar beam. Via a radio link between the radar station and Detachment 2, the USAFSS analysts had access to friendly radar tracking data—the intent being to track and alert friendly fighters on the fighter's daily "MiG Alley" recon sorties up the coast, off Pyongyang.

The 5th Air Force fighter sorties into MiG Alley typically operated on the northern fringe of the aircraft control and warning squadron's radar coverage, whereas Detachment 2 monitored the enemy's own radar operations much closer to the actual sortie tracks. This was, of course, the radar data upon which the enemy MiGs would react. Comparing the friendly versus enemy radar data, Detachment 2's analysts told the AC&W squadron flight commander where "others" thought a given sortie was located, and also advised where and when MiGs were airborne. These tip-offs by Air Force Security Service intelligence specialists in Korea to tactical Air Force users were the first noted use of signals intelligence for tactical direct support during the Cold War.

History credits the lopsided F-86 vs. MiG-15 dogfight kill ratio in Korea to the superior skills and experience of the American pilots; the fact that many of the U.S. Air Force pilots were seasoned World War II veterans was a definite factor, as was the better performance characteristics of the F-86. Nonetheless, the direct support in the form of forewarnings provided by detached Security Service team members at Ewha University, Cho Do, and later on P-Y Do, undoubtedly saved many lives and tilted the kill ratio further in favor of the American pilots.

Airborne Signals Reconnaissance in Korea

The Cho Do and P-Y Do sites were located literally along the front lines, and provided invaluable direct support to the U.N. forces. Yet their range of coverage fell short of the northernmost air combat zones of MiG Alley over northwestern North Korea, along the Yalu River border with Manchuria. Thus was born the requirement for an airborne communications intelligence reconnaissance platform in Korea. Flying over water along the North Korean coast, an ACRP would offer coverage of targets not otherwise available.

In late 1952, Major Bolstridge proposed to modify C-47 transport aircraft to perform the required airborne reconnaissance. Three airframes were made available and equipped with salvaged VHF receivers and wire recorders. The Far East Air Forces assigned the aircraft and flight crews to the 6053d Radio Flight Mobile, and Security Service members attached to Detachment 1, 6920th Security Group manned the airborne intercept positions. Evaluation missions exceeded all expectations.

Operating from Yokota, Japan, the C-47 crews would land at Kimpo Air Base to refuel, fly a mission along the west coast of North Korea, drop their recordings and mission logs in a parachute canister on the beach at Cho Do, refuel at Kimpo, and return to Yokota. In addition to the messages the Cho Do linguists intercepted, they processed and issued reports on materials from the C-47 missions. Later, instead of flying from Yokota, USAFSS linguists attached to Detachment 1, 15th RSM at Ewha University, would travel to Kimpo to board their C-47 missions. On occasion—typically when the aircrew had problems with their parachute canister device—a Blue Sky C-47 would land on the beach at Cho Do, drop off the data collected during the mission, and continue to Kimpo. These landings on the sandy beach at Cho Do aroused no unnecessary suspicions on the part of the North Koreans because other 5th Air Force C-47s made similar landings at Cho Do to deliver mail, food, and supplies. Following the armistice on July 27, 1953, Detachment 2 moved from Cho Do to Paeng Yang Do, and a similar operation continued there.

At first the plane's standard operating procedure had been to land on the beach and literally hand over the classified materials the operators had gathered. But landing and taking off on the beach at P-Y Do was somewhat tricky, especially at high tide and with crosswinds. The "landing strip" was a short expanse of beach on the south shore of the island, with hills at each end of the beach. And the takeoffs were always exciting. The pilot had to get wheels up and immediately bank to avoid a hill at either end of the beach. Because the Blue Sky crews detested landing on the sandy beaches of Cho Do and P-Y Do, a sergeant in the parachute shop at Yokota rigged a small canister and parachute system that could be thrown out the open aircraft door to a waiting ground crew. The ground crew marked the "drop zone" spot with a white bedsheet stretched across the top of a jeep racing along the beach.

Most parachuted packages were recovered intact, but accidents happened. On occasion, recordings were mangled on impact, and in other situations, the mission's intercepted data ended up landing in the sea. There were no security guards or fencing on the beach, and having adults and small kids from the refugee village at the end of the beach running on the beach to meet incoming C-47s for candy and cigarettes always added to the excitement.

At one point a Blue Sky C-47 crashed on takeoff from Yokota, destroying the aircraft. The FEAF commander, concerned at the one-third reduction of his mission capability, gave up his own VIP C-47 as a replacement and asked that it be reconfigured and put into service as soon as possible. Major Bolstridge assembled a Security Service electronic maintenance crew that had the aircraft mission ready in three or four days. The only receivers available in theater were World War II control tower VHF receivers requiring 115-volt, 60-cycle power, and the only potential power source they had was a Homelite ground power unit that produced 115-volt, 400-cycle power. In the shop, they plugged one of the receivers into the Homelite unit, and to their delight it worked just fine.

So a hole was cut in the side of the C-47 for the Homelite unit's exhaust pipe, and the new RC-47 was ready for a mission. Later, when the proper equipment arrived, they swapped out the jury-rigged equipment.

Blue Sky vs. BLUESKY

Though not the first airborne intercept program (Project 502-50/ RB-29A 44-62290 was the first), Project Blue Sky (two words vs. BLUESKY) had the first fully deployed fleet of airborne communications intelligence reconnaissance aircraft. Operationally, Project Blue Sky was a resounding success, but it raised some administrative hackles at the 6920th Security Group during a visit by the USAFSS inspector general. Setting his staff to work on the mundane inspections, the IG zeroed in on his personal interest—Project BLUESKY. Initially, the 6920th felt flattered because they were proud of the program and the important role it continued to play in the Korean War. However, the IG did not delve at all into the operational aspects; he was solely interested in the project's name. "Who," he asked, "named the project?" Major Brady responded, "The FEAF staff." Assured that the 6920th had not named the project, the IG informed them that they were illegally using a one-word code name (BLUESKY) that by definition was a classified term, instead of a two-word nickname (Blue Sky) that is unclassified. In good military fashion, the 6920th immediately had to turn its attention away from operational considerations and toward sifting through all their messages and letters to expunge the offending term. The inspector general was a happy man. Gotcha! Thus the nickname Blue Sky was born. In latter years the project would be known as "Rice Bowl."

Blue Sky Aircrews

A/2C Joseph L. Dean was one of the enlisted men who pioneered the use of the RC-47 intercept platforms. Upon completion of a six-month basic Russian language course at the Army Language School, Presidio of Monterey, California, in 1952, Dean was assigned to the 1st Radio Squadron Mobile, Johnson AB, Japan. He'd hardly unpacked his bags when he was notified that he was being sent to Korea.

Airman Dean arrived at the Ewha University site for his introduction to his new Air Force job as a "radio-telephone (voice) intercept operator." Having studied Russian at language school for six months, in classes with a strong emphasis on military terminology, he and his fellow students had frequently surmised what they were being trained for. Their language professors had, at least officially, not a clue, though they must have made some fairly accurate guesses—the professors were Russian immigrants who'd been hired by the army for their native-language abilities. The students believed during training that they'd probably be translating Russian (perhaps military) documents into English. But reasoned Joe Dean, "Why would the Air Force need a Russian linguist in Korea?"

Receiving a pair of headsets along with his bedding from the unit supply sergeant when he checked in was all the more baffling. The supply sergeant, shrugging his shoulders, advised Dean to take the headsets with him when he reported for work at operations. Only after Airman Dean was introduced to his new supervisor at the ops compound did he learn the significance of his training. Soviet advisers were covertly helping the Koreans and Chinese prosecute the war, and his job would be to monitor the Soviet advisers' communications and determine the extent and precise nature of their involvement. After a short stint with the detachment at Ewha University while learning a little Soviet air force terminology, Dean and a couple of others became the initial cadre of airborne voice intercept operators to start up Blue Sky airborne communications intelligence recon operations in Korea.

The Blue Sky RC-47 missions were an immediate success; Airman Dean and his three-man crew won the support of FEAF intelligence and planning staff by providing tactical intelligence data unavailable from any other source. Starting with three intercept positions, the collection suite was later upgraded to five positions manned by a combination of Russian, Chinese, and Korean linguists. FEAF delegated the scheduling of missions to Air Force Security Service, which meant that indirectly an airman second class, Joe Dean, was telling the 6053rd pilots when and where USAFSS wanted to fly. He'd travel from Ewha University to Kimpo Air Base, arriving in time for his mission. Then, after a mission, he'd rush back to Detachment 1 at Ewha, where he'd often work late into the night sending out reports on messages he'd intercepted during the mission, coordinating the next day's mission, and sometimes contacting his favorite captain at FEAF HQ to add a special mission the following day when no mission had been planned. It never dawned on Dean at the time that he was forging the way for USAFSS airborne communications intelligence recon operations on a worldwide basis.

With the armistice terminating hostilities in Korea signed on July 27, 1953, Airman Dean returned to Yokota for a few days of well-deserved R&R. While at Yokota, he shared a barracks with other Detachment 1, 6920th Security Group airmen. In addition to the linguists and mainte-nance technicians who flew on the Blue Sky C-47s, Detachment 1 pro-vided linguists for flights on photo and electronic intelligence recon missions aboard 91st Strategic Recon Squadron RB-29s and RB-50s.

On July 29, 1953, a mere two days after the "termination of hostili-ties," the Soviets shot down a 91st RB-50 mission over the Sea of Japan. S.Sgt. Donald Hill and A/2C Earl Radlein Jr. from Detachment 1, 6920th SG were among the missing crew members. Dean knew Hill and Radlein; in fact, Sergeant Hill had trained Dean to be an airborne operator on Blue Sky C-47 missions.[58] Hill and Radlein became the first USAFSS airmen killed in the line of duty.

Maj. George I. Mason assigned Dean the task of packing the belong-ings of Hill and Radlein for shipment to their next of kin. Major Mason took the loss of Hill and Radlein especially hard. He knew them person-ally and had supported Hill's efforts to care for children at a Korean or-phanage near Seoul. After a brief rest at Yokota, Airman Dean returned to his flying duties in Korea.

Before the armistice, the prevailing opinion was that the North Ko-reans would again invade South Korea in order to negotiate from a posi-tion of strength. For that reason, Detachment 1, 15th RSM at Ewha University, was ordered moved to a suitable site in the south. Major Bol-stridge surveyed possible sites and selected Osan Ni, on a 7,000-foot mesa not far from the existing Osan Air Base. The expected southward thrust of the North Koreans did not materialize; however, Air Force Security Service would have been forced to move from Ewha University later any-way, and by moving sooner, USAFSS got possession of a prime piece of real estate for its mission. The detachment moved to Osan Ni. (To this day, with no formal peace treaty in place between South and North Korea, a U.S. Air Force Air Intelligence Agency signals intelligence unit—the 303d Intelligence Squadron—remains in Korea monitoring enemy activities north of the Demilitarized zone along the 38th parallel.)

Eventually, the entire RC-47 Blue Sky fleet was upgraded, most notably with Clarke receivers borrowed from America's space program and new magnetic tape recorders. The Blue Sky RC-47 missions continued in Korea until 1966, when the aircraft were reconfigured for an airborne direction-finding mission and sent to Vietnam to support airborne radio direction-finding (ARDF) combat support operations in Southeast Asia during the Vietnam War.

FIVE

—

AIR FORCE RECONNAISSANCE IN EUROPE, 1950s

Events in Eastern Europe and East Asia in the early 1950s made it extremely important that the U.S. and its western allies find new methods to collect intelligence on Stalin's ever-expanding Soviet military forces. The Soviets did such a good job of shutting down the flow of information from behind their borders that U.S. Air Force commanders in Alaska in the early 1950s sent out "beach patrols" during the spring to recover debris washed ashore from Soviet ships that had visited Soviet Arctic ports across the Bering Sea from Alaska. Intelligence by garbage collection was bad enough, but the basic lack of information became even more acute when the Soviet Union began deploying aircraft equipped with VHF radios over Korea in 1952.

The USAFSS reequipped high frequency (HF) intercept sites with VHF radios and antennas, but most of its HF sites were not located close enough to enemy targets to monitor VHF communications. After quickly completed site surveys, USAFSS opened VHF-capable intercept sites, where political boundaries permitted, along the Iron Curtain in Europe and the Bamboo Curtain in the Far East. VHF sites were opened at Oku-Shiri Shima and Wakkanai in Japan; at Shu Lin Kou on Taiwan; on St. Lawrence and Shemya Islands, Alaska; at Sinop, Samsun, and Trabzon, Turkey; at Hof, West Germany, and within West Berlin.

Recognizing the need to fill in gaps in the coverage provided by ground sites, USAFSS used RB-29A 44-62290 to demonstrate the viability of the concept for an airborne communications intelligence reconnaissance platform (ACRP). The substantial success of 290 on exploratory recon missions in the Far East and in Europe in 1952–53 led to the creation of the Blue Sky RC-47s for Korea and a fleet of RB-50 recon aircraft, five RB-50s each for Europe and the Far East. As the RB-50 was one of several new recon platforms being provided to Headquarters, U.S. Air Forces, Europe (USAFE) in the mid-1950s, the USAFE commander assigned them to a newly activated squadron of the 7499th Support Group at Wiesbaden Air Base, Germany.

The 7499th was officially responsible for all tactical air force reconnaissance in Europe, but airborne communication intelligence (COMINT) reconnaissance was an entirely new undertaking, requiring special access security clearances not possessed at the time by 7499th personnel, and neither the 7499th nor USAFE would control the airborne COMINT recon missions. That function would be provided by the United States Air Force Security Service (USAFSS), a newcomer to airborne reconnaissance, under the direction of the National Security Agency. Security Service would not only provide the recon crews, it would control the operational mission of the RB-50 aircraft. An aircrew would consist of the flight crew ("front-enders") and the recon crew ("back-enders"). Assessing facilities to support the RB-50 aircraft and new mission, the 7499th selected nearby Rhein-Main Air Base, near Frankfurt am Main, Germany, to host the new reconnaissance operation. The Security Service would activate a unit at Rhein-Main to support airborne reconnaissance, and USAFE through the 7499th would bring the resources together at Rhein-Main to fly and maintain the fleet of soon-to-arrive RB-50s.

The Front-Enders

The 7499th was activated November 1, 1948, as the 7499th Air Force Squadron, a tactical recon unit located at Fürstenfeldbruck Air Base, Germany.[59] Originally staffed by personnel from the 45th Tactical Recon Squadron, it was redesignated the 7499th Composite Squadron in

1949, relocated to Wiesbaden AB in August 1950, and redesignated the 7499th Support Squadron in October 1954.

The 7499th Support Squadron was organized operationally as three flights—flights A, B, and F. Flight A's primary mission was electronic reconnaissance; its secondary mission was photo reconnaissance of the Soviet and Soviet European Satellite countries. Flight A operated under the direct supervision of the deputy chiefs of staff for intelligence and for operations at Headquarters, USAFE. Additional ELINT mission support was provided by U.S. Navy "Project Shore Line" aircraft from Port Lyautey, French Morocco.

During the early 1950s, Flight B's primary mission was photo reconnaissance. Flights A and B also hauled cargo and passengers—sometimes as actual secondary missions, but in many cases as a cover for their photographic missions.

Flight F, a ground unit, consisted of a photo intelligence section made up of photo interpreters and draftsmen, and a photo laboratory with film developers and photo processors. Flight F's mission was to process aerial film, make prints or transparencies, interpret photos, and write photo intelligence reports.

In March 1955, Colonel Walker, commander of the 7499th, was officially notified that "high priority projects were being formed in the Zone of Interior[60] and were programmed for assignment to the squadron upon their arrival in Europe." By that time, America was responding to the Soviet threat in Europe with increased aerial reconnaissance capabilities.

7499th Support Group

At a meeting at Headquarters USAFE, General Tunner revealed plans to reorganize and enlarge the 7499th; the 7499th Support Squadron would become the 7499th Support Group in charge of three support squadrons. One of the new squadrons, the 7405th, flying out of Wiesbaden, would absorb the original photo and electronic recon mission of the 7499th. Detachment 1, 7499th SS at Rhein-Main, would also be reassigned to the 7405th. The two new squadrons, the 7406th Support Squadron and 7407th Support Squadron, would be activated at Rhein-Main.

The 7406th would have project "Half Track" RB-50D aircraft to support a mission compiling automatic terrain recognition and navigation (ATRAN) data, and project "Dream Boat" RB-50G aircraft for collecting communications intelligence. The other squadron, the 7407th, would consist of RB-57 aircraft to support special photo recon missions. In addition, a detachment of the 7407th, Detachment 1, equipped with three RF-100A "Slick Chick" high performance tactical reconnaissance aircraft, would be based at Bitburg Air Base, Germany.

The reorganization occurred on May 10, 1955. Colonel Walker, former 7499th squadron commander, became group commander and selected Maj. Thomas G. A. Welsh, Capt. William P. Fisher, and Maj. Earl E. Helms as the first commanders for the 7405th, 7406th, and 7407th Support Squadrons, respectively. Col. Clifford J. Moore Jr., assumed command of the 7499th on October 14, 1955.

In January 1955 the 7499th's unit manning document authorized sixty-eight officers and 257 enlisted men to perform the squadron's reconnaissance mission. By December 31, 1959, personnel strength of the 7499th and its three squadrons had grown to 184 officers and 684 enlisted men.

During the transition period (March through May 1955), 7499th recon operations proceeded unabated while the staff carried out concurrent planning for the two new squadrons. On April 14, Colonel Walker dispatched Major Helms and Lieutenant Sensabaugh to Rhein-Main as the 7499th's project directors to prepare for activation of the 7406th and 7407th at Rhein-Main. The 7405th's and 7407th's histories are discussed in Appendix F.

7406th Support Squadron

Activation of the 7406th Support Squadron was a lengthy, drawn out process. The arrival of the 7406th's first aircraft was delayed on a week-to-week basis for seven months, contributing to the confusion brought about by the activation of a unit with a totally new, highly classified mission. Colonel Walker, 7499th commander, assigned Capt. William P. Fisher as the first commander of the 7406th when the squadron was activated on May 10, 1955.[61]

A temporary 7406th office was set up alongside the 7407th office in Quonset hut T-330 at Rhein-Main, and operations unofficially began. The office moved to building T-314 on June 17, 1955 when the first shipment of office equipment arrived. The 7406th Operations office was established in the Quonset hut area in building T-325, moving to a permanent home on the flight line in early 1956.

ATRAN—Automatic Terrain Recognition and Navigation

On May 31, 1955, the 7406th had one officer (Captain Fisher) and one enlisted man assigned, even though their authorized strength was thirty-five officers and sixty-six airmen. Lt. Col. George J. Byars replaced Fisher as 7406th commander on September 13, 1955. Earlier in June two aircrews (most of the squadron personnel) were on temporary duty at the Goodyear Aircraft Corp, Dayton, Ohio, to pick up, check out, and ferry the squadron's first two RB-50Ds to Rhein-Main. Goodyear was outfitting the B-50s with ATRAN (automatic terrain recognition and navigation) equipment. The nickname for these RB-50s was "Half Track."

Major Jesse C. DeHay was the pilot and aircraft commander for one of the 7406th crews—Crew 1.[62] Capt. James W. Kirkbride Jr. headed up Crew 2.[63] Over the next few months, additional airmen and officers arrived for duty in the new squadron.[64] Unit manning had increased to seventeen officers and seventy-one airmen, assigned by December 31, 1955. By December 31, 1956, manning stood at forty-one officers and 161 enlisted men assigned.[65]

During the first few months at Rhein-Main the 7406th was crammed into less than adequate quarters and facilities. The crowded barracks condition was overcome later in 1955 when the 60th Troop Carrier Wing transferred from Rhein-Main, freeing up a former World War II Luftwaffe barracks for enlisted quarters and a 7406th orderly room.

The squadron was divided into two flights—Flight A to fly the Half Track ATRAN missions, and Flight B to fly the Dream Boat airborne communications intelligence recon missions. In typically optimistic fashion, the 7406th expected to receive its two RB-50D Half Track aircraft in August 1955 and five RB-50G Dream Boat aircraft in March 1956. In reality, the first Half Track aircraft arrived on March 6, 1956, and the first Dream Boat RB-50G arrived in December 1956.

In late 1955 delays in getting the 7499th's new recon resources in place resulted in a staff visit back Stateside. While visiting offices in the Pentagon, the Air Material Command and Air Research and Development Command at Wright-Patterson AFB, and Goodyear Aircraft in Ohio, Maj. Melvin H. Andrews sought answers on a series of new airborne recon projects for the 7499th. On Dream Boat, Major Andrews learned that the number of RB-50G-2 aircraft had been reduced from five to two, with scheduled delivery about March 25 and April 25, 1956. And it had been decided that the RB-50Gs would not have aerial refueling capabilities because Security Service said it was not a requirement and because USAFE did not have tankers capable of refueling B-50s. The RB-50Gs would be equipped with radars with an expanded scope.

Based on Major Andrews' trip report, it is obvious that the plan to bring new airborne communications intelligence reconnaissance capabilities to Europe was still evolving in late 1955. The conflicting details regarding the buildup of recon resources for Europe shows the confusion that existed within the Air Force regarding various recon projects. The president's national security advisers were pressuring the Joint Chiefs of Staff for intelligence on the Soviet "bear" that was tormenting Europe, and everyone in the Air Force chain of command was jumping through hoops to make it happen—but not necessarily coordinating their leaps.

The 7406th's first aircraft,[66] a Half Track aircraft, finally arrived on March 6, 1956—seven months late. Pilot training began at Rhein-Main as soon as maintenance had performed an acceptance check.

The second Half Track, RB-50D,[67] arrived on April 3, 1956, after numerous and excessive maintenance delays. But it was in such poor condition that it was immediately cannibalized for parts to keep the other one in commission. The third Half Track[68] arrived on May 26, 1956, flown in from Goodyear by Major DeHay and a 7406th crew. On his arrival at Rhein-Main, DeHay was designated assistant operations officer and commander of Flight A, the flight to which the Half Track RB-50s were assigned. But because of the poor design of the mission and the poor performance of the worn aircraft, the Half Track mission was ended on October 19, 1956.

Meanwhile, in April 1956, Maj. Paul H. V. Swanson arrived on a permanent change of station from Air Force Security Service Headquarters and was assigned duties as the 7406th assistant operations officer and flight commander for Flight B, which would be receiving the Dream Boat communications intelligence RB-50s. On Air Force Project 502-50, Major Swanson had had a USAFSS security clearance and had flown RB-29A 290, the prototype airborne communications intelligence recon platform, on exploratory recon missions in the Far East and in Europe in 1952-53, qualifying him exceptionally well for his new role in the 7406th. However, because it was thought he would not have a "need to know" in his 7406th assignment, which was "merely" a support billet, USAFSS debriefed him (i.e., formally declared him ineligible for such data and formally prohibited him to discuss with anyone what he'd learned when "cleared") before he departed Texas. Thus he could no longer discuss operational mission issues with the USAFSS recon crews that would fly on his aircraft. In Security Service slang, Major Swanson had been "degaussed."

At a planning conference at Wright Air Development Center, Wright-Patterson AFB, Ohio, in October 1956, Swanson learned that some significant decisions had been made on the future of the airborne communications intelligence recon program: the ATRAN mission of the 7406th was cancelled, and the ATRAN-equipped Half Track RB-50Ds would be modified to perform airborne communications intelligence reconnaissance.

From the earliest days, the 7406th was plagued by problems of aircraft maintenance; keeping the RB-50s operational was a challenge because they required a very large number of engine changes. At one point shortly after the RB-50s arrived in 1956, just 245 flying hours had necessitated twenty-one cylinder changes, each change requiring six to nine hours.

Aside from the engine problems, the squadron suffered the growing pains frequently associated with any new flying unit—a general shortage of spare parts and proper ground equipment. The squadron also experienced a severe shortage of personal flying equipment (headphones for helmets, bailout bottles,[69] and oxygen mask microphones).

The maintenance problems severely hampered crew training, and maintenance itself suffered from the mechanics' inexperience. In one case, an apprentice disabled an RB-50 by attaching it to an external power unit with the wrong polarity—the resulting power surge fried several fuel valve motors and instruments.

Moreover, the perennial military modus operandi—"screw the mission; clean the position"—which was all too common in the Air Force, took its toll. The 7406th lost three flying days in December 1956 because the unit had to remove its aircraft from the flight line in order to make room for a farewell parade for U.S. Army General Gruenther, the retiring NATO commander. Adding insult to injury, the young men who would have preferred to have been flying had to shine their shoes, get a haircut, clean up the squadron, stand an inspection, and march in General Gruenther's parade.

Dream Boat

The earliest airborne communications reconnaissance platform (ACRP) project in Europe was an RB-50 that went by the unclassified nickname Dream Boat.[70] The project sponsored by the Air Force Security Service. The 7406th Support Squadron would maintain the ACRP aircraft and provide flight crews (front-enders), and USAFSS would provide reconnaissance crew members (back-enders) to conduct recon missions in Europe. As defined by the 7499th Support Group, the unclassified 7406th mission statement was to "assist in conducting the USAFE portion of the USAF worldwide study of Electromagnetic Wave Propagation." (That was the mission cover story; no one knew what the cover story was supposed to mean because the Air Force never provided the detailed "back story.")

In late October 1956, the task of converting four B-50s to the Dream Boat RB-50 configuration was added to the TEMCO contract under which a single Dream Boat RB-50E had been created. The contract was modified once more, in 1957, to convert five additional B-50s to the Dream Boat configuration. The contract now called for a total of five RB-50s for the 7406th Support Squadron at Rhein-Main AB, and five more for the 6091st Strategic Recon Squadron at Yokota Air Base, Japan.

On December 11, 1956, Major Swanson and a B-Flight crew ferried the 7406th Support Squadron's first Dream Boat RB-50G from the Greenville, Texas, depot to Rhein-Main Air Base, Germany. Decked out in flight suits, cowboy hats, and cowboy boots, Major Swanson and his crew[71] were photographed by their RB-50 on the flight line at Greenville before departing for Rhein-Main.

With the arrival of the first Dream Boat RB-50s in Europe, it seemed that everyone was rushing to get the airborne communications intelligence recon program off the ground. On December 13, 1956, Colonel Byars and Major Herrmann attended a general briefing on the Dream Boat mission at the 7499th Headquarters, and on December 27, Major Swanson described the new Dream Boat at a conference at Headquarters U.S. Air Forces, Europe—attended by key personnel from the 7499th and USAFE, as well as the back-ender "sailors." The 7406th also held several other informal meetings with USAFSS back-ender representatives to discuss Dream Boat operations.

In order to prevent revealing a relationship between themselves and the recon crews, which would be the operational reason for the 7406th's existence, USAFE, the 7499th, and the 7406th could not mention Security Service or USAFSS in public or in unclassified correspondence. So, for routine reference, the RB-50 airborne communications intelligence reconnaissance platform was a Dream Boat, and the Security Service recon crews were its "sailors."

Almost as soon as the first Dream Boat RB-50 arrived at Rhein-Main, both the 7406th and Detachment 1, 6911th Radio Group Mobile sailor maintenance technicians conducted acceptance tests to assure that the aircraft and its reconnaissance equipment suite were fully functional. Since no one in the 7406th had the required special access clearances, the flight crews could only guess at what the sailors would be doing in the back end of the aircraft. After a couple of shakedown transition flights, a crew flew the first Dream Boat mission on January 12, 1957. During the next forty days, combined 7406th and Detachment 1 aircrews flew an enviable 143 hours in their lone Dream Boat RB-50G—becoming the airborne communications intelligence reconnaissance "experts" in Europe.

On January 24, 1957, a 7406th crew headed by Capt. William E Stewart ferried one of the RB-50D ATRAN aircraft from Germany to

Tinker AFB, Oklahoma, for much needed phase maintenance[72] and then on to Majors Field, Greenville, Texas, where it would be converted into a Dream Boat RB-50D. After flight testing the second Dream Boat RB-50G that TEMCO had retrofitted with a communications intelligence recon equipment suite, Captain Stewart's crew ferried the RB-50G to Rhein-Main in mid-February. In late February a second crew returned to Texas aboard another weary ATRAN RB-50D to pick up the squadron's third Dream Boat aircraft and ferry it to Germany. Thus, by March 1957 the 7406th had three Dream Boat recon aircraft and one ATRAN RB-50D that was used for training purposes. Later in 1957 the 7406th acquired its fourth Dream Boat.

RB-50 to C-130A-II Transition

By mid-1957, as everyone was becoming comfortable around the RB-50, the squadron learned that the RB-50s were to be replaced in early 1958 with new C-130A-II Hercules recon aircraft. On December 27, 1957, Capt. James W. Kirkbride Jr. ferried an RB-50 from Rhein-Main to the Greenville, Texas, depot for phase maintenance. The end of the RB-50s era at Rhein-Main was approaching. Men with skills unique to the B-50 (e.g., gunners and aircraft radio operators) would be transferred to other units—the C-130 was unarmed, and its flight crew did not include a radio operator; the pilot and copilot were responsible for radio communications. Others had to be retrained on the C-130.

A conference was held at Headquarters USAFE to address transition into the C-130s. Pilots and flight engineers would undergo transition flight training (sixty days of temporary duty and approximately fifty hours' flying time) in the C-130 at Evreux Air Base, France. Ground maintenance training would be taught to all maintenance technicians. During the six month period of July to December 1957, 7406th aircrews logged 1,693 flying hours in their RB-50s.

The major transitional problem encountered during the first half of 1958 involved finding ways to support C-130 training while concurrently executing the RB-50 missions. The lack of B-50 spare parts also remained a problem, but was alleviated to some extent by cannibalizing one B-50 to keep the mission RB-50s in commission.

On January 6, 1958, two 7406th crews—led by Major Swanson—began the C-130 flight training course in France.[73] After being certified as a C-130A pilot, Major Swanson replaced Colonel Byars as commander of the 7406th. The change of command took place April 2, 1958, coincidentally Swanson's fortieth birthday. Included in the third C-130 flight training course at Evreux was S.Sgt. Laroy Price, the flight engineer who would perish aboard C-130 60528.[74]

Concurrently, 7406th ground maintenance technicians attended C-130 maintenance courses at Evreux in their specialties, and Lieutenant Blemings was sent on temporary duty to the TEMCO plant in Texas to work in-house as the 7406th representative responsible for resolving issues related to receipt of the new C-130 aircraft. Later in April, Staff Sergeant Pittelkau and First Lieutenant Villarreal became the first members of the 7406th to attend combat aircrew survival training—at the USAFE Combat Survival School at Ramstein/Landstuhl AB, Germany. At the time, the 7499th had decreed that completion of an Air Force survival school was a new prerequisite qualification for its recon flight crew members—all 7405th, 7406th, and 7407th crew members would be completing the survival course in small numbers over the next couple of years in order to minimize impact on each squadron's mission. (At that time, it didn't occur to anybody that it might be useful to send the Security Service sailors through the aircrew survival training course, even though they were flying in the same planes on the same missions.)

Nearly all the men associated with the 7406th Support Squadron in 1958 consider it the most memorable year of their lives. But until the tragedy of that September, they thought of the year purely in terms of the transition to the new aircraft.

On June 30, 1958, forty-six officers and 278 enlisted airmen were assigned to the 7406th, compared to thirty-three officers and 111 enlisted on June 30, 1956. The planned transition to the C-130 had caused significant changes in squadron manning. Capts. Rudy J. Swiestra (pilot), Paul E. Duncan (pilot), and Edward J. Jeruss (navigator), plus 1st Lt. John E. Simpson (pilot), arrived in the squadron during the first half of 1958. Swiestra, Duncan, and Simpson were among the twenty-two recon pilots in the squadron in July 1958.[75] The three of them and Jeruss perished aboard C-130 60528 on September 2, 1958.

Notified of aircraft availability, the 7406th sent a crew to Greenville, Texas, in late May 1958 to ferry its first C-130 to Rhein-Main. Satisfied with test flights from the depot at Major Field, Greenville, the crew returned to Rhein-Main in early June aboard the squadron's first "Hercules" aircraft—"Rivet Victor" recon configured C-130A-II, tail number 60484.[76] Transition from RB-50s to C-130A-IIs had finally begun.

On July 8 a crew commanded by Capt. Lewis H. Davis Jr. ferried a RB-50 from Rhein-Main to Greenville and ferried C-130A-II 60525 from Texas to Rhein-Main. 1st Lt. Ricardo M. Villarreal hitched a ride to Texas with Davis's crew, and remained in Texas on a fifteen-day leave when the crew returned to Germany.

The next aircraft ready for pickup at the TEMCO plant was C-130A-II 60528. On July 25, 1958, a crew led by 1st Lt. John E. Simpson (aircraft commander)[77] traveled from Germany to Texas to ferry 60528 back to Rhein-Main. Lieutenant Villarreal, who was on leave in Laredo, Texas, was the second navigator on the C-130 ferry flight to Germany. Simpson's crew conducted the first 7406th flight in 60528 (a round-robin test hop from the TEMCO plant) on July 30, 1958, and ferried the aircraft to Rhein-Main, Germany, on August 3 and 4. In turn, C-130A-IIs 60534, 60530, and 60541 were ferried from Texas to Rhein-Main in August, October, and November, respectively.

Finally, a crew headed by Major Swanson ferried the squadron's last RB-50 to Greenville, Texas, on October 28. He and his crew ferried C-130A-II 60541 to Rhein-Main in late November 1958. The era of the RB-50 Dream Boat program in Europe had ended. The aging bombers would continue flying recon missions in the Far East, but had been fully replaced in Europe by a fleet of more capable C-130A-II aircraft.

In January 1959 a 7406th crew flew to Greenville to pick up, check out, and ferry C-130A-II 60538 to Rhein-Main, completing the initial delivery of C-130A-IIs to the 7406th. At the end of 1959 the 7406th aircraft fleet consisted of seven C-130A-IIs: tail numbers 60484, 60525, 60534, 60530, 60540, 60541, and 60538; aircraft 60540 had arrived the previous October. The following year, in July 1960, a 7406th crew delivered the last C-130A-II, tail number 60535, to Rhein-Main.

Under a program known today as "Big Safari," TEMCO developed the C-130A-II recon platform on the same Air Force contract that was used to develop and maintain the Dream Boat RB-50s.[78] TEMCO received new C-130A model aircraft directly from the Lockheed C-130 factory at Marietta, Georgia, and retrofitted them to a C-130A-II Sun Valley configuration under a contract dated April 2, 1957. Also known as the Rivet Victor configuration, we will use Rivet Victor to reduce confusion.[79] Major modifications made to create the Rivet Victor C-130A-II included: (1) adding a second navigator station on the flight deck, (2) building three compartments (rooms) into the cargo bay, (3) installing ten radio intercept positions in the three compartments, (4) installing four airline-type passenger seats behind compartment three in the rear of aircraft, and (5) building in an electronic maintenance station, a galley with oven, and, to the crews' enormous approval, an airline-type toilet on the sealed-shut rear cargo ramp.

At the end of 1958 the 7406th had completed the transition from RB-50 to C-130A-II recon aircraft, but had paid the severest of flying penalties. When 60528 went down in Soviet Armenia with seventeen men on board, the 7406th realized that it had to modify its flying procedures. After the loss of the plane, 7406th aircrews stood down for an extended period for supplemental ground training, and the concept of the integrated front-end combat crew was applied to the flying personnel of the 7406th.[80] The concept meant that in addition to extensive ground training together, the members of an integrated front-end crew—designated in writing and scheduled to fly together—had to complete five training flights as a group before flying an operational mission, and a primary crew member (pilot or lead navigator) could not be replaced on a flight without replacing the entire crew. During the second half of 1958, 7406th crews logged 2,091 flying hours—only 1,123 of which were mission hours.

As 1958 closed out, the squadron had forty-five officers and 237 enlisted men assigned, reflecting manning adjustments made in response to the transition to a total C-130A-II recon operation. The use of integrated crews required an increase in the number of aircrew members, and by June 30, 1959, sixty-six officers and 239 enlisted men were assigned to the squadron.

Missions over the Baltic Sea and East European perimeter flights operated on a "round-robin" basis from Rhein-Main. In the early days, "Southern" missions generally involved temporary duty to Athens, Greece; Aviano, Italy; Incirlik, Turkey; or Tehran, Iran. Later there were TDYs from Rota, Spain, and Sigonella, Sicily (West Mediterranean missions). For brevity, we will discuss only the southern deployments to Incirlik Air Base, Turkey, the primary TDY base through 1958.

In addition to the Incirlik, Turkey, operating location, the Rhein-Main based C-130 recon resources were used in other areas throughout the Cold War as necessary. On August 25, 1958, Major Swanson commanded a 7406th crew that deployed aboard C-130 60528 to Bodö, Norway—to the same NATO base that Francis Gary Powers was bound for when a Soviet SA-2 missile shot down his U-2 in the Sverdlovsk area of Russia.[81] An Esso fuel receipt dated August 26 shows that S.Sgt. Delbert Johannsen, the mission's flight engineer, purchased 10,550 liters of JP-4 fuel at Bodö to refuel 60528. The crew flew a local mission from Bodö on August 26 (a nonproductive mission—they found few targets of interest in that barren Arctic area), and returned to Rhein-Main on August 27, six days before the same plane was shot down over Armenia.

Having regrouped following the shootdown of C-130 60528, the 7406th resumed normal operations in November 1958. On November 4, Capt. Nelson Halstead (pilot) and his integrated crew conducted the squadron's first deployment to Athens, Greece, for three days on temporary duty (TDY) to fly an operational mission in the Adriatic Sea area abeam Yugoslavia.[82] S.Sgt. Robert H. Bergeron was the Detachment 1, 6911th airborne mission supervisor on the deployment.[83] This was the first C-130 operational deployment after the shootdown, and the first operational TDY mission that included an airborne Morse intercept operator. When C-130 60528 was shot down on September 2, position number nine (the Morse intercept operator position) was not manned. Had it been manned, the plane in all probability would not have strayed into Soviet airspace. From November 1958 on, all operational missions would carry a Morse operator.

Recovering from the loss of an aircraft and crew, the 7406th had a banner year of flying in 1959. In September 1959 the 7406th set an Air Force C-130 record, logging 104 hours average per month for each of the seven assigned aircraft. Then, in October, the squadron broke that record with an average time of 114 flying hours per aircraft. And the heavy flight schedules were accomplished safely. The catastrophic loss of C-130 60528 would be the last major accident involving a 7406th aircrew; the squadron's accident-free record subsequent to 1958 was due, at least in part, to strict adherence to training and safety standards, and high experience levels.[84]

The 7406th continued C-130A-II operations from Rhein-Main, Germany, throughout the 1960s, using its eight assigned aircraft. In addition, the squadron used a C-130A cargo aircraft (tail number 41637) that it acquired in 1961 for flight crew training and logistic support. In mid-1971 the 7406th's C-130A-IIs were replaced by C-130B-II aircraft.

The 7406th Support Squadron continued flying C-130B-II missions from Rhein-Main through June 30, 1973, when the 6916th closed out operations at Rhein-Main and moved to Athens, Greece. Reconnaissance coverage of Soviet and East European satellite targets in the Baltic Sea area (Detachment 1, 6911, aka 6916th missions) was assumed by the 6985th Security Squadron and Detachment 1, 6985th aboard RC-135 aircraft flying missions from RAF Mildenhall, England.

The 7406th aircraft maintenance function remained at Rhein-Main, but its recon missions shifted south. Deploying to Athenai Airport on temporary duty, 7406th flight crews continued flying recon missions from Athens from July 1, 1973, through June 13, 1974. On June 14, 1974, Air Force Strategic Air Command RC-135 aircraft replaced the 7406th C-130B-IIs on recon missions in the East Mediterranean Sea area. Two weeks later the 7406th Support Squadron was deactivated.

TUSLOG, Detachment 72

The highest levels of government had approved the Dream Boat RB-50 recon program as a "gap-filler" source of communications intelligence reconnaissance in Europe, and early missions justified that trust. With the initial deployment base—Incirlik Air Base, Adana, Turkey—selected, the 7406th Support Squadron and Detachment 1, 6911th Radio Group Mobile could extend the range of coverage significantly beyond the range possible from Rhein-Main, Germany. By deploying on temporary duty (TDY) and flying missions from Incirlik, Dream Boat RB-50 crews could cover targets along the southern periphery of the Soviet Union.

Maj. Joseph F. Herrmann Jr., 7406th operations officer, headed the first RB-50 deployment to Incirlik on March 23, 1957.[85] That was a significant milestone for airborne communications intelligence reconnaissance operations in Europe. Later (in 1959–60), when conditions permitted, both the 7406th and Air Force Security Service activated detachments at Incirlik—TUSLOG, Detachment 72 (7406th) and TUSLOG, Detachment 76 (6916th, aka Detachment 1, 6911th)—and assigned small cadres of airmen that were supplemented by crews on temporary duty from Rhein-Main.

As part of State Department efforts to conceal the nature of U.S. military operations in Turkey, all U.S. units were supposedly providing logistic support to Turkey, and in line with the alleged high-level logistical cooperation between Turkey and the U.S., the United States were assigned a "TUSLOG" (Turkish-U.S. Logistics) designator that was used in place of the unit's true identity in open communications.[86] Detachment 1, 7406th became TUSLOG, Detachment 72; and Detachment 1, 6916th, at Incirlik became TUSLOG, Detachment 76.[87] Other reconnaissance-associated detachments included TUSLOG, Detachment 50—the SAC special security office (SSO) detachment that supported RB-47 and ERB-47 operations at Incirlik—and TUSLOG, Detachment 10-10 (a CIA detachment that supported U-2 operations).

Working together, 7499th Support Group and 6900th Security Wing staffs created multiple mission routes in the Black Sea area—all intended to emphasize target coverage while avoiding provocation of the Soviet air defense forces by keeping well away from Soviet airspace. There were two mission routes from Incirlik: the standard Black Sea Central route and the Black Sea East route. On the Black Sea Central route, the crew flew from Adana northeast via Samsun and carried out an east-west figure-eight orbit pattern about sixty miles north of Sinop.[88] On the Black Sea East (east Turkey overland) route—the route on which 60528's crew met its fate—the crew flew from Adana to Trabzon and conducted their figure-eight orbit pattern between Trabzon and Van, Turkey.[89]

Maintenance of the recon aircraft at deployment bases, and the lack of airlift support for ground personnel going to staging areas, proved to be an obstacle. Prior to the first deployment to Incirlik, the 7406th put into place its own supply and maintenance arrangements such that for all practical purposes the squadron developed self-sufficient logistics and maintenance capabilities at Incirlik.

After the shootdown of 528 in September 1958, recon missions were suspended temporarily. The 7406th resumed deployments to Turkey on November 11, 1958, when Capt. William H. Lewis's integrated crew[90] traveled to Incirlik on a fifteen-day deployment.[91]

The 7406th established a formal operating location (TUSLOG, Detachment 72) at Incirlik with one officer and two airmen, authorized in December 1959. 1st Lt. James M. "Jocko" Donlon Jr., a C-130 pilot, served as Detachment 72's commander in 1960 and 1961, rotating from Incirlik in December 1961.

The 7406th continued flying recon missions from Rhein-Main and Incirlik (TUSLOG, Detachment 72) until December 14, 1965, when the loss of a 7407th RB-57F over the Black Sea interrupted American recon missions from Turkey (see chapter two). All U.S. recon missions from Turkish territory ceased on that day.

The "Back-Enders"

In keeping with U.S. Air Force Security Service operations in general, the start-up of airborne communications intelligence reconnaissance in Europe was intentionally low-key. The need for absolute secrecy was drilled into all USAFSS personnel with a level of intensity that bordered on the absurd. The fact that USAFSS airmen would be flying as recon crew members on aircraft belonging to U.S. Air Forces, Europe (i.e., to the 7406th Support Squadron) was not classified, but everyone was cautioned that their relationship was "sensitive." (Unlike the usual classifications of "confidential," "secret," and "top secret," "sensitive" was an ill-defined concept without legislative authority.) "Need to know" was the byword.

The "back-enders" (USAFSS recon crews) would join the "front-enders" (flight crews) at the appointed time at an aircraft for a mission, and after the mission, members of the two units were to pretend that the other did not exist. The USAFSS commander, Maj. Gen. Harold H. Bassett, tasked the 6900th Security Wing to work with Headquarters USAFE and to use existing Security Service resources in Europe to create a new USAFSS airborne unit at Rhein-Main.

Airborne communications intelligence reconnaissance was not only an entirely new mission for USAFSS in Europe; Detachment 1, 6920th Security Group at Yokota Air Base, Japan, was preparing to man such missions in the Far East. Thus, there was no foundation of prior experience on which the new European unit could be built. The 6900th Security Wing, located in Frankfurt's I.G. Farben Building, would work out the details as necessary. Informed in early 1955 that a new airborne recon program nicknamed Dream Boat was to be activated at Rhein-Main, the commander of the 6900th assigned a captain to be the project officer.

Detachment 1, 6911th Radio Squadron Mobile

The 6900th Dream Boat project officer participated in related meetings at Headquarters USAFE through the end of 1955, by which time USAFE had reorganized its 7499th unit at Wiesbaden and activated the 7406th Support Squadron at Rhein-Main. When the 7406th and USAFE began asking operationally oriented questions that the 6900th Dream Boat officer felt ill-at-ease trying to answer, he passed operational responsibility for the USAFSS airborne recon mission to the 6911th Radio Squadron Mobile, Darmstadt, Germany.

The 6911th commander, Lt. Colonel Richard D. Small Jr., selected Capt. Leonard S. Machado, his assistant operations officer, to head up the new airborne reconnaissance task. Like many of his contemporaries Captain Machado—a bomber pilot during World War II—had been recalled to active duty during the Korean War.

To assist him with his new task, Captain Machado selected S.Sgt. Donald H. Riedmiller, a former Morse intercept operator who worked for Machado as a traffic analyst in the 6911th.[92] On February 23, 1956, a 6911th special order designated Captain Machado commander of Detachment 1, 6911th Radio Squadron Mobile at Rhein-Main Air Base and assigned Sergeant Riedmiller to Detachment 1, 6911th as an airborne Morse intercept operator. Within days Machado learned that the new

Dream Boat RB-50s to support Detachment 1's aerial recon mission would not arrive at Rhein-Main for several months, so on March 23, 1956, his and Riedmiller's duty station was changed back to Darmstadt.

By June 1956 the mushy delivery schedule for the first Dream Boat recon aircraft had firmed up enough that Security Service began to assemble staff for airborne operations from Rhein-Main. On June 18, Captain Machado's duty station was once again changed to Rhein-Main. On August 6 he was designated the top-secret control officer (the officer responsible for the safe-keeping of classified documents) for Detachment 1, and signed for equipment to activate a special cryptoclassified teletype circuit between Detachment 1's operations compound at Rhein-Main and the 6900th Security Wing in Frankfurt. The crypto circuit provided the secure means through which Detachment 1 could exchange special intelligence reports with other USAFSS units, the National Security Agency, and other cryptologic agencies.

Detachment 1 was officially activated, and the 6900th Wing published aeronautical order 16 dated August 24, 1956, designating eleven airmen as "noncrew" (see below) but "required to participate frequently and regularly in aerial flight during the period 24 Aug through 30 Sep 1956 in accordance with a USAFSS message dated 3 Aug 1956." The eleven men were on temporary duty from either the 6911th RSM or the 6913th RSM in Bremerhaven, Germany,[93] and they had been selected to be the first airborne intercept operators aboard the new 7406th RB-50s. Despite the awkward fact that it had no aircraft (the first Dream Boat RB-50 would not be delivered to Europe until December 1956), Detachment 1, 6911th was ready to begin flying.

New USAFSS Recon Unit at Rhein-Main

On September 1, 1956, the 6911th Radio Squadron Mobile was redesignated the 6911th Radio *Group* Mobile. The same month, M.Sgt. Jack H. Barnes, T.Sgt. Stanley E. Kresge, and S.Sgt. Raymond E. Sadler were assigned to Detachment 1, 6911th—Barnes as First Sergeant, Kresge as NCO in charge of Operations (NCOIC), and Sadler as NCO in charge of Personnel. Shortly thereafter, Maj. Robert P. Webster arrived to command Detachment 1, and Captain Machado became Detachment 1's operations officer. Machado returned to the U.S in April 1957, replaced by Air Force captain Luther A. Tarbox.

Captain Tarbox was a West Point graduate who chose to be commissioned in the Air Force and became a pilot. He was assigned to the 6911th at Darmstadt in 1955. Effective on May 17, 1957, and without benefit of an overlapping assignment to help smooth the transition, Captain Tarbox was given a chance to excel as operations officer in the Air Force's newest recon unit.

The Air Force began training linguists in 1955 to man the RB-50 recon planes in Europe. In addition, Air Force Security Service planned to draw upon intercept operators then assigned in Europe. Upon completion of a Serbo-Croatian language course at Indiana University, in Bloomington, in June 1956, eleven airmen were assigned to the 6911th at Darmstadt. On December 4, 1956, six of the Serb linguists—Airmen Second Class Richard D. Doto, Lincoln J. Gilbert, Allan M. Hagland, John W. Hamm Jr., Harold T. Kamps, and James C. Kinney—and three Romanian linguists (A/1C Jewell D. Lee, Airmen Second Class Earl J. Moore, and Everett P. Reeves) were transferred from Darmstadt to Rhein-Main to begin their flying careers.

The 6900th issued aeronautical order 27 the same day they arrived at Rhein-Main, placing them on flying status as noncrew members. Because the recon crew members had no flight-related duties, they were "noncrew members" receiving "hazardous duty" pay, a smaller amount than the "flight pay" flight crew members were paid. By January 1, 1957, Detachment 1 had twenty-seven airborne intercept operators (Russian, Czechoslovakian, Serbo-Croatian, Hungarian, Romanian, and Bulgarian linguists) on flying status, and not one of them had ever flown an operational communications intelligence reconnaissance mission.

Prior to the arrival of the first Dream Boat RB-50 in December 1956, 7406th flight crews and Detachment 1 recon crews had flown only transition training missions aboard Half Track RB-50s that did not include the communications intelligence collection equipment (special receivers, antennas, and recorders). The transition training missions acquainted the crews with the RB-50 airframe and airborne operations in general, while the flight crews and recon crews worked together to develop integrated procedures and checklists. But only after the first Dream Boat aircraft arrived in December could the recon crew members begin to familiarize themselves with their intercept equipment.

On January 13, 1957, 7406th and Detachment 1, 6911th crew members flew the first operational airborne communications intelligence reconnaissance mission in Europe—a "perimeter" mission along the East German and Czechoslovakian borders. At last, a back-ender recon crew got a taste of an authentic airborne recon mission. Not one of them had previously flown a mission; in fact, the only person in Detachment 1 who had even set foot in a Dream Boat RB-50 was Technical Sergeant Kresge. Since he'd been introduced to the intercept receivers and recorders in the aircraft at the depot in Texas and had tinkered with the equipment on the long flight from Texas to Rhein-Main, he was the detachment airborne recon expert. As Detachment 1's NCOIC of Operations, Stan Kresge had the monumental task of training a group of utterly inexperienced airmen to be airborne voice intercept operators using equipment that none of them had ever seen or heard of, let alone used, and that he himself had only played with on one flight to Europe. Initially, training was a hit-or-miss affair.

While the 7406th flight crews acquainted themselves with the Dream Boat RB-50, Sergeant Kresge managed to teach a recon crew how to fit and don a parachute harness, how to check and stow a chute itself, how to use the aircraft interphone system, and how to turn on and use their intercept receivers and recorders. At last they were doing the job they'd volunteered for—they were flying recon missions. Moreover, additional airborne intercept operators, mostly inexperienced airmen directly from language school, were arriving weekly.

In January 1957 two airborne Morse intercept operators (Airmen First Class Louis G. Padilla and Gene Swearingen) were placed on aeronautical orders. The use of airborne Morse operators was short-lived; by the end of March 1957, Padilla and Swearingen were shipped back to Darmstadt because neither the 6900 Wing nor Detachment 1 itself saw any real need for an airborne Morse intercept capability.

From day one Detachment 1 got lots of attention and recognition within Air Force Security Service channels, but in practical terms, its lines of communication were badly snarled. Assigned administratively to the 6911th at Darmstadt, the unit got what little technical support and guidance that it received from the 6901st Special Communications Group at Zweibrücken, Germany, and was operationally controlled by the 6900th Security Wing at Frankfurt. The 6911th was charged with providing its Detachment 1 with the resources to accomplish the airborne mission, but had no real incentive to provide those resources. In effect, Detachment 1 was a drain on the 6911th's resources.

As the consolidated USAFSS processing center in Europe, the 6901st laid claim to Detachment 1's analysis and reporting function. Detachment 1 was not to be trusted to analyze intercepted traffic and issue reports because, the 6901st claimed, the detachment's aircrews were inexperienced. Of course, the analysts at the 6901st had never seen, much less analyzed, radio traffic from many of the targets collected by Detachment 1, but the two organizations were involved in a turf battle, and for the time being the 6901st had the sharper spade. The Detachment 1 operators were instructed to "just transcribe the recorded messages and send them to us, and we'll perform the analysis and reporting . . . Oh, and by the way, do *not* carry any written technical working aids aboard the recon platforms because your aircraft might fall into enemy hands." It was okay for an operator to memorize order of battle data—which Soviet units operated out of which airfields, for example—but an operator was expected to forget everything should he be captured.

And so it was that the 6901st provided only minimal technical feedback (military unit identifications, call signs and frequencies, and other order of battle data) for the targets intercepted by Detachment 1, and much of the technical feedback that the '01st (often referred to as the "0-worst" by the sailors) provided was erroneous. The battle was fought for the first several years of Detachment 1 operations before the unit finally received some reporting responsibility. But as long as the 6901st was generating reports and getting favorable feedback, everyone was happy—everyone except for a few Detachment 1 linguists who abhorred having someone else think for them. They created an ad hoc analysis section and prided themselves in "scooping the little ol' ladies in tennis shoes" who professed to be analysts at Zweibrücken. Taking pride in their work and often working sixteen- to eighteen-hour days, they also wanted to be accepted and recognized for their efforts.

Both the front-end and back-end crew members were true pioneers in airborne communications intelligence reconnaissance. Most senior flight crew members had combat experience as bomber pilots, navigator-bombardiers, or engineers during World War II and the Korean War, but none (in fact, no Air Force crew members) had operational experience with communications intelligence recon missions in Europe. A handful of the back-enders (namely T.Sgts. Stanley Kresge and John Kozak, and S.Sgts. William McCormick and Jack Roberts, who were Russian linguists) were "seasoned" voice intercept operators with more than a year's experience at a ground site. Perhaps a half-dozen lower-rank airmen had a few months of ground-site intercept operator experience.

The majority of the operators had six months of language training and no intercept operator training or experience, so for them the airborne mission was a challenge in every respect. Knowledge about the target environment, working aids, and order of battle data were practically nonexistent; the foreign language flight terminology was alien to the novice operators; and there were no qualified trainers.

Trainees learned primarily by trial and error; and training, of necessity, was conducted in a live, hostile environment—life-threatening decisions had to be made instantaneously. Adding to the challenges were a tragicomic lack of training in aircraft emergency procedures and survival techniques, and no standards against which knowledge or success could be measured. Nonetheless, the crews coalesced as a team and contributed "virgin" (otherwise unavailable) communications intelligence from day one. Detachment 1's troops got the job done in spite of the system and without formal operator training.

Staffing for Detachment 1 remained stable during the first half of 1957. On July 1, 1957, thirty-seven airmen (including five maintenance technicians) were on flying status, and except for a few recently arrived (replacement) operators, they were the same group that had begun operational recon missions in January 1957. On July 1, 1957, USAFSS recognized the legitimacy of the role of the airborne recon linguists and maintenance technicians by issuing orders designating the Detachment 1 fliers as "crew members" rather than "noncrew," and defined the aerial flight period as "indefinite" rather than for a specified period, as had been the case previously.

Flight pay had special meaning for the USAFSS crew members. Less than five percent of all Air Force personnel (mostly officers) received flight pay in 1957, and the USAFSS recon flyers made up about one percent of Security Service staffing. With the July 1 orders, they were recognized to be on a par with the front-end crew members, and began receiving flight pay according to rank ($60 to $105 flight pay per month for enlisted men) rather than the hazardous duty pay ($55 per month for enlisted) noncrew members received. Most of Detachment 1's airborne intercept operators were of low rank—airman second class (paygrade E-3) with a base pay of $120 monthly. In addition, they faced an extremely low rate of promotion. Thus, flight pay represented up to a fifty percent pay raise, a godsend for Detachment 1's recon fliers, even with the German mark above 4.0 to the dollar.

On November 18, 1957, the 6900th authorized six airmen to wear the "Aircrew Member Badge" (aircrew wings). At the time, the criterion for award of aircrew wings was completion of 150 hours of flight. T.Sgt. Arthur L. Mello, S.Sgts. Donald P. Connell and Warren H. Hamaker, Airmen First Class William S. Bain and Phillip V. Nowicke, and Airman Third Class Jimmie Reese Jr., were the first USAFSS personnel authorized to wear aircrew wings in Europe. Four of the six (Mello, Connell, Nowicke, and Reese) were airborne maintenance technicians; Hamaker was a Russian linguist, and Bain was a Polish linguist. Each had been on flying status since arriving at Rhein-Main in late 1956.

The excitement of being part of the volunteer cadre of airborne intercept operators within Detachment 1, 6911th offered a ready source of replacements for airmen lost through normal attrition. As Detachment 1 airmen finished their enlistments and were discharged, volunteers waited to fill their airborne slots. A/2C Perry J. Eisenhower was one such. Graduating from the basic six-month Russian language course at Syracuse University in June 1957, Perry arrived for duty with the 6911th at Darmstadt in July 1957. While awaiting his security clearance, Perry learned about and volunteered for airborne duty with Detachment 1 at Rhein-Main. He arrived at Detachment 1 on August 12, 1957, and over the next four decades became a legend in airborne communications intelligence operations.

The second half of 1957 saw a steep increase in the number of airborne intercept operators assigned to Detachment 1, 6911th Radio Group Mobile—with the greatest increase involving inexperienced Russian linguists who arrived directly from language school. On July 1, 1957, only twelve of Detachment 1's thirty-two airborne intercept operators were Russian linguists,[94] The unit's other twenty operators were Polish, Czechoslovakian, Serbo-Croatian, Bulgarian, and Romanian linguists.[95] In addition, the unit had five maintenance technicians on flying status.[96] Shortly after July 4, eleven of Perry Eisenhower's classmates from his Russian language course at Syracuse University reported for duty at the 6911th, Darmstadt, Germany. When offered the opportunity, they volunteered for flying status with Detachment 1 at Rhein-Main.[97] Another Russian language class (ten students from the Army Language School, Monterey, California)[98] arrived at Rhein-Main a few weeks later, and a smaller class arrived from Indiana University[99] about the same time. In addition, John Wilcher, Theodore Klein, and perhaps a couple of other Russian linguists arrived in 1957 from ground sites—tripling the number of Russian linguists assigned to Detachment 1 at the end of 1957.

By January 1, 1958, Detachment 1 had fifty-nine airmen on flying status—more than half of whom were Russian linguists. Needless to say, the primary intelligence target of interest was the Soviet Union. The rapid build-up of airborne intercept operators in 1958 was in anticipation of the replacement of the RB-50 Dream Boat aircraft with C-130A-II aircraft. A typical RB-50 back-end crew included five airborne operators and a maintenance technician to operate five intercept positions, and the C-130 recon aircraft had ten operator positions, doubling intercept-operator requirements on each mission, and the number of missions per month increased. In addition, the need for airborne maintenance technicians increased with two AMTs required on each C-130 mission vs. one on RB-50 missions. At the same time, the C-130s had more capable equipment—some intercept positions had dual receivers and dual recorders, and some included improved demodulators and receivers with increased bandwidth and frequency capabilities. One position (# 9) contained two HF receivers designed specifically to intercept and copy Morse code, which was transmitted on lower frequencies than most air-to-ground voice communications. To support the increased tempo of airborne reconnaissance operations in Europe, eight new C-130A-II recon aircraft were planned to replace five aging RB-50s. Detachment 1 would need to continue growing to support projected airborne communications intelligence recon operations in Europe.

Meanwhile, individual aircrew members were gaining experience: ten men were authorized to wear the Aircrew Member Badge (aircrew wings) on December 30, 1957,[100] and eleven more were authorized to wear the wings on July 1, 1958.[101] The increased experience level was a good thing because the airborne communications intelligence reconnaissance mission was becoming more complex.

TUSLOG, Detachment 76

Having gained experience on local round-robin missions from Rhein-Main during two months of operations, a combined 7406th and Detachment 1 crew deployed to Incirlik, Turkey, on March 23, 1957. T.Sgt. Stan Kresge, Detachment 1's NCOIC, was the airborne mission supervisor (the "admiral") on that historic mission. Other intercept operators included S.Sgt. Jack Roberts and A/2C Leardis G. Rice. T.Sgt. Arthur L. Mello was the airborne maintenance technician on the flight. One airman who was not on the deployment recently recalled:

> They flew in the eastern Mediterranean with Near East targets. I remember that one of the things they got was an army spotter from northern India who was flying a Piper Cub or some such very light aircraft. Stan [Kresge] claimed this was proof of our wonderful capabilities. It was, no doubt, an atmospheric freak.

The "ears" (intercept antennas) on Dream Boat RB-50 136 could not normally detect such distant signals; atmospheric phenomena had played a trick on the airborne intercept crew.

From the forward deployment base at Incirlik, RB-50 recon crews could monitor the training and operations of military targets in the Black Sea area that were not detectable from U.S. and allied ground intercept sites in the area. Deploying for two weeks at a time, Detachment 1's crews initially operated out of the Strategic Air Command's TUSLOG, Detachment 50 Special Security Office (SSO, also referred to as SAC SSO/Incirlik),[102] the only facility at Incirlik with a vault for storing sensitive compartmented information. The SAC detachment also provided Detachment 1 a small work space where the airborne intercept operators could set up minimal processing equipment and transcribe tapes that they recorded during missions.

Detachment 1 did not have any Arabic linguists assigned in the early days, so on occasion, when flying missions from Incirlik over the Mediterranean against Syrian and Egyptian targets, the Detachment 1 aircrews were augmented with British linguists. Two Royal Navy intercept operators who understood Arabic deployed to Incirlik and flew RB-50 missions with the Detachment 1 crews in the eastern Mediterranean in the late 1950s. Until the crisis in Lebanon in 1958, the Middle East had been relatively quiet, and USAFSS scheduled only occasional airborne missions in the Mediterranean Sea area. During the early days of staging from Incirlik, mission emphasis was on Soviet targets along the Black Sea.

One of the results of the loss of 528 and its crew was a change in the chain of command for Detachment 1. The 6900th Security Wing briefly took direct operational control of the airborne recon unit at Rhein-Main—Detachment 1, 6911th became Detachment 1, 6900th Security Wing, which, on January 1, 1960, became the 6916th Radio Squadron Mobile. At the same time, the commander's slot was upgraded to lieutenant colonel. The 6916th then consisted of six officers, fifty-three NCOs, and 122 airmen. On July 13, 1960, Lt. Col. William J. Lynn assumed command of the 6916th from Capt. Luther Tarbox. Captain Tarbox had observed the unit evolve from a detachment with a handful of men to a squadron; now he was going on a permanent change of station to Headquarters USAFSS. The USAFSS airborne recon unit at Rhein-Main had come of age—the men in the squadron now had their own identity. They were no longer assigned to a unit at Darmstadt (6911th) or at Frankfurt (6900th) and detached at Rhein-Main—they were the 6916th Radio Squadron Mobile, based at Rhein-Main.

On April 1, 1960, Detachment 1, 6916th Radio Squadron Mobile was activated at Incirlik as TUSLOG, Detachment 76. It was not much, but thereafter the back-enders had their own compartmented work space and permanent party representation at Incirlik. TUSLOG, Detachment 76 consisted of a small room (approximately twelve by sixteen feet) inside the Detachment 50 (SAC SSO) hangar—providing space for four transcription consoles, a small maintenance bench, a tape rack, a file cabinet, and one analysis and reporting desk. T.Sgt. Louis J. DuLong became the first NCOIC.

TUSLOG, Detachment 76 operated "lean and mean"; the Turkish government strictly controlled the number of American military permitted as permanent party (i.e., permanently stationed) in Turkey, so recon crew members from Rhein-Main continued to perform temporary duty at Incirlik until C-130 airborne communications intelligence recon operations from the Turkish base ceased in December 1965.

After operations from Turkey ceased, the 6916th Security Squadron began deploying on temporary duty to fly missions from Athens, Greece, over the Mediterranean Sea, eventually activating Detachment 1, 6916th SS at Athenai Airport in December 1968. The 6916th continued flying missions from Rhein-Main Air Base until June 30, 1973, at which time it relocated to Athenai Airport. The squadron flew thousands of airborne recon missions from Athens during the period 1966-1990. The 6916th Security Squadron was officially deactivated at Athenai Airport on November 13, 1990. Afterward, responsibility for airborne signals intelligence reconnaissance in Europe shifted to the 6988th Security Squadron at RAF Mildenhall Air Base, England.

SIX

—

GUYS IN THE OUTFIT

The outfit that closed up shop in 1990 must have been vastly different than it had been in its early years. It had three and a half decades of experience to draw on, and having developed a thick set of rules, regulations, and procedures over the years, had become far more efficient. But what was it like before all those regulations came into being—when its personnel were still feeling their way along without the aid of decades of experience?

It was fun. It entailed hard, at times dangerous, work; uncomfortable working and living conditions; and frequent collisions with air base and army authorities. But for a small group of inquisitive adolescents, it was above all fun. One can take some small consolation in the thought that the men who died in 1958 loved what they were doing, both on and off the job.

The outfit had been formed in 1956, and by 1958 it still contained well under a hundred men—kids, for the most part, most of them nineteen or twenty, in a few cases a bit over twenty. The staff sergeants, who seemed almost elder statesmen to the men under them, were in their mid-twenties. A few, the master sergeants and the officers, were in their thirties. But all of them were beginners in the field of airborne voice intercept, which after all had hardly existed before they came to

Detachment 1 in the mid-1950s. They were pioneers, and like so many pioneers, they had several elements in common. They liked excitement, they didn't really quite know what they were doing, since there were very few procedures worked out, and they spent their off-duty hours doing a great deal of drinking and romancing. Among the lower ranks, at least, there was almost no talk of politics or even of their work; talk was of home, of future plans, and above all, of what to do that evening.

Detachment 1 was the single smallest outfit on Rhein-Main Air Base. Moreover, as an intelligence unit, it was not formally part of the base hierarchy; it reported to its parent unit in Darmstadt, not to the Rhein-Main base commander, Colonel Amen. That was the cause of a great deal of distress to the good colonel.

Col. Henry J. Amen was a spit-and-polish officer of the old school, a veteran of World War II and the Korean conflict who saw himself as an upholder of the honorable traditions of the old Army Air Corps. Like a large pet dog, his greatest pleasure seemed to be going for a ride in the family car. He loved to ride around the base in the rear of his chauffeured automobile, his colonel's flag ostentatiously on display on the right front bumper. It must have seemed to him as if officers and even most enlisted men looked a bit sharper, stood a bit taller, as he approached them, and, basking in that belief, he smiled benignly back at them. They were his.

He felt no affection for the 6911th, though. They were an alien presence on his base, a group of men who didn't seem to notice or to care that they were in the Air Force; they gave him more trouble than any other outfit. Despite the fact that they were the smallest unit on the base, they compiled, month after month, the highest number of arrests for drunk and disorderly conduct, and the second highest number of cases of venereal diseases. Of course, they were also better read, knew more about music and art than the other men of their rank or even most of the officers, and were the only outfit on base where most of the men spoke at least a bit of German. But in Colonel Amen's opinion they needed more moral fiber, and he was determined that they should receive at least an occasional dose of that bracing medicine. Periodically, he would call the men of the unit, sergeants and all, into the base movie theater for a lecture on morality, a theme on which he felt he was an expert. He saw himself as a trained, effective public speaker, and his orations were always punctuated with rhetorical ploys meant to win over his audience. "Since you're an intelligence outfit, I assume I can take your intelligence for granted," he invariably began, and then he would move down through the sub-headings of his topic. Transitions were always quite clear—in fact, they were nearly always the same. "Down goes the curtain on excessive drinking, and now up comes the curtain on sexual moderation and caution," he would intone, gliding his open hand down and back up in what he felt was a dramatic, curtainlike movement, to make sure the audience understood. But the sermons never sank in. The men sat there listening politely, and then went right back out and got into trouble again.

Their detachment commander, Maj. Robert P. Webster, didn't seem to care. Major Webster was a good example of the complexity involved in an intelligence outfit. It was quite obvious to everyone that he had very little interest in the 6911th, that he was, in fact, seldom on Rhein-Main. The rumor among the men was that he spent most of his time and energy flying a DC-3 filled with black market liquor down to Saudi Arabia. His operations officer and adjutant, Capt. Luther A. Tarbox, who filled in as the acting commander in Major Webster's absence, was convinced that Webster had something else going on the side. Webster would call Tarbox in on a Friday and inform him that he'd be "out of town and out of touch" for the next few days. Tarbox suspected that he perhaps had a second family or at least a girlfriend somewhere in Germany, and that he spent time with them during his absence from Rhein-Main.

The truth was even more bizarre. Although none of the men, nor even the officers, knew it at the time, Webster had been placed in the outfit merely as a cover for a more important intelligence operation, one that had nothing to do with the Air Force. Being commander of the new Air Force Security Service detachment at Rhein-Main provided a perfect cover for Webster's Central Intelligence Agency operations in Europe.

He made very little attempt to act like a commander, or even, for that matter, to act in a military manner. When his adjutant came to him one Monday morning to report that nearly a dozen men had been caught downtown over the weekend without neckties, and asked him what to do, Webster suggested: "Maybe we should buy them some neckties." Informed by the adjutant that they had the second highest VD rate on the base, Webster remarked laconically that he didn't want his men coming in second in any category.

When that story, inevitably, got back to the men, several of them suggested among themselves that it might be worthwhile getting together a fund to send "the Germ" downtown more often and even drunker. Webster might well have approved of the plan, had he heard of it, or had he known his outfit well enough to have even heard of the Germ or of anyone else under the rank of sergeant.

The Germ had gotten that peculiar nickname by coming back from a weekend in Paris with both gonorrhea and trench mouth. Not only that, he had passed on a case of genital lice to the rest of the outfit three times in a month because he didn't understand what was causing him to itch. The other men admired the Germ's hardiness if not his common sense; they considered him the outfit's star performer in the sexually transmitted disease department.

Major Webster's lamentable lack of moral rigor or of any real interest in the outfit left his adjutant, Captain Tarbox, in a difficult situation. In day-to-day charge of running the outfit, he had to listen to Colonel Amen scream at him over the phone every Monday morning when the police and medical reports came in, and try, against all odds, to keep some form of discipline among the troops. A fundamentally decent, quiet man, Tarbox was a West Pointer in his early thirties who had the look of a bulldog, and although he was not by nature a martinet, he was utterly frustrated by the need to provide some sort of discipline to an amazingly undisciplined group of airmen. There were some small benefits from his impossible task: he liked the fact that the men called him "Nails" behind his back. But he was pretty sure that wasn't what Colonel Amen called him.

One Monday morning, after a particularly nasty call from Colonel Amen, Nails decided it was time for a formal barracks inspection. The bachelor NCOs had been trying for some time to obtain permission to move from the barracks into off-base housing. As the oldest and highest ranking sergeant in the outfit, M.Sgt. Pete Petrochilos had been chosen to present their case before the base commander. Colonel Amen, always suspicious of conditions in the 6911th, told him that before he made a

decision, he wanted to see how well they kept up conditions in the barracks. He had probably been waiting for the right occasion to walk
through the 6911th barracks for a long time by then. He had once been
refused entrance to their unit's work area on the grounds that he lacked
the proper security clearance. He saw that as an insult to his rank and his
position—it was, after all, *his* base. He had eventually gained entrance to
the building, but only under special security precautions. The Detachment 1 officers and NCOs had arranged to cover all the equipment with
sheets. The enlisted men, told that the commander was coming, had
gone a step further: all of them, even the nonsmokers, had bought cigars
for the occasion, and when Amen entered the operations room, the place
looked as if it were on fire. He could barely see or breathe for the smoke,
as the airmen stood at attention around the room, every one of them
with a lit cigar beside him, nearly everyone happily exhaling smoke.
Amen retreated almost immediately, coughing as he went.

The commander was nobody's fool. He could tell when someone was
trying to needle him, and although he said nothing at the time, he nursed
his grievance until he could get back at the outfit. It was payback time.

Accompanied by an increasingly embarrassed Petrochilos, Amen
dropped by the barracks unannounced, and found the living quarters in a
condition that horrified him: empty bottles strewn around the hallway,
vomit on one of the toilet seats, a pair of women's panties hanging from a
door handle. It looked like a brothel after a busy night, and he lit into
Tarbox the next morning on a level that even their normal Monday conversations had never attained before. Within ten minutes of hanging up
the phone, Tarbox had informed the first sergeant of the inspection, to be
held the following Saturday at eight A.M.

The men were shocked; they felt betrayed. One of the advantages
of Air Force airborne intelligence work, they all felt, was that as long
as you did your job, you could feel as unmilitary as possible while still in
uniform. Many of them had not undergone an inspection since basic
training in Texas. Even those who had studied Russian at the army's Presidio in Monterey, California, assumed that inspections were a thing of
the past. They immediately began to devise schemes to mess up the inspection in a manner for which they couldn't be punished. By that noon-
time, after running through a range of suggestions, they had come up

with a workable plan. They fanned out to the stores on base and in Frankfurt that sold popular magazines. By Saturday morning they were ready.

At eight A.M. sharp, Captain Tarbox, followed by First Sergeant Goldenstar, threw open the door to the largest bay of the barracks, in which thirty men slept. The man closest to the door hollered "Attention!" and every airman, in dress uniform, stood by the head of his bunk, eyes straight to the front.

In order to impart at least the illusion of privacy, the men's wall lockers, rather than standing against the wall behind their beds, were arranged in the center of the room. They didn't block the noise of a dozen or more radios and record players blaring away at midnight, but at least they partially blocked the light from whatever all-night card game was taking place on the opposite side of the bay.

In those days there was a custom in the Air Force—not a rule, but an unwritten tradition—that a man could hang a pinup poster in his wall locker as long as it wasn't pornographic. Like young men everywhere, the men of the 6911th had always had more than their share of posters, but by that morning many of them had acquired new ones.

Captain Tarbox, his shoes polished as only a West Pointer can polish them, his back ramrod straight, his expression not fierce, not mistrustful, but sternly professional, strode into the room, made a ninety-degree turn at the head of the first bed, and inspected the man, his bed, and his footlocker with military thoroughness. Uniform, passable; bed, the blanket not really tight enough; footlocker, barely adequate. Then he turned to the man's wall locker and found gazing back at him a poster of Ricky Nelson in a bikini bathing suit. He said nothing, but pretended to rummage through the locker with his baton. His neck, however, began to turn a bit pinker.

Locker after locker, he quickly discovered, was like that. Tab Hunter pouting, Rock Hudson in a skintight outfit, Little Richard making a kissy face at the photographer. Tarbox was an officer and a gentleman; he refused to give expression to his shock. But man by man, bed by bed, the inspection picked up speed and his neck grew redder. At the end he marched out of the room, ramrod straight as ever, Sergeant Goldenstar following him with a puzzled, troubled expression on his face.

Tarbox never held another inspection. He had stared into the abyss once, and he had no desire to do it a second time.

That was one of the stories the men from those early days of Detachment 1 told each other as they sprawled in plastic chairs or leaned against the wall in the "hospitality room" of the Maryland motel in September 1997. They had come from all over the United States to participate in a memorial service for the victims of the Soviet shootdown. Their waistlines had thickened, their hair turned gray and thinned out. In many cases they were unrecognizable to one another after so many years, at least until they started talking. But then, suddenly, sitting around a spartan motel room outside Fort Meade, after a separation of nearly four decades, they were brothers again, united by those years when they could tell no one what they were doing, when they had worked together in an operation so sensitive that not even their families knew they had been involved in it. That sense of stealth, that separation of the group from the rest of the world, had allowed them—forced them, really—to form a separate family among themselves, a family so tight that despite the frequent anger and the occasional fistfight when they were younger, they were bonded together for life: a group of elderly men who sat together off to one side in the bleachers during the memorial service, occasionally whispering a cynical remark during the more flowery portions of the official rhetoric, but too choked with emotion to say anything at all as the "missing man formation" roared suddenly overhead just above the trees, and a single plane peeled off to the right. On the day of the ceremony as well as for the rest of the weekend, they carried themselves with a posture and expression that said quite clearly to anyone who cared to watch them: "We were there; we flew with those lost men or in the years following their deaths; we knew the potential cost."

And back at the motel, sipping beer kept cold in big buckets that were refilled a few times a day, they talked about those days when they were young together, when they hardly ever drank that slowly, the days when they had put their lives on the line several times a week and partied every chance they got. The days before they realized they were mortal.

Tarbox had made a substantial contribution to the morale of the outfit simply by his continuing military zeal. There wasn't much he could

A U.S. Navy electronic warfare and reconnaissance EP-3E Aries II. On April 1, 2001, an EP-3E was harassed in the air by two Chinese Army Air Force fighters while flying a surveillance patrol in international air space off the coast of China. One Chinese fighter collided with the EP-3E, causing the American plane to make an emergency landing on Hainan Island, while the fighter broke up and its pilot was lost at sea. (U.S. Navy)

A Chinese Army Air Force Shenyang F-8 II fighter/interceptor takes off. Based on the Russian Mikoyan Gurevich (MiG) 21, the F-8 is a relatively cheap and simple fighter to produce. One like this was destroyed when its pilot flew into a U.S. Navy EP-3E, setting off an international incident between the United States and China. (USAF)

Nisei linguists—the world's first airborne intercept operators. In 1945, 8th RSM nisei voice intercept operators on Guam flew the first airborne SIGINT recon missions aboard an Army Air Corps RB-24, intercepting Japanese air defense communications during B-29 raids against Japan's main islands. Back row, left to right: Herbert Kawashima, George Hanafusa, pilot, copilot, Mamoru Ishii, T. M. Ishisaka, and Samuel K. S. Hong (OIC). Kneeling: James Okada, James Yoshioka, Yoshio Hoshide, H. Tanouye, and an unidentified crewman. Nisei operators not in photograph: Maseo Deguchi and Yoshio Kimoto. (USAF)

The flight crew and reconnaissance OIC of the prototype airborne signals reconnaissance platform RB-29A 44-62290, based at Yokota Air Base, Japan, August 1952. Kneeling, left to right: 1st Lt. Jimmie J. Benaquis, navigator; 1st Lt. Fred T. Smith, radio maintenance; and 1st Lt. Faran A. R. McClimans, copilot/Crew 2. Standing, left to right: Maj. Paul H. V. Swanson, OIC, pilot/Crew 1; Maj. Theodore W. Bozarth, radar officer; Maj. Fred O. Parrish, pilot/Crew 2; Capt. Herbert G. Fielding, copilot/Crew 1; and Capt. Morris O. Beck, OIC, airborne intercept operator. Major Swanson was the OIC of Project 502-50 in addition to being pilot on Crew 1. Note: Because some missions were 18 to 20 hours in duration, there were two flight crews. (USAF)

S.Sgt. Donald G. Hill, the first USAFSS airborne voice intercept operator killed. He died when the RB-50 he was in was shot down in July 1953. Photo taken in Korea, 1952. (USAF)

An RB-50 based out of Yokota Air Base, Japan, on a mission over the Sea of Japan in 1961. By the late 1950s, RB-50s were being replaced by C-130A-IIs in Europe. (USAF)

Members of Detachment 1, 6911th RGM softball team, 1958. Front row, left to right: Jack "Fat Jack" Price, Russian linguist; Nathaniel "Nate" Moore, airborne maintenance technician; Gerald "Jerry" Medeiros, Russian linguist; Stanley "Stosh" Kresge, Russian linguist/NCOIC Ops; Perry "Ike" Eisenhower, Russian linguist; Richard "Dick" Klingensmith, Russian linguist. Back row, left to right: Stanley "Stosh" Ramsey, airborne maintenance technician; Gerald "Madge" Maggiacomo, Russian linguist; George "Pete" Petrochilos, Romanian linguist; Raymond "Ray" Sadler, administrative clerk/NCOIC orderly room; Robert "Osh" Oshinskie, Romanian linguist; John Argoe, airborne maintenance technician; Robert "Luke" R. Ryan, Russian linguist; William "Bill" McCormick, Russian linguist/airborne mission supervisor; George Schaaf (or Schaef), radio operator on 6900th SW C-54 aircraft; James "Flash" Arnold, Bulgarian linguist; James "Jim" Wiester, Russian linguist; Harold "Harry" Kamps, Serbo-Croatian linguist; and Joel "Joe" Fields, Russian linguist. Softball team members not in picture: James "Jim" Ferguson Jr., Russian linguist; and Robert "Bob" Moore, Bulgarian linguist. Medeiros, Maggiacomo, Petrochilos, Oshinskie, Kamps, Fields, Ferguson, and Moore perished on C-130 60528 on September 2, 1958. (USAF)

One of the many Quonset huts that housed the crews of Detachment 1, 6911th RGM at Incirlik Air Base, Turkey. The huts were notorious for being hot in the summer and cold in the winter. (USAF)

Inside a Quonset hut. An entire recon crew slept in one large open bay. (USAF)

The ill-fated Hercules aircraft. C-130A-II 60528 was the third "Sun Valley" Rivet Victor reconnaissance aircraft assigned to the 7406th Support Squadron. (USAF)

The crew of C-130 60528

Capt. John E. Simpson

A/2C Robert Oshinskie

A/2C Robert Moore

1st Lt. Ricardo
M. Villarreal

S.Sgt. Laroy Price

A/2C James E.
Ferguson Jr.

T.Sgt. Arthur L. Mello

M.Sgt. George P.
Petrochilos

A/2C Gerald C.
Maggiacomo

A/2C Joel Fields

A/2C Gerald H. Medeiros

A/2C Harold T. Kamps

Crewmen not pictured: Capt. Paul E. Duncan, Capt. Rudy J. Swiestra, Capt. Edward J. Jeruss, A/2C Clement O. Mankins, and A/2C Archie T. Bourg Jr. (Photo of George Petrochilos courtesy of Mrs. Theresa Durkin. All other photos from authors' collection)

C-130A-II antenna pod disguised as an external fuel tank. In addition to holding one gallon of fuel, the pod housed VHF/UHF intercept antennas. (USAF)

C-130A standard external fuel tank. Note that it is more slender than the C-130A-II recon antenna pod tank. (USAF)

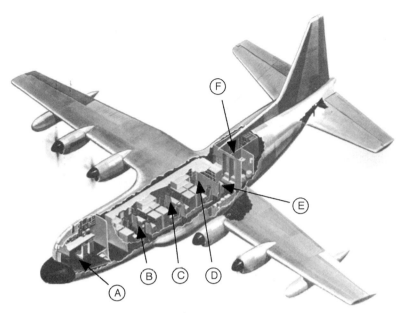

C-130A-II internal configuration. (USAF)
- A   Flight deck—pilot, copilot, flight engineer, and two navigators
- B   Compartment 1—operators 7, 10, 6, and 9
- C   Compartment 2—operators 8, 5, 4, and 3
- D   Compartment 3—operators 1 and 2
- E   Four "airline" seats and galley
- F   Maintenance station and toilet built-in on closed cargo ramp

The cockpit of a C-130A-II showing the pilot and copilot positions. (USAF)

View of the two-position navigator station as installed on C-130 60528. (USAF)

Airborne intercept operator position 10. C-130 60528 had ten such positions, with each operator working at a console similar to this one. (USAF)

The galley of a C-130, which included coffee jugs, refrigerator, ovens, and soup warmers. (USAF)

The lavatory on board a C-130A-II, complete with urinal, sink, and commode. This was built into the rear of the aircraft on the closed cargo ramp. (USAF)

C-130A-II emergency exit (right-side paratroop door) for the recon crew. (USAF)

C-130 60528 in Bödo, Norway, just four days before being shot down over Armenia with the loss of all on board. (USAF)

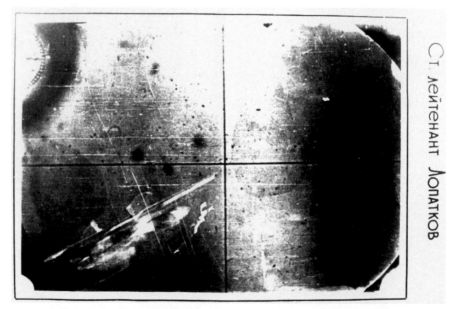

Ст. лейтенант Лопатков

Gun camera photo from Sr. Lt. Lopatkov's MiG-17 as he begins a firing run on 60528. The C-130's right wing, with the disguised antenna pod, is visible in the lower left quadrant of the gunsight. (Russia, PVO Strany)

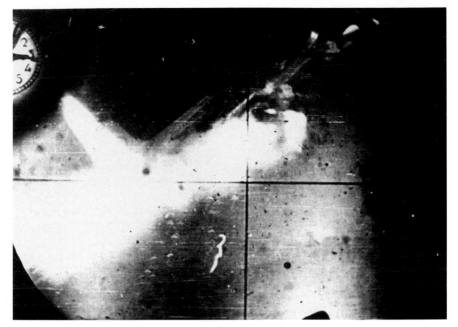

C-130 60528 under attack. Photo taken from the gun camera of an attacking Soviet MiG-17 fighter. 60528 is already on fire with much of the plane obscured by smoke. The altimeter in the upper left portion of the photo indicates the height at 3,000 meters. September 2, 1958, over Armenia. (Russia, PVO Strany)

Ст.лейтенант Кучеряев

Gun camera photo from Sr. Lt. Kucheryaev's MiG-17 as he comes up underneath 60528 to rake the C-130 with cannon fire. (Russia, PVO Strany)

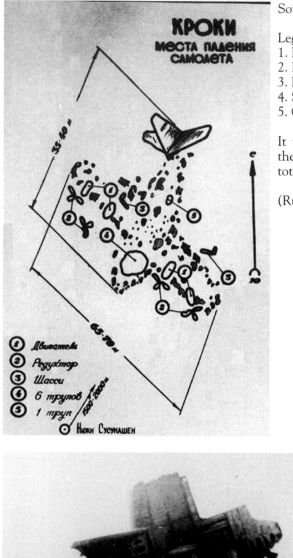

Soviet drawing of crash site.

Legend:
1. Engines
2. Propellers
3. Landing gear
4. Six bodies
5. One body

It was later determined that there were only six bodies in total, not seven.

(Russia, PVO Strany)

Part of the tail stabilizer from C-130 60528 at the crash site near Sasnashen, Armenia. Photo from Soviet air defense archives. (Russia, PVO Strany)

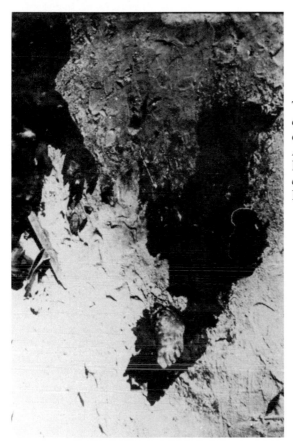

The burned remains from one of the aircrew at the crash site near Sasnashen, Armenia, September 2, 1958. Photo from Soviet air defense archives. (Russia, PVO Strany)

Members of the Memorial Development Committee at the crash site of 60528, July 1997. Pictured are Mike Patterson, Horace Haire, Larry Tart, Martin Kakosian, and Paul Martin. (Authors' collection)

Lorna Bourg, A/2C Archie Bourg Jr.'s sister, at the Armenian *khachkar* memorial honoring the crew of 60528. August 30, 1993, Sasnashen, Armenia. (Authors' collection)

After the original memorial to the downed crew of 60528 was destroyed, a new one was created by sculptor Martin Kakosian and placed in Sasnashen, Armenia. (Authors' collection)

The C-130 60528 memorial display at the National Cryptologic Museum in Fort Meade, Maryland. (Authors' collection)

Last rites for Capt. John Simpson, buried with full military honors at Arlington National Cemetery, September 3, 1997. (Authors' collection)

The hunter and the hunted. In the foreground is a MiG-17 in Soviet Air Force markings, like the ones that shot down C-130 60528. Behind it is the memorial C-130 in 60528's markings. Majors Field, Greenville, Texas, July 1997. (Authors' collection)

A U.S. Armed Forces honor guard showing the colors at the memorial dedication at the National Vigilance Park, Fort Meade, Maryland, September 2, 1997. (Authors' collection)

A replica of the National Security Agency's Wall of Honor at the National Cryptologic Museum, Fort Meade, Maryland. The actual Wall of Honor is located within NSA headquarters and lists 148 cryptologists killed in the line of duty. (Authors' collection)

have done to make the outfit more military. The simple fact was that he needed the men and they knew it; they were very good at their jobs. He could chew them out, he could try desperately and without success to get them to shape up, but he couldn't get rid of them. The mission was not only important, it was dangerous, and the Air Force has too much money invested in training the linguists to replace them.

On occasion Tarbox also repaid the men of the detachment for their hard work by taking them on rest and relaxation trips. On one such excursion, Tarbox, as a pilot needing to maintain flying proficiency, flew a group of off-duty Detachment 1 airmen to Copenhagen in a C-47 transport for the weekend. One of the airmen on that R&R flight discussed his amorous misadventure on the trip:

I went on one of those R&R's to Copenhagen with Tarbox, who had to get his flight time in. I got plastered, and picked up a young lady. I was suspicious, so when we went back to our room, I put my money in my sock. Took off all my clothes but that one sock. I figured that was a fool-proof way of protecting my money. She somehow figured out the situation, and when I awoke, sock and money were missing. Christ, she could at least have left me the sock. Copenhagen in February is cold without a sock!

Another of Tarbox's adventurers must have felt even colder, though: he showed up one morning at the air base main gate at six A.M. in a German taxi. The air policeman on duty did a double take when he peered in and asked the airman in the backseat of the cab for identification. After a night out in Frankfurt, the airman awoke at daybreak in a cheap hotel near the Frankfurt Bahnhof by himself and with no personal belongings other than the jockey shorts on his body—and unfortunately, he had not kept his wallet and money in his shorts.

Except for the athletes, many of whom died in the 1958 shootdown, the men were reported by the flight surgeon to be in terrible physical condition, and the doctor was surely correct. Despite their youth, most of the men in the outfit couldn't have jogged a mile. Yet, given their living and working conditions, it was surprising that they were in as good shape as they were. Their hours were impossible. Men who weren't scheduled for a mission rotated through two shifts—day and evening shifts—later changed to three shifts—day, evening, graveyard—and in the first two years, before the C-130s arrived, they flew two or sometimes three times a week, an eleven hour flight preceded by two hours of preparation and an hour's unloading and debriefing. The lower ranks slept in bays holding either twenty or thirty men, each bay containing men from all shifts and the crew for any given day's flight. Only a group in late adolescence could have slept at all under such conditions.

Of course, the men didn't much care about sleep anyway. When they weren't working, they were usually partying as hard and as long as they could. Then, utterly worn out, often after as much as forty-eight hours without sleep, they would finally return to their bay and try to obtain a little rest in a room with two or three radios playing and a card game going on most of the time. It's a wonder they didn't fall asleep walking to the dining hall.

Many of the elderly men sitting in the motel in September 1997 had known each other from the time they left basic training. Airborne voice intercept operators—the vast majority of airborne recon crew members—are deemed the creme de la creme in the Air Force. Many had one or more years of college, and some had college degrees. Chosen from among the top one percent of enlistees, they had been sent from basic training at Lackland Air Force Base in San Antonio, Texas, to Kelly Air Base right next door. There they had been stuffed for five weeks with Russian grammar and vocabulary, at a rate that no one would have been able to retain for long. Those who made it through the prep (aka pre-language) school went on to a language institute. At the time, there were two big training centers for Russian; one was the Army Language School, Presidio of Monterey, California, and the other attached to Syracuse University, in a set of World War II–era prefabricated huts set out of the way at the foot of the hill where the university ski team practiced their jumps. Until one of the prefab huts burned down in the winter of 1957–58, killing several airmen, very few of the students at Syracuse knew there were a hundred or so servicemen learning Russian in a little-known corner of the university. There were much smaller detachments for the other major Slavic languages, as well as for Chinese, Korean, Arabic, and other languages considered of strategic importance during the Cold War, all of them at schools large enough so that they wouldn't be noticed: George-town, Yale, Cornell, Indiana.[103]

Their training, no matter whether at the Monterey army language school or at one of the universities that cooperated with the National Security Agency's need to provide solid language training for hundreds of men a year, was essentially the same. The men studied language five days a week, starting at eight o'clock in the morning, ending in mid-afternoon, with a few hours of memorization left for homework in the evening. Most of the men in the outfit had undergone six months of that training, and came to Europe with a good basic knowledge of their special language. The Russian course, for example, was termed Basic Russian, and since there was almost no chance, once the six months were over, to actually speak the language, most of the men slowly settled into a rela-tively small, specialized military vocabulary. As one of them complained, "How the hell can you walk into a Russian restaurant and order a bomb-ing run?" But their training was sufficient for the Air Force's needs. They would be sent off to listening stations around the world, to sit at consoles intercepting and transcribing Soviet or other enemy military communi-cations intercepted by huge antenna systems. If they became career NCOs, they were sent, later in their careers, back to intermediate and ad-vanced classes.

In the summer of 1956, airmen had started filtering into Rhein-Main Air Base, a handful at a time, mostly after a stay of a week or two at a ground station in Germany. The NCOs and one or two of the airmen first class had served full hitches at ground listening posts elsewhere in Ger-many or in England. But the biggest pool for volunteers had been the 6911th Radio Group Mobile itself, which had the misfortune to be lo-cated on an army base in Darmstadt, a base under the control of Gen. Ed-win W. Walker, a right-wing zealot who would, in a few years' time, become a planned target for Lee Harvey Oswald before Oswald decided to go for even bigger game.

In the summer of 1957, for example, when eleven new men arrived in Darmstadt from Syracuse, they found that a week earlier, Walker had demoted the second most highly decorated enlisted man in World War II from sergeant down to A/1C for a simple curfew violation. It didn't take much of a recruitment lecture on the part of Captain Tarbox to get them to leave Darmstadt the next day. He talked for ten minutes and then was asked a single question: "Will we have to parachute out of a plane in order to get on flying status?"

"No," the captain assured them, "not unless the plane is on fire; we don't practice that sort of thing in my outfit." And at that assurance, every one of the eleven volunteered. Better a plane on fire than duty under General Walker.

Although it was, and still is, the busiest airport in Germany, Rhein-Main and collocated Frankfurt International Airport always seemed to the men of Detachment 1 a particularly inappropriate location for an air base. From late October to March, at three A.M., they would wake up for a flight and find the base so totally fogged in they could barely make out an automobile in the parking lot. Nevertheless, they would have to take off. They would trudge to the chow hall, wash down their chipped beef on toast—"shit on a shingle," "SOS" in colloquial GI—with enough coffee to bring them into partial consciousness, climb onto the bus, and somehow the driver would find his way slowly to the airplane. After checking out their gear, taking up their positions in the plane, and running through the preflight checklist, they would then resign themselves to an excruciatingly slow crawl out to the runway. The head of the ground crew would walk at a snail's pace in front of the plane with a powerful flashlight, and another crewman would walk just under the tip of each wing with a light. The three men would eventually get the plane on the runway; the pilot would line up on the proper compass heading, the ground crew would get out of the way. There was never any wait once the plane reached the runway because nobody else was crazy enough to fly in such weather. The pilot would rev up the engines, release the brakes, and speed down the runway in complete blindness. Often the aircraft did not break out of the fog until they'd reached 8,000 to 10,000 feet of altitude.

International regulations require that any plane taking off anywhere in the world have a reasonable backup landing field in case of emergency. Because of Western Europe's foul winter weather, it was not unusual for the B-50s to list the Azores, islands west of Portugal in the Atlantic, as a backup air base, and legend had it that there were times when they took off with the backup field in the United States. Luckily they were never called on to use one of those fields.

Most of the pilots in the 7406th were superb. Many of them were veterans of the Korean War and World War II. The commander, however, Lt. Col. George J. "Waxy" Byars, was well beyond his best years. He wore a hearing aid, and legend had it that he had flunked his last driver's license vision test. He was a strong-willed man who refused to listen to even the most timid advice from anyone else in the cockpit. He had several times come in low enough at Rhein-Main to take out a landing light or two, and the men were convinced that he routinely misheard the compass heading for landing runways at other airfields. They often imitated the colonel for one another's entertainment: "Air Force 201, this is Wiesbaden; take up heading two-niner-six."

"Roger, Wiesbaden, this is 201; heading two-niner-four."

Once, unable to stop because he'd touched down too far along the runway, Byars skidded off the end. So, even though he was the commander of the 7406th, he had the men worried. When they heard they were flying with Byars, many of them said a little prayer. But they kept their sense of humor. When he was the pilot, they made sure that they mumbled. Running through the checklist, the copilot would get to the wing flaps, the ailerons, and the elevators. The back-ender response to the movement of the controls would come out something like: "Leffaeronown, srr, lefelruhh, srr." The men pictured Byars sitting up there in the pilot's seat, banging on his hearing aid, and they were as happy as twenty-year-olds can be at four in the morning.

Wherever they came from, none of them had ever made their living flying before, and the new assignment seemed special, infinitely more exciting than sitting at a radio in a building somewhere near the Soviet border, copying military traffic for eight hours at a time. Every man was a volunteer, on a difficult, dangerous assignment, and they quickly developed that sense of brotherhood that comes from belonging to an elite, exclusive, confidential club.

They would develop a great affection for the C-130, but for all its beauty and power, it didn't have the sense of history and romance that their first aircraft possessed. Because in the first two years of the outfit's existence, they flew on actual bombers; and on a bomber, a twenty-year-old could feel like John Wayne.

Until the C-130s began to arrive in the late summer of 1958, they had flown the B-50, an improved version of the B-29 that had been further converted to serve as an airborne communications intelligence (COMINT) reconnaissance platform. The rear bomb bay had been replaced by a module that contained positions for five radio intercept operators and a radio repairman. One man sat in each of two pods where formerly the waist gunners had been stationed. Referred to as scanners, they were the lucky ones with a view. Part of their job was to keep an eye on the nearly constant leakage of oil from the engines on their side of the plane:

"Flight engineer, this is the left scanner. Oil streaming out of engine number two."

"How broad?"

"Six to eight inches."

"Roger, keep an eye on it."

Legend had it that no flight engineer would pay real attention to an oil leak until it had developed into a stream three feet wide. The engines were so worn that they seemed porous, without gaskets of any type. The men were never surprised when the flight engineer had to shut down an engine; it was merely part of the daily routine. They lived with the possibility that they could be shot down by the Soviets. But as far as they were concerned, a far greater possibility was that one of the old crates they flew would crash.

Behind the scanners themselves sat two more operators, and in the rear of the module was the commander of the recon mission (the airborne mission supervisor), a sergeant referred to as the "admiral." The sixth man, the airborne maintenance technician (AMT), sat opposite the admiral, but for much of the time, when the equipment was in good working order, he slept up front, in a shelflike indentation in the front wall of the module.

Grover Campbell, a small, highly popular man from Chicago, could sleep better than most of the other AMTs. He was very good at his job, and once, when one of the Russian operators had caught measles and was scratched from a flight at the last minute, he flew as an intercept operator, and did a good job at that, too. But he liked to sleep. On flights in Turkey, he would sometimes inject oranges with vodka, and by the time the flight was a few hours old, he would be flying higher than the plane or sleeping peacefully.

Once, on a mission out of Rhein-Main, the men decided to play a trick on Grover. They reached up onto the platform where he was sleeping and stole his parachute. They then donned their own chutes and lined up at the emergency exit. The admiral took one of Grover's large wrenches and gave three sharp raps on the emergency bell. Grover jumped up, leaped down from the platform, reached for a chute that wasn't there, and nearly flew around the cabin looking for it, while the men gazed at him solemnly. The men were serious about their jobs, but when the radios were turned off, it was playtime.

The module in which they flew was primitive at best. Toilet facilities consisted of a large pail. Since the first man to use it had to carry it down the ladder and empty it at the end of each mission, all of the men learned heroic bowel control. There was also a "piss tube," a hose with a rather narrow funnel at the end that, at the press of a button, released urine into the outer air with almost no loss of air pressure inside the plane.

The veterans quickly learned to make more creative use of the tube. Since pressing the tube produced a hissing sound, much like the sound of an open microphone, the men developed a script for beginners.

At times they had to break in as many as three men on one day, but whenever possible, they took only one new man on a given mission. Before the aircraft taxied out to the runway, the copilot went through an extensive checklist, item by item, position by position, for about ten minutes. The intercept operators in the module had very little to do with that checklist, the left and right scanners merely reporting on the movement of the controls—but the new man didn't know that. He was told that he played a crucial role in the checklist, and when the copilot called out certain items to be checked, he was to open his "microphone"— actually the piss tube—and give specific answers. He would stand there, nervous at this, his first important duty, his nostrils filled with a rather foul odor, thinking that the mission depended on the accuracy of the answers the veterans had written out for him. More often than not, his stage fright would mean that when he had finished his "checklist," he would then be the first to use the slop bucket. No matter who used it first, even if the new man didn't use it at all, it would be his job to empty it after the mission.

It was no fun being a rookie—a "jeep," as the outfit called their newcomers. "I hate jeeps," Lincoln Gilbert used to snarl at any new man who made even the most innocuous of statements in his presence. He didn't really mean it, nor did any of the others, but Gil's growling was part of the mild hazing that greeted each new man in that elite team.

Of course, in 1958 even the veterans didn't know much about flying. That period has been accurately referred to as the "kick-the-tires-and-go" phase of the outfit's operation. Detachments 1's "Jump School" was representative of the unit's training methodology in the 1950s: new recruits would be given a flight suit, shown how to put on a parachute with both a backpack and a chest pack, taken out to the plane a few at a time, and told to jump from the emergency exit to the ground, bending their knees and rolling to the side as they landed on the tarmac. So much for parachute training. Much later, in the 1960s, they received formal simulated jump training. Finally, by the 1990s, they simply were not issued parachutes at all.

If they had ever jumped from the RB-50s in actual flight conditions, their chances of survival were slim, though they didn't realize it. The emergency exit was located in the belly of the plane. During an emergency, the first man in line to bail out was to stand on the exit plate, pull a rope, and he and the plate would fall from the plane. Then the other five men would follow through the open door.

The problem with the procedure was that a large metal protuberance containing radio antennas was a few feet behind the exit on the belly of the plane. In late 1958, when the RB-50s had finished their service in Europe, they were taken back to the States for phase maintenance and minimal upgrades for use in the Pacific. Rumor had it that during a series of tests, ten 200-pound dummies were dropped through the emergency exit. (Most of the men weighed closer to 150 than to 200 pounds.) The first eight smashed into the dome; the last two made it past the dome, which was by then badly crushed itself. After that test, which proved that the "radome" was fatal, the plane was sent, radome and all, to be used by the unit's sister outfit in Japan.

The rest of the airborne training was as primitive as Jump School.

The men would be taken up, sometimes as many as three at a time, to fly a mission under two of the experienced NCOs. One of the sergeants, usually the radio repairman on the flight, would show them how to operate the intercept radios on the panel in front of them, and how to record on the reel-to-reel tape recorder that each position contained.

In every phase of the work in those early days, training was either inadequate or nonexistent. In part that was because some of the NCOs in charge of the outfit had made a conscious decision to allow their men to know as little as possible—should an intercept operator fall into enemy hands, the less he knew, the better. On the wall of the large operations room was a chart showing the outlines of various Soviet aircraft, but the men never went through recognition drills. They had never listened to or read any information on Soviet—or for that matter, American—air procedures. Their primary function was to capture on tape as much Soviet military chatter as they could get during a given mission, bring it back to Rhein-Main, let the men who were not flying that day transcribe it—not translate it into English, but simply type up as much of the Russian conversations as they could make out through the radio static—and pass along that raw data to the analysis center at the 6901st Special Comms Group, Zweibrücken, Germany. Not until late 1958 did the outfit begin to do any real analysis of the material it intercepted.

Of course, when the plane was actually being shadowed by one or more Soviet fighters, instant analysis became a necessity. The best Russian linguist flew the "defensive" position, listening in on the current fighter attack frequency to see how seriously disturbed the Russians were by the presence of the enemy plane along their border. In most cases there was no great problem, since the Russians were listening in on American air traffic from just outside our border every day. Since, in a sense, the two sides held one another hostage, neither side felt any great sense of urgency—at least not on the lower, operational level.

In *The Puzzle Palace*, his study of the National Security Agency, James Bamford writes:

> [Though the military personnel] had the advantage of providing a cheap labor force, it also had a number of definite disadvantages. One of them was that most operators were young military personnel on short tours of

duty. Because their turnover was high, the risks that one might someday
decide to blow the whistle on the operation was greatly increased.[104]

Cheap help. The men didn't realize it, but nobody in those early
days, either in the military hierarchy or in the NSA itself, felt a strong
need for intensive training when so many men were, in the long view,
simply passing through.

Moreover, the simple newness of the outfit and its mission meant
that the modus operandi was primitive. In any large institution—and the
military is no exception—procedures develop as the result of experience.
Nobody in the 6911th had any experience with the contingencies of flying intelligence-gathering missions, because very few men in the American military had ever flown such missions. The men tried to look
disciplined, at least when on duty, but it didn't always work.

A good example of the problems of those early days was "the
weapon." One man, armed with a .45 caliber pistol, guarded the fenced-
in operations building at all times, and another airman, armed with a .45
or, sometimes, a .38 revolver, guarded the black box full of tapes and mission information to and from the plane for each flight.

But the pistols were a source of trouble because nobody had been
shown how to handle them, let alone fire them. One morning, that day's
guard panicked on guard duty because one of his colleagues, a man he
had known for several months, tried to enter the locked area without
putting on his photo ID badge. The guard threatened to shoot him on the
spot, and the man dared him to do it; they stood there glaring at each
other, the guard sweating and pointing the pistol at his friend's head, until one of the sergeants came out and cooled down the situation. He took
the weapon away from the guard, and the other man put on the badge.

Another of our outfit's "marksmen" sometimes carried the weapon to
and from the aircraft, but out of fear of shooting himself in the foot or
worse, he had never bothered to learn how to load it. He told his buddies
that he would throw the damned thing at anyone who threatened to steal
the black box. Like so much of what went on in the outfit prior to 1958,
the .45 was a toy in a dangerous game played by adolescents.

Then there was the unit's vehicle. It seemed reasonable to the leaders
of the outfit that they should have a vehicle at their disposal, and that all

the men should take turns driving it. They hadn't taken into consideration that a group of skilled linguists did not necessarily make for a group of skilled chauffeurs. After about a year of daily rotation of the driving duties, one of the men made a large blunder. Part of the operating procedure was that the driver for the day should start by filling the tank with gasoline and checking the fluid levels. Having gassed up, one of the less mechanically skilled chauffeurs checked the levels, found that the radiator was low, and poured in two quarts of motor oil. The base motor pool quickly decided it was too dangerous to allow Detachment 1 to have its own vehicle.

Despite nearly constant horseplay, the men worked hard at their jobs. But they worked every bit as hard at their off-duty pursuits, which consisted primarily in drinking and picking up women.

Part of the attraction of Detachment 1 was the fact that the men got paid $55 extra a month in hazardous duty pay, and got to spend that extra money in one of the cosmopolitan centers of West Germany—Frankfurt, a place with first-rate opera, the finest jazz scene in Germany, several wonderful art museums lining the Main River, and, most important, hundreds of prostitutes and other young women looking for sexual companionship. The Städtele Museum contained a highly impressive Rembrandt painting of Delilah smiling triumphantly as the Philistine soldiers blind and shackle Samson, but the men of Detachment 1 paid no more attention to the moral of that painting than they did to Colonel Amen's sermonettes. They liked women. Since the army units throughout Germany, and most of the other Air Force outfits as well, had to obey an eleven o'clock curfew, Detachment 1 swing shifters, for example, could head downtown at midnight, after their army compatriots had bought their girls liquor all evening, and move in to take advantage of the situation.

The detachment was therefore at odds with the entire army and much of the Air Force a good deal of the time. There were constant brawls over women, as well as a good number of fights caused by the fact that the intelligence outfit was socially as well as formally integrated racially. If you sat in the Royal Bar or the Fischerstube, where the prostitutes hung out, or frequented the King Bar, the primary location for picking up girls looking for a good time, you were bound to get into trouble sooner or later—mostly sooner. But that was part of the game, and the occasional black eye or broken nose was a cheap price to pay for the good clean fun the men had. Hell, Samson had paid with his eyes.

The Café Royal, right across the street from the train station, served as unofficial detachment headquarters. When the King Bar closed for the night, and the Fischerstube began to smell too bad, everyone headed for the Café Royal. At times, a dozen or more of the men could be found there at four-thirty in the morning. At one point, a sergeant went on leave, planning to travel to a few of the major cities of Europe, and ended up spending his entire two-week vacation in the Café Royal. The men brought him changes of clothes every few days, and cheered on his ability to stay awake. Instead of taking pictures of the tourist sites of, say, Amsterdam, he came back to the base with a picture of the clock on the Bahnhof tower taken every hour for an entire twenty-four-hour period. He became yet another legend, a figure to be admired and emulated by the younger men who served under him.

The Fischerstube was a bit more than a block away, and if it was at all possible, was scurvier than the Café Royal. None of the men—except maybe the Germ—would have thought of picking up a prostitute in the Fischerstube. But the atmosphere was pleasant, homey, and there were always little surprises to liven up a dull evening—like the time one of the prostitutes gave birth in the ladies' room.

Once, the board of governors of the Rhein-Main Airmen Club decided to create a more family atmosphere by scheduling a "Bring your wife to the Airmen Club" evening. When many of the bachelors on the base complained of the restriction, that quickly got modified to a "Bring your wife or your girlfriend to the Airmen Club." Three of the Detachment 1 airmen decided to liven things up. That afternoon they went to the Fischerstube, picked out the three loudest, drunkest, prostitutes they could find, and escorted them to the club in early evening.

As the evening went on and the drinking grew heavier, the three young ladies grew louder and more obnoxious. By nine o'clock they were screaming obscenities at the other women, the band, and the waiters who were trying to quiet them down. The Air Police not only threw all three couples out of the club, they escorted them to the gate. It must have been one of the few times that an airman was thrown off his own base.

On a hot summer day in Frankfurt a few months later, a group of the men decided to use the ornamental fountain in front of the main train station as a beer cooler. A busy, central intersection of a major German city turned out not to be a good place for a picnic. It didn't take long for the Military Police to notice that there were several cases of beer in the fountain, or that a small group of American drunks was happily seated on the road in front of the fountain, drinking cool beer. They arrested the entire group and brought them to the main MP station in town, a location that most of the men knew well. Luckily, Goldenstar was still the first sergeant in those early days, and he drank about as heavily as the rest of the outfit. He received the call from an irate MP captain, and managed to bury the deficiency reports before Captain Tarbox saw them.

One of the constant problems for anyone stationed in Germany in those days was neckties. The necktie order was a stupid U.S. Army regulation, the primary purpose of which seemed to be to make GIs stand out like sore thumbs. All military personnel in civilian clothes had to wear a tie after six P.M. It could be, and quite normally was, a tie that had nothing at all to do with the rest of your outfit. About the only men who tried hard to look traditionally well-dressed in town were the black guys. But even the most stupid tie, one with a picture of Mickey Mouse or a forest fire, would keep a GI out of trouble. The lack of a tie, on the other hand, would get him arrested and put a Discrepancy Report on your record; and a DR was a DR, whether it was for mayhem or for a missing tie. Accumulate enough DRs and you got busted one rank. Therefore, when the lookout outside the King Bar, for example, reported that the MPs were coming up the road, every man without a tie ran for the back door or a window. Once, a lieutenant tried to hold the men in the bar for the MPs by flashing his ID card and shouting that he was an officer; he got kicked in the stomach for his troubles.

West Germany's currency reform had only taken place a few years earlier, and the country had yet to undergo even the beginnings of the *Wirtschaftswunder* that would turn it once again into one of the industrial and financial powers of the world. The dollar was worth 4.20 Deutschmarks, which meant that a beer cost perhaps a quarter, a good meal less than five dollars, and the best-looking prostitute in the Royal Bar maybe $25. Five dollars was the going rate for the average prostitute, and penicillin was of course free at the dispensary on base. It was a good time to be an American overseas, a great time to be a young man in Frankfurt with a pocketful of money and no curfew.

The command structure was rather remote from the day-to-day workings of the outfit. The commander, the operations officer, and the first sergeant took care of the promotions—and frequent demotions—and kept track of the records, the necessary bureaucratic work of the outfit. But the mission itself, as far as the men could see, at any rate, was in the very capable hands of T.Sgt. Stanley Kresge. One of the older men in the outfit, somewhere in his early thirties, Kresge looked like everybody's conception of a sergeant. A rather short man, he possessed a fireplug body and a face like a fist. He spent a fair amount of time shouting, but most of the men liked or at least respected him. He seemed to possess reams of arcane knowledge about the field of intelligence gathering, which gave him—at least until the fall of 1958—an aura of infallibility. No wonder: Kresge was a man who never told anyone anything if he could help it. It was not simply that he had spent his career in intelligence, where the "need to know" is the central rule of access to information; it was also part of his personal character, that refusal to share what he knew in more than the occasional, apparently offhand, remark.

Kresge had been in the service long enough to know that in any bureaucracy, private knowledge is the key to power. And he thrived on power. Captain Tarbox was nearly as old as Kresge, and Major Webster even older, but neither of them could approach Kresge's intimate knowledge of the details of 6911th's mission. In effect, though of course not in rank, Kresge was the day-to-day commander of the outfit.

M.Sgt. Pete Petrochilos was the only noncommissioned officer in Operations who outranked Kresge. Petrochilos, a bachelor, had enlisted in 1940, and had seen service through the entire war and then the Korean conflict as well. Everyone was a bit in awe of Pete. He was far and away the best poker player in an outfit filled with good card players. Legend had it that Pete could sit and read a book until it came time for his bet. At its most extreme form, the myth was that Pete could finish three books in the course of a card game and still come out way ahead. If Kresge was the center of power, Pete was the father figure.

And there was Bruce Henderson, a man approaching forty who should have been an officer. Henderson was an avid bridge player, and a

regular participant in the poker and blackjack games in the Incirlik
Quonset huts. He was careful, however, not to win too much, or take advantage of the young "high rollers" who frequently got in well over their
heads in those games. He seemed to have a paternal instinct not to abuse
the young troops; he didn't really need the money, and played cards with
the gang mostly for entertainment and socializing.

A married man, Henderson had been a bomber pilot in World
War II, and he had stories about the giant sorties from England over the
German territory in which he was now stationed. He knew, for example,
how dangerous the tail gunner's position had been. He told the men
about the number of American tail gunners killed by friendly fire in those
enormous formations, and they listened to him with a respect bordering
on awe.

They felt sorry for him, too, however. Henderson had been a captain
up until a few months before he joined the outfit, but he had been passed
over one time too many for promotion to major, and was "riffed" down to
his permanent rank of airman first class; later he was promoted to staff
sergeant. He had no choice but to accept the insult; he was too close to
retirement (after which his retirement pay would be calculated based on
his officer rank). Sometimes, early in the morning when the entire plane
crew was waiting for a repair to be finished, he would leave the group of
back-enders standing near the back, and approach the officers standing
beside the cockpit. It never worked; they never accepted him. He would
say a few words to them, realize they wanted nothing to do with him, and
then he would stroll back to the men as though he had not just been
insulted.

The officers were probably afraid of him, probably saw him as a mirror of what could happen to them at any time. The late 1950s were a difficult time to be an officer. There were too many of them with too much
time in the service. Promotion was extremely difficult for an officer or
even a sergeant, because there was a glut at the top. The Vietnam War
would eliminate that problem.

Then there were the younger noncoms. Kozak, from Pennsylvania, a
technical sergeant and fellow Pole, was not really young, but he wor-
shiped Kresge as if Kresge had been his younger brother. "Stash," he
called him, using the Polish familiar form for Stanley. Most of the men

liked Kozak. A bachelor in his late thirties, he confided to his second-in-command during one flight home that once, during high school, he had something approaching a love affair. "Lord, that girl was classy, and she loved sex," he recalled nostalgically. "She couldn't get enough of it, and I made sure she got it . . . but my old man found out about it and hit me over the head with a ball-peen hammer . . . That straightened me right out . . . My old man really knew a lot about life." Apparently, Kozak Senior had effective teaching methods, too. On recovering from the blow to the skull, Kozak had entered the military, where he belonged, where women were at best casual acquaintances.

Not all the sergeants were drinkers. Some, like S.Sgt. Bob Bergeron, were quiet family men. Bergeron, who spoke French as well as Russian, was a dependable, decent human being who managed to get along with a group full of heavy drinkers because of his generally unassuming nature. Like all of the noncoms, he was a career man, who loved the Air Force and believed in Detachment 1's mission passionately. He was a good man to fly with; you knew he wasn't going to be hung over, and although he was newer to the mission than many of the men he outranked, he managed to give his crews the feeling that they were under a reasonably reliable leader. Married, he had relatively little to do with the men socially, but they liked him.

The men were closer to the bachelor noncoms who drank, though, for obvious reasons. One of the outfit's legendary stories, like so much of 6911th lore, had to do with Captain Tarbox. Several times a year officers were allowed into the NCO Club. It was like ladies' night, or Bring Your Daughter to Work Day; it was expected that the noncoms would invite their commanders for a drink. When Tarbox became commander, he was invited, but he made the mistake of arriving late, after his NCOs had had time to get quite a few too many snorts under their belts. He walked over to the table where a half dozen of them were seated, and in an attempt to break the ice, remarked: "Men, just treat me like one of the guys." One of the drunker sergeants growled: "I don't see any frigging stripes on your sleeve." The night was not a success—at least not in the expected manner.

Although the noncoms who headed up the maintenance section of the outfit held themselves aloof from their men socially, the majority of the language-specialist NCOs made little distinction between the ranks. They drank with the men as intensively as they worked with them, and the men loved them for it.

S.Sgt. Jack Roberts bore the nickname "Fang." As far as one could tell, it was because he was an utterly gentle human being, one of the kindest, most intelligent men in the outfit, with an appearance, even at twenty-five, that gave the false impression of slight frailty. Fang was an utterly dependable human being. Like his friend Mac, he hung out with the enlisted men. Rarely totally drunk, seldom close to sober during the frequent all-night sessions in the Royal Bar or the Fischerstube, he watched the "younger" men make utter asses of themselves night after night, thoroughly enjoying the spectacle. But aside from a dignified stagger to the men's room and a tendency to slur his words by, say, three o'clock in the morning, he showed relatively few signs of inebriation—at least by the standards of Detachment 1. Years later, at the end of his career, he would be voted into the Freedom Through Vigilance Association Hall of Honor.

His good friend S.Sgt. Bill McCormick made up for Fang's quietness with the manner of a drunken rooster. Of all the noncoms, Mac was the loudest and the most fun. It was he who christened half the outfit with a series of nicknames—Weasel, Fang, Slick, Little Turk, Big Dumb, etc. In July 1957 he took Dumb, Slick, and Joel Fields up on their first mission. "I taught you babies everything," he would bellow to Slick years later in Maryland. "Turned you into men!" Once, when he had taken Big Dumb and Joel on their first mission, he decided to celebrate by taking them to Heidelberg and getting them drunk in new surroundings. By late that evening the new men were plastered, but Mac was even worse off. Driving away from the center of town in an ostentatiously unsteady manner, they found themselves chased by the Heidelberg MPs. Mac, at the wheel of his Volkswagen, decided on a quick evasive maneuver: he made a ninety-degree right turn into an alley, unfortunately without noticing how close together the buildings were. The Beetle ended up wedged between the two houses, its front end several inches narrower than it had been a minute before.

Most of the men in the outfit were heavy drinkers, guzzlers who could sit next to Fang or Mac for twenty-four hours or more and hold their own. The department record for beer-drinking was held by Barney Rakestraw, of Little Rock, Arkansas, a small man who managed to put away thirty-seven glasses of draft beer before fading off into a well-deserved sleep. His record was nearly matched a few months later by Big Dumb, several inches taller and fifty pounds heavier than Barney. Dumb drank thirty-five glasses within less than three hours, and seemed well on his way to the championship when a German acquaintance walked into the bar and, spotting Dumb, bought him a shot of schnapps. Never one to turn down a free drink, Dumb lifted the glass to his acquaintance's good health, swallowed the contents at a gulp, and fell over onto the floor.

Dumb's luck was always bad like that, from the time he entered the Air Force until the day he left. During pre-language school at Kelly Air Force Base, in San Antonio, he found himself alone one evening in his three-man room and entertained himself by occasionally tossing a firecracker out the window. Nothing dangerous, but he enjoyed the sound. After a half hour or so of throwing them into the parking lot, he decided the blast would sound even louder if he exploded one in the hall. A cautious man who didn't want to get into trouble, he lit the fuse before he opened the door, then adroitly stepped into the hall ready to toss the cracker and found himself confronted by two Air Policemen. That was the first of several times when he lost a stripe.

He gained his nickname not through anything actually stupid—he was actually quite intelligent—but, again, because of his almost inevitable bad luck. He was busy talking to two friends one summer day as they entered the base cafeteria at Rhein-Main. Looking back at them, he failed to notice that the glass door was in fact closed, and he stepped with complete dignity through an absolute shower of glass fragments. Big Dumb seemed a fitting name for a large man who could do that, no matter how smart he was.

He hated the name, despised it. On his last day at Rhein-Main, scheduled to fly back to the States and civilian life at two P.M., he rushed around, making final preparations, gathering his stuff together at the last moment as his friends stood around and watched, even occasionally helped him. "I'm going to miss you guys a lot," he remarked, "but there's one thing I won't miss a bit: that damned nickname!" He should not have brought up that subject. Having no time left to mail his final packages, he left two wrapped cartons with his friends. They accompanied him to his flight, then returned to the barracks, unwrapped the boxes, and put fresh wrapping on them addressed to "Big Dumb," with his address below.

Even among a group of heavy drinkers, one man stood out: Moe. He was not a tough human being; no one had ever seen him in a fight. But let him once get drunk—and he was drunk a good deal of the time—and he took great glee in insulting men who were much bigger or much more powerful socially than he was. He sat in the Airmen Club at Rhein-Main one evening, listing heavily to one side, when a group of men from another outfit sat down at the next table. Moe immediately began heckling the biggest of them, very quietly but steadily. "Asshole, your brain's in your crotch . . . silly looking bastard . . . haven't had a thought since high school, if you ever got to high school."

Luckily for Moe, the man was gentler than he looked. But nobody can keep his temper forever. After about a half hour the man stood up, grabbed Moe by the shoulder and growled, "One more word and I'll beat the living shit out of you."

Moe didn't even bother looking up. In the same quiet voice, he answered, "Yeah, but you'll still be an asshole when you're finished with me." The man and his friends moved to another table. Clearly, at Rhein-Main brains were not limited to the detachment.

Several months later Moe and a friend were sitting, or at least trying hard to sit, in the Royal Bar, which boasted that it closed for a total of one hour a week, in order to tidy up. It was four o'clock on a Monday morning and they were the only customers left in the bar. The owner suggested that they leave, but they felt they hadn't finished drinking. He had known them for a year, and he finally agreed to let them stay, but only if they kept their mouths shut, because the top gangster in Frankfurt, who was apparently a silent partner in the bar, was coming in to have a chat with some other crooks. Since his friend was too drunk to talk at all, and Moe was not much better, the two airmen nodded in silent agreement.

The two of them together didn't weigh 300 pounds, and neither of them could fight even when sober. They sat there at the back of the room, smiling stupidly at one another, as five gangsters walked in. One of them, obviously the leader, was a small man in his late fifties. The other four were much younger, and huge. They looked like professional wrestlers, though they all wore expensive suits.

It took Moe about five minutes to go into his quiet routine: "Stupid bastard, about the size of the average dick, doesn't look like he could run a bratwurst stand . . . " His friend began to feel that he had only a few more minutes to live, but he was too stupefied to do more than ponder his coming end philosophically. Moe just kept on talking. Finally two of the thugs walked over, one for each airman. They picked them up with surprising gentleness, carried them out, and placed them on the sidewalk as if they were that week's garbage, then went back inside to sit with their boss again.

After September 1958, when the plane had been shot down and the mood of the outfit turned bleak, Moe began drinking even heavier, and he lost his clearance. Perhaps it was no coincidence that his best friend, Dick, who could look stupider than anyone else in the outfit when he was drunk, later became an officer; perhaps the friend turned Moe in for some infraction. That sort of thing could make officers sit up and take notice of your potential to become an officer and a gentleman.

Certainly none of the rest of the men would have seen Dick as officer material. One night Moe and the future officer came in around nine-thirty in the evening, already wasted from a day's drinking in Frankfurt. Dick fell, fully clothed, into bed, but Moe was suddenly overcome by the need to tidy up his area. While twenty or so men looked on at the unexpected entertainment, Moe fetched the big industrial buffer from the hallway, plugged it in, and began to buff the floor around his bunk. Dick, who bunked next to him, found Moe's sudden neatness hilarious, and started to giggle. Moe took affront at his lack of proper gravity, picked up the buffer and began to buff his bunkmate. The other men struggled for several minutes to get the buffer away from Moe and to untangle Dick from the machine. Dick was still giggling. Even forty years later it seems amazing that anyone who drank as heavily as that man did could have sobered up long enough to get through Officers Candidate School.

At any rate, whether through the ministrations of his friend or simply through his own habitual drunkenness, Moe lost his clearance. He was busted down to airman basic (the lowest pay grade), taken off flight status, and banned from the operations building. He was not, however, transferred from the outfit; presumably, since he had only a few months left in the Air Force, the command structure figured it would not be worth the paperwork. Instead he was assigned to the base woodwork hobby shop and told to make tables.

Moe had about as much ability to build a table as he had to maintain a truck. He never successfully put together two boards in his six months or so in the hobby shop. Early one morning, well before dawn, the base sirens went off, signaling a rare, unannounced alert. Grumbling and moaning, the men fell out of bed, dressed, and straggled outside the building into something like a military formation. Within a half hour or so Captain Tarbox had arrived from his off-base housing. The first sergeant called the men to attention, Tarbox strode out of his car, all spit and polish, and barked loudly, "All men to their duty stations!"

From the back of the ranks came Moe's voice, as serious in its own way as his commander's: "Sir, the base hobby shop doesn't open till ten A.M." Another defeat for Captain Nails.

Of course, not every man was a heavy drinker. There were teetotalers--whom the rest of the outfit largely avoided—and there were some who were, by the unit's high standards, light drinkers. Joel Fields was one of the most popular men in the entire outfit, and on most nights he got by with less alcohol than his friends. Once, following a squadron picnic, seven or eight of the men had continued their celebration at a bar a few hundred yards from the front gate of the base. Unfortunately for them, they had just seen *The Bridge on the River Kwai* a few days earlier, and they decided, instead of simply walking back to the barracks, to march back and insist on their rights "as officers." They marched up to the front gate in civilian clothes whistling the theme song of the movie, and refused the guard's reasonable request to see identification. After about ten minutes of almost pleading with them, while Moe hollered continually, "Officers do not have to work on the bridge!" the guard felt compelled to arrest them. They were hauled over to the Air Police headquarters in the back of a truck, lined up against the wall and searched. Joel brought from his pockets a collection of weapons that said a lot about him: two lollipops and a package of chewing gum. That's how straight Joel was. But he was living proof that you could be popular without being a lush. Everybody liked and respected Joel, from the commander on down. A good-looking, rather small man from a town north of Lexington, Kentucky, he had been class president of his high school; he and two of his friends had formed a doo-wop trio that lipsynched the hits of the day and became the showbiz stars of their hometown. He never told the others in the outfit about that aspect of his background, never talked about himself at all, for that matter. But if you got into trouble, you could always count on Joel either to be in trouble with you or to provide a sympathetic ear as you told him how unfair the police had been.

If Joel represented the extreme peaceful fringe in the outfit, John Argoe represented the other side. Argoe, about six-foot-one, 195 pounds of muscle, had wandered into the base gym one day and found himself invited to spar with the light-heavyweight champion of the U.S. Air Forces, Europe Command. He knocked the man out in the second round.

But you didn't have to be an amateur boxer to find yourself in a fight with John; you didn't even have to weigh more than 130 or so pounds. He was far and away the meanest drunk in the outfit—in fact the only really mean drunk. Once he got three or four beers under his belt, you began moving away from him. He would sit there, sulking, and begin to look for trouble. Anybody who made eye contact with him was liable to become his enemy. "You staring at me?" he would ask, and there wasn't any safe answer. He would get up, or simply reach across the table, and knock you cold. Once in a wine town on the Rhein, he coldcocked a German who happened to glance his way, then knocked five of his mates flat as, one after the other, they piled on his back.

The only man he had any fear of was Warren (Lennie) Hamaker. Lennie, a highly intelligent man, had received his nickname by being as big as the simpleton in Steinbeck's *Of Mice and Men*. He was enormous, with a barrel-shaped chest and huge biceps. He was also one of the nicest men in the entire outfit—perhaps because he could afford to be.

It was inevitable; sooner or later Argoe was going to get drunk enough to get over his avoidance of Lennie and try him out. One night at the King Bar, Lennie glanced at him at the wrong time, and the battle began. They fought each other up and down the bar, across the dance floor, out the door, fell over the railing onto the sidewalk and pummeled each other ultimately to a draw. John was far and away the better boxer, amazingly quick with his fists, and, as always, had gotten in the first punch—which in most cases would have been enough. But Lennie was just too tough for him, could absorb anything John could hand out. John never fought him again. Within a week they were reasonably close friends again.

Every once in a while, instead of getting simply belligerent after a few drinks, John got religion, which unfortunately became for him merely a more complicated form of belligerency. One hot afternoon in Turkey, when most of the men were lying on their bunks reading, John staggered in plastered and went into his South Carolina Baptist harangue. "There's no book worth anything but the Bible," he roared at nobody in particular. "All that shit you guys read ain't gonna last but a few weeks. Bible lasted hundreds a years, and you guys just read shit." John was not a reading man himself, not even if it was the Bible. But he was filled with drunken piety. He snatched a book from the hands of the man nearest him. Unfortunately for his argument, it was a collection of the writings of Aristotle. "Look at this crap—Aristol," and he pronounced it as if it were a spray can, "been out about two weeks, best-seller probably, gonna be gone in about another ten days." The men all nodded sagely. That's about all you could do when John got religion.

You could tell that John Argoe wasn't going to make it to middle age. Sooner or later he was going to get shot, or knifed, maybe bludgeoned to death by a jealous boyfriend of one of the dozens of women he picked up. Yet his death, not long after 528 was shot down, shocked the outfit a little—to the extent that it could still be shocked. On one of those incredibly foggy nights that Frankfurt experienced with great regularity all winter, John was a passenger in a car heading back to the base. An unseen truck pulled out from a highway rest stop, and the small car drove right under it, crushing the right side. John was beheaded. The outfit hardly mourned him; they had lost too many men too recently to mourn yet another loss. Death seemed something to be taken for granted in the months following September 1958.

The men who served in the early days of the outfit are getting old now. Newspapers reporting on the memorial service in September 1997 referred to the two hundred or so 6911th veterans sitting in a separate section of the bleachers as "aging warriors." The term seemed amazing to all of them on that weekend when they had sat together telling war stories of their youth—but it was accurate enough. In fact the only ones still young are the men who died that autumn afternoon in 1958—and John, who died soon thereafter. The rest of them have grown gray, put on weight over the years, married, divorced, produced children, in many cases even grandchildren. And then they look at their photo albums, and there they are, still young. Joel Fields sliding home on a close play while Petrochilos waves him in as a good coach should. Maggiacomo, his horn-rimmed glasses riding low on his nose as usual, holding Ferguson's baby girl—Debra. Debra is a mother now. But Fields and Maggiacomo and Ferguson have never grown old, never had time to reach maturity either in the military or in civilian life. Never even made it past airmen second class.

A year or so after the shootdown, one of the lost airmen's friends in the squadron was promoted to airman first class. He dreamt that night that Joel Fields came to him silently, a look of strong disapproval on his face. The dreamer attempted to placate him, to get him to stay; he told him he would give him that extra new stripe if he would only remain. Joel's face retained its stony expression, and he slowly moved off into the distance and disappeared.

One of the men who didn't make it to the memorial dedication in 1997 was Wimpy Belmont. He was at home in Canyon Lake, Texas, waiting for a heart transplant that never came. As the end approached a few months later, his daughter sat by his side in the hospital. Wimpy died well, keeping up his daughter's spirits. He didn't want a sad wake and funeral, he told her; he wanted people laughing and talking about the good things in his life. As an example, he told her a story of "a guy named Slick" and his "death" and resurrection from the Detachment 1 days. Its festive stages took place, fittingly enough, in the Royal Bar. Later she would hear a fuller version of the story from Slick himself.

It happened only a few weeks after 528 had been shot down, in the awful emptiness of the period when the outfit was grounded, a time when there was still some hope that at least some of the men on the plane might be alive.

Most of the men in the outfit were angry at the Russians, at the

American brass, at everyone in the world who was not part of Detach-ment 1. And they weren't real happy about their own officers and NCOs either. During that period, the outfit gathered every weekday morning for a briefing in which they were told nothing, and then had the rest of the day off. After the briefing one Friday morning, Moe and Slick decided to take the train from Frankfurt to Rüdesheim, a tourist village on the Rhein. They arrived in the town around one in the afternoon, and by sundown were already just barely able to walk.

Somehow, they managed to keep drinking all night. In the morning, they found themselves staggering along the dike between the railroad tracks and the river, waiting for the train to take them back to Frankfurt. They had reached a point opposite the station when the train appeared around the corner, perhaps two hundred yards away. "Let's run," Moe hollered, and staggered as rapidly as possible toward the overpass that led to the right side of the tracks. Slick just casually let himself fall over the restraining fence, rolled down the hillside, managed to roll across the tracks a few feet in front of the oncoming train, crawl up onto the empty platform, and then, tired from the combination of hard drinking and strenuous exertion, he curled up under a bench and immediately fell into something between sleep and a coma.

Moe had seen what he interpreted as the train running over his buddy. When he arrived a moment or two later on the platform, he looked around under the tracks and could find no body parts. But then, he found no live Slick, either. He boarded the train, and when he arrived in Frankfurt an hour or so later, he crossed to the Royal and announced to the half-dozen or so Detachment 1 troops gathered there for their Sat-urday morning refreshment the manner of Slick's passing.

Death was pretty familiar to the men by then. They ordered another round and began a semiformal celebration of the man's short life, each telling a story or two about his adventures. The affair had its solemn side, but there was a good deal of laughter.

Meanwhile, as the next train was ready to pull into Rüdesheim, the railroad authorities had discovered the drunk under the bench. They were not happy. They poured him onto the train to Frankfurt and told him not to come back. Arriving in Frankfurt, Slick of course immediately headed toward the Royal, and found himself in the middle of his own wake. He joined in with gusto, telling a few stories of his own in a somewhat slurred voice, and the party turned from a wake into a celebration of life without skipping a beat. No wonder that Wimpy, a few moments from death, would think back on that one drunken morning.

It was like that in Detachment 1. Like soldiers in any war, the men who engaged in the Silent War were very young, both sentimental and cynical, very serious both about their job and about getting just as much fun as possible out of their free time. They had seen, that September, just how short life can be, and just how dangerous their occupation really was. But they carried on. And they would have carried on even if their losses had been much heavier. They were a fine group of men, and Wimpy was right to fix his mind on them at the end. Probably, when the others from that group lie dying, many of them will think back on those strange, wonderful years when they were separate from a world at peace, when they were part of a small group carrying on their own little war.

SEVEN

60528'S LAST CREW

In March 1957 the 7406th Support Squadron and Detachment 1, 6911th Radio Group Mobile, despite the fact that they were based in Germany, commenced flying recon missions over the Black Sea. To support those missions, each unit kept aircrews deployed on temporary duty at Incirlik Air Base, just outside Adana, a city in south-central Turkey. The units also flew "local" missions from Rhein-Main Air Base and started deploying to bases other than Incirlik in 1958. The deployments to Turkey had become routine—at any given time, a 7406th flight crew and a Detachment 1 Security Service recon crew were on temporary duty for approximately two weeks at Incirlik to fly missions in the Black Sea area. Typically, the men served away from home on a rotating basis, spending approximately two of every six to eight weeks on temporary duty in Turkey. C-130 60528's seventeen crew members during the fateful shootdown on September 2, 1958, are listed in Figure Three. The plane was manned by a six-member flight crew that flew the aircraft and eleven recon crew members whose mission it was to intercept military communications emanating from the Soviet Union.

Figure Three—C-130 60528's Last Crew

Flight Crew—7406th Support Squadron

Rank	Name	Age	Position
Capt.	Rudy J. Swiestra	38	aircraft commander
Capt.	Paul E. Duncan	35	standboard pilot
Capt.[105]	John E. Simpson	27	copilot
1st Lt.	Ricardo M. Villarreal	24	lead navigator
Capt.	Edward J. Jeruss	33	second navigator
S.Sgt.	Laroy Price	29	flight engineer

Recon Crew—Detachment 1, 6911th RGM

Rank	Name	Age	Posn.	Language or Specialty
M.Sgt.	George P. Petrochilos	38	1	Romanian
A/2C	Gerald C. Maggiacomo	20	2	Russian
A/2C	Clement O. Mankins	19	3	Russian
A/2C	Harold T. Kamps	22	4	Serbo-Croatian
A/2C	James E. Ferguson Jr.	20	5	Russian
A/2C	Joel H. Fields	20	6	Russian
A/2C	Robert H. Moore	21	7	Bulgarian
A/2C	Gerald H. Medeiros	20	8	Russian
	(none aboard on mission)		9	Morse operator
A/1C	Robert J. Oshinskie	23		Romanian
T.Sgt.	Arthur L. Mello	31	AMT	airborne maint. tech.
A/2C	Archie T. Bourg Jr.	21	AMT	airborne maint. tech.

60528's Flight Crew

The standard 7406th flight crew for the C-130A-II consisted of a pilot, copilot, two navigators, and a flight engineer. The flight crew aboard 60528 on September 2 included an extra "standboard" pilot—Capt. Paul Duncan, who was evaluating and certifying the qualifications of 7406th C-130 flight crews on recon missions operating from Incirlik AB, Turkey.

Captain Duncan

Capt. Paul E. Duncan was the senior pilot aboard C-130 60528 when it was shot down. A bomber pilot during World War II, he had been re-called to active Air Force duty during the Korean War. Having served as a C-130 instructor pilot at Evreux AB, France, before arriving in the

7406th in 1958, Captain Duncan had trained many of the 7406th C-130 pilots and was the most experienced C-130 pilot in the squadron. He was designated a reconnaissance pilot in the 7406th in July 1958. When the 60528 catastrophe occurred, Duncan was evaluating the proficiency of (i.e., standboarding) Captain Swiestra as a C-130 aircraft commander in the East Turkey recon mission area.

Captain Swiestra

Capt. Rudy J. Swiestra was christened Ruurd Johannes Swierstra at birth. Born to Dutch parents Bartele Johannes and Wouthera Swierstra, who had emigrated from the Netherlands to America in 1920, Rudy had changed his name. After serving as a U.S. Army Air Corps pilot in World War II, he was flying as an airline captain with KLM Royal Dutch Airlines when recalled to active duty during the Korean conflict. After the Korean Armistice in 1953, he ended up in a nonflying Air Force assignment—grounded, like many contemporaries, due to a surplus of Air Force pilots at the end of Korean hostilities. In 1957, Captain Swiestra was commander of a U.S. Air Force Air Police squadron at RAF Molesworth Air Base in England when offered a new flying assignment. After attending C-130 aircrew conversion training at Evreux AB, France, he was assigned to the 7406th as a reconnaissance pilot in March 1958. Captain Swiestra was the aircraft commander on September 2.

Captain Simpson

Many of the senior officers in the 7406th viewed Capt. John E. Simpson[106] as an "up and coming" career officer—destined someday to become an Air Force general. Simpson held a regular commission in the Air Force, whereas most of the officers in the squadron, and all of 60528's other officer flight crew on September 2, 1958, were reserve Air Force officers on active duty.[107] Commissioned as a second lieutenant in 1953 after graduating from the University of Texas at Austin, he completed basic pilot training at Bartow, Florida, and jet fighter pilot training at Bryan Air Force Base (Jet Fighter School Class 55-F). The phase-down of the Korean War created a surplus of fighter pilots, and Simpson cross-trained to transport aircraft. By 1958 he was a C-118 aircraft commander with the Military Air Transport Service (MATS) at Rhein-Main Air Base. Learning about a new requirement for C-130 recon pilots in the 7406th, Captain Simpson volunteered, completed C-130 aircrew conversion training at Evreux AB, France, and was reassigned to the 7406th in mid-1958.

Lieutenant Villarreal

1st Lt. Ricardo M. Villarreal, the youngest of eight children, graduated from Martin High School, Laredo, Texas, where he was a student officer in the high school ROTC program. He was voted the best all-around male in his high school senior class and received a degree in engineering from the University of Texas before entering the Air Force in 1955. Villarreal graduated from navigator-observer school at Mather Air Force Base, California, and was assigned to the 7406th as a second lieutenant in July 1956.[108] A small, cheerful man at five feet five inches tall and 135 pounds, he was a good athlete—an excellent second baseman—who was well-liked and respected by his peers and superiors.

Assigned as a navigator-trainee on the squadron's RB-50s, he never missed an opportunity to fly a mission and quickly became the most experienced young navigator in the squadron. Lieutenant Villarreal was the lead navigator on the recon mission on September 2 and was introducing Capt. Edward Jeruss to navigation operations on recon missions along the Turkish-Armenian border.

Captain Jeruss

Capt. Edward J. Jeruss grew up in Connecticut, possessed a near-genius IQ of 165, and had won a scholarship to Yale University when World War II interrupted his plans for college. Captain Jeruss's widow, Irene, discussed her late husband in 1996:

> Feeling patriotic, as a 17-year old he considered it more important to defend his country than attend college, so he joined the Navy and served as a tail gunner on Naval aircraft during World War II. After the war he graduated from the University of Connecticut, entered the Air Force and

became a navigator-bombardier. We met at Travis AFB, California, in
1951 and married in 1952. After 18 months as a B-57 navigator at
Laon AB, France, we transferred to a new squadron [7406th] in Ger-
many. Eddie had only been in Germany a few months and was on his
first flight of a C-130 from Turkey.

Captain Jeruss was an experienced navigator. He transferred to the
7406th in Germany in the summer of 1958 in conjunction with the
phase-out of U.S. bases in France. He began his first temporary duty deployment to Turkey on September 1, 1958. He was the second navigator—
undergoing recon area familiarization training under Lieutenant Villarreal.

Staff Sergeant Price

S.Sgt. Laroy Price grew up in Kentucky and enlisted in the Air Force
after high school. Trained as an aircraft mechanic, he was assigned to the
7406th at Rhein-Main AB, Germany, in 1957. With extensive training
and experience in aircraft maintenance, he volunteered to go on flying
status as a flight engineer. He had been providing ground maintenance
support on the squadron's RB-50 aircraft. In March 1958 he traveled on
temporary duty (TDY) to Evreux AB, France, for sixty days to complete
flight training in C-130 Hercules aircraft operations.[109] He arrived back
in Germany in early May, a few weeks before the 7406th received its first
C-130A-II recon aircraft in early June 1958. He gained additional experience as a C-130 flight engineer during transition training missions at
Rhein-Main and by ferrying a new C-130 from Greenville, Texas, to Germany. By August 19, Sergeant Price was one of ten 7406th C-130 flight
engineers.[110] In addition to flight engineer duties, each of the ten were
authorized "to inspect and certify that repairs and work accomplished to
remedy a red cross [not operationally ready] condition on assigned aircraft is [sic] satisfactory." He was on his first deployment to Turkey as a
C-130 flight engineer and on his first recon mission along the Turkish-
Armenian border on September 2.

On the fateful flight, Sergeant Price remembered at the last minute
that he'd forgotten the small tool kit that he carried on flights. As the
flight crew's chief technician, he prided himself in keeping his plane in

tiptop shape; he might need a wrench or screwdriver from his tool kit while airborne. Rather than trekking over to the 7406th Quonset hut for his tool kit, he decided to borrow one from ground maintenance. One of his bowling league partners and friends, A/2C Ralph (Bo) Palmer, part of 60528's ground team, was on the flight line, and the two men chatted for a few minutes. Palmer loaned Price his Air Force–issue toolbox. He would later have lots of explaining to do before the accident review board: "How do we know that your toolbox was on that aircraft; maybe you sold it to a Turk or were careless and let someone steal it, and now you're trying to get out of reimbursing the government for it?" Then, more frighteningly: "Were you trying to sabotage that mission? . . . Did you have a bomb in your toolbox?" In the end, Bo Palmer was deemed innocent, and the Air Force replaced his toolbox free of charge after scaring the pants off him. Palmer was the last person left behind in Turkey who talked to Laroy Price.

60528's Recon Crew

The recon crew consisted of nine airborne intercept operators (five Russian linguists, two Romanian linguists, one Serbo-Croatian linguist, and one Bulgarian linguist), plus two airborne maintenance technicians. Although C-130A-II airborne communications intelligence recon platforms had ten airborne intercepts positions, position number nine (Morse intercept operator position) was not manned during 60528's first (and last) mission in eastern Turkey on September 2, 1958. Prior to the shootdown of 60528, the normal crew makeup for Detachment 1, 6911th recon crews did not include a Morse operator—one of several factors contributing directly to the shootdown.[111]

Master Sergeant Petrochilos—the "Admiral"

Born in Scranton, Pennsylvania, on August 4, 1920, M.Sgt. George P. Petrochilos graduated from Hazelton High School in 1939 and enlisted in the U.S. Army Air Corps in June 1940. During World War II he served as a supply specialist with the 9th Bomber Division in England—

supporting the air offensive in Europe at Normandy, in northern France, and in the Rhineland. He was awarded the Bronze Star in 1945.

Discharged in September 1945, Petrochilos completed two years of college, majoring in electrical engineering, before reenlisting in the Air Force in July 1948. During the Korean War, he served in Japan and Korea. In 1956 he was accepted into the Air Force foreign language training program. He completed a nine-month Romanian language training program at Cornell in early 1957 and a nine-week voice intercept training course (specialized operational training course #601) at the National Security Agency on June 21, 1957. Later in August 1957 he was assigned to Detachment 1, 6911th Radio Group Mobile and began his new career as an airborne voice intercept operator—his first assignment in communications intelligence work.

"Pete," as he was known to the squadron's NCOs and airmen in nonmilitary settings, quickly assimilated into the unit. He was a good athlete who played and coached on the squadron's softball team for the remainder of the 1957 season and throughout the 1958 season. Single and living in the barracks with additional duties as the barracks chief, he developed an immediate rapport with Detachment 1's young airmen At thirty-eight years old, he was a father figure to many airmen in the unit.

Master Sergeant Petrochilos had a knack for languages and had picked up some working knowledge of German through a self-taught course, in addition to gaining proficiency as a Romanian intercept operator. At the same time, he was proclaimed an airborne mission supervisor. As an AMS, his job was to coordinate mission activities with the aircraft commander and direct the intelligence (reconnaissance) aspects of airborne missions: (1) assign to intercept operators signals to search for and copy, (2) search for and copy signals himself, (3) make decisions on the significance of intercepted communications, (4) coordinate onboard recon equipment repairs with his airborne maintenance crew, and, most important, (5) recognize and forewarn the aircraft commander of any hostile intent toward their mission aircraft. While Sergeant Petrochilos was relatively new in the intelligence field and voice intercept operations, his peers and subordinates viewed him as a capable airborne mission supervisor—relied on by everyone to get the job done.

Technical Sergeant Mello

Shortly after graduating from Erie Technical High School in Pennsylvania in 1945, T.Sgt. Arthur L. Mello enlisted in the Army Air Corps, where he received training in electronic (radio and radar) maintenance. He was assigned to Detachment 1, 6911th at Rhein-Main in December 1956, within days of the arrival of the first RB-50 airborne communications intelligence reconnaissance platform at Rhein-Main. Sergeant Mello began his flying career on the RB-50s in February 1957. On July 1, 1957, he was one of the first six U.S. Air Force Security Service airmen in Europe to be awarded the aircrew member badge,[112] making him one of the most experienced fliers in his unit. He was the senior airborne maintenance technician aboard the September 2 flight. Airman Bourg was the other onboard maintenance technician.

Airman Bourg

A/2C Archie T. Bourg Jr. graduated from high school in Baton Rouge, Louisiana, in 1955 and enlisted in the Air Force. After completing an electronics repairman course at Keesler AFB, Mississippi, in September 1956, his first duty assignment was working on avionics systems on B-47s at Lake Charles AFB, Louisiana. Ron McCann, who later flew reconnaissance missions in the C-130A-II aircraft at Rhein-Main, Germany, was Bourg's roommate, classmate, and buddy at Keesler. He remembered Bourg as an all-around great person, a good student in their electronics course, and an excellent shortstop in intramural fast pitch softball at Keesler. McCann recalled that Bourg was overjoyed at his assignment to Lake Charles—less than 150 miles from his home in Baton Rouge—while McCann was assigned to an RB-66 recon squadron in Japan. In the summer of 1958, Bourg volunteered for an airborne flying assignment with Detachment 1, 6911th at Rhein-Main. As an airborne maintenance technician (AMT), his job in the 6911th entailed troubleshooting and repairing the Security Service intelligence collection equipment (intercept receivers, antennas, demodulators, tape recorders, private interphone, signal patching equipment, et al.) aboard the RB-50 and C-130 recon aircraft.[113] Anxious to get his flying career under way,

Bourg volunteered for a deployment to Incirlik AB, Turkey, where he'd have the opportunity to fly a series of missions in a training capacity under the watchful eye of Sergeant Mello, the squadron's most experienced AMT.

Airman Kamps

At twenty-two years old, A/2C Harold T. Kamps was a senior airman among young contemporaries in his squadron at Rhein-Main and aboard C-130 60528 on September 2, 1958. He grew up on a farm in Coleman, Wisconsin, joined the Wisconsin Army National Guard in December 1953, graduated from Lena High School in 1954, and enlisted in the Air Force in February 1955. Airman Kamps, together with eleven other airmen, completed the first Serbo-Croatian language course at Indiana University, Bloomington, in June 1956. He and ten of the twelve new linguists received follow-on assignments to the 6911th Radio Squadron Mobile, Darmstadt, Germany. Arriving at Darmstadt in August, Kamps and five of his classmates volunteered to transfer to the squadron's Detachment 1 at Rhein-Main as airborne Serbo-Croatian voice intercept operators,[114] arriving at Rhein-Main on December 4, 1956. They received aeronautical orders assigning them flying duties the same date— making Kamps the most experienced airborne intercept operator on the September 2 flight. Kamps also played softball on the detachment team in 1957 and 1958.

Airman Fields

A/2C Joel H. Fields, although a mere twenty years old, was the most seasoned airborne Russian voice intercept operator aboard C-130 60528 when Soviet MiG pilots shot it down in 1958. In all probability, he was monitoring the conversations of the pilots who shot down his aircraft. We can never know at what point he recognized the significance of those conversations. Fields and Jackie Price palled around together in school in Cynthiana, Kentucky, and after graduating from high school in 1956, joined the Air Force. After basic training at Lackland AFB, Texas, they transferred together to Security Service Headquarters less than five miles away at Kelly AFB. After completing pre-language school at Kelly,[115] they were split up for the first time ever—Price studied Russian at the Army Language School, Monterey, California, and Fields completed the six-month Russian language course at Syracuse University, graduating in mid-1957. Their careers joined again at Rhein-Main, Germany, in the summer of 1957; Fields arrived at Rhein-Main in August, Price followed in September, and they flew a few missions together before Fields's fateful mission on September 2. Highly popular with everyone in Detachment 1, Joel Fields was a member of the unit's softball team in 1957 and 1958.

Airman Ferguson

At six feet four inches tall, A/2C James E. Ferguson Jr. had been a high school star in LaPorte, Indiana, from 1953 to 1956—winning seventy-five ribbons for basketball and track victories. He likewise excelled as a member of his unit's basketball and softball teams at Rhein-Main in 1958. After graduating from Union Township High School in 1956, Jim Ferguson enlisted in the Air Force and became an airborne Russian voice intercept operator. Ferguson, after basic training, became a classmate of Gerald Maggiacomo, Jackie Price, and several other young airmen who completed the six-month Russian language course at the Army Language School at Monterey in 1957. Like them, he arrived at Rhein-Main in September 1957. Although he had been flying local missions from Rhein-Main for the better part of a year, he was on his first deployment to Incirlik, Turkey, when he lost his life.

Airman Maggiacomo

A/2C Gerald C. Maggiacomo enlisted in the Air Force in July 1956 after completing high school in Everett, Massachusetts. Selected on the basis of a high score on aptitude qualification tests during basic training, Airman Maggiacomo attended the standard five-week pre-language course at U.S. Air Force Security Service Headquarters, Kelly AFB, Texas, in late 1956. He then completed the Army Language School's six-month Russian language course at Monterey in June 1957. Carl Van

Ness, a good friend and classmate of Maggiacomo during language training at Monterey, discussed "Madge" with Larry Tart in October 2000. Carl and Madge spent many hours shooting straight (one-up rotation) pool in the on-base recreation center at Monterey. Calling Madge a keen competitor and dear friend, Carl joked that neither bankrupted the other with their penny-a-point pool bets. Receiving different follow-on assignments from Monterey, they exchanged a couple of letters before Madge's fateful flight in 1958.

In the "small world" department, Van Ness and Larry Tart worked together as Russian voice intercept operators with the 6950th Radio Group Mobile at RAF Chicksands, England, and partied together in London during the late 1950s. In August 1957, Van Ness reported to Chicksands, and Maggiacomo was assigned to the 6911th Radio Group Mobile, Darmstadt, Germany. Responding to a request for volunteers to go airborne, Maggiacomo transferred to Detachment 1, 6911th at Rhein-Main in September 1957. Like most of the other recon crew members on 528, he played on Detachment 1's intramural softball team in 1958.

Airman Medeiros

A/2C Gerald H. Medeiros grew up in New Bedford, Massachusetts, graduating from high school in 1956. Like the four other Russian linguists aboard 60528 on that fateful mission, he learned Russian at an Air Force sponsored school—Airman Medeiros and Barney Rakestraw, another Russian airborne intercept operator in Detachment 1, 6911th, completed one of the first Russian language courses taught at Indiana University, Bloomington, in the fall of 1957. They were assigned directly to Detachment 1 from language school. Like most of the other recon crew members aboard 60528's last flight, Medeiros was a member of the detachment's softball team in 1958.

Airman Mankins

Born on March 16, 1939, A/2C Clement O. Mankins—at nineteen years old—was the youngest member of the C-130 crew. He was born in

Point Marion, Pennsylvania, and joined the Air Force after graduating from Point Marion High School in 1957. After completing a Russian language course, Airman Mankins was assigned to Detachment 1 during the summer of 1958 and was on his first deployment to Turkey when the shootdown occurred. Tragically, he wasn't even in the outfit long enough to become well-known.

Airman Moore

A/2C Robert H. Moore grew up in West Monroe, Louisiana. After high school, Moore enlisted in the Air Force, studied Bulgarian at an Air Force sponsored language school, and entered Security Service as a voice intercept operator. After language school in 1957, his first operational assignment was with the 6931st Radio Squadron Mobile, a Security Service intercept site at Iraklion on the Greek island of Crete. In mid-1958—just days before the end of his tour on Crete—Moore volunteered to be an airborne Bulgarian voice intercept operator and transferred directly to Detachment 1, 6911th at Rhein-Main, Germany. Moore played softball with his unit's team during the summer of '58. Like many of the other recon crew members, he was on his first deployment to Turkey in September 1958.

Airman Oshinskie

A/1C Robert J. Oshinskie, twenty-three, was an Air Force old-timer among his fellow recon crew mates aboard 60528. However, he was relatively new to airborne communications intelligence reconnaissance. Oshinskie graduated from high school in Shamokin, Pennsylvania, in 1953 and enlisted in the Air Force in November 1954. Upon graduation from Romanian language school at Cornell in October 1955—the same course that crew mate Master Sergeant Petrochilos finished in 1957—Oshinskie was promoted to airman second class and assigned to a Security Service ground intercept site at Landshut, Germany.[116] He was promoted to A/1C effective March 1, 1957. Former Air Force linguists who served with Oshinskie at Landshut, bowled with him, and played basketball and softball with him, describe him as "tall and athletic—an all around good guy." In

January 2000, Robert Sprankle, Oshinskie's roommate at Landshut, reminisced about their days together in Germany:

> *Bob and I spent a lot of time together at Landshut—bowling, playing cards and sports. Bob was looking forward to getting out of the Air Force and completing his college degree. Early in 1958 just before I departed Germany, he decided to extend his enlistment and transfer to the flying unit at Rhein-Main. With the additional flight pay, he could save lots of money toward his college education.*

Oshinskie transferred to Detachment 1, 6911th at Rhein-Main during the summer of 1958—arriving in time to participate in his unit's 1958 softball season. He may have been on his first operational mission to Turkey that day.

Families of 60528's Last Crew

The mothers, fathers, sisters, brothers, wives, and children of the seventeen men who perished aboard C-130 60528 are a cross section of the families of the men assigned to the 7406th and Detachment 1, 6911th in 1958. Older than the recon crew members, the six flight crew members were married. Four of the six had their families with them in Germany; one's family (the Swiestras) remained in England, and one (Lieutenant Villarreal) was a newlywed who was in the process of bringing his new bride, Laurentina, from Texas to Germany.[117] Three of the recon crew members—Mello, Bourg, and Ferguson—were married but had to live in German apartments in villages around the base, rather than in on-base housing. Several of the wives were pregnant, and most had small children.

Capt. Rudy Swiestra left behind a wife and two sons: nine-year-old Ronald and eight-year-old Dennis. They were living in military family housing at RAF Molesworth, England, Swiestra's previous duty station, waiting for the next available military family quarters at Rhein-Main. Capt. Paul Duncan had his wife Pauline and five children with him in Germany. Capt. John Simpson's wife Delores and two sons, John Jr. and Mark, lived in family housing at Rhein-Main; Mark was only four months old when he lost his father. Lt. Ricardo Villarreal's new bride of two months, Laurie, had planned to arrive in Germany from Texas in late September 1958; she was living with her parents in Laredo. Capt. Edward Jeruss and his wife, Irene, lived with their six-year-old son, Paul, in a small German apartment. Irene was three months pregnant with her second son, Steven Edward. S.Sgt. Laroy Price and his wife Marion lived in the Gateway Gardens Military Housing Complex adjacent to Rhein-Main AB with their young sons Michael and Richard.

Jim Ferguson Jr. was the only one of the recon crew airborne intercept operators who was married. He and his wife Rita were high school sweethearts who married shortly after graduation, before he enlisted in the Air Force. Because of his low rank (A/2C), the Air Force would not pay travel expenses to bring Ferguson's family to Germany. Nonetheless, Jim and Rita scrimped and saved enough nickels and dimes while he attended Russian language school and during the first couple of months he was in Germany to buy a ticket for Rita and their daughter Debra. They joined him at Rhein-Main in late 1957 and lived in a German apartment in Mörfelden, seven miles from Rhein-Main.

An automobile was a necessity to travel to base at odd hours for early morning missions, to shop in the base exchange and commissary, and to keep doctors' appointments at the dispensary. Airman Bob Barrow had the solution for Ferguson. Prior to Rita's arrival, Barrow sold Ferguson his four-door 1950 American Chevy sedan, for $300. A former *Stars and Stripes* staff car—the old Chevy still had faint markings of the newspaper's logo on its front doors—it was at least reliable transportation.

Their daughter Debra, two years old, was with Rita, who was five and a half months pregnant, when Rita drove Ferguson to the base for his first trip to Turkey on August 25. Rita and Debra Ferguson had already been shipped back home to Indiana when Keith was born, on December 14, 1958, and Jim Ferguson's younger brother, nineteen-year-old Ken—himself an airman third class in the Air Force—became Keith's godfather at the christening.

T.Sgt. Arthur Mello, one of two airborne maintenance technicians on the flight, had returned to civilian life for a short time at the end of his first three-year Air Force enlistment. His mother, Mary Wagner, of Erie, Pennsylvania, recalled in 1959 a conversation she had with him when he decided to reenlist: "If I go back in now [in 1948], I'll be young when I can retire." Mrs. Wagner added, "He's thirty-two now [1959], if . . . he's still living. Will I ever live long enough to know?" After reenlisting, Mello met and married his wife Ila while assigned with the Air Force in South Carolina. Ila had accompanied him to Rhein-Main, and they, together with daughters Mary, three, and Margaret, one, lived in a small German apartment in Mörfelden, not too far from the Fergusons. Ila was five months pregnant with daughter Brenda when her husband disappeared. Brenda was born on January 2, 1959, exactly four months after her father's aircraft was shot down, and coincidentally, on Arthur Mello's birthday.

Like Jim Ferguson, A/2C Archie Bourg Jr., the other maintenance man, had married his high school sweetheart—in late 1956 after Archie completed technical training at Biloxi, Mississippi, and received his first operational assignment at Lake Charles AFB, Louisiana. Archie got married in his dress blue uniform and posed at the reception in Baton Rouge for a family photograph with his parents, his sister Lorna, his brother James, and his new bride Mary.

Archie and Mary lived in a small apartment in Lake Charles during their first year of marriage, and daughter Vickie was born in Lake Charles. Finding it difficult to feed his family on an airman's pay (about $100 per month plus about $150 in food and housing allowances), Archie volunteered to transfer to Rhein-Main to fly missions aboard reconnaissance aircraft. He traveled to Germany alone, leaving Mary and Vickie with her family in Baton Rouge. As soon as he could make arrangements, he paid for his wife and daughter to fly to Germany to join him. In September 1958 they were living off base in a small German apartment, and Mary was three months pregnant with their son Mitchell.

The eight single airmen had close family ties with parents and siblings, although they had seen their families infrequently since enlisting in the Air Force. Many had younger siblings at home whom they missed, and found comfort in the comradeship that they developed with other airmen whom they ate, slept, worked, and palled around with. With the exception of M.Sgt. George Petrochilos, who'd been in the Air Force eighteen years, they were all first-term airmen, overseas in unfamiliar settings for the first time. Petrochilos had never married and was extremely close to his sister, Theresa Durkin, in Levittown, Pennsylvania. He listed Theresa on his emergency records as his next of kin. In 1957—the last time Theresa saw George—he was already planning for retirement from the Air Force. He was saving his money to finance a Greek restaurant that the two of them would open, using their Greek heritage to leverage his retirement nest egg into a business venture.

Harry Kamps was proud of his family for its closeness, love, and size. His parents, Louis and Elsie Kamps, had thirteen children, and three of Harold's sisters and eight brothers are alive and relatively healthy at the dawn of the twenty-first century. Needless to say, Harry had no trouble adapting to close living conditions and getting along with others in the Air Force. One of his best friends at Rhein-Main was Lincoln J. Gilbert. He and Lincoln had been inseparable since becoming acquainted at language school in 1956.

Robert Moore had a younger brother Michael who, at eight years old, looked up to and adored his big brother. Robert Oshinskie, similarly, had a close relationship with his mother Julia and nine-year-old sister Rose. He was also very close to his brothers: John, Edward, and Leonard. Joel Fields and Clement Mankins likewise left behind sisters (Phyllis Wilson and Maxine Mankins) with whom they had close relationships. Gerald Maggiacomo was the sole son of Margaret DiLoreto. By the time the United States government finally released full details of the mission and the shootdown, nearly forty years after the fact, very few of the parents of the seventeen men were still alive, and those were in frail health. Most of the parents died not knowing how and why their sons died.

The Crew That Almost Was

Imagine being an aircrew member whose life is spared when a fellow flier replaces you on a mission that turns fatal. That was the lot for many 7406th and Detachment 1, 6911th fliers who—but for last minute crew changes—would have been aboard C-130 60528 on September 2, 1958. Both squadrons were engrossed in transitioning from a recon fleet of RB-50s to new C-130 aircraft, and aircrew scheduling during the best of times is a dynamic process. Typical reasons to replace a crew member include: medical (DNIF, a flight-surgeon-directed Duty Not to Include

Flying), conflicting official and personal commitments, and even conflicting team sports schedules. The makeup of 528's crew on September 2 was affected by those and other factors.

The 7406th and Detachment 1 routinely juggled aircrew schedules, but 1958 posed special challenges. The 7406th scheduling officer had to schedule crews for both RB-50 and C-130 flights—replacing an RB-50 crew with a C-130 crew when an RB-50 failed a preflight checkout, and providing flight crews for both C-130 transition training and operational missions. Some flight crew members were qualified in both the RB-50 and the C-130, others were not. The Detachment 1 scheduling NCO had different but likewise challenging scheduling priorities. Language specialty was a key factor. Romanian linguists were not needed on missions in the Baltic Sea area, and Polish linguists did not typically fly on "southern" missions; Russian linguists were used in all areas. Airborne voice intercept operators were deemed equally qualified for RB-50 and C-130 missions, but a C-130 recon mission required twice as many operators—five intercept operator positions on the RB-50 versus ten on the C-130. Last minute scrambles to man a C-130 flight originally scheduled as an RB-50 mission were not unusual. Assigned ground duties and even extracurricular activities also weighed heavily on which recon crew members flew where and when.

In August, in the midst of a heavy C-130 transition training program, an add-on C-130 deployment to a new operating area—to Bodö, Norway—impacted already scarce aircraft and aircrew resources. Although it was a onetime deployment, the 7406th scheduling officer had to plan a crew for an August 25 to 27 Bodö deployment while taking into consideration a scheduled deployment to Incirlik, Turkey, on August 28. Lt. James Edds was scheduled as the lead navigator on the August 28 deployment to Turkey, conflicting with plans for a birthday party. Shirley Edds had planned a party for her husband for August 29, and Jim, who had palled around with Lt. Ricardo Villarreal since their days as aviation cadets in 1954, switched flights with Villarreal. Edds took the C-130 mission to Bodö on August 25, and Villarreal's trip to Turkey was rescheduled to September 1 so that 60528—the C-130 that flew to Norway—could be used for the deployment to Turkey.

During the last two weeks of August, S.Sgt. Laroy Price toured

Europe on leave with wife Marion and their sons Mike and Richard, including a visit to the World's Fair in Brussels. The 7406th scheduling officer had no way of contacting Sergeant Price, who was due back at work on Monday, September 1, so he alerted S.Sgt. Del Johannsen to be available for the deployment to Turkey if Price did not sign back into the squadron over the weekend. Had Price not signed in from leave Friday night to save two days' leave time, Johannsen would have been the flight engineer aboard 60528 on September 2, 1958.

The Detachment 1 scheduling NCO's job was even more chaotic than 7406th scheduling. Unlike the flight crews whose primary (and only full-time) job was flying, the recon crewmen had full-time jobs on the ground. When not flying, most of the linguists worked eight-hour shifts transcribing communications intercepted on previous missions. In addition, many of the linguists attended University of Maryland night classes locally, pursuing a college degree. The scheduling NCO took this off-duty education into consideration when assigning linguists to fly—avoiding, when possible, conflicts between an individual's flights and scheduled class exams. The overwhelming majority of Detachment 1's men were young—twenty to twenty-one years old, on average—and single. The men helped one another; the single airmen volunteered for deployments on temporary duty away from Rhein-Main, and the young married airmen like Jim Ferguson and Archie Bourg generally flew local missions that permitted them to be home with their families at night. Most of the recon crew members loved to fly, and the scheduling NCO had an abundance of volunteers willing to fly missions on short notice. Finally, nearly everyone in Detachment 1 was involved in Rhein-Main's intramural softball league, either as a player or spectator, and softball presented the scheduling NCO its own set of flight scheduling idiosyncrasies.

Although only a tenant unit on Rhein-Main and significantly smaller than primary squadrons on base, Detachment 1 led the softball league throughout the summer in 1958, due in large part to the juggling of recon crew flight schedules to make Detachment 1's softball players available for key games. During the season, airmen who would otherwise have completed one or more deployments to Turkey remained home at Rhein-Main—flying local missions and playing softball. Volunteers who did not play softball replaced them on deployments. With the base softball championship tournament scheduled from late August to early September, the Detachment 1 scheduling NCO penciled in a recon crew that excluded softball players for the deployment to Turkey on August 29, and the mission was subsequently pushed forward to September 1. But the Detachment 1 softball team—the team to beat, the team that had played in championship form all season—was eliminated from tournament play early in the playoffs, making the team eligible for all flying assignments and deployments. The informal policy of not sending married airmen on temporary duty deployments was lifted at the same time; everyone would pull his share of deployments on a rotating basis.

Following the new scheduling guidelines, the scheduling NCO essentially erased the names of the recon crew originally scheduled to fly to Turkey on August 25, replacing the crew almost entirely with members of the detachment's softball team. The replacement airborne mission supervisor was Master Sergeant Petrochilos, player and coach on the softball team. Seven of Petrochilos's eight airborne voice intercept operators on the deployment—Oshinskie, Fields, Ferguson, Maggiacomo, Medeiros, Kamps, and Moore—had played softball with him during the summer, as had Archie Bourg, airborne maintenance technician. Bourg replaced T.Sgt. Allan MacDougall on the deployment. MacDougall, who at the time had not flown his first airborne recon mission, was removed from the scheduled deployment to Turkey when the base flight surgeon would not grant him a medical waiver for an eye/vision problem. It is not clear whether Arthur Mello, the primary AMT on the mission, had been scheduled with the original deployment crew or if he replaced another AMT. The other intercept operator on the deployment was Clement Mankins, who was included on the crew at the last minute for his first deployment from Rhein-Main.

The airmen originally scheduled for the temporary duty (TDY) deployment but subsequently replaced by members of the softball team can recall vividly to this day how, but for fate, they would have been aboard 60528 on September 2, 1958. S.Sgt. Robert Bergeron had been scheduled originally to be the admiral (airborne missions supervisor) on the deployment to Turkey on August 25, but Sergeant Petrochilos replaced him. Instead, Bergeron was the admiral on the next C-130 mission to Turkey, a two-day trip on September 1 and 2. From the parking ramp at Incirlik,

Sergeant Bergeron and his crew waved good-bye to Petrochilos and his crew as the latter crew boarded C-130 60528 shortly before noon on September 2.

Harold Kamps replaced James Kinney on the TDY; Kinney had attended Serbo-Croatian language school with Kamps. Bob Barrow, a Czech linguist, had been tasked to go on the TDY, but his name was removed from the scheduling board when he expressed intent to marry a German national, and it was decided that he should remain at Rhein-Main to train new Czech linguists who'd just arrived in the squadron. Bob Oshinskie, who bunked next to Barrow, had inadvertently taken Barrow's Air Force raincoat with him to Turkey, leaving his own raincoat on Barrow's cot.

Two other linguists who were originally scheduled for the TDY trip and replaced were John (Turk) Wilcher and Perry Eisenhower—both single and both softball players. Wilcher recalls that he was replaced by an operator who had not been to Turkey before, probably Clement Mankins. Eisenhower was scheduled for the deployment as part of the replacement crew of softball players, but was removed from the crew list because he had multiple dental appointments already scheduled that otherwise would have to be cancelled. Robert Trainor, a Czechoslovakian linguist, had also been scheduled initially for the TDY, but was removed from the trip when the decision was made to staff the trip with members of the softball team.

S.Sgt. George Rubel was not permitted to deploy to Turkey with the crew because of delays in receiving the necessary passport and visa required for entry into Turkey. To this day Rubel and others who because of sheer luck were not aboard C-130 60528 on September 2, 1958, are haunted by the randomness of their survival, and in many ways feel a tinge of guilt. "Why them and not me?" Some, including Rubel, believe that had they been on that mission, they would have recognized prior to the point where the C-130 entered enemy airspace—in time for the flight crew to have turned away—that the aircraft and crew were in peril. And in the case of Rubel, this is probably right.

EIGHT

—

THE AFTERMATH

C-130 60528 was the first American reconnaissance aircraft to crash on Soviet soil after being shot down by Soviet air defense forces—all other American aircraft forced down by the Soviets crashed in water. The shoot-down also represented the first serious incident with loss of aircraft and crew for the 7406th Support Squadron that owned the C-130 and flight crew, and Detachment 1, 6911th Radio Group Mobile, the recon crew members' unit. Why did an unarmed U.S. Air Force reconnaissance aircraft violate denied Soviet airspace? The short answer is that the aircraft was off course and the airspace violation was unintentional. The persons most surprised by the inadvertent overflight and loss of aircrew were the fellow members of the 7406th and Detachment 1.[118] They found it unbelievable that such a catastrophe could happen. Their infallibility had been violated.

To the Soviet air force MiG-17 pilots who shot down the intruding aircraft, it was all in a day's work—their mission was to defend Soviet airspace. The Western world viewed the Soviet actions as the cold-blooded murder of seventeen men aboard an unarmed aircraft, while from a Soviet perspective an intruder had violated sovereign Soviet airspace and attempted to escape back across the border. Following their controller's orders, the MiG pilots blasted the intruding aircraft out of the sky—their first live-fire encounter with an enemy.

In 1993, retired Soviet General Valentin Soznov, former air defense district commander, and former Senior Lt. Viktor Lopatkov, flight leader of one pair of the attacking MiGs, discussed the incident with a television production company. General Soznov stated, "It [the American aircraft] usually flew on a straight course along the border, but this time, it was hugging the border, but not crossing it . . . I ordered a pair of MiGs to scramble and keep watch."

Lieutenant Lopatkov recalled that it was a very hot day in Yerevan, and he was on duty with the alert flight: "I believe we were playing dominoes [when the Klaxon sounded]." Lopatkov's pair of MiGs reached the border area just in time to intercept the intruder as it lumbered into Soviet Armenian airspace. Lopatkov fired warning shots, resulting in the intruder's attempting to turn back toward the border.

"At this point," the general continued, "my next command was: 'Shoot it down!' "

Lieutenant Lopatkov remarked, "I fired with all the ammunition I had."

In June 1994, Lopatkov provided additional details about the attack in a meeting with the U.S.-Russian Joint Commission on POW/MIAs.

In 1958, I was stationed at Yerevan when a pair of us—myself and Kucheryaev—were sent up to intercept a plane that had violated the border. There was another pair sent up from Leninakan. The plane was south of Leninakan, toward Yerevan. I gave a warning shot across the bow. Kucheryaev approached him on the other side. We got the order to destroy the aircraft. I was on the right side of the plane as I approached it. As the other pair shot into the plane, it descended to about 1,400 meters. Then Kucheryaev attacked, and as he did, I also turned toward the plane and fired. The plane turned nose up, at about a 30 degree angle. I then got caught in the plane's slipstream, and had to fight to get out of it. In any case, I couldn't see him anymore. I didn't see him crash; I only saw the smoke. I heard that the plane crashed; the wing came off. I landed back in Leninakan. I talked to General Tsedrik—he was the one who gave the order to shoot down the plane. Other guys from my unit went to the crash site, but I didn't go.

We learned that there was a six-person crew, that there was radio-

*technical equipment aboard. The plane flew along the border from the
Black Sea trying to get the locations of Soviet radars.*

The four MiG pilots took turns—two firing passes each—in what
amounted to target practice against the unarmed transport plane. At the
end of the engagement, one of the MiG pilots summed up the fate of the
C-130 and its crew: "The target has lost control; it's going down." While
the interception occurred close enough to the border for Turkish border
guards to witness the MiG attacks, the C-130 crashed twenty-five miles
inside the Armenian border—near the village of Sasnashen in the Aragat Mountain foothills. If any of the four pilots felt any guilt at all, there
has never been any evidence in their statements, either at the time or decades later. Their job was to kill, and they did their job thoroughly.

C-130 60528 Is Overdue

Back in Turkey and Germany, the ground controllers to whom C-130
tail number 60528 reported were beginning to worry. (It must be remembered that although Air Force Security Service ground-based Morse intercept operators were listening to the catastrophe as it unfolded, they
had no means of contacting "normal" air traffic controllers.) Ankara control tracked all flights in Turkey, and 528's copilot had reported his craft
over Trabzon at 12:42 P.M., at an altitude of 25,000 feet. He made the
same report to "Homeplate," 7499th Support Group in Wiesbaden, Germany, parent organization of the 7406th. Neither Ankara nor Wiesbaden
would hear another word from 60528. Later in the afternoon, Homeplate
would grow worried as hour after hour it received no in-flight progress reports from the plane. A phone call to the 7406th duty officer at Rhein-
Main proved futile. By mid-evening the officers at group were alarmed. It
is quite normal for a plane to miss a single mandatory report due to
weather conditions or equipment malfunctions, but too long had gone by.
They would have to do a mandatory ramp check at Incirlik and other
likely airfields to make sure that the plane hadn't landed unannounced
somewhere, but their worst fears seemed likely—the fuel range of 60528
had long since passed, and the aircraft had to be down somewhere.

The authorities back in Germany were anxious and confused. For the first time in their two years of uneasy coexistence, the two separate command structures—the hierarchy in charge of the plane and the reconnaissance bureaucracy in charge of the mission—needed straight information from one another, and the lines of communication didn't exist. Very worried, the 7499th Group operations officer phoned 6900 Security Wing's action officer. No knowledge.

In reality, Security Wing was receiving sketchy details about the encounter from Security Service ground sites, but no one had a good handle on what had occurred at that point, and security restrictions did not permit the wing to share the special access information with the 7499th. Over secure teletype, Security Wing contacted the 6901st Special Comm Group at Zweibrücken and the 6911th Group at Darmstadt, to which Detachment 1 belonged. The initial "Critic" Report and Lateral Critic merely said the C-130 had been attacked; additional details were lacking.[119] Security Wing's executive officer, Colonel William Rice, telephoned Capt. Luther Tarbox, operations officer and acting commander of Detachment 1. Tarbox, sitting in his office at Rhein-Main, in direct if distant command of the men who had been shot down, knew less than Colonel Rice. With only a limited secure "ops-comm" teletype circuit to the 6900th Security Wing, Detachment 1 did not even receive the Critic or Lateral Critic reports. Tarbox should have received notification from wing on the ops-comm circuit, but Detachment 1's low-grade, worn-out teletype machine quickly became overloaded when traffic got heavy; in other words, it was usable except when it was needed. Reports of the shootdown were being transmitted from unit to unit within Security Service, but the outfit directly involved was caught in the electronic jumble of Detachment 1's ancient communications circuits. Besides, the 6901st rigidly controlled information flow to Detachment 1, so Detachment 1 would not have received technical details about the shootdown even if its circuits had been operating properly.

Tarbox telephoned Major Swanson, 7406th commander, on the other side of the base, to see if he knew anything. Everyone was calling everyone else, and nobody had any answers.

To be fair to Tarbox, it has to be pointed out that he was not authorized to tell the 7406th and others what was being reported in Security

Service channels. The Air Force Special Security Officer at Headquarters U.S. Air Forces, Europe (AFSSO, USAFE) had that job and was receiving whatever information the Security Service field units were reporting. The AFSSO had the responsibility to pass such information on to appropriate USAFE officials, and in all probability did inform the USAFE hierarchy. At any rate, whatever information was being shared at the top, very little filtered down to the 7406th, and confusion reigned.

The Cover-Up

The lies began shortly thereafter. Later in the day, the operations officer of the 7499th Group called the duty officer of the 7406th to ask if he had received any information yet. He hadn't, so he called Tarbox to see if he knew anything. At that moment, things started to fall apart.

Tarbox had indeed heard about the aircraft's fate by then. The 6901st had received the Critic Report reporting the hostile attack and passed on the information to Tarbox. But nobody outside special security channels—not even the outfit whose flight crew actually flew the C-130—had the appropriate security clearance, the "need to know." Tarbox had no permission to give out the truth. So he lied. He told the 7406th operations officer that he did not know what had happened to the missing aircraft and crew. Luther Tarbox was an honorable, upright man, and he didn't lie easily. But in the next week he would find himself boxed into a corner where lying seemed the only alternative to breaching security. The truth of the matter was that in those early hours subsequent to the downing of the aircraft, he knew little more about the incident than did his 7406th counterpart; both had received notification that the C-130 was down, but no amplifying information. Details about the actual shootdown would come later.

Tarbox and his key NCOs caucused in his office the night of September 2 to assess the situation and devise a plan. They decided that it would be best to keep a tight lid on the incident and withhold information—even from their own men. The American cover-up had begun.

Headquarters, U.S. Air Forces, Europe, finally announced publicly on September 3 that a C-130 was missing. The European *Stars and Stripes* military newspaper carried the story under the headline c-130 LOST IN TURKEY, 17 ABOARD.

> WIESBADEN, Germany (AP)—USAFE HQ Wednesday night reported a transport plane with 17 persons aboard has been missing since Tuesday on a flight from Adana, Turkey.
>
> The Air Force said the C-130 Hercules transport took off from Incirlik Air Base at Adana Tuesday on a study of radio wave propagation—part of a worldwide wave study.
>
> It last reported at 12:42 p.m. Tuesday and has failed to return to the base where it was scheduled to arrive at 7:40 Tuesday night.
>
> An intensive search was started after the plane became overdue.
>
> The plane belonged to the 7406th Support SQ based at Rhein-Main Air Base at Frankfurt, the Air Force said.

Headquarters reported that the transport plane had failed to make its scheduled two P.M. report that it was crossing the Lake Van beacon. Nothing had been heard from it since, and it was presumed down somewhere in the mountains of eastern Turkey. For the next week that missing plane report served as the official story of the United States Air Force.

Not simply for public consumption, the story was designed to fool everyone without the need to know—and that included everyone in the 7406th and nearly everyone in the 6911th. Wives, children, buddies—everyone believed, and needed to believe, that the plane had crashed in friendly territory. Tarbox himself held out some meager hope that maybe some of his men were alive. After all, it could be that some of the crew had parachuted to safety; a couple of months earlier, in the Soviet shootdown of an Air Force C-118 in the same general area, five of the C-118's nine crew members had parachuted safely and been captured. No one in Germany knew precisely where the C-130 had gone down. That hope, and the need to maintain security no matter what, lay at the base of a useless betrayal that would sour the lives of several dozen men and women for the next forty years.

The military bureaucracy had long before fallen into a terrible if understandable foul-up. No emergency procedures had ever been developed either by the 7406th or by the 6911th. Given the clumsy security policy and dual, somewhat ambiguous chains of command under which the units operated, it is hard to imagine they could have developed joint procedures even if they had wanted to. Neither USAFE Headquarters nor USAFSS (Air Force Security Service) had bothered to put together or force subordinate units to create, let alone exercise, a contingency plan addressing such a catastrophe. Other than flying on the same aircraft, the 7406th and Detachment 1, 6911th had very little in common.

The cockpit crews from the 7406th, for example, had been thoroughly trained in emergency procedures, and some had been through survival and interrogation training. The 6911th sailors, on the other hand, had never opened a parachute, never even heard a lecture on survival. All they knew about endurance in enemy territory was what they had seen in John Wayne films. They had not even been provided a proper cover story in case of capture by the Soviets. After the crew failed to return, Headquarters, USAFE, provided the standard explanation— "conducting an electromagnetic wave propagation study"—to the press, and that became the cover story for future recon missions. Crews could say that they were involved in the study of the propagation of radio waves in conjunction with the geophysical year, but no one told them what "propagation" meant or what a "geophysical year" was. The real function of the cover story, it would seem, was to allow youthful minds to feel that they were safe from harm. It was as if the upper levels of the Air Force hoped that none of its flight crews would survive a crash in Soviet territory. Like U-2 pilot Gary Powers eighteen months later, live sailors would have proved an embarrassment to the United States.

But the 7406th and the 6911th did not share that cruel hope; they wanted their men alive. Overnight on September 2 the 7406th devised a plan. They had few details, but they had by then received collateral information that the Soviets had shot down an American transport plane along the Turkish-Armenian border, at around two P.M. Incirlik time. They could assume the plane was theirs, and, given the lack of information, could further hope that, as in the shootdown of the C-118 in late June, at least some men had managed to parachute to safety.

The 7406th would send RB-50 and C-130 aircraft and crews to Incirlik to conduct search operations over a wide swath of the Turkish mountains along the Soviet border. In the middle of the night, the 7406th duty officer informed Captain Tarbox at Detachment 1 of the plan and requested that he provide sailors to participate in the effort. A C-130 would depart as soon as a crew could be assembled, and an RB-50 would deploy to Incirlik the following day.

The Search Crews

T.Sgt. Jack Roberts took a USAFSS search crew to Incirlik on the C-130 early in the morning of September 3. S.Sgt. Robert Bergeron— the NCO who had given up his assigned place on the downed aircraft to George Petrochilos—would follow on Thursday, September 4, with a second crew aboard the RB-50. While Roberts drove home to pack a bag, T.Sgt. Stan Kresge, NCO in charge of operations, ordered another NCO to round up a crew. Walking through the largest open bay in the barracks, a room holding thirty men, the NCO simply woke up the first men he found and told them to don their flight suits, grab their shaving kits and a change of clothes, and report to the operations office for a briefing.

A/2C Robert Keefe's bunk was right next to the door of one of the bays; he had just fallen into a heavy, much-needed sleep. He had been flying three missions per week for a month in Turkey until his best friend, Joel Fields, relieved him, and had been back in Germany only a few hours. Now, settling in for a solid twelve or more hours of sleep, he was rousted out of bed to search for a downed plane that contained his friends.

In the darkness of the large room, he could see the shadows of a half-dozen other men struggling into their flight suits. It was a routine they could—and sometimes did—perform in their sleep by then; get up at three A.M., dress, shuffle over to the mess hall for chipped beef on toast, drive to the hangar, check out parachute, check out aircraft, then in the air by five. But this time it was different. All of them were fully awake immediately. They weren't despondent yet, or if they were, they didn't realize it. But there was a fevered excitement in the air, a need to talk without letup, to cover up the catastrophe in soothing words.

Normally, the men spent the long flight down the flank of the Soviet bloc monitoring air traffic, but on this day, September 3, 1958, they sat on the carpeted floor of the brand new C-130 and chattered endlessly at one another, imagining various scenarios of the crash and devising happy endings. They had been told nothing whatever beyond the bare fact—or, rather, bare lie—that the plane was down in eastern Turkey, so their imaginations were free to roam through their memories of movies they had seen, movies that ended with the rescued pilot embracing his woman.

By some twist of fate, A/2C Jackie Price, who came from Joel Fields's hometown in Kentucky and had enlisted with him, was one of the crew. He sat there cross-legged, a twisted little grin on his face, telling the others that they were going to see all seventeen men standing around beside the wreckage on some godforsaken plateau—maybe even Mount Ararat, like Noah and his family—and he was going to tell Joel he was a dumb shit for letting himself crash like that. The others agreed wholeheartedly. They didn't know what to do if they couldn't keep on believing that the men were alive. No one seated in that circle was over twenty-two. They knew of death as an abstraction, but they weren't yet on intimate terms with it. They were still a few days away from reality.

Family Notification

As the C-130 and, later, the RB-50 were heading for Incirlik, the commanders of the two units were faced with the hideous task of notifying the wives of the victims. For the commander of the 7406th, Major Swanson, the blow he had to deliver was softened a bit by his lack of knowledge. For Captain Tarbox, on the other hand, the message was even more difficult because he realized he was probably lying; he knew or at least strongly suspected that the plane had gone down in Armenia. Neither could mention that the crew had been involved in intelligence gathering or reconnaissance. Both men told the same frightening story: a plane is missing, and your husband was on it. Whether he is alive or dead is something we still don't know. Planes are searching the area where the mission was operating, and as soon as we know the status of your husband, we will let you know. Again and again the two officers repeated the story, knowing they would probably never let the wives know the truth—not then, not ever.

All six men of the 7406th cockpit crew were married, and Major

Swanson drove to four homes that night to inform four women that their husbands were missing: Captains Duncan and Jeruss, First Lieutenant Simpson, and S.Sgt. Laroy Price. Captain Jeruss's wife Irene was three months pregnant, and Lieutenant Simpson's wife Delores was five months pregnant. Swanson's wife assisted with the care of the women, who moved in with other 7406th families at Rhein-Main pending receipt of additional information on the missing men. Ultimately, the wives were sent back to their U.S. homes of record in late September to await further word about the fate of their husbands. Captain Swiestra's wife was notified by Air Force officials at RAF Molesworth Air Base, England. Lieutenant Villarreal's new bride Laurie, who had been busily packing in Laredo, Texas, to join her husband in Germany later in September, was notified by a telegram from Headquarters, U.S. Air Force.

Accompanied by Captain Tarbox, Colonel H. V. Hartbrodt, the 6911th's commander, had the unpleasant task of notifying the wives of the three Detachment 1 airmen who were married and had their families with them in Germany. The two officers visited Mrs. Ila Earlene Mello first on Martin Lutherstrasse in Mörfelden, arriving about six on the evening of September 3. As they informed Mrs. Mello, T.Sgt. Kenneth Simonson and his wife arrived and spent several hours with the frightened woman and her two daughters. Like two other Detachment 1 wives, Mrs. Mello was pregnant at the time. Later, she and her children moved in with A/2C Earl Moore and his wife Jeanne.

Hartbrodt and Tarbox were next driven to Heinzstrasse in Mörfelden, arriving at about six-twenty. Rita Ferguson had joined her husband Jim in Germany in March. Five and a half months pregnant, she was alone with her toddler, Debra, when the two officers and Staff Sergeant Bergeron's mother arrived. Mrs. Bergeron remained with Rita, and persuaded her later that evening to move in with Technical Sergeant Kresge and his wife, Margaret, in base family housing.

Archie Bourg Jr.'s wife Mary, who was also pregnant, took the news more stoically than the others. Bergeron's wife, Lillian, was with her when the officers arrived. Tarbox and his wife Betty tried to persuade Mary to move in with them, but she refused. A neighbor stayed with her that first night, and on September 4 she relented and moved in with the Tarbox family.

The families of the other men received the news through Western Union. Mrs. Theresa Durkin in Levittown, Pennsylvania, was getting ready for work on September 3 when a florist service vehicle drove into her driveway. Mrs. Durkin wondered who could be sending her flowers. It was a telegram from Major General R. J. Reeves, Director of Military Personnel:

> *It is with deep regret that I officially inform you that your brother, Master Sgt. George P. Petrochilos, has been missing in flight since 2 September 1958 in Turkey. When further information is received you will be notified immediately. A letter containing further details will be forwarded to you at the earliest possible date. Please accept my sincere sympathy in this time of anxiety.*

One week later, General Reeves followed up with the promised letter on Headquarters Air Force letterhead:

> *. . . Sgt. Petrochilos was a passenger of a C-130 transport aircraft on a routine flight from Incirlik Air Base, Adana, Turkey, and return. In order that you may be fully advised concerning the circumstances under which your brother became missing, we have arranged for his commander to write you a letter containing more detailed information. The letter will be dispatched when the results of the search are known.*

Immediately after the loss of the C-130, the 7406th and the 6911th grounded all other aircraft except for the two planes that had headed to Turkey for the search.

The Air Searches

The RB-50 and the C-130, along with specially equipped search and rescue aircraft, flew through valley after valley of eastern Turkey for nearly a week in a search that, it turned out, had no meaning whatsoever, since both the Russian and, at some level, the American command structures were quite aware that the plane had crashed in Armenia. As the American search craft flew, Russian listening stations picked up their troubled conversations with one another.

The American crew members were certain they were involved in an actual hunt for the downed aircraft. The officers and men of the 7406th had no idea that the wreckage was not in Turkey, and the leaders of the 6911th were not much better informed, at least in the first couple of days. The men spent the daylight hours trying desperately to spot a glint of metal that would indicate where the plane went down. They were dozens of miles from the wreck, but as the days went by and the American analysts realized that the plane was without question in Armenia, the search served other purposes for the American government. Conducting the search complemented the Air Force cover story and bought time for the American side. Hopefully, the Russians might tip their hand with a public statement or by official contact with the American embassy in Moscow. So, keeping the crews in the dark was, in the final analysis, part of an intelligence game.

Not to have searched would have meant admitting to the Russians that American ground stations had been eavesdropping on their military conversations as they shot down the plane. Of course, we had been listening, just as the Soviets were then intercepting communications between the American search aircraft. But no matter; in the looking-glass war of military intelligence, each side would dance through a complex ritual designed to demonstrate that it had no knowledge of a plane's being shot down. The search crews had the bad luck to be the dancers for our side.

For the men who took part in the search, that week was one of the strangest of their lives. Visually, it was lovely. The late summer landscape was starkly beautiful, the weather perfect, and the planes flew as close to the ground as they dared, skimming in and out of valley after valley. As spotters, the men on the C-130 sat strapped down in the open "jump" doors on each side of the plane. They were in awe of the wild countryside. Bands of horses galloping under the roar and shadow of the strange machine over their heads, fields of gleaming white cloth stretched out beside the rivers to bleach and dry in the sun—it was a world they had been unaware of during their months of high-altitude flying, an exotic world like nothing they had ever seen. But there was no sight of a downed plane.

At night they would come home to the Quonset hut, too depressed to do much more than stare at the floor, avoiding one another's eyes. Kept in a state of ignorance by their officers, the men had begun their mission with a good deal of hope. By the third day that hope was gone and there was nothing left to say to one another.

The Associated Press summarized the search activities on Friday, September 5, in a story headlined: AF HUNTS LOST C-130 WITH 17— TURKEY'S MOUNTAINS HIDE PLANE'S FATE.

> ADANA, Turkey (AP)—U.S. Air Force search plane crews scanned the mountainous country about 110 miles from the Soviet border Thursday for a military transport that disappeared two days ago with 17 men.
>
> The C-130 Hercules turboprop transport last was reported over Trabzon, a Black Sea port in northeast Turkey at 12:42 A.M. Trabzon is about 100 miles from Batumi on the Soviet border.
>
> The pilot's next radio report was due about an hour later over Lake Van in eastern Turkey, about 110 miles from Soviet Armenia . . .
>
> Six mountains of 10,000 feet or more altitude are within a radius of 50 miles of the lake . . . The transport disappeared somewhere near Soviet Armenia . . .
>
> A U.S. cargo plane flying from Germany to Pakistan became lost in bad weather over the Van area on June 27 and strayed into Armenia. Two Soviet jet fighters shot it down. The nine American fliers aboard were held for 10 days before being turned over to U.S. military authorities.
>
> Air Force authorities would not comment on the possibility that the C-130 had strayed into Soviet territory . . . Its failure to return or report triggered an intensive air rescue operation that included SC-54s, C-130s, and B-50s. Two paramedic teams also were along with the search planes. Search operations were veiled in secrecy.

The press account also said the C-130 was involved in an Air Force worldwide radio wave study when it disappeared—true enough; it merely left out what sorts of radio waves the plane's crew was studying. The comments about the release of nine American crewmen whom Soviet pilots shot down in a C-118 in June no doubt gave false hope that some of the seventeen men aboard the C-130 had survived. At best, the searches might reveal some clues about the fate of the missing crew; at worst, it was a stalling tactic.

Disguising the Cover-Up

The cover-up had begun in earnest. Air Force leadership had been caught in a dire predicament in which logic and common sense fell by the wayside in the interest of a disguise that fooled nobody but the American public. How do you explain the use of a U.S. Air Force Security Service reconnaissance crew aboard a lost cargo plane while denying to the world that the plane was on a reconnaissance mission?

Everyone in Security Service was aware that the Soviets knew the role of USAFSS ground sites around the world. Radio Moscow often said as much in stories broadcast in English to the West—sometimes giving the names of Air Force students who, according to the broadcasts, were "studying Russian at Syracuse University to become spies against the Soviet Union." To admit that eleven of the men aboard the 7406th C-130 were assigned to Security Service would amount to admitting that the aircraft was on a spy mission. The solution—retroactively transfer the eleven men from the 6911th to the 7406th.[120] Posthumous transfers must have been a bit unusual, but it probably seemed a brilliant scheme to the intelligence officers who concocted it.

Having made the decision to obscure the identity of the men, Detachment 1, 6911th personnel worked all night on September 3 to retroactively assign each of their eleven missing airmen to the other squadron. "Unit of assignment" on all records in each airman's personnel file was changed to show that the man had been originally assigned to the 7406th Support Squadron. Then, on September 4, Captain Tarbox headed a team that physically inventoried and transferred the belongings of the bachelor airmen who lived in the barracks to the 7406th airmen's quarters at the other end of the same building and handed over the men's personnel files. From that day forward, Detachment 1, 6911th Radio Group Mobile would deny all knowledge of these men.

To emphasize the finality of that change of assignment, Detachment 1's enlisted men were forbidden to even communicate with the wives of the missing airmen. The effect of these maneuvers was to deny to the men of the 6911th all opportunity to honor their fallen brothers, or to console the wives. It created a bitterness in the men that has lasted to this day.

As 7406th commander, Major Swanson had a commitment to forward "a letter containing additional information" to next of kin who were not residing in Germany. In a letter dated September 9, 1958, Major Swanson provided T.Sgt. Arthur Mello's mother the obligatory letter—essentially a repeat of the original notification telegram's text on 7406th letterhead with Major Swanson's name, title, and signature. She also received a letter of condolence dated September 10, 1958, from her congressman. Sergeant Mello's mother and the next of kin of other Detachment 1 men—those receiving that 7406th "form" letter, and later other official correspondence—were never told that their relatives had been retroactively transferred to the 7406th Support Squadron in the middle of the night.

A few weeks after the men had died and been transferred, a young German woman presented herself at the Detachment 1 orderly room and asked Captain Tarbox for the whereabouts of A/2C Medeiros, one of the missing men. She explained that she was his live-in girlfriend and that he had failed to come home since leaving for Turkey the previous month. She knew he was assigned to Detachment 1, 6911th because he had told her so, and she had driven him to his barracks many times in her car for flights. Captain Tarbox informed her there was no Airman Medeiros in his unit and never had been. He directed her to the other end of the barracks; perhaps the 7406th would have heard of him. Tarbox was not proud when the woman left his office that day. His actions didn't seem very manly to him. He was a West Point graduate, however, and he was carrying out an order.

Captain Tarbox took the order from above not to fraternize with the 7406th literally. He told Major Swanson and others in the 7406th that he'd be avoiding them in the Officers Club and other public areas: "It's best if we don't acknowledge or speak to each other until this thing blows over. . . . We're not supposed to know each other." And so the officers and the top NCOs carried out their charade. It was of course useless. Everyone on Rhein-Main was probably aware that the plane that had gone down was involved in intelligence, and nearly everyone must have known that the missing men belonged to the 6911th. Their transfer merely highlighted the relationship between the back-enders and the unit that flew the planes. As so often happens in the military, the emperor was wearing no clothes.

Reality Sets In

The air search over Turkey was called off at the end of the week, and the men flew back to Germany. They returned to a thoroughly demoralized group of comrades. Both Captain Tarbox and Sergeant Kresge spoke at the debriefing. Tarbox informed the men for the first time that 60528 was down in Armenia and that the status of those aboard was unknown. Kresge added that all operational flights were grounded until further notice.

The men had been gone from Rhein-Main for a week, and so did not yet know that the missing men were no longer to be considered part of their outfit. Airman Keefe wanted to know about the wives. He asked where they were staying, and requested permission to visit Rita Ferguson. Request denied. He and the others were warned that the wives were off limits to all but the officers and NCOs with whose families they were staying.

That denial would become one of the bitterest bones of contention between the men of the 6911th and their leaders. One night a week later, Keefe and his friend A/2C Moehringer grew angry enough—and drunk enough—to decide to act. Keefe drew up a full-page complaint concerning the lack of information in general and the sequestration of the wives in particular. The next day he polished it, and he and Moehringer began collecting signatures. By late that morning, after having collected the signatures of nearly half the men in the outfit, they were called into Kresge's office and threatened with court-martial for mutiny unless they immediately destroyed the petition. They ripped it up, and the anger of the men who had signed it grew deeper, the gulf between them and their leaders even wider. From that day, several of the men even refused to salute officers properly.

It never occurred to their leaders to have an open meeting at which some of the complaints could be aired. The men who had returned from the search believed falsely that the search had been an act of betrayal, that Tarbox and Kresge had sent them on what they both knew was a wild goose chase. That belief was wrong; the two men had held out some hope, at least in the beginning. They had gone through the same process of increasing despair. But they felt no need to explain that to their troops. It was the 1950s, and leaders were not supposed to show emotion. The officers and men of the 6911th did their mourning in sullen, rancorous silence.

Some of the men of 6911th tried surreptitiously (to avoid having their security clearances revoked) to get psychiatric help, but they were laughed at. In the 1950s, real men didn't have nervous breakdowns, and the term "post-traumatic stress" didn't come into common usage until after the Vietnam War. But it clearly was present in 1958. Jonathan Shay, in Achilles in Vietnam, writes: "Moral injury is an essential part of any combat trauma that leads to lifelong psychological injury . . . Veterans can usually recover from horror, fear, and grief once they return to civilian life, so long as 'what's right' has not also been violated."

The public lies, the surreptitious transfer of the dead men to another outfit, the total lack of information, the sequestration and then secret removal of the wives from Germany—all these actions constituted a violation of trust between the leaders of the 6911th and the men under them. The self-destructive behavior, even wilder and more reckless than before, that the officers and NCOs observed in their men in the autumn of 1958 might have been considered the result of moral weakness. It was not. It was the inevitable breakdown of discipline that occurs when those imposing it have demonstrated insufficient regard for "what is right." It would take several years for the unit at Rhein-Main to recover its morale. For at least some of the survivors of the September 2 tragedy, it would take a lifetime.

Insofar as possible, Detachment 1 tried to resume normal operations after the loss of C-130 60528, but with eleven Detachment 1 airmen among the missing in action, everyone in the unit was on edge. The atmosphere in the unit remained bleak, hopeless. Many of the men now saw their leadership as the enemy. The rate of drunkenness, always high, grew even higher. Details about the shootdown were shrouded in secrecy, and the veil of secrecy took its toll on morale. Unable to express their grief publicly, the unit's airmen coped as best they could—burying themselves in their work, and drinking and carousing harder when not working. In March 1959, A/2C John B. Argoe, after a night of heavy drinking, was decapitated in an auto accident, taking a further toll on unit morale.

What Did the Soviet Government Know and When?

In the September 2, 1958, incident, the Russians were conducting their own investigation from the moment their air force fighters shot down the American C-130. The same day, Soviet air defense headquarters, Moscow, informed the Communist Party Central Committee about the incident. The report that follows is from Soviet air defense archives:

> On 2 September 1958 at 15:06, the state border of the USSR was violated in an area 15 kilometers southwest of LENINAKAN.
>
> Coming from TURKEY, the intruding aircraft penetrated 45 kilometers into the territory of the USSR at an altitude of 10,000 meters and a speed of 650 to 720 kilometers per hour.
>
> A "scrambled" fighter pilot, Senior Lieutenant LOPATKOV, intercepted the violator at 15:10 and shot it down at 15:12.
>
> According to the pilot's preliminary report, the intruding aircraft had four engines and American markings.
>
> The burning aircraft fell on our territory in the vicinity of MASTARA, 20 kilometers southeast of LENINAKAN. Measures are being taken to search the downed aircraft. A more detailed report will follow.

> Headquarters PVO of USSR
> Major General of Aviation
> [Signature] Stukalov
> 2 September 1958

A separate report said: "Observations from the ground and the air indicated that the crew did not parachute out of the aircraft." In its followup report to the central committee on September 3, air defense headquarters stated that two pairs of MiGs intercepted the intruder and provided the following additional details:

> . . . Upon approach of the fighters, the violator began to withdraw to the state border of the USSR with a sharp descent and turn to the right, not responding to warning shots of our fighters. On command of a Transcaucasian Air Defense Corps command post, the fighters shot to kill.
>
> The violator aircraft was hit and went down in a region 55 kilometers northwest of Yerevan. On impact with the ground, the aircraft exploded.
>
> Established at the aircraft impact point were:

- The violator aircraft is an American military transport aircraft of the type C-130 "Hercules" with four turboprop engines.

- According to gun camera film, the aircraft had USAF markings and tail number 60528.

- Factory No. 337824271, series 3137 was found on a piece of plastic.

- The aircrew died. Five bodies so far have been detected in the impact area. Two identification cards issued by the Department of the Air Force of the USA to Captain Rudy J. Swiestra and Lieutenant Ricardo Manuel Villarreal were found. In a certificate [military temporary duty orders] was a list of five persons:

  Captain Rudy J. Swiestra
  Captain Edward J. Jeruss
  Lieutenant Ricardo M. Villarreal
  Lieutenant John E. Simpson
  Master Sgt. Laroy Price

- Observation from the ground and air indicated that the crew did not parachute out of the aircraft.

- According to radio intercept, the Americans are conducting a search for a downed aircraft type C-130, tail number 60528 that had taken off from

Adana airfield [Turkey], apparently equipped with the newest reconnaissance apparatus.

The remains of the broken and charred aircraft are under guard.

The Transcaucasian Military District command staff was given a report about the related interment of aircrew remains.

Further investigation of the aircraft remains continues.

I. Konev
S. Biryuzov
Witnessed: Lt. Col. Muvetkov
3 September 1958

On September 4, in a detailed report addressed to Marshal of the Soviet Union, Comrade S. S. Biryuzov, commander, PVO (Soviet Air Defense Forces), General Lieutenant I. Pavlovskij, acting commander, Transcaucasian Military District, provided an investigative commission's report on the border violation and shootdown:

STATEMENT
Investigation of Violation of State Border of the USSR
By a foreign aircraft in an area 20 kilometers
South of Leninakan, Armenian SSR
on 2 September 1958

Investigative commission consisted of:

- *General Major of Aviation, K. T. Tsedrik, chairman and acting commander, 34th Air Army*

- *Colonel V. V. Andreev, deputy commander for combat training, Transcaucasian PVO Corps*

- *Colonel, KGB, attached to Council of Ministers, USSR, A. I. Nesterov, chief, special branch, 34th Air Army*

- Lt. Colonel A. A. Sarkisyan, senior engineer, 236th IAD [Fighter Aviation Division]

- Lt. Colonel A. A. Mel'nik, deputy commander, 29th RTP [Radio Technical Regiment], PVO.

Col. Mel'nik prepared this statement. Through a personal on-site investigation, the commission has established:

1. On 2 September 1958 at 14:32 hours, on Turkish territory in an area 50 kilometers south of Rize, air target no. 7845, a single foreign aircraft at an altitude of 7,500 meters, was detected by radar of the Transcaucasian Corps of the PVO. The target proceeded from this area in a northeasterly direction. Twenty kilometers south of the city of Batumi, the target turned and with a climb, began flying along the state border of the USSR along the route: Artvin, 15 kilometers south of Ardakhan, 20 kilometers north of Kars with an approach to the state border of the USSR, 20 kilometers south of the city Leninakan.
    The target was steadily tracked by seven radar stations of the 29th RTP PVO [Radio Technical Regiment, Air Defense] of the Transcaucasian PVO Corps.

2. With the goal of not allowing a foreign aircraft to violate the state border, at 14:47 hours, on command of the 236th IAD [Fighter Air Division] command post, a pair of MiG-17 aircraft from the 25th IAP [fighter air regiment] was launched from Yerevan airfield. The flight leader was senior pilot, Senior Lieutenant LOPATKOV, V.V.; his wingman was senior pilot, Sr. Lt. GAVRILOV, N. At 14:54 hours, a second pair of MiG-17 aircraft from the 117th Guards IAP was scrambled from the Leninakan airfield. The formation commander was Sr. Lt. KUCHERYAEV, I.P.; his wingman was senior pilot, Sr. Lt. IVANOV, V.D. The fighter pairs were dispatched to the state border and they patrolled in an air sector where a possible border violation by the foreign aircraft could occur.

3. At 15:06 hours, the foreign aircraft violated the state border at an altitude of 10,000 meters in an area 20 kilometers south of Leninakan, and following a course of 120 degrees, penetrated 45 kilometers into Soviet territory.

The weather in the area of the border violation was: cloud cover 1-3 of average layer, visibility 15-20 kilometers. The state border along the natural water boundary—the river Arpa-Chaj—was clearly visible from the air.

The flight pair of Sr. Lt. LOPATKOV intercepted the foreign aircraft at 15:07, immediately after it violated the state border. At 15:09, the foreign aircraft was intercepted by the second pair of aircraft, that of flight commander Sr. Lt. KUCHERYAEV.

During the approach of the fighters to the foreign aircraft, the latter made a sharp dive and turned to the right toward the state border. The leader of the first pair of fighters, Sr. Lt. LOPATKOV, approached the foreign aircraft and fired two warning shots to which the foreign aircraft did not respond and continued its descent toward the state border. Following this, in accordance with order number 0049 of the minister of defense of the USSR dated 4 July 1958, the fighters, under direction of the command post of the 236th IAD and at the command of the Acting Commander of the 34th VA, attacked the violating aircraft, carrying out two attacks each in succession. As a result of the fighter attacks, the violating aircraft caught fire, began to come apart in the air, and fell in an area 11 kilometers east of the populated area Verkhnij Talin, 44 kilometers south of the city of Leninakan.

4. After personal observation of the crash site, the committee established:

• According to identifying markings, plates on assemblies of the aircraft, and gun camera photographs, the violating aircraft was a USAF C-130A Hercules, with four turboprop engines, each engine having 6 cylinders, a one-stage turbine, and a three-bladed propeller of metal construction. The tail number was 60528. Upon impact with the *ground the plane exploded and burned. Separated pieces of the aircraft were spread over a 300 to 350 meter area.*

- *On the plane were found burned and scorched remains of radio recon-naissance equipment: according to labels they were determined to be reconnaissance radio receivers type [in English] "AN/YRR-35C and TN-128/APR-9," and charred and completely scorched instructions for operation of radio receiver type [in English] "R-484/APR-14" used for monitoring radio communications.*

- *The burned remains of seven human bodies were found at the crash site. An investigation into the identities of the bodies is not possible due to the bodies being severely mangled, charred, and some body parts completely consumed by fire. In addition to the seven established corpses, there may also be other bodies fully burned or mixed in with the bodily remains found.*[121]

During the inspection of the crash site, the following item was found:

USAF order number 194 dated 28 August 1958, by which one can conclude that the destroyed aircraft belonged to the 7406th Support Squadron. From this order, it is also evident that the plane, its officers and airmen, were to fly on 1 September from Germany to the city of Adana, Turkey, to serve as crew members on aircraft performing an op-erational mission.

The following military members are listed in the order:

- *Captain Edward J. Jeruss, AO 1905185*

- *Captain Rudy J. Swiestra, AO 781703*

- *1st Lieutenant John E. Simpson, 25642A*

- *1st Lieutenant Ricardo M. Villarreal, AO 3064233*

• *Sergeant Laroy Price, AF 15436645*

Among the bodily remains were found two ID cards in the names of Villarreal, Ricardo M., AO 3064233, and Rudy J. Swiestra, AO 781703, as well as a dog tag with the name of Duncan, Paul, AO 940196 T51.

Partially burned foreign currency was also found: American dollars— four bills for a total of 31 dollars; West German marks—four bills for a total of 50 marks; French francs—one bill for a total of 1000 francs; Dutch guilders—one bill for a total of 10 guilders; Turkish lira—5 bills for a total of 175 lire.

Also found was a pistol serial number 1769459 made by the Ithaca Company, New York State.

CONCLUSIONS

1. *USAF C-130A tail number 60528 deliberately violated the state border of the USSR and conducted a reconnaissance flight over the territory of the USSR. This is established by existence of radio communications intercept equipment on board the aircraft, the route of the aircraft along the Soviet border, its intrusion into the boundaries of the USSR, and the presence of operational mission orders.*

2. *The existence of a good reference point, the river Arpa-Chaj and a canyon that defines the state border, and other large, clearly visible reference points, as well as good visibility at the time of the violation, and the existence of modern radio-navigational equipment on board the aircraft completely rules out accidental violation of the state border of the USSR by said aircraft.*

3. *The actions of the 236th IAD and the 29th RTP of the PVO during the intercept of the foreign violating aircraft were correct and in accordance with the orders for defense of the USSR's air borders.*

The evidence that the aircraft was on a reconnaissance mission in all probability had an impact on how the Soviet government treated the incident when dealing with the U.S. government. Signed by each commission member, the report also included eight enclosures: air intercept command post diagram; gun camera photographs and interpretation; map, sketch, and photographs of crash site; forensic report; and photographs of aircrew remains. The gun camera interpretation included score cards for each of the four pilots who expended live ammunition, giving number of rounds expended, target, target distance, altitude, and other specifics, plus an effectiveness rating for the pilot. Three of the pilots received an excellent rating (*otlichno* in Russian) while the fourth pilot rated a *khorosho* (good).

Soviet Forensic Investigation of Remains

The day after the crash, a team of Soviet Army doctors conducted a forensic investigation of human remains recovered from the crash site. In a report dated September 4, 1958, that became part of the comprehensive Soviet investigative document on the incident, Lt. Colonel B. V. Krukovskij, Medical Services doctor, described the results of a forensic investigation that he conducted at the crash site:

At the request of the Acting Commander of the 34th Air Army, General-Major of Aviation K. T. Tsedrik, a forensic investigation on the remains of the foreign aircraft crew was conducted at the crash site on 3 Sep 58. It occurred at 17:00 hours on a clear, sunny day in an open field at a point 44 kilometers south of the city of Leninakan. The investigation was conducted by Lt. Col. of Medical Services B. V. Krukovskij, the chief of PAL No. 2 of the ZAKVO [Transcaucasian Military District], in the presence of chief of the Medical Services Department, ZAKVO, Colonel of Medical Services M. L. Sklyarenko and physician-specialist Lt. Col. of Medical Services I. L. Vernik of the 35th PSEhO.

Preliminary Information

    The foreign aircraft, shot down over Soviet territory on 2 Sep 58 at 15:06 hours, began to burn, started to disintegrate while in the air and fell in flames to the earth 44 kilometers south of the city of Leninakan. The aircraft continued to burn on the ground. Remains of the first four bodies were recovered from under the burned fragments during the evening of 2 Sep. The remains of two more bodies were recovered on the morning of 3 Sep, and the remains of one body on 3 Sep at 17:00 hours.[122]

External Examination of the Remains

    On the ground next to the smoldering wreckage of the aircraft lay the charred remains of human bodies having the appearance of shapeless black lumps. The following corpses were identified through analysis of the remains:

- Charred part of a corpse with intact bones of the shoulder girdle, part of the vertebrae and bones of the base of the skull.

- Charred, grossly deformed, headless torso with charred upper and lower extremities; only the right foot was not charred. The skin had the appearance of a smooth shiny crust with red spots.

- Grossly deformed, charred torso with charred upper extremities and charred thighs. Lower legs and feet are missing.

- Charred upper torso with remains of the head, right upper extremity, and left shoulder. Left forearm and left hand missing.

- Grossly deformed and broken, charred torso with remains of the skull and upper extremities. Lower extremities are missing.

- *Grossly deformed, charred torso with charred upper extremities and charred thighs. Lower legs are missing.*

- *Grossly deformed, charred upper torso with remains of the head (lower jaw with teeth completely intact) and right upper extremities.*

In addition, the following separate charred remains of bodies were identified:

- *Charred muscle with a section of the right iliac bone and upper section of a right thigh bone.*

- *Charred muscle with pieces of ribs from the upper thoracic cavity.*

- *Charred left lower extremity with a section of the left iliac bone.*

- *Grossly deformed, broken and charred lower section of a torso with the lower extremities.*

- *Charred section of a pelvis with the upper section of the right thigh.*

- *Charred section of a pelvis with pieces of the iliac bone and head of the thigh bone.*

Conclusions

Based on the examination of the remains of the foreign aircraft aircrew, I ascertain that the charred remains of the human bodies at the crash site of the aircraft are those of seven human corpses.

Identification of the dead is not possible due to the massive destruction of the corpses from charring and complete burning of body parts.

Of significance is the fact that the Soviet forensic team had no knowledge at the time about the number of crew members aboard the crashed C-130. In addition, the charred, extremely mutilated body parts made it difficult to accurately determine the number of corpses represented by the remains. By September 12, when the Soviet foreign ministry informed the American embassy that human remains had been found at the crash site, the number of corpses had been adjusted to six. American forensic experts would attempt to identify the six remains as soon as the Russians returned them. Unbeknownst to Russian investigators, eleven missing crew members were merely ashes and tiny bone fragments strewn about on the side of an Armenian mountain.

When the dust settled and the fiery heat of the burning aircraft subsided at the crash site, the Soviet Union clearly had the upper hand in the war of words that was sure to follow. In addition to the remains of the intruding aircraft and aircrew, the crash site was inaccessible to the Americans, and the odds were in Russia's favor that there were no American witnesses—right? Soviet field reports had informed Kremlin leaders unambiguously that the entire C-130 crew perished.

There was one fallacy in the Soviet assessment—Soviet intelligence had underestimated the capabilities of Western signals intelligence sites to monitor Soviet air surveillance radar tracking and aircraft communications in Armenia.

What Did the American Government Know and When?

By monitoring Soviet air defense communications in Armenia—internal Soviet radio networks—U.S. and Allied signals intelligence collection sites in Europe had access to the same Soviet radar data and aircraft communications that Soviet command posts used to direct air defense operations. At U.S. Air Force Security Service sites in Germany, England, and Turkey, Morse intercept operators monitored HF communications to determine which aircraft Soviet radar stations were tracking and where the tracked aircraft were flying; the radar stations tracked both friendly (Soviet) and hostile planes.

Voice intercept operators at a site in the eastern Black Sea area complemented the intercepted Morse tracking data by monitoring VHF radio communications between Soviet aircraft and ground controllers. However, this was a non-American voice intercept site—a "second-party source"—that shared special intelligence with the U.S. intelligence community, but not on a real-time basis. It would be a couple of days after the shootdown before the existence of a tape recording of conversations of the attacking Soviet MiG pilots became known to U.S. authorities, complicating an already complex international incident. This recording is discussed later in this chapter.

Morse Intercept

On September 2, S.Sgt. George W. Rubel, Morse intercept operator, reported for work at the 6911th Radio Group Mobile intercept site at Darmstadt, Germany, eager to get back to work after an eight-week temporary duty assignment at Detachment 1's airborne operations at Rhein-Main. Checking the operations flight schedule board for planned recon missions in the European area, he noted that a C-130 mission was scheduled to depart Incirlik, Turkey, at five A.M. (Zulu time/six A.M. Incirlik time), a makeup mission for an incomplete mission that aborted the previous day. He wished he were aboard the C-130; copying Morse code at 28,000 feet altitude was more exciting than ground duties, but at least he'd be able to "flight-follow" the crew on the day's mission over eastern Turkey.

Monitoring the same radio frequencies that the Soviet air defense command and control center at Leninakan airfield, Armenia, was monitoring to receive radar tracking position reports on Soviet and non-Soviet aircraft flying in the vicinity of the Turkish-Armenian border, Sergeant Rubel observed all radar tracks that were being reported, but the Soviet air defense operators reflected no unusual flight activity.

He knew the routine; normally, Soviet radars in Armenia would acquire American communications intelligence recon missions about thirty miles or so south of Trabzon on the Black Sea, identify the track as "hostile," and pass updated position reports on the hostile target every couple of minutes as long as the U.S. mission remained within range of a Soviet radar station. The logical reason that they had not reported detecting the flight was that departure of the C-130 had been delayed. Sometime later Rubel learned from one of the analysts in the ops-comm area that the C-130 mission had departed at 10:21 A.M. Rubel thought about how tired the crew on the C-130 must be after such a long delay. Nonetheless, he would have liked to be with them. He resumed monitoring his intercepted radio net; the Soviets should be detecting the airborne reconnaissance platform soon.

At 11:32 the Soviets detected track number 7845, identified as a single "hostile" aircraft at altitude 7,500 meters approximately fifty kilometers south of Rize, Turkey—fifty or so kilometers southeast of Trabzon. At first Rubel didn't believe this hostile track could be the C-130 recon aircraft; the track was not following the C-130's planned flight path. However, as he continued copying the Morse traffic, he realized 7845 was the only hostile track the Soviets were observing. The Soviet radar stations continued tracking the hostile target and reported that it climbed to an altitude of 10,000 (meters) while headed northeastward toward Batumi, in Soviet Georgia. The track's reported altitude was somewhat high; the speed (about 450 kph) was okay for a C-130, but the flight route was wrong. Twenty kilometers south of Batumi—just outside the Georgian border—the track assumed a course of roughly 120 degrees heading directly toward Armenia.

Soviet air defense authorities also found the actions of track 7845 strange and reacted by scrambling a pair of fighters from Yerevan airfield, Armenia. Rubel's Morse tracking reports showed the fighters flying northwest toward Leninakan, and track 7845 continued southeastward toward the Turkish-Armenian border—toward a point south-southwest of Leninakan. George Rubel listened in shock as the Soviets scrambled two more fighters from Leninakan, tracking them southwestward. The large plotting board showed the four fighter aircraft and hostile track 7845 merging on the Turkish-Armenian border.

Rubel had sensed much earlier that track 7845 was probably the C-130, and that for unknown reasons its crew had strayed very far off course. He attempted to drive those thoughts from his mind, but they kept returning. He felt helpless; if only he were aboard the C-130, he'd have informed the airborne mission supervisor of the error eons ago, and the plane's navigators would have corrected the aircraft heading long before the aircraft approached the Armenian border. Rubel, his flight commander who had been notified, and the entire group of analysts on duty in the "recon mission monitoring area" recognized the gravity of the situation, but they had no way of alerting the plane, and it was too late to save the C-130 crew. The Soviet air defense network ceased tracking 7845, and reported that track 7845 had been destroyed and that the four fighters had landed. The analysts issued a "Critic Report" and Lateral Critic informing other signals intelligence sites in Europe; the Special Security Officer at Headquarters U.S. Air Forces, Europe; the National Security Agency; Central Intelligence Agency; State and Defense Departments; and the White House about the attack. The fate of the aircraft and crew was unknown.

Rubel's relief on the swing shift arrived to take over as he sat mesmerized in front of his SP-600 intercept receivers. Rubel went to the Army NCO Club at Cambrai-Fritsch Kaserne and got drunk. He could not discuss his anxiety and anguish with anyone; the alternative was to drown his sorrows in Henninger Pils.

The following morning when he arrived at work, Sergeant Rubel confirmed that the C-130 had indeed gone down—from all indications, in Armenia. Based on the tracking data, U.S. intelligence analysts could surmise that Soviet fighter pilots had downed the American plane near the border, but the fate of the crew was unknown. He felt distraught, helpless, disgusted, and outraged. He blamed bureaucratic incompetence and himself personally for the loss of the recon aircraft. But for foot-dragging of the incompetent bastards in the American consulate who were obtaining his passport and Turkish visa, he would have been on that plane. And, had he been on the plane, the entire tragedy would have been avoided. Rubel wondered why God let him live while his friends aboard that aircraft perished.

Informing the President

In a memorandum for record dated September 9, 1958, General Andrew J. Goodpaster, President Eisenhower's national security adviser, provided insight into the information on the shootdown that had been briefed to the president—information that in all probability had been received via the Pentagon from an Air Force Security Service ground intercept site in Europe:

On the evening of 2 September, General White [Thomas D. White, Air Force chief of staff] told me he had just received information indicating that a C-130 equipped for electronic reconnaissance had apparently been shot down somewhere along the Turkish-Soviet border earlier that day. He said the report was inexplicable, in that the course of the plane as planned was never closer than 85 miles to the Soviet border. He phoned me the next day, indicating that there was no further public information, a C-130 was unreported. He sent General Walsh [Air Force assistant chief of staff for Intelligence] over, with a report indicating that the aircraft had been off course, had crossed the Soviet border (possibly lured by a false radio beacon) and that it had been shot down.

General White said that he had taken several steps to tighten up further the conduct and supervision of such reconnaissance flights. He sent over copies of instructions aimed at assuring that the aircraft do not, even through navigation error, leave friendly territory. At his request, I reported the matter to the president and secretary of state in Newport on 4 September, and discussed it further with the president on 6 September. He thought the instructions were about all that could be done, but stressed the necessity of command emphasis and supervision. I so informed General White.

Air Force intelligence officers had briefed General Goodpaster and the president on the missing C-130 earlier on September 3. In March 1998 retired Air Force Colonel Jack Morris discussed the early hours following the shootdown. Then a captain and "current briefing officer" in the Pentagon, Morris recalled that the first message said little more than "the aircraft is overdue . . . Messages from Fort Meade were sparse initially, then about two, three, or four o'clock in the morning message traffic (intelligence reports from the NSA) picked up—the C-130 had crossed the border into Soviet Armenia, had been met by Soviet fighters and was apparently shot down." He said that one report suggested that the C-130 may have been "lured across the border by a Soviet beacon, and that made sense to me because I knew where the Yerevan [airfield] beacon was located."

Preparing a briefing quickly ("two pages and a hand-drawn map"), Morris briefed General Walsh, who made a couple of phone calls. In a matter of minutes Morris had briefed the Air Force assistant chief of staff for Operations, the Air Force vice chief and chief of staff. In turn, General White (chief of staff) called the secretary of defense, who informed General Goodpaster. By that time Morris and General Walsh were in a staff car bound for the White House, where Morris briefed Goodpaster. Goodpaster felt that the "boss" needed to hear the briefing, so Morris briefed President Eisenhower in a small dining area near the president's office. The president was "pretty upset," saying that we could not go to war over this, but that we can raise a strong protest with the Russians. Ironically, the State Department was not "in on the initial briefing." Morris did not discuss intercepted communications of the attacking Soviet fighter pilots in his initial briefing, but he recalled that the Current Intelligence Section where he worked learned about those MiG pilot conversations about the same time.

Turkish Investigations and Results

Immediately following the incident, the Turkish government had more firsthand information on the shootdown than did the United States government. Turkish army border guards and peasants working in fields along the Turkish-Armenian border had witnessed the C-130 approaching the border from the direction of Kars, Turkey. In a question and answer session for a sworn affidavit in 1959, Turkish Lt. Nurettin Bahul described the border violation and MiG attacks:

The aircraft fell near your post. Did you see it? Please tell me the true story of what you saw, what happened, the whole story.

I [Lt. Bahul] was commander of the Kinegi post; I was in charge that day and was going to inspect the Ani post. From the direction of Dumanlida, in other words from Cala, I saw a plane. I called up my post on the phone. They told me that they had seen the plane and that they were following it. The weather was a little foggy and partly cloudy. The plane was coming directly to the Russian territory. He passed the boundary two or three kilometers into Russia. As soon as he passed, from the Aragat Mountain there came first two jet airplanes and then one more. These

three jets got the big plane between them. One of the jets went up above the big plane and began shooting. At this time, I heard some automatic weapons noise ... At this time, the plane fell downwards twice in the air, and on the second fall, I think the plane had been hit and he came down to the ground directly without turning over, and went nose down. In the place where I was watching there were a few mountains, so I could not see where the plane fell to the ground. When the plane struck the ground we heard a big noise ... I saw cars with soldiers going to the place of the accident. These cars were coming from all the villages in the Russian territory. When I came to my post, the guards on the other side, in the Russian post, some soldiers there were making hand signs to show me that they had got the plane down. When I looked up at the planes in the sky with my binoculars, on the tail of the big plane I saw a flag which was red ... The altitude of the plane was about 600 or 900 meters.

When you first heard the sound of the airplane, did you have binoculars with you?

Yes, I had them.

When you looked up and saw the plane coming, toward what place in the Soviet Union was the plane flying?

The plane was flying toward the Aragat Mountains.

When you saw the plane cross the Soviet frontier into the Soviet Union, how soon in time was it before that plane was encountered by the jets?

I cannot tell the exact time, but the only thing I can say is that the American plane crossed over just about 500 meters when the jet planes encountered that American plane.

When you saw the soldiers on the other side just after the plane came down, were you still at Ani or were you on the road?

I was riding my horse toward Kinegi when I saw with the binoculars the military vehicles going toward the scene of the crash. There are three villages in the Russian territory, and from all those three villages came soldiers.

Using information from Lieutenant Bahul and other army commanders whose posts had witnessed the shootdown, the Turkish General Staff compiled and forwarded a summary of the incident to NATO COMSIX-ATAF (Commander, Sixth Allied Tactical Air Force):

It was observed that on 2 September at 14:00, a transport aircraft of unknown nationality coming from the direction of Yah Niler Mountain (40:36N 43:24E) was flying to the east in the direction of UC Tepeler, and that when the plane came over the boundary, it was met by three Russian jet aircraft and when they had flown away in the direction of the Aragat Mountain (40:31N 44:12E), after a time an explosion was heard and following this it was seen that a huge smoke column was rising from the rear of the hills to the east of Kizil Kilise (40:33N 43:43E) located in the Russian territory, and five minutes later it was also perceived that the Russian jeeps and cavalries were moving toward the place of incident quickly. It was believed that this was an American C-130 transport plane, and was not lost in the area of Trabzon/Van, was shot down by the Russian fighters over the Russian territory indicated above.

The United States based much of its subsequent protests to the Soviet Union on information derived from this message.

Voice Intercept—MiGs Monitored Intercepting C-130

From the moment the C-130 disappeared on September 2, there was conclusive and irrefutable evidence that Russian fighter pilots had attacked and downed its aircraft, but U.S. Intelligence agencies were not privy to that evidence immediately. Linguists at a non-American intercept site in Turkey copied the voice communications of the Russian MiG-17 pilots as they intercepted and attacked the transport.

The linguists recognized the MiG attack as it occurred, and forwarded a report through their intelligence channels—a report that eventually made its way to a U.S. Intelligence agency. The source of the information was a dilemma. All communications intelligence data is highly classified and normally not releasable outside special channels, but the sensitive source of this data limited its distribution even further. In a matter of days, a copy of the transcript of the MiG pilot shootdown communications was made available on a strict need-to-know basis to a few recipients—including Detachment 1, 6911th at Rhein-Main. Detachment 1 intercept operators needed to fully comprehend what was being said in the recorded pilot conversations for self-protection during future recon missions. The Air Force and State Department were careful not to reveal sources when discussing aspects of the incident with the public or with the Soviets.

Turkish military border guards and Turkish farmers working in fields along the border also witnessed the MiG interception and downing of the C-130. What neither U.S. officials nor the public knew was why the recon aircraft violated the border, details surrounding the actual crash of the C-130, or the status of the C-130s crew members—answers most sought by families of the crew.

Initially, Turkish witnesses were said to be the basis for United States charges that Soviet MiGs intercepted and downed the C-130, apparently lulling the Soviet government into a false sense of security that the U.S. had no real proof beyond the Turkish witnesses. After all, the American witnesses who'd been aboard the downed aircraft had certainly been silenced. Such a ploy had worked for the Soviets on April 18, 1955, when a pair of MiGs shot down a U.S. Air Force RB-47 off Kamchatka—the U.S. government had no proof that the RB-47 had been attacked, and never raised the issue with the Soviet foreign ministry.

Airborne Voice Intercept

We'll never know what the Security Service recon crew aboard C-130 60528 knew or when they knew they were being intercepted and attacked, but we know the capabilities of the signal intercept equipment aboard the C-130. The aircraft was equipped with nine voice intercept positions, at least eight of which were capable of monitoring and recording one or more VHF voice communications channels at a time. In addition there was a tenth (unmanned) intercept position equipped with dual HF receivers capable of copying and recording Morse or voice signals. With the C-130 flying at altitudes of 25,000 feet and higher, reception of VHF voice communications such as the conversations of the attacking MiGs would have been excellent—loud and clear. To the recon crew, the MiG pilots would have sounded as if they were right off the wing tip of their C-130.

One can surmise that none of the nine onboard voice intercept operators recognized the seriousness of the threat prior to being intercepted by the MiGs. One or more of the linguists (two Romanian, one Bulgarian, a Serbo-Croatian, and five Russian) may have been monitoring the fighter pilots' conversations, but a former airborne voice intercept operator who served in Detachment 1 at the time speculates otherwise:

> I think it's possible they [the intercept operators] never detected the traffic. Search procedures were unrefined and rudimentary. I doubt that anyone —or at most only one—operator actually heard the activity. It [the MiG pilot conversations] occurred on a single special activity frequency and they [the crew] may not have known which frequency was used for special activity . . . They had just turned on the primary leg [of the mission], plus search and [signal] acquisition capabilities were not great . . . "Hearability" was not too good; no pre-amps and lots of RFI [radio frequency interference]. None of the receivers had SDUs [signal display units], and there was only one Pan [panoramic search receiver] for 100-150 megahertz—above position #2—and it was at best, unreliable. In those days, many crews did not even bother to turn it on since they didn't know how to use it.

Why wouldn't the linguists have sensed the danger at hand? As the former operator points out, it is conceivable that no one heard the MiG pilots' conversations, and there are many other possibilities—exhaustion (their takeoff time delayed a few hours), their youthful sense of invincibility and complacency (the fact that their C-130 could be off course, and violating the Soviet border was unthinkable), the possibility that they did not recognize that they themselves were the plane spoken of as the target of the fighter interception. Assuming the C-130 crew believed they were on course according to the Trabzon-to-Van flight plan, if the recon crew was monitoring the MiG conversations, they probably thought in the early stages of the fighter interception mission that the fighters were either engaged in practice ground-controlled intercept missions or that the fighters were responding to an unidentified target along the border. By the time an intercept operator realized that his own aircraft was the target, it was too late.

Airborne Morse Intercept

Ground-based Morse intercept operators had been intercepting air defense data since World War II, but the Air Force Security Service had used Morse intercept operators aboard recon aircraft only sparingly before the shootdown of C-130 60528. Prior to the loss of that plane, no one appreciated the importance of using an airborne Morse intercept operator to monitor the movement and location of the airborne reconnaissance platform itself. When the disaster struck, the downed aircraft's crew did not include a Morse operator; the unit manning document neither authorized nor required Morse operators on airborne recon missions. An evaluation was being made to determine what role, if any, a Morse operator should play in C-130 airborne reconnaissance in Europe. U.S. Air Force Security Service Headquarters had tasked its 6900th Security Wing to evaluate the use of Morse intercept operators on the C-130, and Major Richard Machelski, 6900th airborne COMINT recon platform project officer, had selected Staff Sergeant Rubel as the USAFSS Morse intercept operator to participate in the evaluation.

Sergeant Rubel was an ideal candidate for the project. From 1952 to 1954 he'd pioneered airborne COMINT reconnaissance operations aboard RB-29 290. For the previous two years, he'd been intercepting Soviet air defense Morse communications at Darmstadt. On July 7, 1958, he was detached from Darmstadt for temporary duty with Detachment 1 at Rhein-Main.

Enthusiastic about another crack at flying recon missions, Rubel departed Darmstadt's Cambrai-Fritsch Kaserne early on Monday morning,

July 7, and headed out on Autobahn E-451 toward Frankfurt. Since he was on TDY for sixty days, it would be convenient to have his car with him. He exited the autobahn at the Rhein-Main Air Base exit and drove directly to Detachment 1 operations, where he met with Technical Sergeant Kresge. He also said hello to Bill McCormick and some of the others he'd known at Darmstadt before they transferred to Rhein-Main late in 1956.

They assigned Sergeant Rubel a bunk in the Detachment 1 barracks and accompanied him to the 7406th personal equipment shop and Base Supply to outfit him with flying gear. At the end of the day, the NCOs retired to the stag bar at the NCO Club around the corner in Building 353 to unwind. The next day, Rubel visited the Rhein-Main dispensary to obtain a cholera shot and schedule an "emergency" Category III flight physical so he'd again meet aircrew qualifications. He also filled out an application for a U.S. passport and visa that would permit him to travel to Turkey. The remainder of the week was pretty quiet; Rubel got a guided tour of C-130 60484, but did not fly any missions. The 6900th issued aeronautical orders designating him a crew member.[123] Finally, the big day arrived. On July 15, George Rubel flew his first mission in four years—a local transition training mission; it felt good to be flying again.

That first mission turned out okay, but he didn't intercept anything spectacular. For that matter, Rubel had no real guidance as to his tasking during the mission—"just come along and do your thing, whatever that is." No one in Detachment 1 was clamoring to have a Morse intercept operator on missions. On previous airborne missions, Morse intercept operators, Rubel included, had copied aircraft air-to-ground Morse communications and other military traffic, with little emphasis on Soviet radar tracking.

Truth be known, at the time, none of the airborne voice intercept operators had any real understanding of or appreciation for Morse tracking. The radio stations (HF) that the airborne Morse operator monitored could be intercepted just as easily from a Security Service ground site. As Rubel said, "And, why have a Morse operator on board to track ourselves? . . . We have two navigators to keep us on track, and we have no faith in Soviet radar tracking anyway." It never dawned on anyone that what mattered most was where the *Russians thought* the reconnaissance C-130 was located; that, after all, was how the Russians determined the status of airborne targets. And the question of whether the Soviets felt an American plane was a direct threat was crucial, whether they were correct or not. But with no one championing the airborne Morse operator cause—Rubel's vote essentially didn't count—the evaluation was destined for failure.

No one stepped forward to authorize Rubel to carry essential classified tracking grid codes on missions. Detachment 1 was absolutely forbidden to carry any classified materials aboard recon aircraft. Throughout its short history, the unit had been in a pissing contest with the National Security Agency, USAFSS, and everyone else in the chain of command, over which technical materials aircrews could or could not carry on missions. The 6901st processing center refused to provide Detachment 1 any technical order of battle information, reasoning that the unit had no need for technical feedback because its job was to provide raw data, not to analyze or report on it. And, by the same reasoning, the unit did not have a reporting mission because its intercept operators did not have the expertise to do analysis and send out reports. So why provide order of battle data to the operators when it would only tempt them to illegally carry the materials on missions? It was a vicious cycle. Any classified information carried aboard mission aircraft would be solely in the minds of the operators. Prevalent reasoning in management was that in the event that an intercept operator became a prisoner of the Russians, it would be best if the operator didn't know anything.

To support his mission, Rubel had his supervisor at Darmstadt send classified tracking grid readouts via the crypto ops-comm circuit to Detachment 1, and immediately prior to departure on a mission he'd memorize the grids he'd need during the flight. He used a small section of an Air Force ONC navigation chart as a map covered with a piece of clear acetate (plastic) so he could write the grids and tracking information on his map with a grease pencil. Then, at the end of a mission and before departing the aircraft, he'd erase the grease-pencil markings from his map, keeping everyone happy.

Rubel flew a couple of additional local missions during July and August, and looked forward to deploying to Turkey on the first C-130 mission to Incirlik on August 25, 1958. The local missions had for the most part involved transitional training for the front-end flight crews, and had provided very little opportunity for Rubel to show the airborne mission supervisor how a Morse operator could contribute to the mission. That opportunity would come during the southern missions in the Black Sea area during his temporary duty trip to Turkey.

However, his deployment to Incirlik on August 25 was cancelled at the last minute, when he had not received the passport and visa that he'd applied for in July. No sweat; if the passport and visa arrived within the next week, he'd fly down to Incirlik on September 1 on the next C-130 mission to Turkey. The 6900th amended his aeronautical orders, extending the duration of his crew member status to October 9, 1958. August 31 arrived and still no passport—Sergeant Rubel dejectedly returned home to Darmstadt.

Meanwhile, Major Machelski faced a deadline in his ongoing evaluation of the value of having a Morse operator onboard the C-130s. He'd received no positive feedback on any increased intercept capabilities that an airborne Morse intercept operator would provide, and the defensive advantage that Morse would give the C-130—the ability to monitor the Russian radar stations that were in turn monitoring the American aircraft—simply did not occur to him despite the fact that a plane without a Morse operator had just been shot down. At the same time, U.S. Air Force Headquarters, Europe decreed a stand down of C-130 recon missions for an indefinite period to assess the causes of the loss of the C-130 and to implement corrective measures.

After pondering the Morse operator decision, and with no known relationship between a Morse intercept operator and the crisis situation involving the loss of the C-130, Major Machelski decided to cancel further C-130 Morse operator evaluations. (In fairness to Machelski, when the evaluation commenced, Soviet radar tracking data was viewed as a minor target, a small part of the Morse operator's intercept mission, which placed greater emphasis on monitoring air-to-ground Morse communications.)

Adding insult to Sergeant Rubel's already pained state, Machelski informed Rubel of his decision and sent out a message to USAFSS Headquarters, 6911th and Detachment 1 stating that based on evaluation results, Morse airborne intercept operators were not needed on C-130 missions in Europe. Contacting Rubel by phone, Machelski said, the "ACRP Morse operator evaluation" had been terminated, and thanked him for participating in the flights. There did not appear to be a valid mission for a Morse operator on C-130 recon missions. Sergeant Rubel would not be needed for additional flights.

Rubel was dumbfounded but unable to discuss the issues with Major Machelski since their conversation occurred on an open telephone. He acknowledged the major's message and vowed to himself to leave Air Force Security Service. Sergeant Rubel visited his first sergeant the following day and completed an application to marry his German girlfriend, Marie. His security clearance was revoked effective immediately, and Rubel never worked again as a Morse intercept operator. He married Marie and completed his Air Force career as a radar operator in aircraft control and warning squadrons.

Fixing the Problems

The loss of C-130 60528 had a sobering effect on both the 7406th and Detachment 1. For the remainder of September and October both units and their respective higher headquarters reassessed their flying programs and implemented new procedures that would improve flying safety. The 7499th Support Group, parent organization of the 7406th, headed up investigations involving aircraft maintenance, the mechanical condition of aircraft 528 on its last flight, ground crew and flight crew training and competence, flying safety, and airborne operating procedures. USAFSS Headquarters investigated all mission-related aspects of its airborne reconnaissance program—seeking answers to why 528's recon crew had not recognized imminent danger and forewarned the aircraft commander before the MiGs attacked. Drastic changes affected operations within both the 7406th and Detachment 1, 6911th.

Tightening Up Aircraft Maintenance and Operating Procedures

Without admitting any mistakes—indeed, no one was charged with wrongdoing or incompetence—the 7406th implemented several changes resulting in improvements in flying safety. Many of the changes involved safe navigation, i.e., avoiding enemy airspace. The criteria for aborting missions were better defined and included a mandatory mission abort if the APN-99 radar was marginal or inoperative. At the same time, a factory-trained civilian radar maintenance technician was assigned to the squadron to boost the reliability of the APN-59 and APN-99 radar systems. The use of integrated crews, discussed in chapter five, was also begun, which improved crew cohesiveness. Increased emphasis was also placed on in-flight emergency procedures training and survival training for downed crews. All aircrew members had to pass written emergency procedures tests and had to practice handling in-flight emergencies. By the early 1960s, the Security Service recon flyers had begun attending the same Air Force survival schools and escape and evasion courses that were mandatory for flight crews, who participated in airborne signals intelligence reconnaissance missions.

The Evolving USAFSS Airborne Reconnaissance Program

For Air Force Security Service, airborne reconnaissance operations would have matured over time, but the loss of its eleven crew members aboard C-130 60528 undoubtedly expedited the process. Some changes occurred immediately; others evolved over time. The most obvious change for Detachment 1 was the inclusion of a Morse operator on all operational missions on flight routes along the periphery of the Soviet Union and East European satellite countries.

Airborne Morse Defensive Operator on All Flights

It was unfortunate that George Rubel was not permitted to remain a Morse intercept operator in Security Service, but his legacy lived on. Whether C-130 60528 would have strayed off course and been shot down if Rubel had been on the mission is moot, but there was an official change in policy. As investigators sorted out details and sought preventive measures that would enhance the safety of Security Service recon crews, it became very clear that a Morse intercept operator did indeed have a crucial defensive function to perform. Headquarters USAFSS decreed in October 1958 that all Security Service airborne recon crews would include an airborne Morse intercept operator. The edict was effective immediately and applied to Detachment 1, 6911th operations at Rhein-Main and Detachment 1, 6988th operations at Yokota Air Base, Japan.

A scramble ensued to recruit qualified Morse operators who would volunteer for flying status and move to Rhein-Main immediately. The 7406th and Detachment 1 concentrated on implementing the safest possible flying program aboard their C-130 recon fleet.

Replacement Crew Members

During a two-month stand down in flights, the 7406th and 6911th assessed personnel requirements and redefined crew needs commensurate with new operating policies. In addition to replacing the six lost flight crew members, the 7406th required additional crewmen if it was to reorganize with integrated combat flight crews. Replacements for the 7406th would be pilots, navigators, and flight engineers already qualified in airborne operations. Filling the Security Service Detachment 1, 6911th crew needs was not as simple; no available airborne-qualified Air Force linguists and Morse operators existed. Linguists and Morse operators who were recruited from Security Service ground intercept sites in Europe were trained on the job with Detachment 1 for their new airborne duties. Twelve Russian linguists were reassigned from the 6913th Radio Squadron Mobile, Bremerhaven, Germany, to Detachment 1 effective October 6, 1958.[124] The initial cadre of Detachment 1's new airborne Morse operators transferred from the 6911th at Darmstadt.[125]

Resuming Recon Missions After the Shootdown

The 7406th and Detachment 1 eased back into deployments on recon missions with a three-day trip to Athens, Greece, on November 5,

1958.[126] S.Sgt. Braxton Lockett, one of the first Morse intercept operators permanently assigned to Detachment 1, 6911th, flew as a Morse operator on the first operational mission, setting the stage for all future C-130A-II recon operations at Rhein-Main Air Base. Thereafter, lack of a qualified airborne Morse intercept operator was grounds to cancel or abort a Security Service airborne SIGINT recon mission.

On November 11 an all-volunteer C-130 crew deployed to Incirlik to resume normal operations from Turkey. T.Sgt. John J. Kozak headed up the reconnaissance crew as the airborne mission supervisor. The crew consisted of ten airborne voice intercept operators, including Sergeant Kozak, two airborne Morse intercept operators, and two airborne maintenance technicians.[127]

In light of the shootdown of 528, higher headquarters had defined an interim internal advisory program with specified criteria under which the airborne mission supervisor (admiral) would inform the aircraft commander (AC) if potential danger arose that warranted abort of the mission. Naturally, the crew was alert and worried during the first mission that they flew from Incirlik a couple of days after deploying. Departing Incirlik on a planned "Central Black Sea" mission, they flew northwest via Samsun, Turkey, to a point over the Black Sea at 43:00N (point Alpha) and continued to the intended northernmost and easternmost point (point Bravo). They would then orbit in a figure-eight pattern between points Alpha and Bravo—on a course viewed as nonprovocative by the C-130 crew—and well outside Soviet airspace. (Even before the shootdown of 528, the unit's recon flights made a point of orbiting on figure-eight flight legs—always reversing course by turning away from the Soviet landmass to avoid the appearance of being provocative.) The primary targets of the Central Black Sea orbit were military units in the Crimean area, the southwestern Soviet Union, Romania, and Bulgaria. Reaching point Bravo, the C-130 made a 180-degree turn and headed back toward point Alpha.

On edge throughout this, their first mission out of Turkey since the shootdown, the recon crew was determined not to be surprised by any MiGs approaching their flight path from the north or east. In the same manner that Soviet air defense radar stations had tracked 60528's flight path on September 2, radar stations along the Soviet coastline detected the current C-130 flight and tracked its flight path to points Alpha and Bravo, where it reversed course. The Soviet air defense facilities identified the C-130 track as a "hostile" target. The air defense radar stations were also tracking several additional aircraft over the Black Sea as "friendly" (Soviet) tracks that came out over water from the Soviet mainland and were on an intersecting course with the C-130.

At that point the scenario was not unlike the situation on September 2, in that Soviet aircraft were heading toward the C-130, but the C-130 was clearly outside Soviet airspace. Seeing from the Soviet radar-tracking data that the tracks of unidentified aircraft were heading toward their flight path, the airborne Morse intercept operators immediately tipped off Kozak, who assigned Bob Keefe, one of the Russian linguist intercept operators, to monitor the VHF voice radio channel that would most likely be used by Soviet fighter aircraft sent out to intercept the C-130 aircraft. Himself a Russian linguist, Kozak also searched for any associated Soviet fighter communications. Although neither Keefe nor Kozak detected any suspicious voice communications, aircraft were nonetheless being tracked toward their flight path.

With September 2 clearly etched in his mind, and having very tenuous criteria and guidance against which to respond, Sergeant Kozak took the safe approach, contacted Captain Lewis, the aircraft commander, on the aircraft interphone and told him: "AC, I have a Condition Alpha. There are unidentified-type Soviet aircraft approaching us from the north, let's get the hell out of here!" Banking sharply to the right, extending the flaps and landing gear, Captain Lewis literally dove the C-130 from their 28,000 feet position to 500 feet in record time and proceeded at maximum throttle on a course of 180 degrees toward the Turkish coast. But the radar tracking showed that the Soviet aircraft were still closing, so Sergeant Kozak called Captain Lewis on the interphone and said, "AC, this is the admiral. Kick 'er in the ass! . . . They're gaining on us." The banking/diving maneuver put such stress on the aircraft that popped rivets on its skin were found during inspection back at Incirlik.

The 500-foot altitude was too low for the Soviet radar station operators to detect and track the C-130. The unidentified Soviet aircraft may well have been bombers that were known to practice navigational training over the Black Sea. As the C-130 continued southward, the Morse intercept operators continued to observe confusion on the Morse tracking network, which still tried unsuccessfully to detect the "hostile" target that it had lost over the Black Sea. The entire Sevastopol air defense sector must have feared being sent to a concentration camp in Siberia for permitting an enemy aircraft to penetrate their borders without retribution.

When Captain Lewis and crew arrived back at Incirlik, a major investigation ensued. Apparently feeling they needed a scapegoat for the aborted mission, 6900th Security Wing managers at first attempted to "hang" Sergeant Kozak for his actions, but as one and another defended his actions, all disciplinary considerations were dropped. They could not punish him for following orders, no matter that the orders were less than clear. Captain Lewis's crew flew several more missions over the Black Sea without incident.

The 7406th and Detachment 1 resumed normal deployments and operations out of Incirlik following Kozak's "Condition Alpha" abort in early November 1958. T.Sgt. Bruce Henderson headed up a crew that arrived at Incirlik on November 26 to replace Kozak's crew.[128] Subsequently, C-130 recon crews increased the pace of operations, with two crews frequently on station at Incirlik concurrently.

Other Changes in USAFSS Airborne Operations

Responding to an ever-changing operating environment, Detachment 1, 6911th Radio Group Mobile built upon the few established procedures in place when recon operations resumed subsequent to the shootdown— changing those procedures as necessary to meet newly imposed requirements, and defining and implementing new procedures.

First Echelon Analysis

Reluctantly, the National Security Agency and Detachment 1's intermediate headquarters accepted the fact that the airborne intercept operators required current enemy technical order of battle information (radio frequencies, call signs, and air surveillance tracking grids, for example) to effectively do their jobs. Denying recon crews permission to take classified technical materials aboard missions—in effect, forcing intercept operators to memorize classified enemy order of battle data or work without needed OB data—was no longer an acceptable solution. To keep abreast of its reconnaissance aircraft's location based on the signals that its intercept operators were intercepting, the recon crews were permitted to carry classified (secret-level) working aids on airborne recon missions. Eventually, one of the voice intercept positions (position number two) evolved into an airborne analyst position; the analyst on position two maintained the technical order of battle data carried on missions and assisted the airborne mission supervisor in the identification of intercepted traffic. These first echelon analysis functions resulted in the creation of a small analysis section within Detachment 1 operations. When not flying as an airborne analyst (there was one analyst aboard each mission), the analysts studied traffic intercepted on previous missions to keep the airborne working aids up-to-date. As Detachment 1's analysts gained expertise, NSA and the 6901st Special Comms Group (Security Service's second-echelon analysis center in Europe) tasked Detachment 1 with technical reporting. Now, with a combined analysis and reporting section, Detachment 1 was growing, both in terms of expertise and responsibility.

Airborne Intercept Operator Training

From the earliest days, the Security Service had recognized the need to provide "intercept" training for its Morse intercept operators, but had found it difficult to provide voice intercept operator training for its linguists. Morse intercept operators received formal Morse intercept training at Keesler AFB, Mississippi, before arriving for their first assignment at a Security Service intercept site. Most voice intercept operators, on the other hand, were posted directly to their first USAFSS intercept site after completing a basic language course. With a severe shortage of linguists and long (six to twelve month) language courses, Security Service believed it could not afford the luxury of formally training its linguists in voice intercept processing techniques; the task of training new voice intercept operators fell upon individual intercept sites. (This policy would be short-lived.)

With airborne voice intercept operators, there was the added burden of mastering intercept assignments in an alien airborne environment. While fundamentals are essentially the same, the airborne intercept tasks are significantly more varied and complex than comparable intercept operator duties at a ground-based intercept site. By 1958 (even before the 528 shootdown), the lack of formal voice intercept operator training had been recognized as a deficiency that needed to be corrected. The loss of 528's crew under undetermined circumstances may have expedited decisions to create a formal voice intercept processing training program. In any event, by late 1958, Security Service had established a voice intercept processing course (a twelve-week course) at the USAFSS School at Goodfellow AFB, Texas.

Using recorded intercepted foreign air force voice communications—primarily communications between pilots and ground controllers—new language school graduates were taught voice intercept processing techniques. In addition to becoming familiar with relevant military terminology, they learned how to tune intercept receivers and operate tape recorders. In addition they learned how to hand-scan (write down pertinent voice traffic) while monitoring intercepted voice communications, and how to transcribe recorded voice communications. While the training did not initially address the specific problems of airborne voice intercept operators, this generalized training in voice intercept processing techniques helped airborne voice intercept operators adapt to their new jobs easier and quicker.

Finally, in 1960, 1st Lt. Doyle E. Larson[129] and T.Sgt. Waldo C. Kline set up at the Goodfellow-based school an airborne voice intercept operator course (six weeks in duration) that was specifically designed to train new airborne intercept operators. Linguists selected to become airborne intercept operators attended the airborne training course immediately after completing their basic voice intercept training course. Working with recorded voice signals that had been intercepted on airborne missions, the airborne operator-trainees practiced functioning as an airborne crew under the tutelage of training instructors, who were themselves former airborne voice intercept operators.

During an airborne training lesson conducted as a simulated airborne reconnaissance mission, an operator-trainee on training position number one functioned as the airborne mission supervisor (AMS), managing the "intercept" mission and controlling the intercept tasks assigned to the other operator-trainees. Using receivers, signal demodulators, and tape recorders identical to those installed in C-130 recon aircraft—in operator positions like those in actual use in 1958—the students were taught to perform as an airborne recon crew:

1. Tune their receivers

2. Search for and intercept signals of interest

3. Recognize the type of voice traffic and inform the AMS

4. Record signals of interest as directed by the AMS

5. Hand-copy (hand-scan) transmissions in their foreign language (Russian, Polish, etc.)

6. Recognize the significance of copied traffic and tip off the AMS

A training mission in the airborne intercept training simulator at Goodfellow AFB was the next best training experience to an actual training mission on a C-130 recon aircraft.

Training position number nine in the simulator (just like intercept operator position nine on 528 and on the other C-130 recon aircraft) provided HF receivers and a signal environment to train an airborne Morse intercept operator. Manning position nine during simulated missions, the airborne Morse intercept operator-trainee practiced intercepting Morse tracking data and "plotting the track" of the simulated airborne mission, taking care to keep the AMS informed of the location of their mission aircraft relative to denied airspace. The recording of the Soviet MiG pilots communicating among themselves and with their controllers while they shot down 528 was one of the key recordings used in the airborne voice intercept operator training course. Learning to immediately recognize the nature and significance of those pilots' conversations and similar Soviet air force terminology was a prerequisite for

Russian linguists before they were permitted to fly operational recon missions. Such training for the crew who perished aboard 528 in 1958 could have helped the crew's linguists better comprehend the conversations they were monitoring, but we do not know if the crew was monitoring the MiG pilots who shot them down. Whether better crew training might have precluded the shootdown will never be known.

Growing Pains—Detachment Elevated to Squadron

Because of its evolving mission, swift increase of size, inadequate operational preparation of its linguists, the switchover from RB-50s to C-130s, and murky lines of command and control with its higher echelons, Detachment 1, 6911th had been experiencing growing pains since its inception. That became clear when, in early 1959, the unit underwent its first ever unit inspection by a USAFSS inspector general team. The IG team identified significant discrepancies in every functional area—most of which were beyond the detachment's control. Detachment 1 was at the mercy of the 6911th for administrative support and of the 6900th for operational control, and neither unit was doing a good job of supporting Detachment 1's needs. The inspection found that the detachment was not properly managed, but that it was nevertheless somehow meeting operational requirement in spite of the lack of support. Most of the action items to correct discrepancies were levied upon the 6911th and the 6900th.

Working through the IG write-ups, it became clear to the 6900th that a realignment of responsibilities was in order, and on July 1, 1959, Detachment 1, 6911th Radio Group Mobile became Detachment 1, 6900th Security Wing. Six months later, on January 1, 1960, Detachment 1, 6900th Wing became the 6916th Radio Squadron Mobile,[130] a more appropriate designation for its operational airborne reconnaissance mission. Growing from a handful of men who started Detachment 1 in 1956, when C-130 60528 was shot down in September 1958 the unit consisted of significantly less than a hundred men—fifty-nine Detachment 1 airmen were on flying status in January 1958. Two years later (December 31, 1959), six officers, fifty-three NCOs, and 122 airmen were assigned to the unit.

Many of the initial cadre of squadron personnel who had lost best friends aboard 60528 in September 1958 suffered in silence during 1959 as investigations of the incident continued. Regrettably, the squadron and the nation knew no more about the fate of the eleven missing men a year after the shootdown—thirty years, for that matter—than they knew in September 1958. Many of the changes highlighted in this section are discussed in additional detail in chapter ten.

NINE

DIPLOMACY: FAMILIES ARE POLITICAL PAWNS

Alexandr Semyonovich Orlov was very busy during the first week following the downing of the American aircraft; he headed a Soviet Army OSNAZ (signals intelligence) radio reconnaissance and jamming element involved in monitoring U.S. Air Force search efforts for the downed C-130. Born in 1924, Orlov served in the Red Army in World War II before graduating from the Military Institute of Foreign Languages and radio intercept school in 1952. After serving with the GRU (Soviet Army Intelligence) as an English voice intercept operator in Korea, he was serving within the Baku Air Defense District in 1958.

Orlov's unit had played only a minor role in the C-118 shootdown incident in June 1958, since there had been no related U.S. search operations—the Soviet Union admitted downing the aircraft within twenty-four hours. He had been involved in transferring the nine airmen who'd been aboard the C-118 to Baku and interrogating them before they were returned to American authorities ten days later.

The C-130 incident in September was different. Two to three American aircraft searched over eastern Turkey for the C-130 daily for almost a week, with Orlov's voice intercept operators monitoring all of their air-to-air and air-to-ground communications. Monitoring the American search aircraft's communications confirmed that they were searching for

C-130 60528, and that the United States did not know where 528 crashed or why it crashed. If anything, the vague but open and frank discussions between the U.S. search crews probably convinced Soviet authorities that the United States was in the dark about Soviet MiG involvement in the disappearance of its missing aircraft. Orlov was interviewed about the incident in 1993. To his knowledge, there were no survivors in the C-130 crash.[131]

During the ninety-six hours following the downing of the C-130, the sides maintained diplomatic silence—each waiting for the other to raise the issue and reveal its strategy. For the Soviets, the wait provided ample time to gather facts; for the Americans, waiting was more a stall while attempting to create a strategy.

Diplomatic Exchanges—Round One

Finally, on Saturday, September 6, 1958, the American embassy in Moscow delivered a note to the Soviet Ministry of Foreign Affairs seeking any available information on the missing plane:

> It has been ascertained that an unarmed United States Air Force C-130 transport plane on a roundtrip flight from Adana to Trabzon and Van, Turkey, is missing. Departing Adana at 10:21 GMT [Greenwich Mean Time] on September 2, 1958, the aircraft was last reported over Trabzon at 11:42 GMT and is unreported at Van. A crew of seventeen was on board.
>
> In view of the foregoing, the United States government would appreciate receiving any information which might become available to the Soviet government concerning the missing United States aircraft and its crew. A similar inquiry is being addressed to the Iranian government.[132]

This was the first indication to the Soviet government that seventeen crew members, not six or seven, were aboard the missing C-130. On a diplomatic "fishing trip," a Soviet bureaucrat orally informed the American embassy on September 8 that the Soviet official who was conducting an investigation desired to know in what region the plane might have approached the Soviet border—the Soviet side clearly wanted to know what the Americans knew before they responded. Finally, in a phone call with the American chargé d'affaires in Moscow, Richard H. Davis, on the same date, an official in the Soviet foreign ministry denied any knowledge of the incident.

On September 12 the Soviet foreign ministry delivered a note to the American embassy in Moscow acknowledging that a U.S. Air Force aircraft had indeed crashed in Soviet Armenia. The U.S. State Department recapped relevant details of the Soviet note in a press release on September 12:

> The Soviet Ministry of Foreign Affairs informed the American Embassy at Moscow today that the remnants of a destroyed and burned airplane have been found at a point 55 kilometers northwest of Yerevan, the capital of the Armenian Soviet Socialist Republic, and that judging by remains discovered there, it may be assumed that six of the members of the crew perished.
>
> The Soviet Ministry of Foreign Affairs further declared that there was no doubt that the airplane belongs to the United States Air Force. It alleged that the aircraft had penetrated for a significant distance into Soviet airspace and had fallen within Soviet territory and had thus intentionally violated the Soviet border.[133]

The note gave no indication how the plane came down. In response to oral questions, the foreign ministry spokesman stated that he had no information to add to that given in the note.

Chargé d'Affaires Davis requested that a further search for eleven missing crew members be made, pointing out that seventeen American airmen were aboard the missing aircraft. He also sought permission for an officer from the U.S. Embassy to visit the crash site and asked that arrangements be made to transfer the remains of the plane's six crew members to American authorities. On Friday, September 12, an Associated Press report summarized the State Department press release:

> WASHINGTON (AP)—Russia notified the United States Friday an American Air Force C-130 transport plane had crashed in Soviet Armenia killing six of a 17-man crew.

The State Department said in an announcement Friday night that Soviet fighter planes intercepted it in the area of the Turkish-Soviet border near Kars, a point some 35 miles inside Turkey.

. . . The State Department did not accuse the Soviets of shooting down the plane even though it reported Soviet fighters intercepted it.

POINT NOT CLEAR

The department did not clear up the point whether Soviet fighters crossed over the Soviet frontier. A spokesman when asked about this said he did not know the answer.

The State Department press release on September 12 was the first public acknowledgment that Soviet fighter aircraft had intercepted the missing C-130. The *New York Times* interpreted the department's statement as implicitly charging that Soviet fighters shot the plane down. The U.S. Air Force also released the names and hometowns of the seventeen crew members on September 12. In Moscow, the Soviets offered no explanation for the crash, saying merely that the aircraft had "fallen" within Soviet territory. A *New York Times* article, "Soviet Explanation Lacking," elaborated on the Soviet note:

MOSCOW, Sept 12—There was no indication in the Soviet note today as to what had caused the crash of the United States plane. The Soviet government used its note to register a "decisive protest" against what it called this "new crude violation by a United States military plane of the state borders of the USSR"

The Soviet note recalled that the Soviet government had protested earlier against violations of its airspace by United States planes and called for strict measures to be taken to prevent any repetition.

That was the aftermath of an incident in which a United States transport was forced down near Soviet Armenia and its nine crewmen held for several weeks. The Soviet note said the new incident showed that the United States had not taken the necessary measures to prevent violations of Soviet airspace. It charged that "such a policy by the United States

could not be interpreted except as being aimed at sharpening relations be-
tween the United States and the USSR."

The earlier "incident" was of course the Soviet attack on the C-118 aircraft that had inadvertently violated the Turkish-Armenian border on June 27, 1958. The Soviets notified the U.S. Embassy in Moscow about that incident the following day. The American government denied that the C-118 border violation in June was intentional, and the Soviets re-leased its nine crewmen ten days after that shootdown.

The *New York Times* commented from Moscow on September 13 that diplomats were puzzled by the absence of comments by Soviet authorities about the eleven missing men:

> *In announcing the incident in the Soviet press this morning, Moscow gave the full text of its note, but only a summary of the U.S. request for a search. Thus, the Russian reader would know nothing about the eleven unaccounted for crew members.*

Diplomatic Exchanges—Round Two

The American chargé d'affaires promptly delivered a new "urgent" note to the Soviet foreign ministry on September 13:

> *The Soviet note states that the wreckage of a burned and destroyed American Air Force plane had been found . . . and that the bodies of six members of the crew had been discovered on the spot. The Ministry was informed in the embassy's note of Sept 6 that the crew of the plane totaled 17 persons, but no mention is made of the whereabouts or fate of the re-maining eleven airmen. Information on the whereabouts and condition is urgently requested. If these men have not been located, it is requested that every effort be made to find them. The United States government expects full cooperation from the Soviet government in granting access to the crewmen in the custody of the Soviet authorities and in returning them at the earliest possible moment.*
> *The Ministry's note does not identify the bodies found with the wrecked*

plane. The United States government requests that representatives of the embassy accompanied by such technical experts as may be required to investigate the circumstances of the crash be permitted to visit the scene of the crash of this plane and that facilities be extended to them for effecting identification of the victims of the crash and arranging for the transfer of their remains to appropriate United States authorities.

There is no foundation for the charges contained in the Soviet note that the C-130 aircraft intentionally violated the frontier of the Soviet Union, and the United States government rejects the Soviet government's protest in this regard . . .

The investigation conducted by the United States Air Force in Europe (USAFE) in connection with the disappearance of this plane has elicited information to the effect that it was intercepted by three Soviet fighter aircraft at about 2:00 p.m. September 2, 1958, in the region of the Turkish-Soviet border near Kars, and that following interception, the American plane proceeded eastward under control of the Soviet aircraft. Shortly after this, an explosion was heard and a large column of smoke was observed rising at a point within Soviet territory.

The United States government emphasizes that the missing C-130 aircraft was an unarmed transport aircraft clearly marked and operating on an instrument flight plan duly filed in advance in accordance with the regulations of the International Civil Aviation Organization. As the Government of the Union of Soviet Socialist Republics is aware, it is recognized international custom when intercepting an unarmed aircraft to indicate by signals that the intercepted aircraft shall follow the intercepting aircraft to the nearest appropriate airfield for investigation. As information available to this government indicates that the C-130 aircraft was intercepted by Soviet air force planes, the United States government expects that complete information as to the circumstances surrounding and following the interception will be made available to it without further delay.

Denying that the border violation was intentional, the note expressed surprise and lack of understanding—"in view of the involvement of Soviet aircraft"—that the Soviet government had earlier denied any knowledge of the incident and had delayed its response for six days. No word was mentioned about Soviet pilot communications being intercepted.

What the State Department note did not say is as important as the note's contents. In the event that an enemy fighter demonstrated the international signs to "follow me" while over either international or hostile airspace, aircraft commanders of U.S. recon aircraft had standing orders to turn away from unfriendly airspace and avoid surrendering their aircraft and crew. They were briefed to evade rather than to follow intercepting fighters to an enemy airfield—a procedure sure to provoke a confrontation if an intercepting fighter pilot was ordered to force the recon aircraft to land.

Stating (intentionally or not) that the interception occurred "near Kars" had a deleterious effect on further U.S.-Soviet discussions of the incident. Kars, Turkey, is located about thirty-five miles from the state border, and the Soviets no doubt interpreted the diplomatic note as accusing their fighter aircraft of intercepting the C-130 over Turkish airspace.

On September 15, Chargé d'Affaires Davis asked Acting Soviet Foreign Minister Vasili V. Kuznetsov in a phone call when a reply to his American note dated September 13 would be forthcoming and if he had any additional details on the missing men. Davis pointed out the anguish suffered by the missing crew members' relatives. Kuznetsov replied that he had no further information, that a reply would be expedited, and that such unpleasant affairs would be avoided if American planes would stop penetrating Soviet airspace. Two days later Soviet Deputy Foreign Minister Nikolai Firyubin repeated the same answers to the same two questions from Chargé d'Affaires Davis.

Maintaining silence for six days, the Soviet foreign ministry finally responded to the U.S. note on September 19—the Soviets had no additional information on the eleven missing airmen, and they were willing to transfer the six remains to American authorities. But they denied intercepting the C-130 "near the Turkish-Soviet border around Kars." As addressed in an internal message from Acting Foreign Minister Kuznetsov to the Communist Party Central Committee, the Soviet hierarchy felt maligned by the tone of the American diplomatic note:

On 12 September of this year, the MID [foreign ministry] of the USSR passed a demarche to the U.S. Embassy concerning the American plane that crashed 55 kilometers northwest of the city of Yerevan.

On 13 September, the U.S. Embassy sent a replying demarche in which an attempt is made to portray the incident as if Soviet fighters inter-cepted the American plane on the Turkish-Soviet border near Kars. A re-quest was also made for information concerning the 17 crew members, and asks permission for an embassy representative accompanied by tech-nical experts to investigate the circumstances of the accident at the crash site, identify the bodies, and make arrangements for the transfer of the re-mains of the crew members to the proper American authorities. That re-ply takes an obviously provocative tone.

The MID of the USSR, the ministry of defense, and the Committee for State Security [KGB] prepared a draft of the reply to the American note. Our reply strongly refutes the fabrications in the embassy's note. The American's request about landing at the crash site is being ignored in our reply. Bear in mind that the area where the plane went down is a re-stricted border zone where foreigners are not allowed. Therefore, the Americans are not to be given access to this area.

As concerns the embassy's request for the transfer of the remains of the crew to the American side, it would be reasonable to fulfill this request and task the Committee for State Security [KGB] to carry out the transfer of the bodies of the dead crew members.

The draft is attached for your perusal.

V. Kuznetsov

The central committee approved the response and directed that its text be printed in the Soviet press, with a short account of the American demarche from September 13. The text of the Soviet demarche dated September 19 follows:

In response to U.S. Embassy note # 270 dated 13 September 1958, the Ministry of Foreign Affairs of the USSR calls attention to its note dated 12 September about the U.S. Air Force plane that intentionally crossed the state border of the USSR and went down 55 kilometers north-west of Yerevan. The ministry's note reported that this aircraft crashed and burned, and the remains of bodies were found at the crash site. It was determined from the remains that six crew members perished. The Soviet side does not possess any other information about crew members.

An assertion made in the U.S. Embassy's note purports that Soviet fighters intercepted this aircraft near the Soviet-Turkish border around Kars. The Soviet government strongly rejects this assertion as groundless and provocative in nature. Such an unworthy attempt to lay the blame for the loss of the American aircraft and its crew on the Soviet side has apparently been made in order to justify the very obvious fact that this aircraft intentionally crossed the state border of the USSR.

The Soviet government has repeatedly stated that the U.S. government is fully responsible for the consequences of U.S. aircraft illegally crossing the Soviet state border. There is one thing that the U.S. government must do. It must once and for all prohibit its air force from illegally crossing the state border of the USSR. It is precisely these types of measures that the Soviet government expects from the U.S. government.

As far as the embassy's request to transfer the remains of the six crew members from the burned aircraft, appropriate Soviet authorities are ready to transfer them to a representative of the American government.

There are two key points in its response: (1) Soviet investigators recovered only six remains from the crash site and had no other information on other crew members, and (2) the Soviet government considered the assertion that Soviet fighters intercepted the American aircraft "around Kars" as provocative. As indicated in a news article on September 20, the *New York Times* (and other news media) interpreted the Soviet response as a flat-out denial of Soviet involvement in the downing of the C-130. Western media also for the most part ignored references to Kars, Turkey:

WASHINGTON, Sept. 19—The Soviet Union has denied shooting down a United States Air Force plane that crashed near the Soviet-Turkish frontier Sept. 2.

. . . The State Department had no comment on the new note and would not publish the text.

Though not announced by the U.S. government, the facts were that although it was an unarmed transport, a C-130 had crossed the Soviet border illegally and refused to land—the second such border violation by a U.S. military aircraft in two months. The intercepted voice communications of the Soviet MiG pilots during the C-130 shootdown neither negated nor confirmed the use of warning shots or other international "follow me" signals, but the attacking pilots told their controller that the intruding aircraft was attempting to escape toward the border, and their attack did in fact keep the C-130 from leaving Armenian airspace. The Soviet air defense system had reacted legally in the sense that a sovereign government has a right to defend its airspace, so why all the secrecy and denials by the Soviets?

One logical explanation is that the Soviet government clearly had the upper hand and wanted to teach the American government a lesson. The Soviet attitude was, "Either you keep your aircraft out of our airspace or we'll shoot 'em down." As with the shootdown of the RB-47 near Kamchatka in 1955, the Soviet leadership probably decided to withhold relevant details about the incident because they believed it was not to their advantage to cooperate; there were no survivors in the C-130 crash, and they controlled access to the crash site. A good bet is that the Soviet government wanted to keep the Americans guessing, and the U.S. government had no recourse.

Responding to the urgent U.S. diplomatic note, dated September 13, was the Soviet government denying involvement in downing the aircraft or denying that the interception took place "near Kars" (over Turkish airspace)? Probably the latter at that point; in other border violation incidents the Soviets had readily admitted attacking intruders after they violated its airspace. Semantically, the Soviet foreign ministry answered half the assertion correctly; Soviet fighters intercepted the C-130 at the Armenian border, not thirty-five miles westward near Kars. Later, the Soviet government dug in its heels and lied consistently, unable to reconcile the earlier denial and admit the shootdown without losing face in the world of public opinion.

Because of misinterpretation relative to "near Kars," the Kremlin leaders believed that the United States was attempting to place blame for the incident on the Soviets. Whereas the international community viewed the downing of an unarmed transport aircraft as unconscionable and barbaric, if not illegal, under Soviet law—ministry of defense order number 0049 dated July 4, 1958—downing the C-130 over Soviet territory was not only legal, it was official policy. Coming on the heels of the downing of the C-118 and subsequent release of its crew in June 1958, order number 0049 emphasized the duty and obligation of Soviet antiaircraft air defense crews to act decisively against border violators.

Soviet-American relations were approaching a Cold War low, and each side perceived the other as lying. There had been three air incidents along the Soviet Union's southern borders in just months—the C-118 forced down in June, a U.S. recon mission chased from the Caspian Sea area in August, and the C-130 shootdown over Armenia in September. The Soviets claimed the C-130 had intentionally violated its border on September 2, and the Americans had undeniable evidence that Soviet fighters shot down the C-130. The Soviets said they'd recovered only six bodies from the crash site and knew nothing about eleven other crew members, points that seemed inconceivable to Americans.

On September 21 the *Stars and Stripes* military newspaper raised questions that bothered most Americans regarding the latest Soviet response:

> *The Soviet note left many questions still unanswered. One of the most puzzling and worrisome to Americans in Moscow is why the Soviet government waited 10 days after the crash, and six days after the U.S. lodged an official request for information on it, to make its first report on the incident. An even more puzzling question is how 11 other American crew members could have disappeared into thin air.*

Chargé d'Affaires Davis again verbally pressed the Soviet foreign ministry for information about the eleven missing men, but was told that the Soviet government had no information on them. Davis also reiterated the American request that American officials be permitted to examine the wreckage at the crash site, but that request was again denied. The acting Soviet foreign minister told Davis that he had nothing to add to what was in the note.

Diplomatic Exchanges—Round Three

Davis delivered the third formal note to the Soviet foreign ministry on September 21, again requesting information on the missing eleven crewmen, and seeking to facilitate without delay the transfer of the remains, identification tags, and other materials that would aid in the identification of the six airmen who were known to have perished. The *New York Times* reported on the U.S. State Department's note:

> MOSCOW, Sept. 22—*The United States appealed to the Soviet government on humanitarian grounds today for some information about eleven fliers missing since their transport crashed near the Soviet-Turkish frontier nineteen days ago.*
>
> . . . *The United States message was reported to have appealed to the Soviet authorities on behalf of the families of the seventeen fliers involved. It explained that for nearly three weeks, they had been without a clue to the whereabouts of the fliers and even without information as to which six men had perished.*

No additional information was forthcoming on the eleven missing men, but the Soviets agreed to hand over the six remains and related personal effects recovered from the C-130 wreckage. Finally, the two adversaries worked out a plan for transferring the remains to American authorities.

Picking Up the Pieces—Moving On

The Soviet announcement, ten days after the C-130 and its crew were declared missing, that the aircraft had crashed in Armenia and six corpses had been recovered had a sobering effect on the 7406th and Detachment 1, 6911th. Commanders, senior NCOs, apprentice aircraft mechanics, newly arrived linguists/airborne intercept operators—everyone in the two units—were in shock. The death of six comrades added finality to the calamity, yet the mission had to go on, and there were family members to take care of.

Seven of the missing men had their families with them in Germany; these families had moved in with fellow officers and NCOs in the units.

They were well taken care of, but announcement of corpses and missing men—no known survivors—changed the family atmosphere. Each wife had to consider a life without her husband. All the wives wanted to believe their husbands were alive and among the missing, but they feared that the worst had happened. Some felt a family obligation to remain in Germany, waiting for a husband's return; others wanted to return to America, where they could be comforted by family members while awaiting further word from the Air Force. By the end of September each of the families had accepted Air Force offers to relocate it to its home of record in the United States.

Transferring the families to the States had its pros and cons. For the wives, their families consoled them as best they could, but they also missed the camaraderie and closeness of local Air Force contact; the wives had to deal with government bureaucrats, rather than the friendly fellow officers and airmen they had known in Germany. For the officers and NCOs in the 7406th and 6911th, sending the families "home" was an operational necessity. Everyone wanted only the best care and consideration for the families, but the outlook was not good. Feedback from the Russians that six bodies had been recovered, coupled with knowledge that MiGs had shot down the aircraft, suggested that resolution of the case of the eleven missing airmen would be a difficult and prolonged process. The likelihood that the eleven missing men would be returned alive in the near future was extremely low. Considering the circumstances, and the fact that the units had to resume operational recon missions, it was best for the families and the Air Force to move the families back to America.

But for the enlisted men of Detachment 1, who were not informed of the families' departure until after they were gone, not even given the chance to say good-bye, the move was yet another proof that the men were being betrayed, that they were being treated simply as pawns. For nearly four decades, several of the wives felt that their husbands' friends had simply abandoned them. It was a wound that would never heal.

Taking Care of the Families

"The Air Force takes care of its own" is a slogan that men in airborne reconnaissance take to heart. It was more than a slogan to S.Sgt. George

Pittelkau, flight engineer in the 7406th in 1958. Pittelkau had trained and flown with the men lost aboard 528, and but for fate, could have been aboard when disaster struck. He had partnered with Lieutenant Villarreal in combat survival training in April 1958, had ferried 60528 from the recon depot in Texas to Germany with Lieutenant Simpson in July, and had deployed to Incirlik on August 25 with Captain Duncan on the first C-130 deployment to Turkey. Duncan, a flight examiner, flew missions with Pittelkau's crew along the Turkish-Armenian border on August 26 and 28, and they aborted a mission on September 1.

Duncan remained behind in Turkey to conduct a crew performance evaluation on the new crew arriving from Germany on September 1— Captain Swiestra, Captain Simpson, Lieutenant Villarreal, Captain Jeruss, and Staff Sergeant Price. Sergeant Pittelkau returned to Germany with his crew on September 2, while Swiestra's crew departed Incirlik aboard 60528 on a "makeup" flight—to complete the mission that Pittelkau's crew had aborted the previous day. On September 3, Pittelkau returned to Turkey as a member of a C-130 search crew. His crew flew search missions over eastern Turkey on September 4 and 5 before flying back to Germany on September 6. During the next three weeks, Pittelkau helped Marion Price (Sergeant Price's wife) and other wives with Air Force paperwork, and with shipping cars and household goods back to America.

Scheduled to travel to Greenville, Texas, to ferry another C-130 aircraft to Rhein-Main, Pittelkau arranged to accompany Mrs. Price and her two sons, Michael and Richard, home. On September 27 he escorted Mrs. Price and her sons to Dallas, Texas. He also paid his respects to Capt. John Simpson's extended family, who also lived in Dallas. Simpson's wife had recently arrived from Germany.

In mid-October, while en route back to Germany aboard a new C-130, Pittelkau spent a night at Lajes Field, Azores. While there, an Air Force C-121 transporting the six sets of remains from Germany to Washington, D.C., was parked on the ramp next to Pittelkau's C-130 and he said a silent prayer for them.

Remains of Six Crew Members Returned

As an Air Force pilot assigned to the U.S. air attaché's office, American embassy, Ankara, Turkey, in 1958, Major Joseph Faulkner provided air logistics support for the collocated American Embassy and JUS-MAAG (Joint U.S. Military Advisory Assistance Group) in Turkey. The remoteness of Turkish sites that he flew into called for a bush pilot's skills—landing in pistachio and olive groves—anywhere with wing clearance to set down a small military transport. So Faulkner was not fazed at all when the call came to transport the remains of the C-130 crewmen from the Turkish-Armenian border to Incirlik AB, Adana, Turkey.

When the air attaché was notified that release of the remains was imminent, the American embassy in Moscow sought Soviet permission to land a small transport—a C-47—in Soviet Armenia, but the request was refused. A request to drive a truck across the border to pick up the bodies was likewise denied; the Soviets would deliver the remains to the Turkish-Armenian border near Leninakan, Armenia.

On September 24, Faulkner piloted a C-47 that landed in an open field at Kars, the closest major Turkish city to the Soviet Akhurik border post on the Turkish-Armenian border adjacent to Leninakan, Armenia. At the border post, Soviet authorities repatriated the remains to the U.S. air attaché to Turkey, Col. John S. Chalfant. As Chalfant explained in a memo for record, the transfer of the remains did not begin well:

> *Together with the American delegation, we went to the eastern border gate of Tiknis on the date and hour that had been arranged by the American and Russian governments ahead of time (on 24 September at 12:00 by Ankara time) in order to receive the crew of the United States government aircraft that had been shot down on 2 September 1958. The Russian military specialist at the gate said that he knew nothing about it and that he would ask his commanding officer.*
>
> *After waiting for two hours we were informed that the delivery could be made only at 4:00 p.m. At the appointed time Governor Hilmi Degcioglu, the Border Commissioner of the Kars zone, and Koulik, the Border Commissioner of the Leninakan Zone of the USSR, had the gates opened, and the remains of the American personnel, which were in six*

caskets together with documents that were on the plane, were delivered and received . . .

. . . The remains were brought to Kars for a special ceremony with the participation of the honor guard.

The transfer of the remains was covered in a *New York Times* article, BODIES OF 6 FLIERS RELEASED BY SOVIETS:

ISTANBUL, Turkey, Sept. 24 (UPI)—The bodies of six United States airmen whose unarmed transport crashed in Soviet Armenia Sept. 2 were turned over to the United States at a Soviet border town today.

There still was no word on the fate of eleven other crewmen aboard the plane. The United States State Department has charged Soviet interceptors forced the plane over Soviet Armenia where it crashed.

Col. John S. Chalfant, United States Air Attaché, and Governor Hilmi Degcioglu of the Turkish province of Kars accepted the bodies at Leninakan on the Turkish border with Soviet Armenia, and took them to Kars, about 35 miles inside Turkey.

The Soviet officials said they had not seen the eleven other crewmen in the plane. The officials said they had no information and knew only about the six bodies they returned today.

Col. Chalfant stayed in the Russian town for about an hour before leaving for Kars with the bodies, each in an individual coffin. At Kars, the United States Air Force had a transport waiting to fly the bodies to Adana, Turkey.

The news statement—"charged Soviet interceptors forced the plane over Soviet Armenia"—was a common misconception in the West, an accusation that severely agitated the Soviet government. A more correct portrayal is that the C-130 inadvertently flew into Armenian airspace where Soviet MiGs intercepted it and prevented it from escaping back to the safety of Turkish airspace. The KGB statement of transfer describes the remains and other materials that were delivered to the air attaché:

. . . surrender in six coffins, the remains of the bodies of the crew members of an aircraft of the Air Force of the United States of America,

discovered under and extracted from beneath the wreckage of the aircraft
that crashed and burned 55 kilometers northwest of the city of Yerevan,
Armenian Soviet Socialist Republic on 2 September 1958 . . .

The list of documents, weapon, and foreign currency returned by the KGB is found in appendix A. In addition to the six sets of human remains, Soviet investigators recovered and returned the partially burned contents of two wallets, an identification tag, American and foreign currency, a set of 7406th Support Squadron special orders for the flight crew's temporary duty travel to Turkey, a partially burned notebook, a partially burned navigation aid, and a burned .38 caliber American pistol. The detritus of disaster; nothing of much value to either air force. Significantly, what were not returned or mentioned were the reconnaissance receivers or associated APR-14 receiver operator's manual that investigators recovered from the crash site.

The 7406th TDY orders (appendix B) recovered by Soviet investigators—special order No. 194 dated August 28, 1958—lists the five primary flight crew members (Swiestra, Simpson, Villarreal, Jeruss, and Price). The sixth flight crew member aboard the C-130 downed on September 2, 1958, Captain Paul Duncan, third pilot and "flight route checker" (flight examiner), had deployed to Turkey on August 25 with a different crew.[134]

Although the U.S. air attaché's party was not permitted to visit the crash site, Major Faulkner commented recently that the crash site was clearly visible to pilots flying at altitude along the Turkish side of the Turkish-Armenian border: "The crash site appeared as a seared black spot on the Armenian horizon where the C-130 had pancaked in." The air attaché signed for the six bodies in unopened wooden coffins. Arriving back in Kars late on September 24, the six bodies were stored in a morgue overnight. Major Faulkner flew the bodies to Incirlik the following morning, and an Air Force C-130 transported them to Rhein-Main AB, Germany.

Identification of Remains at Army Mortuary in Germany

Upon arrival in Germany on September 25, the six flag-draped coffins were transferred to the U.S. Army Quartermaster Mortuary in

Frankfurt. A mortuary identification laboratory report dated October 9, 1958, describes the remains and personal effects received from the Soviets:

> At 21:00 hours 25 September 1958, six (6) wooden caskets were received at the Identification Laboratory of this headquarters along with an envelope containing personal effects for two (2) airmen and the identification tag for a third (3rd). Subject caskets contained the remains of six (6) crewmen recovered from the C-130 crash site in Armenia near the Turkish border as reported by the Soviet authorities.
>
> Items received were as follows:
>
> Captain Rudy J. Swiestra—Wallet contents, including various identification and membership cards, and family photos.
>
> First Lt. Ricardo M. Villarreal—Wallet contents, including various identification and membership cards, immunization record and family photos.
>
> Captain Paul E. Duncan—Burned identification tag only.
>
> A preliminary examination of the remains revealed that no attempt had been made at preservation. The remains were shattered, burned and incomplete in varying degrees. The heads were completely missing on two (2), portions of skull base only were found on three (3), and several shattered skull portions were on one (1). Charred fragments of USAF flying suits were found on all bodies. A portion of upper jaw containing identifiable teeth was found intact with one (1) remains, and one (1) identifiable tooth was found intact with a second remains.

Using identification techniques available in 1958—primarily individual medical and dental records and physical characteristics assessments—the mortuary identification lab in Frankfurt identified the two remains with teeth as "forward crew members, namely: Capt. Edward Jeruss and Lt. Ricardo Villarreal," the two navigators on the mission. The next two paragraphs in the ID lab report probably weighed heavily in the lab's identification process:

> At this stage of processing, it was becoming increasingly apparent that the six (6) returned bodies were probably those of the crew members stationed in the forward portion of the plane and not those of crewmen occupying the rear compartments. This theory was strengthened when it was further determined that three (3) more of the bodies were found to have physical characteristics in excellent agreement with forward crewmen but were negative in two or more respects when compared with the characteristics of the rear compartment crew members. Those associations are as follows:

> Captain Rudy J. Swiestra, pilot

> Captain Paul E. Duncan, [pilot and] flight route checker

> Staff Sgt. Laroy Price, engineer

> The sixth (6th) and final remains consisted of such a limited portion of the upper torso that it was impossible to determine factors of age, height, weight or hair details. This sixth (6th) remains, however, did exhibit a large "hairy mole" near the middle of the back between the shoulders, which has been recognized and described by two fellow officers of subject plane crew's unit as a "hairy mole noticed on the back of the remaining forward crew member, namely First Lt. John E. Simpson, copilot."

Using a compiled physical characteristics chart listing age, height, weight, and hair color, the ID lab experts did a comparative analysis of all crew members vs. the five sets of remains for which those traits could be hypothesized. According to the lab report, fillings in teeth and physical characteristics supported the identification of Jeruss and Villarreal for remains X-1 and X-2, and a longer left clavicle vs. right and the sternal articulation showing a larger and smoother contour—more usage of the left shoulder (and arm) than the right—agreed with records indicating that

Captain Swiestra was the only "left-handed" crew member aboard; providing tentative identification of remains X-3.

There were possible associations between Lieutenant Simpson and remains X-4, but longer and darker hair with X-4 could not be associated with Simpson, who had blond hair and a crew cut. Additionally, the right ear for remains X-4 did not flare out; it fit closely against the head. "Pictures examined for all crew members indicated this feature was best associated with Capt. Duncan." Thus, the lab identified remains X-4 as Captain Duncan.

The lab was more tenuous about the identification of remains X-5. In discussing the identification of X-5, the lab report offered possibly contradictory evidence, but in the end identified the remains as Lieutenant Simpson.:

> . . . This remains suffered greater burning and charring than the other recovered crew members. The anterior area of the torso is burned completely away, exposing the back portions of the ribs and the anterior surface of the upper spinal column. For some time during the processing, it was felt that this more severely burned remains could best be associated with Capt. Duncan. This was not on the basis of any physical characteristics, but on the theory that Capt. Duncan, in his position as Flight Route Checker, was the only forward crew member who was more or less roving in the plane and was not protected by strong seats or instrument panels. Supporting this theory was the burned identification tag received for Capt. Duncan . . . Subject theory was abandoned when the "hairy mole" found near the upper middle back of this remains was favorably associated with Lt. Simpson . . . The excellent association of remains X-4 with Capt. Duncan also indicated that this remains (X-5) cannot be associated with Capt. Duncan.

The identification of remains X-6 was likewise tenuous. The estimated height (sixty-seven inches) was based on the left femur only, while the available clavicle indicated an age of twenty-four to twenty-eight, and "the pubic syphysis gives an excellent age range of 27 to 30." The axillary hair was light brown and the pubic hair was dark reddish brown. An autopsy had been performed in Armenia by making a medial cut through the neck area. After comparing all the crew members' features, the army lab identified remains X-6 as S.Sgt. Laroy Price. The lab report's summary provided rationale for the identifications:

Summary: *There appears to be no doubt concerning the identification of crew members Jeruss and Villarreal where identifiable teeth were found intact with the remains and several other favorable factors of identification are present and no negative factors to be considered.*

In the cases of remains associated with crew members Swiestra, Duncan and Price, all physical characteristics are in excellent agreement while attempts to associate these remains with other crew members resulted in several negative factors being encountered.

In the case of X-5 exhibiting very limited clues, but being associated with crew member Simpson, we have a situation wherein identification would not normally be acceptable. The identifiable factor being a "hairy mole," which is not indicated in the medical records of any crew member and has been recognized by associate officers who "believe" this marking coincides with one they have noticed on Lt. Simpson. This cannot preclude the possibility of a situation where such a "hairy mole" may also be present on another crew member and didn't happen to be noticed by fellow associates.

The finding of personal effects for three (3) out of the six (6) forward crew members and no personal effects for any of the eleven (11) rear compartment crew members gives a good indication that the six (6) returned bodies do represent the forward crew. The identifications and excellent associations of five (5) of the six (6) bodies strengthens this conclusion to a great degree. The absolute lack of evidence concerning the nine (9) younger (ages 19-25) rear crewmen further adds to the preponderance of evidence at hand that indicates that none of the eleven (11) rear crewmen are amongst the six (6) remains returned from this air crash by the Soviet authorities in Armenia.

The army mortuary in Frankfurt classified its "Identification Laboratory Report" CONFIDENTIAL—denying family members of the seventeen crew members the basis upon which identification of the six remains was made.

On October 17, 1958, the Air Force transported the six remains to Bolling AFB, Washington, D.C., where pathologists from the Armed Forces Institute of Pathology, Walter Reed Army Medical Center, conducted an examination. This examination resulted in the transfer of the remains to the Aerial Port Mortuary, Dover AFB, Delaware, where identification reprocessing was accomplished between October 23 and 31, 1958.

Identification of Remains at Dover AFB, Delaware

On October 16, Robert W. Ralston, an Air Force identification specialist based in Dayton, Ohio, received a request from Headquarters, USAF, for identification assistance in connection with the corpses. In a trip report dated November 13, 1958, he described the purpose of his related temporary duty trip to Bolling AFB and Dover AFB:

> Identification assistance was requested for reprocessing this group by Headquarters USAF since two remains were identified, four were designated "believed to be" with names assigned, and eleven individuals, known to have been aboard the aircraft, were unaccounted for by the Russian authorities.

Ralston's trip report stated that Headquarters USAF had requested assistance after reviewing the initial identification report from overseas. The trip report describes his task in a section titled "Circumstances":

> . . . A detailed study of the overseas processing report by the AMC [Air Material Command] identification specialist [Ralston] supported these conclusions that the identification of two remains were not firmly established and only circumstantial evidence appeared to be the supporting evidence for identification of the other four remains. Initial examination conducted by the AMC identification specialist disclosed that the condition of all remains made it mandatory to suggest that these remains be completely reprocessed. This contention was further supported by collecting tissue specimens for blood typing tests. Results of these blood typing tests proved there was commingling of remains.

This fact was made known to the Mortuary Branch, Headquarters, USAF, who took action to transfer the remains to the Aerial Port Mortuary, Dover Air Force Base, Delaware, for complete reprocessing since ample space was not available for this type of processing at the Armed Forces Institute of Pathology. The remains were transported to Dover AFB, arriving there on 22 October 1958. Reprocessing activities were started on 23 October 1958.

Ralston described the problem, actions taken, and conclusions in succeeding sections of his report:

PROBLEM

Seventeen individuals were aboard the aircraft on take-off; six crew members and eleven highly skilled passengers. Personal effects for two airmen and one identification tag for a third individual apparently led overseas identification personnel to believe through circumstantial evidence that the remains returned to U.S. control were the remains of the crew members. However, review of the overseas identification processing report does not completely substantiate this fact. Therefore, the problem in this case was to attempt to establish firm identification for the remains based upon the most reliable scientific means.

Certain questions posed by Headquarters USAF were of great significance and answers to these questions were wanted as quickly as possible by the White House and Department of State. These questions were: first, were there more than six individuals contained in the group; second, if there were only six individuals contained in this group, were they the remains of the crew members; third, could these remains be of both crew members and passengers or just the passenger complement.

ACTIONS TAKEN

Post-mortem examinations of the remains were conducted to evaluate and record all identification media. To accomplish this phase of the processing activities, dental comparisons were made, when possible, stature and body build estimations were estimated, hair characteristics were determined, ages were estimated from skeletal remains, each remains was x-rayed and tissue specimens were tested to determine blood types. In addition to these identification media, fingerprint comparisons were used and the remains were examined closely for healed scars or other anti-mortem marks. Photographs of the individual remains and the important skeletal and dental anatomy were photographed for each case. Photographs were taken of the charts showing the overseas and zone of interior processing activities that simplified recording of known physical and dental characteristics and identification media found with the remains.

CONCLUSIONS

Upon completion of the identification reprocessing at Dover AFB, it was concluded that four of the six remains could be firmly identified and two remains could not be identified. (See attached Identification Statement).

It was also established that this group contained only the remains of six individuals since there was no evidence of duplication of anatomical structures. (See attached Identification Statement).

The identification specialists at Dover AFB changed the identifications for four remains, accepting the overseas mortuary's identification for Lieutenants Villarreal and Simpson. The following changes in identification and unknown designations were made during reprocessing examinations at Dover AFB:

Remains	Overseas	Remains	Dover AFB
X-1	Capt. Jeruss	X-1	Capt. Swiestra
X-2	1st Lt. Villarreal	X-2	1st Lt. Villarreal
X-3	Capt. Swiestra	X-3	Unknown
X-4	Capt. Duncan	X-4	Capt. Jeruss
X-5	1st Lt. Simpson	X-5	1st Lt. Simpson
X-6	S.Sgt. Price	X-6	Unknown

The referenced "attached Identification Statement" describes the employed identification methods and techniques and provides a detailed explanation regarding the new identities of the six remains. Reidentifying remains X-1 as Captain Swiestra was based on dental records comparison for the seventeen crew members—correcting the overseas comparison, stature and body build comparisons, hair color, aging criteria, blood type, and FBI fingerprint identification. Multiple feature comparisons supported the identification of remains X-2 as Lieutenant Villarreal, and comparison of a postmortem dental chart with dental records for all seventeen crew members resulted in identical agreement with Villarreal's dental records. Identification of remains X-3 was listed as unknown "since the stature and body build too closely parallel the medical records of Capt. Paul Duncan and M.Sgt. George Petrochilos. Blood type A of X-3 is identical with the recorded blood types of Capt. Duncan and Sgt. Petrochilos."

The reidentification of remains X-4 as Captain Jeruss was based on stature and body build, an abundance of dark brown hair over the chest, shoulders, back, and lower arms, as confirmed by Mrs. Jeruss, estimated age (thirty to thirty-five), and blood type B in agreement with the blood type on Captain Jeruss's medical records. Although the identity of remains X-5 was not changed, the basis for continuing to identify the remains as belonging to Lieutenant Simpson changed. Body stature and build for X-5 were not in agreement with Lieutenant Simpson's medical records, but blond body hair was found that agreed with hair color for both Captain Swiestra and Lieutenant Simpson. No "hairy mole" was evident, possibly because it had been removed during the examination in Germany. X-5's age was estimated at twenty-five to twenty-nine; Simpson was twenty-seven. X rays of the first and second cervical vertebrae showed several slight sclerotic areas that could cause discomfort on extension or rotation of the head, and Lieutenant Simpson's medical records contained reports of complaints of repeated stiffness and soreness in the neck region. X-5's blood type (O) agreed with the type entered on Simpson's medical records. Comparing the X rays of the cervical vertebrae and blood type results of remains X-5 with Simpson's medical records, the identification specialists decided that remains X-5 belonged to Lieutenant Simpson.

In comparing identifying characteristics of remains X-6—estimated height 67 ³/₈ inches, slight body build, estimated age of twenty-seven to thirty, light brown hair, and blood type A based on an absorption test— to the heights, weights, and body builds, blood type and hair color of S.Sgt. Laroy Price and T.Sgt. Arthur L. Mello, the matches were so close as to preclude any reliable basis of identification for X-6. Based on the identification results as recorded in Ralston's trip report, it was recommended "that X-3 and X-6 not be identified at the present time."

During the two months since the seventeen airmen disappeared, the United States had shared essentially no meaningful information with the aircrew's families. The sad truth was that the U.S. government had no data that would shed any light on the men. It had told the families in September that six bodies had been recovered and were being identified. Now, in early November, the Air Force had some definitive information for the families—actually, for four of the seventeen families. For the other thirteen families, the two unidentified corpses offered little consolation. Now there were two possible fates to worry about—adding to the pain, suffering, and confusion. As time passed their despair grew, and having received no substantial information, family members grew suspicious that their own government was withholding information from them. They were right.

Giving Diplomacy a Chance to Work—Round Four

Throughout September 1958 the State Department tried most tactics at its disposal in dealing with the Soviet foreign ministry, working from various perspectives in an attempt to acquire information on the eleven missing men and to get the Soviets to acknowledge involvement in the downing of the C-130. On October 3, U. S. ambassador Llewelyn E. Thompson Jr. continued the diplomacy with a note to Acting Foreign Minister Kuznetsov requesting further information on the interception of the C-130 by Soviet fighters.

> . . . Investigations undertaken by the Headquarters United States Air Forces in Europe (USAFE) and by the appropriate Turkish authorities establish that the C-130 aircraft was intercepted at about 2:00 P.M. on

September 2 by Soviet fighter aircraft in the area of the Turkish-Soviet frontier west of the Aragat Mountain (Gora Aragats). The investigations also disclose that this C-130 aircraft was last seen flying on an easterly course in the direction of the mountain and that the Soviet aircraft were then in close proximity to it. A few minutes after the aircraft disappeared, an explosion occurred and a large column of smoke was seen rising from behind hills in Soviet territory in the direction of Aragat Mountain. In view of the proximity of the Soviet fighter planes to the C-130 aircraft, it must be assumed that the pilots of the Soviet aircraft involved in this interception had knowledge of the circumstances surrounding the crash of this unarmed American aircraft.

The Government of the United States, therefore, is still unable to understand the assertions by the Soviet government that it has no knowledge of the circumstances surrounding the crash of the American aircraft. Nor does the United States government understand why the Soviet government appears unable to furnish any information regarding the whereabouts and condition of eleven members of the crew of this aircraft who are unaccounted for and still missing. The United States is prepared to extend whatever assistance the Soviet government might consider helpful in the search for these missing airmen.

As stated in the embassy's note of September 13, the United States government categorically rejects the ministry's charge that this American aircraft intentionally violated Soviet airspace . . . The commanding officer of the aircraft was under strict, standing orders not to violate Soviet airspace, and the Government of the United States is convinced that he did not knowingly commit such a violation.

Under these circumstances, the Government of the United States repeats its request that complete information be furnished regarding the whereabouts and condition of the eleven members of the crew of the aircraft who are still missing . . . The United States government reserves the right to full compensation for the loss of life incurred and for the loss of this aircraft and its equipment.

Three days later, in the course of a conversation with Soviet Ambassador Menshikov on another matter, Deputy Under Secretary of State Robert D. Murphy requested information on the missing eleven men and access by U.S. authorities to the crash site. The ambassador stated that the Soviet government had no further information on the matter and that "since the crash site is probably in a restricted frontier area, the United States was asking to visit a closed area in the Soviet Union." Murphy asked Menshikov to inform the Soviet government of his comments, adding that the United States "has evidence that the C-130 was shot down."

The Soviets remained silent on the C-130 incident until October 16, when Acting Foreign Minister Kuznetsov handed Ambassador Thompson a response in Moscow. The *New York Times* addressed the Soviet response on October 18:

> MOSCOW, Oct. 17—A new Soviet note has destroyed the hopes of Americans here for the lives of eleven United States fliers missing for more than six weeks.
>
> In response to a third United States plea for possible clues to the whereabouts of the Americans, the Soviet foreign ministry said again that it had no further information.
>
> Moscow also indicated that it regarded continued correspondence on the subject as distasteful. The sharp tone of the note and recent Soviet complaints of border violations by United States military planes have led observers here to the conclusion that Moscow intends to do everything possible to discourage fliers from approaching Soviet borders. In view of the Soviet government's persistent position that it knows nothing about the eleven men, few here were left with any hope this evening that the fliers might be recovered . . .
>
> In the note delivered yesterday, Moscow said even more strongly that it felt no responsibility for the fate of the plane or of its crew.
>
> Replying to a United States appeal that information about the missing fliers be supplied for humanitarian reasons, the government said:
>
> "The Soviet people understand the sufferings of the American citizens who have lost relatives and close friends. But, it is not the USSR that should be asked to reply to those people. We recommend asking those who gave the order to the United States plane to violate the border of the USSR to invade its airspace. They and only they are responsible for the plane's catastrophe as well as the fate of the crew members. And namely,

they should be responsible to the relatives of those who were killed and to all the American people. Who gave them the right to play so flippantly with the lives and destinies of the people in their command?

"*If the Government of the United States will take strict measures not to permit any violation of Soviet borders by American planes in the future, it will thus eliminate one of the constant sources of irritation of relations between the USSR and the United States, and will simultaneously spare the Soviet government the necessity of conducting correspondence on such matters.*"

Any chance of obtaining Soviet cooperation to solve the mystery of the missing eleven airmen or of getting a Soviet explanation of what happened the day that Soviet MiGs shot down the C-130 evaporated with the Soviet response of October 16.

Soviets Protest Border Violations in Far East

On the same date, Moscow lodged a "strong protest" against what it said were deliberate violations of Soviet airspace in the Far East in July, August, and September. The protest note specifically charged that a U.S. military aircraft overflew the Soviet Ratmanov (Big Diomede) Island west of Alaska and the Chukotka Peninsula, which protrudes toward Alaska in the Bering Sea area, on September 30. The note said that it was Moscow's fourth complaint since June that United States aircraft had violated Soviet borders, and added that the Soviet government "cannot overlook that the new violation [on September 30] had occurred while the United States was strongly denying Soviet charges of deliberate intrusions over the southern Soviet border earlier this year." In closing, the note reiterated the Soviet position on frontier violations:

The Soviet government has declared more than once and is hereby stating again that the responsibility for violations of the Soviet airspace by American aircraft and for the consequences of such violations will lie entirely with the Government of the United States.

On November 13 the United States rejected the Soviet complaint, denying that one of its aircraft violated Soviet airspace over the Bering

Strait on September 30. The U.S. note said the only United States aircraft in the area on September 30 was a Navy patrol plane operating in international airspace, never flying over Ratmanov Island or any other Soviet territory.

In a related matter, the United States protested to the Soviet Union in early November that Soviet planes attacked one RB-47 flying over the Baltic Sea and made provocative "simulated" attacks on another RB-47 over the Sea of Japan. The U.S. protest note said both incidents occurred within hours of each other on November 7, and that both American aircraft were flying in international airspace more than sixty miles from Soviet territory at the time. In neither case was the American plane damaged, but in the second incident, the Soviet fighter maneuvered across the bow of the American recon aircraft at an uncomfortably close distance of a hundred feet. The Soviet government appeared determined to drive American reconnaissance aircraft out of international airspace along its borders, and the United States was just as emphatic in claiming its right to fly unimpeded over international territories.

Calling Soviet Bluff

In an effort to bring the issue of the eleven missing airmen back to the diplomatic table, the Eisenhower administration decided to unveil a recording of Soviet MiG pilots' conversations as they attacked the C-130. Release of the highly classified recordings required presidential approval, but the country wanted information on the fate of the missing eleven airmen. The government first tried quiet diplomacy; Deputy Under Secretary of State Murphy summoned Ambassador Menshikov to his office on November 13, asking him to bring along Soviet Air Attaché Major Gen. Mikhail N. Kostiouk. Menshikov arrived with General Kostiouk in tow. Murphy wasted little time getting to the business at hand. The meeting is described in a State Department press release:

> Mr. Murphy recalled Ambassador Menshikov's past statements regarding his desire to promote improved U.S.-USSR relations and better understanding between the two countries. He then referred to the loss of

the U.S. Air Force C-130 in Armenia as a cause of grave misunderstanding. He expressed the hope that the ambassador would cooperate in removing this misunderstanding.

Mr. Murphy told the ambassador that it was difficult for the United States government to understand why the Soviet government had supplied no information regarding the crash until ten days after the incident had occurred and then had furnished only a fragmentary report. Mr. Murphy reviewed the facts in this case and informed the ambassador that it appeared to the United States government that the American pilot, as a result of the signals transmitted by radio beacons in Soviet Georgia and Armenia, had probably made a navigational error, which resulted in his unintentionally crossing the Soviet border. The plane, having thus flown into Soviet territory, had been shot down by Soviet fighter aircraft without regard to the rules of civilized international practice, as though it were an enemy aircraft. The tail assembly had been shot off and the plane had fallen out of control.

There had been seventeen men in the plane, but the remains of only six men had been returned to the American authorities. Accordingly, the United States government was making this demarche to the Soviet government through Ambassador Menshikov for information in the possession of the Soviet government regarding the men who were still missing. Mr. Murphy said that he could not emphasize enough the gravity with which the United States government viewed this case. The United States government wants the facts. It wanted to know what happened to the men.

TAPE RECORDING OFFERED

Since the ambassador questioned Mr. Murphy's statement that the United States plane had been shot down by Soviet fighter aircraft, Mr. Murphy offered to have played for the ambassador a recording of the radio communications between the Soviet pilots who had shot down the C-130. The ambassador declined to listen to this recording, saying that he was not competent to assess it from a technical point of view. Mr. Murphy explained that it was for that reason that the Soviet Air Attaché,

General Kostiouk, an aviation expert, had been invited to accompany the ambassador on his call.

Mr. Murphy explained that the ambassador had been summoned in order that facts known to the United States government might be communicated to him as Soviet ambassador to the United States for conveyance to his government. Mr. Murphy said that it was Ambassador Menshikov's responsibility, as Soviet ambassador to the United States, to listen to the representations that were being made to him. The Soviet ambassador nonetheless refused to listen to the tape recording. Mr. Murphy then gave the ambassador a transcript in Russian of the recording.

Ambassador Menshikov stated that the Soviet government had replied to the notes addressed to it by the United States government on this matter and suggested that these replies represented all the information available to the Soviet government.

Mr. Murphy replied that evidence in the possession of the United States government indicated that additional and very important information was available, and added that it was the intention of the United States government to pursue this case further. Mr. Murphy said that the United States government wished a settlement on this case. He emphasized that some of our men had been killed, that there were certain rules of conduct in the civilized world, and that the United States government hoped the desired information regarding the missing men would be promptly forthcoming.

SOVIET ARTICLE READ

Mr. Murphy then briefly reviewed the case once more, pointing out that the operation of Soviet radio beacons in the area might easily have induced a navigational error on the part of the pilot. He said that the plane had entered Soviet airspace in error, and not intentionally.

Mr. Murphy then read most of a translation of an article entitled "Great Skill: A Swift Attack," which had been published in Soviet Aviation, the newspaper of the Soviet air force, on September 20, 1958. When he had concluded, the Soviet ambassador asked Mr. Murphy whether what had been read was fiction. Mr. Murphy then handed the ambassador photostatic copies of the article and a preceding one on the same subject. Mr. Murphy once more told the ambassador that the United States government regarded this case with extreme gravity.

Ambassador Menshikov said that he would convey the details of this representation to his government.[135]

The ambassador and air attaché hurried from Murphy's office, and reported the meeting to the Soviet foreign ministry.[136]

Soviet Response—Nothing Further to Report

Responding to Menshikov's assessment of his meeting with Murphy, Soviet Foreign Minister Andrei Gromyko recommended the next course of action to the Communist Party Central Committee on December 6, 1958. His recommendation as reflected in an internal Kremlin document—do nothing:

SECRET
MID [Ministry of Foreign Affairs] of USSR
Countries of America Department
Entry 2596, 7 Dec 58
TO: CC CPSU

Comrade Menshikov, ambassador of USSR to the USA, reported that he was invited to the State Department by Deputy Assistant Secretary of State Murphy, who gave him an oral presentation about the American aircraft that violated the border of the USSR near Yerevan on 2 Sep of this year (Telegram No. 2196 from Washington).

During his presentation, Murphy asserted that the aircraft, which crossed into Soviet airspace, was supposedly following a Soviet radar beacon and was downed by Soviet fighters. "Eyewitnesses" supposedly saw parachutists jump from the plane.

Murphy also said that since the remains of only six crew members of the aircraft have been sent to the Americans, and there were 17 persons on board, there should still be 11 individuals on Soviet territory, some of whom are possibly still alive.

Murphy further announced that the 19 and 20 September issues of the newspaper Sovetskaya Aviatsiya [Soviet Aviation] *published articles written by Major A. Meshkov entitled, "Vysokoe Masterstvo" "Great Skill," which, in Murphy's opinion, confirm the fact that the American aircraft was downed by Soviet fighters. Murphy announced that the Americans allegedly have a taped recording of the conversation between the Soviet fighter pilots and ground controllers.*

Comrade Menshikov declined to discuss the issue raised by Murphy and announced that as concerns the American aircraft that violated the border of the USSR near Yerevan on 2 Sep, the appropriate answer was already given by the Soviet side in Moscow. He categorically denied Murphy's assertions that Soviet pilots shot down this American aircraft, refused to listen to the taped recording fabricated by the Americans, and rejected the Americans' conjectures relating to the article in the newspaper Sovetskaya Aviatsiya.

It is completely obvious that the American side is using various fabrications to draw us into a new discussion of this issue in order to rid themselves of the guilt for the American aircraft that violated the border of the USSR and also to lay the blame on the Soviet side.

The position of the Soviet government on this issue has already been detailed in three demarches sent to the U.S. Embassy and published in the Soviet press. Therefore, the MID of the USSR believes it would not be expedient to enter into a discussion of this issue with the Americans at the present time and will limit itself to the reply that was given by comrade Menshikov in his discussion with Murphy. If the Americans should mention this matter, they should be told that the demarche sent by the Soviet side on this issue, as well as the reply to Murphy's announcement by Ambassador Menshikov on 13 Nov, completely settled the matter and the Soviet side has nothing additional to add.

Please review.

original signed by A. Gromyko
6 Dec 58

Menshikov and Gromyko seem to treat the American accusation about the Soviet beacons as a simple lie, as frivolous as the claim that parachutes were seen in the air. The fact is, though, that C-130 60528 apparently *had* followed Soviet beacons, and that the Soviet beacons were transmitting on or very close to the Turkish beacons at Trabzon and Van, Turkey. Menshikov and Gromyko clearly believed that the border violation had been intentional, and that the U.S. was still attempting to pass off blame for the incident on the Soviet government . The November meeting between Murphy and Menshikov was not publicized until the State Department issued its press release twelve weeks later, on February 5, 1959.

The Soviet government permitted itself to be backed into a corner from which there was no escape short of admitting that it had been lying from the start—it never admitted any involvement in the incident whatsoever. The American plane had simply crossed the border illegally and "fallen."

Great Skill—The Target Is Detected and Swift Attack

Given the fanaticism of the Soviet leadership concerning secrecy and its need to keep all sensitive issues out of Soviet open source materials, it is surprising that a major piece of the evidence showing Soviet MiGs shooting down the C-130 was published in *Sovetskaya Aviatsiya*, the official Soviet air force newspaper. During the Cold War, the American embassy in Moscow gleaned morsels of intelligence from major Soviet periodicals, especially military newspapers, journals, and magazines. Perhaps ninety-nine percent of the stories in the periodicals were extraordinarily unhelpful (not to mention badly written), but an occasional nugget made scanning them worthwhile.

While the Soviet foreign ministry was working overtime to withhold information about the shootdown from the American State Department, Soviet air force Major A. Meshkov innocently authored a two-part article in *Soviet Aviation* about how Soviet air defense forces defended Soviet airspace against intruding enemy aircraft. Finding the interception and shootdown of the defenseless C-130 irresistible as a classic example of Soviet air defense forces prowess, Major Meshkov covered the story in blow-by-blow detail.

In the September 19, 1958 edition of *Soviet Aviation*—in an article titled "Great Skill, Part 1, The Target Is Detected"—he described in meticulous detail how "the vigilant fighting men at one of the antiaircraft air defense posts detected an aerial target." In turn, he discussed how each vigilant fighter in the air defense radar target detection and tracking function carried out the unit's functions: target assigned a track number, warning sent out, intensified observation of air situation, target annotated and tracked on command post plotting board, fighter pilots scrambled and vectored on intersecting course to combat air patrol area of state border immediately across the border from the target track. For added realism, Meshkov addressed participants in the story by name, rank, and duty title, and included photographs of targets being plotted. The first part of the story ended with Meshkov describing how Captain Romanyuta, the ground intercept controller, had made precise and accurate calculations to vector the fighters into the right area for the intercept:

> Steadily the fighter aircraft were approaching the indicated area. Tension within the command post became even greater. It was necessary to direct the pilots into an initial position that was advantageous for attack and to ensure reliable control of the air "battle."
>
> It was a busy time in the command post.

The second part of the story—"Great Skill, Part 2, A Swift Attack"—published in the newspaper on September 20, began with duty officer Kulnikov directing a second pair of alert duty pilots to go on "combat readiness," while one pair was already heading toward an interception of the target. The fighter pilot call signs (three-digit numbers) that Meshkov used in his article are identical to the call signs of the pilots who intercepted the C-130 on September 2, as noted by the second-party signals intelligence site in Turkey that recorded their communications. Meshkov used the phrases: "201, take off in a pair" and "582, take off in a pair" (scramble commands) in the article, and pilots 201 and 582 were flight leaders of the two pairs of MiGs recorded by the voice intercept operators who monitored and recorded the shootdown-related pilot conversations. In a manner similar to part one of the article, Meshkov identified the four fighter pilots by name and described the interception and attack:

Course 360, altitude 11 [000].
The target is in front of you, to the right, below.
I see the target.

At this point, Meshkov describes the attack—as if he were following the transcript of the pilot conversations intercepted by the voice intercept operators.

The leader, Lopatkov, dashed in to attack first and switched on his gun camera. After him, officer Gavrilov attacked the "enemy." He succeeded in making three passes. When the wingman made a combat turn and broke off the attack, the second pair of fighter aircraft entered the "battle." These were Senior Lieutenants Kucheryaev and Ivanov. After them, the first pair carried out another successful attack on the target.

The story concluded with the fighters landing—one at his reserve airfield because the pilot was low on fuel. Excited and tired after the just completed interception, the pilots gathered together. The commanding general drove up to the pilots, shook their hands warmly and thanked them for their successful execution of the mission.

"We serve the USSR," the officers responded simultaneously.

"That was fine," said Gavrilov quickly. "Just as in actual combat . . . To be sure, the flight was instructive," said Kucheryaev. Author Meshkov had attempted to disguise the scene as a hypothetical target interception training exercise.

Third-Party Feedback from Premier Khrushchev

The U.S. government was sometimes successful in obtaining information through unofficial channels from American businessmen who had had meetings with Soviet leaders while on visits to Russia during the Cold War. A review of presidential correspondence recently found in the Eisenhower Library reveals feedback provided by Eric Johnston, president of the Motion Picture Association of America, after cultural exchange visits to the Soviet Union in September and October 1958. Johnston "made copious notes" of conversations he had with Premier Khrushchev on October 6 and left an accounting of the Khrushchev meeting with the American embassy before leaving Moscow. The tone of the Khrushchev-Johnston discussions suggests that the premier used Johnston as an unofficial courier—anticipating that Johnston would report the meeting to American authorities—to convey Soviet displeasure with American policy in some areas. After expressing Soviet ire toward U.S. policy vis-à-vis Sino-Soviet relations, Khrushchev raised the issue of American reconnaissance along Soviet borders:

> "And another cause of irritations," he said, "is you are constantly flying your planes around our borders . . . When a neighbor pulls his blinds down, you don't try to peek around the corner . . . We have shot down several of your planes in the East and West, and we are going to continue to shoot them down when you get around our borders."
>
> "Just recently," he continued, "you had a reconnaissance plane on our border and it crashed in flames . . . We returned six bodies to you . . . Now you claim there are eleven more men, but we don't know anything about those men. We never saw them."
>
> I asked him if I heard him correctly—that he had never seen these eleven men and did not now have them.
>
> He said, "Yes, you heard me correctly . . . We have never seen the men; we do not now have them . . . We do not even know that there were eleven men aboard. If they were, we do not know what happened to them."
>
> I said, "Have you told our embassy?"
>
> He replied, "Yes. Now you claim that this was a plane en route from Germany, but we know that isn't true . . . We know the base of the plane in Turkey . . . Your plane was on reconnaissance trying to find out about a new radar warning system that we have installed . . . I want to tell you that we are going to continue to shoot down any planes that violate our borders . . . When we have guests in our country, we treat them well, but we are not going to tolerate unwelcome guests, and furthermore, I don't know what you are bothering with Turkey for . . . I'll let you in on a secret . . . We have no navy in the Black Sea and no sub-

marines in the Black Sea, and we are not going to put them there . . .
Our missiles could wipe out Turkey in fifteen minutes . . . We have sent
a note to Turkey, and we are going to make a claim against Turkey for
these plane incidents."

This was a subject that I was not prepared to discuss, and not desiring
to pursue it further, I changed the subject.

The "strong statement made by Khrushchev to Eric Johnston" resulted in a conference between Deputy Under Secretary of State Robert
Murphy and the Defense Department's Joint Chiefs of Staff. Murphy
asked the JCS, "What possible countermeasures could be taken to discourage the Soviet Union from shooting down American recon missions?" He also asked the JCS to reevaluate its reconnaissance activities
to be sure that none of the incidents occurring were a result of our own
carelessness or neglect. The discussion on possible countermeasures was
inconclusive.

General Nathan Twining, Chairman of the JCS, indicated that in his
opinion the recent events did not indicate a new pattern.

We are now flying many more missions than in the past. We have lost
at least twelve aircraft, probably more, since [World War II]. The loss of
two of them could be considered as "our fault." This reconnaissance,
moreover, is essential for our intelligence on the USSR and we must also
assure that we assert our right to fly over international waters. We must
increase this type of reconnaissance flights, and we must take steps to
educate the American public on the necessities for doing so.

General Curtis LeMay, then vice chief of staff, U.S. Air Force, added
that there was not normally too much interference with the U.S. flights:

The Russians know the nature of the missions and identify them. They
are, of course, very touchy about penetration of Soviet airspace.

After Admiral James Russell, Vice Chief of Naval Operations, discounted the possibility of carrying out countermeasures against Soviet

submarines and surface craft with "anything short of piracy," LeMay, typically, mentioned "the possibility of following aggressive aircraft into the base and shooting up the base." He pointed out: "This has been done before." There were no responsive suggestions concerning other countermeasures that could be effectively applied.

Long Wait—No Response

The Soviet government had made it quite clear in its last response, on October 16, to America's fourth diplomatic note on the C-130 incident that it desired no further discussions on the subject—"spare the Soviet government the necessity of conducting correspondence on such matters." Thus, the State Department did not expect a quick response to Deputy Under Secretary Murphy's discussions with Ambassador Menshikov four weeks later. Four rounds of written diplomatic representations had failed to break the impasse. The Soviet government refused to elaborate beyond its original statement, in effect saying, "Your military aircraft intentionally violated our airspace and fell in our territory—we returned six remains and have no information on other crew members; stop bothering us about the incident." A standoff ensued, from which the Soviet Union refused to budge. The standoff continued into 1959.

In January 1959, Deputy Premier Anastas I. Mikoyan visited Washington, D.C. Seeking to thaw Soviet-American relations, which had hit rock bottom, and hoping to elicit information on the eleven missing airmen, official Washington afforded Mikoyan first-class treatment. Senators and congressmen wined and dined him, and treated him royally. In February a State Department press release described a private meeting between Mikoyan and Vice President Richard Nixon:

> On January 7, 1959, the Vice President of the United States [Richard Nixon] received the First Deputy Chairman of the Council of Ministers of the USSR, Mr. Anastas I. Mikoyan. During the course of their conversation, the vice president raised the question of the eleven missing crew members from the C-130. Referring to the desirability of reducing tensions between the United States and the Soviet Union, the vice president said it would be useful to make progress on matters like this one. He said

it would be helpful if the Soviet government gave the United States government an indication or a statement about what had happened to the men involved. The vice president said that the C-130 case has great emotional impact in the United States. Great concern is felt about this case by the American people.

Mr. Mikoyan replied that the Soviet government had given all the information it had. He said that there was no sense in their trying to hide anything and wondered why the Americans were so suspicious about this.

The same State Department press release discussed a meeting between Secretary of State John Foster Dulles and Mikoyan during his American visit:

The secretary of state took up with Mr. Mikoyan on January 16, 1959, the destruction by Soviet planes of the unarmed C-130, and asked for information regarding the eleven missing crew members. He pointed out that response by the Soviet government to our representations would help satisfy serious anxieties felt by the American people, who want the missing men returned, and that a meaningful response would be a helpful step from the standpoint of United States–Soviet relations.

Mr. Mikoyan said that the Soviet government had done all that it could, that all the bodies had been returned, and that the Soviet government did not know about any other personnel. Mr. Mikoyan protested that there would be no point in the Soviet government holding any bodies or living crewmen, and he expressed the Soviet government's lack of understanding and irritation over the U.S. government's insistence concerning this case. He denied that the plane had been shot down, asserting that it crashed.[137]

In other meetings with senators and congressmen, Mikoyan likewise stated that the Soviets had found the plane and returned the six bodies; they possessed no information on eleven unaccounted for airmen. Mikoyan commented to one senator: "You have no faith in us." In effect, Mikoyan lied outright and confirmed explicitly what had been implied since mid-September—the Soviet government was denying directly that Soviet aircraft shot down the C-130, and did not want to discuss the incident further.

Ruse Unveiled—MiG Air Attack Tape Revealed

The State Department waited two weeks after Mr. Mikoyan's return before abandoning hope of a Soviet reply. Convinced that diplomatic discussions with the Soviets about the fate of the eleven missing airmen had reached an impasse, on February 5, 1959, the Eisenhower administration released a recording and transcript (see appendix C) that documented how the Soviet pilots shot down the C-130 over Armenia. One of the most damaging pieces of evidence in the recording is a statement by a fighter pilot that "the target is a four-engine transport." In their statements, the Soviets had referred to the downed aircraft only as a military or a U.S. aircraft—never as a transport or unarmed aircraft.

State Department press officer Lincoln White explained why the recording was being released: "It is clear that we are not going to get a rational explanation despite the fact that they know we have the facts . . . The period of grace has now run out."

Release of the recording represented a major milestone; the State Department decided to release its evidence only after Russia refused to say anything about the eleven missing airmen. Though not expressed at the time, officials in the State Department and Air Force had virtually given up hope of ever learning what happened to the eleven men. The timing was also connected with a mounting crisis over the "German question."

There was speculation that at a time when voices in Congress and in some Western capitals were urging flexibility in making counterproposals to the Soviet Union, Secretary of State Dulles welcomed the opportunity to document the lack of credibility he attached to Soviet words. Soviet lies about involvement in the shootdown were occurring precisely at the same time that Premier Khrushchev was telling the world that the Soviet Union wanted to end the Cold War. The release of the recording came as British Prime Minister Harold Macmillan was arranging talks with Moscow, and as Secretary of State Dulles was traveling to Europe for talks with British, French, and West German leaders on Soviet threats in Berlin.

While denying a tie-in between the timing of the release of the recording and some perceived beliefs that a thaw in East-West relations was imminent, the State Department cited the persistent Soviet attitude in the case over the previous five months as anything but the actions of a nation seeking a thaw in the Cold War. "Reliable sources" also insisted that the State Department had given serious consideration to making the evidence of the Soviet air attack public two months earlier. However, while it was contemplating the release, the visit of First Deputy Premier Mikoyan to the U.S. was scheduled, and officials held off on publishing the recorded transcript in the hope that in talks with him, the Russians could be persuaded to provide more information.

Release of the recording had an immediate impact around the world. The U.S. ambassador to the United Nations played it at a U.N. Security Council meeting, and TV networks echoed the recording during newscasts. A German recording company even produced a 45 RPM record of the "shootdown communications." Several months later A/2C Horace F. (Joe) Bissett, a Russian linguist, and several language school classmates who had arrived at Rhein-Main in April 1959, listened to the German-made recording at Rick Parendes's apartment in Neu Isenburg. As they listened to the shootdown of 528, they became very angry, and Joe Bissett remembers that the recording changed his feelings from "it's a job" to "the mission." With that as his motivation, he reenlisted and served twenty years in Security Service, most as an airborne voice intercept operator.

The tape recording was front-page news in major U.S. and overseas Western newspapers. The *Washington Post* captured much of world opinion in a February 6 headline, INTERCEPTED CONVERSATION THROWS DOUBTS ON VALUE OF ANY STATEMENTS BY REDS. The *Post* article emphasized total distrust of Soviet statements and actions, and at the same time displayed a degree of skepticism toward the motives of the U.S. government:

> *The Eisenhower administration chose yesterday to introduce a complicating new factor into the Cold War that had been showing signs of a thaw.*

This factor was the strange and far from fully explained case of the American transport carrying 17 airmen, shot down by Soviet fighter planes some 20 or 30 miles over the Turkish border inside Soviet Armenia. The evidence indicates the Russians have been caught in a bald-faced lie about the plane's fate.

The disclosure here came only after the speeches at the Soviet Communist Party Congress by Premier Nikita Khrushchev and his deputy, Anastas I. Mikoyan.

The effect of the disclosures could be to discredit Mikoyan whose peace-and-trade talk to American businessmen here last month had caused some alarm at the State Department. In a larger sense, the disclosures tend to discredit the Soviet word on any subject—and the Soviet reputation was none too high in many quarters both here and elsewhere in the free world . . .

Why had there been no disclosure of the tape recording until now of conversations among the Soviet fighter pilots who shot down the plane? American officials have been saying privately for some time they had at least a hope that some of the 11 men unaccounted for might have gotten out of the plane alive. These officials thought it at least possible the airmen were in Soviet hands, subject to harsh interrogation and quite likely to be shot rather than returned home if there was too much public pressure from Washington.

Release of the information yesterday seems to indicate that there is now little hope any are alive . . .

To the dismay of the National Security Agency, there was little mystery as to how the United States obtained the tape recording. A UPI press story described how Western "ears" were monitoring Soviet communications in Europe:

LONDON, Feb. 7 (UPI)—An allied network of electronic sentries is eavesdropping against surprise attack all along communism's "Iron Curtain" in Europe.

The efficiency of the Western radio listening posts was publicly disclosed this week when the State Department released a tape recording of the Soviet attack on an unarmed U.S. Air Force transport along the Turkish-Soviet frontier last September.

This network of radio posts surrounds the Soviet Union. Night and day, Russian language experts tune in on every frequency used by the Red forces on land, sea and air. Details are top secret, but this much can be said on excellent military authority:

The Western "ears" operate in Britain, Canada, West Germany, Turkey, Cyprus and certain other allied areas fronting the communist bloc. Mobile units operate in planes and ships. Big "panoramic" radio receivers scan whole bands of wave lengths for signs of communications activity. Russian-speaking operators zero in on all transmissions.

Direction finders pinpoint the location of a communist transmitter. Measuring instruments gauge its size. Shorthand and tape recorders take down voice and code messages.

Most military traffic is in code. But aside from code-cracking machines and speedy cryptographers, the West believes it can hear enough plain-language traffic to keep itself posted on communist military plans.

Not far from the main U.S. Air Force headquarters in West Germany, a typical listening post monitors the Soviet and East German air force channels. Short-distance communications between Red Army units on the ground are similarly monitored.

In releasing the recording, the State Department for the first time publicly accused Russia of shooting down the C-130, and by implication accused Soviet Deputy Premier Mikoyan of lying about the incident. The release of the tape recording came while families of the thirteen fliers unaccounted for were gathering in Washington, D.C., for a memorial service honoring two unidentified airmen who had perished aboard the downed American aircraft.

Memorial Services for the Crew

On November 4, 1958, the families were notified that four of the six bodies that the Soviets returned six weeks earlier had been identified. The four identified bodies—of Captains Swiestra and Jeruss, Lieutenants

Villarreal and Simpson—were handed over to their families for memorial services of their choosing. The Jeruss family decided on a military funeral and burial in the Arlington National Cemetery in Virginia for Captain Jeruss. The Simpson family conducted memorial services and interred Lieutenant Simpson in a private grave in Austin, Texas. The Swiestra and Villarreal families held private memorial services for Captain Swiestra and Lieutenant Villarreal in late 1958.

Following notification that four of the remains returned by the Soviets had been identified, the Air Force personnel director, Major General Reeves, sent a personal letter to the next of kin of the thirteen missing airmen on November 8. The letter to Mrs. Mary Wagner confirmed "the recent message informing you that your son, Technical Sergeant Arthur L. Mello, is still missing." The message continued with a review of what had occurred to date since the aircraft was declared missing on September 2 and procedures the Air Force would follow pursuant to the Missing Person Act. Efforts on behalf "of your son have received the close personal attention of the chief of staff and secretary of the air force, the secretary of defense and the secretary of state." In his closing remarks, General Reeves expressed his heartfelt sympathy during that period of uncertainty.

Memorial services for the two unidentified remains came later. After coordinating arrangements with the families of the thirteen unaccounted for crew members, the Air Force honored the two unidentified remains with full military memorial services and burial in Arlington National Cemetery on Friday, February 6, 1959. Members of most of the thirteen families of the missing airmen were present for the services. The *Washington Post* newspaper addressed the memorial services in a front-page story on February 7:

> *Two unidentified soldiers who died in the Cold War were buried yesterday on a wind swept slope of Arlington National Cemetery.*
>
> *High ranking State and Defense Department officials, generals, senators and congressmen came to honor them.*
>
> *There was also a slight young woman who sobbed quietly within herself at the graveside. She was Mrs. Arthur L. Mello, whose husband was one of the 17 crew members on the unarmed Air Force transport lost September 2 near the Russian-Turkish border . . .*

Yesterday, the little colonial chapel at Fort Myers [adjacent to the cemetery] was filled with men in Air Force blue uniforms. A contingent of men came on their own from Bolling Air Force Base. Along one side of the chapel, a line of master sergeants, most with decorations from World War II and the Korean War, stood silently for the services. A three-star Marine general sat in the back row. Not far away was a Navy lieutenant.

Both Protestant and Catholic services were held over the two flag-draped caskets. Then, with muffled beat of black-draped drums, the funeral procession moved slowly through the wooded cemetery to the graves. The two Arlington graves will be marked simply "Unknown."

Family members sobbed quietly in the chapel and at the graveside. Having heard nothing definitive since the crew failed to return five months earlier, they could not know if their loved one was in one of the two adjacent graves.[138] In their hearts, each wanted to believe that somehow the eleven missing men had survived and would come home soon. For them, closure would come only after the thirteen unaccounted for men had been accounted for.

Grieving

The memorial services served as an outlet for family members to unburden pent-up feelings of grief and despair. For the first time since the Air Force had notified families about the missing crew, the Air Force sponsored a formal ceremony honoring and paying tribute to the lost men. But try as it might, the U.S. government could offer little comfort or bring real closure for any of the seventeen families; the information the families sought simply was not available. The Soviets were not going to offer any explanation or accept any responsibility; nor would they cooperate in the one way that could have brought some relief for family members—American access to the crash site. That inability to examine the crash site itself precluded finding clues to the eleven missing crewmen and an explanation of how the men had died. At the same time, the six returned remains were so severely mangled and incomplete that opening caskets for viewing by family members was not an option. Requests by some family members to open caskets were denied, bringing suspicions that information was being withheld from the families intentionally. This feeling was especially true by February 1959 when the two unidentified remains were interred, and no additional data was forthcoming on the missing men.

By then many family members were feeling they had been abandoned by their government and began speaking out to a press eager for news, any news, about the C-130 incident. The New York *Sunday News* devoted over three pages of its February 8, 1959, issue to coverage of the frustrations of the families. In a story titled BEHIND PLANE ATTACK STORY, the *Sunday News* said that release of the "damning tape-recorded dialogue among Soviet pilots—'Attack, Attack! . . . I will finish him off, boys!'—was to have been bared weeks ago, but was abruptly held up by the 'good will' visit of First Deputy Soviet Premier Anastas I. Mikoyan." The story captured the mood, sentiments, and hopes of many affected family members.

The State Department withheld its white paper for weeks. During that time, mysterious and unsubstantiated rumors about intelligence missions against the Eastern bloc surfaced, along with other pieces of questionable information, like official statements that said nothing concrete, neither truly confirming or denying anything. Added to this was plain old faith, which served to give the families of the missing airmen hope that their kin might still be alive. The airmen's wives and parents saw the release of the tapes and charges made by the State Department as support for their beliefs that some of the missing were alive and being held by the Russians.

It was made clear by Deputy Undersecretary of State Murphy that at least some of the men had been killed, leaving questions in the families' minds: Did any of the crew survive, perhaps by bailing out of the stricken airplane before it crashed and burned? If some did manage to parachute to safety, had the Russians captured all of them, or only some of them? Were friendly Armenians even now harboring the downed airmen and keeping them safe from Russian search parties?

But hardest of all was the fear and longing to know which two men from 60528 were now buried in Arlington National Cemetery. It was known that of the dead crewmen identified, there were four of the five officers on the lost C-130. Many wondered if this was a coincidence.

Despite that the fact that one of the officers, Capt. Edward J. Jeruss, thirty-three, was buried November 12 in Arlington, his mother, Mrs. Hyman

Jeruss, still wasn't positive that her son had died. Her reasoning was based on a faint but real hope. She had continued to receive a telegram every three days from Oct. 7 through Oct. 31 telling her that all the remains had not yet been processed and that therefore all the identities of the dead were not known. It wasn't until Nov. 2 that she and the other parents received confirmation that one of the bodies had been confirmed as being their son.

The coffin for Captain Jeruss arrived sealed, and the Air Force refused to allow it to be opened despite the wishes of Jeruss's father. He wanted to be sure he was really burying his son, but without that simple token of proof, a lingering doubt remained that the body of the dead airman might not be their son.

Mr. Jeruss perceived the Air Force as withholding information. He felt it had not done all that it could to clear up the mystery by which it had finally identified his son—the whole thing appeared to be veiled in a shroud of secrecy that served to keep the parents from knowing the truth.

For A/26 Archie Bourg Jr., twenty-one, flying the mission had been a way to earn some extra money in flight pay. It wasn't to be. Archie's father still had hope, believing, much as many of the other families, that his son was in fact alive and a prisoner behind the Iron Curtain.

T.Sgt. Arthur Mello, airborne maintenance technician on the plane, had first enlisted in the Air Force in 1945 and married his wife, Ila, after reenlisting. She became convinced that Arthur was being held prisoner by the Russians.

A-2C James E. Ferguson Jr.'s family was left wondering how "Jim," once star of his high school's basketball team in La Porte, Indiana, had ended up flying secret and dangerous Air Force missions. They knew the Air Force had sent Jim to school to learn Russian and stationed him in Frankfurt, Germany. Rita, his wife, commented that he often left home early in the morning for flights, but he never told her what it was he did. The limited information she had received from the Air Force led her to believe that Jim's body had not been one of those found and therefore he was still missing. She knew too that Jim had been some kind of passenger, not a "crewmen," which is who the bodies seemed to be. And so she continued to write to Jim regularly, even though she knew he wasn't receiving any of her letters.

Grief and anger over the fate of his son, A-2C Robert H. Moore, prompted Mr. Cecil Moore to write President Eisenhower to seek some answers. He expressed his frustrations with the lack of information about Robert's status. How, he wondered, could the U.S. government not continue to search for answers when the matter involved such an expensive plane and, more important, the fate of the crew. "Men die or men disappear in wartime, and I can understand it. But we are not at war . . . Eisenhower won't do anything about it. All he's interested in is playing golf or fishing."

A U.S. official told the *News* that the Russians were deliberately and maliciously hurting the families of the dead and missing men because they had a point to prove. He strongly believed that the cruel disregard for the suffering of the families by the Russians was all a ploy to make the United States stay farther away from Soviet borders in the future.

Despite the burial of the two unknowns at Arlington, questions about the shootdown still remained. Attempts to get information from the Russians would continue as the families of those missing and dead waited throughout America, hoping for some kind of answer. As one of the Air Forces telegrams said: "The State Department is continuing to make every effort to obtain further information."

For the families of the men lost on 60528, the words sounded hollow indeed.

Cecil Moore's feeling that the government had abandoned the missing men and their families was typical of most family members by February 1959. The identification of the six returned corpses as four flight crew members and two unknowns—plus Air Force reference to the eleven Security Service (recon) crew members as "passengers"—led to scuttlebutt that the Russians "sent the bodies of the front-end crew home and kept the back-enders," implying that the Soviet government handled the situation in that brutal manner to send a message. (That was also the belief of nearly every man in Detachment 1, 6911th.)

Theresa Durkin, Master Sergeant Petrochilos's sister, contacted each new administration for nearly four decades trying to get them to release something—anything—that would give her a sense of why her brother, after surviving World War II and the Korean War, had died so violently in peacetime. Sadly, there were no answers.

Rita Ferguson believed fervently that her husband was alive. She wrote to Eisenhower himself in 1959 in a desperate plea for information. She received no answer. Ila Mello was quoted making similar remarks:

"I'm convinced my husband is still alive . . . None of the bodies the Russians sent back were those of my husband's buddies." Out of hopelessness, the Security Service families readily accepted speculation of KGB captivity as "proof" that their relatives were alive, imprisoned in Russia.

The State Department and Air Force maintained contact with next of kin continually during the first two months—through the identification cycle for the returned remains—and on a less frequent basis up to the memorial services for the two unidentified fliers in February 1959. The problem was simply the nonexistence of information under the circumstances that would bring closure for the families.

Mrs. Margaret DiLoretto, mother of A/2C Gerald Maggiacomo, appealed directly to President Eisenhower in a handwritten letter on November 19, 1958:

Dear President Eisenhower:

I want to thank you for your letter dated Oct. 29th. I was very disappointed as I was waiting for some good news. Again this year, I will be praying and hoping that my son will be home for Christmas. It would be a good deed if they did send the prisoners home.

I hope that while you are traveling the eleven nations, you will be able to release the eleven airmen. They are around somewhere and they need help now and not later.

I pray every day for his safe return home. He is my only child, and I will not give him up. Where are the airmen that parachuted out of the plane? They were not returned with the six which only means that they are prisoners.

Besides you, there is only Khrushchev and between the two of you, they should be released.

Please help me, and you know what it means to me as you have children of your own, and they mean a great deal to you. I know you will receive this letter before you leave on Dec. 3rd.

Wishing you lots of luck in your mission and also best of health. Make this a Merrier Christmas for us and send my son back home to live with us once more.

God Bless You.

An internal White House memorandum directed an aide to reply to Mrs. DiLoretto's letter: "The president said she should have some acknowledgement, not Presidential." Accordingly, a deputy assistant to the president wrote to Mrs. DiLoretto on December 15, 1959:

> *I regret that there is nothing new that I can add at this time to the president's letter informing you of the reply that Mr. Khrushchev had made to his request . . .*
>
> *This government does not consider the case closed and will continue to do everything that can usefully be done to determine the fate of the missing men.*

When Larry Tart located Mrs. DiLoretto in March 1997, she was still in mourning, and still waiting to learn what happened to her son.

By 1960, relatives were openly questioning whether their government was withholding information about the incident from the families. In May—after the shootdown of Gary Powers's U-2—Moses Fields wrote a letter to President Eisenhower:

> *This is in reference to your letter of October 29, 1959, and is in request of further information concerning my son, Joel Fields . . .*
>
> *With the latest development in the news concerning the matter of planes and personnel crossing the Soviet borders, I am wondering if there might be some information which, perhaps for reasons of national security, has been withheld which can now be shared with the parents of those boys who were aboard the ill-fated transport.*
>
> *Mr. President, I am sure that you are aware of the fact that even a knowledge of my son's death is better than knowing nothing of his fate. I am a father; I love my son. But I do not know how to give my love to him—whether in grief or in anxious prayer for his safety. Certainly every man is entitled to know this much about those he loves.*
>
> *My son went into the service of his country, as did the sons and daughters of many citizens, with a loyal conviction that his country merited his very life. I do not quarrel with this. I share the conviction. Even now, I am not bitter. I simply want to know. My mind has been clouded, my heart torn in two for almost two years. Dare I ask for a reply?*

An Air Force aide to the president answered Mr. Fields's letter:

I have been asked to reply to your letter to the president concerning your son, Airman Joel Fields.

It is my earnest desire to furnish you actual details of the fate of your beloved son which might lessen the anxiety and anguish caused by this long period of uncertainty. Regrettably, I am unable to do so, since no additional information has been learned since my letter of 29 October 1959.

Raymond Kamps, brother of A/2C Harold Kamps, attempted over the years with little success to obtain information on his brother's fate from his congressman, others in the United States government, and anyone else who would listen to his pleas. In a letter to Congressman Melvin Laird on April 28, 1960, Kamps discussed recent correspondence with an author who had published a story about the shootdown:

Enclosed you will find photostatic copies of the article "Mademoiselle Jardine and America's 17 Decoyed Airmen" which was written by Emile C. Schurmacher, and appeared in the March issue of For Men Only. *I am forwarding these copies since you may have difficulty in obtaining an issue of the publication. Also, enclosed you will find a copy of the letter I received from the author in February.*

As you can note, I asked the author where he got his information from and tried to pin down how accurate it was. The story, of course, makes good reading, and has probably some sex appeal, etc., written into it. The thing that intrigued me with this article is the accuracy of the facts that I am aware of. Many articles I've read regarding this incident, and others, generally are way off base regarding the facts, dates, etc.

It is this article, plus correspondence, plus visiting with other people on this case that brings up my question whether the State Department knows a lot more than they are telling us.

I'd like to bring to your attention the fourth paragraph of Schurmacher's letter, stating that the State Department wasn't too cooperative in giving him data on this case. I can understand their position, knowing a little more of the picture through my visit with you and them.

I would appreciate it if you could find out whether this secret radio station was actually a fact, and whether an American was actually sent there to locate it and did, as the story tells us. If this is true, it would then indicate that our government is working in more ways than one, to try to get the answers we're looking for. As you probably know, I try to read every article pertaining to this "incident" and try to find out anything I can from anybody who may have a little information. It doesn't seem right for me to merely forget that my brother and those men ever existed, and close the case in our minds. I also strongly feel that if the relatives aren't interested in their loved ones, our State Department and government officials might soon lose interest, except for the official facts for the record.

I appreciated having an opportunity to talk to you at great length over the telephone the other day, and hope that I didn't upset your schedule too much.

Our family and I definitely want you to continue to do everything you can to bring about an accounting of what happened to these men. If we are to find out that they died in this crash, we would be satisfied with that, if there were proof of it. On the other hand, we don't like to accept this fact until some concrete evidence has been brought to light.

I want to thank you for your past efforts and hope that you can continue to work with us until we get the information we want.

While interesting, no additional details about the "secret radio station" are available, although it may have involved a leaked reference to the intercept site that recorded the communications of the MiG pilots as they attacked and shot down the C-130 aircraft. Amazingly, no news reporter is known to have ever asked questions of the U.S. government about the location of the intercept site that intercepted those MiG pilot conversations.

Later in October 1960, Raymond Kamps wrote letters to Senator John F. Kennedy and Vice President Richard Nixon—U.S. presidential candidates in the upcoming election—seeking actions each would take to find the eleven unaccounted for airmen missing in the C-130 shootdown:

I have followed the TV debates between you and the other principal candidate for the next president of the United States of America . . .

We have been promised our government will do everything humanly

possible for these men. However, we have had no results. Therefore,
"What specific measures" will you take to find out if my brother is a pris-
oner or not, and "What specific measures" will you take in getting the
known prisoners released?

I would like very much to have this question answered before Novem-
ber 8th, and perhaps debated as the biggest issue confronting our nation
today.

Kamps also indicated in the letter that a similar request had been
made to the candidate of the other party, and he provided a copy of the
letters to his local newspaper. In addition he provided a copy to
Congressman Laird, asking him to urge Vice President Nixon to adopt "a
very aggressive approach to this problem." "I don't advocate an armed
conflict, but anything short of it would be agreeable."

Senator Kennedy responded on November 4, 1960, on JOHN F.
KENNEDY FOR PRESIDENT letterhead:

Thank you very much for your recent letter.

It is lamentable that more has not been done to help secure the release
of American citizens imprisoned by the communists. Let me assure you
that in the event that I am elected to the Presidency, I will use the
full powers and prestige of that high office to try to free these unjustly de-
tained men.

An executive assistant to Vice President Nixon responded; Nixon
was too busy campaigning to respond personally:

In the absence of the vice president who is campaigning, I wish to
thank you for your letter of October 25 . . .

You may be sure that he shares the strong feelings of all Americans
over the deplorable and outrageous detention of our men as prisoners by
the communists. He has supported all of our efforts toward their release.
He personally demanded it of Khrushchev when he talked to him. With
respect to the future, however, he believes it would be most unwise to re-
veal in advance what tactics he would adopt to obtain their freedom, lest
countermeasures be prepared and the advantage of surprise be lost.

I know the vice president would want me to send his best wishes to you and your family.

The sad facts are that both candidates (or their surrogates) implicitly suggested that the eleven unaccounted for crew members were Soviet prisoners, giving false hope of repatriation when there was no evidence to support that conclusion.

In 1961, Kamps wrote a number of letters to the new Kennedy administration and to his congressman, Melvin Laird. Supposedly, Kennedy promised him in a meeting in Wisconsin in late 1960 during a campaign stop in the state that if elected, he would seek the release of the eleven missing airmen in his first summit conference with Premier Khrushchev. Kamps discussed that promise in a letter to Laird in August 1961:

Enclosed you will find a letter to Lawrence F. O'Brien together with two carbon copies of previous letters written by he and myself. I would appreciate it if you would forward my letter to him together with these two carbons.

After you sent me this carbon of his letter of August 7th, I was so angry that I did not want to write to you or he until quite a little time had elapsed. My letter of June 28th to you was not intended to put President Kennedy on the spot. I merely wanted to know if he would keep the promise made to me before his election. I think he had a wonderful opportunity at Vienna to bring up this subject . . .

Acting as an intermediary, Laird forwarded a letter to Kamps on November 1, 1961, from the State Department—from Richard H. Davis, Deputy Assistant Secretary for European Affairs:

Mr. O'Brien has asked me to reply to your letter of August 24, 1961 to him regarding your brother, Mr. Harold T. Kamps.

Very careful consideration was given your request that the president raise the case of the missing C-130 crew members, including your brother, with Mr. Khrushchev in Vienna. Because of the nature of this first meeting between the president and Mr. Khrushchev and the international situation at the time, it appeared to the Department that this was not a propitious occasion to raise the matter and that to do so might in fact worsen rather than improve the chances of obtaining any information from the Soviet government regarding the fate of your brother and the other missing men. Consequently, the Department of State made the determination that this question should not be on the agenda of problems to be discussed between the president and the Soviet premier.

As you doubtless know, since 1958 the president, vice president and Secretary of State, as well as other high officials of the United States government, have intervened with the highest Soviet authorities, including frequent occasions with Chairman Khrushchev, in an effort to elicit information in regard to the missing crew members of the C-130. These efforts have unfortunately been fruitless. The record does not in fact encourage the hope that the Soviet government will alter its oft-repeated assertions that it has no further information.

Despite Soviet intransigence in this matter, the Department will continue its efforts to ascertain the fate of the missing men, and you may be sure that the families concerned will be informed immediately of any new developments in the matter. Moreover, the president has made it clear that he is prepared to intervene personally whenever developments might promise some positive results.

A month later—on November 16, 1961—Kamps received a letter from the Department of the Air Force officially notifying him of the termination of the missing status of his brother, A/2C Harold T. Kamps. The letter said in part:

Although the Soviet authorities have returned the remains of the six personnel of the C-130, they have consistently denied any knowledge of the remaining personnel that were aboard. In the past 38 months, the Department of the Air Force has received no positive intelligence which would substantiate a belief that anyone successfully abandoned the C-130 prior to the crash, or survived the indicated extremely violent impact of the C-130 with the ground . . .

Consideration of these facts and circumstances compels the regrettable conclusion that all personnel aboard crashed with the C-130 and died as a result of the impact.

The Air Force sent each of the families of the missing crew members a similar version of the same letter.

Soviet intransigence made impossible a joint U.S.-Soviet investigation of the crash site immediately after the shootdown, the one scenario that could have made a difference. Form letters stating that there was nothing new to report but the government was making every effort to learn what happened to a husband (son, brother, etc.) only added to lack of confidence in the government, causing additional pain, despair, and grief. The State Department release of evidence that Soviet pilots downed their relatives' aircraft—a recording transcript provided to families of the seventeen fliers—boosted morale momentarily and increased the thirst for a detailed accounting of what happened.

Air-Attack Tape Faked, Soviets Claim

"We hope that in the light of the revelation of the facts and the shock of world opinion that it has produced, the Soviet government will come forward with facts on this case." That State Department comment about the release of the recording probably expressed the feelings of most Americans. But the public release of the damning evidence had the opposite effect on the Soviet government. Calling the United States act a "sensational farce," Moscow countercharged that the air-attack tape was faked. The Kremlin said the State Department's aim was to poison East-West relations and undo the favorable impression made on the American people by the visit of Anastas I. Mikoyan.

In broadcasts beamed around the world on February 7 in English and other non-Slavic languages, Radio Moscow commentators described the tape as "clumsy" and "staged," and again denied any attack on the U.S. plane. The broadcasts reiterated previous Soviet statements that the plane had crashed while flying "a long way over Soviet territory," adding that the State Department now has "made up another untrue version of the incident that the U.S. aircraft was alleged to have been shot down by Soviet fighters":

To support this version, one more false piece of evidence was invented . . . It is typical that the State Department has refused to inform the press how the U.S. authorities got hold of this recording. The facts are perfectly clear: No such recording exists.

The fake is so transparent that a child could see through it. The script sounds as if it were written in Hollywood by someone who knew nothing of contemporary Russian language or even fighter tactics.

Just listen to this, "I am attacking . . . There is a hit . . . The target is burning . . . The target is banking . . . Look at him, he is already falling . . . I will finish him off, boys."

Whoever heard such nonsense. U.S. pilots might use such language. They might address each other as boys. Soviet pilots address each other as comrade. The State Department ought to employ better script writers for their forgeries.

The commentators also asked why the United States waited five months and exchanged a series of notes with Russia seeking information on the crash if it had a tape recording all the time. "After all, recordings are made instantaneously or not at all."

No one in America questioned the authenticity of the recording, but reaction to the release of the information was mixed. The intelligence community found it inconceivable that such sensitive classified information was being released publicly—period. From a security perspective, willfully sharing such special intelligence data with a person not possessing an appropriate security clearance was punishable by a $10,000 fine and ten years imprisonment.

Relatives of the seventeen airmen wondered if the State Department was withholding other relevant information, and several senators and congressmen complained publicly because they first learned about the recording from a television news program. Congressman Wayne Hays expressed congressional ire to news reporters: "If we had known the facts, the congressional reception for visiting Soviet Deputy Premier Anastas Mikoyan would have been much different." A week later the State Department apologized for failing to tell the House Foreign Affairs Committee in advance that it had the tape, admitting to the committee in a secret session that it was a "slip-up."

Whereas the public in the West knew about the recording and U.S. charges of a Soviet cover-up, neither the Soviet press nor domestic broadcasts told the Russian people about Moscow's denunciation of the tape recording. About the incident, the average Russian knew only that a U.S. aircraft—never described in the Soviet press as unarmed or as a transport—had crashed deep inside Soviet territory, and that six crew members who perished in the crash were returned to U.S. authorities. Nor did the Moscow broadcasts in English and other Western languages ever note that the American plane was an unarmed transport—it was a "military plane" or an "American plane."

The State Department described Radio Moscow's charge of United States fakery "transparent" and "shocking." It expressed hope that the broadcast denial "does not reflect the considered attitude of the Soviet government." It asked that Moscow "reconsider its inflexible attitude in this case." On Monday, February 10, State Department press officer Lincoln White again challenged the Russians to listen to the recording. Noting that Radio Moscow had broadcast charges of American fakery in languages other than Russian, he also dared the Kremlin to tell the Soviet people about the recording, charging that the Russians had avoided informing Soviet citizens.

Diplomacy Failed—Fate of Eleven A Mystery

Release of the recording showing the Russians to be bald-faced liars lined up world opinion on the U.S. side of a diplomatic shouting match, but failed in its attempt to restart a dialogue with the Russians about the fate of the eleven missing airmen. Most American newspapers believed the U.S. government's claim that the seventeen men, a crew and passengers on an innocent transport flight, had been shot down and probably murdered by the Soviets. The following article in the *Erie Daily Times*, Pennsylvania (Sergeant Mello's hometown), on February 12, 1959, is typical:

> *The United States government has again caught the Soviet government in a willful lie about the murderous attack on 17 Americans traveling in an unarmed transport plane last September. Moscow claims that the tape recording issued by the State Department is a fake—but that is nonsense and the Russians know it.*

. . . The Soviet government was offered a chance to listen to the tape last November 13. Why didn't they call it a fake before? They had three months to say so publicly—or privately—to the U.S. government.

The transcript of the episode, which cost 17 American airmen their lives as Soviet patrols shot down the unarmed transport plane, was checked and double checked.

. . . Portions of the tape now have been played on the radio in this country and abroad so that anyone who understands the Russian language can make his own translation and decide for himself . . .

Officials are astounded at the flatness of the Russian denial of the authenticity of the tape recording. The only way they can figure it out at all is to assume that the Soviets, once having taken a position of complete innocence, do not dare now to change their minds. All the American airmen presumably are dead—so the Russians think the issue cannot ever be resolved.

In an editorial later in 1959, the *Erie Daily Times* went further in urging the U.S. government to exert more pressure on Russia to learn whether "these eleven men are dead or alive, and so end the heartbreaking anxiety their families wake up and go to bed with every day . . . Why continue diplomatic relations with a country that refuses to abide by the dictates of international law and the norms of common decency?"

The lack of progress in obtaining additional information on the eleven missing airmen resulted in letter writing campaigns by both family members and U.S. government officials. President Eisenhower sent a personal note to Nikita Khrushchev via Ambassador Thompson in May 1959. Deputy Foreign Minister V. Kuznetsov forwarded Eisenhower's note with a draft resolution to the Communist Party Central Committee:

On 4 May of this year, American ambassador Thompson delivered a note to Comrade N. S. Khrushchev that expresses the anxiety of the President of the United States with the fate of the 11 American fliers who were supposedly on an American C-130 that violated the state border of the USSR on 2 Sept. 58 and crashed near Yerevan. The possibility that the Americans will publish their note cannot be excluded.

Accordingly, the MID [foreign ministry] of the USSR considers that it

*would be expedient to deliver our note on this matter to Chargé d'Affaires
Davis. It could be published if necessary. It would follow that the answer
given by Comrade Khrushchev to the U.S. ambassador Thompson
should be stated in our note.*

A draft of the resolution is attached for your perusal.
Please review.

V. Kuznetsov
15 May 59

Later, Vice President Richard Nixon sent a personal letter to
Khrushchev on August 1, 1959, upon his return from a visit to Moscow
in July. Foreign Minister Gromyko coordinated Khrushchev's response
with the Communist Party Central Committee:

*On 1 August of this year U.S. Vice-President Richard Nixon sent
Comrade N. S. Khrushchev a letter in which a request has been made to
provide information on the fate of the 11 Americans who supposedly were
on board the USAF aircraft that crashed on 2 September 1958 in the
area of Yerevan. In his letter Mr. Nixon raises the issue of the fate of the
11 crew members of this aircraft as a "serious impediment" to improving
relations between the USSR and the USA.*

*In accordance with its instructions, the Ministry of Foreign Affairs of
the USSR is presenting Comrade N. S. Khrushchev's draft answer to
Nixon's letter mentioned above.*

The draft decree is attached.
Please examine it.

[original signed] A. Gromyko
17 Aug 59

Khrushchev's response reveals the continued hostility that the Kremlin felt toward American reconnaissance eleven months after the C-130
incident:

DRAFT

Dear Mr. Nixon,

I have familiarized myself with your 1 August 59 letter in which you again raised the issue of the USAF plane that crashed on 2 September 1958, 55 kilometers northwest of Yerevan.

I will tell you candidly that the fact that you have raised this issue after the Soviet government has done all it possibly could to clarify the circumstances of this crash and has fully informed the American side of the findings of its inquiries, must at the very minimum cause perplexity on our part. We cannot view this as anything but an attempt to artificially create barriers toward improving U.S.-Soviet relations.

The government of the United States has already been informed that on 2 September no Soviet fighter downed an American aircraft and that on that day a U.S. military aircraft crashed near Yerevan. At the site the remains of corpses were discovered. After an examination of the remains, which were sent to the American side on 24 September 1958, it was possible to conclude that six crew members perished. No other American airmen from the indicated aircraft were found in the USSR and therefore we don't have them.

I understand the feelings of the relatives of those who perished when the plane crashed. However, it is completely obvious that those who are in charge of such flights of American aircraft are responsible for them to the American public and to the relatives of those who perished.

I would like to point out to you, Mr. Vice-President, that such issues would not ever come up in the relations between our two countries if U.S. military aircraft did not fly so close to the Soviet border and did not cross the border for purposes that are incompatible with improving Soviet-American relations. Moreover, such flights of American airplanes and their illegal crossings of the Soviet border are still taking place. In particular, these flights were recorded in the eastern sector by our country virtually on the eve of your visit to the USSR.

I inform you of this with the hope that the American side will curtail such activities that, without doubt, will make a very important contribution toward developing and improving relations between our countries. In other words, curtailing such activities will be conducive to achieving the noble goals of "ending the Cold War" and reinforcing peace, discussions of which we and you have devoted many hours to during your stay in our country.

Very sincerely,
N. Khrushchev

The Air Force discussed Nixon's visit to the Soviet Union in a letter dated September 9, 1959, to next of kin of each missing airman. The letter ignored (or was unaware of) the Nixon-Khrushchev letter exchange:

. . . You will be interested to know that the question of missing crew members was raised by Vice President Nixon during his recent visit with Premier Khrushchev in the Soviet Union. Mr. Khrushchev was asked to provide the United States with full information regarding the missing airmen. His response failed to supply any new information pertaining to their status, and the USSR continues to deny any knowledge of these persons.

The Air Force sent the letter to next of kin after conducting an annual review pursuant to the status of missing personnel under the "Missing Persons Act."[139] In the letter to Arthur Mello's mother, the Air Force director of military personnel expressed "sincere regret that the fate of your son is still uncertain after a year's absence and to notify you that he is to be continued in a missing status for the reasons explained below." Among the reasons:

. . . A full review of all available information is required when a 12 month period of absence in missing status is about to expire. It authorizes either a continuance of the missing status or a presumptive finding of death, whichever is warranted by the available information.
The law requires that a person be retained in a missing status as long as he "may reasonably be presumed to be alive."
. . . While the effort of the Department of Defense and Department of State have thus far failed to establish that any member did survive, there

is also a lack of firm information to the contrary . . . Your son will continue to be officially recorded in a missing status until circumstances indicate that a change is required. Meanwhile, pay and allowances will continue . . .

I realize how disheartening it is to learn nothing more about your son after these many months. You may be assured that our government is continuing to utilize its resources to obtain the facts concerning the fate of the personnel who are unaccounted for. You will be notified of any new information that may become known.

On October 1, 1959, Eisenhower attempted once more—this time in a personal letter to Khrushchev—to solicit information on the missing airmen:

I am writing to you to raise one question, which in our concentration on other matters, I did not take up with you during our talks at Camp David. This is the question of the fate of the eleven men who are still missing since September 2, 1958 from the C-130 United States Air Force transport aircraft.

I know you will understand the deep concern of the families of these men who continue to hope that some indication of their fate will yet be uncovered . . .

I want to express my hope that the appropriate Soviet services will again look into this question to see if there is further information which I can provide to the families of the missing men. I am encouraged to renew this personal appeal because of the fine and understanding attitude you took toward such human problems during our talks at Camp David.

The letter received "presidential handling" and was not reported in the press. A State Department memorandum of conversation documents receipt of an answer to the president's letter—a personal letter from Khrushchev dated October 10, 1959:

In his letter, Mr. Khrushchev acknowledged President Eisenhower's letter of October 1, 1959, and assured the president that he understood the feelings of the relatives of those who perished in the crash of the C-130 plane. He referred to the letter of August 22 to Vice President Nixon, and stated that it contained all the information at the disposal of the Soviet authorities. This information was based on a most careful investigation carried out on the personal order of Mr. Khrushchev. Recalling the case of the American plane which violated the Soviet frontier in June 1958, Mr. Khrushchev said that, as in that case, any American fliers or their bodies found on Soviet territory would have been immediately turned over to the American authorities. Mr. Khrushchev advanced the sincere hope that both sides will do everything possible to avoid anything that could adversely affect the development of relations between the two countries. In concluding, he referred to the continuing fresh impression he has of the frank and extremely useful conversations which he had with the president at Camp David on questions affecting not only the peoples of both countries, but all of mankind.

The Soviet diplomat who delivered the letter to the State Department declined to reveal the subject of his visit with Deputy Assistant Secretary Murphy. Khrushchev's response to Eisenhower convinced high-level diplomats in the State Department that no additional information would be forthcoming, as evidenced by an internal memorandum from Foy D. Kohler to the Secretary of State:

We have been asked for recommendations regarding any further action on the C-130 case. In the light of Khrushchev's negative reply to the president's inquiry, we believe it is now clear that the Soviet government, barring a radical internal development or drastic change in our relations, will never concede that they have any knowledge of the eleven men still missing from this plane.

We therefore believe that no purpose would be served by a further communication to them, at least at the present. However, Mr. Klaus [special legal assistant in State Department] is proceeding with the collection of evidence with a view to the submission of this case to the ICJ [International Court of Justice] as has been our normal practice in other similar cases after the exhaustion of direct communication with the Soviet government.

A six-page declassified Headquarters Air Force twelve-month status review document dated August 31, 1959, details what the Air Force knew about the incident when the twelve-month review was completed. An "Additional Information" section included "unconfirmed and unverified reports that have developed concerning the fate of the unaccounted for":

(1) A United States national, a registered nurse, visiting in Yerevan in October 1958, reported that (information is third-handed) an Armenian witness had seen the C-130 flying in and out of the thin clouds being attacked by Soviet fighter aircraft that shot off the C-130's right wing. The transport aircraft crashed, exploded and burned. Subsequent probing of the debris, after the fire had burned out, revealed a total of 18 bodies, 12 of which were burned beyond recognition.

(2) Reports obtained by personnel of the Department of State have been reviewed and indicate, in one instance, that a Turkish officer and two soldiers viewed the attack of the C-130 through binoculars. They reported seeing the aircraft attacked by three Russian fighter aircraft, but saw no evidence of the tail assembly having separated from it, nor did they observe any parachutes come from the transport. Another report indicates three farmers along the Turkish border also observed the attack on the C-130, and they too reported they did not see any of its personnel escape by parachutes.

(3) While attending a social function in Armenia, a United States national tourist of Armenian extraction heard that the C-130 aircraft was scattered in pieces over a wide area and that the bodies of the crew were destroyed beyond recognition. His impression was that few people in Armenia knew any of the actual facts about the incident. He did not recall having heard any mention of the number of bodies in the aircraft or the possibility of survivors.

(4) A Soviet farmer, who defected in late October 1958, reported that he heard, presumably from persons who had visited the scene of the crash, that six bodies were recovered, including that of a woman. The defector had been a member of a patrol established to search all roads in the vicinity of the crash since the border guards reported that either parachutes or

weather balloons had been dropped from the C-130. However, he neither saw nor heard rumors of any survivors.

(5) A Turkish officer indicates that he witnessed two Soviet aircraft intercept the C-130. At an altitude of approximately 2,000 feet, two parachutes were seen to come from the transport and then it was fired upon by the attacking aircraft. The C-130 spiraled earthward and crashed to the ground rather lightly, but almost immediately thereafter exploded violently.

(6) An elderly housewife, a United States national of Armenian extraction, was visiting her sister in Yerevan in October 1958. She was informed by her sister of the rumor circulating among numerous residents of Yerevan that two of the persons on board the C-130 were alive and being held by the Soviets.

(7) A letter from a Polish national implies that she has information (third-handed) concerning the C-130 crash in Armenia. Her sources of information indicate that an American airplane was forced to land on an Armenian airfield. Since it was a carrier (possible refers to transport) type aircraft, the crew was taken for examination. Some days later, six of the crew were killed by dropping them to the ground from a Soviet aircraft in flight. The other ten crew members were taken to specialists for further examination. Three of these persons later died, and the remainder were placed in concentration camps.

The document continued, "All leads have been actively pursued, but to date none of the reports have been confirmed." The document also included a section titled "Locations of Personnel Positions and Means of Abandoning the C-130 in an Emergency":

The positions of the six flight crew were on the flight deck. Within the rear compartment were ten special operator positions installed in three separate cubicles and a maintenance area for the one other special operator farther aft. All operator positions were located on the right side of the aircraft. A hallway about three feet wide ran the length of the aircraft from the flight crew compartment aft to the rear escape door on the left side of the fuselage. A corresponding door was on the right side, reached by a lateral corridor. Both doors were designed to be used as paratroop ex-

its. Each of the cubicles had a door opening into the common hallway, allowing easy and expeditious access to the exit doors for the special operators. The crew had been briefed to wear parachutes throughout the mission. The special operators could have exited the aircraft through either side paratroop door. The flight crew could have left the C-130 in flight through the front crew entrance door or through the rear exits. In an emergency situation the flight crew would undoubtedly be occupied with control of the aircraft. The special operators would be free to exit immediately upon direction from the pilot by warning bell, of which ten were installed, or by voice signal. Operational personnel estimate that it would require only 30 seconds after warning for the eleven special operators to bail out using all available escape exits. The time interval of approximately five minutes that the aircraft was estimated to be under attack would allow ample time for the eleven special operators to abandon the C-130 before it crashed.

Under a section titled "Discussion," the document provides the rationale for maintaining the "missing status" for the unaccounted for men:

Since the report from the Polish national is at such great variance with the substantiated fact that the C-130 exploded upon impact with the ground, it appears that little credence can be attached to the report. Some doubts must also be expressed in accepting as entirely reliable the reports of the witnesses viewing the attack and indicating that no one abandoned the aircraft prior to its crash. The history of aircrew escape and survival is filled with eye-witnessed incidents in which the observers indicated no person could possibly have escaped from the aircraft after its being hit severely by anti-aircraft or gunfire, and that often times disintegrate in mid-air. Yet crew members of these aircraft were later recovered from prison camps or evaded and returned to military control. The accounts of the crash of the C-130 and the conditions of the remains recovered reveal that the impact was of great explosive force and that fire was also present. This appears to substantiate an assumption that any persons aboard at the time of the crash of the C-130 could not have survived. However, the evidence in this case is insufficient to confirm as fact that all personnel aboard the C-130 were in the aircraft at the time it crashed. Sufficient *time was available, from the beginning of the attack, for personnel to have parachuted. Three reports from different sources indicate that at least two parachutes may have come from the C-130 while in flight. The absence of a report that these persons were taken into custody and detained by the government of the USSR is no indication that such is not the case.*

Past experience has demonstrated that the USSR has deliberately withheld or distorted information concerning the whereabouts or fate of U.S. personnel who have disappeared in territory controlled by communist countries. Any decision to terminate the missing status of the personnel who were aboard the C-130 until the State Department and the intelligence agencies have explored and exhausted all available means to procure the complete details or the whereabouts and fate of these men would be premature. Therefore, until positive proof becomes available that members of the crew were not detained or other events occur that disclose their non-survival, it may reasonably be presumed, pursuant to the provisions of the Missing Persons Act, that the personnel herein considered may be living and that any change in their status on this date is beyond the safe calculated risk of error.

The Air Force conducted a "Re-review of Missing Status" for the thirteen missing or unidentified airmen one year later with similar findings—no additional significant details had surfaced, and the review board recommended that each of the thirteen continue to be listed as missing in September 1960.

False Hopes and Unwarranted Optimism

Eager for information—anything—that offered hope that a loved one was still alive, family members accepted as fact a secondhand story in a Soviet magazine in January 1961 that the eleven missing men were imprisoned in Russia. In the magazine article, Wolfgang Schreyer, an East German propagandist, also wrote about the U-2 and RB-47 missions that had been shot down in May and July 1960, and about National Security Agency defectors: William H. Martin and Bernon F. Mitchell—pointing out that Martin and Mitchell said that the C-130 had been on a spy mission over Armenia.

As soon as the article appeared in the Soviet magazine *Ogonyok*, the American ambassador in Moscow delivered a note to the Soviet foreign ministry requesting clarification. The U.S. note dated January 18, 1961, said, in part:

> . . . *The attention of the United States government has been drawn to the publication in the January 15 issue of the Soviet publication* Ogonyok *of an article by Wolfgang Schreyer in which the following statement is made with regard to the shooting down of a United States airplane over Soviet Armenia on September 2, 1958: "On September 2, 1958, a spy plane was shot down over the territory of the Armenian SSR and burned in the mountains. It was equipped with radar and special apparatus for radio interception. It was a heavy aircraft . . . On board, there were seventeen persons. The plane was based in Turkey. Since the Americans thought that the USSR did not have any evidence of the spy character of this flight, they, as usual in such cases, tried to present the affair in a distorted light.*
>
> *"The State Department of John F. Dulles even summoned up the insolence to deliver a note in which it accused the Russian pilots of 'deliberate enticement' of the American plane onto Soviet territory, and of 'savage reprisal on an innocent aircraft.' But the Soviet government exposed the falsificators with annihilating facts. Even before pursuit in the air of the intruding American plane was undertaken, eleven of the seventeen members of its crew were parachuted onto Soviet territory; they were captured in the vicinity of Yerevan."*
>
> *As the Ministry knows, the United States government has repeatedly requested the Soviet government to furnish information concerning the eleven men who were unaccounted for after the shooting down of the C-130 aircraft, and the Soviet government has repeatedly denied that it had any information about the fate of these men.*
>
> *In view of the fact that the magazine* Ogonyok, *which is a product of the Pravda Publishing House, as a matter of practice bears the indication that it has been authorized for publication—in the present instance,*

authorized for publication on January 11, 1961—and having in mind the existence of an organ of government subordinate to the Council of Ministers of the USSR known as the Main Administration for Safeguarding Military and State Secrets in the Press, the United States government cannot fail to ascribe importance to the information contained in issue No. 3 of Ogonyok of January 15.

If the eleven men to whom reference is made are presently in the USSR, in custody or otherwise, the United States government expects that the embassy will be granted immediate access to them. The United States government further will expect their return without delay to the United States authorities. In the meantime, the United States government expects to be informed immediately of the welfare and whereabouts of these men in order that their families may be notified.

In its response, dated January 25, the Soviet government repeated earlier claims that it had nothing to add to information provided previously regarding the crash of the C-130 on Soviet territory. The foreign ministry also accepted no responsibility for incorrect information provided by the East German writer:

Concerning the references contained in the embassy's note to an article by the German writer W. Schreyer in the magazine Ogonyok, according to facts transmitted to the Ministry by the Editorial Collegium of the magazine Ogonyok, this article by W. Schreyer was republished from the magazine Neue Berliner Illustrierte, published by the German Democratic Republic, and an incorrect presentation of the facts concerning the C-130 aircraft was committed by the author of the article.

Naturally, the Soviet government cannot take any responsibility for this sort of publication.

In an article titled U.S. FLIERS DOWNED IN '58 HELD IN SOVIET, MOSCOW JOURNAL HINTS, the *New York Times* offered a glimmer of hope that the eleven unaccounted for men might still be alive:

MOSCOW, Jan. 23—A Soviet magazine has reported that eleven crewmen of a United States reconnaissance plane shot down by Soviet fighters near the Turkish border in September 1958, parachuted safely and were captured.

This was the first acknowledgement that the American airmen, part of a crew of seventeen aboard the Air Force C-130 transport plane that flew across the Soviet-Turkish border, had been taken alive by Soviet authorities . . .

The report was buried in Ogonyok, a Soviet popular magazine, in the second installment of a long article by an East German writer named Wolfgang Schreyer. The editors of Ogonyok said the article had been picked up and translated from an East Berlin magazine, Neue Berliner Illustrierte . . .

Despite this unusual source for information on the fate of the American fliers, it bore the stamp of authority in view of the fact that the magazine is published in the printing house of Pravda, the Communist Party paper, and presumably was given official approval.

. . . After describing the flight of the United States aircraft, which, the writer said, was on an espionage mission over the USSR, the article said that even before the Soviet fighters closed in on the plane, "eleven of the seventeen members of the crew were dropped by parachutes on Soviet territory . . . They were caught in the outskirts of Yerevan," the article added.

This was part of the writer's long list of incidents and collected information designed to support the thesis that the United States had taken up where Hitler left off in an all-out campaign of espionage against the USSR and the East European allies . . .

Coverage of the "new" information in the *New York Times* produced a flood of letters from family members to the White House. In a letter dated March 16, 1961, a State Department political affairs officer responded to a letter from Mrs. Joseph Lindy:

Dear Mrs. Lindy:

The White House has asked the Department of State to reply to your letter of January 28, 1961, concerning your brother, Technical Sergeant Arthur L. Mello, who was aboard the United States C-130 aircraft shot down over Soviet Armenia on September 2, 1958.

You stated that you had been apprised of a magazine article asserting that eleven members of the crew parachuted to earth and were captured and of the subsequent Soviet denial. I am enclosing a press release that contains the texts of the notes exchanged between the United States and the USSR on this subject.

Additionally, the January 29 issue of Ogonyok, *the Soviet magazine, which published the story that the eleven men had been captured alive, stated that the article containing this information had been republished from the East German magazine* Neue Berliner Illustrierte *and that "the incorrect version in it of the facts concerning the circumstances of the crash of the American C-130 aircraft was committed by the author of this article." According to a Reuters dispatch from Berlin, on January 31, the editor of the East German magazine in question told a reporter that the magazine had published "incorrect facts" about the fate of the crew of the C-130. He said the author of the article, Wolfgang Schreyer, had made the error due to the misreading of newspaper clippings published at the time the plane was shot down, which he had had no means of checking . . .*

The article in *Ogonyok*—though totally false with regards to the eleven missing crew members—momentarily renewed optimism and raised false hopes among the missing airmen's families. As usual, the State Department letter expressed sincere sympathy and stated that the families would be advised immediately "if there are any further developments in the case."

Samuel Klaus Dossier on C-130 Shootdown

Sam Klaus, a Special Assistant to the Legal Advisor in the U.S. Department of State from 1946 to 1963, had responsibility for gathering evidence and building cases against the Soviet Union for adjudication in the International Court of Justice. Klaus was a meticulous record keeper, and his files were placed in storage after he retired—all 106 boxes of personal memoranda and message exchanges on international air incidents that occurred during his tenure. The U.S.-Russian Joint Commission on

POW/MIAs uncovered the Klaus files in 1992, arranged declassification actions, and made the files available in the National Archives for public use. His declassified files are one of the most detailed sources of American information on Cold War Soviet-American shootdown incidents.

In early February 1959, Klaus developed an intragovernment position paper that outlined steps he proposed to take to prepare a possible claim of the "C-130 case" against the Soviet government in the International Court of Justice (ICJ). He drafted a letter to the U.S. Defense Department asking for its cooperation in an investigation and proposed to investigate the radio beacon problem and weather conditions during the September 1958 mission and obtain affidavits—legally admissible evidence—from witnesses to the incident. Klaus's files reveal an often acrimonious relationship and less than stellar cooperation that existed among the State and Defense Departments and the Central Intelligence Agency throughout his investigations. At the same time, Klaus faced often insurmountable odds with the unsophisticated witnesses from whom he attempted to obtain meaningful affidavits.

He met his first challenges on the case in March 1959 while attempting to discuss the incident with officers on the Turkish military staff. He documented one discussion with a Turkish officer about the beacon problem in a memorandum:

> It appeared that he [the Turkish officer] did not understand what a radio beacon was. He said that he had ascertained at Trabzon that the station was working at the time of the incident but that perhaps they were in conversation with Ankara and could not be disturbed for conversation with an airplane in the air . . .
>
> When I explained to him what a radio beacon was, he called THY (Turkish Airlines] and finally got someone who would seem to be the office director who he said told him that he would look the matter up.

Later, the Turkish General Director of Airports confirmed that the Trabzon radio beacon suffered a power failure on September 1, but the power was restored at nine-ten the following morning. About the Van beacon, Klaus wrote:

I then asked him about the radio beacon at Van. He said I had not asked him about that before, and he had made no inquiry. I said that I thought I had, and he said he was sure that that beacon was in constant operation because it was on the international air route to Iran, and if there were a failure there, it would be reported by the airlines at least to their home offices. He indicated that I should inquire of the airlines who pass through Van.

I said that it was quite clear that the C-130 was being directed toward Yerevan when the incident happened, although it was presumably looking for Van. He said it must be that since he had heard no report of any international airplane being diverted by Yerevan that the Russians had a lure beacon near Yerevan, which they put on for military aircraft such as ours and did not put on when normal international traffic going to and from Iran passed over that point.

I asked him to keep us informed by special affidavits as to any experiences of this kind in the future. He said if it came to his attention, he would keep the FAA [Federal Aviation Agency] informed and the FAA would undoubtedly let me know. I emphasized again that what we needed was not information but affidavits. He acknowledged my statement but I could not reach the conclusion that he was going to attempt to do anything of this kind.

So much for affidavits and admissible evidence! During 1959, Klaus interviewed nine Turkish eyewitnesses—four village peasants (two who could not read or write) and five border guards—to the shootdown and obtained affidavits. The eyewitness recollections corroborate the voice messages of the Soviet pilots. Each eyewitness reported essentially the same story—they saw a pair of MiG-17s "herding" the C-130 while two other MiGs carried out attacks from behind and above the C-130.

The Turkish witnesses insisted that the MiG pilots intercepted the large transport the instant the American plane crossed the border ("just about 100 to 150 meters inside the second fence"). They stated that the large plane approached the border from the direction of Kars, Turkey, corroborating the Soviet tracking data. Hearing the sound of an airplane, two Turks at a border outpost looked around and saw an airplane coming out of a dense cloud that extended up to the border. Following the plane's movements, a short time later "four Russian planes suddenly appeared and began moving around the plane that was entering their territory— moving on its right, on its left, above it and under it." As the intruding aircraft continued on its way, the witnesses heard an explosion resembling a cannon, and a minute or two later heard the same sound again. At that point the American plane burst into flames and, turning over a number of times in the air, fell to the ground. Most of the attacks were carried out at relatively low altitudes—some Turkish witnesses observed accurately that the tail stabilizer and underside of the wings of the transport plane were painted red. One Turkish border guard testified that the C-130 crossed the border near the Turkish Kinegi and Kizilay border posts and then flew over Kosarak village, Armenia. Over Kosarak it started to descend rapidly, "to fall like it hit an air pocket" according to the Turkish witness. Another witness observed the same scenario: "As the American plane flew over Kosarak village it suddenly lost altitude at the same time that three Russian planes came out of the clouds and started to fly around, under, and over the American plane. The American plane was brought down by the fire of the Russian plane that was above it."

Two witnesses had seen the C-130 near the border but had not seen the MiG attacks themselves, and all had misjudged distance (estimating the crash site to be 500 to 2,500 meters from the border instead of an actual distance of approximately twenty-five kilometers). None had seen the C-130 impact with the ground (it fell behind a hill), and none had seen any parachutes, although one had seen three shiny objects in the sky (three of the attacking MiGs at a distance)—hardly the witnesses or level of evidence Klaus required to score big in world opinion and before the International Court of Justice.

In an internal memorandum soliciting State Department support, Klaus pointed out that he needed to find and interview other Turkish witnesses as well as Armenian witnesses, if possible, who had witnessed the MiG attacks. He also felt the need to conduct a careful analysis of the attack itself and compare the time elapsed with the time of crash:

> The witnesses indicate that the crash took place "within a few cigarette puffs" in time from interception of the plane.

I have already asked Colonel Smith of the Air Force to produce the so-called log which the Russians returned and which I learned in Turkey was not a log but a sheet of scratch paper with what appeared to be penciled calculations by the navigator, presumably trying to figure out where he was from certain data. This is an important factor . . .

The Assistant to the Governor of Trabzon told me personally that he was sitting in his home on September 2 shortly after 1:00, and in the fog heard an airplane, which is a rare thing in Trabzon at that season, circle three times over the city and then take off east toward the Soviet border.

If this is what the Soviet radar and radios showed, then we can not argue about unpredicted winds pushing the airplane away from Trabzon toward Batumi. More likely, the pilot's instruments failed and, having circled Trabzon and being unable to make contact with the beacon, he went up toward Batumi, figuring he was over Trabzon, and so reported to the ground stations, which relayed it to Athens.

It is important that we know this in proper time. This would make it the Yerevan beacon, particularly if the Van beacon was not working, as it may not have been. This conclusion is subject to the receipt of an affidavit from the Turkish officer in charge at Van at the time in question, which I have requested.

In addition to the time analysis study, Klaus advocated the use of the tape recording of the MiG pilots' communications during the attack on the C-130 to lend credence to his presentation before the ICJ. He also wanted the intercept operator who copied the Russian pilot communications to testify as a witness to verify the authenticity of the recording. On both accounts, the Central Intelligence Agency stonewalled and refused to cooperate—it considered the sensitivity of the source of the recording sacrosanct, not releasable under any conditions. By 1960 the CIA and some Air Force officials were pressing Klaus to discontinue attempts to bring the case before the international court.

Without the recording, intercept operator's testimony, and affidavits from additional eyewitnesses, Klaus believed that his case was too weak to adjudicate in the ICJ. He documented phone discussions about the case on March 10, 1960:

I called Mr. McAfee [senior State Department officer] this afternoon to keep him apprised . . . He knew that Mr. Service [political affairs officer] was leaving soon. I told him that this meant that there would be no one in the political section who had been actively concerned with the case. Mr. Service was concerned about this because if another incident took place, which was not unlikely, the C-130 [case] would split open and the political desk would have to reply . . . Mr. McAfee said that this was exactly what he wanted to hear. If Mr. Service was sufficiently concerned, he, McAfee, could raise the matter more strongly with his own people, pointing out the embarrassment of the political desk and Service's concern with what appeared to be the lack of cooperation of the Intelligence people . . .

If the case was going to be dropped I would tell all the facts in justification of not dropping the case. I would point out that there were many witnesses who had not been interviewed and that the case did not need to rest on the recording alone. I also explained again to Mr. McAfee that while Service stressed the recording problem, I stressed the eyewitness problem since the recording would become of minor importance if we got more eyewitnesses. I said I knew there were many more eyewitnesses since I had talked to the few the Turks produced . . . I reiterated to McAfee that I would be willing to go back to Turkey, if I had the cooperation of the Turkish authorities and the Intelligence people, and supervise on-the-spot the interviewing of many more Turkish eyewitnesses. McAfee made the point that he would be enabled with this approach to make his people state flatly whether they had or had not exhausted all available sources so there could be a definite answer . . . Mr. McAfee said that if Mr. Service got "off the hook," it would be easier for McAfee to deal with his own people.

The investigation of the C-130 shootdown incident had in effect become a political football. On March 11, Klaus discussed the status of the C-130 case with Colonel Smith of the Air Force:

I emphasized that we needed a maximum of eyewitnesses as well as the verification of the recording. I told him that if there were another case,

*the C-130 [case] would explode, and we would have to answer. He said
that the whole thing was now in the hands of the State Department, and
he realized that I myself was not responsible . . .*

*I told him that I stood ready to go to Turkey with Air Force help and
the Intelligence cooperation to direct on-the-spot coverage of the entire
border but that the Intelligence people must be persuaded to cooperate.
He said that their concern was that the interception program might be interrupted. We both agreed, however, that the publication of the intercept
had already disclosed to the Soviets that we had monitored that particular
frequency. He said, of course, this was well-known to both sides. Nevertheless, he said, there were intermediaries between him and the top in the
Defense Department that were concerned with this problem and were also
siding with the Intelligence approach.*

Klaus exchanged views with Mr. Service on the C-130 case on
April 25:

*He [Service] told me that Richard Davis, his supervisor, had gone over
this case a good deal and had apparently come to the conclusion that if we
brought a case in the ICJ and the Soviets accepted or were forced into accepting jurisdiction, we could then take up with CIA the question of the
tape recording certification . . . I argued that this seemed to be a fair
compromise—the real question was proving the incident by eyewitnesses,
increasing the number of eyewitnesses, and the areas from which they
came. This, I said, would make the recording less determinative of the
outcome, although, of course, we would want, in any final proceeding, to
get that in.*

The situation dragged on through the summer of 1960, and on September 13, Colonel Raymond (Air Force Operations) called Klaus to
his office. Raymond had intervened earlier with Richard Davis, Deputy
Assistant Secretary of State for European Affairs, in an attempt to terminate pursuit of the C-130 case in the ICJ. He asked Klaus to prepare a
memorandum that Raymond could provide to Davis outlining the evidence that was currently available and what additional actions Klaus pro-

posed to complete the case. Klaus documented their conversation in a memorandum:

> He [Raymond] had expressed to Davis his own personal opinion, he said, that we should not continue bringing cases to the International Court of Justice since we obtained no satisfaction in Court. We might, of course, he said, exchange diplomatic notes to a given point, but he questioned the advisability of going beyond that. He wished Davis to consider the problem further . . .
>
> I pointed out to Colonel Raymond—the program for going to the International Court of Justice—that we would not merely engage in diplomatic correspondence but would prepare a case, ready for submission, so that if we were called on, we could prove what we asserted without further delay. A mere exchange of notes was not what we had in mind. The idea of going to the ICJ itself was to obtain a historical record of both our assertions and of the Soviet refusal to submit to the Court.

The following day, Klaus sent Colonel Raymond the requested memorandum providing background on the shootdown incident and the project's current status. He concluded the report with a personal assessment:

> It was my conclusion that while we have seven witnesses who could testify that the Soviet story was false as to the cause of the crash and the falsity could be shown as willful (the witnesses saw ground soldiers drive to the scene of the crash), the existence of survivors was a matter for further investigation . . . The tape recording, while dramatic, was of less importance but had to be sustained now that the credibility of the President of the United States was placed in question by Khrushchev.
>
> Khrushchev had in substance told the president that we had made up the facts. We were, therefore, in a position where we had to go ahead, particularly since the facts were on our side. However, the Intelligence people were afraid that the source of intelligence information, like the tape recording, would be made available. I took the position that the tape recording was unnecessarily emphasized since, with witnesses, we

might be able to prove exactly what we thought the tape recording showed.

Furthermore, we might even have evidence of survivors. We could not disregard rumors that we constantly heard about three survivors, even though they were not in the form of admissible evidence nor were the survivors identified by name. We nevertheless might have witnesses from Armenia in the near future who might be able even then to show that there were survivors, as well as the nature of the shooting, and Congress or public opinion might criticize us for not going into a deeper investigation than merely the exchange of notes.

This [verification of the recording] could presumably be now established, in order merely to show that we were not foregoing the original diplomatic assertion by having available as a basis for any further legal assertions the affidavit of any person who took the original recording. This might involve a few persons, but it would not be necessary, in my view, to disclose their precise base, although it is now universally clear that the base was somewhere in a limited radius from the Soviet-Armenian frontier. Nor would it be necessary to disclose more, in any pleading stage, than the conclusions that we were, and must be, prepared to prove.

According to Klaus, the National Security Council and OCB (Operations Coordinating Board) had decided to bring the cases—the C-130 and RB-47 cases—to the ICJ; this was established policy. Klaus found some support for his plan to continue with the C-130 investigation in Colonel Lee Smith, with whom he discussed the case on September 27, 1960:

He [Smith] said he had handled the C-130 case only because he wished to keep the investigation out of certain channels. I assumed he meant that he wanted the investigation to keep out of electronics problems, although I was not sure . . . He said he stayed on the C-130 case merely because he liked me. He was prepared to submit a letter, addressed to the State Department, asking us to fish or cut bait. I said he knew this was not our decision but that of another agency to which he had access. He said he would consider what he could do. He knew that he and I could get along and that we saw eye to eye, but there were some people in the State Department that he had difficulty with . . .

Bureaucracy was clearly keeping the investigations from moving forward. By then Klaus had begun to develop a case file on the Soviet July 1, 1960, shootdown of the RB-47 in the Barents Sea and had requested a point of contact within the Air Force for operational support on the RB-47 case. He discussed the support issue with Colonel Smith on October 3. Smith told him it looked as though Klaus "would get nobody to work with because of the same security problem that arose in the C-130, namely, an unwillingness on the part of the CIA to permit access to what they had classified and did not wish to reopen." (The Air Force also had a recording of communications between a Soviet ground controller and the MiG pilot who shot down the RB-47.) Klaus documented ways that Colonel Smith had discussed to work around the problem:

He said he had talked to the Director of Policy for the Air Force, Colonel A. Williams, who is the boss of both Colonel Tuttle and Colonel Smith. He is the man who is most in control in the Air Force on the B-47 case. He was told that the State Department should write a letter to the Defense Department and that the document would undoubtedly come back to Colonel Tuttle, who had been trying to evade responsibility. He said he had been told that he, Smith, would not be named and reiterated the C-130 offer. He said I could take it as official, since he had it from the chief of staff, that the Air Force was prepared to supply complete logistic support for the fuller inquiry in Turkey.

In the course of the earlier conversation he mentioned a Colonel Rawlings of the International Affairs Section, largely with reference to the C-130 case. The drive in the Air Force, he suggested, was to drop the case because we did not prosecute. However, he said, he understood my difficulty. I told him I had heard the opposite from Colonel Ball.

It seemed that everyone was pointing fingers; no one was completing any actions to further the investigations of the shootdown and its aftermath. By January 1961 the case of the C-130 had taken a back seat to the homecoming of Captains Olmstead and McKone, the RB-47 crew members who had been imprisoned in Moscow for the previous seven months. Klaus was then working both the C-130 and RB-47 cases. On March 29, 1961, he discussed the cases with McAfee in a State Department hallway:

> . . . SOV [Soviet Affairs Section] wished to be let out of the channel of direction in the case. The project which I outlined was approved, he said, subject to clearance with the agency which he was trying to get. He said that SOV had expressed doubt that the eleven men were picked up alive and indicated that perhaps others had expressed doubt about what he said was my proposition. I said we simply had not checked that fact out and until it was checked out we were not in a position to say whether they were taken alive or whether any of them were alive . . .
>
> McAfee said he had also checked with the Air Force and found what I said was true—the Air Force would give full logistic support . . . I should therefore be patient, and he would have an answer for me shortly.

Klaus waited a month, and McAfee still had not followed up with him; he called McAfee on April 28:

> He said there was some delay in the agency. The desk officer for Turkey was away and was expected back soon. He said he had not only, in the meantime, arranged to bypass the Soviet desk, but also the Turkish desk, in the Department. Some opinion had been expressed, he said, that we might not get the cooperation that I expected because Turkey had shown signs of bending in the winds. I said I was aware of what he was talking about.[140] . . He said that he would keep after this and let me know.

The spring of '61 came and went with no meaningful action taken toward developing further eyewitness accounts of an incident that had, by then, occurred two and a half years earlier. Foot-dragging, incompetence, and bureaucracy had won out; a memorandum for record dated August 1, 1961, stated that Col. Foster L. Smith, the Air Force officer who was monitoring the C-130 case, had been reassigned and his replacement had "tentatively approved the proposed actions on 24 July 1961."

With the third anniversary of the shootdown approaching, the Air Force had to make a decision on the status of the thirteen missing crew members. Samuel Klaus had been broadsided; the memorandum for record announced that investigations into the shootdown and status of the missing crew members were being discontinued:

> The Department of State was active in collecting data with regard to the loss of the aircraft and it was anticipated that they would present through the International Court of Justice a claim against the USSR for damages. Telephone conversation between Mr. Obertone, this office, and Mr. Robert Klaus [actually Samuel Klaus], the individual in the State Department handling this case, indicates that evidence is insufficient to present a claim against the USSR and, in all probability, no further information can be developed.
>
> Believe this action necessary to comply with intent of Missing Persons Act and to record the State Department's official position regarding their attitude with respect to active investigation and possibility of getting further information on the status of the personnel involved.

The memorandum for record was signed by Lt. Colonel James G. Scurlock from the Air Force Casualty Branch. For those wanting to close out the C-130 case, three years of stonewalling had paid off; there would be no further investigations. On August 9, Colonel Scurlock circulated within Air Force Headquarters for coordination and approval a letter addressed to the Secretary of State regarding the status of C-130 60528's thirteen missing airmen:

> 1. Thirteen Air Force personnel aboard the C-130 transport aircraft shot down over Soviet Armenia on 2 September 1958, are still carried in an official missing status. On 3 September 1959, at the time of the mandatory review pursuant to the Missing Persons Act, a determination was made to continue these persons in the missing status. This action was taken primarily to provide time for the State Department and Intelligence agencies of the United States to fully explore and exhaust all available

sources which might provide definite details concerning the fate or where-abouts of these crew members.

2. No information has been received in the Department of the Air Force in the almost three year period since this incident occurred which would substantiate that any of the missing personnel survived the crash and are still alive. It therefore appears that all available information in this case should be currently reviewed and, if warranted, the missing status terminated under the provisions of the Act.

3. Since the loss of this aircraft created an international incident, the State Department should be given the opportunity to express their attitude on our contemplated action. Also, the State Department may have additional information which should be considered in the review of the status.

RECOMMENDATION

4. That the attached letter to the Secretary of State be signed.

The letter, dated August 21, 1961, and addressed to Secretary of State Dean Rusk, said in part:

The Department of the Air Force proposes to review all available information concerning these Air Force crew members. Should the facts and circumstances warrant such action, we propose to change their status from missing to dead . . .

In view of the international implications of this case, request whether your Department has any objection to this action. If you concur with our proposed action, further request that the State Department files concerning this incident be made available to representatives of the Air Force Casualty Branch so that the information may be considered in the review and determination of these persons' status.

An Air Force Casualty Branch review team showed up at Klaus's office on September 25, 1961, to review Klaus's C-130 case files:

Pursuant to arrangement made last week, Colonel Scurlock and Mr. Obertone of the Casualty Branch of the Air Force arrived this morning. We talked for about an hour and a half on the various aspects of the case. I stressed the fact that I was not satisfied on the evidence as to the eleven men. I said that if the Air Force wished, for its own purposes, to make a finding of death, that was its own business.

Obertone and Scurlock, however, said that the matter was not that simple in their views; they wished to see the evidence I had before they made a finding. Obertone said that he and Colonel Scurlock's predecessor, Colonel Heard, had seen my files before, that is, the testimony of the Turkish witnesses, and he now wished to re-read them. He was not interested in the Intelligence information nor in the other interrogations which I had conducted . . .

Obertone stressed Soviet propaganda purposes as bearing on this and the notion that the Soviets would never let the men stay alive or deliver them to us in view of the propaganda position the Soviets have taken. He also referred to Khrushchev's statements to Eisenhower on this subject. I said to him that I assumed those statements were general and possibly false, particularly since Khrushchev and others continued to assert that the airplane had merely been found on the ground, and it had not been shot down . . .

I said to them that the changes in the Turkish government might affect our ability to get additional testimony one way or the other. I pointed out that Colonel Smith and I did not necessarily adopt Berman's conclusions [that it would not have been possible for the recon crew members to have parachuted from the plane before it crashed], and that perhaps the Casualty Branch might have more influence in the reopening of the investigation than the Intelligence people had.

I said I could not disregard the hearsay statements even though some of them were obviously unreliable. The possibility that there were parachutes was indicated by at least one witness, and the matter should not be dropped if we wished to ascertain the truth. I certainly could not concur that I had proof that the men were all killed. I indicated that I had suggested that it would be possible to get the Soviets committed to an answer on whether they had held anybody a spy, or otherwise detained, who looked like the missing men, in this area, or who purported to be Americans and whom the Soviets had deliberately disassociated from the aircraft. I noted also that the Soviets had never returned to us ECM operators.

Klaus had also interviewed several Armenian-Americans who had picked up rumors about the crash during visits to Armenia. He was correct in his assessment that the Soviet government had not returned any intelligence specialists—airborne intercept operators—from reconnaissance missions that Soviet air defense forces had shot down. The only returned crew members had been Francis Gary Powers, U-2 pilot shot down on May 1, 1960, and Captains Freeman B. Olmstead and John R. McKone, copilot and navigator aboard the RB-47 shot down on July 1, 1960. Later, on November 2, 1961, Klaus documented a discussion with Mr. Owen, another State Department officer who had reviewed the C-130 case with Colonel Scurlock and Mr. Obertone:

He said they had talked with him about half an hour before coming to see me. He said to them that he understood that their interest was confined to performing their duty under the statute of missing persons, whereas we were concerned with another subject. I told Owen that they had agreed with me to keep the matter quiet in order to avoid adverse publicity or adverse treatment by the Soviets of any survivors. If the matter got out, the press would be after us. He said that if the press came here he would send the press to the Air Force. I reiterated to him that I did not feel that we had got sufficient evidence to justify the starting of a claim since we had only a few Turkish witnesses out of several thousand who witnessed the incident from the Turkish side and the great many who witnessed it from the Armenian side.

Samuel Klaus was a lawyer to the bone, and he was unwilling to accept a determination of death for the eleven missing C-130 crew members without convincing proof of death. However, he was one voice in the bureaucratic morass that we call the United States government.

Letters of Sympathy

During 1959, 1960, and 1961, next of kin received letters of sympathy from various government officials—from President Eisenhower down—usually in response to an event of interest or as a reply to a personal letter. The president sent Theresa Durkin a personal letter in October 1959.

The White House
Washington
October 29, 1959
Dear Mrs. Durkin:

As you know, several times during the past year I have taken up with the Soviet government the case of the C-130 Air Force transport plane shot down over Soviet Armenia on September 2, 1958. In each instance, the answers have revealed no new facts.

After meeting Mr. Khrushchev in Washington, I again reminded him of the grief and the anxieties of the families of those still missing from this plane, and of the continuing hope held by the families that some indication of the fate of these men would yet be uncovered. I requested him, as Vice President Nixon had done in an earlier message, to ask the appropriate Soviet authorities to look again into this question with a view to providing further information that I could furnish to you.

To my deep regret, Mr. Khrushchev's reply has failed once again to provide any new information. This means that the possibilities of obtaining any information from the Soviet government now appear meager indeed. In spite of this, I assure you that the Government of the United States will continue to do everything that can be done to determine the fate of these missing men.

I know that there is no consolation that I can offer you in your sorrow, but I want to express to you on behalf of the American people my heartfelt sympathy.

Sincerely

The letter carried no signature block, but when you are the president, a signature only is apropos. The letter was signed *"Dwight D. Eisenhower."*

The following year, Mrs. Durkin wrote a personal letter to Khrushchev, for which she received a response from Mikhail A. Menshikov, Soviet ambassador to the United States:

> Dear Madam,
> This is to acknowledge receipt of your letter and to advise you that Nikita S. Khrushchev, Chairman of the USSR Council of Ministers, has been informed about your request. Upon his instructions, your letter has been forwarded to the appropriate Soviet authorities for their consideration.

Unfortunately, Mrs. Durkin received no further amplification from the Soviets.

Thirteen Missing Declared Dead in November 1961

The next letdown for the families would involve a change in the status of the thirteen crew members unaccounted for: based on available "evidence" (or lack thereof to the contrary). At the third annual review conducted in November 1961, the review board recommended that the thirteen missing men be declared dead. The board's report, classified secret and dated November 9, 1961, provides the Air Force rationale for its decision:

> 1. a. Pursuant to the provisions of the "Missing Persons Act," reconsideration has been given to the facts and circumstances surrounding the disappearance of the Air Force personnel listed below, who were initially reported missing aboard a C-130 transport aircraft on 2 September 1958 . . .

> Captain Paul E. Duncan
> Master Sergeant George P. Petrochilos
> Technical Sergeant Arthur L. Mello
> Staff Sergeant Laroy Price
> Airman First Class Robert J. Oshinskie

Airman Second Class Archie T. Bourg Jr.
Airman Second Class James E. Ferguson Jr.
Airman Second Class Joel H. Fields
Airman Second Class Harold T. Kamps
Airman Second Class Gerald C. Maggiacomo
Airman Second Class Clement O. Mankins
Airman Second Class Gerald H. Medeiros
Airman Second Class Robert H. Moore

b. *Following the mandatory full review of the status of the above named personnel pursuant to Section 5 of the Act, they were continued in the missing status on 3 September 1959, the expiration of the initial 12 month period of absence . . .*

2. a. More detailed information from the seven Turkish eyewitnesses to the Soviet fighter attack on the C-130, after its inadvertent border-crossing, follows: The C-130 crossed the border into Soviet territory in the vicinity of Kinegi, Turkey. Within seconds after the crossing was made, three Soviet jet aircraft attacked the transport. Two jets maneuvered on either side of the transport while the third jet took a position above the transport. The third jet began a diving run on the C-130 and shot or dropped missiles, which may have been bombs or rockets since the report sounded like cannon-fire. The first missed the C-130, but the second scored a direct hit, apparently in the forward part of the fuselage. The C-130 continued on a straight course, caught fire, wavered and then began a nose-down descent wavering from side to side. The witnesses claim that the C-130 crashed and burned for hours at a location given at various points ranging from 500 meters to 2½ kilometers inside Soviet Armenia. They all indicate that they did not actually see the crash since it occurred beyond a distant hill. The aircraft, at the time it was attacked, was at a relatively high altitude (approximately 20,000 feet) as the multiple engines of the C-130 and the color of its tail section (red) were apparently distinguishable only by the use of binoculars. The witnesses who were using these binoculars state they did not observe anyone emerge from the C-130 during the engagement, nor did any see a parachute billow out in the sky. One witness reported seeing three white things that he thought were parachutes, but later his companion, using binoculars, informed him that what he saw were the fighter aircraft. (Parachutes available to the personnel aboard the C-130 were made up of alternating orange and white colored panels.) All the witnesses are in agreement that they did not observe the C-130 break-up or lose its fuselage or tail section.

b. When the six remains from the C-130 were returned, the Soviet authorities provided a document receipt that appears to offer an indication of the actual area in which the transport crashed. The document reveals that the Soviet commission officiating at the ceremony included a medical expert and the Chairman and Deputy Chairman of the Talin region Executive Committee Worker's Deputies. Talin [Leninakan] is a city approximately 18 miles from the Turkish border and 55 kilometers northwest of Yerevan. Considering the time element, the cruising speed of the C-130 and its apparent straight line flight after crossing the border, the foregoing appears to justify the placing of the actual crash area in the vicinity of Talin and not as close to the border as the Turkish witnesses indicate. The place of crash is further substantiated by the information received from the United States registered nurse. Her source of information placed the crash in the vicinity of Talia (40°20'N 43°51'E), the identical coordinates for the city of Talin . . .

c. Examination of the six remains reveals that the cause of death in each case could not be determined. However, the multiple extreme injuries, fragmentation of remains, and the carbon monoxide content of lung tissues are consistent with injuries experienced in aircraft accidents involving high speed impact preceded by fire. It is a valid determination that any person in the aircraft at the time of the crash could not have survived.

d. Radio conversation of the fighter pilots who participated in the attack on the C-130 were monitored. A translation of the transcript of these conversations from the time of the attack to the time the C-130 went out of control follows: "201, I am attacking the target . . . Open fire . . . The target has lost control, it is going down." The time consumed for these conversations was 130 seconds, a little over two minutes.

e. The State Department has made available for this review all its information pertinent to the status of this crew through the office of the Special Assistant to the Department's Legal Advisor. In reply to a Department of the Air Force query regarding our intention of reviewing this case pursuant to the provision of the Missing Persons Act, the State Department stated that they perceive no objection to a determination of the missing status of these persons.

f. The Soviet magazine Ogonyok contained an article in its 15 January 1961 issue that indicated that the eleven personnel parachuted before the pursuit was undertaken and were caught in the outskirts of Yerevan. In reply to our State Department's request for clarification, the Soviet government replied: (1) They had previously furnished all information possessed and there was nothing new to add, and (2) the Soviet government was not responsible for the incorrect presentation of facts concerning the C-130 by the author of the magazine article.

g. Nikita Khrushchev, Deputy Premier Anastas I. Mikoyan and other Soviet government officials have consistently and emphatically denied that they have any knowledge of any other members of the C-130 not returned as remains. The official Soviet response is to deny the interception of the USAF C-130 transport aircraft or shooting it down.

3. The following are summarizations of international incidents within the past ten years that involved Air Force personnel and the USSR or its satellite countries: [Eight air incidents from 1951 to 1960 listed in which known survivors were returned; missing status for MIAs was terminated by a presumptive finding of death; and to date no positive intelligence received that any missing crew members survived and were, or are still, being held alive by the Soviet communists.]

4. A similar pertinent international incident occurred on 1 May 1960 when a United States U-2 aircraft, used by NASA as a photo-reconnaissance plane, was downed in Soviet territory in the vicinity of Sverdlovsk, 900 miles east of Moscow. The pilot was Francis Gary Powers. The USSR propagandized the incident as espionage and aggression of the Soviet airspace. Also, they publicized that the pilot would be tried under Soviet laws. Powers's trial for espionage and aggressive action against the USSR was dramatically publicized. It terminated in his being judged guilty and receiving a ten-year sentence.

5. The Air Force assistant chief of staff, Intelligence and chief of Plans have no additional information pertinent to a determination of the status of the subject personnel.

DISCUSSION

6. Consideration of the information available to the Department of the Air Force and factors involved appear to lead to no other logical conclusion than that the subject personnel crashed with the C-130. This conclusion is supported by the following:

a. No evidence had been received to substantiate that parachutes were used, despite the fact that their color would have made them readily visible.

b. There was no great amount of debris seen either by the Turkish eyewitnesses or by the attacking pilots. This eliminates the possibility of explosive decompression blowing the personnel out of the C-130 and their exit being camouflaged by flying debris.

c. The C-130 was under attack for only a little over two minutes before it went out of control. It is questionable whether personnel were wearing oxygen masks and their parachutes. The surprise of the attack and the short time that elapsed before the C-130 went into an uncontrolled descent was not conducive to their abandonment of the aircraft.

d. Had any person parachuted from the C-130 between the time of initial attack and the time it went out of control, it probably would have been commented on by the attacking pilots as the radio monitoring of their conversations indicates they were keeping the C-130 in view and were commenting on all minute happenings to the target aircraft.

e. The forces present in the uncontrolled descent, such as indicated in this case, appear to preclude the possibility that any personnel left the C-130 during its partially unwitnessed uncontrolled descent.

f. An evaluation of incidents similar to this one in the past ten years, particularly those immediately preceding and following, appear to justify a conclusion that it was of Soviet design to create incidents of overflights for propaganda purposes. It would be advantageous, as later proved to be the case with the U-2 and the RB-47 aircraft, for the Russians to exploit the incident throughout the world by putting on trial living participants of the incident. Therefore, it appears that no personnel of the C-130 survived since it is logical to assume, considering the time and following events, that any survivor would have also been exploited in the same manner as were the surviving personnel of the U-2 and the RB-47.

g. Over the past ten years there have been other Air Force incidents similar to this one and beliefs that the Soviets may have held the personnel. However, there has been no positive intelligence from any source in the past ten years to establish that any of the persons involved survived and were, or are now, alive.

h. The lapse of more than 38 months without receipt of any positive intelligence to establish that any personnel of the C-130 survived the incident lends credence to the preceding individual conclusions.

7. The conditions of the six remains establishes beyond a doubt that no one in the aircraft could have survived the impact of the crash. Since it is established beyond a reasonable doubt that no personnel abandoned the C-130 from the time of attack to the time of its crash, it can only be concluded that they died in the crash of the C-130. The fact that only six remains were returned appears to be the main reason for doubt that these men died in the crash of the C-130. The following are two plausible reasons for their non-return by the Soviets:

a. The Soviets have refused to admit to the world that they shot down the C-130 aircraft. Therefore, they could not allow the return of remains of personnel from the fuselage if they contained fragments of metal from the missile that would provide irrefutable evidence of the act.

b. In the crash of any aircraft in a steep angle dive, parts of the remains of its crew members in the forward portion of the aircraft are found in or adjacent to the impact crater. In the instant case, it may be noted that the identified remains (recovered from beneath the wreckage) were members of the flight crew with positions in the forward part of the aircraft. Further, experience reveals that personnel in other portions of the aircraft are thrown out and would be in the outer crash and aircraft disintegration area. These remains normally would be in small fragments. The Soviets could have overlooked these fragmentations, if they were very small, or they may have preferred not to bother with the recovery of such fragmentary remains.

8. Based upon the information set forth herein, it can only be logically concluded that the personnel under consideration died 2 September 1958 as the result of the crash of the C-130 aircraft in Soviet Armenia, approximately 55 kilometers northwest of Yerevan.

Based on the materials discussed above, the review board recommended that the Air Force accept the foregoing information "as an official report of death," resulting in a "Report of Casualty" being issued stating that "the personnel died (non-battle) on September 2, 1958 as the result of an aircraft accident in Soviet Armenia, approximately 55 kilometers northwest of Yerevan." The recommendation continued, "Death occurred while in pay and duty status, and while a crew member was receiving incentive pay . . . Evidence of death will be considered to have been received on the date of approval of this review." The assistant chief of staff, Air Force Personnel, approved the recommendation on November 16, 1961.

With the presumptive finding of death on November 16, the Air Force washed its hands of the shootdown of C-130 60528 and of accountability for its missing crew members. Shortly thereafter the Air Force notified the next of kin of each of the thirteen missing men by mail, sending each a Report of Casualty (DD Form 1300). In addition to identification data (name, date of birth, date entered Air Force, etc.), the casualty report listed—falsely in eleven of the seventeen cases—military unit of assignment (7406th Support Squadron) and casualty status (nonbattle death in military aircraft accident in Armenia), and contained a "Remarks Section" that summarized the actions taken and what the actions meant:

REMARKS—Pursuant to the authority contained in the Missing Persons Act, Title 50, U.S. Code, app. 1001-1015, this individual is held to have been in status of missing for period commencing 2 September 1958, and until such absence was terminated on 16 November 1961, the date on which evidence received in the Department of the Air Force was considered sufficient to conclusively establish the death pursuant to Section 9 of the Act.

Note: This form may be used to facilitate the cashing of bonds, the

*payment of commercial insurance, or in the settlement of any other claim
in which proof of death is required.*

Because the Air Force letter justifying the finding was classified secret, the basis for the declaration of presumptive death was not shared
with families. Once more, the families felt abandoned.

Theresa Durkin learned that her brother had been declared dead in a
letter from General Curtis E. LeMay:

DEPARTMENT OF THE AIR FORCE
Office of the Chief of Staff
United States Air Force
Washington, D.C.
November 22, 1961

My Dear Mrs. Durkin:

*We of the Air Force share your sorrow in the untimely death of your
brother, Master Sergeant George P. Petrochilos.*

*This loss, I know, is especially hard to bear after the long period of
uncertainty concerning your loved one's fate. Yet it is my hope that as
time lessens the burden of your grief, you will find comfort in the knowledge that your brother's courage and dauntless spirit inspired all who
knew him.*

*My heartfelt sympathy is extended to you and the other members of the
family in your sorrow.*

Sincerely,
Curtis E. LeMay
Chief of Staff

Thus, the Air Force officially closed out the shootdown incident in
November 1961. Four decades later, family members are still seeking
closure.

TEN

—

FACTORS CONTRIBUTING TO 60528'S SHOOTDOWN

At nineteen years old, Clement Oscar Mankins was the youngest of the seventeen men who perished aboard C-130 60528 in September 1958. Four decades later his ninety-year-old father still had two questions that he "would like cleared up":

> *Why did our plane intrude into Soviet airspace? Didn't they know that they would get shot down? Someone in charge of the flight screwed up somewhere.*

The elder Mr. Mankins raises valid questions that the U.S. Air Force has never satisfactorily answered. The crew was well aware that the Soviet air force would shoot down the aircraft if they overflew Soviet territory. The intrusion was inadvertent, caused by a series of unrelated but contributing factors. The given circumstances—extreme Cold War tensions, illegally implemented Soviet radio navigation beacons, a "kick the tires and fly" mentality, and lack of full preparation for the transition to the new C-130A-II aircraft—all added up to an accident waiting to happen.

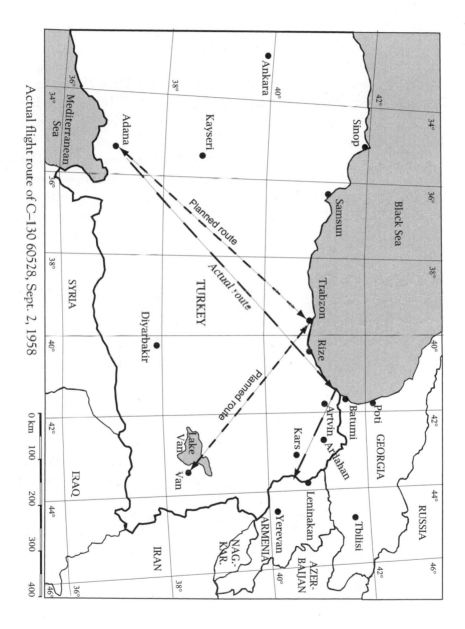

Actual flight route of C-130 60528, Sept. 2, 1958

Cold War Tensions

By 1958 the ideological differences between the Soviet Union and the United States were such that the two nations essentially disagreed on every possible topic. The closed society created by the Iron Curtain ringing the Soviet Union and its satellite countries forced the West to resort to airborne reconnaissance, legal and illegal, to "see" behind the Iron Curtain, and the Soviets used violent methods to counter Western recon missions along its borders.

During the late 1940s and early 1950s the United States and Great Britain conducted a number of overflights of Soviet territory—more or less with impunity—all the while infuriating the Soviet leadership. The Soviet Communist Party Central Committee had a zero tolerance policy; if a foreign aircraft violated Soviet airspace and refused to comply with international signals to land (wing waggling, shots across the bow, etc.), it was to be shot down without further question. Soviet air defense generals and subordinates were purged if their forces did not stop reconnaissance aircraft violating Soviet airspace.

It didn't matter to the Soviets whether an intruding aircraft was unarmed or even a commercial aircraft; it had to be stopped. On the opposing side, early Cold War American recon aircraft had, for the most part, begun life as bombers, and many retained a machine gun as defensive armament. The Soviet air defense forces had no way of knowing whether a U.S. Air Force RB-29 was carrying atomic bombs or cameras.

Attacks on American reconnaissance aircraft along Soviet borders (all over water, except the C-130 shootdown over Armenia) resulted in charges and countercharges. With U.S. authorities claiming that Soviet attacks took place over international waters, the Soviets counterclaimed in each case that the attack occurred in their airspace. In the RB-47 shootdown over the Barents Sea in 1960, the U.S. presented tracking charts derived at least in part from Soviet air defense tracking data before a United Nations Security Council meeting as proof that the RB-47 never violated Soviet airspace. The Soviets offered no refuting evidence before the council.

In many incidents, the Soviet interceptor pilot claimed to have fired warning shots—the international "follow me" signal—and only after the

American aircraft attempted to escape did the fighter pilot attack. Captain Polyakov, who shot down the RB-47 in 1960, testified as a witness against RB-47 crewmen McKone and Olmstead during their pretrial investigations in Moscow that he waggled his wings alongside their RB-47, signaling them to "follow me." McKone and Olmstead claimed to have not seen Polyakov's follow-me signal, but would have considered it illegal anyway: (1) the follow-me signal that Polyakov claimed to use was the incorrect one, and (2) the recognized follow-me signal has no authority in international airspace. Claims regarding "follow me" instructions—warning shots or otherwise—remain unsubstantiated. (Some former Soviet MiG pilots have stated that the interceptor aircraft they flew were armed with live ammunition only, no tracer rounds that could be used for warning shots.) Soviet pilots claimed they returned fire after being fired on, and American recon crews likewise claimed they were fired on without provocation. Given the acrimony between the Soviet and American military, if a MiG pilot did intend the rounds he fired to be warning shots, it is quite feasible that a gunner on a reconnaissance bomber might have misinterpreted intent and returned fire.

Tensions built up—the "pucker" factor experienced by every recon crew member—each time a Soviet fighter pilot intercepted a recon crew, whether shots were exchanged or not.

Finally, on April 8, 1950, Soviet fighters shot down a U.S. Navy PB4Y-2 Privateer recon aircraft operating over the Baltic Sea. Tensions continued to build between the Soviet Union and the United States as the frequency of U.S. recon missions increased and Soviet air defense capabilities improved. Within the next five years, the Soviets shot down five additional American recon aircraft. The Soviet government claimed the recon aircraft were violating its airspace, while the U.S. government countered that its aircraft were attacked over international airspace—all the downed aircraft prior to the downing of 60528 crashed at sea, complicating evidence as to whether an intrusion into denied airspace had occurred.

The shootdown of C-130 60528 on September 2, 1958, further complicated Soviet-American relations and increased international tensions. The shootdown occurred over land in a sensitive border area of Soviet Armenia, barely two months after Soviet fighters had shot down another

U.S. Air Force aircraft (a C-118) in the same general area. Adding to the tensions was a Soviet protest that a U.S. reconnaissance aircraft had been chased from Soviet airspace over the Caspian Sea weeks earlier, in August.

Unlike most earlier shootdowns where the Soviet government readily admitted—often bragged—that its fighters had shot down an intruder, the Soviet party line was that the C-130 "fell" on its own in Armenia after intentionally penetrating deeply into Soviet airspace. In a manner that only increased distrust, Soviet leaders denied emphatically that their fighters had intercepted and attacked the unarmed transport.

Soviet-American diplomacy reached a new low—a virtual impasse—over the C-130 incident, and release of the tape recording of fighter pilot shootdown communications cast doubt on the truth of Soviet statements in the world arena. By that time American citizens, politicians, and journalists were urging the U.S. government to break diplomatic relations with the Soviet Union. In an editorial in the February 13, 1959, issue of *U.S. News & World Report*, editor David Lawrence echoed the feelings of many Americans:

> The time has come for the United States to take the lead in cutting off diplomatic relations with the barbaric dynasty that rules in Moscow.
> The time has come for the United States to urge all its allies to do likewise and to embargo all trade with the Soviet empire.
> There is no need to go to war—ostracism is a salutary alternative . . .
> . . . America has been studiously patient. The facts about the tape recording were available to the Soviet government as far back as last November. The United States tried for months, quietly and without publicity or the display of public emotion, to get the Soviet government to cooperate at least in establishing the facts—the responsibility for the error of the unarmed transport could come later.
> Most insulting of all, however, was the attitude of Ambassador Menshikov in his meeting with Deputy Under Secretary of State Robert Murphy on November 13 last.
> Mr. Murphy said that it was Ambassador Menshikov's responsibility, as Soviet ambassador to the United States, to listen to the representations

that were being made to him . . . The Soviet ambassador nonetheless refused to listen to the tape recording.

Why should the United States continue to deal with any ambassador who shows such discourtesy to the government to which he is accredited? Why should we keep an American ambassador in Moscow who is refused information about the cold-blooded murder of 17 American citizens?

Millions of Americans would answer: Send Menshikov home—recall our ambassador!

An American attempt to explain how the C-130 crew made a navigational error by inadvertently locking onto and following the beam of a Soviet radio beacon into Armenian airspace created yet another phase of rhetorical jousting. Soviet Foreign Minister Gromyko viewed this admission of error as an attempt by "the American side to use various fabrications to draw us into a new discussion of this issue in order to rid themselves of the guilt for the American aircraft that violated the border of the USSR and also to lay the blame on the Soviet side."

Soviet Deception Beacons

The simplest way to navigate, as long as the ground signals are functioning properly, is to "home in" on a radio beacon, that is, to follow the sound of that beacon as you would follow the sight of a road. In the 1950s all countries used omnidirectional radio stations to facilitate air and naval navigation. Low-powered radios transmitted continuously on an internationally allocated frequency, typically repeating a station identifier in Morse code. On September 2, 1958, C-130 60528 was supposed to fly a figure-eight (orbiting) pattern between Trabzon (station identifier TZ) and Van (identifier VN). The Trabzon radio beacon transmitted on 365 KHz and the Van station on 397 KHz. In other words, an aircrew flying within reception range of Trabzon could tune a navigation receiver to 365 KHz, and if it was flying on instruments, onboard navigation equipment would home in on the Trabzon beacon signal and steer the aircraft to Trabzon. The same homing process was true for Van's beacon. An aircraft's onboard receiver would home in on a signal—any signal—being transmitted on or very close to the transmitters' frequency, 365 KHz at

Trabzon and 397 KHz at Van. If the airborne receiver detected more than one signal, it would simply lock on to the stronger signal.

The International Telecommunications Convention of 1952 defined the approach for allocating radio station identifiers and frequencies such that each station's transmitted beacon signal would not interfere with signals from other local stations, similar to the way in which commercial radio station broadcast frequencies are allocated. The Soviet Union, the United States, Turkey, and most other nations are signatories to this convention, agreeing not to operate stations in a manner that interferes with navigation in neighboring countries. But that is precisely what the Soviet Union was doing in 1958, transmitting navigation beacon signals on 365 KHz and other frequencies that, by international convention, rightfully were reserved for use by Turkish radios.

Two misleading signals, in two different locations, disregarding international law entirely: the Soviets had at some time in the past set up an internal navigation system in Georgia and Armenia that had dangerously—and illegally—usurped beacon radio frequencies allocated to Turkey by the International Civil Aviation Organization for use by Turkish beacons just across the border. The Soviet refusal to comply with ICAO standards of flight safety meant that the Soviet radio beacons constituted a clear and present danger to foreign planes flying just outside the Soviet border. If tuned to a frequency used by one of the Soviet beacons—even if a pilot or navigator believed he were tuning in the Trabzon or Van beacon—his plane's navigational radio could lock onto one of the stronger Russian beacons and head straight for the Soviet border.[141]

Believing the worst from their Soviet counterparts, many U.S. Air Force and U.S. government managers accused the Russians of willfully transmitting "decoy" signals to intentionally lure U.S. pilots operating near Soviet borders into hostile territory where Soviet fighter pilots could shoot them down. In a *New York Times* article, President Eisenhower alluded to such a hypothesis for the C-130 downing at a news conference on February 10, 1959. The news article said in part:

> . . . *On the C-130 incident, the president said he thought the Sept. 2 incident—meaning the straying of the plane—had been accidental. But he offered two reasons why American planes might wander off course.*

Occasionally, he said, there are errors in navigation, and sometimes there are storms and other weather disturbances.

"Once in a while, we believe there are false radio signals that will take a plane off course," the president said . . .

. . . In reviewing the flight of the American plane on Sept. 2, officials cited tricky radio conditions.

The flight plan called for a northeast course from Adana to Trabzon, thence southeast to Van, and a return over the same course . . .

. . . In this region, two Soviet radio beacons can be heard, one from Batumi and the other from Poti [Soviet port cities on the Black Sea]. Their frequencies are identical with those of the Turkish radio station at Trabzon.

Another strong Soviet station at Yerevan has a frequency only 20 kilohertz above that of the station at Van, Turkey.

The existence of the Soviet radio stations and the fact that they interfered with navigation—in particular, instrument flying—along the Turkish-Soviet border was no mystery to the flight crews of the 7406th Support Squadron. In fact, the 7406th forbade its aircrews to rely on radio stations for navigation in the area precisely because of the dangers of being lured off course.

In the back of his mind, Vincent Bracci, 7406th navigator from 1956 to 1959, knew as soon as he learned about the C-130 being down in Armenia that the C-130s crew had been lured into enemy airspace by what he called "false Soviet radio beacons in Armenia." In a declassified affidavit to an Air Force investigator in March 1959, he recalled a discussion he had the night before 528 was shot down with Lieutenant Villarreal, C-130 60528's lead navigator:

SECRET

. . . I had talked to the primary navigator, Lt. Villarreal, the night before they took off from Adana for their mission. I left the same morning for Rhein-Main on another airplane. I told him—which he already knew—that the radio facilities on this particular route were unreliable.

He had done the route fifty times, but just for discussion, we were sitting at dinner, and I just repeated to him because I am a little older and a little more experienced, navigation-wise.

When we passed over the radio beacon at Trabzon, in particular when we came over the station and headed south to Van—I flew that particular route about four or five days prior—my radio [compass] still pointed to 90 degrees after I passed the station, which it should not have done. It should have swung around behind me. It proved to me that somebody [some signal] was overriding the station—somewhere there was a stronger, higher-powered station on approximately the same frequency.

We do not use radio [beacons] as the primary means of navigation. In my conversation with him, I said it was unreliable, because in making the turn at Trabzon to Van, I found my compass still pointing toward the Soviet zone to be specific, and from that I concluded that the Soviets must have another radio [station] or that the Trabzon radio station was not working properly . . .

. . . I think I also told him that there was trouble at the Van station. I indicated that the bearing needle indicator was pointing toward Yerevan in Armenia . . . .

In other words, again, there was an overpowering station. So I advised him not to use that at all, but to use radar navigation—either visually or through his radar set. He said to me that he had had the same experience, that he knew that because he had flown that route more than I had.

Bracci also stated in the affidavit that he'd experienced the radio beacon interference problems on missions with Captain Duncan, senior pilot aboard 60528 when it was shot down over Armenia:

. . . Captain Duncan was my former AC, and I had flown the same route with Captain Duncan probably about a week before. On that occasion, I had trouble with it, and Captain Duncan knew about it. He called me up on the interphone and said, "Have you gone over the station?" I said, "We sure have." He said, "The needle still is pointing to zero degrees." And I said, "Yes, but I don't pay any attention to it." That was prior to reaching Van—say roughly 60 to 70 miles out I had tuned in the

[Van] station. He had tuned in to try to pick it up, and I said, "Look where that needle is pointing."

On my flight with Captain Duncan, before we approached Van, or on the way to Trabzon, the needle was not pointing toward Van, but indicating toward Yerevan. By the bearing, which I could plot from my positioning reciprocal, I knew approximately where the signal was coming from.

So of the two men aboard the C-130 that had gotten into difficulty, Captain Duncan knew about it and Villarreal knew about it. I have a faint recollection that other members of the crew were present during this discussion. Whether they overheard what we said, I cannot now say.

. . . In my opinion, the two navigators on board the C-130 that crashed were very highly qualified . . .

Vincent J. Bracci
Captain, USAF
2 March 1959

Suspecting intentional Soviet deception and believing that navigational radio beacons had a role in causing the C-130 to fly into Armenia, the U.S. Air Force initiated an investigation of radio beacon operations along the Turkish-Soviet border shortly after the shootdown.

In a secret message dated September 4, 1958, the U.S. air attaché in Turkey reported on the status of the Trabzon and Van radios. According to the attaché's report, the Trabzon radio was out of commission on September 1, but had been operating normally since nine o'clock on September 2. The radio beacons at Kars and Van had been in continuous operation throughout the period. The attaché's report also stated that the Trabzon beacon and a Soviet beacon at Poti in Soviet Georgia transmitted on the same frequency, with an estimate that the Soviet beacon was 15 to 20 watts stronger than the Trabzon beacon.

The U.S. Air Force investigated radio navigation interference along the Turkish-Armenian border as suspected "spoofing"—the surreptitious transmission of decoy radio signals to interfere with navigation. In other words, the Air Force suspected and investigated whether the Soviets had intentionally transmitted radio beacon signals from within Armenia or

Georgia specifically to lure the C-130 or other allied planes into Soviet territory.

Recently declassified segments of U.S. Air Force messages dated October 6 and 7, 1958, shed light on the investigation. Prior to the C-130 shootdown, no formal study of the Trabzon and Van radio beacons had been conducted, but the frequencies used by the two radios were "covered daily and various signals have been heard on or near those frequencies." Those navigation beacons were owned and operated by Turkish civil authorities. Although interference to the facilities had existed for some time, the Air Force communications frequency management office that conducted the investigation learned about the problem only after the shootdown, and recommended to appropriate Turkish authorities that Trabzon's radio frequency be changed. The frequency was ultimately changed.

On September 10 and 11, 1958, using a specially configured 7405th Support Squadron C-54, the 7499th Support Group[142] conducted missions over the exact route the lost C-130 had embarked on the day it was shot down—Adana, Trabzon, Van, and return. The purpose of the missions was to find out just why the C-130 crew had wandered so far off course. With a receiver tuned to 365 KHz, observers on the C-54 expected to hear the Trabzon Morse code identifier "TZ ... TZ ... TZ ..." in their earphones—with the signal growing louder and stronger as they approached Trabzon.

As their aircraft approached Trabzon from the southwest (magnetic heading 034 degrees), the two onboard observers were surprised—the radio compass gave steady bearings through Trabzon, but they did not hear the TZ station identifier. It was a clear day and they saw Trabzon below them, but their onboard compass did not show the aircraft passing the station's homing beacon. As they left Trabzon, the quivering needle on their radio compass did not swing around and point back toward Trabzon as it should have if it were homing properly on the Trabzon beacon. Instead the needle kept pointing northeast along the coast of the Black Sea. Their radio was locked on to an unmodulated, non-Morse carrier signal on 365 KHz emanating from Soviet territory northeast of Trabzon.

After they turned over Trabzon, to a heading along the Black Sea coast (075 degrees), the compass held steady at approximately the aircraft heading. Those compass indications generally passed through Batumi in Soviet Georgia. Approaching a point within sight of the border and using their sensitive direction-finding equipment, the evaluation crew determined that the unmodulated signal was coming from the vicinity of either Poti or Batumi, beckoning them toward the Soviet border. Had they been flying on instruments—following their radio compass indicator—they would have entered Soviet airspace.

On the September 11 mission the evaluation crew heard the TZ station identifier, and the radio compass indicated passage of the station only when directly over Trabzon. Otherwise the test results in the Trabzon area were essentially the same on both dates. Air Force investigators elaborated on the unmodulated signal in their October message:

> The use of an unmodulated carrier signal may possibly indicate a Soviet attempt to lure USAF aircraft. A commercial broadcast station operating on 362 KHz was plotted in the vicinity of Yerevan.

In other words, the evaluators noticed two signals that could have interfered with the C-130 crew's navigation on September 2.

The crew continued their evaluation on September 10 and 11 by flying southeast from Trabzon to Van. After turning toward Van (magnetic heading 134 degrees), with the radio still tuned to 365 KHz the compass indicator pointed generally toward Mount Ararat (about twenty-five miles southwest of Yerevan). Additional Air Force comments on the Trabzon beacon:

> The results are consistent with other reports and evidence indicating one or more strong Soviet stations in the Batumi/Poti area transmitting within two kilohertz of the Trabzon beacon frequency. The source of the signal heard on the Trabzon-Van leg cannot be definitely established. A previous report indicates that a station in the Leninakan area transmits on 363 KHz. A probability exists that the beacon at Tabriz may have played a part in affecting the radio compass.

The Royal Air Force radio facility chart for Africa and the Middle East listed a radio beacon at Tabriz, Iran (about 130 miles east-southeast of Van, Turkey) with call sign TZ, power 1,000 watts, and frequency 365 KHz.

The Air Force investigators next discussed their analysis of the Van beacon. Several observations of the Van beacon (call sign VN on 397 KHz) were made on September 10, and only two bearings were taken on that beacon on September 11. On September 10, bearings taken while heading directly toward Van indicated a good signal from the Van beacon; however, on an aircraft heading of 106 degrees—approximately 045 degrees to the left of Van—strong heading indicators were received by one observer on the same heading as the aircraft, in fact leading the plane toward Armenia. At the same time, the other observer received indications from 10 to 30 degrees to the right of the aircraft heading, in other words showing the correct Van beacon. Air Force comments regarding the Van beacon:

> *In view of the limited and inconsistent data received on the Van beacon frequency, it is not possible to draw any firm conclusions. A previous report indicates that the Van beacon may go off the air for short periods of time. Such an occurrence might account for the results observed. Frequency publications of the International Telecommunications Union contain no listing that would account for any of the above interference.*

Formal reports filed by other pilots flying the commercial air corridor through the Van area and within Iran corroborated the navigation interference around Van and in western Iran. On July 31, 1958, a pilot in the vicinity of the Rezayeh, Iran, beacon reported that he observed an overriding signal with call sign TZ when he tuned to Rezayeh's beacon (370 KHz). The pilot's onboard equipment indicated that the interfering signal was emanating from the Soviet Union.

Another pilot reported interference involving the Van beacon on September 9. While flying on a heading of 090 degrees inbound toward the Van beacon at altitude 25,000 feet, the beacon signal was clearly identified and the radio compass needle indicated straight ahead (090 degrees). Approximately seventy nautical miles west of the Van beacon—while still approaching—the needle suddenly moved to a bearing of approximately 020 degrees, but the station signal could not be heard audibly. Using the large lake west of Van visually to confirm passage of the Van station, the pilot noted that the radio compass needle did not indicate passage of the Van beacon; the compass continued to point in a northerly direction. A rough fix on the unknown station placed it roughly 150 to 200 miles due north of Van, i.e., in Soviet Armenia.

An Iranian Airways pilot on a flight from Frankfurt to Tehran via Turkey experienced similar interference with the Van beacon in June 1959. En route from Ankara to Van on an easterly heading, the pilot had his radio tuned to 397 KHz. At position 38:10N 41:06E (110 miles west of Van), his radio compass indicated a steady bearing of 061 degrees, but there was no clean identifier for Van (no Morse code identifier). Continuing eastward, at 38:28N 42:15E (about fifty miles west of Van) his compass plotted the signal on a steady bearing of 058; still no clean identifier for Van. Finally, at position 38:25N 42:45E (about thirty miles west of Van) he was receiving a steady bearing of 078 degrees and a weak identifier for Van. Reliable bearings from the Van beacon ceased eleven miles east of the beacon. Later, eighty miles east of Van, he had a strong signal at 397 KHz, and his radio compass showed a steady bearing emanating north of his current location; however, no identifier for Van was heard. The pilot stated that he flew that route frequently, had made other checks on this beacon anomaly, and strongly felt that a powerful radio station transmitting on or near 397 KHz was located north of Van in Soviet Armenia.

The final results of the two Air Force evaluation flights on September 10 and 11, 1958, were published in a U.S. Air Forces, Europe unit history in 1959. The evaluation established that the Trabzon navigational beacon and a Soviet beacon at Poti transmitted on the same frequency (365 KHz), with the Soviet beacon an estimated 15 or 20 watts stronger. Preliminary tests indicated that Soviet beacons might be exerting an effect on radio compasses of aircraft overflying the Trabzon-Van area. However, in view of limited and inconsistent data, no conclusions were drawn. To minimize problems caused by interference with low-frequency navigation beacons in eastern Turkey, the U.S. Air Force installed more effective TACAN navigation facilities at Trabzon and Diyarbakir, Turkey, in late 1958. In addition, the ban on use of radio beacons by 7406th C-130 crews for navigation along the Turkish-Armenian border was reemphasized.

Deception or Not?

A bold headline in *Reader's Digest* for June 1959 asked the question that officially remained a mystery throughout the Cold War: "Are the Russians Decoying Our Planes?" The *Digest* story by Allen Rankin was titled "One of Our Planes Is Missing—Again," and contained an appropriate subtitle: "Has cold-blooded murder been committed along the Russian-Turkish border? Consider the evidence . . ."

Rankin summarized the shootdown and addressed in detail results of the evaluation flights that attempted to determine if the Soviets used decoy beacons to lure the lost C-130 crew into a trap and certain death. According to Rankin, one U.S. Air Force pilot told him that "decoy" radio signals in the area were nothing new:

> As early as 1956, when I flew through Turkey, there was a notice, "Beware of confusing radio signals." We all knew whose signals were meant. Today every pilot who flies through that part of the world where the C-130 went astray is warned to watch his step, his dead reckoning and his radar.

Rankin defined the suspected Soviet deceptive tactics as "spoofing," adding that the mildest thing that could be said about spoofing was that it was illegal. "At best, interfering radio signals are criminally dangerous entanglements capable of tripping the most skillful pilots in bad weather . . . At worst, the Soviet kind amounts to cold-blooded murder—a calculated terrorism aimed at harassing airmen who fly free-world air routes near Soviet territory." In February 1959 an Associated Press story described how the Soviet radio beacons were violating a "Safe Air Navigation Pact":

> WASHINGTON, Feb. 7 (AP)—State Department officials say Russia has violated international principles of safe air navigation in the area of the Soviet-Turkish border.
>
> This is the area in which an unarmed U.S. Air Force transport, carrying 17 men, crashed last September 2 . . .

Signals Confused

It was traveling in an area where, officials said, pilots have long been told that confusing radio beacon broadcasts from across the Soviet border make it difficult to distinguish radio signals from Trabzon and Van.

In an effort to determine whether this could have figured in the off-course flight of the ill-fated transport over the Soviet border, a test plane on September 8 flew the same route that craft had mapped out.

Officials said this plane found there was only one kilocycle difference between the beacon signal from Trabzon and signals from Batumi or Poti, in Soviet territory . . .

Russians Agreed to System

State Department officials said the Soviet government subscribes to the principles of the International Telecommunications Union. These specify that signals must be identified, that they must have a wide spread of kilocycles between stations in the same area, and that they must not be broadcast with so much power that one set of signals interferes with another.

All three of these principles, State Department officials said, were violated in the case of the Soviet beacons in the border area. They added that the beacons in Turkish territory were operating on frequencies and other conditions in keeping with international agreements.

So, did the Soviets intentionally—and specifically—lure the C-130 into Soviet Armenia so Russian pilots could destroy the reconnaissance aircraft and crew? The facts suggest otherwise. Although there is clear evidence of the Soviets ignoring the international convention on allocation of radio beacons, there is no evidence to support deliberate "spoofing."

The Soviets were indeed transmitting signals (an unmodulated solid tone rather than a repetitive Morse identifier) on frequencies set aside by the International Telecommunications Union for use by Turkish radio navigation stations. But though illegal, these were not "decoy" signals in the normal sense of the term. They were operational Soviet air force radio stations used by Soviet pilots to navigate within Soviet territory.

Soviet paranoia probably explains in part their use of an unmodulated signal vs. a Morse identifier for their radio navigation signals. An enemy bomber cannot immediately recognize an unmodulated signal as the beacon for a specific city or air base, precisely because the signal lacks an "identifier."

Disregarding international protocols to which they were themselves a signatory, the Soviets transmitted on whatever frequencies worked best for them. If their pilots experienced interference from nearby Turkish stations, Soviet engineers probably revved up the output wattage on their transmitters—never mind that their stronger transmitters interfered with radio stations in neighboring Turkey. Civil aviation air corridors between southern Europe and southwest Asia traversed Turkey and Iran along the southern Soviet periphery, and Soviet beacons in that area routinely interfered with the navigation of Western pilots who attempted to use Turkish radio beacons.

The fact that such Soviet radio beacons had been operating in that area for years and always appeared to be on the air—that is, they were not selectively turned on only when recon missions were in the area—is further evidence that the Soviet stations were for internal use rather than for spoofing. To believe otherwise would mean that the Soviet government was intentionally trying to lure all Western aircraft flying in the area, commercial and military crews alike, into Soviet airspace in order to shoot them down. Not even its most vocal critics have accused the Soviet empire of that.

Kick-the-Tires-and-Fly Mentality

In fairness to U.S. Air Force managers involved in the activation, planning, and management of the airborne signals intelligence reconnaissance operations in Europe (worldwide for that matter), it must be said that they and their subordinates were pioneers in uncharted territory. When the first RB-50 aircraft arrived at Rhein-Main in 1956, most of the men in the 7406th and Detachment 1, 6911th had never seen a B-50 up close, and only Major Swanson in the 7406th had ever flown a

SIGINT recon mission. Detachment 1's commander and operations officer were the only men in that unit who had logged crew-member flying hours on any military aircraft. Some of the enlisted men had traveled overseas by military troopship and had never even flown as a passenger on a military aircraft.

At the same time, the 7499th and Headquarters, U.S. Air Forces, Europe (the 7406th's immediate headquarters) and Security Service management (6911th at Darmstadt, 6901st at Zweibrücken, 6900th at Frankfurt and HQs, USAFSS in San Antonio, Texas) likewise had no airborne SIGINT reconnaissance experience. Everyone was a novice and all were working to create a fledgling airborne reconnaissance program from scratch.

Given so little background, mistakes were inevitable, and some mistakes and poor decisions ended in the 60528 tragedy. Starting with a lack of realistic training objectives and flying safety standards, both the 7406th and Detachment 1 implemented airborne operations plans fraught with errors of omission and commission that affected flying safety. A "kick the tires and fly" mentality is not a far fetched description of airborne reconnaissance in those early days.

No one took the threat of being shot down seriously; shootdowns happened only to crazy electronic intelligence (ELINT) recon crews who flew irregular flight patterns and occasionally cut across a Soviet border; the 7406th and Detachment 1 missions flew on planned fixed SIGINT recon mission routes at a safe standoff distance from hostile borders. Recon aircraft flying the same mission route points (Trabzon to Van) over eastern Turkey for the previous eighteen months had acclimated Soviet air defense forces to their flight path and orbital habits and simultaneously built up crew confidence and experience.

Each RB-50, and later each C-130, was equipped with two fully independent navigator positions, the philosophy being that two navigators usually using different navigation methodologies would continuously double check each other's calculations. If their navigation results did not agree, they'd quickly resolve differences and remain on track. Thus, together with the pilot who also followed a mission's flight path closely, the two navigators would assure fail-safe navigation. In addition, the new C-130A-II aircraft were equipped with the APN-59 radar and APN-99

Doppler radar, providing the flight crew with state-of-the-art navigation technology. How could any errors slip into such a plan?

One problem area was that abort criteria were loosely defined. Prior to the shootdown, there were few defined aircraft equipment outage conditions that called for an automatic mission abort. The decision to abort rested squarely on the pilot's shoulders—the aircraft commander decided if and when to abort and had little written guidance. If a radar component failed and the AC felt that flight safety was at risk, he could abort his mission; if, on the other hand, the radar failed and he believed that other available navigation capabilities were adequate for mission safety, he could continue the mission. There was an edict forbidding flight crews to use radio stations like Trabzon and Van as primary navigation tools, but both the RB-50 and C-130A-II aircraft had a plethora of navigation aids to help the flight crew keep on track. The navigators did use the radio stations and dead reckoning to confirm other calculations. After the shootdown, the lack of an operational APN-99 radar became an automatic abort criterion for C-130A-II recon missions along communist borders.

The Detachment 1 recon crews had even fewer directives outlining how to plan for and carry out airborne reconnaissance. When the detachment was formed, the NCO in charge of operations (NCOIC) essentially ran operations with the acquiescence of the operations officer. The operations officer had more than he could handle fighting "brushfires" related to a new, evolving Air Force flying unit and filling in for his commander who was often away piloting the 6900th Security Wing's C-54 on liaison missions throughout Europe. Complicating the unit startup, there were no definitive Air Force or Security Service regulations or manuals outlining specific guidelines and procedures for conducting airborne SIGINT reconnaissance.

The Operations NCOIC traveled to Texas in December 1956 and returned aboard the first RB-50 Dream Boat SIGINT recon aircraft assigned to the 7406th, and that qualified him as the SIGINT airborne reconnaissance expert in Europe. At the time, he was the only USAFSS airman in Europe who had logged flying hours on the Dream Boat RB-50.

Airborne intercept operator training was accomplished on the fly with no written guidance, recognized standards, or qualified trainers. Fortunately, the original cadre of NCO linguists (all Russian linguists) at least had intercept operator experience at a Security Service ground intercept site. By virtue of rank, those NCOs became airborne mission supervisors, and were charged with training newly assigned linguists—most of whom had arrived in the unit after six months of basic language training but with no intercept operator training.

One NCO who arrived in Detachment 1 shortly before the C-130 shootdown explained his airborne intercept operator training as "one four-hour transition training mission during the summer of 1958." With a 7406th RB-50 flight crew conducting takeoffs and landings, and other transition training in a newly arrived C-130, the NCO managed to turn on and operate the equipment on one of the C-130's intercept positions— to twiddle a few receiver and recorder knobs for a couple of hours although he did not intercept any target signals. He was to have been an airborne mission supervisor (AMS) trainee—training under the Ops NCOIC—on his next scheduled flight, an operational mission over the Baltic Sea. When he showed up for that mission's premission briefing, the Ops NCOIC told him that due to a last minute conflict, he (the Ops NCOIC) had to scratch himself from the mission to fight a "brushfire" in Operations that day: "You're the AMS for today's mission; I just certified you as qualified."

In fairness to the Ops NCOIC, that scheduling conflict was no doubt beyond his control. He and the operations officer received less than stellar support from intermediate headquarters when support and guidance would have been most beneficial. All operator training was not as helter-skelter as the NCOs "instant certification" as an AMS, but that example illustrates typical growing pains during Detachment 1's first couple of years. Fortunately, some of the NCOs and young linguists quickly taught themselves, and many became superb linguists and airborne intercept operators.

General inexperience within Detachment 1 operations at Rhein-Main, and lack of knowledge about the Security Service mission—in particular regarding Soviet air surveillance radar tracking—may have directly impacted on 60528's inadvertent overflight of Armenia. One of the detachment's former NCOs recently said that several of the unit's more experienced Russian operators knew about and had on occasion intercepted voice traffic containing Soviet air surveillance tracking data on the route along the Turkish-Armenian border prior to the shootdown. The problem, as he put it, was that such tracking data received the lowest of mission priorities because, naively, no one in Detachment 1 operations at the time attributed any importance to the tracking. And, analysts at higher headquarters (6901st at Zweibrücken and NSA) had not tasked the unit to copy air surveillance tracking. The operators knew they could determine from the tracking the location of their mission aircraft, but why bother? If the airborne mission supervisor wanted to know the location of their aircraft, he only had to ask a navigator on interphone. To consider that their C-130 with two navigators would ever venture off course and violate Soviet airspace was unthinkable.

They saw no need for an airborne Morse intercept operator for the same reason. Recall that there was no Morse intercept operator aboard C-130 60528 when it violated Armenian airspace and was shot down. Needless to say, that attitude changed following the shootdown.

It would be unfair, however, to blame Detachment 1's naiveté on its officers and NCOs since the 6901st special processing center at Zweibrücken, the Security Service intermediate analysis center in Europe, kept the detachment pretty much in the dark regarding the USAFSS mission. The 6901st did not permit the detachment's linguists to analyze or report the traffic they were intercepting during the first couple of years of the detachment's existence—a bureaucratic battle that kept the detachment from doing its job more effectively.

After the shootdown, some contemporaries informally pointed to the lack of experience of the Detachment 1 recon crew on 60528's fateful mission. Admittedly, it was a relatively inexperienced recon crew—a weak recon crew—but the crew composition certainly met existing aircrew scheduling requirements, albeit defined requirements were minimal. The airborne mission supervisor was an outstanding NCO, a well-liked master sergeant with well-honed management skills that he had acquired during decorated service in World War II and the Korean War. He was not, however, the ideal choice for mission supervisor on that particular run. After sixteen years as a nontechnical Air Force supply specialist, he completed a basic Romanian language course in mid-1957 and joined

Detachment 1, his first Security Service assignment. Given the mission's target environment, an NCO *Russian* linguist would have been a better match as airborne mission supervisor along the Turkish-Armenian border, but there were no rules stipulating that only qualified Russian linguist NCOs would serve as the airborne mission supervisor in that area. The recon crew did include five Russian voice intercept operators, but only one, Joel Fields, had more than a year's experience as an intercept operator.

Eight of the nine airborne intercept operators were members of the detachment softball team. Since they had flown fewer missions during the recently concluded softball season than contemporaries, and had not flown along the Turkish-Armenian border during the summer, their operator skills may have been a bit rusty. In all probability, however, without using intercepted Soviet radar tracking data to ascertain their aircraft's location, no intercept crew, no matter how experienced, would have realized in time that the plane being stalked by Soviet fighters was their own C-130, miles away from its presumed course.

Some of the same comments apply to flight crew members. For example, the second navigator was flying his inaugural recon mission in the Turkish-Armenian border area. In addition, no one in the 7406th or Detachment 1 had more than a handful of flights on the newly arrived C-130A-II recon platform, and most of the C-130 flights they had logged were RB-50 to C-130 transition training flights rather than operational missions. Finally, having arrived in Turkey only the day before, the flight crew, except for the "stan/eval route checker" senior pilot, was flying its first C-130 recon mission along the Turkish-Armenian border when the shootdown occurred. Nonetheless, all aircrew members met minimum requirements as then defined. Investigators found no aircrew inadequacies; nor did they find that any regulations had been violated.

One other factor that may have contributed to the incident involves crew cohesiveness, especially with regards to the flight crews. The flight crew for a C-130A-II recon mission consisted of a pilot (aircraft commander), copilot, lead navigator, second navigator, and flight engineer. Each had to meet standard Air Force qualifications for the C-130, and had to have completed transition training in the C-130A-II (a couple of flights). In addition, the aircraft commander and lead navigator had to be certified in the mission area being flown. Flying a C-130, especially on reconnaissance routes, requires a coordinated crew effort; the members of the flight crew work better as a team if they always fly together as a crew. The 7406th did not use integrated crews prior to the shootdown, and that in itself may have contributed to costly errors on the fatal flight.

Although no chargeable infractions of Air Force regulations were cited postmortem, and no Air Force managers lost their jobs as a result of the incident, the investigation's many observations of factors which might have caused or contributed to the border crossing resulted in changes that ultimately improved flying safety for future airborne signals intelligence reconnaissance missions.

Ill-Prepared Transition to C-130

Had the 7406th Support Squadron managed to complete its first year of flying the C-130A-II reconnaissance aircraft without a serious accident, an inadvertent overflight such as happened on September 2, 1958, might never have happened. That is not to say there would not have been a serious accident, but transitioning to the new C-130A-II aircraft from RB-50s was definitely a factor—probably a major factor—in the inadvertent overflight.

The transition was challenging for both the 7406th and Detachment 1, 6911th—more so for the 7406th—and successful transition to the C-130 by the 7406th was more critical for flight safety. A Detachment 1 operator might make an error routing a voice signal to a tape recorder and end up with a blank recording; that is not a flight safety problem. By comparison, if 7406th electronics maintenance technicians misaligned the C-130's APN-59 or APN-99 radars, or if the flight crew did not understand the radar systems well enough to activate and use them properly, the crew could commit a critical in-flight error. And, whatever the reason, on September 2, 1958, navigation errors cost 60528's seventeen crew members their lives.

Were 60528's Navigation Systems Functional on September 2, 1958?

There are strong indications that a lack of understanding of the C-130's navigation system by 7406th personnel contributed to that fatal error. Major Joseph C. Wheeler, 7499th Support Group staff electronics maintenance officer, investigated the status of 60528's navigation equipment and documented his findings in 1959 in a secret (since declassified) affidavit.

He described 60528's navigation equipment as consisting of the APN-59 radar navigation set, APN-99 Doppler navigation system, ARN-6 radio compass, and the ARN-14 OMNI range navigation equipment. Using radarscopes, the APN-59 could display a pictorial radar indication of landmass over which the aircraft was flying up to a range of two hundred miles. Range marks were displayed on the scope, varying according to the scale selected for operation. The APN-59 functioned in either of two modes: one in which the top of the scope is always North, with the heading mark displayed according to the aircraft track; and the other with the heading mark at the top of the scope, and North then being dependent on the aircraft heading.

After viewing maintenance records for C-130 60528 and discussing "certain problems" relating to the aircraft's radar systems, the investigator concluded that 528's radar systems may have been inoperative or marginal on the aircraft's last flight. In addition he concluded that 7406th personnel—maintenance technicians and flight crews alike—did not fully understand the aircraft's APN-59 and APN-99 radar systems. Major Wheeler said:

> I have looked into this case from the electronics standpoint, have had conversations with maintenance personnel, and looked into maintenance records on the C-130. In view of certain problems that apparently arose before the airplane became airborne at Adana on its last trip, I would like to make the following comments. There had been trouble with the antenna tilt, and Sgt. Rigsby [electronics maintenance technician at Incirlik AB by Adana] worked all that night in Adana with the assistance of Airman Miller, changing the antenna.
>
> I believe it is important from a maintenance standpoint to note that,

according to the aircraft maintenance forms, the APN-59 on 528 was inoperative from 7 August 1958, at which time both scopes and the receiver-transmitter were removed, until 21 August 1958, when they were replaced. The aircraft was flight tested without the APN-59 on 20 August after a periodic inspection. The APN-59 was carried as out of commission on 22 August 1958, and an entry on 23 August 1958 indicates that both radarscopes were replaced again. On 27 August 1958, the APN-59 was written up after flight for failure of the antenna tilt system, and was cleared on 28 August 1958 by "ground check OK" after one hour's operation on the ground. The antenna tilt failed again on the flight to Adana on 1 September 1958, at which time the antenna was changed.

I should explain that the antenna tilt system permits the antenna to be adjusted for various attitudes of the aircraft. For example, if the aircraft is in an extreme nose high attitude, such as in a climb; if the antenna could not be tilted down, it would be pointing more at the sky than the ground, and no return would be received from the ground immediately in front of the aircraft. Conversely, if due to malfunction, the antenna tilted down in level flight, the range would be considerably decreased because the antenna would be looking immediately in front of the aircraft . . .

The receiver-transmitter in 528 was the RT-289. All RT-289s have been modified since that time to the 289-A . . . The modification fixed a problem involving instability and arcing that would cause failure of the system entirely or poor and intermittent scope presentations.

Referring to the antenna change made at Adana, Sgt. Rigsby told me that after installation, he was unable to obtain a correct heading mark position in the second type operation of the APN-59. The heading mark was approximately 20 degrees off. However, this error was said to have been explained to the crew.

It is my personal opinion that the APN-59 installed in 528 on 2 September 1958 was in marginal condition on 2 September 1958. I say this from experience that once a radar system such as the APN-59 is inoperative for a period of time and various components have been changed, it will normally require several flights to get all the bugs out. The possibility of intermittent, partial, or complete failure of the APN-59 on 2 September 1958 appears likely from the maintenance history. However, I am informed that if the APN-59 was not fully operating, it was the pilot's duty to turn around and return to base. I assume, therefore, that if there was radar trouble with 528, it was in the pilot's opinion only of intermittent character and not sufficiently bad that he could not maintain a continuous observation of his flight course.

The APN-99, a Doppler navigation system, gives drift ground speed and geographical coordinates. The APN-99 installed in the C-130 at the time of this accident had been reported as either inoperative or malfunctioning on every flight made by 528 from 3 August 1958 through 28 August 1958, including the test flight on 20 August 1958. A corrective action of "repositioned two switches" was entered in the form of 28 August, and I was told that the APN-99 operated satisfactorily on the trip down to Adana.

As regards the performance of this equipment, inquiries with maintenance and operations personnel indicated to me that operators and maintenance personnel were not thoroughly familiar with the system as of 2 September 1958. A civilian technical representative was not assigned to the organization until late September 1958.

It is important to note that the only satisfactory check of the APN-99 system must be made in the air. This situation requires that both operations and maintenance personnel be thoroughly familiar with the system for proper maintenance.

Assuming that the crew attempted to use the Doppler system, the chances of failure, which might be reflected in the deviation of the aircraft from its course, would arise out of numerous component factors in the equipment. Previous write-ups indicated both drift and ground speed as being off. If there were a failure in the Doppler equipment during flight, it would require a mechanic to work on the equipment, adjusting or substituting new components as necessary. I am not aware that 528 had anybody onboard capable of maintenance or any spare equipment. Therefore, if the Doppler equipment stopped working at any time, it probably was not workable thereafter . . . If the radar equipment was intermittent or not continuously functioning, this would not necessarily affect the Doppler system or vice versa.

There is, of course, the fundamental piece of navigation aid, the radio compass that is in common use in all aircraft. I have been informed that the crews that fly in Turkey are informed in advance of the unreliability of some of the local beacons and of the difficulty near Trabzon with interference from the Soviet Union. However, this is not an exceptional situation. Everybody that flies an aircraft has to be concerned about interference with the radio compass from many sources: either other stations that are emitting on related frequencies or interference from thunderstorms and other weather conditions.

With regards to thunderstorms, it may be useful to remember that the APN-59 is generally used to give a navigator and pilot a good view in advance of the approaching thunderstorm areas. This enables them to take a course away from the thunderstorm. Should the airplane nevertheless enter the thunderstorm, the effect would be for the cloud formations and turbulence to interfere with the picture on the radarscope. In the case of 528, if it were assumed that near or over Trabzon, thunderstorms were encountered, in my opinion, the passage of the thunderstorm would be so rapid as not to interfere with the visual observation through the radarscope of most of the terrain. The pilot therefore should not have been disturbed by any thunderstorm insofar as the radarscope is concerned. He might have other reasons for wanting to avoid the thunderstorm, such as the safety of the aircraft, but that would not affect the operation of his radarscope.

I should of course point out that where a pilot sees a series of thunderstorms or a line of them ahead of him on his path, he may deviate from his course to the extent of trying to find a way through the thunderstorm area that would permit him to go ahead on his original course without damage to the aircraft . . .

The squadron had three C-130s by 1 September 1958 that had flown a total of 314 hours according to the records of the squadron. The numbers of these aircraft were [56]0484, 0525, and 0528. Plane 484 was received by the squadron May 28, 1958, 525 on June 17, 1958, and 528 on July 30, 1958. The maintenance records for 528 indicate that the aircraft was used primarily for pilot transition training. I say this because of the period of time the APN-59 and APN-99 were carried as inoperative, or the equipment was removed from the aircraft. In this respect, I believe it is important to note that the period May through September 1958 was a transition period for maintenance personnel and aircrews of the 7406th Support Squadron on the C-130.

It is my opinion that the APN-59 and APN-99 navigation equipment onboard aircraft 528 were in marginal condition on 2 September 1958. My opinion is based on review of aircraft and shop maintenance records.

There is little doubt that 528's navigation equipment problems contributed to the inadvertent overflight of Soviet territory on September 2.

Documented APN-59 and APN-99 Problems

An extract of electronic write-ups from 60528's "Form 1A" that Major Wheeler attached to his affidavit suggests that the APN-59 and APN-99 navigation equipment never functioned properly after the 7406th accepted 528 at TEMCO's aircraft depot in Greenville, Texas. In the same manner that a person's medical records list ailments, diagnoses, and treatments, an aircraft's Form 1A provides a flight-by-flight accounting of equipment write-ups and corrective actions as long as the aircraft remains in the inventory.

Aircraft 528's Form 1A showed "No electronic write-ups" for a flight on July 30, 1958, the first flight on 528 for 7406th personnel. Coincidentally, Lt. John Simpson—528's copilot during the fatal encounter—was the pilot on that first flight, an acceptance test flight at TEMCO's Greenville facility. It is logical to assume that contractor maintenance personnel had all aircraft systems in shipshape for acceptance testing, and that factory electronics engineers accompanied the crew on the acceptance test flight, thus ensuring that the 7406th crew could set up, check out, and operate the new APN-59 and APN-99 equipment. That turned out to be the last time that 528's Form 1A indicated a clean bill of health for the aircraft's navigation system. On the very next flight—ferry flight to Germany on August 3 and 4—Lieutenant Simpson wrote up the APN-99 as inoperative, and the pilot's APN-59 radarscope was out for three hours during flight. As documented in the 528 Form 1A, this navigation equipment plagued squadron personnel to the end. Given the history of the problems, the trustworthiness of 528's APN-59 and APN-99 systems would have been, at best, questionable on September 2.

Major Wheeler's investigation uncovered two major factors in the inadvertent overflight of Soviet territory. Aircraft 528's APN-59 and

APN-99 navigation equipment was "in marginal condition on September 2, 1958," and 7406th flight crew and maintenance personnel "were not thoroughly familiar with the [C-130A-II navigation] system as of September 2, 1958."

It is interesting that no meaningful comparison exists between the failure rate of 528's APN-59 and APN-99 systems and those on the squadron's other two C-130A-IIs (60484 and 60525) at the time. If 484 and 525 were relatively problem-free, why all the problems with 528? Forms 1A for 484 and 525 are not available for review, but a table provided by Major Wheeler offers some historical failure report data. Incomplete data for June show forty-one C-130 hours flown (all transition training missions) and an undetermined number of radar failures. The data for July show four APN-59 failures with 134 C-130 hours logged (almost all transition training missions). The first operational C-130 airborne signals intelligence recon mission was flown—in the Baltic area—on July 30, 1958. The reported failure rate increased dramatically in August; thirty-three APN-59 failures reported, and 139 flight hours logged. With 7406th aircrews completing as many as twenty flights in 60528 in August, most of the squadron's C-130 flying hours during August were logged in 528. The excessive number of APN-59 failures (thirty-three) during August suggests that almost all C-130 flights in August experienced an APN-59 failure. Inadequate data makes it impossible to carry out a similar comparison of APN-99 failures on the other aircraft during the last six months of 1958.

A civilian technical representative trained in APN-59 and APN-99 electronics was assigned to the 7406th subsequent to the loss of 60528, and the number of APN-59 failures per month decreased—twenty in September, nine in October, twelve in November, and ten in December—while flying hours per month increased. It is unfortunate that the civilian tech rep was not assigned to the squadron with the arrival of the first C-130 in June 1958. With someone available who could have helped the 7406th ground and air crews better understand the new C-130 navigation systems, introduction of C-130 operations would undoubtedly have gone smoother, with reduced risk of an inadvertent overflight of denied territory.

Was 60528 Mechanically Ready on September 2, 1958?

Although the investigator, Major Wheeler, did not state directly in his affidavit that C-130 60528 should not have been flying an operational mission the day of the inadvertent overflight and shootdown, his conclusions suggest as much. Prior to that last fatal flight, the 7406th had been using 528 almost exclusively for flight crew transition training—many of the transition training missions were flown with the APN-59 and APN-99 equipment not even installed in the aircraft, meaning that the crews acquired little experience during training in setup and use of the new navigation systems. Aircraft 528 had arrived at Adana on September 1, bringing to Turkey a replacement crew. The 7406th flight schedule for September 2, 1958, called for the replaced crew to return to Germany aboard 60528, and for aircraft 60525 to be used for a local mission along the Turkish-Armenian border.

The plan went awry on September 1 when Captain Nelson Halstead's crew aborted its mission in the same area aboard 525 due to aircraft pressurization problems. After working all night on the problem, ground maintenance informed operations in early morning, September 2, that 525 would have to fly nonmission back to Rhein-Main for repairs. It was later learned that the problem with 525's pressurization was a control switch in an incorrect position, an indication of the unfamiliarity of 7406th personnel with the C-130A-II airframe. With no other aircraft available in Turkey, it was decided to use 60528 for operational missions there until another C-130 deployed from Germany to replace it.

With the decision to swap aircraft made, 7406th ground maintenance redirected all efforts to preflight 60528 for the operational mission. Except for its radar systems, preflight checks deemed 528 a hundred percent mission-ready. Radar maintenance technicians replaced a defective APN-59 antenna, but the radar still failed the preflight check in one of its two operating modes—the heading mark was 20 degrees out of alignment in one mode. The navigators, Lieutenant Villarreal and Captain Jeruss, were advised accordingly. One of the navigators told radar maintenance that the APN-59 was good enough for search, or words to that effect, and that they'd give it a thorough checkout once airborne.

Whether 528's APN-99 was operational on September 2 is suspect.

Major Wheeler says he was told that the APN-99 operated satisfactorily on the trip down to Adana. Air Force records show that 528's APN-99 had not functioned properly on any flight (as many as nineteen flights) between August 3 and 28, and 7406th ground maintenance at Incirlik (Adana) probably lacked the equipment to perform even a cursory check of the APN-99.

Lack of an operational APN-99 was not a defined abort condition. Major Wheeler's opinion that the "APN-59 and APN-99 navigation equipment onboard 528 were marginal on September 2, 1958" would seem to be an understatement. Abort criteria were tightened after the loss of 528, making mission abort mandatory if the APN-99 was not fully operational.

There were also unsubstantiated reports that 528's radio compass indicated three degrees off; in response to an investigator's question, a radio maintenance technician indicated that a three-degree variance was within accepted tolerances but said that he could not recall if the compass was three degrees off. There was also unconfirmed speculation of problems with 528's N-1 compass system. While aircraft 60528's navigation systems may have been within "official" tolerances on September 2, 1958, there is little doubt that the condition of the navigation equipment, together with the 7406th's unfamiliarity with the C-130A-II, were major factors in the inadvertent overflight that day. Add to those crucial equipment problems the interference from the illegal Soviet navigation beacons, and the crew's fate was sealed.

On September 5, 1958, Headquarters, U.S. Air Forces, Europe grounded its C-130 ACRP fleet. Its RB-50s, though not officially grounded, were not used again for missions in Europe because the 7406th was phasing them out. Thus, 7406th flight crews stood down for a few weeks to reassess flying safety and conduct additional training, including integrated combat crew training.

USAFSS Investigations Associated with the Crash

As a result of the shootdown, General James H. Walsh, Air Force deputy chief of staff for Intelligence, tasked Air Force Security Service to provide a detailed evaluation of the entire Air Force airborne signals intelligence reconnaissance platform program. At the time, USAFSS recon crews were flying ACRP missions in Europe, the Far East, and Alaska— the Alaskan missions being performed by crews from Yokota, Japan, on periodic temporary duty to Alaska. A declassified USAFSS Headquarters history, dated 1959, discusses details related to the shootdown and subsequent investigations. Of particular interest is an entry that states, in part, "USAFE [U.S. Air Forces, Europe] removed all C-130 aircraft from ACRP missions until navigational equipment could be corrected."

Because of publicity surrounding the crash, HQ USAFSS had, in effect, to rejustify to General Walsh why ACRP missions were required, i.e., why the intelligence collected by the recon aircraft was not available from other sources. USAFSS also evaluated airborne procedures in Europe to determine how to improve the safety of recon aircrews.

One area of investigation receiving special attention was an attempt to answer the question: "Did the Soviets intentionally lure 528's crew into Armenia?" The USAFSS Headquarters history alludes to a couple of instances of suspected Soviet "spoofing" against U.S. aircraft operating over West Germany, but offers no solid proof that any intentional spoofing or luring occurred. On October 15, after the 7406th overhauled its operations to improve flying safety, USAFE lifted the ban on C-130 recon operations. Meanwhile, HQ USAFSS investigators probed its European units' management of airborne operations aboard the C-130s.

Coincidentally, the Headquarters, USAFSS airborne recon project officer was in Europe during the shootdown (August 24 through September 22), familiarizing himself with ACRP operations in Europe.

The shootdown also brought to a head another question involving the method and degree of coordination within USAFE regarding ACRP mission requirements and mission areas. During discussions of the incident, General Walsh asked Major General Gordon A. Blake, USAFSS commander, if the USAFSS 6900th Security Wing at Frankfurt determined the orbits for ACRP missions in Europe. USAFSS answered General Walsh with quoted paragraphs from two C-130A-II operating directives:

The theater air commander concerned will be responsible for: aircraft flight clearances, including overflights and landing privileges.

> USAF Security Service, in coordination with the proper USAF agencies, will be responsible for: (1) Determination of mission requirements. Route coverage will originate in the respective senior USAFSS theater unit and will be passed to the reconnaissance unit for execution with the approval of the theater air commander . . .

The operating directives went on to describe the coordination process and the organizations involved, explaining that representatives from affected units in Europe got together monthly to discuss requirements and create a monthly mission forecast that was in turn forwarded to headquarters having a requirement for the monthly forecast. Strictly speaking, that answer was correct in theory, but the practice was much more informal, as the USAFSS ACRP project officer later described the process upon his return from Europe:

> The ACRP missions are planned and established at the beginning of each month at a "Monthly Reconnaissance Board Meeting." . . . The operations officer of Detachment 1, 6911th RGM informed me that up until August 1958, the 6900th Security Wing and 6901st Special Communications Group were seldom in attendance and even then, the 6901st was usually represented by an Airman First Class. I attended a couple of these meetings during my TDY and was astounded to learn that no alternate missions were planned in the event of a cancelled scheduled mission. Rather, it was left up to the discretion of Detachment 1, 6911th to determine the alternate mission although Detachment 1 has no knowledge of overall theater requirements in any given instance.

M.Sgt. George Petrochilos, airborne mission supervisor on 60528's last mission, had taken the initiative to reschedule the mission aborted along the Turkish-Armenian border on September 1, 1958, resulting in the rescheduled mission's being shot down on September 2. The USAFSS history cites this inappropriate application of directives—as claimed by Detachment 1 personnel—as evidence that Detachment 1 was receiving only minimal support and guidance from the 6901st SCG. In addition, Detachment 1 cited repeated requests to the 6901st for technical information that were never acknowledged. Responsibility for providing technical support and operational control over Detachment 1 was shared by the 6901st and the 6900th. The history points out that "the 6900th SW had an ACRP section that dealt with Detachment 1, but the 6901st was not always aware of actions taken—the reverse of this situation was also true . . . According to Detachment 1 personnel, this situation had existed for more than a year." Commenting on the situation, the USAFSS ACRP project officer added:

> A discussion with 6900th SW and 6901st SCG ACRP personnel confirms this; however, I was assured that this situation is rapidly being remedied by the assignment of new and interested personnel. It is extremely interesting to note that operations personnel of Detachment 1, 6911th RGM have never seen copies of USAF Directive Letters governing RB-50-2 and C-130A-II ACRP operations although the 6900th SW has a copy of each. Discussions with both 6900th SW and detachment personnel have resulted in promises for closer coordination between Detachment 1, 6911th RGM, 6900th SW and 6901st SCG.

Comments in the USAFSS history document much of the "kick the tires and fly" philosophy that permeated RB-50 and C-130 ACRP operations prior to the loss of 60528 and seventeen crew members. A concluding comment in the USAFSS history assesses the impact that loose management had on the incident: "Although it had not been proven that this situation had a direct bearing on the shootdown of the C-130, it was obvious that closer ACRP coordination and planning among USAFSS units was required . . . The 6900th SW promised that this would be accomplished."

It is interesting that not one person in either chain of command—in USAFE (aircraft and flight crew management)—or in USAFSS (recon crew management) lost his or her job because of the lax management practices that might have led up to the catastrophe.

Security Issues

In an open society, safeguarding classified information is always an issue, and during the Cold War the intelligence community often went overboard trying to keep information about airborne reconnaissance from the public. The fact that Air Force Security Service airmen flew missions aboard aircraft of other Air Force commands was unclassified but was nevertheless considered "sensitive." The 7406th Support Squadron and Detachment 1, 6911th downplayed the relationship between their two squadrons; any questions about reconnaissance to members of either squadron would draw a sharp "No comment." Security may have factored into the inadvertent overflight, and there are indications that unflattering, unclassified investigative findings may have been shielded in "secret" reports.

Because of security issues, the 7406th and Detachment 1, 6911th operated with onboard walls (compartments) separating flight crews from recon crews aboard the C-130 recon aircraft. The security barrier extended further, to tight restrictions on what type and how much information the USAFSS airborne mission supervisor could share via aircraft interphones with the aircraft commander. The separation manifested itself in each unit's training and ground operations as well—men from two separate organizations were thrown together for airborne missions where flight crew and recon crew needed to work closely together for aircrew safety but weren't. In fact, even in Turkey, on a relatively isolated air base, the two outfits had almost nothing to do with each other, either on the ground or in the air.

Security Service ground sites monitored Soviet air surveillance coverage (tracking) of American reconnaissance missions, but those monitoring efforts were even compartmented within each USAFSS site—performed in a "black room" where entry was permitted only to those with real "need to know." The wall of secrecy extended to operations within the 6901st analysis center and 6900th Security Wing; each had a small recon section that operated in isolation from other intelligence operations. That isolation also extended to technical support that the 6901st was obligated to provide to Detachment 1, 6911th. Prior to the shootdown, the 6900th and 6901st had not sat down with Detachment 1's operations officer and NCOIC and explained why and how airborne recon crews should be monitoring Soviet air surveillance tracking of their recon aircraft. Had the recon crew been monitoring Soviet tracking, the recon crew could have warned the aircraft commander a half hour or so before the border violation that the C-130 had deviated from its planned course.

Tasking the recon crew to intercept Russian tracking data in order to keep abreast of where the Russians believed the recon aircraft to be would have provided a fail-safe against inadvertent overflight. The fact that security rules prohibited recon crews to carry classified materials aboard the recon aircraft explains, at least in part, why recon crews had not been briefed on the role Soviet tracking could play on the safety of the recon aircraft. At the time, some opinions within Security Service held that the less classified information aircrews were exposed to, the better it would be for crew members should they fall into the hands of the Soviets.

The lack of closer aircrew coordination between the aircraft commander and the recon crew may have also factored into the tragic incident. In one scenario that is not farfetched, the Russian-language intercept operators aboard 528's last mission would have intercepted the communications of the MiG pilots who scrambled to intercept an intruder at the Armenian border. Chances are also excellent that an intercept operator recognized associated Russian pilot communications as being unusual.

Certainly the excitement and stress reflected in the voices of the Russian pilots would have been enough to tip off the intercept operators that what they were monitoring was not routine ground-controlled intercept training. The operators probably did not recognize that they were themselves the MiG pilots' target, however, and by the time the C-130 crossed the border, it was too late. Immediately, a MiG began firing. From that point two scenarios are imaginable. In the first, the recon crew began to suspect that they were heading into trouble, but the security rules that forbade discussing the recon mission with the flight crew would have kept Sergeant Petrochilos, the airborne mission supervisor, from informing the aircraft commander unless he was positive of the threat. In the second scenario, the recon crew simply did not recognize the danger in time to react; as far as they knew, they were miles west of the border.

We'll never know whether overstrict security compartmentation played a role in the recon crew's not apprising the AC of pending dangers, but security definitely played a role in postincident investigations and in information the government passed to family members. Any evidence of an intentional cover-up or of attempts to shield unclassified information in classified reports is strictly circumstantial. However, all investigations were shrouded in secrecy, and no outside agencies or independent investigators that might have asked the "hard questions" probed the incident. Shielded behind the tight security afforded airborne reconnaissance, Air Force managers seemed to want to sweep past the incident and start anew. Even four decades later, some related documents released by the government are very thoroughly sanitized of classified materials, and other related documents are still not releasable to the public.

The incident itself was tragic, and the fact that essential information could not be provided to affected family members added to the tragedy. But it is a sad truth that throughout the Cold War the U.S. civilian government did not have access to information sought by the families, especially regarding what happened to the eleven missing crew members. The Air Force callously withheld some information. But without Soviet cooperation in permitting a visit to the crash site immediately following the shootdown, it is unlikely that even a disclosure of all available Air Force files would have brought peace of mind to the families.

Nonetheless, without compromising security, the Air Force could have told the families more; for example, that marginal navigation equipment aboard C-130 60528 probably contributed to an inadvertent overflight that led to the shootdown. Those unclassified facts, documented in the aircraft's unclassified Form 1A maintenance record, were protected from public scrutiny in an investigator's report that was stamped "Secret." At the same time, all public (unclassified) records for aircraft 60528 were purged from all Air Force and aircraft depot maintenance contractor files. It is in the nature of all bureaucracies to protect their reputation. Military establishments are, among other things, large bureaucracies. It was more convenient—and bureaucratically safer—for the U.S. and Soviet air forces to blame one another for the downing of 528 than for either to publicly admit their own shortcomings. The families of the seventeen men would be left in the dark for another four decades.

ELEVEN

END OF THE COLD WAR

The families waited almost four decades before finally learning a few scant details about what happened to their loved ones on that fateful afternoon on Tuesday, September 2, 1958. By the third anniversary of the shootdown, the U.S. Air Force and almost everyone except the families had concluded that the eleven missing airmen had perished in the crash. In November 1961 the Air Force issued a "Report of Casualty" to each family whose loved one was unaccounted for. The casualty report for A/2C Harold T. Kamps succinctly closed his military records: "Report number 3145 and Final, completes report number 3114."

Throughout the Cold War, family members of the missing wrote letters to each new presidential administration, always receiving the same type of response: "Sorry; our condolences; no additional information." The question of any form of official recognition for the lost crew never seems to have come up at any level of government.

Discreet Recognition

The 7406th Support Squadron quickly acquired a replacement C-130A-II for tail number 60528 and replacement flight crew members; the Cold War, after all, would continue for another thirty years. Within the squadron, the personal friends of the six lost flight crewmen completed their tours of duty in the squadron and went their separate ways as is the military custom—taking with them their personal knowledge of futile search missions and of other details about the incident. Many who had originally been scheduled for that mission, had worked on the aircraft before its last flight or had a role in authorizing the mission, went through life carrying a personal burden that they dared not share with anyone. A few maintained correspondence—usually on special occasions—with spouses of the lost crew, but even that infrequent contact evaporated after a few years. Due to the sensitivity of its mission, the squadron was not permitted to create any kind of a memorial honoring the lost crew, and within a decade the shootdown was ancient history within the squadron.

The situation was certainly no better—in significant ways it was actually worse—regarding squadron recognition of the eleven missing U.S. Air Force Security Service recon crew members. Immediately following the shootdown, Detachment 1, 6911th Radio Group Mobile falsified the military records for its eleven missing men, erasing all references to Detachment 1 and transferring the airmen on paper to the 7406th Support Squadron. Family members were never informed of the "paper" transfer. Squadron records bearing the names of the men, for example, file copies of military orders, were likewise purged. From September 3, 1958 (date of the paper transfer) forward, Detachment 1, 6911th was to pretend that the men had never been part of the squadron. Due to security paranoia, Security Service was supposed to disown eleven of its men and move on—business as usual.

No one in the unit agreed with the philosophy, but orders were orders, and security was deemed to be at stake. Not only would there be no memorials to their lost squadron brothers, the men of Detachment 1 were to wipe from memory the eleven men and their families. Denied the right to discuss the incident because of security, many of the younger squadron members who'd lost good friends in the shootdown considered their leaders' actions traitorous and despicable.

Between 1958 and 1963, Detachment 1, 6911th grew from a small unit of about seventy-five men, to approximately two hundred airmen, and was redesignated the 6916th Security Squadron. Most, but not all, of the corporate memory about the shootdown was lost. There was a nearly complete personnel turnover, but some airmen who were present during the shootdown in 1958 had left and returned after additional language training. Others had transferred from Rhein-Main to the squadron's detachment at Incirlik AB, Turkey. Those "old-timers" sometimes answered questions from young airmen about the incident, but only if asked and only in the secure area at work.

Seeking to boost morale, including his own, Lt. Col. Russell J. McElroy, 6916th operations officer, decided in 1963 to honor C-130 60528's lost crew with a memorial. Since security regulations forbade any recognition in public, he created a simple plaque that read: "IN MEMORIAM OF THESE SEVENTEEN AIRMEN, September 2, 1958." The names of the seventeen men and a silhouette of their C-130 were engraved on a brass plaque. Colonel McElroy mounted the plaque on a wall inside the squadron briefing room within Operations. Only those with special security clearances had access to the briefing room and plaque.

Colonel McElroy's intentions were genuine and heartfelt, but because the 6916th had not retained any official records on the lost crew members, three of the seventeen names on the plaque were misspelled. While the outside world had largely forgotten about the shootdown, the recon fliers took comfort in being able to pay tribute to their predecessors at pre- and postmission briefings. The plaque was a morale booster and remained a permanent fixture in its briefing room until the squadron was deactivated in 1990.

The idea for placing plaques honoring lost Security Service recon aircrew members in closed operations areas caught on, and security restrictions eased up somewhat. In 1976 during Armed Forces week, Brigadier General Kenneth D. Burns, Security Service commander, dedicated two plaques to seventeen members of the command who lost their lives in two separate aircraft accidents: the C-130 shootdown and the loss of an RC-135 crew that disappeared in flight over the Bering Sea on June 5, 1969. A story covering the memorial service and dedication of the plaques appeared in the Security Service *Spokesman* magazine for June 1976, a rare acknowledgment in unclassified media that the eleven recon crew members aboard the C-130 were once—until they died—assigned to Security Service.

A similar plaque had been dedicated in 1973 honoring Security Ser-vice airmen killed in the Vietnam War. Later, the Electronic Security Command (formerly USAFSS) in San Antonio dedicated two more plaques honoring command airmen lost in recon aircraft accidents. The plaques are displayed on an "In Memoriam" wall in the Hall of Honor within the command briefing room inside the secure headquarters opera-tions compound on "Security Hill," Kelly AFB, Texas. Maintaining the command's low profile, the outside press was not invited to the dedica-tion ceremonies. Neither were family members of the lost airmen.

Due to errors in some of the plaques—including three misspelled names on that for 528's recon crew—attendance by family members could have been embarrassing, and one of the errors on it was unforgivable—a USAFSS crew member's name had been omitted, replaced by that of the 7406th flight engineer on the mission. A former member of the 6916th who personally knew the eleven USAFSS men lost in the C-130 down-ing recognized the mistake and got it corrected in 1987.

The inaccuracies—the misspelled names and the names left off the plaques entirely—are symptomatic of the 1950s, when Security Service was not above falsifying official government records to conceal its involve-ment in airborne reconnaissance. Another related incident in which the command lost track entirely of members killed or missing in the line of duty involves a crew lost aboard an RB-50G on September 10, 1956. Commenting on the RB-50G loss in 1994, a command history office statement illustrates just how little information the command has re-tained on its lost recon crew members:

> An RB-50G was lost at sea with seven USAFSS personnel aboard. The History Office obtained a copy of a page from a SAC history that listed names of casualties, but it did not state which ones were USAFSS personnel. We are certain only of Major Disbrow because he was com-mander of the 6988th Security Squadron (Yokota AB, Japan) from January 1956 until the incident. We have no clues as to the other six USAFSS members.

The personnel records for the seven Security Service crew members had probably been falsified, transferring the seven men to the Strategic

Air Command immediately following the disappearance of their flight. The official Air Force investigative report for the RB-50G that disappeared during its mission over the Sea of Japan lists the seven USAFSS crew members as: Major Lorin C. Disbrow; S.Sgts. Raymond D. Johnson, Paul W. Swinehart, and Theodorus J. Trias; Airmen First Class William H. Ellis, Harry S. Maxwell Jr., and Leo J. Sloan. Purging the names of the lost USAFSS recon fliers—disowning its own men—was unconscionable, especially since the fact that USAFSS airmen flew missions aboard aircraft of other commands was not classified information.

The discrepancies in the USAFSS/ESC plaques resulted in similar errors to the National Security Agency's "Wall of Honor." That memorial, located at NSA Headquarters, lists 148 American cryptologists [intelligence specialists] killed in the line of duty between 1945 and 1995. The list inadvertently excludes the seven USAFSS airmen lost aboard the RB-50G in 1956, and includes the same spelling errors found on the C-130 memorial plaque in San Antonio.

Bringing the C-130 Incident Out of the Closet

As the Cold War droned on into the 1980s, restrictions on associating Air Force Security Service and the Electronic Security Command (formerly USAFSS) with airborne signals intelligence reconnaissance relaxed to the point that ESC squadrons began publicly honoring squadron members lost while flying missions aboard aircraft of other commands. In March 1988 the 6911th Electronic Security Squadron sought assistance and guidance from ESC Headquarters regarding squadron plans to commemorate the thirtieth anniversary of the shootdown of C-130 60528. At the same time, the 6916th ESS requested headquarters permission to include details about the shootdown in an unclassified squadron "fact sheet." Both requests reached ESC at the same time, and were obvious indications that some of the impenetrable intelligence security wall was crumbling.

The 6911th and 6916th messages created a furor within Headquarters ESC regarding association of the command with the C-130 incident. The ESC command section assigned the ESC chief of intelligence as the action officer to coordinate a command response to the squadrons;

coordinating offices included ESC chief of staff, Operations, Plans, Security, History Office, and Public Affairs—the response required concurrence of each office.

A secret "Talking Paper" summarized relevant details about the shootdown and related contemporary events. In addition to the squadron requests, two newspaper reporters had recently requested all information concerning the shootdown from the National Security Agency. The unclassified 6911th message built a case that made it difficult for the command to deny the squadron's request:

> We are currently planning several events to commemorate our MIAs. To do a proper job, we request your assistance in several areas. We need to know what official ESC/Air Force history says on the topic. We need guidance on what aspects of the C-130 mission can be released to the general public. We need to know the names of the crew, those assigned to the 6911th Security Squadron and also to the 7406th Support Squadron. We also need to know the missing crew members' official status: Is it MIA, KIA or something else?
>
> This unit's company grade officers' council is planning several events to mark this occasion: among them, a dining out, a retreat and a flyover on 2 September 1988, procuring a suitable plaque or monument with the eleven MIAs names engraved, an open house for unit members and dependents, and a series of articles in various appropriate publications (Air Force Times, Stars & Stripes, Air Force Magazine). In order to properly commemorate our MIAs, we request your help in providing the best information on the subject.
>
> Most of our information has come from open sources and a former member of the 6911th Security Squadron who knew of the incident first hand. That member is our civilian operations analyst, Perry Eisenhower (Chief Master Sgt., retired). He has also provided us with several Stars & Stripes articles from 30 years ago on the C-130 shootdown. While interesting, we realize this is not the final official version of the incident. To ensure that an accurate accounting of the shootdown is given during our commemoration activities, it is essential we have the official history of the incident.
>
> We see these activities as representing a tremendous opportunity to

honor our missing comrades of [sic] the long tradition of USAFSS/ESC
service to the theater and our nation. Request guidance and information
at your earliest convenience. As we need to get a lot of work done if we
are to meet publishing deadlines, any assistance and additional informa-
tion on this matter will be gratefully received and appreciated. We will re-
quest approval for an open house via separate message.

The 6911th message reflects the American version of what former
Soviet Premier Mikhail Gorbachev called "Glasnost"—openness or candor in dealing with the public. An ESC response package consisting of
the 6911th and 6916th messages, a C-130 Shootdown Incident "Talking
Paper," a half-dozen thirty-year-old newspaper articles on the shootdown,
a brief history on the 6916th, and a 6916th fact sheet entered the coordination cycle within ESC Headquarters. Comments by the reviewers of
ESC's response offer insight into how far Security Service/Electronic Security Command had come—and how far it still had to go—in thirty
years, relative to openly sharing perhaps sensitive but unclassified information with the public.

Colonel William Bender, director of Operations, pointed out that the
6916th, not the 6911th, was the rightful owner of the unit to which the
C-130 recon crew was assigned. The ESC director of Security's immediate recommendation was brusque: "Recommend we not associate the
command with this incident." In a note to the command historian, the
ESC chief of staff made two basically incompatible points:

Jim, I need you to review the package, my thoughts are: 1. We are
over-classifying, and 2. Mention of a shootdown in a unit fact sheet is in-
appropriate; not what any unit puts in its handouts.

Guess which position the historian took? The ESC historian offered
solutions echoing the chief of staff's thoughts, but not all parties agreed:

Colonel Bender is correct. The 6911th ESS has no claim to the lineage
of the unit (Det 1, 6911th RGM). This unit eventually became the
6916th ESS. Legally, the 6911th ESS goes back only to 1 July 1963 . . .
We've already publicly commemorated those crew members with a

plaque here at the headquarters, so I see no problem with the 6911th ESS commemorating them again as long as they do not claim they were members of the 6911th. Perhaps they could handle it the same way the 6920th ESG did recently when they commemorated ARDF [airborne radio direction-finding] crew members who lost their lives in Vietnam. Those men were not members of the 6920th ESG, but the group still commemorated them.

However, if we permit the 6911th to commemorate the 11 crew members, we need to make sure they are not commemorated as MIAs as the 6911th suggests in their message. Officially, this command does not have any MIAs [our emphasis]. Nota bene—underlined.

The shootdown is not mentioned in the current 6916th ESS fact sheet and rightfully it should not be. The "history" portion of the fact sheet should be limited to a brief lineage of the unit.

In commenting that the command does not have any MIAs, the historian was splitting hairs; the Air Force officially declared the missing crew members dead in November 1961 although no bodies were recovered, and the men were therefore still, actually if not legally, "missing."

The chief of Plans supported a plan honoring the men:

I agree with the concept of honoring those who have given their lives in the line of duty; we should be able to do this . . .

The 6911th could simply discuss the role of all airmen in peace to be prepared, etc. Even in peace the ultimate sacrifice is required . . . Today we honor several who met that challenge . . .

Later, the chief of Plans clarified his position to Security: he did not want the C-130 associated with the 6916th, but saw no problem associating it with the 6911th. The security officer, on the other hand, held firm, recommending that "neither unit be associated with the C-130 shootdown." Applying logic and common sense, the public affairs officer took yet another position: he saw no reason to withhold related information:

a. Nothing in the fact sheet or commemoration disputes what was reported in the past.

b. The recommendation does not call into question any of the unit mission statements or fact sheets.

c. Neither is classified.

After further discussions between the public affairs officer and Security, the security officer stated in a note to the Director of Intelligence:

The public affairs officer is adamant in his non-concurrence since the information is unclassified and has appeared in the Spokesman. *He feels the units should be authorized to publicize their association.*

The information that was unclassified in 1988—the relationship between the eleven Security Service airborne recon fliers and C-130, on which they gave their lives—was just as unclassified in 1958. The Air Force scheme for Security Service to disown its eleven crew members in 1958 was disingenuous and served no useful purpose. Thirty years later in 1988, chinks in a once impregnable security wall that impeded any honest exchange of information with families of lost Cold War recon crew members were growing, similar to fissures that were developing in the Berlin Wall and the Soviet-dominated Iron Curtain around Eastern Europe.

The walls—the physical, the political, and to some extent the bureaucratic walls—of the Cold War began to tumble in 1989 when the East European countries, one after another, threw off their shackles and Berliners tore down the Berlin Wall. Two years later, in December 1991, the Soviet Union was officially declared defunct—ending the Cold War. At last, new investigations could be opened into missing-in-action U.S. military forces who disappeared during the Cold War.

After the Cold War

Relations between the first postcommunist leader of Russia, Boris Yeltsin, and the first ex-CIA American president, George Bush, were surprisingly cordial, though hardly trouble free. An important though little known part of their work together involved Russian cooperation with the United States in searching for American and Russian missing-in-action and prisoner-of-war casualties from the Cold War era. The cooperation of Yeltsin's government in the area of POW and MIA accountability has helped bring closure for families of many American military men who disappeared on missions during the Cold War.

United States–Russian Joint Commission on POW/MIAs

On December 31, 1991, during a summit in Washington between Russian President Boris Yeltsin and U.S. President George Bush, Yeltsin proposed the formation of a joint commission between the United States and Russia. The commission would investigate the loss of American servicemen in territory either on or adjacent to the former Soviet Union, or under its control from 1945 to 1991. The commission would also search for former Russian military men missing in action. It was to be a humanitarian effort beneficial to both countries. For the United States, information would be sought on Americans lost during World War II, the Cold War, the Korean War, and the Vietnam War; and for Russia, those Russians unaccounted for in Cold War activities and during the Afghanistan conflict in the 1980s. In February 1992, U.S. Secretary of State James Baker responded favorably to Yeltsin's proposal, formally establishing the "United States–Russian Joint Commission on POW/MIAs" (Prisoners of War and Missing in Action). No time limit was set for the tenure of the joint commission.

The commission held its inaugural meeting in Moscow in March 1992. Malcolm Toon, former U.S. ambassador to the Soviet Union, headed the U.S. delegation. Other U.S. members of the delegation included the Deputy Assistant Secretary of Defense for POW-MIA Affairs, the Defense Intelligence Agency chief of staff, two Department of State assistant secretaries, two senators, two congressmen, and the assistant national archivist. Yeltsin's senior military adviser, Col. Gen. Dmitri Volkogonov, served as Russia's cochairman. Russian commission members included parliamentarians, the heads of major archives, and officials of the Ministries of Defense, Foreign Affairs, the Interior, and security services. Commission meetings were held in Moscow and Washington, D.C.

During the first plenary session, each side obtained a general understanding of the other. The commission organized itself by conflict, forming separate working groups for World War II, the Cold War, the Korean War, and the Vietnam War. Though it began as an operation managed by the U.S. Army, the U.S. Defense Department formed the Defense POW/MIA Office (DPMO) within the Office of the Secretary of Defense, consolidating all Washington, D.C.–based agencies dealing specifically with the POW/MIA issue into one operation headed by the Deputy Assistant Secretary of Defense for POW/MIA Affairs.

The Defense POW/MIA Office serves as a focal point for guiding research requirements and assuring transmittal of commission-related documents to commissioners, family members, and the public. On-site support was rendered by a Task Force Russia (TFR) group in Moscow, later renamed the Joint Commission Support Branch. The JCSB maintained day-to-day contact with Russian commission members, coordinated research, interviewed Russian citizens, and examined archival records.

The Joint Commission's Cold War Working Group was charged with investigating incidents in which U.S. Navy and U.S. Air Force aircrews were declared missing in action during airborne missions adjacent to former Soviet territory. Most but not all of the incidents involved the shootdown of American military aircraft by Soviet pilots. To the extent possible, all relevant military documents in former Soviet archives and U.S. government archives have been declassified. Pertinent documents and information have been passed to family members of the MIAs, and declassified documents were placed in the National Archives and Library of Congress for public use. The joint commission uncovered and facilitated declassification of most of the documents cited in this book.

On the eve of the fiftieth anniversary of the end of World War II in Europe (May 8, 1995), the joint commission submitted an interim report declaring that "no American citizens, either military or civilian, are being held against their will on the territory of Russia today." The report also pointed out that the commission had done extensive work to resolve questions related to ten U.S. aircraft losses during the Cold War period—those air incidents in which U.S. servicemen were unaccounted for. The shootdown of C-130 528 over Armenia in 1958 was one of the ten incidents investigated by the commission. As pointed out in the interim report in 1995, the work of the joint commission continues:

The Commission must continue its work until every lead is exhausted, leaving no stone left unturned. Those who the Commission serves—the families of the missing, the American and Russian people, and all past, present, and future military service members who put their lives at risk— deserve no less.

Thanks to the end of the Cold War, the joint commission was made possible, and thanks to it, an accounting for America's Cold War prisoners of war and missing in action is being carried out. The most active efforts at present involve locating and repatriating remains of airmen lost during the Korean War and the Vietnam War. The commission completed most investigations of POW and MIA issues associated with the end of World War II and Cold War U.S.-Soviet incidents during its first three years; efforts continue on a few more difficult issues. From 1992 to 1994 the joint commission unveiled and facilitated declassification of a treasure trove of Russian and American documents related to the shootdown of C-130 60528. The commission also sponsored an excavation of the C-130 crash site in Armenia and interviewed several witnesses to the shootdown, lending credence to the supposition that the C-130's entire seventeen-man crew perished in the crash on September 2, 1958.

Investigations at Crash Site—1992

Preparations commenced in early 1992 to investigate the C-130 shootdown at the crash site in Armenia. In February, while visiting the site—in the village of Sasnashen (in the Aragat Mountain foothills)— the chargé d'affaires from the American embassy in Yerevan interviewed several eyewitnesses who gave detailed accounts of the shootdown and crash. An embassy message describes those eyewitness accounts:

On the afternoon of September 2, 1958, villagers saw three MiGs flying from the direction of the border in pursuit of a larger aircraft. The MiGs flanked the aircraft on left and right, with one MiG at a lower level aft. The villagers had the impression that the MiGs were attempting to force the intruding aircraft down. The aircraft tried repeated evasive maneuvers at a low level between the villages of Sasnashen and Mastara

(10 kilometers distant). The aircraft then opened fire on the fighters, and one abandoned the pursuit. The remaining MiGs fired on the intruding aircraft . . . [Since the C-130 was unarmed, the witnesses probably heard a fourth MiG fire on the C-130.] . . . Smoke and flames were visible, and it lost altitude and crashed in vacant land, approximately 500 meters from the village center.

The two MiGs departed, flying north toward Leninakan. Villagers went to the crash site and saw a large fire with explosions. One villager was wounded in the leg by exploding debris. Rescue attempts failed because of the intensity of the fire. No one survived the crash, and parts of bodies were scattered over the area. Observers saw only one intact body, that of a "stout" crew member. Parachutes were strapped to the bodies/torsos . . . Eyewitnesses claim that the debris was left unattended overnight.

The following day, a group of soldiers and KGB personnel arrived. They maintained guard over the scene, removed all remaining bodies and parts, and sifted the debris. The bodies were placed in coffins and taken from the scene in military vehicles. Eyewitnesses agree that only seven coffins were taken from the scene—one containing the "stout" flier and the rest containing parts of bodies . . .

A woman aboard? It is an article of faith among the villagers that one of the crew members was a woman. Tangible evidence for this appears to be slim thus far: one eyewitness claims that a woman's shoe was recovered from the wreckage. According to the villagers, the woman was an Armenian-American radio specialist. There is a rumor that this person's mother travels to Echmiadzin (seat of the Armenian Orthodox Church) to light candles for her daughter, and it is alleged that the mother visited Sasnashen two years ago.

Aircraft fragments: We recovered a one-meter piece of wreckage (possibly part of an aileron or flap) and are pouching it to OSD [Office of Secretary of Defense] so that any interested addressees may have a chance to examine it. Larger pieces of the aircraft remain in the village and are also available for examination.

Sasnashen inhabitants have contacted the Armenian charitable organization "GTUTIUN" to erect a memorial to the fliers. They request that the USG [U.S. government] provide the full names of all personnel killed

*in the crash for placement on the memorial. They also request that the
USG inform the crew's families of their plans. They would like the families to visit and are seeking to have the memorial in place by the next
anniversary of the shootdown.*

*COMMENT: Are the reports credible? The stories were sponta-
neously and emotionally related, and ring true in the telling since Armenia is now a free and independent nation. We have no reason to suspect
government intimidation . . . There is a discrepancy between the seven
coffins reportedly transferred and the six bodies that USG records list as
received . . . The accounts appear to establish that all personnel on board
were killed on impact . . .*

There is no doubt that all aboard the C-130 were killed on impact,
and the villagers' recollection about seven coffins is consistent with a report prepared by the Soviet military pathologist at the crash site. But
later examination determined that only six corpses were involved. The
American chargé d'affaires did not take villager comments about one of
the crew members being a woman seriously.

Witnesses to the 60528 Shootdown Come Forward—1993

As part of a publicity campaign to locate eyewitnesses to shootdown
incidents, the Moscow-based office of the joint commission advertised in
local newspapers. Six Armenian citizens came forward and detailed their
accounts of the shootdown of C-130 60528 to the American embassy
staff in Yerevan in the spring of 1993. An embassy message dated May
1993 summarizes those eyewitness accounts:

*. . . Embassy has located and separately interviewed six eyewitnesses
to the shootdown of a C-130 transport on September 2, 1958 near the
Armenian-Turkish border. Their accounts disagree in several respects
with Soviet account in referenced telegram and with accounts in the Soviet press. All witnesses agree that the plane was flying low when it was
shot down, that no one was seen parachuting, and that no one was
known to have survived the crash.*

THE OVERFLIGHT, CHASE AND SHOOTDOWN

One eyewitness of the shootdown was Martin Kakosian, a construction firm director who was then a university student. He was riding a bus to Yerevan on the day of the incident. His bus stopped, and the passengers watched the entire incident. Second witness is Artosi Avdalyan, now retired, then a driver for a collective farm near the crash site who witnessed the entire shootdown and went to the scene immediately afterwards. A third witness was Albert Avaryan, now a physicist, then a university student who was visiting a village near the incident and witnessed the crash and shootdown. Fourth witness was Yurik Bogdazartan who lived in a local village and was eleven years old at the time and saw the crash and shootdown. Fifth witness was Marsbed Averyan who was fifteen at the time. He watched the chase and shootdown, and visited the crash site an hour later. Sixth witness was Henrik Petrosyan, a journalist who was eighteen at the time. He lived in the next village to the crash site. He witnessed the shootdown and arrived at the crash site a few minutes after the crash.

Avdalyan said that the plane was flying very low when he first saw it from his farm in Bagravyan village in the Ani region near the Turkish border. The incident took place about 10 kilometers from Leninakan, not 20 as stated in referenced telegram. It was between two and three p.m., in bright and sunny weather. The plane, which he said was the color of dry leaves, was flying parallel to the railway. Suddenly two MiG-17s appeared. Witness Kakosian said he knew they were MiG-17s because he had built models of them. Then two more MiGs appeared. The MiGs flew very close to the C-130, almost touching, apparently trying to force it to go with them.

Witness Kakosian began watching the incident from the bus at this point. He said the plane was low enough to see the stars on the fuselage and wings. Witness Petrosyan also saw the star emblems on the plane. The planes flew behind Mount Aragat and reappeared, heading toward the border. The chase lasted in all as long as fifteen minutes.

At this point, there was one MiG above the C-130, one on either side, and one behind. Witness Averyan said it looked like an eagle surrounded by four birds. At this point, witnesses Albert Avaryan, Marsbed Averyan and Henrik Petrosyan say that the C-130 fired on the plane behind and that the MiG behind—smoking—turned away and flew toward Leninakan. COMMENT: Since the C-130 presumably was unarmed, either the witnesses were mistaken or a crew member of the C-130 fired from the rear doors at the plane, or it was the MiG firing, or the MiG simply had engine trouble.

Averyan said the C-130 turned ninety degrees and tried to gain altitude to escape the MiGs. Kakosian said the plane was at an altitude of about 300 meters. Avdalyan estimated no more than 1,000 meters. The journalist Petrosyan said 800 meters. The mathematician Averyan thought about 1,000 meters. None was close to the 25,000 feet as in referenced telegram. One MiG came underneath extremely close and began shooting. One engine on the right side caught fire, then half the plane was burning. Kakosian said the plane descended and went behind a hill out of his sight, and he saw flames and smoke.

Witness Averyan, the mathematician, saw the plane smoking as it descended, and dropping pieces of metal, but no one emerged. Witness Petrosyan, the journalist, said he expected to see someone jump, but no one did.

Witness Petrosyan lived in the village of Veri (Upper) Sasnashen, not far from the crash site. The crash site is flat and rocky, on the edge of a deep ravine. After watching the chase and shootdown, he saw the plane pass just over a low hill, and then saw smoke and flames. He ran from his house to the crash site, arriving in about four minutes. The wreckage was burning, and there was a very bad smell from the flames. A large portion of the tail was intact, and some of the fuselage. He saw one badly burned body near the wreckage.

Witness Avdalyan jumped in his car and drove to the crash site. He arrived just as the fire was being put out. He said the tail section was intact about fifteen meters from the scattered wreckage of the rest of the plane. He helped the villagers collect what remained of the bodies. He said they gathered about six bodies, but none of them were intact. He picked up a leg and a body with badly burned head and no feet. He also picked up a folder that contained papers and a photograph of a man in civilian clothes with a wife and three children.

Witness Averyan arrived about the same time. He said that by that time, there were approximately 25 people at the crash site from the nearby villages. The ground was burning. He saw three bodies lined up, all burned. One villager took a wallet with documents and dollars—the first dollars any of them had ever seen—from one of the bodies.

About an hour after the crash, Russian pilots arrived in a jeep, apparently the same pilots who had shot down the plane, coming from the airfield in Leninakan. Shortly afterward, MVD and KGB forces arrived with dogs and sealed off the area, taking away the folder and photograph. The villager who had taken the documents and dollars gave them to the pilot.

THE AFTERMATH

The next morning Kakosian and Avdalyan both went to the crash site. The area was surrounded by troops and dogs. Avdalyan said there were two trucks on the site with six coffins. Villagers told him they had seen from a distance bodies being taken out of the plane. Kakosian picked up a souvenir—a piece of white synthetic fabric, charred by fire. Avdalyan took pieces of the same fabric. Other witnesses took similar fabric and remarked that it didn't seem to burn. They have since lost the fragments.

Averyan said that the day after the crash, a major or colonel came to his school and asked for students from the eighth to tenth classes to join in a search in the area around the site. Asked what they were looking for, they were told "anything you find." He found three large bullets and five smaller bullets that he handed over to the officer.

Petrosyan said he visited the site after the authorities had left, and found a gold wedding band, a second ring and a wristwatch. He later gave them to his mother and to his teacher. He said other villagers had found pistols and radio equipment. One villager took away a large piece of fuselage, which he still has.

Kakosian said the area was sealed off for ten days, and buses were searched during that period. Five days after the incident, there was a brief article in Pravda *saying that the border had been violated and an aircraft shot down, but mentioning only "the southern region" without mentioning Armenia.*

COMMENT: *If POW/MIA team wishes, we can visit the crash site or arrange for them to visit the site. We also can place a second press release or article asking for the return of any personal effects.*

So far, all witnesses agree that the plane was flying at an altitude of less than a thousand meters when it was fired upon, that it was smoking when it descended, and that no one jumped out before it crashed. No one saw survivors at the crash site. All testimony seems to confirm that, unfortunately, no one survived the crash.

There is a logical explanation for the discrepancy between the altitude of the C-130 as noted in a referenced Soviet report (25,000 feet) and the low altitudes observed by both Turkish and Armenian witnesses (approximately 1,000 to 3,000 feet). The C-130 copilot had reported being at altitude 25,500 feet in his last radio contact, and Soviet radars showed the transport to be climbing as it flew from Turkey into Armenian airspace. When the first MiG pilot saw the intruding aircraft, he reported to his ground controller that the target aircraft was flying at an altitude of 10,000 meters (32,800 feet). Seeing the lead MiG pilot fire shots, the logical response—in fact the only feasible defensive response—of the C-130 aircraft commander would have been to evade; bank sharply, descend rapidly to an altitude of a few hundred feet, and attempt to fly away from Armenian airspace. The intercepted communications of the Soviet MiG pilots who shot down the C-130 confirm the evasive actions of the C-130 crew.

Three months after the American embassy issued its message detailing the eyewitness reports, a U.S. crash site excavation team arrived in Armenia.

Crash Site Excavation—August–September 1993

Between August 29 and September 16, 1993, a team from the U.S. Army's Central Identification Laboratory, Hawaii (CILHI) successfully excavated a total area of approximately 350 square meters at the crash site in Armenia. The army team of mortuary affairs specialists and an anthropologist—similar to teams that have excavated dozens of Vietnam-era crash sites in Southeast Asia—spent two weeks methodically digging and sifting through the earth and debris at the crash site.

The site associated with the crash is situated upon gently sloping terrain that is extremely rocky and contains several small washes that serve to drain the area in times of heavy rainfall. Surface vegetation is very sparse, with scrub thorn bushes predominating the landscape. With the exception of a graded dirt road that encroaches on the western boundary of the site, the nearby village of Nerkin (Lower) Sasnashen had not seriously disturbed the crash site. The artifact-bearing soil, for the most part, was gray to black in color, the result of the fierce fire caused by the plane's crash; the burned soil differed in thickness throughout the site. The team could easily differentiate between the dark artifact-rich layer and the sterile base clay layer that was extremely dense and light brown to brown in color.

Standard archaeological methods were used to control for provenance and to maximize recovery of all human remains, personal effects, and pertinent aircraft wreckage. Prior to excavation, the project area was cleared of most of the vegetation, as well as many of the small rocks. Excavation involved the removal of all relevant soil by hand implements and the subsequent screening of all that soil through one-eighth-inch mesh wire screen.

The excavation team recovered approximately two thousand small human skeletal bone fragments, thousands of pieces of aircraft wreckage and personal effects of crew members. The bone fragments, most of which were smaller than two centimeters in diameter, generally exhibited effects of fire and were not sufficient to establish forensic identification through DNA analysis.

Although the excavation did not account for all of 60528's missing crew members, it recovered significant artifacts directly associated with the missing crew. The team recovered two identification tags (dog tags) for crew members (Robert H. Moore and Joel H. Fields), plus a metal "serial number" data plate for C-130A-II 60528. The team also recovered an array of watches and watchband fragments, ten U.S. coins (nickels, dimes, and pennies dating from 1943 to 1958), and several keys (some for Streamlite and Samsonite suitcases). The dog tags for Paul E. Duncan (unaccounted for) and Archie T. Bourg Jr. had been recovered at the crash site earlier.

Armenian Khachkar *Memorial Dedicated—August 1993*

When the Sasnashen villagers discussed the shootdown with American embassy personnel in early 1992, they had been serious about dedicating a memorial honoring the men killed in their village. Martin Kakosian, an Armenian eyewitness to the shootdown and a talented sculptor, collaborated with the villagers to create a memorial honoring an unknown American crew that had died unceremoniously at the edge of their village during the Cold War. Kakosian sculpted a *khachkar* (a type of Armenian memorial stone), and together with the villagers and Lorna Bourg, sister of one of the crew members, dedicated the *khachkar* in late August 1993, commemorating the thirty-fifth anniversary of the shootdown. The *khachkar* was just a simple stone monument—without crew member names, since the American government had not provided the names of the crew members for inclusion on the memorial.

Irony—Families—Hostages of Strict Security System

It seems ironic that citizens of Armenia, a former Soviet republic, came forward and honored a lost Cold War American reconnaissance aircrew before American military leaders permitted the same crew to be similarly honored in the United States. The Cold War was over, but American Intelligence was not yet ready to associate "dirty words" like COMINT and SIGINT—communications intelligence and signals intelligence—with reconnaissance platforms such as C-130 60528. In other words, America still considered the issue too sensitive to acknowledge that 60528 was performing intelligence collection when its crew inadvertently violated Soviet airspace and got shot down.

A National Security Agency policy memorandum dated July 11, 1997, finally declassified the relationship between SIGINT and U.S. airborne reconnaissance platforms. The NSA memorandum states in part:

> . . . *Effective immediately, the "fact of" airborne SIGINT and the SIGINT mission of the following current and historic "SIGINT-capable" airborne platform designators are declassified:*

RB-17	Flying Fortress
RB-29	Super Fortress
RB-47	Stratojet
RB-50	Super Fortress
RC-7	De Havilland Dash 7
RC-12	Beech King Air
E/RC-130	Hercules[143]
E/RC-135	Stratolifter
EC-47	Skytrain
EP-3E	Orion
SR-71	Blackbird
U-2	Dragon Lady
PB4Y-2	Privateer
P2V	Neptune

The Cold War security wall has not completely crumbled on either side, but in many ways the American wall is now more akin to a sheer security curtain that permits an open discussion to a certain point. While withholding sensitive technical details, in today's world of tight, competitive defense budgets, intelligence managers openly "sell" the operational capabilities of their reconnaissance platforms. An article appearing in the May 2000 issue of the Air Force Association's *Air Force Magazine* touts the capabilities of the RC-135 Rivet Joint SIGINT collection platform, the modern day equivalent of C-130 60528 in 1958:

RIVET JOINT—RECON READY

The year is 2005 and a military linguist at Battle Station 4 intercepts enemy plans to fire rockets at a friendly jet. An electronic warfare officer at the Raven 2 position uncovers the weapon's location. The reconnaissance data streams to a B-2 full of satellite-guided Joint Direct Attack Munitions, but the pilot needs only one to vaporize the enemy's artillery.

The recon-ready RC-135 Rivet Joint aircraft crew agrees: their airmanship—determining position, timing and warning—was "spot on."

You won't overhear Rivet Joint airmen detailing expeditions like this over blood-red steaks at a local restaurant when they return to Offutt Air Force Base Nebraska, for such crew procedures are proprietary information. It's safe to acknowledge: For decades, the "RJ" airmen fired a weapon that, in its own way, is as powerful as smart bombs or lasers during battle. It's called information—data that wins wars.

"We search for activity and report it. Most crews get information to the ultimate consumer in seconds," Technical Sgt. D.J. Matthews said. He supervises signals intelligence and language-trained airmen on the RJ. "The end-product of a collection mission goes directly from our airplane to the hands of the national command authority."

Interesting! Today they call it "information—data that wins wars," and discuss "it" more or less openly. In the old days we called it "intelligence," and intelligence was a nasty word that just wasn't discussed in public. Such open discussions—commercial advertisements, really— about recon missions in 1958 would not have saved the crew of C-130 60528, but more openness and candor with the families of 528's crew could have meant the difference between some degree of closure and continuing anguish for the families of the men who died on that day in Armenia.

TWELVE

PAYING TRIBUTE
FOUR DECADES LATER

In February 1994, Malcolm Toon, former U.S. ambassador to the Soviet Union and cochairman of the U.S.-Russian Joint Commission on POW/MIAs, welcomed the commission's Russian delegation to the eighth plenary session of the commission in Washington, D.C. Charged with resolving issues involving missing-in-action and prisoner-of-war issues between the Soviet Union and the United States during the Cold War, the commission had held plenary meetings approximately quarterly since the first session convened two years earlier. The February 1994 plenary session—the first plenary session in the United States—was special. The meeting was being held in the Pentagon; families of the Cold War MIAs would be meeting with commission members; and Col. Gen. Dmitri Volkogonov, Russian cochairman of the commission, brought from Russia a commemorative gift for the American people.

At the sixth plenary session in Moscow six months earlier, Ambassador Toon had paid tribute to Soviet MIAs by presenting to Volkogonov a ship's bell from a Soviet Golf-class submarine that disappeared in the Pacific Ocean in 1968. Believing that the Soviet sub had collided with an American sub, Russia requested through the joint commission any available information on the missing submarine. Although the U.S. Navy had not been involved in the disappearance of the missing Soviet vessel—an onboard explosion had sunk the sub—U.S. Intelligence knew about the catastrophe. Moreover, the Central Intelligence Agency had recovered a portion of the Soviet ballistic missile sub from three-mile-deep waters 1,700 miles west of Hawaii in 1974. Toon also provided Volkogonov two dog tags of Soviet sailors who perished aboard the sub, and a video recording documenting an at-sea burial of six of the sub's sailors whose remains had been recovered. Responding with deep appreciation, Volkogonov replied, "We will tell the relatives . . . I'm deeply gratified . . . It's an important memorial . . . We'll find a place for it in a museum."

Now, during the meeting in Washington, commission members met with families of U.S. Cold War MIAs, giving the family members an opportunity to question Russian commission members directly. Pointing out that millions of Russian citizens had seen the story about the American government handing over the Soviet submarine bell and watched the *At-Sea Burial Service* for the missing Soviet submariners on Russian television, Volkogonov broke the news about the gift he'd brought from Russia:

> The bell, which the American services raised from the Soviet submarine, occupies a place of honor in the Military Museum of Russia.
>
> Just as you presented us with the bell, we would like to pass to you a fragment from the Lockheed aircraft shot down by a Soviet rocket many years ago as a common memento so that those times will never return. This is a photograph of the rocket, or more precisely the rocket launcher that launched the rocket that brought down the plane.

"Is this the U-2?"

"Yes, Powers's plane."

"Could we show this at the press conference?"

"Yes, of course!"

"Thank you."

National Cryptologic Museum

In 1995, Dr. David A. Hatch, the National Security Agency Historian, was conducting a guided tour for visitors to NSA's National Crypto-

logic Museum at Fort Meade, Maryland. Standing before a display commemorating the "U-2 incident," Dr. Hatch provided his audience an
overview of the U-2 shootdown:

> On 1 May 1960, while flying over Sverdlovsk, deep in Soviet terri-
> tory, American pilot Francis Gary Powers was shot down in a U-2 high-
> altitude reconnaissance aircraft. The Soviets accomplished the shootdown
> with fourteen SA-2 missiles and [with] MiG-19 interceptors. All four-
> teen SA-2's reached altitude and exploded at the same time; the shock-
> waves damaged the U-2 and one of the MiGs.
>
> On 7 May, Soviet premier Nikita Khrushchev held a news conference
> in which he displayed Powers and accused the United States of spying.
> The resulting international political turmoil caused the cancellation of a
> summit meeting scheduled in Paris between President Dwight Eisenhower
> and the Soviet premier.
>
> Powers was sentenced to ten years in a Soviet prison. However, he
> was released after only twenty-one months, when the Soviets exchanged
> him for convicted spy Rudolph Abel, who was in a U.S. prison. Powers
> died in August 1977 in Los Angeles, when the traffic helicopter he flew
> ran out of fuel and crashed.
>
> Last year, two Russian officers, including a lieutenant general, paid a
> private visit to the National Cryptologic Museum. In token of their visit,
> they presented the museum with a fragment from the U-2 piloted by
> Francis Powers.

The U-2 fragment is a central part of the cryptologic museum's memorial display. Other museum guides often enrich the story by identifying
the Russian U-2 fragment benefactor as a KGB general who visited the
museum.[144]

The U-2 display is one of many Cold War intelligence-related topics
on display in the museum that the NSA opened to the public in December 1993. The extensive museum collection of cryptologic and intelligence displays includes a collection of rare books on cryptology—one
published in 1518; a functional German Enigma cipher machine from
World War II; a Japanese Purple cipher machine; a USS Liberty display

about the American Intelligence ship attacked by Israeli defense forces in the Mediterranean Sea in June 1967; a display containing photographs from the KGB Museum in Moscow; and a display about the "Venona" program under which U.S. Intelligence collected and exploited Soviet diplomatic communications showing that Julius and Ethel Rosenberg were guilty of espionage for passing secrets to Soviet agents about the Manhattan Project—the American effort to develop the atomic bomb in World War II.

A Belated Recognition

On August 19, 1995, Larry Tart listened somewhat aghast at the openness with which Dr. Hatch, National Cryptologic Museum tour guide, discussed the National Security Agency's success in intercepting and decoding foreign communications. For decades the NSA had operated in silence—over the years, many jokingly commented that the letters NSA stood for "No Such Agency." But in 1995 the NSA historian was openly discussing how Soviet SA-2 missiles shot down Gary Powers's U-2. Listening to the public discussion of a plane that had flown out of Incirlik Air Base, the same base from which the C-130 had taken off on September 2, 1958, Tart realized that the time had come to honor C-130 60528's crew, which, twenty months earlier than Powers, had paid an even higher price during another intelligence recon mission.

Thanking Hatch for his excellent guided tour, Tart asked why the museum did not have a display honoring other American airborne signals intelligence recon crews that had been shot down—for example, the C-130 crew that Soviet MiG pilots shot down over Armenia in 1958? Dr. Hatch responded that the museum had no artifacts associated with such shootdown incidents.

Returning home, Tart wrote a personal letter to Dr. Hatch. Explaining that he had flown signals intelligence recon missions on C-130 and RC-135 aircraft for ten years, Tart offered to assist with the acquisition of artifacts for a cryptologic museum display honoring the seventeen aircrew members who lost their lives aboard C-130 60528 on September 2, 1958:

I'd like to see some type of memorial to our airborne brothers in the National Cryptologic Museum . . .

Are you interested in receiving artifacts with the intention of establishing a display dedicated to airborne SIGINT activities?

Dr. Hatch sent a courteous response, but declined Tart's offer of memorabilia for an airborne reconnaissance display:

Thank you for the kind words about the National Cryptologic Museum in your letter of 24 October. As a matter of fact, I do remember discussing with a tour member the question of displays for airborne reconnaissance.

We appreciate your generous offer of photographs and articles about the C-130 incident of 1958, but the Museum does not at this time have any plans for a display about airborne reconnaissance . . .

Disappointed, Tart decided to begin networking with former Air Force acquaintances, and at the same time began mailing letters to relevant Air Force and U.S. Intelligence agencies seeking associated information under the Freedom of Information Act (FOIA). The Air Force Casualty Office assisted by forwarding a letter from Tart to the last address of record for next of kin of the lost crew. The Internet also aided his searches. A CD-ROM version of a national phone directory—100 million listings—facilitated phone searches. A typical phone call uncovered two or three additional names of Air Force veterans with knowledge, related photographs, and newspaper articles from 1958 to 1960 about the shootdown. Tart followed up phone calls to family members and former Air Force recon fliers with letters. Nearly every contact led to more names and phone numbers.

Many of those contacted had known the lost crew members personally, and all willingly provided copies of associated memorabilia. Networking led to contacts with family members of the lost crew, engineers who had equipped the C-130 for reconnaissance, investigators from the U.S.-Russian Joint Commission on POW/MIAs, an Armenian eyewitness to the shootdown, and a few hundred former Air Force recon fliers.

The search also turned up many former 7406th Support Squadron and Detachment 1, 6911th Security Group crew members who had been personal friends of 60528's lost flight crew.

One such is Robert Keefe, coauthor of this book. Keefe had lost his best friend, Joel Fields, in the shootdown, and volunteered to be a part of any commemorative effort paying tribute to his lost Air Force friends. The search resulted in the creation of the "Prop Wash Gang," a close-knit fraternal group of more than three hundred former USAFSS and current Air Intelligence Agency "Silent Warrior" airborne recon fliers. Everyone who was contacted encouraged pursuit of a memorial within the National Cryptologic Museum.

Learning about the joint commission's searching for Cold War MIAs opened other avenues for relevant information, and uncovered a massive group of declassified Soviet and American reports related to the shootdown. By February 1996, next of kin of lost crew members were offering access to their own files dating from 1958 to the present. Some of the available materials were spectacular: a transcript of Soviet MiG pilot communications as they shot down the C-130; MiG-17 gun camera photographs of the shot-up C-130 seconds before it crashed; interviews with the Soviet pilots; ammunition expenditure score cards of the attacking pilots; photographs of the crashed C-130; and videotape footage of Armenian villagers dedicating a memorial to the lost American crew at the crash site in 1993.

Tart created a briefing package and provided copies to key persons in government intelligence organizations and related civilian contractor groups. A copy of Tart's "C-130 60528 Crew Memorial" briefing found its way into the in-basket of the NSA Director, Air Force Lt. General Kenneth A. Minihan. General Minihan, who had dedicated the "EC-47 Memorial" at the Air Intelligence Agency in San Antonio, Texas, in September 1994 while commanding the AIA, had been looking for an approach to honor American fliers who had lost their lives on airborne reconnaissance during the Cold War.

Reviewing the 60528 briefing package, General Minihan announced at a director's staff meeting on November 18, 1996, that he wanted the NSA to honor with an Aerial Reconnaissance Memorial the C-130 crew that had been shot down over Armenia in 1958. His staff responded enthusiastically. They felt that a display inside the museum would be a superb addition.

General Minihan explained that he had much more than that in mind. He envisioned the memorial as a full-size C-130 aircraft set up in one of the parking lots, and he wanted to dedicate the memorial on the following anniversary of the C-130 shootdown—in September 1997. "Can we make that deadline?"

When a general asks that sort of question, the answer is inevitable: "Yes sir! No question; we can make it by September." Many staffers were no doubt thinking to themselves, "Where the hell does the director think we can find a C-130 for his parking lot?"

Minutes after the staff meeting, General Minihan called Colonel Wyatt C. (Chris) Cook, 694th Intelligence Group commander at Fort Meade, with an offer too good for the colonel to pass up. "Chris, Ken Minihan here . . . I've committed NSA to create a memorial honoring SIGINT aircrews who lost their lives on Cold War aerial recon missions . . . Can your group get us a C-130 and have it in place here at Fort Meade as the centerpiece of an aerial recon memorial in time for a dedication ceremony next September?" Colonel Cook, who had previously commanded the Electronic Security Command airborne SIGINT recon squadron in Panama, accepted the challenge, and was more than likely thinking all the while to himself, "Where does the general think we can find a C-130 for his parking lot?" Amazingly, everyone associated with the NSA—including Dr. David Hatch—suddenly felt that an aerial reconnaissance memorial was a great idea.

National Vigilance Park and Aerial Reconnaissance Memorial

Larry Tart got a call from Air Force Senior M.Sgt. Frederick Ferrer, whom Colonel Cook had assigned as the Air Force project manager for the aerial recon memorial project. "Larry, are you sitting down? . . . I have some great news; General Minihan has approved a memorial for the C-130 crew . . . Get this—he not only wants a memorial display in the museum; he wants to dedicate a real C-130 memorial in his parking lot

next September 2 . . . Can the Prop Wash Gang help us find a C-130?"
The stage was set to create "National Vigilance Park," permanent home
for the Aerial Reconnaissance Memorial.

Creation of NVP and the aerial recon memorial took on a life of its
own. Literally hundreds of volunteers donated thousands of hours toward
bringing the project to fruition. Through Kirk Carpenter, a Prop Wash
Gang member in Tucson, in late November 1996, Tart located a surplus C-130 aircraft in the Air Force "boneyard" storage facility at Davis-
Monthan AFB, Arizona. Meanwhile, William Grimes, director of the Air
Force "Big Safari" RC-135 Program Office—the same program office that
outfitted C-130 60528 for reconnaissance in 1958—offered assistance in
acquiring a C-130 for the memorial.

Michael Patterson, Big Safari RC-135 program manager, assumed responsibility for acquisition and delivery of a restored C-130 to National
Vigilance Park at Fort Meade. Several defense contractors offered their
support. Raytheon E-Systems (Greenville, Texas), with employees volun-
teering hundreds of off-duty hours, refurbished a "flyable" C-130A from
storage, providing it with the original 1958 paint scheme and outside appearance of C-130A-II 60528. An Air Combat Command C-130A flight
crew from Eglin AFB, Florida, ferried the C-130 from Arizona to Texas,
and flew it to Maryland on July 22, 1997, landing on a 3,000-foot runway
at Tipton Field, two miles from Vigilance Park. Volunteers from the
Maryland Air National Guard, assisted by volunteer active duty Air
Force personnel from Fort Meade, partially disassembled the aircraft and
moved it to Vigilance Park, where they reassembled it in its final configuration. Seeing a C-130 with a third of each wing and its tail stabilizer removed being towed along Fort Meade's streets to Vigilance Park was an
eye-opening experience for local Maryland commuters in early August.

Honoring 60528's Lost Crew in Armenia

Learning that significant pieces of 60528 wreckage remained at the
crash site in Armenia four decades after the shootdown, Air Force Big
Safari program director Bill Grimes deemed it fitting that the materials
be returned home to America. While plans for the trip to Armenia were
evolving, Larry Tart located Martin Kakosian, an Armenian witness to the

shootdown. Kakosian and his wife had, not long before, emigrated from Armenia to Long Island, New York. Kakosian had visited the crash site many times and had sculpted the memorial monument at the crash site in 1993. He said he'd welcome an opportunity to help memorialize the C-130 crew in America.

In February 1997, Tart visited the Kakosians in their home on Long Island and arranged for Martin Kakosian to escort an American team on a visit to the crash site. Between July 9 and 16, 1997, the team—Mike Patterson, Paul Martin, Horace (Red) Haire, Larry Tart, and Martin Kakosian—spent a week in and around Yerevan, Armenia.

Visiting the crash site by Sasnashen village, the team learned that the sandstone memorial that Kakosian had sculpted in 1993 had fallen over (or been dislodged by a grazing cow), and was irreparably damaged. Kakosian vowed to replace it, and he remained in Armenia to sculpt a new one that he, Bill Grimes, American and Armenian government officials, and Sasnashen villagers dedicated at the crash site later in 1997.

During the July visit, the Sasnashen villagers warmly welcomed the American team. The village mayor hosted an extensive luncheon shared by the team and the villagers. Some villagers were using larger pieces of C-130 debris—one- to two-meter-long pieces of a wing, stabilizer, or fuselage—to shore up open mesh fences by their dwellings. The villagers gladly gave up the C-130 fragments, and one villager handed Tart a small patch of white nylon that he had recovered immediately following the crash in 1958. Patterson arranged to ship the retrieved C-130 debris home to America for use in museums and memorials honoring lost recon crew members.

Memorial Recon Displays in National Cryptologic Museum

Sergeant Ferrer and Tart worked with the National Cryptologic Museum curator, Jack Ingram, to create three museum displays devoted to aerial reconnaissance. Sergeant Ferrer provided photographs and memorabilia for a "Cold Warrior" display honoring all American aircrew members killed or missing in action on airborne signals intelligence recon missions during the Cold War. The second display contains memorabilia provided by Mrs. Theresa Durkin, sister of M.Sgt. George P. Petrochilos, the Security Service airborne mission supervisor on 60528's last mission. Sergeant Petrochilos remains unaccounted for. His Class A blue uniform—complete with aircrew wings, ribbons, and name tag—as it hung in his locker in 1958, is the centerpiece of the second display.

Tart gathered the artifacts and chronicled the events depicted in the third "60528 memorial" display. Describing the shootdown of the C-130 and paying tribute to its crew, this display includes a memorial plaque with the names of the destroyed C-130's seventeen crew members and an extensive collection of memorabilia donated by former Silent Warrior recon fliers. In addition, the 60528 memorial display includes a fragment of the aircraft and the white nylon swath of material that Tart hand-carried from the Armenian crash site in July 1997.

The carved walnut plaque, shaped like a C-130, bears nameplates for each of the seventeen-man crew, placed in the positions in which they were seated when the plane was attacked. In addition, a pair of aircrew wings—donated by former airborne SIGINT recon fliers, many who had lost personal friends aboard the C-130 —is displayed on the plaque above each nameplate. During the weekend of the memorial dedication, one of the donors of the wings, who had had the reputation as one of the toughest men in the outfit, was chatting with Tart and Keefe. Suddenly, while laughing over old times, the man's eyes filled with tears and he said: "Larry, can you tell me which of the lost crew members is wearing my wings?" The tone of that simple, poignant question said everything about the meaning of the memorial for the men who had been there in 1958.

Helping Families with Travel Expenses

The memorial development volunteer group actively sought out family members of 60528's lost crew and invited them to attend the dedication ceremony planned for September 2, 1997. The Defense Department's POW/MIA office provided limited assistance with travel expenses but could not cover the expenses of all family members—one of the missing-in-action crew members left behind twelve siblings, ten of whom attended the dedication ceremony with their own families. Additionally, three large bronze plaques for the recon memorial and incidental costs not covered by corporate gifts had to be paid for.

Dan Hearn, president of the Intelligence Reconnaissance Fund of the Intelligence Scholarship Foundation, came to the rescue by offering use of the IRS-approved nonprofit fund as a mechanism for opening a tax-deductible fund-raising account. A massive fund-raising effort ensued. Overall, the memorial committee raised about $65,000, roughly one-third contributed by corporations and defense-related associations. Former recon fliers, current and former intelligence specialists, defense contractor employees, active duty military, and civilians wanting to help honor airmen who never returned from missions donated the remainder. After paying for the three plaques and incidental bills, the finance committee split the remaining funds (about $60,000) among qualifying family members of the honored crew—about ninety persons—to help offset travel expenses.

Silent Warriors' Reunion

Larry Tart arranged a "Silent Warriors' Reunion" for former Air Force recon fliers and their families, inviting family members of 60528's lost crew as honored guests. On Sunday, August 31, 1997, four hundred guests—two hundred of them seasoned, former recon fliers—gathered in a German restaurant near Fort Meade for camaraderie, remembrances, and repast. Some brought photographs and photo albums of their Air Force days, including photos of comrades who perished aboard 60528. Many former fliers, out of touch with each other for three to four decades, had lots of catching up to do, reliving the earlier, carefree days of their youth. Many former NCOs simply picked up on stag bar conversations from thirty-five years earlier as if they were "debriefing" at the Rhein-Main Rocket Club after a local C-130 recon mission.

The "mission debriefings" continued nightly in the hospitality suite at the former fliers' reunion motel, where more than a hundred couples enjoyed a memorable, extended weekend. Many shared remembrances involving 60528 crew members, stories that intrigued visiting family members of the honored crew. Sons and daughters who have no memory of their fathers were mesmerized and occasionally awestruck to hear stories about Dad from men who'd lived, worked, and partied with their fathers forty years earlier when they all were young—frequently half the age of the children they were speaking to. They also eagerly looked at photos of their fathers—photos they'd never seen before. Widows and siblings likewise found common ground for reminiscing with the former fliers. Several of the widows renewed old acquaintances with contemporaries of their husbands, old friends they had lost track of after 1958. Preferring the camaraderie of former fliers who knew their loved ones, several family members bypassed formally planned Air Force functions to spend more time with the former fliers. The family of one 60528 honored crew member even went so far as to move from the motel that the Air Force had reserved into the old fliers' reunion motel. Discussions between former fliers and 60528 family members brought healing and some closure to the shootdown incident for both groups.

Dedicating the Memorial

Tuesday, September 2, 1997, dawned as a typical warm, hazy, humid day. Overcast skies cleared as the sun burned away ground fog; it was a perfect day to christen America's first major memorial honoring airborne reconnaissance crews. After a three-day Labor Day weekend, local commuters jammed parkways and local roads, heading to work. Another group with a more important calling added to the morning traffic. Two thousand guests crowded into National Vigilance Park at Fort Meade, Maryland, at nine A.M. to dedicate the new park and Aerial Reconnaissance Memorial.

Most of the guests arrived at NVP early to visit with old friends before the ceremony. Designated seating—an area for the general public, a VIP section for honored family members and dignitaries, and a section reserved for former airborne recon fliers—permitted old friends to find each other in the gathered masses. Two hundred former airborne recon Silent Warriors, most with spouses and many from as far away as Washington State, California, Texas, Florida, Maine, Nebraska, and even England, gathered to pay tribute to fellow Silent Warriors who did not return from their last mission.

As the honored guests arrived, the U.S. Air Force Ceremonial Brass Band played softly. Everyone stood and faced the flagpole as the band struck up the "Star Spangled Banner," and the flag was raised in National

Vigilance Park for the first time. Immediately prior to the ceremony, seven geese appeared over the park, formed up in a vee formation, and disappeared in the blue sky.

As the geese flew off, Lonnie Henderson, one of the former recon fliers attending the ceremony, thought about his Air Force brothers who had not returned from their mission thirty-nine years earlier. As he glanced at his fellow recon veterans—described by one newspaper as "a grizzled group of veterans of the aerial reconnaissance campaign"—Henderson reminisced silently about the hundreds of recon missions he'd flown with many of those gathered on that morning. Two days after the ceremony, he eloquently wrote about the ceremony in an e-mail message to his Prop Wash Gang recon friends:

> On September 2, 1958, the crew of 60528 sat through a routine briefing as they got ready for yet another mission. A couple of crew members were talking softly to each other as Master Sgt. Petrochilos completed his pre-mission briefing. They were not ignoring the airborne mission supervisor; they had just heard it all before.
>
> Words that at one time had seemed riveting, which still held the rapt attention of the jeeps—the "Yenis" on board—were not lost to these old-timers. They talked about wives and girlfriends back at Rhein-Main; some nursed a slight hangover from the previous day's celebrations; others dozed slightly, half listening. Just a routine mission. After the briefing, they prepared for take-off as the pilot completed his checklist. Some of them were talking about the B-B-Q they were going to have that night, and everyone complained for the umpteenth time about just how rotten Turkish beer is. At oh-dark thirty, the plane rumbled down the runway, banked north and disappeared into history.
>
> On September 2, 1997, another crew assembled—airborne mission supervisors, two-operators [analysts], tac-rats [tactical voice intercept operators], wirebenders [airborne maintenance technicians], pilots, navigators, crew chiefs—gathered to pay tribute to fellow fliers and offer belated condolences to the families of 17 men who never returned from that mission 39 years ago.
>
> Before the dedication began, a flight of geese flew over the memorial grounds where another C-130, tail number 60528, stood in silent and

eternal tribute. During the ceremony, a hawk circled slowly overhead. Skip DeRousse pointed out the hawk, and mentioned that we could pretend that it was an eagle. The first hawk was soon joined by another, and I imagined that these were eagles, circling slowly, riding the winds.

Sitting there in the September sun were airborne legends in their own time, and airborne legends in their own minds. I saw some in uniform, in the uniform they wore at their retirement ceremonies. I wistfully mused that the only part of my uniform that still fits is my socks. As I looked at this group of a couple of hundred fliers, I imagined other briefings, other missions in all parts of the world.

I thought of a lifetime of briefings and a lifetime of friends brought together by a common bond. I thought of being alone, and unarmed, and afraid. I thought of 17 men whose Air Medals were a long time coming. I thought of the countless hundreds of Air Medals earned by our group of two hundred or so former fliers. I sat there with gray hair and fat belly, and looked around at other gray-haired men with fat bellies. And all of a sudden, as they stood in salute to their comrades, the hair changed color; the bellies disappeared; the men stood tall, sleek, slim and trim, and just for a moment, those fliers were ready for one more flight.

Today, we are back delivering the mail, teaching school, appraising real estate, raising peppers, consulting, maybe just fishing and taking it easy. The moment is over, over at least until I hear the drone of a C-130 as it flies low and slow over my house.

And then, I'll look up, render a silent salute, and remember...
September 4, 1997
Lonnie Henderson and
The Prop Wash Gang

Henderson—an ordained minister in Oklahoma and "Chief" to his friends due to his Comanche heritage—caught the essence of other Prop Wash Gang members in his tribute. Others attached personal meaning to the flock of geese at the dedication ceremony. Morris Levine wrote, "For the extremely observant, you will have noticed that when the geese first entered the area from the left, they were not yet in formation . . . It was as they passed over the C-130 that they assumed formation . . . Spooky, and inspiring."

Jack Harden's response: "Well said . . . I'm obviously not the only one who saw the symbolism when the honkers made their pass Tuesday . . . Somehow I suspect that Larry Tart made the arrangements."

And from Tart: "Guys, having the geese fall into formation was certainly a nice way to kick off the ceremony . . . I though that maybe our 'Chief' had ushered them in to start our day off right." Never at a loss for words, "Chief" Henderson had the perfect explanation:

> Gang:
> I talked with My Boss before the ceremony and although I didn't specifically ask for that formation to fly over, He knew what to do, and He arranged it all.
> Chief

As the geese faded away, Lt. General Kenneth A. Minihan, director of the National Security Agency, welcomed the crowd to NVP:

> We're honored to be here today to dedicate National Vigilance Park and to tell you why National Vigilance Park and the Aerial Reconnaissance Memorial are so significant to all of us. We're also honored to host the family members of the reconnaissance crew here today who were shot down over Armenia September 2, 1958 . . . And, we want to publicly acknowledge to the families and to the nation that we will never forget their sacrifice.
>
> Our presence here today is to celebrate the opening of the National Vigilance Park. The Aerial Reconnaissance Memorial is particularly meaningful and important to that celebration. We are taking a major step to publicly recognize and remember the sacrifices and dedication of aerial reconnaissance service men and women from all branches of the armed services throughout the Cold War . . .
>
> In the era before satellites and space-based systems, and worldwide interconnected communications, service members flying aerial reconnaissance missions were a critical source of information for our decision makers, writing a history of bravery and hope. As the Cold War raged on, more than 40 reconnaissance aircraft were lost on every frontier of the Cold War . . . The danger was real, and the price of peace and freedom was paid in American lives . . .

Of the 152 cryptologists from all services who lost their lives during the Cold War, 64 of them—over one-third—gave their lives in the conduct of this aerial reconnaissance mission.

The centerpiece of National Vigilance Park is the Aerial Reconnaissance Memorial, a refurbished C-130 "Hercules" aircraft to symbolize the mission ended in the line of duty 39 years ago today. This aircraft is the first exhibit in the park, and should be viewed as symbolic of the ultimate price paid by reconnaissance crews of the army, navy, marines, and air force. This symbolic resting place for this aircraft is marked by eighteen evergreen trees. Each tree represents a reconnaissance type of aircraft lost during the Cold War . . .

We will never forget the sacrifice and courage of those who went before us. The National Vigilance Park and Aerial Reconnaissance Memorial is our way of permanently and publicly honoring those Americans and all Americans who risked their lives daily defending the peace and maintaining our national security for this great nation . . .

Members of eleven of the seventeen families of C-130 60528's crew attended the dedication. Those family members were told that their loved ones' contributions "could not be acknowledged at the time because of the necessity to maintain secrecy with respect to their activities." Calling reconnaissance crews "Silent Warriors," Air Force Deputy Chief of Staff, General Ralph E. Eberhart, noted that "recognition is long overdue," and acknowledged that some recon missions violated enemy airspace:

Although we had a gentlemen's agreement to avoid penetrating each other's borders, occasionally, we would stray into prohibited air space. We flew probing missions—"ferret" missions they were called—to test Soviet defense capabilities. In addition, the navigation aids at that time were imprecise. These factors, combined with aggressive Soviet fighter pilots, led to a mission fraught with danger . . .

The reconnaissance crews' constant vigilance and frequent probes of the Soviet defenses allowed American planners to prepare for the worst case scenario—thank God, a scenario that never unfolded—an all-out war with the Soviet Union . . .

Today, we pause to reflect on the sacrifices of those brave reconnais-

sance crew members and to remember especially the crew of aircraft 60528. On September 2, 1958, six crew members from the United States Air Forces, Europe, and eleven operators from the U.S. Air Force Security Service took off on aircraft 60528 for what they would term a routine mission, a routine mission back then that seems far from routine today. They flew over Turkey within 100 miles of the border, and once they strayed—this unarmed aircraft strayed into prohibited airspace—it was attacked by Soviet fighter aircraft. After repeated attacks and re-peated passes, it fell to the earth, killing all seventeen crew members on board. Today, we humbly dedicate this memorial to their memory and the ultimate price they paid for their country . . .

General Eberhart presented posthumous Air Medals to the families of 60528's crew in recognition of their loved ones' "heroism, courage, and gallantry." To the accompaniment of a bagpiper's dirge, a joint-service honor guard also presented each family a U.S. flag that had flown over the NSA and that had flown aboard the final flight of memorial C-130 60528 from Greenville, Texas, to Maryland.

Right on cue after the flags were presented, a formation of three Maryland Air National Guard C-130 aircraft approached National Vigi-lance Park. As the lead C-130 banked to the right, creating a "missing crew" formation while approaching the park, the peculiar, inimitable drone of the C-130 engines brought tears to the eyes of the two hundred Silent Warriors in the park—most of whom had flown recon missions aboard C-130s. They were not men who cried often. But they had heard those engines so often, had heard them when they were airmen, and could never hear them thereafter without stopping for a moment to pay attention to that sound from long ago. Every one of them could tell the drone of those turboprop engines immediately. Now the tears flowed, un-questionably in recognition of the missing men, whom their comrades had loved—and still loved—but also perhaps in recognition of a time when they all, the dead and the living, had been part of a very special team, a time when they had been young, and brave, and wild together. There were no dry eyes in the former recon fliers' seating section at NVP. Following a twenty-one-gun salute by a seven-person drill team, the cere-mony ended solemnly with a bugler playing Taps.

EPILOGUE

—

Around the end of the Cold War, advances in DNA[145] analysis techniques made it possible to identify heretofore unidentifiable remains associated with U.S. military missing in action. When the Soviet government returned six sets of remains in 1958, the U.S. Air Force assigned designators X-1 through X-6 to the remains. Subsequently, remains X-1, X-2, X-4, and X-5 were identified and honored with memorial services in accordance with family requests. The U.S. Air Force interred the two unidentified sets of remains (X-3 and X-6) with full military honors in separate graves in Arlington National Cemetery in February 1959.

In 1992 the family of A/2C Archie T. Bourg Jr., an MIA in the shootdown, requested the Air Force to exhume the two unidentified remains for DNA analysis. DNA specialists—an Armed Forces DNA Identification Laboratory (AFDIL) group in Maryland and a civilian group in California—conducted independent DNA sequence matching tests, comparing DNA from Bourg family blood samples to DNA from bone samples from remains X-3 and X-6.

The AFDIL analyses showed a match between unidentified remains X-6 and the Bourg DNA samples in 1993, but conclusions reached in 1994 by the DNA specialists in California did not confirm the match with remains X-6. This discrepancy prompted the U.S. Army to commission a study of the effectiveness of mitochondrial DNA (mtDNA) assisted identifications. Meanwhile, the Defense Department imposed a moratorium on the use of DNA for identifications.

To resolve the discrepancy, in March 1994 the army sent another bone sample from remains X-6 and Bourg family blood samples to an impartial, third-party laboratory in England. In April 1994 other bone samples from remains X-6 were resubmitted to the AFDIL as "blind samples," i.e., with no name or incident association. Later, in May 1995, another bone sample from X-6 was submitted to AFDIL as another blind sample. The AFDIL specialists found the two blind bone samples to match Bourg family DNA samples. A report prepared by the British-based DNA specialists confirmed the AFDIL findings. Accordingly, the Defense Department lifted the moratorium on DNA analysis and reaffirmed the usefulness and reliability of DNA analysis for the identification of human remains. On August, 27, 1996, the Defense Casualty and Memorial Affairs Board of Officers approved an army recommendation that remains X-6 be identified as Airman Bourg.

Memorial Services for Archie T. Bourg Jr.

Notified that Airman Bourg's remains had been identified, the Bourg family requested a memorial service and reburial. On April 2, 1997, memorial services with full military honors were held for Airman Bourg in the Fort Myers, Virginia, post chapel. His remains were returned to the same grave site from which remains X-6 had been disinterred. An Associated Press story describes the memorial service:

Nearly 39 years after U.S. Airman Archie "Boogie" Bourg's plane was shot down during the Cold War, his family finally had a chance to say goodbye.

For more than three decades, Bourg was buried in Arlington National Cemetery as an unknown. On Wednesday, his remains finally identified because of the persistence of his sister, he was reburied with full military honors.

About a dozen family members and friends attended the service. Bourg's sister, Lorna Bourg of New Iberia, Louisiana, said the nation had finally given her brother and the 16 men who died with him the honor they deserved.

"Today is an important day not just for my brother, it's an important day for our country to understand how many people served in our armed forces and made sacrifices, sometimes in secret," she said, her voice breaking. "People don't really understand and know that the Cold War was a real war with real casualties . . . Real people died."

Members of the Air Force 694th Intelligence Group attended the memorial services and hosted the Bourg family during a visit to the National Cryptologic Museum at Fort Meade following memorial services for Airman Bourg in Arlington. Meanwhile, an announcement was pending regarding the identification of remains X-3—the last of the unidentified 60528 remains that the Soviets recovered from the crash site in 1958.

Memorial Services for John E. Simpson

On April 3, 1997, the day after Archie T. Bourg Jr. was laid to rest, the Air Force informed Mark Simpson, himself by then an Air Force major, that based on DNA analysis, remains X-3—the other set of unidentified remains—belonged to his father, Captain John E., which was problematic since the Air Force had identified remains X-5 in 1958 as Captain Simpson. Based on tenuous evidence and without the benefit of DNA analysis, identification of remains X-5 in 1958 had been inconclusive, a fact that the Air Force did not share with the Simpson family. The Simpson family and the Air Force accorded remains X-5 full military honors and interred the body in a cemetery in Austin, Texas, in late 1958.

Four decades later, with a firm DNA identification of remains X-3 as Captain Simpson, the Air Force obtained the Simpson family's permission to disinter remains X-5 for DNA analysis. At the same time, plans were worked out to honor Captain Simpson with a new memorial service.

On September 3, 1997, the Simpson family and many of Captain Simpson's friends who had paid tribute to 60528's crew at Fort Meade,

Maryland, the previous day traveled to Arlington, Virginia, to pay homage to Captain Simpson. After a funeral service in the Fort Myers post chapel and graveside services, Captain Simpson was laid to rest in Arlington National Cemetery—in the same grave from which his remains (X-3) had been removed for identification. Fittingly, the graves of Captain Simpson and Airman Bourg are adjacent.

The aerial recon memorial dedication in Maryland and memorial services for his grandfather, Capt. John E. Simpson, in Virginia had a special impact on John E. Simpson III. Young John Simpson felt a "calling" and enlisted in the U.S. Air Force. Currently a Spanish linguist with the 97th Intelligence Squadron at Offutt AFB, Nebraska, Airman Simpson volunteered for airborne recon missions, as did his grandfather, father, and uncle. He recently shared his feelings in an e-mail message:

Dear Mr. Tart,

My name is John E. Simpson III, and I believe we met in Sept. '97 up at NSA. I'm interested in membership in the Prop Wash Gang, and although I'm not quite a former ESC flier, I think I have a unique association in that my grandfather copiloted the 60528 flight. Although I never met my grandfather, and didn't feel the direct impact of his early death, I have certainly seen the emotional scars in my father, his brother, and his mother.

It pains me to imagine what my family must have gone through, all without ever knowing what my grandfather really sacrificed his life for, or even the now obvious importance of his mission. However, I believe that the actions that blossomed into the NVP, and the volunteerism that accompanied its dedication, were perhaps the best act of good faith, comfort, and closure that I am aware of to date.

After I returned to Houston from Baltimore, it took me about two weeks to decide that if what I had attended was what the Air Force was about, then I wanted to be a part of it. Coincidentally, or maybe not, I am now a member of the 97th IS [Intelligence Squadron] at Offutt, in spin-up linguistic training to fly on the RJ [Rivet Joint RC-135 aircraft].

I am proud of my Air Force heritage from my grandfather, to my father and uncle—John Simpson Jr. and Lt. Col. Mark Simpson—both

*of whom I'm sure you know; but I am always anxious to hear more
about the events leading up to and after my grandfather's plane was
downed, and always anxious to correspond with folks that appreciate his
sacrifice . . .*

A/1C John Simpson III

Airman Simpson is the youngest member of the Prop Wash Gang .
On September 29, 2000, Lt. Col. Mark Simpson had the honor of pin-
ning aircrew wings on his nephew, A/1C John Simpson III, at a ceremony
at Offutt AFB, Nebraska.

Remains X-5 Found to Be Gerald H. Medeiros

On November 28, 1997, DNA analysis showed that the remains originally identified as those of Captain Simpson (X-5) were in fact the remains of A/2C Gerald H. Medeiros. Working with Medeiros's family, the
Air Force honored him with a memorial service. With the six sets of remains recovered from the crash site in 1958 identified, only the remains
(the thousands of minuscule bone and tooth fragments) excavated from
the crash site in 1993 remained unidentified.

Final Memorial Services for 60528's Crew

The major objective of the excavation of the crash site in Armenia
in 1993 was to resolve issues involving 60528's unaccounted for crew
members. A U.S. Army missing-in-action recovery team recovered "over
2,000 bone and tooth fragments, thousands of fragments of aircraft
wreckage, life support equipment, and personal effects—including two
identification tags for Moore and Fields." Anthropological analysis of
the human remains revealed that the remains were "those of at least
one adult." The analysis also showed evidence of "high-temperature
perimortem incineration"—the bodies had been cremated in an inferno
created by the crash of the fuel-laden C-130 aircraft.

The six sets of remains recovered from the crash site in 1958 (originally designated X-1 through X-6) were only partially complete; none

were complete bodies. The human remains collected at the crash site in 1993 were so badly damaged by fire that they did not yield useful DNA; identification specialists could not match those remains to specific airmen killed in the crash:

> The size and condition of the remains preclude the use of mtDNA analysis given the current state of that technology.

CONCLUSION

Available evidence indicates that Capt. Rudy J. Swiestra and his 16-man crew died in Soviet Armenia following the crash of their C-130 aircraft. Partial remains repatriated by the Soviet Union to the U.S. in 1958 were ultimately identified as those of Capt. Swiestra, 1st Lt. Villarreal, Capt. Simpson, Capt. Jeruss, A2C Medeiros and A2C Bourg. Human remains recovered from the crash site in 1993 show evidence of perimortem trauma consistent with incineration related to an aircraft crash. Given the incomplete nature of the remains of the six men previously identified from this incident, it is possible that the remains recovered from the crash site represent any or all of the manifested crew.

Based on laboratory analysis and available circumstantial evidence, the Air Force identified the remains recovered in 1993 as "Group Remains" from the incident and listed the seventeen crew members:

Capt. Paul Ernest Duncan
Capt. Edward Joseph Jeruss
Capt. John Edwin Simpson
1st Lt. Ricardo Manuel Villarreal
M Sgt. George Peter Petrochilos
S Sgt. Laroy Price
T Sgt. Arthur Leroy Mello
A1C Robert Joseph Oshinskie
A2C Archie Theo Bourg Jr.
A2C James Edward Ferguson Jr.
A2C Joel Hughes Fields

A2C *Harold Theodore Kamps*
A2C *Gerald Carmine Maggiacomo*
A2C *Clement Oscar Mankins*
A2C *Gerald Herve Medeiros*
A2C *Robert Henry Moore*

On September 2, 1998—forty years to the day after the shootdown—the "Group Remains" for 60528's last crew were buried with full military honors in Arlington National Cemetery. The Air Force hosted those families of crew members who were able to attend. A seven-member Air Force drill team honored the crew with a twenty-one-gun salute; each family was provided an American flag, and a C-130 aircraft paid tribute to the crew with a flyover.

A Pentagon press release pointed out that the remains being buried "represent all of the crewmen . . . Such burials have taken place at Arlington before in similar instances."

In a news section on Cold War Casualties, the *Air Force Times* newspaper titled its story about the memorial services: A LONG TRIP HOME — C-130 CREW LAID TO REST FORTY YEARS AFTER BEING DOWNED BY SOVIETS.

Four decades. That is a long time in the life of a human being—twice as long as the majority of the men on that plane had lived. Their parents outlived them, in nearly every case dying without ever hearing anything specific enough about the circumstances of their son's death.

This book has told a story of camaraderie, of bravery, of mutual distrust and hatred, of human and mechanical error. But at its core it is a story of seventeen men, most of them very young. Those twenty-year-olds on 528 had not enlisted to go to war; they had joined to learn a skill they could use in later life, or to see the world, or simply to grow into manhood in a broader setting than their hometowns. The flight crew—most of whom had experienced Korea and some the Second World War—knew a great deal about death, as did Pete Petrochilos, who had enlisted a couple of years after most of his crew were born. Perhaps those older crew members set out with a hard-won sense of the precariousness of life. But the others were too young. Though they boarded the plane that morning exhausted as usual, they probably carried with them very little sense of personal mortality; instead, we can assume they were filled with that youthful feeling of sheer adventure they possessed every time they flew. They were doing something their parents, their high school classmates, even their wives and girlfriends, knew nothing about. Their mission that day, and every day before it, was special, dangerous, secret; they could picture themselves describing those missions to their children and then their grandchildren in their old age.

But they didn't have time to grow old. They burned to cinders that afternoon in the midst of their youth, victims of the Cold War, and the rubble was left on a barren hillside in Soviet Armenia. Even their ashes took forty years to come home.

APPENDIX A

—

MATERIALS RETURNED BY SOVIETS WITH REMAINS

List dated September 24, 1958, of documents, weapon, and currency that the Soviet KGB returned to American authorities with the six sets of human remains.

1. Identity card of 1st Lt. Ricardo M. Villarreal

2. Identification card of Ricardo Villarreal

3. Membership card of Reserve Officers Association made out to R. Villarreal

4. Driver's license and three photographs

5. Note with address

6. Fourteen postage stamps

7. Book of fuel coupons

8. Driver's license for West Germany

9. Tabular sports calendar

10. Calling card bearing the name Beni Khuks

11. Insurance policy

12. Card No. 23567 bearing the name Ricardo

13. Inoculation card

14. Physiological training card

15. Identity card bearing the name R. Swiestra

16. Membership card of the Reserve Officers Association made out to Swiestra

17. Boy Scout membership card

18. 28-year calendar

19. Driver's license made out to Swiestra

20. Insurance policy

21. Radio operator's certificate made out to Swiestra

22. Pilot's class card made out to Swiestra

23. Mutual Aid membership card made out to Swiestra

24. Membership card of California Association

25. Driver's license

26. Fragments of partly burned documents numbering seven sheets

27. Two snapshots

28. Special order No. 194, dated August 28, 1958, of the 7406th Squadron of the United States Air Force

29. Partly burned United States currency, four bills, thirty-one dollars

30. Partly burned Turkish lira, five bills, 175 lira

31. Partly burned West German marks, three bills, 50 marks

32. Partly burned French francs, one bill, 1,000 francs

33. Partly burned Dutch guilders, one bill, 10 guilders

34. Partly burned Austrian shillings, one bill, 10 shillings

35. Remnants of burned notebook

36. Partly burned navigation guide

37. Metal identification tag bearing the name Paul E. Duncan

38. Burned pistol of American make, Ithaca, No. 1769459

APPENDIX B

—

FLIGHT CREW TDY ORDERS TO INCIRLIK, TURKEY*

7406TH SUPPORT SQUADRON (USAFE)
UNITED STATES AIR FORCE
[APO 57], US FORCES

SPECIAL ORDERS AUGUST 28, 1958
NUMBER 194

Following named officers and airman, this unit, will proceed on or about 1 Sep 58 from Rhein Main AB, Germany, to Adana, Incirlik, Turkey, on TDY for approximately 10 days for the purpose of acting as crew members on aircraft performing an operational mission. TDN. 551-5795400 980- . . . P458.99 S67.300-0211. Items 1, 2, 3, 4b (with the exception of SSGT PRICE, who is cleared for access to classified material up to and including SECRET), 5, 6, 7, 8, 9, 11, 12 and 15 (on the reverse side) are applicable. Authority: USAFE Reg 30-13, as amended and AFM 35-11.

* The Soviets translated original S.O. #194 into Russian after finding the orders at the crash site. This translation back into English by Larry Tart. *Note: Capt.* Paul E. Duncan, the other pilot on flight on Sept. 2, 1958, deployed to Turkey on August 25, 1958, on S.O. #191, and eleven U.S. Air Force Security Service crewmen were on separate TDY orders.

519

CAPT   EDWARD J JERUSS, AO1905185
CAPT   RUDY J SWIESTRA, AO0781703
1STLT JOHN E SIMPSON, 25642A
1STLT RICARDO M VILLARREAL, AO3064233
SSGT   LAROY PRICE, AF15436645
FOR THE COMMANDER:

[signature]
JACK G. FERRELL
Captain, USAF
Asst Admin Officer

APPENDIX C

—

TRANSCRIPT OF MIG PILOTS
SHOOTING DOWN C-130 60528

Transcript of a tape-recorded radio conversation among Soviet
fighter pilots who participated in the attack on C-130 60528 over Armenia on September 2, 1958. The parenthetical and bracketed material has
been added in explanation.

I am at maximum speed.
Roger.
What is yours?
3,000 [meters].
583, I read you excellently. [583 is pilot call sign]
I read excellently.
I read 18 excellently. [18 is either ground controller or pilot (2)18]
Understood. Altitude 100 [10,000 meters].
Understood.
In the northwest, about 7 balls here. [70 percent undercast or cloud
cover]
Very poor, almost none.
130? [compass course].
Roger, 330.
582, I have taken course 330, altitude 80. [altitude 8,000 meters]

Roger, I am taking.

You are understood. Altitude 90. [9,000 meters]

Roger, 40 kilometers. [not clear; possibly distance from take-off]

. . . [. . . means break in transcript, signal too weak to read]

Poor. I cannot see the orientation point yet.

No, not visible. It does not matter.

. . .

45. . . .

180 I have taken [course].

201, passed the second. [201 is one of the Russian pilots]

I am 201. I can see the fence well. [barbed-wire fence inside border between Turkey and Soviet Armenia].

Roger.

Roger. Proceed in a slight climb toward your point.

. . .

Altitude 100. [10,000 meters]

My course is 200.

Roger.

Roger.

Roger.

. . .

. . .

. . .

I have already turned toward the point, over 136. Now I am turning to 180 [course]. [136 is checkpoint on the ground]

I am turning toward 135. [checkpoint]

Yes, I am over 136 now.

Roger.

Roger, I am approaching your point.

I am turning to 180. I am taking . . . to 135.

Roger. . . . .

Roger. I am approaching your point.

My altitude is 110. [11,000 meters]

Roger. I am looking.

I am climbing. I am 201; I am climbing.

Roger.

No. I . . . .

. . .

Roger, ... 582.

I am looking.

To the south there is 2–3 balls. [20–30 percent cloud cover]

582, I see the target; to the right.

I see the target; a large one.

Its altitude is 100 as you said. [10,000 meters]

I am 201. I see the target. Attack!

I am 201. I am attacking the target.

You are understood.

I am attacking the target.

Stand by.

The target is a large one.

Roger.

Attack; attack. 218 attack.

Stand by.

582. . . . .

Roger.

. . .

. . .

Roger.

Attack by four-fourths. [evidently the quarter of attack from the indicated course; from the left rear].

. . .

The target is a transport, four engine.

Roger.

Roger.

. . .

. . .

201. I am attacking the target.

. . .

218. . . . .

. . . . 201.

Target speed is 300 [KPH or 180 MPH]. I am going along with it. It is
turning toward the fence. [border]

. . . . The target is burning.

There is a hit.

. . .

The target is burning. 582.

The target is banking.

It is going toward the fence. [border]

. . . . Open fire. . . .

218. Are you attacking?

Yes. Yes. I.

The target is burning. . . .

The tail assembly is falling off the target.

82, Do you see me? I am in front of the target.

. . .

. . . . Look!

Oh!

Look at him. He will not get away. He is already falling.

Yes. He is falling. I will finish him off, boys. I will finish him off on the run.

The target has lost control. It is going down.

Now the target will fall. . . .

82. A little to the right.

The target has turned over. . . .

. . .

The target is falling. . . .

218. . . . . No?

Do you see me?

. . . . Form up. . . .

82. I see. I am watching the target. I see.

Aha. You see. It is falling.

Yes. . . . . Form up; go home.

After my third pass, the target started burning.

. . . . In succession.

. . .

Roger. I am turning. . . .

Roger.

16. 577. Give the altitude, mission. [16 is ground station; 577 is a pilot]

Who asked? I did not understand.

. . .

577.

Altitude 100, toward 135. [10,000 meters; 135 is a checkpoint].

Roger.

Repeat. Where are you?

On the left, on the left; below.

Well, let's form up. Follow. Let's go.

The remainder of the transcript recounted conversations between the pilots, control points, and control tower as the fighters made their way back to base.

APPENDIX D

—

INTERNATIONAL AIR INCIDENTS COMPARED TO THE C-130 INCIDENT VIS-À-VIS THE MISSING PERSONS ACT

a. On 19 November 1951, a USAF C-47 aircraft was forced down by Soviet fighter aircraft near Papa, Hungary. The four crew members were held for 39 days by the Hungarian communists and then released to duty.

b. On 13 June 1952, a USAF B-29 aircraft was lost while performing a mission over the Sea of Japan. [Twelve crew members were MIA; missing status terminated by a presumptive finding of death on 15 November 1955; to date no positive intelligence received that any crew member survived and were, or are still, being held alive by the Soviet communists.]

c. On 7 October 1952, another USAF B-29 aircraft was shot down by a Soviet fighter in the vicinity of Hokkaido, Japan. [Eight crew members MIA; missing status terminated by a presumptive finding of death on 15 November 1955; to date no positive intelligence received that any crew member survived and were, or are still, being held alive by the Soviet communists.]

d. On 29 July 1953, a USAF RB-50 aircraft with a crew of 17 performing a mission over the Sea of Japan was shot down by Russian MiG-15 type aircraft approximately 40 miles east of the Siberian coast. [One survivor rescued, three bodies accounted for and 13 MIAs; missing status terminated by a presumptive finding of death on 15 November

1955; to date no positive intelligence received that any missing crew members survived and were, or are still, being held alive by the Soviet communists.]

e. On 23 December 1957, a USAF T-33 trainer disappeared en route from Chateauroux, France, to Naples, Italy. On 7 January 1958, the communists reported that the T-33 was forced to land in Albania. The pilot was granted a Yugoslavian visa and released to travel commercial airlines. He returned to military control on 11 January 1958.

f. On the evening of 19 May 1958, after an off-base party, three airmen crossed the East–West German border near Hof, Germany. The communists returned these three airmen to duty on 26 May 1958.

g. On 27 June 1958, a USAF C-118 aircraft with a crew of nine was shot at and forced down near Yerevan, Armenia, by Soviet fighter aircraft . . . Shortly after the personnel cleared the grounded C-118, it exploded. On 28 June 1958, the Soviets announced the incident and commenced a propaganda campaign branding the incident as a "crude violation" of Soviet airspace. On 7 July 1958, the Soviets released the entire crew of nine.

h. On 1 July 1960, a USAF RB-47 aircraft with a crew of six was shot down by Soviet aircraft while over international waters of the Barents Sea off the coast of USSR. On 11 July 1960, the Soviet Union announced they had shot down the RB-47 and had rescued two survivors. The Soviets propagandized this mission as an aggressive intrusion of the Soviet airspace and threatened to judge the rescued personnel according to the fullest severity of Soviet laws. The Soviets stated that, on 4 July 1960, they recovered from the waters north of Cape Svyatoi Nos, the remains of one crew member. His remains were returned to the United States authorities on 23 July 1960. The Soviets denied any knowledge of the other three crew members. After exploitation of the incident the Soviets released the two survivors in January 1961 without actually having tried them. Based upon information received from the two survivors, the missing status of the three other crew members of the RB-47 was terminated by a determination that they died 1 July 1960 as the result of the aircraft incident.

APPENDIX E

ACRONYMS AND ABBREVIATIONS

Acronym/ Abbreviation	Meaning
'06th	7406th Support Squadron
'99th	7499th Support Group
6911th RSM	6911th Radio Squadron Mobile
6911th RGM	6911th Radio Group Mobile
7406th	7406th Support Squadron
7499th	7499th Support Group
aka	also known as
AAA	antiaircraft artillery
AAC	U.S. Army Air Corps, forerunner of U.S. Air Force
AAF	U.S. Army Air Forces
AC	aircraft commander
AC&W squadron	aircraft control and warning squadron
ACRP	airborne communications intelligence reconnaissance platform
admiral	cover name for Air Force Security Service airborne mission supervisor on recon missions in Europe
AFB	Air Force Base
AFDIL	Armed Forces DNA Identification Laboratory

AFSA	Armed Forces Security Agency, forerunner of NSA
AFSS	U.S. Air Force Security Service
AFSSO	Air Force Special Security Office
AMC	Air Material Command
AMT	airborne maintenance technician
AMTI	airborne moving target indicator
AOB	air order of battle
AP	Associated Press
APN-59	airborne search radar on C-130A aircraft
APN-81	airborne search radar on C-130A aircraft
APN-99	airborne Doppler radar on C-130A aircraft
apparatchiki	bureaucrats, managers (Russian)
AR	army regulation
ARDF	airborne radio direction-finding
ATRAN	automated terrain recognition and navigation
Aunt Sue	project name for USAFE ATRAN recon mission in the 1950s
back-ender	recon crew specialist on a recon mission
Bahnhof	train station (German)
bat	airborne intercept operator on Yokota, Japan–based ACRP aircraft
Betty Lou	Air Force project name for USAFE RB-50D ATRAN recon aircraft in the 1950s
Blue Sky	project name for RC-47 operations in Korea in the 1950s; later became project Rice Bowl
Capt.	captain
CIA	Central Intelligence Agency
CILHI	U.S. Army Central Identification Laboratory, Hawaii
Col.	colonel
COMINT	communications intelligence
COMSEC	communications security
CONOP	concept of operations
Cpl.	corporal
Creek Grass	USAFE project name for C-130A-II and B-II recon aircraft and missions
CW	continuous wave, Morse code

DC	District of Columbia
DCS/Intelligence	deputy chief of staff for Intelligence
DCS/Ops (Operations)	deputy chief of staff for Operations
demarche	protest, note, representation (Russian)
Detachment 1	Detachment 1, 6911th Radio Group Mobile
DF	direction-finding
DNA	deoxyribonucleic acid
DNIF	duty not to include flying
DPMO	Defense [Department] POW/MIA Office
DR	discrepancy report
Dream Boat	project name for USAFE RB-50 ACRP aircraft in the 1950s
ELINT	electronic intelligence
EOB	electronic order of battle
ESC	Electronic Security Command
ESG	Electronic Security Group
ESS	Electronic Security Squadron
FAA	Federal Aviation Authority
FEAF	Far East Air Forces
ferret	reconnaissance mission
FRG	Federal Republic of Germany (West Germany during the Cold War)
front-ender	cockpit (flight) crew member on recon mission
GI	government issue; slang for military or military troop
GCI	ground-controlled intercept
GDR	German Democratic Republic (East Germany during the Cold War)
Gen.	general
GMT	Greenwich Mean Time, aka Zulu time
GRU	Soviet army intelligence
Half Track	project name for USAFE RB-50D photo-mapping aircraft in the 1950s
Hay Stack	Air Force project name for USAFE RB-50 ACRP aircraft (also known as Dream Boat)

Heart Throb	project name for USAFE RB-57A photo recon aircraft in the 1950s
HF	high frequency
Hot Pepper	project name for USAFE 7405th RC-54 photo/electronic recon aircraft in the 1950s
HQ	headquarters
HUMINT	human intelligence
IAD	fighter aviation division
IAP	fighter aviation regiment, Soviet air force
ICAO	International Civil Aviation Organization
ICJ	International Court of Justice
ID	identification
IFF	identification friend or foe
IG	inspector general
IG	intelligence group
IRAN	inspection and replacement as necessary
IS	intelligence squadron
IW	intelligence wing
JCS	Joint Chiefs of Staff
JCSB	Joint Commission Support Branch
JUSMAAG	Joint U.S. Military Advisory Assistance Group
KGB	Soviet secret police
KIA	killed in action
LRAA	Soviet Long-Range Air Force
Lt.	lieutenant
Lulu Belle	project name for USAFE 7405th RC-54 ATRAN recon aircraft in the 1950s
Maj.	major
MATS	Military Air Transport Service
MIA	missing in action
MID	Ministerstvo Inostrannykh Del (Russian), Ministry of Foreign Affairs
MP	military police
MVD	Soviet Ministry of Internal Security
NATO	North Atlantic Treaty Organization
NCO	noncommissioned officer

NCOIC	noncommissioned officer in charge
nisei	second generation Japanese Americans
NSA	National Security Agency
NVP	National Vigilance Park at Fort Meade, Maryland
OB	order of battle
OCB	Operations Coordinating Board; part of the NSC
OL	operating location
ONC	operating navigation chart
Ops NCOIC	noncommissioned officer in charge of operations
OSD	Office of Secretary of Defense
OSNAZ	Soviet signals intelligence
PAL	pathological and anatomical laboratory
pan	panoramic display receiver
PARPRO	Peacetime Aerial Reconnaissance Program
Pfc.	private first class
PHOTINT	photo intelligence
Pie Face	project name for USAFE 7405th YC-97A photo recon aircraft in the 1950s
POW	prisoner of war
POW/MIAs	prisoners of war and missing in action persons
Pretty Girl I and II	USAFE ELINT/PHOTINT recon RC-54 aircraft in the 1950s
PSEhO	*podrazdelenie canitarno-ehpidemichecheskoj otrabotki,* (Russian), sanitation and epidemiological treatment section
PVO	*protivo-vozhdushnaya oborona* (Russian), antiaircraft air defense
R&R duty	rest and relaxation
RAF	British Royal Air Force
raven	electronic warfare officer on Strategic Air Command recon aircraft
RBN	radio beacon
Red Owl	project name for USAFE 7405th photo recon support for U.S. Army in Europe in the 1950s
RFI	radio frequency interference
RGM	Radio Group Mobile

Rice Bowl	project name for RC-47 operations in Korea in the late 1950s and early 1960s; earlier called Blue Sky
Rivet Victor	project name for C-130A-II and B-II ACRP aircraft in the late 1950s and 1960s
RJ	Rivet Joint RC-135 airborne signals intelligence reconnaissance platform
RPM	revolutions per minute
RSM	Radio Squadron Mobile
RTP	radio technical regiment
SAC	Strategic Air Command
sailor	cover name for Air Force Security Service recon crew member in Europe
SALT	Strategic Arms Limitation Treaty
SCG	Special Communications Group
SDU	signal display unit
SG	Support Group
Sgt.	sergeant
Sharp Cut	project name for USAFE RB-57A photo/electronic recon aircraft in the 1950s
SIGINT	signals intelligence
SIOP	single integrated operations plan
Slick Chick	project name for USAFE RF-100A photo recon aircraft in the 1950s
Slot	project name for USAFE 7405th RB-26 photo recon aircraft in the 1950s
SQ/Sqdn	squadron
SRS	strategic reconnaissance squadron
SS	Support Squadron
SSM	surface-to-surface missile
SSO	special security office
Sun Valley	project name for C-130A-II and B-II ACRP aircraft in the mid-1950s; later redesignated Rivet Victor
TAC	Tactical Air Command
TASS	official Soviet news agency
TDY	temporary duty
TFR	Task Force Russia

TRD	thermal heat device (infrared)
U.S./USA	United States/United States of America
USSR	Union of Soviet Socialist Republics
U.N.	United Nations
UPI	United Press International
USAF	United States Air Force/U.S. Air Force
USAFE	United States Air Forces, Europe
USAFSS	United States Air Force Security Service
USG	United States Government
VA	*vozdushnaya armiya* (Russian), air army
VD	venereal disease
VHF	very high frequency
VIP	very important person
WD	war department
Willy	project name for USAFE 7405th RC-47 photo recon aircraft in the 1950s
ZAKVO	Transcaucasian Military District
ZI	Zone of Interior (continental United States)

APPENDIX F

BRIEF HISTORIES OF 7405TH AND 7407TH SUPPORT SQUADRONS

7405th Support Squadron

The buildup of new recon capabilities within the 7499th Support Group in the mid-1950s shows the emphasis that the U.S. Air Force placed on gathering intelligence on Soviet and East European targets behind the Iron Curtain. In early 1955, the 7499th was a photo and electronic recon squadron, about to expand its aircraft inventory and capabilities.

At the monthly commander's call in June 1955, Major Welsh, 7405th commander, approached the 7499th expansion and reorganization with a "business as usual" speech to his troops, who had transferred on paper from the 7499th to the 7405th on May 10. The 7405th mission involved undertaking aerial photographic missions, conducting courier and freight flights, supporting Flight C, and providing administrative and logistic support to the 7499th group.[146] It was a broad spectrum of demands.

The 7405th (exclusive of Flight C activities) operated as two flights: Flights A and B. Personnel were assigned to either Flight A or Flight B depending on job specialty. The squadron supported a hodgepodge of operational missions. Flight A continued flying its electronic reconnaissance of the Soviet European satellite countries using two C-54 aircraft, Pretty Girl I and II. Headquarters USAFE directed that 7405th Pretty

Girl ELINT missions along the Soviet and East European satellite borders remain at least twenty miles from the borders at all times.

The Flight B mission was broader in scope than the Flight A mission. In addition to its primary photo reconnaissance mission, Flight B supported other 7499th units by transporting personnel and cargo, and flew its share of training missions. On special missions and training missions, Flight B flew to virtually all North Atlantic Treaty Organization (NATO) bases and USAF installations in Western Europe, plus the occasional "embassy run" to U.S. embassy locations behind the Iron Curtain.

To perform its mission in 1955, Flight B had four B-26Cs, three C-47 A and D model aircraft, and two RC-54Ds—all with special equipment modifications. The B-26s and the C-47s formed the Red Owl section, using vertical photography (the camera lenses are mounted vertical with the horizon) and overflying target areas to photograph objects of interest. The C-54s formed two projects: Hot Pepper and Lulu Belle. Hot Pepper's primary mission was oblique photography (using side-looking cameras to photograph target areas from a stand-off position), with a secondary ELINT recon mission, and Lulu Belle was tasked with the ATRAN mission, along with other photography and support missions.[147]

In August 1956, a limited "ferret" capability was provided aboard Hot Pepper with the installation of a radio and radar intercept equipment suite. The equipment, which could be installed and removed as required, was used on flights through the Berlin corridors and on missions through Austria and Yugoslavia and along the Albanian border. An operator borrowed from A Flight manned the ferret (ELINT) intercept position on such missions. The ferret capability was not employed on all missions.

To support ATRAN (automatic terrain recognition and navigation) and its other missions, the Project Lulu Belle RC-54 had undergone extensive special equipment modifications.[148] The same type of ATRAN equipment was being installed in Half Track RB-50D aircraft destined for the 7406th. Adding linguistic confusion, Aunt Sue was the project name covering all ATRAN activities in the 7499th; Aunt Sue was composed of Lulu Belle and Half Track, and the special orders for the two 7406th aircrews on temporary duty at Goodyear stated that they were supporting project Betty Lou. (Soviet intelligence officers probably went bonkers trying to keep track of all the project nicknames.)

Detachment 1, 7405th Support Squadron

Detachment 1, 7405th Support Squadron at Rhein-Main Air Base conducted operations in utmost secrecy. The now declassified histories for the 7405th still include statements such as: "Detachment 1, Rhein-Main AB, Germany (Due to the nature of Detachment 1 and its mission, it is not included in this history.)." The detachment already existed in May 1955 (Flight C, 7499th SS) when the reorganization transformed the 7499th into a group.[149] Using a YC-97A (Pie Face) aircraft, Detachment 1 flew special missions with the standard 7499th cover story of being a freight and passenger carrying unit.

The unit supported sensitive covert operations, conducted photo recon, and, more prosaically, carried passengers and highly classified cargo on both unscheduled and scheduled courier missions. The primary mission of the Pie Face C-97 was long-range oblique photography. Detachment 1, 7405th Support Squadron was disbanded on August 20, 1959.

Flight C, 7405th Support Squadron Special Project

Except for an innocuous entry in the squadron mission statement in the 7405th unit history—"provide logistical and administrative support to Flight C"—little mention was made of the 7405th's Flight C. Flight C's mission was carried out by the 7405th, but operational control was retained by the 7499th commander or his designated representative. Flight C—also known as the 7405th Special Project—was in reality a Central Intelligence Agency operation. Flight C had a single C-118 aircraft, a military version of the Douglas DC-6 civilian airliner. The C-118 was attached to the 7405th for maintenance and accountability. Flight C personnel were also attached to the 7405th for logistics and administrative support and flew special missions under the standard 7405th cover story of being a freight and passenger carrying unit. On June 27, 1958, while on a flight from Cyprus to Tehran, Iran, a 7405th Special Project

C-118 flew into Soviet airspace and was forced down in southern Azerbaijan by Soviet MiG-17 fighters—this shootdown incident is described in chapter two.

7407th Support Squadron

Start-up of the 7406th and 7407th Support Squadrons was accomplished concurrently. Major Helms[150] and Lieutenant Sensabaugh from the 7499th met with Colonel Harry S. Bishop, Rhein-Main Air Base commander, on April 15, 1955, to brief Colonel Bishop and his staff on plans for activating the two new squadrons.[150]

Activation of the 7406th and 7407th (and a 7407th detachment at Bitburg) posed some real challenges. Facilities at Rhein-Main were grim in May 1955. The only available space for the 7406th and 7407th was in the "Hutment" area, which consisted of temporary Quonset hut–type buildings created to support the Berlin Airlift in 1948–1949. Not only were the buildings in a sad state of repair, they were filled with overflow from the base supply warehouse, and it would require time to empty any of them.

Because of the imminent arrival of RB-57 aircraft for the 7407th, initial emphasis was placed on satisfying housing, maintenance support, and other needs for that unit since the 7406th did not expect its RB-50s until August 1955. At start-up, maintenance shops for the 7406th and 7407th were combined in a "lean-to" building on the north side of hangar 16. Hangar space was so critical at the time that none could be assigned permanently; hangar usage for secure operations was possible by appointment only.

Choosing to first line up necessary support for the 7407th was the correct decision; by June 30, 1955, the 7407th had received its first Project Sharp Cut RB-57A and was already flying actual missions. By August 1955, the 7407th was fully operational with its one Sharp Cut RB-57A, six Heart Throb RB-57As, and crews to support missions in the seven aircraft.

The difference between the two variants involved their capabilities. Sharp Cut included an electronic intercept and a photo capability; Heart Throb was photocapable only. The squadron retained its Heart Throb aircraft until June 1959 when six RB-57Ds arrived to replace them. The RB-57D had much longer wings, and the squadron parking ramp area had to be rearranged to accommodate them.

On December 14, 1965, a 7407th RB-57F with two crew members disappeared during a mission over the Black Sea. The loss of the RB-57F and its crew is discussed in chapter two.

With the advent of the U-2 reconnaissance aircraft, and the later launching of reconnaissance satellites, the RB-57 recon aircraft were eventually deemed obsolete. The 7407th Support Squadron was deactivated in the late 1960s.

Detachment 1, 7407th Support Squadron

The activation of Detachment 1, 7407th was even more expeditious than was the activation of its parent unit. Detachment 1 was the outgrowth of Project Slick Chick, which was established by Headquarters USAF on December 7, 1954, to fulfill a USAFE requirement for high-performance jet reconnaissance aircraft for special projects. In March 1955, three pilots and six maintenance personnel began factory training on the F-100 fighter at the North American Aviation factory in California and transition training at Edwards AFB. After training the men would be assigned to Detachment 1 at Bitburg AB.

The arrival of the Slick Chick RF-100 aircraft at Bitburg AB on May 16, 1955, marked a significant milestone; they were the first U.S. Air Force supersonic aircraft in Europe and the first in any overseas command.

Major Dowdy became the first commander of Detachment 1, 7407th. He and his other two pilots completed 145 flights by December 31, 1955, proving the value of high-performance tactical photo recon in continental Europe. Detachment 1 and its RF-100 contingent continued to support the USAFE tactical recon mission until July 1, 1958, when the unit was deactivated.

APPENDIX G: U.S. MILITARY RANKS AND GRADES

Note: O = Officer   E = Enlisted   W = Warrant Officer

Service Grade	Army	Air Force	Marine Corps	Navy	Coast Guard
O1	2nd Lieutenant	2nd Lieutenant	2nd Lieutenant	Ensign	Ensign
O2	1st Lieutenant	1st Lieutenant	1st Lieutenant	Lieutenant Junior Grade	Lieutenant Junior Grade
O3	Captain	Captain	Captain	Lieutenant	Lieutenant
O4	Major	Major	Major	Lieutenant Commander	Lieutenant Commander
O5	Lieutenant Colonel	Lieutenant Colonel	Lieutenant Colonel	Commander	Commander
O6	Colonel	Colonel	Colonel	Captain	Captain
O7	Brigadier General	Brigadier General	Brigadier General	Rear Admiral (Lower Half)	Rear Admiral (Lower Half)
O8	Major General	Major General	Major General	Rear Admiral (Upper Half)	Rear Admiral (Upper Half)
O9	Lieutenant General	Lieutenant General	Lieutenant General	Vice Admiral	Vice Admiral
O10	General	General	General	Admiral	Admiral
O11*	General of the Army	NA	NA	Fleet Admiral	NA
O12	Chairman of the Joint Chiefs of Staff				
W1**	Warrant Officer 1				
W2	Warrant Officer 2		Chief Warrant Officer 2	Chief Warrant Officer-2	Chief Warrant Officer 2
W3	Warrant Officer 3		Chief Warrant Officer 3	Chief Warrant Officer-3	Chief Warrant Officer 3
W4	Chief Warrant Officer 4		Chief Warrant Officer 4	Chief Warrant Officer-3	
E1	Private E-1	Airman Basic	Private	Seaman Recruit	Seaman Recruit
E2	Private E-2	Airman	Private First Class	Seaman Apprentice	Seaman Apprentice
E3	Private First Class	A/1C	Lance Corporal	Seaman	Seaman
E4	Specialist 4 or Corporal	Sergeant	Corporal	Petty Officer 3d Class	Petty Officer 3d Class
E5	Sergeant	Sergeant	Staff Sergeant	Petty Officer 2d Class	Petty Officer 2d Class
E6	Staff Sergeant	Technical Sergeant	Staff Sergeant	Petty Officer 1st Class	Petty Officer 1st Class
E7	Sergeant First Class	Master Sergeant	Gunnery Sergeant	Chief Petty Officer	Chief Petty Officer
E8**	Master Sergeant	Senior Master Sergeant	Master Sergeant	Senior Chief Petty Officer	Senior Chief Petty Officer
E9**	Sergeant Major	Chief Master Sergeant	Sergeant Major	Master Chief Petty Officer	Master Chief Petty Officer
E10	Sergeant Major of the Army	Chief Master Sergeant of the Air Force	Sergeant Major of the Marine Corps	Master Chief Petty Officer of the Navy	Master Chief Petty Officer of the Coast Guard

*General of the Army and Fleet Admiral ranks have not been filled since World War II

**E8 and E9 ranks were introduced in late 1950s, and the Air Force phased out Warrant Officer ranks in early 1960s.

NOTES

———

1 Lieutenant Osborn's EP-3 crew included the following U.S. Navy personnel: Richard Bensing, Steven Blocher, Bradford Borland, David Cecka, John Comerford, Shawn Coursen, Jeremy Crandall, Josef Edmunds, Brandon Funk, Scott Guidry, Jason Hanser, Patrick Honeck, Regina Kauffman, Nicholas Mellos, Ramon Mercado, Shane Osborn, Richard Payne, Kenneth Richter, Marcia Sonon, Jeffery Vignery, Wendy Westbrook, and Rodney Young; plus Richard Pray (U.S. Marine) and Curtis Towne (USAF airman). Kauffman, Sonon, and Westbrook were female members of the crew.
2 From the *People's Daily* Strong Country Forum, April 16, 2001.
3 Cold War Era Air Aces homepage, compiled by Allan Magnus.
4 U.S. Foreign Broadcasting Information Service Daily Report: Communist China, 12 and 17 February 1970.
5 National Archives, SN 70-73, Pol Chicom-US.
6 Series of "Hot Skies" articles in *Aviation World (Mir Aviatsii)* No. 1(11) 1996.
7 U.S. Navy "All Hands" publication dated April 1954.
8 For the most part, the Chinese government has not cooperated with the United States in efforts to resolve MIA cases associated with Sino-American Cold War incidents.
9 Retired Commander Perry related the story in a retirement newsletter in 1992.
10 *History of China's Aviation*, Jun Yao et. al., Beijing, China, 1998.
11 Fecteau was released on December 13, 1971.
12 Internet Web site on ROCAF U-2 operations.
13 Although the Soviets reported the C-130s altitude as 32,800 feet (10,000 meters), the typical mission altitude for the C-130A-II missions in 1958 was 26,000 to 28,000 feet.
14 Approximately five meters from the Arpa-Chaj River that forms the border between Turkey and Armenia, the KGB maintained a lightly plowed strip that would show the footsteps of anyone passing, and one hundred meters beyond the plowed strip was a barbed wire fence about one meter high. The fence was composed of four strands of barbed-wire—on posts, one strand above the other—crisscrossed with strands between. In addition, fifty meters beyond the first fence was another fence of closely woven barbed wire. The fences were guarded by armed sentries in towers at approximately forty-yard intervals.

15 A Cuban SA-2 missile shot down a U-2 over Cuba on October 27, 1962, killing the pilot, Maj. Rudolf Anderson.

16 Rivet Amber is the project nickname of the missile-monitoring RC-135 platform lost in this crash.

17 Cobra Ball was another missile-monitoring RC-135 platform.

18 A U.S. Air Force RC-135 had been operating over the Pacific Ocean east of Kamchatka earlier that day.

19 Yuri Island, the nearest island to the Russo-Japanese border, is a small remote outpost about thirty kilometers from the border. About twenty-five Russians are stationed on the island, which is about twenty kilometers square with rocky terrain.

20 Dunham was promoted posthumously to captain after the shootdown.

21 Irmelshausen is a small border village seventy miles northwest of Nuremberg.

22 In dealing with the press during the early 1950s, peacetime aerial reconnaissance missions were called weather reconnaissance missions.

23 Marrying a foreign national was often grounds for suspension of an American's special intelligence security clearance.

24 Capt. G. F. Svetlichnikov and B. F. Zakharov claim to be the MiG-17P pilots who shot down the C-118 on July 27, 1958. *Cold War Era* by Allan Magnus.

25 The six officers were promoted to these ranks subsequent to the shootdown on July 1, 1960.

26 Russian magazine *Aviation World (Mir Aviatsii)* No. 1 (11), 1996.

27 With the advent of DNA identification techniques in the 1990s, the unidentified sets of remains were exhumed; the last set of those remains was identified in 1998, leaving eleven of the C-130 crew members unaccounted for.

28 Paul Lashmar, *Spy Flights of the Cold War* (Sutton Publishing; Phoenix Mill, England, 1996) p. 109.

29 Quoted from *The Puzzle Palace* by James Bamford (p. 475).

30 This was in support of the SIOP (Single Integrated Operations Plan) that the Strategic Air Command used for combat mission planning—a major part of SAC's war plans involved strikes over the North Pole into the Soviet Union's heartland.

31 Cold War Era Air Aces homepage, compiled by Allan Magnus.

32 "The Bloody Border" by James Oberg, chapter 3 of *Uncovering Soviet Disasters*, Random House, 1988.

33 *Khrushchev Remembers: The Last Testament* by Nikita Khrushchev; Little Brown and Co, Boston, 1970, p. 210.

34 *Aviation World.*

35 After the end of the Cold War, the reason for the Russian refusal became clear: " 'Open Skies' was rejected because in those days Khrushchev was playing a game of bluff. He made public statements that claimed that the Soviet Union was absolutely equal and not lagging behind, although in reality they had to make great efforts to overtake or even to equal [the] Americans" (Russian historian Colonel Orlov, quoted in *Spy Flights of the Cold War*, p. 109).

36 As a direct result of the U-2 and B-47 overflights, American estimates of the number of Soviet bombers dropped steadily. The 1958 estimate was 50 percent lower than 1957, the 1959 estimate another 20 percent below 1958. In 1955, the NIE (National Intelligence Estimate) had estimated that the Soviets would possess 600 bombers by the end of the decade, half Bisons and half Bears; in 1960, the NIE for Soviet bombers of all types was between 125 and 185. Nevertheless, Congress continued to vote the funds for the fighters we "needed" to fight off all those bombers we had previously believed the Soviets would possess (see *Spy Flights of the Cold War*, p. 144).

37 "Alaska: Cold War's Strategic Frontier, 1945–1991" by Richard K. Korb, *VFW Magazine*, April 1998.

38 The HF radio spectrum is .3 to 30 Megahertz, although not all HF radios cover the entire spectrum.

39 Aircraft VHF radios operate in the 100 to 150 Megahertz frequency range.

40 Corporal Fordham was one of ninety-five enlisted men who transferred from the Army to the Air Force per 2d RSM Special Order 56 dated 15 July 1949.

41 The 10th, 12th, and 41st Radio Squadrons Mobile were actually activated at U.S. Air Force Security Service Headquarters, Brooks AFB, Texas, and deployed to their respective overseas lo-

cations in December 1950, early 1951, and December 1951, respectively. Detachment C, 2d RSM was integrated into the 41st RSM.

42 The 34th and 37th RSMs were also activated at Brooks AFB. The 34th RSM arrived at Wheelus Air Base, Libya, in 1951, and the 37th deployed to Kirknewton, Scotland, in June 1952.

43 Activated at Brooks AFB, Texas, in July 1953, the 6901st Special Communications Group was redesignated the Air Force Special Comms Center when the unit moved to Kelly AFB in August 1953. Subsequently, the 6901st SCG was reactivated and deployed to Landsberg, Germany, in 1955.

44 Activated at Brooks AFB, Texas, in July 1953, the 6901st Special Communications Group was redesignated the Air Force Special Comms Center when the unit moved to Kelly AFB in August 1953.

45 Meritorious Unit Commendation awarded to 1st RSM per FEAF GO # 411 dated Aug. 29, 1951.

46 Drew Field later became Tampa International Airport.

47 The history of the 8th RSM in World War II is documented in a unit history "The Story of the Flying Eight Ball" prepared by Ed Bradfield and other members of the squadron in 1945.

48 More than 6,000 U.S. Marines and an estimated 20,000 Japanese lost their lives in the battles for control of Iwo Jima, with the Marines enduring the most severe fighting in the history of the Corps while invading the island between February 19 and March 16, 1945.

49 Mamoru Ishii, a college student in Hawaii when the Japanese attacked Pearl Harbor in 1941, is a retired University of Hawaii professor of agriculture.

50 A waist-gunner turret and guns were retained on the RB-24.

51 The Japanese airfield at Chitose, Hokkaido, had a 10,000 feet runway, and an American general, General LeMay, wanted to establish a new world flight record by flying nonstop from Japan to Washington, D.C. After the general departed Chitose in a B-29 that was fully loaded with fuel, Ishii and the supporting party departed Japan.

52 David Kahn, *The Codebreakers* (The Macmillan Company, New York, 1967) p. 578. After the war, the Army Air Corps moved the 1st RSM to Johnson Air Base, Japan. In 1949, the 1st RSM was transferred to the United States Air Force Security Service.

53 First RSM nisei voice intercept operators who supported Army Air Corps operations in the southwest Pacific during World War II included Thomas Y. Doi, Minoru Y. Doi, Minoru Hamada, Hideo Ihara, Alata Ikebe, Bennett M. Ikeda, Harry T. Inouye, Yoshito Kawabe, Hisashi Matsuo, Tsugio Miyamoto, Edward K. Nakagawa, Kenji Nakahara, Shoichi Nakahara, Edward N. Nakamura, George Okamoto, Thomas T. Omura, Johnny S. Onoda, Kazuo Oshiki, Yoshiyuki Sakai, Takeo Sakuma, Kenichiro Sekiguchi, Yoshitsugu Shiraishi, Nobuyoshi Terao, Yonetada Watanabe, Shizuo Yuamada, and Keiji Yotsuya.

54 Unfortunately for the U.S. Air Force, Lt. Samuel Hong elected to remain with the Army Security Agency when the Air Force Security Service was created in 1948; thus Security Service was not aware of the earlier airborne nisei voice intercept missions that had been flown in 1945.

55 The flight crews included (from USAFSS) Maj. Paul H. V. Swanson, Capt. Herbert G Fielding, Capt. Fred O. Parrish, and 1st Lt. Faran A. R. McClimans (pilots); M.Sgts. Benjamin W. Faulkner and Emil J. Bacak (flight engineers); T.Sgt. Francis W. Baker and S.Sgt. Bobby C. Fisher (aircraft radio operators); plus Maj. Theodore W. Bozarth and 1st Lt. Jimmie J. Benaquis (navigators on temporary duty from Eglin AFB, Florida).

56 The executive order extended the enlistment of most U.S. military forces to support the Korean War.

57 Detachment C, 1st RSM was redesignated Detachment 13, 1st RSM 39 on February 1, 1951.

58 Hill, Radlein, and Leo Sloan had also flown missions aboard Strategic Air Command RB-45s from Yokota by July 1953, and Airman Richard "Perry" Hain was one of the replacement voice intercept operators on later RB-45 missions.

59 Documented in the 7499th unit history dated 1955.

60 Zone of Interior was a military term for the continental United States at the time.

61 Activation of the 7406th Support Squadron is documented in the unit history dated 1955.

62 As aircraft commander, Maj. Jesse C. DeHay's crew included 2d Lt. George G. Berg, Capt. Robert

O. Stephens, Capt. Robert O. Murdock, M.Sgt. Frank C. Martin Jr., T.Sgt. Richard D. Carlson, S.Sgt. John D. Mulkey, and A/2C Richard LaSota.

63 Capt. James W. Kirkbride Jr. (pilot) had on Crew #2: 1st Lt. Henry J. Jeremica, Capt. Marvin L. Pinkerton, 1st Lt. Richard L. Leming, M.Sgt. Howard H. McKinney, S.Sgt.. Clarence J. Klinkbeil, A/2C Sheldon Z. Myers, and S.Sgt.. Edwin T. Murray.

64 Early assignees to the 7406th Support Squadron included 2d Lts. Charles V. Davis Jr., William D. Rogers, and Lawrence L. Lively (navigators straight out of school), S.Sgt.. Wallace D. Sumner and M.Sgt. Lawrence Gumenski (aircraft gunners), T.Sgt. Daniel R. Anders (first sergeant), Capt. Stanley B. Klein (training officer), Maj. John R. Smith and Capt. Francis B. Shaffer (navigator bombardiers), and Maj. Joseph F. Herrmann (operations officer).

65 M.Sgt. Harry Johnson assumed the first sergeant duties on August 1, 1956.

66 RB-50D #49312 was the first aircraft received by the 7406th Support Squadron on March 6, 1956.

67 The 7406th SS received its second aircraft, RB-50D #127, on April 3, 1956.

68 The 7406th SS received its third aircraft, RB-50D #307, on May 26, 1956.

69 A bailout bottle is a high-pressure portable oxygen container that is packaged with a parachute to provide a supply of oxygen to airmen parachuting from an aircraft at high altitudes.

70 In December 1955, the Air Force, through its Oklahoma City Air Material Area office, contracted with TEMCO for depot maintenance and installation of special electronic surveillance equipment in one B-50E aircraft. That project, nicknamed "Hay Stack" in Air Force procurement channels, was sponsored by Air Force Security Service and was known as Dream Boat in Europe.

71 The crew included Maj. Paul H. V. Swanson (pilot), Capt. Fred L. McDowell Jr. (copilot), 2d Lt. Lawrence L. Lively (navigator), Maj. Francis B. Shaffer (navigator), M.Sgt. Frank C. Martin, Sr. (flight engineer), S.Sgt. John D. Mulkey (aircraft radio operator), M.Sgt. Lawrence Gumenski (gunner/scanner), S.Sgt. Neil W. Hurley (gunner/scanner), and T.Sgt. Stanley E. Kresge (Detachment 1, 6911th Radio Group Mobile Operations NCOIC).

72 Phase maintenance is a preventive maintenance program under which most or all aircraft systems are inspected, serviced, and repaired according to defined guidelines after the aircraft has flown a predefined number of hours.

73 Two 7406th crews—Major Swanson (pilot and 7406th ops officer), 1st Lt. Douglas A. Blemings (pilot), and S.Sgt. George B. Pittelkau (flight engineer), and Capt. William H. Lewis (pilot), 1st Lt. Richard E. McDevitt (pilot), and T.Sgt. Asencion Gonzales (flight engineer)—began the C-130 flight training course.

74 The third C-130 flight training course commenced on March 10, 1958, for 1st Lts. James H. Carter Jr., Vernon Conway, Melvin N. Ledbetter, and Charles U. Williams II (pilots) and S.Sgts. Owen J. Long and Laroy Price (flight engineers).

75 Per 7406th Personnel Action Memorandum dated July 17, 1958.

76 In its attempt, no doubt, to confuse the Soviet KGB, the U.S. Air Force also referred to the C-130A-II Rivet Victor I as a "Sun Valley I" aircraft.

77 Simpson was a qualified C-130 pilot but lacked the experience on operational missions needed to be upgraded to aircraft commander status on recon missions.

78 The C-130A-II was developed on Air Force Project "Big Five," the same contract under which TEMCO developed and maintained the Hay Stack (Dream Boat) RB-50s. Later, Project Big Five was moved into the Big Safari Program, under which Air Force reconnaissance aircraft are developed to the present day.

79 Adding to project nom de guerre confusion, the Sun Valley I C-130A-II was called "Rivet Victor I" in some Air Force channels, and the unclassified USAFE nickname for C-130 recon missions in Europe was "Creek Grass."

80 As part of an "integrated crew," if either the lead pilot or lead navigator were unavailable for a mission, the entire crew would have to be replaced with another integrated crew.

81 Other crew members on the deployment to Bodö, Norway, included Capt. David A Stewart (pilot), 1st Lt. Richard E. McDevitt (copilot), Capt. Marvin L. Pinkerton (navigator), James T. Edds (navigator), S.Sgts. Delbert C. Johannsen and Jackie R. Knight (flight engineers), and Capt. Harold H. Kinder (material officer).

82 The first flight crew that deployed to Athens, Greece, included Capt. Nelson Halstead (pilot), 1st Lt. Douglas A. Blemings (copilot), Capts. Gerald W. Monier and Lonnie C. Sitts (navigators), and George B. Pittelkau (flight engineer).

83 Other Detachment 1(Security Service) crew members included the following airborne voice intercept operators: Airmen First Class Earl J. Moore and Warren H. Meyer, Airmen Second Class Allan M. Hegland, Robert L. Trainor, Minthorne D. Norton, Wayne G. Kenyon, Leo L. Simms, Howard L. Meyer, and Richard D. Doto. S.Sgt. Braxton Lockett was the airborne Morse operator, and the airborne maintenance technicians on the trip were T.Sgt. Kenneth D. Simonson and A/2C Joseph A. Silcott.

84 The 7406th Support Squadron suffered a minor aircraft accident on August 24, 1956, when Lt. Col. George J. Byars, the squadron commander, landed "long" in B-50D 49307 at Rhein-Main AB. Touching down halfway down the runway, he and his copilot, 2d Lt. James H. Carter Jr., were unable to stop the aircraft in time and skidded sideways off the end of the runway. Fortunately, no one was injured and the aircraft suffered little damage.

85 The 7406th SS crew who deployed to Incirlik AB, Turkey, in March 1957 included three pilots (Herrmann, Capt. Allen C. Rozsa, and 2d Lt. James H Carter Jr.), three navigators (Capts. Vincent J. Bracci and Robert O. Murdock, and 2d Lt. Ricardo M. Villarreal), M.Sgt. Frank C. Martin Jr. (flight engineer), S.Sgt.. Clarence J. Klinkbeil (aircraft radio operator) and two scanner/gunners (S.Sgts. Curtis F. Shuman and Robert A. Nankivell); ref 7499th SO # 55, dated March 22, 1957.

86 In the 1950s and 1960s, U.S. military unit designators for units in Turkey were classified; in lieu of true unit designator, each was identified as a Turkish U.S. Logistics Group (TUSLOG) detachment.

87 TUSLOG, Detachment 76 was also known as TUSLOG, Detachment 10-1 for a short period.

88 The Black Sea Central orbit points were at latitude 42:30N between 33:00E and 36:00E longitudes (north of Sinop, Turkey); later changed in the early 1960s to 34:00E and 37:00E.

89 Initial orbit points for the Black Sea East route was later changed to a point northeast of Trabzon (42:20N 40:00E) as north point (Alpha) with the south point (Bravo) at Erzurum.

90 The integrated crew included Capt. William H. Lewis, Jr. (pilot), 1st Lt. George G. Berg (copilot), Capts. Marvin L. Pinkerton and Victor P. Farris (navigators), and T.Sgt. Robert L. DeGrasse (flight engineer).

91 One result of the investigation of 60528's inadvertent violation of enemy airspace and subsequent downing was that only "integrated flight crews" could fly missions; if a key member of such a crew (lead pilot or lead navigator) was unavailable for a mission, the entire crew had to be replaced.

92 S.Sgt.. Reidmiller had flown recon missions as a Morse operator on RB-29 62290 in Europe in 1953.

93 The first USAFSS airmen assigned on aeronautical orders in Europe were S.Sgts. Donald H. Riedmiller and George W. Rubel, Airmen First Class Ronald S. Bassford and Warren H. Hamaker, and Airmen Second Class Richard T. Frederick, Thomas Joseph Jr., Robert E. Payne, James K. Bumgardner, Donald L Horger, Billy G. Payne, and Louis G. Padilla.

94 Detachment 1's Russian linguists included Stan Kresge, John Kozak, Bill McCormick, Jack Roberts, Ronald Bassford, James Bumgardner, Donald Dunnagan, Warren Hamaker, Donald Horger, Robert Moran, Billy Payne, and Leardis Rice.

95 Detachment 1's "other" twenty operators-linguists in July 1957 included Bill Bain, Charles Clark, James Booth, James Moehringer, David Parker, and James Wright (Polish); Bobby Barrow, Robert Berry, and Nathan Britt (Czechoslovakian); Lincoln Gilbert, Richard Doto, John Hamm, Allan Hegland, Harold Kamps, and James Kinney (Serbo-Croatian); Thomas Joseph Jr., Robert Payne, and Virgil Wethington (Bulgarian); and Earl Moore and Everett Reeves (Romanian).

96 Airborne maintenance technicians included Robert Deuster Jr., Arthur Mellow, Donald Connell, Phillip Nowicke, and Jimmie Reese Jr.

97 Detachment 1's new Russian linguists arriving from Syracuse in July 1957 included Perry Eisenhower, Sam Clark II, Dennison Cottrell, Bill Cunningham Jr., Joel Fields, Gary Hizer, Wayne Kenyon, Robert Keefe, Dick Klingensmith, Albert Lott, Joe Martineau, James Morris, and Minthorne Norton.

98 In late 1957 another Russian language class (Terry Faubus, James Ferguson Jr., Richard Garrigan,

Joseph Kramer, Gerald Maggiacomo, Harrold Patterson, Jackie Price, Robert Ryan, Leo Simms, and David Southern) arrived at Rhein-Main from the Army Language School, Monterey, California.

99 Gerald Medeiros and Barney Rakestraw were among the Russian linguists arriving from Indiana University.

100 The following airmen were authorized to wear aircrew wings on December 31, 1957: William H. McCormick, Jack Roberts, Charles E. Clark, Billy G. Payne, Leardis G. Rice, John B. Argoe, James M. Booth, Grover L. Campbell, James T. Moehringer, and James D. Wright.

101 The eleven airmen authorized to wear aircrew wings on July 1, 1958, were Lucius Baker, Theodore Klein, James Arnold, William Cunningham Jr., Richard Garrigan, Wayne Kenyan, Earl Moore, Jackie Price, Harrold Patterson, James Weister, and John Wilcher.

102 TUSLOG, Det 50 was Detachment 1, 7th Air Division (SAC).

103 Among the larger programs, Yale played a major role in Chinese language training, Indiana taught airmen Serbo-Croatian (and later Russian), and many of the Romanian linguists received their training at Cornell.

104 James Bamford, *The Puzzle Palace*, p. 334.

105 Lieutenant Simpson was promoted posthumously to captain effective September 1958.

106 John Simpson was promoted posthumously from first lieutenant to captain effective September 1, 1958.

107 The type of officer commission—regular vs. reserve—was a discriminator in promotion and personnel policy; regular officer status was similar to tenure in the college teaching professions.

108 Others graduating with Lieutenant Villarreal and being assigned to the 7406th included Maj. Frank Redler and 2d Lts. Vernon Amundson and James Edds—per special orders dated July 21, 1956.

109 Pilots and flight engineers on TDY to France per 7499th special order #85 dated March 6, 1958. Others in the C-130A training with Sergeant Price on SO #85 included 1st Lts. James H. Carter Jr., Vernon Conway, Melvin N. Ledbetter, Charles U. Williams III, and S.Sgt. Owen J. Long.

110 7406th special order #188 dated August 19, 1958, listed ten C-130 flight engineers: Robert De-Grasse, Asencion Gonzales, Donald Van Horn, Donald Conrad, Fredrick Fredrickson, Delbert Johannsen, Owen Long, George Pittelkau, Bobby Pruett, and Laroy Price.

111 Prior to the shootdown of 60528, there was no official requirement that a Morse operator be aboard Air Force airborne communications intelligence recon missions operating in Europe.

112 At the time, aircrew members had to fly 150 hours to qualify for the aircrew member badge (aircrew wings).

113 The airborne maintenance technicians had a maintenance station in the back of the C-130 where they accomplished in-flight repairs of malfunctioning equipment.

114 The first six Serbo-Croatian airborne voice intercept operators were Harold T. Kamps, Lincoln J. Gilbert, John W. Hamm Jr., Richard D. Doto, Allan M. Hegland, and James C. Kinney.

115 For a few years in the mid-1950s, completion of an intensive introductory (prelanguage) course in Russian was a prerequisite for qualifying to attend an Air Force sponsored Russian language school.

116 Oshinskie was assigned to Detachment 1, 6912th Radio Squadron Mobile at Landshut, Germany, and the unit was redesignated Detachment 4, 6910th Radio Group Mobile in September 1957.

117 The number of military family housing units at Rhein-Main versus the number of requests for family quarters resulted in a lengthy waiting list. Officers and enlisted who qualified could defer bringing families to Germany until housing became available, or receive a housing allowance and live in German rental quarters. Several of the families of 60528's crew members were living in apartments on the German economy.

118 Even in the lower levels of NSA, there were men who thought the incursion had been deliberate. Bernon F. Mitchell and William H. Martin, having grown disenchanted with U.S. violations of Soviet borders, defected to the Soviet Union in June 1960. In a Moscow press conference, the two men listed the C-130 overflight as one of the provocations "that could be the cause of war" (*The Puzzle Palace*, p. 190). The author of *The Puzzle Palace* still believed, in 1983, that the plane had crossed into Armenia deliberately.

119 Multiple USAFSS ground sites would have been tracking the progress of C-130 60528's mission; however, details about which site forwarded the initial Critic Report are not available.

120 The Report of Casualty (DD Form 1300) for each of the seventeen lost men lists the crew member's organization as 7406th Support Squadron.

121 The Soviets later determined that there were only six remains, not the seven reported initially.

122 Ibid.

123 Aeronautical orders #18 dated July 22, 1958, designated Sergeant Rubel a crew member effective July 15, 1958, covering the first mission he'd flown the previous Tuesday.

124 Per special orders No. A-443 dated September 23, 1958, the following airmen were reassigned from the 6913th RSM to Detachment 1, 6911th RSM on October 6, 1958: S.Sgt. Billy M. Grant, Airmen Second Class Bobby J. Gilpatrick, Jerry L. Harper, Joseph F. Horcher, Cyrus K. Huneycutt Jr., David F. Kelly, Terrence G. Kenny, Donald H. Lee, Thomas A. Ozoroski, Robert N. R. Paradis, and James B. Whitaker, plus Airman Third Class James E. Hensley.

125 The initial cadre of Morse intercept operators who were assigned to Detachment 1, 6911th in 1958 included Austin H. Humbles Jr., Braxton Lockett, William L. Looney, Ralph D. Johnstun, Estel H. Callebs, Curtis E. Cross, S.M.M. "Sam" Craver, Arlen R. Van Fossen, and Ray K. Stokes.

126 Per special orders No. 326, the following Detachment 1, 6911th airmen deployed to Athens for three days on November 5, 1958: S.Sgts. Robert H. Bergeron and Braxton Lockett, T.Sgt. Kenneth D. Simonson, Airmen First Class Earl J. Moore and Warren H. Meyer, and Airmen Second Class Allan M. Hegland, Robert L. Trainor, Minthorne D. Norton, Wayne G. Kenyon, Leo L. Simms, Howard L. Meyer, Joseph A. Silcott, and Richard D. Doto.

127 In addition to Kozak, the reconnaissance crew for this first deployment to Turkey after the stand down included Airmen Second Class airborne voice intercept operators John W. Hamm Jr., Raymond F. Posladek, Ferdinand J. Metzger, James C. Weister, Robert Keefe, Joseph P. E. Martineau, Jackie A. Price, Robert F. Peck Jr., and Thomas E. Tucker, plus airborne Morse intercept operators S.Sgt. William F. Looney and A/2C Curtis E. Cross, and airborne maintenance technicians Airmen Second Class Grover L. Campbell and Fred A. Bellew.

128 The crew that deployed to Incirlik, Turkey, on November 26, 1958, included T.Sgt. Bruce Henderson, S.Sgt. Braxton Lockett, and Airmen Second Class Nathaniel Moore, Joseph Silcott, Sammy Butler, Donald Roesner, Gerald Lynch, William Cunningham Jr., Wayne Kenyon, and Harrold Patterson.

129 Promoted to captain, Doyle E. Larson left Goodfellow AFB in 1962 to activate and become the first commander of the USAFSS 6985th Radio Squadron Mobile at Eielson AFB, Alaska. Seventeen years later, as a major general, Larson was the last commander of Air Force Security Service and first commander of the Electronic Security Command when USAFSS was transformed into ESC in 1979.

130 The 6916th RSM became the 6916th Security Squadron in August 1963.

131 Aleksei Orlov was working as a professor for the Institute of Military History in Moscow when the Task Force Russia component of the U.S.–Russian Joint Commission on POW/MIA issues interviewed him in search of information on Cold War MIAs.

132 U.S. State Department press release #518 dated September 6, 1958.

133 U.S. State Department press release #534 dated September 12, 1958.

134 7406th Special Order No. 191 dated August 21, 1958.

135 Press release No. 93 dated February 5, 1959.

136 Telegram No. 2196 from Washington.

137 Press release No. 93 dated February 5, 1959.

138 The two unknown corpses (designated X-3 and X-6) were interred in Arlington National Cemetery on February 6, 1959, in grave sites ANC 34-4779 and ANC 34-4778, respectively.

139 Public Law 490, 77th Congress as amended, more widely known as the Missing Persons Act.

140 In 1960, Turkish army units led by Gen. Cemal Gursel seized control of the government and set up a provisional government.

141 By listening to a beacon, a person with a knowledge of Morse code can identify the beacon by its unique (usually two- or three-letter) identifier, but aircraft navigation systems lock onto any signal transmitted on the frequency to which its receiver is tuned—receiving the stronger signal if more than one signal is being transmitted.

142 7499th Support Group was the parent organization of 7406th SSH, to which C-130 60528 was assigned.

143 The C-130A-II (aka 60528) and C-130B-II recon aircraft were never officially designated as E- or RC- variants of the C-130.

144 A Russian army colonel from the Russian Armed Forces Museum, Moscow, and a Russian Army lieutenant general, Chief of the Russian Army Personnel Directorate, presented this fragment of Powers's U-2 to NCM curator Jack Ingram on October 5, 1994.

145 DNA is deoxyribonucleic acid.

146 The 7405th mission as defined in 7499th group regulation 23-1 dated June 1, 1955, was to: a) perform such aerial photographic missions as may be directed by commander in chief, US-AFE; b) perform priority administrative, courier, and freight flights; c) provide logistical and administrative support to Flight C; and d) provide administrative and logistical support to the 7499th group. In further elaboration of the unclassified mission cited in regulation 23-1, the 7405th was responsible for Projects Red Owl, Pie Face, and Hot Pepper photography as outlined in USAFE target lists and reconnaissance requests; the visual reconnaissance program to satisfy U.S. Army and U.S. Air Force requirements; the ATRAN program; the USAFE heat-mapping program; AMTI radar recon; and the USAFE ferret reconnaissance program. (USAFE euphemistically identified electronic reconnaissance as "ferret" missions.)

147 Among its other missions, the Red Owl section worked closely with U.S. Army Europe intelligence liaison teams to support army targeting with "Willy" C-47 missions and "Slot" B-26 missions.

148 Project Lulu Belle's special equipment modifications included: 1) ATRAN (automatic terrain recognition and navigation); 2) AMTI (APS-27 airborne moving target indicator radar); 3) TRD (a thermal reconnaissance device used to capture an image based on heat given off by an object on the ground); 4) Wild Waves (modified Loran receiver); and 5) vertical camera T-11 or K-17. The TRD and APS-27 equipment had been installed at Convair/Fort Worth during the period July to September 1955.

149 Detachment 1, 7405th command staff are included in the unit histories. Maj. Carl E. Norman was Detachment 1's first commander. Capt. Robert H. Copple was his assistant; 1st Lts. Kenneth D. Long and Florenz J. Mansmann were still photography officers; and 2d Lt. Michael J. Rega was the detachment navigator in May 1955. Capt. Copple replaced Maj. Norman when the major rotated back to the States later in 1955, and Maj. George C. Berner replaced Captain Copple by early 1956. Maj. Paul E. Hanamire succeeded Major Berner as the Detachment 1 commander in March 1957.

150 Major Helms, first commander of the 7407th, was in effect an interim commander; he returned to the 7405th at Wiesbaden in mid-1955, replaced by Maj. Walter J. Raynor. Lt. Col. Raymond L. Fitzgerald, a veteran bomber pilot with seventy-two combat missions in North Africa and Southern Europe during World War II, replaced Major Raynor as 7407th commander in November 1955.

INDEX

549

ABOUT THE AUTHORS

LARRY TART and his wife, Diane, reside in State College, Pennsylvania. In his post-military career, he worked over sixteen years for a defense contractor, designing and building surveillance and reconnaissance systems. In the U.S. Air Force, Larry completed the Defense Language Institute's basic, intermediate, and advanced Russian language courses and holds a B.A. in Russian. He served in the United States Air Force Security Service (USAFSS) for twenty-one years, retiring in 1977 as a senior master sergeant. Trained as a Russian cryptologic linguist, he served on overseas tours in England, Germany, and Japan before going airborne in 1967. Between March 1967 and June 1976, he logged approximately 3,000 hours aboard C-130 and RC-135 aircraft, conducting aerial signals intelligence reconnaissance missions. His military awards include eleven Air Medals and two Meritorious Service Medals. In September 2000, the Air Force Air Intelligence Agency inducted Larry into its Hall of Honor.

During his flying career, he served in the 6916th Security Squadron—the same unit to which the eleven recon crew members who perished aboard C-130 60528 on September 2, 1958, were assigned.

As initiator of a proposal to honor 60528's lost crew, Larry is recognized as the "father" of the Aerial Reconnaissance (C-130) Memorial. He played a major role in creating the memorial, dedicated in National Vigilance Park at Fort Meade, Maryland, on September 2, 1997.

You can visit his Web site at www.larrytart.com.

ROBERT KEEFE is a professor of English at the University of Massachusetts in Amherst. He was trained as a Russian linguist in 1956–57 at Syracuse University and subsequently became one of the first airborne Russian-German linguists in Europe. In four years in Germany, he logged about 2,000 hours of flight time. He was a close friend of many of the recon crew members of aircraft 60528 when it was shot down.

After his discharge from the Air Force in 1961, he attended Brandeis University on a full scholarship, earning his B.A. in three years. Having won both a Woodrow Wilson and a Danforth Fellowship, he earned his Ph.D. at Princeton, again in three years. At UMass, he served for nearly a decade as director of English graduate studies. He has spent four separate years as a visiting professor at the University of Freiburg in Germany and has published widely both in his field, Victorian literature, and on current affairs.